...OK

...SA

...pyright Bruce Whipperman, 2001.

...opyright
...2001.

...ations are used by permission
...he original copyright owners.

...r: Erin Van Rheenen
...ins
...lissa Sherowski
..., Marie J.T. Vigil, Kelly Pendragon
...s
...enfeld, Kat Kalamaras, Chris Folks, Ben Pease

...ith C. Haden; jhaden@halcyou.com

...pperman unless otherwise noted.

...States and Canada by Publishers Group West

...Colorcraft Ltd., Hong Kong

Please send all comments,
corrections, additions,
amendments, and critiques to:

**MOON HANDBOOKS:
OAXACA
AVALON TRAVEL PUBLISHING
5855 BEAUDRY ST.
EMERYVILLE, CA, USA
email: info@travelmatters.com
www.travelmatters.com**

Printing History
1st edition—January 2000
2nd edition—September 2001
5 4 3 2 1

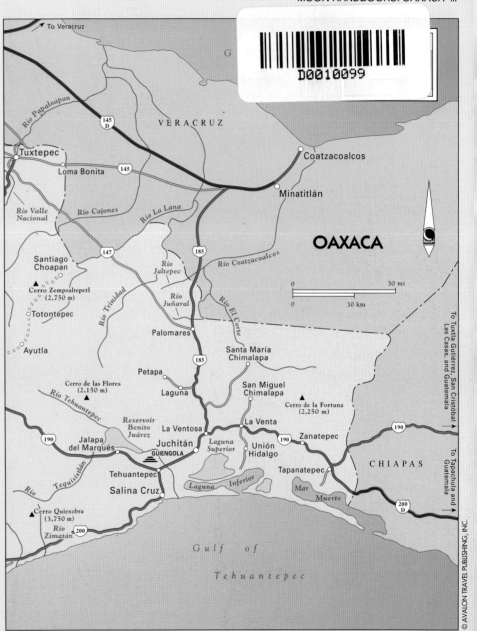

OAXACA

MOON

OA

MOUNTA
ARCHAEOLOGICAL

BRUC

OAXACA HANDBO
SECOND EDITION

Bruce Whipperman

Published by
 Avalon Travel Publishir
 5855 Beaudry St.
 Emeryville, CA 94608,

Text and photographs © c
All rights reserved.

Illustrations and maps © c
Avalon Travel Publishing,
All rights reserved.

 Some photos and illus
 and are the property o

ISBN: 1-56691-331-4
ISSN: 1533-3949

Editor and Series Mana⌐
Copy Editor: Carolyn Pe
Graphics Coordinator: N
Production: Amber Pirk⌐
Map Editor: Naomi Dan⌐
Cartography: Mike Morↄ
Index: Emily Lunceford

Front cover photo: © Ju

All photos by Bruce Wh

Distributed in the Unite

Printed in China throuↄ

All rights reserved. No
by a reviewer for the p

Although every effort ↖
 the author and publish
 age caused by errors,
 whether such errors o

A ⌐
T ꜰ

To those valiant Oaxacan people who,
inspired by Benito Juárez's immortal words—
"Respect for the Right of All Is Peace"—
give their all in the struggle for justice.

CONTENTS

INTRODUCTION **1–67**

Land and Sea 1–4
  Climate

Flora and Fauna 4–17
  Vegetation Zones; Mammals; Birds; Reptiles and Amphibians; Fish

History 17–42
  Early Civilization; The Conquest; New Spain; Colonial Oaxaca;
  Independence; Reform, Civil War, and Invasion; Order and Progress;
  Revolution and Stabilization; Contemporary Mexico and Oaxaca

Economy, Government, and Politics 42–49

People 50–67
  Population; Ethnic Groups; Shared Oaxacan Customs; Religion;
  Language; Indigenous Groups

SPECIAL TOPICS

Oaxaca Summary 3
Cochineal— 26
  Nature's Richest Red Dye
Population Changes 27
  in New Spain
Porfirio Díaz 32–33
Socioeconomic Statistics: 43
  Oaxaca vs. Mexico vs. The U.S.

Income Distribution— 45
  Regional vs. National
Economic Activity— 46
  Regional vs. National
Mesoamerican Calendar 52–53
The Virgin of Guadalupe 56
Indigenous Languages 57
Taking People Pictures 64

ON THE ROAD **68–121**

Sports and Recreation 58–76
  On the Beach; Water Sports; Power Sports; Tennis and Golf; Fishing;
  Festivals and Events

Arts and Crafts 76–81
  Basketry and Woven Crafts; Clothing, Embroidery, and Leather; Glass
  and Stonework; Jewelry; Woodcarving and Musical Instruments;
  Metalwork; Paper and Papier-Mâché; Pottery and Ceramics; Woolen
  Woven Goods

Accommodations 82–88
  Guesthouses, Bed and Breakfasts, and Homestays; Apartments and
  House Rentals; Tourist Yu'u; Local Hotels; International-Class Resorts;
  Camping, *Palapas,* and Trailer Parks

Food and Drink 88–91

Getting There 91–101
  By Air; By Bus; By Car or RV; By Tour

Getting Around 102–106
  By Air; By Bus; By Train; By Car, Taxi, Tour, or Hitchhiking

Other Practicalities. 107–121

Entry and Exit Regulations; Money; Shopping; Communications; Staying Healthy; Conduct and Customs; Specialty Travel; What to Take

SPECIAL TOPICS

Fish 70-71
Fiestas 73-75
Where to Find Tourist Yu'u 83
Resort Toll-Free 85
  Numbers and Websites
Trailer Parks and Camping 86-87
Catch of the Day 89
A Trove of Fruits and Nuts. 90
Airlines Serving Oaxaca 92
Road Safety 96
Detour into a Cornfield. 98

Highway Routes from 99
  the U.S. Border to Oaxaca
Car-Rental Agency 106
  Toll-Free Numbers and Websites
Mexico Tourism Board Offices. . . . 108
Tianguis 112
Medical Tags and Air Evacuation . . 116
Machismo. 117
Packing Checklist. 119
Packing Checklist for Campers . . . 120

OAXACA: THE CITY 122–159
History 122–125
Sights 126–133

Around the *Zócalo*; Andador de Macedonio Alcalá; North End
Accommodations 134–142

Hotels; Bed and Breakfasts, Guesthouses, and Apartments; Trailer Parks and Camping
Food 142–146

Snacks, Foodstalls, and Coffeehouses; Cafés and Restaurants
Entertainment and Events 147–148
Sports and Recreation 149
Shopping 149–152
Other Practicalities. 153–159

Services; Information; Getting There and Away

SPECIAL TOPICS

Margarita Maza 124-125
Oaxaca City 136-137
  Accommodations by Price

A Oaxacan Menu 144

AROUND THE VALLEY OF OAXACA 163–192
Getting Around
East Side: The Textile Route 163–175

Dainzu and Lambityeco Archaeological Sites; Teotitlán del Valle; Santa Ana del Valle; Tlacolula; Yagul Archaeological Zone; San Bartolomé Quialana and San Marcos Tlapazola; Mitla; Hierve El Agua Mineral Springs

South and Southwest of Oaxaca City 175–183
Ocotlán; Ejutla; Down Highway 131; Southwest Side
West and Northwest of the City: The Archaeological Route 184–192
Monte Albán; Santa María Atzompa; San José El Mogote; Etla;
Suchilquitongo and Cerro de La Campana Archaeological Zone

SPECIAL TOPICS
....

Town Names . . . . *162*   *The Story of Donaji* *188*
Building Churches *178-179*

PACIFIC RESORTS AND SOUTHERN SIERRA **193–262**
Puerto Ángel and Vicinity 194–210
Beaches and Sights; Accommodations; Food; Entertainment and Sports;
Shopping; Services and Information; Getting There and Away; Upland
Excursions from Puerto Ángel
The Bays of Huatulco and Vicinity 211–229
History; Sights; Accommodations; Food; Entertainment; Sports and
Recreation; Shopping; Services; Information; Getting There and Away;
Upland Excursions from the Bays of Huatulco: Coffee Country; East
toward the Isthmus: Chontal Country
Puerto Escondido and Vicinity 230–245
Around Town; Beaches and Activities; Sights out of Town;
Accommodations; Food; Entertainment and Events; Sports and
Recreation; Shopping; Services; Information; Getting There and Away
Upland Excursion into Chatino Country 246–251
Santos Reyes Nopala; Santa Catarina Juquila: Shrine for All Seasons
West to the Mixtec Coast 252–257
Lagunas de Chacagua National Park and Vicinity; San Pedro Tututepec;
Charquito Atotonilco Hot Springs; Santiago Jamiltepec; West of
Jamiltepec
Pinotepa Nacional and Vicinity 258–262
Excursions North of Pinotepa; Excursions South of Pinotepa

SPECIAL TOPICS
....

A Turtle Arrives at . . . . . . *202–203*   *Trouble in Chatino Country* *249*
    Playa La Ventanilla   *Pozahuancos* *259*

THE MIXTECA **263–310**
Northwest from Oaxaca City 265–271
Nochixtlán; Forgotten Kingdoms; Oaxaca's Shangri-La: The Vale of
Apoala
Dominican Route South 271–278
Tamazulapan and Vicinity; Teposcolula; Yucunama; Yanhuitlán
Dominican Route North 279–284
Coixtlahuaca; San Miguel Tequixtepec; Tepelmeme de Morelos

Land of the Sun: The Mixteca Baja 284–298
Huajuapan de León and Vicinity; North of Huajuapan: Into the Ñuiñe
Region; South of Huajuapan: Along the High Road to the Mixteca Alta;
Santiago Juxtlahuaca and Vicinity
Roof of Oaxaca: The Mixteca Alta 298–310
Asunción Tlaxiaco; South of Tlaxiaco; East of Tlaxiaco; West of Tlaxiaco;
Putla de Guerrero: Land of Water

NORTHERN OAXACA 311–341
Northern Sierra 312–319
Up from the Valley: Benito Juárez and Cuajimoloyas; Along the Road to
Ixtlán; At the Summit: Ixtlán de Juárez and Vicinity
Into the Papaloapan 320–332
Valle Nacional: Land of Springs; Santa María Jacatepec; San José
Chiltepec; Tuxtepec: River Country; Temascal and Miguel Alemán Dam
and Reservoir; San Pedro Ixcatlán and the Islands; San Lucas Ojitlán
The Mazateca 332–337
Jalapa de Díaz and Vicinity: The Low Mazateca; Huatla de Jiménez and
Vicinity: The High Mazateca
The Cañada: Canyon Country 338–341
Teotitlán del Camino; Cuicatlán
SPECIAL TOPIC

Benito Juárez *318*

THE ISTHMUS: LAND OF PLENTY 342–375
Santo Domingo Tehuantepec and Vicinity 343–355
History; Sights; Accommodations; Food; Services; Getting There and
Away; Excursions West of Tehuantepec
Juchitán and Vicinity 356–361
Sights; Accommodations; Food; Entertainment and Events; Services;
Information; Getting There and Away
North of Juchitán 361–364
The Springs at Tlacotepec and Laollaga; Lagunas: Company Town;
Santo Domingo Petapa: Limestone Cave
East of Juchitán 364–367
La Venta; Unión de Hidalgo; Playa Copalito and San Dionisio del Mar;
Santo Domingo Zanatepec; San Pedro Tapanatepec; Rincón Juárez and
the Calm Sea
Salina Cruz and Vicinity 368–375
Sights; Accommodations; Food; Entertainment and Events; Services and
Information; Getting There and Away; Playa La Ventosa; Excursion East
of Salina Cruz: Huave Country
SPECIAL TOPICS

Velas *of the Isthmus* . . . . *348*   *Juana Catalina Romero* *352*
Motocarros *351*

RESOURCES

Glossary 375–377

Pronunciation Guide 378

English-Spanish Phrasebook 379–384

Suggested Reading 385–390

Internet Resources 391–392

INDEXES

Accommodations Index 393–394

Restaurant Index 395–396

General Index 397–413

About the Author

ABBREVIATIONS

a/c—air-conditioned
ATM—automatic teller machine
Av.—Avenida
Blv.—Búlevar (boulevard)
C—Celsius
Calz.—*Calzada* (thoroughfare, main road)
d—double occupancy
Fracc.—Fraccionimiento (subdivision)
Fco.—Francisco (proper name, as in "Fco. Villa")
Hwy.—Highway
km—kilometer

Km—kilometer marker
kph—kilometers per hour
IAMAT—International Association for Medical Assistance to Travelers
Nte.—Norte (north)
Ote.—Oriente (east)
Pte.—Poniente (west)
s—single occupancy
s/n—*sin número* (no street number)
t—triple occupancy
tel.—telephone number

LET US HEAR FROM YOU

We're especially interested in hearing from solo female travelers, handicapped travelers, people who've traveled with children, RVers, hikers, campers, and residents, both foreign and Oaxacan. We welcome the comments of business and professional people—hotel and restaurant owners, travel agents, government tourism staff—who serve Oaxaca travelers.

We welcome submissions of unusually good photos and drawings for possible use in future editions. If photos, send duplicate slides or slides from negatives; if drawings, send clear photocopies. Please include a self-addressed stamped envelope if you'd like your material returned. If we use it, we'll cite your contribution. Please address your responses to:

Moon Handbooks: Oaxaca
Avalon Travel Publishing
5855 Beaudry St.
Emeryville, CA 94608
email: info@travelmatters.com

MAPS

Oaxaca . . . . ii–iii

INTRODUCTION
The Land of Oaxaca 2
Vegetation Zones of Oaxaca 5
Oaxaca Regions, Governmental Districts,
and Capitals 44
Mesoamerica and Oaxaca 51
Native Peoples of Oaxaca 58

ON THE ROAD
Driving and Busing to Oaxaca 94
Driving and Busing within Oaxaca 103

OAXACA: THE CITY
Oaxaca City 128–129
Oaxaca City Downtown 130

AROUND THE VALLEY OF OAXACA
Valley of Oaxaca 161
Mitla Archaeological Zone 171
Monte Albán Archaeological Zone 186

PACIFIC RESORTS AND SOUTHERN SIERRA
Pacific Resorts and Southern Sierra . . 194–195

Puerto Ángel Area 196
Puerto Ángel 198
Bahías de Huatulco 212
Crucecita 214
Santa Cruz de Huatulco 216
Puerto Escondido 232–233
Laguna Manialtepec 234
Lagunas de Chacahua National Park 253

THE MIXTECA
The Mixteca 264–265
Nochixtlán 266
Tamazulapan 272
Huajuapan de León 286–287
Asunción Tlaxiaco 299

NORTHERN OAXACA
Northern Oaxaca 313
Tuxtepec 324–325
Huatla de Jiménez 334
Teotitlán del Camino 339

THE ISTHMUS: LAND OF PLENTY
The Isthmus 344–345
Tehuantepec 346
Downtown Juchitán 357
Salina Cruz 369

HANDBOOK DIVISIONS

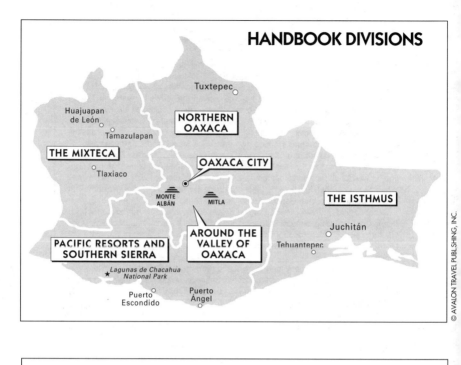

© AVALON TRAVEL PUBLISHING, INC.

MAP SYMBOLS

═══ Divided Highway	⊙ Capital City	✗ International Airport
══ Primary Road	○ City	🛢 Gas
══ Secondary Road	○ Town	⚑ Golf Course
═ ═ ═ Unpaved Road	★ Point of Interest	∧ Campground
- - - - Trail	• Accommodation	≜ Archaeological Zone
·········· Ferry	▾ Restaurant/Bar	▲ Mountain
⊢−⊢−⊣ Railroad	▪ Other Location	☇ Waterfall
◯ Mexico Route	♟ Church	+ Unique Natural Feature
◯ Mexico State Route	ⓉⓅ Trailer Park	⁘⁘ Mangrove

ACKNOWLEDGMENTS

Without the help of a host of kind Oaxacan people, this book would not have been possible. In Oaxaca City I owe a mountain of thanks to Martín Ruiz Camino, former Secretary of Tourism Development, and the present Secretary, Oscar Holm, and his excellent staff for the load of support they have given me. I owe the same to Teresa Morales and Patricia Ramírez at the Community Museums of Oaxaca. Likewise, I'm in debt to both "Chencho" Velasco at the Posada de Chencho and the sympathetic staffs of the Hotel Señorial and Hotel Rivera del Ángel, my headquarters in Oaxaca City for the first edition, and my friend Marí, the kind owner of Villas María where I stayed while researching the second edition. I owe a load of thanks to Jane and Thornton Robisson, owners of Casa Colonial, for their kind hospitality. I owe the same to guide Juan Montes Lara and his wife for sharing some of their deep knowledge of Oaxaca with me. I'm similarly in debt to author, chef, and cooking teacher Susana Trilling for the friendly welcome that she extended to me at her Rancho Aurora cooking school.

Farther afield, in the Valley of Oaxaca, I owe a big debt to Dr. Ignacio J. del Río Dueñas for introducing me to the cultivation of cochineal at his farm, Tlapanochestli. Much the same is due to Hector Joel Cruz and Victoria Jiménez Jiménez at San José del Mogote for taking the time to guide me around their town's community museum and archaeological site.

On the Pacific Coast, many thanks are due to Cali López of Posada Cañon Devata in Puerto Ángel and Gloria Esperanza Johnson of Shambala in Zipolite for their warmth and hospitality. I owe the same to my gentle guides, Gregorio Cruz Cruz, at Xadani, and Frédy Zárate, at Nopala.

In the Mixteca, I owe a big debt to Juan Cruz Reyes, Community Museum President at San Miguel Tequixtepec, for taking care of me, and to Elvia and Cari Cordoba Reyes for their kindness and excellent cooking. The same goes for sculptor Manuel Ruiz-Garcia, President of the Teposcolula Community Museum, and his *simpatico* friend, Amancio Odriozola. I feel equal gratitude to dance master and Municipal President Antonio Martínez Sánchez for his hospitality and excellent explanation of Yucunama's museum collection. Much credit is also due to Jesus Ramírez at Yucuita and Francisco Simon Reyes at San Miguel de Progreso for taking time to explain their museum collections to me.

In the north, at Huatla de Jiménez, I owe a load of thanks to Inez and Juvenal Cortez Rodríguez for taking time out to show me around their town and the same to Leonardo Altamirano and Catalina Casamiro of the Hotel Rinconcito for their kindness and hospitality.

In the Isthmus, my gratitude goes out to my guide José Luis Toral Sánchez, who went way beyond the call of duty to lead me to the Guiengola ruin at dusk, when the owls were hooting and the bats were fluttering about. The same is due to Casimiro Cano Alvarado, manager of the Lagunas company hostel, for his kindness and hospitality and to Salvador Mendoza at La Palapa de Chiva, for his patient explanation of the history of Playa La Ventosa.

Back in my hometown, I owe a mountain of thanks to the kind and sympathetic workers at my office-away-from-home, the Café Espresso Roma, where espresso maestro Miguel's famous lattes have become integral to my writing projects.

I give many thanks, moreover, to my friend and business partner, Halcea Valdes, who sympathetically adjusts her schedule to manage for me while I am on the road writing Moon Handbooks.

Finally, the most thanks of all go to my wife, Linda, who puts up with me being gone for long stretches, who comes to Mexico to join me for little vacations, and who skillfully manages our home front when I'm gone.

PREFACE

The once-neglected state of Oaxaca is now fulfilling its promise. Its capital has become one of Mexico's most enjoyable colonial cities. By day, people relax at plaza-front sidewalk cafés beneath shady arches and take in a seemingly slow-motion scene, reflecting the best of old Mexico. By night, the same plaza comes alive with entertainment, from mimes and crafts and dessert stalls to folkloric dance shows and band concerts.

Within a few blocks of the plaza, good restaurants and hotels, traditional markets, and a host of handicrafts shops and galleries offer a feast of food, comforts, and shopping opportunities.

The list goes on. Visitors who venture into the surrounding Valley of Oaxaca can sample much more—regal ruined cities, crafts villages, colorful native markets, beloved old churches, small community museums, and comfortable tourist Yu'u accommodations.

Farther afield, the delights of Oaxaca's regions beckon. Head south and explore the tufted strands of the Pacific coastal resorts of Huatulco, Puerto Ángel, and Puerto Escondido. Here visitors opt for a trove of outdoor adventures, from fishing and river rafting to paddling wildlife-rich coastal mangrove lagoons and hiking butterfly- and flower-bedecked tropical forest trails.

Travel northwest from Oaxaca City to the Mixteca to explore its magnificent old Dominican churches, ancient Mixtec kingdoms, waterfalls, limestone caves, great cypress groves, crystal springs, and colorful country markets. Or head to northern Oaxaca and the pine-tufted, wildlife-rich Sierra heights and beyond, to the fertile, tropical river country of the Papaloapan basin and Tuxtepec, Oaxaca's second city.

As a finale, head southeast to the Isthmus, the rich land of vivid, bustling markets and near-continuous festivals. Here virtually everyone enjoys an abundance of food and dancing—to the lovely, lilting strains of the beloved *Sandunga,* melody of the Isthmus.

Whatever options you choose, Oaxaca offers excitement, lots of friendly folks, relatively low prices, and a host of traditional Mexican delights. Regardless of the route you prefer, whether by back-road adventure or via the lap of luxury or a little bit of both, Oaxaca offers it. This book will show the way.

INTRODUCTION

LAND AND SEA

On the map of North America, Mexico's state of Oaxaca (wah-HAH-kah) makes up the southern bulge of Mexico, the region where the Mexican coastline thrusts into the Pacific like the belly of a frolicking Pacific dolphin. Oaxaca is a sizable place—with about 36,800 square miles (95,400 square km)—Mexico's fifth largest state, as big as a midsize U.S. state, such as Indiana, or an entire small European country, such as Portugal.

As in Mexico as a whole, mountains rule Oaxaca's landscape. From the U.S. border, Mexico's grand pair of mother ranges, the Sierra Madre Oriental in the east and Sierra Madre Occidental in the west, sweep southward a thousand miles until they reach Oaxaca, where they bend eastward and practically merge. In Oaxaca, the ranges, respectively called the Sierra Madre de Oaxaca and the Sierra Madre del Sur, form a broad, rumpled, pine-tufted landscape, dotted with 20 peaks in excess of 10,000 feet (3,000 meters). Only the mostly narrow southern coastal plain, one large valley, and a few scattered lesser vales provide enough level cropland to support large towns. From those few valleys, a handful of streams, blocked and forced by the mountains to twist through deep canyons, make their way to the sea.

A Closer Look

Imagine navigating a high-altitude airship, borne by the tropical breezes, over Oaxaca's vivid shoreline, mountain, and valley panorama. Start your adventure in the southwest, at Oaxaca's coastal border with its neighboring state of Guerrero. Here, as you drift eastward above the green coastal plain directly below, the broad estuary of the **Río Verde** empties into the sea. The mightiest river system entirely within in the state, the Río Verde's tributaries drain a major fraction of western Oaxaca, including the central valley, where it is known as the Río Atoyac.

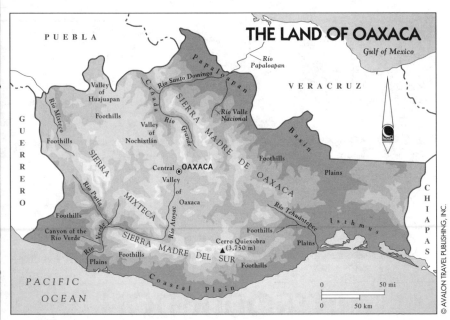

THE LAND OF OAXACA

PUEBLA

Gulf of Mexico

Río Papaloapan

VERACRUZ

Valley of Huajuapan

Río Santo Domingo

Río Valle Nacional

GUERRERO

Foothills

Foothills

Valley of Nochixtlán

Río Grande

SIERRA MADRE DE OAXACA

Basin

Foothills

Plains

Central OAXACA

Valley of Oaxaca

MIXTECA

Río Atoyac

Río Tehuántepec

Isthmus

CHIAPAS

Foothills

Canyon of the Río Verde

Río Verde

SIERRA MADRE DEL SUR

Foothills

Cerro Quiexobra (3,750 m)

Plains

Plains

Foothills

Foothills

PACIFIC OCEAN

Coastal Plain

0   50 mi

0   50 km

As you continue easterly, the forest-swathed peaks of the Sierra Madre del Sur stretch ahead, cresting at cloud-capped 12,300-foot (3,750-meter) **Cerro Quiexobra,** Oaxaca's tallest mountain. To your right far below, Pacific waves wash a coastline indented with small bays and lined with wildlife-rich mangrove wetlands and pearly, palm-tufted strands. In succession, you pass over the small resorts of **Puerto Escondido, Puerto Ángel,** and the **Bays of Huatulco,** where visitors flock year-round to enjoy the delights of South Seas Mexico.

To the Isthmus and North

As you continue, the coastal plain gradually broadens as the Sierra shrinks to mere foothills at the **Isthmus of Tehuantepec,** the neck of land where Mexico (and indeed the entire American continent) shrivels to a scant 125 miles (200 km) in width. East beyond the Isthmus, in the remote region Oaxacans call the **Chimalapas,** you spot a new range of mountains, the **Sierra Atravesada,** rising and stretching east into the neighboring state of Chiapas. The Atravesadas' isolated, rugged, summits, sylvan forests, and

deep gorges shelter one of Mexico's last remaining troves of endangered plants, birds, mammals, and reptiles.

From the Isthmus, other Oaxaca regions beckon. Turning around to the left and heading your airship northwest, you follow the valley of the **Río Tehuantepec,** passing over the bustling, tradition-rich small cities of Juchitán and Tehuantepec and their luxuriant hinterlands of fruit, corn, and cotton. Soon, on your right toward the north, rises the grand **Sierra Madre de Oaxaca.** You see a succession of peaks stretching west a hundred miles, from the rugged homeland of the indigenous **Mixe** (MEE-shay) people in Oaxaca's northeast to the equally mountainous domain of their neighbors, the Sierra **Zapotec** at the northern center of the state.

Drawn by what you might find beyond the mountain crest, you navigate your airship due north, over the Mixe country, above the gigantic massif of **Zempoaltepetl** (only 9,000 feet, but composed nevertheless of a score of separate peaks), the Mixes' holy mountain. Beyond that, the mountains gradually drop to foothills, where you see a great river-laced plain of tropical forest checkered with pasture, farms, and small towns, stretching north past Oaxaca's northern lowland border with the state of Veracruz all the way to the Gulf of Mexico. The Oaxaca portion, known as the **Papaloapan** (pah-pah-loh-AH-pahn) for the great river system that drains it, encompasses the **Chinantla** and the **Mazateca,** homelands of the indigenous Chinantec and Mazatec peoples.

The Central Valley of Oaxaca and the Mixteca

Continue your breeze-blown journey, now turning southwest, over the mountain Zapotec country to the **Valley of Oaxaca,** the heartland of the Zapotec people and Oaxacan civilization for more than 3,000 years. Below you spreads Oaxaca's great highland central valley complex: farms, pastures, towns, and villages, radiating in three 50-mile fingers (east, northwest, and south) from the capital city, Oaxaca.

Drawn on by the mystery of the mist-shroud-

the view from Isla Soyaltepec, with cloud-capped Cerro Rabón in the background

---

OAXACA SUMMARY

Land area: 36,860 square miles, or 95,470 square kilometers (fifth largest among 31 Mexican states and the federal district)

Tallest mountain: Cerro Quiexobra, 12,300 feet (3,750 meters)

Population (1995): 3,224,000 (tenth largest among Mexican states)

Indigenous population: 50 percent of the total

Population density: 88 per square mile, 34 per square kilometer

Average daily income per active worker: US$4.60

Average school grade attained per person: 5.4

Illiteracy: 23 percent

---

ed western mountains, you continue a hundred miles northwest, following the valley of the upper **Río Atoyac,** where the Sierra de Oaxaca rises again. There, you gaze down on a broad mountain and high plateau landscape, much of it tragically eroded. Oaxacans call this the Mixteca, the domain of the Mixtec people, proud transmitters of a major share of Oaxaca's ancient tradition. From your high vista, you see a landscape as creased as an old chopping board, dotted with tiny settlements scattered atop rugged mesas and tucked into deep gorges.

A closer look reveals natural divisions in the land. In the center you see the **Mixteca Alta—** high, cool, and cloud-shadowed. To the northwest, bordering the states of Guerrero and Puebla, lies the **Mixteca Baja,** a lower, desert plateau-land of cactus, maguey, and dwarf palm. To the south, toward the Pacific, at the place where your imaginary journey began, the mountains drop to the verdant, jungle-draped foothills, lush river canyons, and coastal farms of the **Mixteca de la Costa** (Mixtec coastal region).

CLIMATE

Despite its deep southern latitude, Oaxaca's elevation, cooling sea breezes, and summer rain showers moderate the heat of its plentiful sunshine. Most of the state, excepting the remote mountain summits, basks in the tropics, never feeling the bite of frost.

The seashore and coastal plain, including all of the Isthmus, is truly a land of endless summer. Winter days are typically warm and rainless, peaking at 82–88°F (28–31°C) and dropping to 65–75°F (18–24°C) by midnight

Summers on the Oaxaca beaches are warmer and wetter. Mornings are usually bright and balmy, warming to around 90°F (32°C). Early afternoons, clouds often gather and bring short, sometimes heavy, cooling showers. Later, the sun reappears, drying the beaches and warming the breeze just in time to enjoy a dazzling Oaxaca *puesta del sol* (sunset).

Visitors to Oaxaca City experience similar but more temperate seasons. Midwinter days are mild, typically peaking between 70 and 75°F (21–24°C). Expect cool but frost-free winter nights between 45 and 60°F (9–16°C). Oaxaca City summers are delightful, with afternoons typically in the mid- to upper 80s (28–32°C) and pleas-ant evenings in the mid-70s (24–26°C), perfect for strolling. May, before the rains, is usually the warmest, with June, July, and August, highs being moderated by afternoon showers.

Visitors should take note that Oaxaca's rainfall, like all of Mexico's, is strongly seasonal. Most years, nearly all the rainfall accumulates during the summer and early fall. Rains taper off in October and November and don't usually return until June. May, before the rains, is typically Mexico's warmest month. Relief comes with the cooling summer showers.

Many trees, especially along the coast, respond to the winter-spring drought by losing their leaves by February. This might make a typical late winter-early spring Oaxaca landscape appear barren to the visitor in March even though the same area will be blooming with greenery by July or August. If you prefer lush, jungle verdure to be part of your Mexico experience, you'll enjoy plenty if you visit during the seven months from July through January.

FLORA AND FAUNA

Luxuriant tropical foliage is one of the reasons that visitors are pleasantly surprised when they visit Oaxaca during the rainy summer-fall season. Then excursions through Oaxaca's forest hinterlands offer an exotic experience. Leafy trees are swathed with mats of vines; giant-leafed philodendrons climb toward the canopy, while tropical hangers-on, such as spiny, pineapple-like red bromeliads and big, white-flowered orchids perch atop available branches.

Forests are not the only places that bloom. Wildflowers sprout everywhere, especially on upland plateaus. There, summer rains bring carpets of roadside blossoms—petite purple daisies, blue and yellow lupine, morning glories, tiny magenta sweet peas, and dozens more.

The dry winter-spring season also brings its surprising rewards. Many trees, especially along the coast, having lost their leaves, flower in February. Hundreds of varieties of the pea family bloom in riotous red, pink, yellow, and white. Now and then visitors stop, attracted by something remarkable, such as a host of white flowers blooming from the apparently dead branches of the appropriately named *palo de muerto* (tree of the dead). Other times, strikingly beautiful tree blossoms, such as the yellow, roselike *rosa amarilla,* tempt one's poetic imagination.

In dry country, cactus-like plants rule. Dotted all over the state, fields of maguey in ranks and files like obedient botanical battalions wait to be harvested for *mescal.* In other places, you will often see farmyards fenced with bulging nopal (prickly pear) cacti, their thick leaves studded with red tunas (cactus apples). And, on the road some drowsy afternoon, when you least expect it, a big candelabra cactus might appear around a bend, bristling with a house-size row of dozens of upright fluted green columns.

VEGETATION ZONES

Plants must adapt to the soil, sun, and rain, and Oaxaca's astonishingly diverse plant population reflects the state's varied landscape. Of Mexico's 14 major vegetation zones, ranging from high desert to tropical rainforest, at least eight occur in Oaxaca.

Directly along Oaxaca's paved national high-

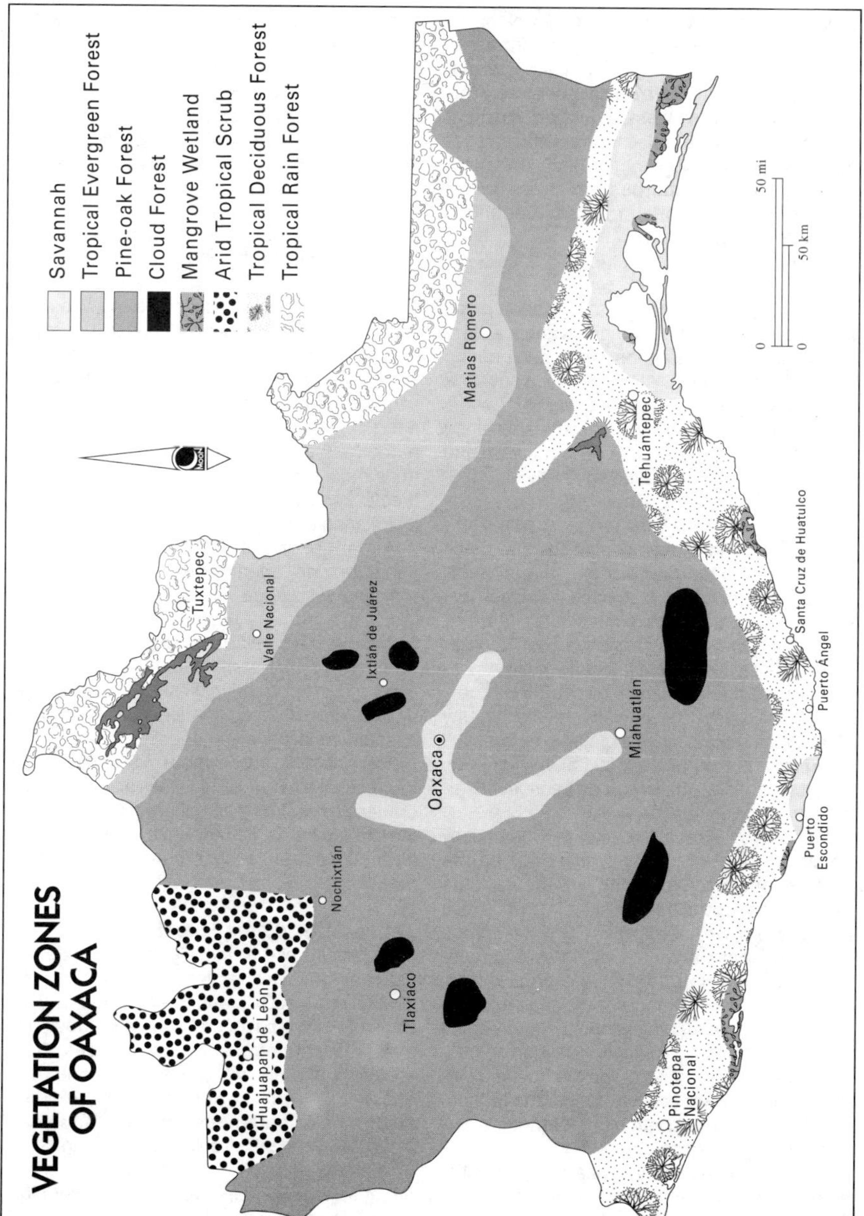

© AVALON TRAVEL PUBLISHING, INC.

VEGETATION ZONES OF OAXACA

Savannah

Tropical Evergreen Forest

Pine-oak Forest

Cloud Forest

Mangrove Wetland

Arid Tropical Scrub

Tropical Deciduous Forest

Tropical Rain Forest

50 mi

50 km

0

0

Tuxtepec

Valle Nacional

Matías Romero

Tehuántepec

Ixtlán de Juárez

Oaxaca

Miahuatlán

Santa Cruz de Huatulco

Puerto Ángel

Nochixtlán

Puerto Escondido

Huajuapan de León

Tlaxiaco

Pinotepa Nacional

ways you can visit six of these zones: Near the seacoast lie extensive swaths of **savanna, deciduous tropical forest,** and **pine-oak forest.** Inland you can add the **tropical evergreen forest, tropical rainforest,** and **arid tropical scrub** to your botanical itinerary. Oaxaca's remaining major two vegetation zones, the **cloud forest** and **high coniferous forest,** are accessible only on high, often roadless, mountain slopes and summits.

Savanna

In their natural state, Oaxaca's savanna lands appear as flat, palm-dotted grasslands, watery during the summer and dry and brown during the winter and spring. Although much savanna has been converted to pasture or farmland, some pristine stretches lie along coast, notably along Hwy. 200 near the Lagunas de Chacahua and along the Isthmus shoreline south of Hwy. 190, east of Juchitán.

Although grass rules the savanna, palms give it character. One of the most familiar in Oaxaca is the **Mexican fan palm,** or *palma real (Sabal Mexicana),* seasonally festooned with black fruit with leaves spread flat like a señorita's fan. The *palma real,* sometimes called the Oaxaca palm, resembles its cousin, the palmetto of the American southeast. The *palma real,* moreover, doesn't limit itself to the savanna. It appears in many other Oaxaca landscapes, notably in picturesque dwarf form in the cactus forest alongside Hwy. 190, just north of Huajuapan de León, in deserty northwest Oaxaca.

Visitors to Oaxaca's coastal resorts usually enjoy the sight of plenty of **coconut palms** *(Cocos nucifera),* by many measures the world's most useful tree. Local folks, who call it the *cocotero,* use nearly all of its parts: fronds for thatch, mats, and baskets; lumber for construction; and nuts for cooling drinks, fruit, candy, and oil. Nothing seems to symbolize the tropics more than a coconut palm drooping lazily over the beach or its fronds rustling gently in the tropical breeze. The coconut is completely benign with one exception: falling coconuts are no joke. Watch out for them, especially during a breeze.

Another interesting savanna resident is the **sea grape** *(Coccolobis uvifera),* a genuine, although unusual, grape, often found growing on or behind seashore sand dunes. Like many true grapes, its vines sprout large round leaves and edible reddish-purple berries, which are probably too sour and astringent for wine.

If you see what look like several grapefruits sprouting from a tree trunk, you are probably looking at a **gourd tree,** or *calabaza (Crescentia alata).* The mature gourds, brown and hard, were handsomely carved and fitted with gold handles for Aztec emperors to drink chocolate out of. Oaxacans, who still call them by the ancient name *jícaras,* use them as bowls (notably women, on the west Oaxaca coast, who carry them all day at market on their heads, like a hat).

Its petite, pumpkin-shaped gourds both identify and name the **sandbox tree,** or *jabillo,* because they once served as desktop boxes full of sand for drying ink. The Aztecs, however, named it the exploding tree, because its ripe fruits burst their seeds forth with a bang like a firecracker. Beware of its poisonous seeds and its irritating sap.

A **mangrove wetland** *(manglar),* a vegetation sub-zone, often borders a savanna's watery seaward edge. Healthy mangrove wetlands are primary nurseries for uncounted forms of aquatic plants and animals. While a number of prime spots exist, Laguna Manialtepec, a half-hour drive west of Puerto Escondido, is one of Oaxaca's richest and most accessible mangrove wetlands.

The plant both synonymous with and essential to the mangrove wetland is the **red mangrove,** or *mangle colorado,* a tree that seems to stand in the water on stilts. Its new roots grow downward from above; a time-lapse photo would show it marching, as if on stilts, into the lagoon.

Tropical Deciduous Forest

Great swaths of this "friendly" or "short-tree" forest coat Oaxaca's coastline, especially along coastal Hwy. 200 around Puerto Ángel and the Bays of Huatulco. As the label "deciduous" implies, this is the forest where the trees, in response to the dry winter weather, go dormant and lose their leaves. For visitors, the upside to all the winter barrenness is that many trees' leaves show bright fall colors; then, at the height of winter bleakness, they sprout profusions of bright red, yellow, pink, and white winter blossoms from apparently lifeless branches.

One of the most strikingly beautiful of these is the *rosa amarilla*, or yellowsilk shellseed (*Cochlospermum vitifolium*). Although not a rose, it looks every bit like a wild yellow rose when its big flowers sprout from bare branches in the early spring. After the flowers fall, leaves bud and apple-shaped green fruit grows, turning brown into pods, which pop open and release silky fluff.

The **silk cotton tree** *(Ceiba pentandra)*, another of the tropical deciduous forest's major actors, yields a form of lightweight, cottony kapok fiber. Local folks, who call it the *cuajilote,* prize it for its spectacular large white (or red in cultivated varieties) blossoms with big, brushy pink stamens. In dense forest the silk cotton tree stays relatively short, but isolated it can grow to a wide-crowned giant with bulging buttresses on the lower trunk.

Lovers of Hawaii will be pleasantly surprised to find that a number of their favorite island plants are Mexican natives. The **frangipani** or **plumeria,** prized by native Mexicans for its heavenly orange-blossom-like fragrance, was first classified and named as *Plumeria acutifolia* by French botanist Plumier. Pick some of its white, pink, or yellow whorl-lobed five-petaled flowers and put one behind your ear to get yourself into the mañana mood.

In Oaxaca as in Hawaii, you always know Christmas is coming because of another famous Mexico native, the **poinsettia** or *catarina (Euphorbia pulcherrima),* first classified in 1828 by Joel R. Poinsett, an early ambassador to Mexico. Interestingly, the poinsettia's red blooms, in great abundance at Oaxaca City's Christmas fiestas, are not actually flower petals, but green leaves turned red, known technically as bracts.

Not nearly so benign is the *mala mujer* (bad woman), southern Mexico's poison ivy bush *(Cnidoscolus urens)*. Before venturing out through the Oaxaca coastal forest, ask someone to point out its drooping, oak-like, five-lobed leaves and tiny flowers. Otherwise, you might risk a stinging rash from the nettle-like hairs on the leaf surfaces and the long stalks.

If you go out on your hike but forget your makeup kit, you can improvise with the **lipstick tree** or *achiote (Bicha orellana)*. It appears as an ordinary shrub, but marked with brownish-green soft burrs above long, heart-shaped leaves. The surprise comes when you crush the burrs and discover their bright red-orange pulp, source of annatto dye, which warriors used to make themselves look fierce and which manufacturers now use to color cheese, silk, and lipstick.

One of the showiest of roadside inhabitants is *mata ratón* (mouse killer, *Gliricidia sepium*), a plant that lives up to its name. Despite its fragrant spring swirls of pink and white pea-like blossoms, Oaxacans grind its bark and leaves with cooked corn for a very effective rat and mouse poison (which, beware, is also poisonous to dogs). It can be further identified by its four- to six-inch-long seedpods.

Pine-Oak Forest

About an hour's drive inland, at elevations of about 5,000 feet, the tropics give way to the cooling heights of the pine-oak forest, Oaxaca's most extensive vegetation zone.

Although pine-oak forest once covered half of Oaxaca's landscape, people, beginning thousands of years ago with Oaxaca's original farmers, cleared much of it for fields, especially in the central valley and surrounding mountainsides. Nevertheless, extensive upland tracts of pine-oak forest still remain, doing their beneficent work, storing moisture, anchoring soil against erosion, and providing food and shelter for hosts of animals.

As you enter the pine-oak forest from lower elevations, you usually see the oaks first, occurring in two broad families. Mexicans identify them as either the *encino* (evergreen, small-leafed) or the *roble* (deciduous, large-leafed), both resembling oaks that dot the hills and valleys of California and the U.S. Southwest. Clustered in their branches and scattered in the shade are the *bellota* (acorns), which unmistakably mark them as oaks.

At higher elevations the oaks gradually give way to pines, which, in Oaxaca, often grow in pure stands above six or seven thousand feet. Pines are easy to identify, because of their long needle-like leaves, which grow in bundles, in contrast to the shorter needles of other conifers, such as spruce and fir, which commonly grow feather-shaped leaves made of rows of needles individually attached to the leaf stem.

Although pines are easily distinguished from other tree families, individual pine species are

Tonalá's old sabino grove

often hard to differentiate from each other. Nevertheless, examining the cones (which often conceal edible, tasty nuts) and the needles may yield identifying clues to at least a few members of this populous and very useful Mexican tree family.

Among the varieties you may encounter is the **Mexican white pine** *(Pinus ayachuite),* similar to the white pine of the western United States. Local folks, who call it the *pinabete* or *ayacahuite,* know it by its very large (more than eight inches, 20 centimeters) cones and long, four- to six-inch needles, which hang in clusters of five.

Others you might see are the **Montezuma pine,** locally called the *ocote macho* (dark three- to nine-inch dark cones, long, drooping needles, five to a bundle) or the **Aztec pine** or *pino real* (shiny, small brown one- to two-inch cones and long, bright green needles in bundles of three—very useful for turpentine, tar, soap, and medicines).

Often associated in the same territory as pines and oaks is Mexico's renowned national tree, the ***ahuehuete*** (ah-way-WAY-tay) or *sabino.* Nearly every visitor to Oaxaca City sees the country's most famous specimen, at the village of Santa María del Tule, half an hour east of the city, where droves of visitors arrive, some on bended knee, to wonder at what is know locally as El Tule. Probably the most massive tree in Latin America, it's as big around at the trunk as it is high: approximately 150 feet (46 meters).

Other more modest but still impressive *ahue-huete* specimens occur in outlying areas, often in majestic groves near water, which accounts for its name, which translates as "old one of the water." When traveling through the inland countryside, especially along stream bottoms in the Mixteca (northwest Oaxaca), you may be able to spot an old *ahuehuete* by its general appearance, unusual for Mexico: a thick, deep green crown and reddish-brown, vertically grooved bark, not unlike a California redwood. Up close you will identify it by its round, reticulated two-inch cones and its feathery green spruce-like leaves (which led botanists to classify it as a type of cypress, namely the Montezuma bald cypress, *Taxodium mucronatum).*

Tropical Evergreen Forest

In rainy foothill and low mountain areas, especially along the north Gulf slope, the lush, dense undergrowth and tall, leaf-crowned trees of the tropical evergreen forest decorate the hillsides. Here, most extensively in the north along Hwy. 175 around Valle Nacional, and, to a lesser extent, in the southern Sierra foothills along highways north from the Pacific Coast, huge trees and vine-strewn thickets often overhang the highway. As the road curls through a dark, isolated, liana-draped canyon, momentarily I often feel as if I am traversing a forgotten corner of some prehistoric lost world, where a last remnant dinosaur might rear up at any moment.

But the bright visions of the tropical evergreen forest invariably dissipate such Jurassic Park images and jolt me back to its vivid jungle realities: a green iguana, looking every bit as primitive as a dinosaur, slithers across the road; a screeching swarm of bright green parrots swoops overhead; or a big, bird-size butterfly flutters in a roadside patch of sunlight. Overhead, huge-leafed climbing plants, such as the **ceriman** *(Monstera deliciosa),* hang by thick ropy vines on the trunks of accommodating trees. Local people, who know the ceriman as the *piñanona,* enjoy its sweet, juicy, corn cob-shaped fruit and find relief from aches and pains by drinking a tea brewed from its leaves.

No Oaxaca jungle trip would be complete without experiencing the **strangler fig,** known by the hideously accurate local label *matapalo* (killer tree). A strangler fig seed, once it sprouts in the crotch of a victim tree, will grow, finally entwining its host in a suffocating embrace. By then the strangler fig will have planted hairy "air roots" for ground support and will most likely go on living long after its victim has died. In a peculiarly national quirk of character, many Mexicans prize such dead victim-tree trunks. Workers scour the forests, cutting, gathering and polishing these death embraces, to decorate living room corners or support elaborate outdoor *palapa* roofs, especially in fancy open-air restaurants.

In numerous stretches of Oaxaca's tropical evergreen forest, local folks cultivate coffee beneath the shady canopy. Even if coffee *(Coffea arabica),* known to its Mexican growers as *cafeto,* weren't commercially important, people could still enjoy it as an attractive ornamental, with its shiny, ribbed green leaves and red holly-like berries. Even though coffee shrubs are quite common in Oaxaca's jungly foothills, you have to look carefully for them, because they grow best in the deep shade beneath taller trees. If you don't spot the ripe red berries, look instead for the white flowers, which are as fragrant as those of coffee's cousin, the gardenia.

Another popular import to Oaxaca's tropical forestland is the **African tulip tree** *(Spathodea campanulata).* Often seen right at roadside, a host of spectacular big red blooms caps a lush leafy crown like a host of heavenly scarlet bells.

Nearly as spectacular in its own exotic way is that cousin of the banana, the **heliconia** *(Heliconia latispatha).* Because of the resemblance, Mexicans call it the *platanillo,* or "little banana." In contrast to the fruit of the banana, the heliconia's golden-orange flower-like leaves (bracts), reminiscent of bird-of-paradise blossoms, are the main attraction. To happen upon one for the first time in a garden or in the wild—hanging amongst the greenery in descending golden-orange segments like a ladder for leprechauns—is an experience rarely forgotten.

Tropical Rainforest

This is the "forest primeval" of legend, where heavy rains nourish grand evergreen hardwoods whose great leafy crowns tower up to 200 feet (60 meters) over layers of lesser trees. Here and there, rays of sunlight shine through and nurture a luxuriant undergrowth of palms, bamboo, orchids, and bromeliads.

The rainforest gives rise to many unique, sometimes bizarre, adaptations. The big trees fortify themselves against their top-heavy bulk by developing ponderous buttresses, reaching up to a dozen feet from the ground and spreading six or eight feet from the trunk. On the other hand, shorter, lower-canopy trees commonly drop fibrous filaments, which eventually root and grow into strange, stilt-like side-trunks as far as 50 feet (15 meters) from the original trunk.

bamboo thriving in the rainforest

Oaxaca's rainforests, which once spread in a continuous green swath along its northern border with the state of Veracruz, are steadily being logged and replaced by farms and ranches. Nevertheless, sizable tracts still remain, much in roadless areas on both sides of Hwy. 175 around Valle Nacional, Isthmus Hwy. 185, and its offshoot, Hwy. 147, which runs northwest, through lowland Mixe territory, paralleling the Veracruz border.

The acknowledged king of the Mexican rainforest community is the **mahogany,** which local people, who call it the *caoba,* often point to with pride. The label refers to a number of similar trees of the genus *Swietenia,* which grow throughout the Mexican and Central American rainforests. Although the original mahogany *(Swietenia mahogani)* does not grow in Mexico, some of its cousins, such as *Swietenia macrophylla,* do. Oaxacans prize it for its handsome reddish wood, much valued for furniture. You can identify it by its half-foot-long slender leaves and four-inch woody fruits, curved like a vulture's head, thus the tongue-twisting indigenous label *zopilo zontecomacuahuitl* (buzzard-head tree).

If along the roadside you spot a tall tree with diagonal slashes on its bark (for gathering sap), it's most likely either a rubber tree or the chewing-gum tree, the **chicle,** locally known as the *chicozapote.* Chewing gum, made from the chicle's sap (notice the Chiclets in every store), spread all over the world during the early 20th century and continues to gum up sidewalks and schoolroom desks from San Francisco to Samarkand. Additionally, chicle trees, known to botanists as *Acrasuzapote,* yield hard, very durable wood and, from small pinkish-white flowers, luscious round, cream-colored fruits.

Of both commercial and decorative importance is the **rubber tree** *(Castilla elastica),* the source of so-called Panama rubber, once made (before synthetics) for raincoats, tennis balls, and tires. Indigenous Mexicans, who still call it the *hule* (OO-lay), have used it for millennia for making the ball for the ceremonial game of *tlatchtli.* Besides the diagonal grooves (which guide the milky sap into cups) on the trunk, you can identify the rubber tree by its foot-long, elliptical, leathery dark-green leaves, shiny on the top side and hairy underneath.

Among Oaxaca's most useful rainforest natives is the **chocolate tree** *(Theobromo cacao),* the "food of the gods" of the preconquest kings of Mexico. Before the conquest *cacao* seeds served as currency. Although these days most people don't like to think of such things, historical records indicate that a healthy slave usually traded for about 100 beans; a small animal, for perhaps about five. Most likely you'll identify the *cacao,* growing as a smallish tree beneath the forest canopy, by spotting its 10-inch (25-centimeter) pods, which sprout right from the trunk. Workers break open the ripe, leathery yellow pods to harvest the trove of beans inside.

Arid Tropical Scrub

Although it looks a lot like a desert, Oaxaca's arid tropical scrub vegetation zone, along its northwest border with the state of Puebla, averages as much rainfall as San Francisco. In Oaxaca, however, the rain comes within a few summer months, often in cloudburst deluges that quickly drain away, leaving the people, animals, and plants to cope with six months of winter-spring drought.

The arid tropical scrub zone's most successful plants, succulents such as the cactuses and their cousins the agaves, cope by storing moisture in fleshy leaves, trunks, and stems. None is more successful or important than the **prickly pear** *(Opuntia tuna),* which, from its role in Aztec legend and consequent presence on the Mexican flag, is an important national symbol. Moreover, it is especially useful as a fence plant, for cattle food, and, most of all, for its delicious red tunas, "cactus apple" fruit, which festoon its fleshy leaves.

The prickly pear is but one member of a broad look-alike family, known in Mexico generally as the *nopal.* Another, especially benign relative, known to botanists as *Platyopuntia,* is cultivated both for its tasty, spine-free leaves and, in Oaxaca, for red **cochineal** dye. Although once commercially very important but now largely supplanted by synthetics, cochineal is still produced in a few Valley of Oaxaca communities. It turns out that a certain scale insect, *Dactylopius coccus,* loves to munch on the *Platyopuntia* cactus leaves. When the insects have eaten their fill, the people gather, dry, and crush their bodies, which yield a brilliant scarlet dye prized by weavers.

Another useful domesticated member of the arid tropical scrub community is the **maguey** (mah-GAY), or century plant, so-called because it's said to bloom once, then die, after 100 years of growth, although its lifetime is usually closer to 50 years. The maguey, moreover, has a number of well-known relatives. These include the very useful *mescal*, renowned for distilled liquor; *lechuguilla*, for *ixtle* fiber; and sisal, also useful for fiber. All of these, of the genus *Agave*, mature as a rose-like cluster of leathery, long, pointed gray-green leaves, from which a single flower stalk eventually blooms.

Wondrous gardens of wild cacti proliferate in the arid tropical scrub zone of northwest Oaxaca. Hard to miss is the **bravo** *(Neobuxbaumia mexcalaensis)*, which often appears right at roadside, rising as pencil-shaped fluted columns. Bravos frequently grow in spectacular grand forests stretching to far rocky horizons.

Often growing in the same habitat is the *candelabro,* or **candelabra cactus** (Stenoceris weberi), which, most likely, you will see in a community of spectacular many-columned giants, like house-size menorahs, dotting the landscape for miles.

Cloud Forest and High Coniferous Forest

Oaxaca's two rarest plant and wildlife communities lie on the slopes and summits of high, remote mountains. The easiest, safest route is to hire a guide who can take you to isolated, dewy mountainsides where, beginning around 6,000 feet, you will first meet the plant and wildlife community of the cloud forest. Most botanists believe the cloud forest plants to be Ice Age remnants of a time when Mexico's climate was much cooler than today. The proof is in the unusual specimens, many of which appear to have been transported directly across the Gulf of Mexico from the mountain forests of Georgia or North Carolina. In Oaxacan cloud forests, you may see the brilliant reds and oranges of **liquidambar,** the lovely white flowers of **dogwood,** or the white bark and tan falling leaves of **beech.**

Besides those, you might experience some of the cloud forest's even more ancient vestiges, dating from the age of the dinosaurs. They include the giant Mexican **tree ferns** *(Cyathea mexicana)* with their long feathery fronds, dotted underside with ranks of brown spores. New fronds, which are born curling out of the treetops, account for the tree fern's local name, *rabo de mico* (monkey's tail).

Other such relics are the bromeliads and orchids, which as epiphytes merely enjoy physical support in their hosts' branches (unlike parasites, which feed on their hosts). **Bromeliads,** members of the pineapple family, love the drippy cloud forest environment, collecting water in their cup-like leaf folds. Of the dozens of Mexican species, one of the best known is the showy *piñuela (Guzmannia lingulata),* whose roseate central leaf cluster matures from green to red, finally appearing as an exotic scarlet flower.

Among the **orchids** you will most likely first see the very widespread *bayoneta* or *pata de paloma* (dove's foot), which thrives in every humid Oaxaca environment from mangrove lagoons to cloud forests. You can recognize the *bazyoneta* by its clusters of fleshy, drooping green leaves, topped by showy white flowers that age to a mellow golden hue.

Follow your guide even higher and you will reach the zone of **high coniferous forest,** which in Oaxaca probably exists only as a few scattered roadless, cloud-swathed green alpine islands, with vegetation resembling upper Rocky Mountain slopes in the United States and Canada. In Oaxaca, as you climb above about 9,000 feet (2,700 meters), you will likely pass through a zone of mixed pines, alders, and firs, reigned over by the regal **Montezuma pine** *Pinus montezumae,* distinguished by its long, pendulous cones and rough, ruddy bark, reminiscent of the sugar pine of the western United States

Ascending still higher, you may pass through pure stands of **sacred fir** (Abies religiosa), which your guide will probably know as *oyamel* or *abeto.* You can identify them by lovely violet-blue cones and typical fir-like needles, which grow in rows along the branches. Even higher, the firs will eventually thin out, giving way to bunchgrass and bushy **Mexican juniper** *(monticola),* with its edible, waxy blue berries.

For more details of Oaxaca's marvelous plants, consult M. Walter Pesman's delightfully readable *Meet Flora Mexicana* (which, unfortunately, is out of print, but major libraries often have a copy). Also informative is the popular paperback *Handbook of Mexican Roadside*

Flora, by Charles T. Mason Jr. and Patricia B. Mason. (See Suggested Reading.)

MAMMALS

Although thousands of years of human hunting and habitat encroachment have generally reduced their numbers, many of Oaxaca's native animal species still thrive in the wild. While some animals sensitive to human presence, such as jaguars, howler monkeys, and tapirs, are now rarely seen in Oaxaca, others, such as foxes, coyotes, coatimundis, and peccaries, seem unaffected by, and sometimes even appear to benefit from, human presence.

The exciting reality of animals in the wild is the reward of visitors who take time to visit them in their own wilderness home grounds. Sylvan stretches, such as the pine-oak woodlands coating mountainsides both north and south of Oaxaca City, the thick forests of the Huatulco preserve, or the rich Manialtepec mangrove wetland near Puerto Escondido, are ripe with wildlife-viewing opportunities for those willing to get off the beaten track and quietly watch and wait.

peccary

BOB RACE

Armadillos, Coatimundis, Peccaries, and Bats

The benefits of quiet isolation once came to me when, lazing on a tropical beach, I spotted my first armadillo *(Dasypus novemcinctus).* Although it behaved much like the familiar opossum, I was struck by its reptilian-like shell. The armadillo was going about its business, nosing through the forest-edge leaf cover nearby. Not seeming to possess particularly good eyesight, the pre-occupied armadillo didn't notice when I crept in for a closer look. He waddled right up and sniffed my shoe, which evidently gave him such a scare that he scuttled back into the woods in a flash.

One of the Mexicans' favorite animals is the raccoon–like **coatimundi** *(Nasua narica),* known in Mexico as *coati,* or *tejon,* the Spanish name for badger. While many city Mexicans, charmed by the coatimundi's acrobatic antics and inquisitive nature, keep them as pets, hungry country folks enjoy them for culinary reasons. You can identify one by its long nose and straight, usually vertically held tail. Watch for them at country markets.

The pig-like **collared peccary** *(Tayassu tajacu)* is definitely *not* one of Oaxaca's endangered species. Known locally as the *jabalí,* the Spanish name for the much larger European wild boar, it eats most anything and thrives in nearly all environments—often not far from towns and villages. The gray-to-brown, short-haired *jabalís,* although normally shy when encountered alone, sometimes congregate in large groups and become aggressive. People have occasionally reported being chased and, in one case, forced up a tree, by collared peccaries.

Bats *(murciélagos)* are widespread in Oaxaca, home to around two or three times as many bat species as the entire United States. In Oaxaca, bats were once widely worshipped, and even today, as everywhere, they are both feared and misunderstood. Shortly before sundown, bats emerge from their cave and forest roosts and silently flit through the air in search of insects. Most people, sitting outside enjoying the early evening, will mistake their darting silhouettes for those of birds who, except for owls, don't generally fly at night.

The nonvampire Oaxacan bats carry their vampire cousins' odious reputation with forbearance. They go about their good works, pollinating flowers, clearing the air of pesky gnats and mosquitoes, ridding cornfields of mice, and dropping seeds, thereby restoring forests.

Monkeys

Oaxaca's remote mountains and jungles, notably in the Chimalapas region in the eastern Isthmus of Tehuantepec, still shelter a number of rare and endangered species. Accompanied by a competent tracker and suitably equipped with a jeep and a week's worth of supplies, you may be lucky enough to catch glimpses of Mexico's two seldom-seen primates, the **spider** and **howler monkeys.** The black spider monkey, whom your tracker will probably know as the *chango* or *mono de araña,* congregates in groups and uses its spindly arms and legs (thus the "spider" label) and its prehensile tail to reach its favorite wild fruits. Although its entertaining antics and endearingly mischievous ways have earned the *chango* a place as a pet in many Mexican homes, its present rarity is due in large part to its contribution to the diet of many poor indigenous families.

The even rarer howler monkey, called locally *saraguato* or *aullador,* is, by contrast, extremely shy and retiring. Seldom seen even in captivity, howler monkeys *(Alouatta palliata)* withdraw far into the forest as man encroaches. Consider yourself lucky if somewhere in Oaxaca's eastern jungle fastness you can draw close enough to hear a big male howler's far-off booming call. Consider yourself doubly fortunate if, on such an excursion, you also hear the chesty cry of a jaguar, the fabled *tigre.*

El Tigre

The jaguar's cunning, stealth, and strength are the stuff of Mexican legend. In ancient times the jaguar was the supreme source from whom kings, princes, and warriors drew their power. And when Mexicans recall the old proverb etched in their memories that "Each hill has its own *tigre,*" they remember that untamable presence out there beyond the campfire, the gate, the town limits, lurking somewhere in the darkness.

The legend is well deserved; at 250 pounds and six feet in length, the jaguar *(Felis onca)* is America's largest, most powerful cat. With dark reticulated spots over a tan coat, the jaguar resembles a beefy, short-legged leopard. Although hunting and human encroachment have driven jaguars into Oaxaca's deepest forest reaches, a few still live

on, mostly in the southern coast and Sierra and the northeastern isthmus, where they hunt along thickly forested stream bottoms and foothills. Unlike its more common cousin, the mountain lion, or *león,* the jaguar will eat any game. They have even been known to wait patiently for fish in rivers and stalk beaches for turtle and egg dinners. If they have a favorite food, it is probably the pig-like collared peccary.

Although government rules strictly prohibit jaguar hunting, the temptation for a poor *campesino* to earn a year's wages by shooting a jaguar and clandestinely selling its pelt is too great for the jaguar to survive for many more years in the wild in Oaxaca.

Despite their fearsome reputation and the demonstrated fact that they will fight back when cornered, little or no evidence indicates that jaguars are deliberate man-eaters.

Ocelots, Margays, and Jaguarundis

Although jaguars are extremely endangered, other Mexican cats are less so. Besides the bobcat and mountain lion, both familiar north of the border, Oaxaca is home to three other wild cat species. In descending order of size, first comes the ocelot *(Felis pardalis).* Its appearance, like a miniature jaguar, with a spotted yellowish-tan coat and stout legs, reflects its Mexican name, *tigrillo.* Full-grown male ocelots measure about 25 pounds (10 kilograms) and three feet in length. Its soft, fine fur, highly valued as a pelt, has unfortunately led to the ocelot's near-disappearance from Oaxaca's forests.

Approaching large house cat size is the **jaguarundi** or *leoncillo,* which, full-grown, weighs in at around 13 pounds (five kilograms). Although its species label *(Felis jaguarundi)* with its elongated head, appears somewhat otterlike.

With its spots and diminutive size, a full-grown **margay** appears at first glance to be a baby jaguar. A closer look, however, reveals spots more aligned in rows than

jaguar

AISUNN RACE

the jaguar's. Moreover, a domesticated margay, in contrast to the untamable jaguar, can be as endearing as your own family cat.

Like their larger cousins, the jaguarundi and margay are gradually disappearing from Oaxaca's forest wildlands. They hunt mostly along stream banks in deep remote valleys and roadless mountainsides. They feast on small game, birds, and fish, and, as a matter of self-preservation, make it their business to see you before you see them.

BIRDS

Oaxaca's coastal wetlands and upland forests straddle the southern zone of the great Pacific Flyway, the major western pathway for hosts of birds migrating south from the United States and Canada. These familiar winter visitors, such as Canada geese and ducks, including the Muscovy, black-bellied whistler, gadwall, baldpate, and shoveler, arrive and join an already-rich resident population of ibis, parrots, jacanas, egrets, herons, and anhingas, swelling the numbers into the millions.

Some of the most commonly seen residents are also the most spectacular and entertaining. The cootlike, blackish **northern jacana** *(Jacana spinosa)* amuses bird-watchers by appearing to walk on water. Actually, its clownishly large feet allow it to scoot across gardens of water-borne lily pads as if they were solid land, earning it the label "lily walker."

Always impressive is the graceful swoop of a **great blue heron** *(Ardea herodius)* gliding to rest in a Oaxacan wetland. Unmistakable because of its regal six-foot wing-

blue-footed booby

BOB RACE

spread and blue-gray coloring, the male great blue heron also sports a proud blue head plume. In the same marshland you will also probably spot its smaller (about two feet long), more numerous cousin, the **snowy egret** *(Egretta thula),* pure white except for its black beak. Although differing sharply in appearance, both species single-mindedly stalk through a pond ever so slowly, freezing rock still when prey is spotted. After several seconds, pop! down goes the bill, snaring a hapless crab, fish, or frog.

Try not to confuse the snowy egret with the smaller (18-inch) yellow-billed **cattle egret** *(Bubulcus ibis),* an African native that began appearing in Mexico around 1900. True to their name, cattle egrets usually flock around cow pastures, where they feed on the hordes of bugs that follow livestock. Local Mexican people generally identify all herons and egrets collectively as *garzas.*

Seabirds

Oaxaca's prime beach-bird actors, in addition to the swarms of gulls, terns, sandpipers, and boobies, are **brown pelicans** and big, black-and-white **frigate birds.** Their collective feed-

Canada goose

BOB RACE

ing rituals, although quite distinct, are equally entertaining. That of the brown *pelícano* (pay-LEE-cah-noh) is the most deliberate. After spotting a school of their preferred prey, the pelicans, singly or in pairs, circle once or twice, then dive headlong into the billows, usually coming up with fish in their gullet. They rest, bobbing over the waves for a spell, seemingly waiting for their comrades to take their turns.

Frigate birds *(fragatas),* by contrast, prefer either being fed or stealing food to hunting for themselves. They often reap bonuses from the efforts of villagers who haul in nets of fish right on the beach. Once the salable part of the catch is gone, kids have great fun throwing the residue overhead to a gaggle of wheeling frigate birds. In contrast to the pelicans' mannerly behavior, it's every frigate bird for itself. Frigates who miss a tossed morsel often try to snatch their fellow's prize.

Parrots

Flocks of small parrots screech, shriek, swoop, chatter, and swarm above Oaxaca's coastal mangrove lagoons and tropical foothills. The best places to spot them are in fields or pastures adjacent to thick forests, far from town. Half a dozen species—mostly green, with a patch of color on their throat or forehead—are common. If you don't get far enough into the country to see them, ask where *péricos* (PAY-ree-kohs) are for sale in big markets such as Oaxaca City, Tlacolula, Etla, Tehuantepec, Tuxtepec, Pinotepa Nacional, and Valle Nacional.

Although you might be tempted to buy such a market parrot, don't. Like all wild animals, parrots outside of their forest homelands present manifold difficulties. For starters, they quickly chew their way out of bamboo cages. Later, your airline will probably require that you buy a special "parrot ticket" for the flight back home. Moreover, after you arrive, parrots are all but impossible to get through customs. On the other hand, if you must have a pet parrot, best buy a pair of (never a single) certified healthy birds from a pet shop back home.

Among the parrots you're most likely to encounter in Oaxaca is the foot-long **green parakeet** *(Aratinga holochlora).* A long tail and a red throat further mark the species, whose members prefer to flock in the drier woodlands above

3,000 feet (1,000 meters). Another, commonly seen in tropical lowlands, is the **Aztec parakeet** *(Aratinga astec),* at nine inches, (23 centimeters), all green with olive-brown throat. For colored drawings and details, consult Roger Tory Peterson's *Field Guide to Mexican Birds.* (See the Booklist.)

REPTILES AND AMPHIBIANS

Snakes

Of Oaxaca's many dozens of snake species, the great majority couldn't harm you even if they tried. Furthermore, most snakes are shy and will clear out if they you give them plenty of warning. In Oaxaca, poisonous snakes have been largely driven out of city and tourist areas. In the bush or jungle, however, carry a stick and beat the shrubbery in front of you while watching where you put your feet. When hiking or rock-climbing in the country, don't put your hands in niches you can't see.

While such precautions minimize potential hazards, outback travelers should be prepared to encounter members of Oaxaca's most notorious snake families, the **rattlesnakes** and the **fer-de-lances.** Each occurs in a number of species, all potently venomous and generally aggressive. Mexican rattlesnakes or *cascabeles* (kahs-kah-BAY-lays), with the same warning rattle and the diamondback markings as their north-of-the-border American relatives, need little introduction. Their tropical viper-cousins, the fer-de-lances *(Bothrops atrox),* are known locally by various names, such as *nauyaca, cuatro narices, palanca,* and *barba amarilla.* Although about the same size (to six feet) and general appearance as rattlesnakes, fer-de-lances lack warning rattles and are consequently even more dangerous. On treks into the jungle, where the fer-de-lance commonly lives, **guard** against them by wearing high-topped leather boots and watching carefully where you put your feet.

Snakes in the tropics are not confined to land. Although very unlikely, it is possible that you may encounter a **sea snake** *(culebra marina)* while swimming offshore at an isolated Oaxaca beach. If small, yellow, and black, it will be certainly the *Pelamis platurus,* which, although shy, lives in groups and has been reported to inflict a serious, venomous bite. Some **eels,** which resemble snakes but have gills like fish and inhabit rocky crevices, can inflict nonpoisonous bites and should also be avoided.

The Oaxacan land counterpart of the poisonous sea snake is the **coral snake** *(coralillo),* which occurs in several species, all with multicolored bright bands that always include red. Although relatively rare, small, and shy, coral snakes occasionally bite, sometimes fatally.

Gila Monsters, Iguanas, and Geckos
The Gila monster (confined in Mexico to northern Sonora) and its southern tropical relative, the black-with-yellow-spots *escorpión,* are the world's only poisonous lizards. Despite its beaded skin and menacing, fleshy appearance, the *escorpión (Heloderma horridum)* bites only when severely provoked; even then, its venom is rarely, if ever, fatal.

The rest of Oaxaca's many lizard species are much more benign; some are even endearing. Of them, the **iguana,** locally called the *garrobo,* is most popular, mainly because of its tasty flesh. Although usually masked in the bush by its spotted green camouflage, you may glimpse an iguana scurrying, in a flash of green, across the road in front of your car or bus. Despite their fierce dinosaurian aspect, iguanas are peaceful vegetarians, often munching flowers in a favorite treetop.

One of Oaxaca's most endearing reptilian residents is the **gecko,** known affectionately as *guerita* (blondie) in the coastal towns and villages where they are common. Visitors usually encounter them in their hotel rooms. If you hear their homey clicking sound (for which residents affectionately call them *besucona,* the "kissing one"), don't be alarmed. Quite the contrary, for each room cannot be without its resident gecko to properly cleanse it of gnats and mosquitoes. If your room doesn't have one, ask the management to find a *guerita* for you.

Crocodiles
The crocodile, *cocodrilo* or *caiman,* once prized for its meat and hide, came close to vanishing in Oaxaca's coastal lagoons until the government stepped in to ensure its survival. Now officially protected, a few isolated breeding populations live in the wild, while government and private hatcheries are breeding more for the eventual repopulation of lagoons where they once were common. A hatchery open for touring is located in Lagunas de Chacagua.

Two crocodile species are native to Oaxaca. The true crocodile *(Crocodilus acutus)* has a narrower snout than its local cousin *(Caiman crocodilus fuscus),* a type of alligator *(lagarto).* Although past individuals have been recorded up to 15 feet long, wild native crocodiles are usually young and a few feet or less in length.

Sea Turtles
The story of Mexican sea turtles is similar. They once swarmed ashore on Mexican beaches to lay their eggs. Prized for their meat, eggs, hide, and shell, the turtles were severely devastated. Now officially protected, growing numbers of sea turtles are hatching and returning to the sea from Oaxaca's beaches, thanks to the increasing ranks of eco-volunteers who guard against poachers. Very accessible Oaxaca turtle sanctuaries include the entire Bays of Huatulco, Playa Escobilla, not far from Puerto Escondido, and Playa Mazunte, near Puerto Ángel, where a government turtle aquarium and hatchery occupies the site of a former turtle processing factory.

Of the several locally occurring species, the olive ridley *(tortuga golfina)* and the green turtle *(tortuga verde)* are the most common. From tour boats, the green turtle can often be seen grazing on sea grass offshore from Puerto Escondido and the Bays of Huatulco.

For more details of Mexico's mammals and birds in general, check out Starker Leopold's very readable (but unfortunately out-of-print) classic, *Wildlife of Mexico,* and other works in the Suggested Reading section.

FISH

Shoals of fish abound in Oaxacan waters. Four billfish species are found in deep-sea grounds several miles offshore: **swordfish, sailfish,** and **blue and black marlin.** All are spirited fighters, though the sailfish and marlin are generally the toughest to bring in. The blue marlin is the biggest of the four. Although 10-foot, 1,000-pound fish used to be occasionally brought in, four feet and 200 pounds for a marlin, 100 pounds for a sailfish are recently more typical. Recognizing the need for conservation, forward-looking captains now encourage victorious anglers to return these magnificent "tigers of the sea" (especially the sinewy, poor-eating sailfish and blue marlin) to the deep after they've won the battle.

Billfish are not the only prizes of the sea. Serious fish lovers also seek varieties of tunalike **jack,** such as **yellowtail, Pacific amberjack, pompano, jack crevalle,** and the tenacious **roosterfish,** named for the "comb" atop its head. These and the **yellowfin tuna, mackerel,** and *dorado,* which Hawaiians call mahimahi, are among the delicacies sought in Oaxaca waters.

Accessible from small boats offshore and by casting from shoreline rocks are varieties of **snapper** *(huachinango, pargo)* and **sea bass** *(cabrilla).* Closer to shore, **croaker, mullet,** and **jewfish** often can be found foraging along sandy bottoms and in rocky crevices.

Sharks and **rays** inhabit nearly all depths, with smaller fry venturing into beach shallows and lagoons. Sometimes, huge **Pacific manta rays** appear to be frolicking, their great wings flapping like birds, not far off Oaxacan shores. Just beyond the waves, local fisherfolk bring in **hammerhead, thresher,** and **leopard sharks.**

Also common is the **stingray,** which can inflict a painful wound with its barbed tail. Experienced swimmers and waders avoid injury by both shuffling (rather than stepping) and watching their feet in shallow, sandy bottoms.

Captains from marinas at Santa Cruz de Huatulco, Puerto Ángel, and Salina Cruz routinely pilot big boats equipped for four or five anglers to try for the big marlin, sailfish, and swordfish. Launches and tackle, suitable for smaller but still exciting catches, can be hired at those same marinas, in addition to Puerto Escondido and a number of other beach villages along the Oaxacan coast.

For more fish details, including a chart of species encountered in Oaxacan waters, turn ahead to Sports and Recreation in the On the Road chapter, following.

HISTORY

An age ago—perhaps as long as 20,000 years—small bands of hardy people, ancestors of the adventurers who had crossed the Arctic land bridge from Siberia thousands of years earlier, were hunting and foraging in what is now the Valley of Oaxaca. The forests and meadows abounded with edible plants and game—from squirrels and rabbits to great Ice Age herds of camels, horses, and mammoths. Supplied with abundant food, the people multiplied.

But by around 7000 B.C. the climate had warmed several degrees, and the great game animals were extinct. Perhaps in response, the people began to sow seeds of their favorite edible wild grains, legumes, vegetables, and fruits. As their descendants still do today, those ancient Oaxacans picked out the biggest and healthiest seeds to plant for the succeeding year's crop. After many generations, their fields were blooming with domesticated beans, squash, corn, and avocados nearly as robust as those enjoyed today.

EARLY CIVILIZATION

The Village Era
Millennia later, about 2000 B.C., those early Oaxacans, supplied with the bounty of their fields, no longer had to wander in search of food and were settling into permanent villages. Although initially small—typically only a dozen houses—the villages prospered and grew. Discovered remains reveal that many aspects of Oaxacan village life have remained fundamentally unchanged. Then, as now, planting, harvesting, and preparation of food occupied most of the day. Men used flint ax-heads hafted to wooden handles to clear brush, which they would burn in preparation for seeding. Women ground corn with the familiar *mano* and *metate,* combination roller-crusher. They patted tortillas and baked them on the flat clay *comal* griddle and stewed meats, beans, and chili sauces in round clay pots.

Excavated ceramic figurines reveal the villagers' dress: for women, woven cloth or frond skirts, fiber or leather sandals, and long, often attractively braided hair, earrings, and necklaces. Men ordinarily wore a simple loincloth and sandals.

Village people buried their dead family members, laid out flat, in graves near their houses. A few offerings for the afterlife accompanied the deceased: a bowl with food, drinks, favored personal objects, and jewelry, including a semiprecious stone placed in the mouth.

Gradually, population increased. By 500 B.C. some villages, such as at San José Mogote about 10 miles (16 km) northwest of Oaxaca City, had grown into small towns, with as many as 500 residents. Here investigators have uncovered early evidence of social classes—large, regally elevated houses—and specialization, in the form of a factory where workers polished iron-rich magnetite into small mirrors, which were traded hundreds of miles away.

Gradually during the few thousand years as villages were growing into towns, abundant food and burgeoning commercial wealth had lifted a small but significant fraction of Oaxacans to a privileged leisure status. They had become the artists, architects, warriors, and ruler-priests—with time to think and create. Over time, they devised symbols, writing, and a calendar that tied the constant wheel of the firmament to life on earth, defining the days to plant, to harvest, to feast, travel, and trade. Eventually, a grand city arose.

Archaeologists have gradually uncovered the remains of a sizable early urban stage (circa 500 B.C.) town at San José Mogote, 20 minutes drive north of Oaxaca City.

Monte Albán

Around 500 B.C. ancestors of Oaxaca's present-day Zapotec peoples founded what many experts believe to have been the Americas' earliest metropolis. On the central valley summit known today as Monte Albán, they raised monumental platforms, pyramids, palaces, and ceremonial ball courts. These they decorated with inscriptions, in a language yet to be deciphered, recording the exploits of their god-kings. The ordinary family homes of adobe bricks, arranged around central patios, occupied the hillside just below the ceremonial summit.

For centuries, Monte Albán flourished, overflowing halfway down its hillsides. Although starting from a population of only 2,000 at its founding, Monte Albán flourished to a city of as

many as 40,000 at its height a thousand years later. By A.D. 500 Monte Albán encompassed three square miles (seven square km), interlaced with vegetable and flower gardens and spreading to several monumental neighborhood sub-centers downhill.

Although Monte Albán ruled, upwards of two dozen subsidiary cities administered local areas throughout Oaxaca. Their ruins litter the present-day state: sites such as Yucuita and Yucuñudahui in the Mixteca Alta, Cerro de las Minas in the Mixteca Baja, and Dainzu and Lambityeco in the central valley. War appears to have been a scourge of Oaxaca's early cities. Like Monte Albán, and in contrast to most village-era sites, most cities lay atop defensible hilltops.

Monte Albán's days were nevertheless numbered. After dominating Oaxaca and beyond for more than a thousand years, its power was fading fast by around A.D. 750. Although experts argue over what combination of drought, disease, war, or overpopulation ended Monte Albán's glory days, they agree that it was virtually abandoned by A.D. 1000 and eclipsed by a crowd of tussling city-states. A similar mysterious fate befell other southern and central Mexican cities, most notably Teotihuacán, Monte Albán's great rival metropolis in the north.

Teotihuacán

Although founded half a millennium later than Monte Albán, Teotihuacán grew rapidly, attaining population and wealth on a par with the ancient world's great cities by A.D. 300. Its epic pyramids still stand, not far north of Mexico City, along a grand avenue of fearsome, ruby-eyed stone effigies of Quetzalcoatl, the feathered serpent king of gods.

After Teotihuacán was abandoned around A.D. 700, a host of its former vassal cities rose to power, among them Xochicalco, in the highlands in the present state of Morelos, an hour's drive south of Mexico City.

The Living Quetzalcoatl

Xochicalco became renowned as a center of learning, where noble families sent their sons to study the healing arts, astronomy, architecture, and agriculture. A prominent student among them was Topiltzín (literally, "Our Prince"), who left Xochicalco in A.D. 968 to found his own city-state, Tula, north of old Teotihuacán.

After an enlightened 20-year rule, Topiltzín became so revered that his people began to know him as the living incarnation of Quetzalcoatl, the plumed god of gods. He was not universally loved, however. Jealous priests, who hated Quetzalcoatl-Topiltzín's persuasive opposition to their bloody rites of human sacrifice, drugged him with alcohol. He awoke, bleary-eyed, in bed with his sister. Devastated by shame, Quetzalcoatl-Topiltzín banished himself from Tula with a band of retainers. In A.D. 987, they headed east, toward Yucatán. Although he sent word he would reclaim his kingdom during the 52-year cyclical calendar year of his birth, Ce Acatl, Quetzalcoatl-Topiltzín never returned. Legends say that he sailed east and rose to heaven as the morning star.

The Rise of Oaxacan City-States

By A.D. 1000, the power vacuum left by the demise of Monte Albán had been filled by its dozens of former tributary cities, whose rulers carved out their own little kingdoms, mostly in the central valley and the Mixteca. Each had a dominant town, typically with a population of 5,000-10,000, which ruled a dispersed walking-distance village hinterland of about 100 square miles (250 square km) and 10,000 or 20,000 people. Some of these, notably Zaachila and Mitla near present-day Oaxaca City, remain thriving towns, still dominating their districts, while others, such as Yagul, near Mitla; Huijazoo, in the Etla Valley northeast of Oaxaca City; and Guiengola, in the Isthmus west of Tehuantepec, are uninhabited ruins.

8-Deer and the Mixtec Invasion

In A.D. 1011, not long after the great Quetzalcoatl-Topiltzín had trekked east, another renowned noble, known to historians as 8-Deer, the calendar name-date of his birth, was born in Oaxaca. Scholars have learned details of his life through preconquest hieroglyphic documents, collectively called **codices** (or singularly "codex"). Although most were destroyed by Spanish priests all over Mexico early in the conquest, eight Oaxaca codices, folded deerskin picture books whitened with lime, survived, all from the Mixtec region of Oaxaca: respectively called Becker I, Becker II, Bodley, Colombino, Nuttall, Sánchez Solis, Selden, and Vienna. Six of these eight Mixtec codices commemorate 8-Deer's adventures. Among the most enlightening, codex Nuttall records 8-Deer's given name as "Tiger Claw," portending his ruthless exploits.

As Monte Albán's power faded, the Mixtec city-states, west and northwest of the central valley, thrived. But overpopulation, and perhaps pressure from Xochicalco and the Toltecs ("People of Tula"), forced ambitious Mixtec nobles to look southward at the fertile lands of the Oaxaca central valley.

The stage for Mixtec expansion was set when 8-Deer Tiger Claw came of age. He moved quickly, forming alliances and setting his rivals against one another. Codex Nuttall depicts one of 8-Deer Tiger Claw's expeditions. It shows him, along with two allies, 4-Tiger and 9-Water, spears and shields in hand, crossing a lake by

This depiction of the sacrifice of 8-Deer ("Tiger Claw") was taken from the Bodley codex.

AISUNN RACE

canoe toward an island, the Hill of Mixtlatl. The document records the expedition's three consecutive dates: 10-Serpent, 11-Death, and 12-Deer, of A.D..1046, when 8-Deer was in his 35-year-old fighting prime.

After bringing the entire Mixteca, from the Tehuacán Valley in the north to the coastal stronghold at Tututepec, under his control, 8-Deer led Mixtec armies southeast from his capital at Tilantongo and defeated a number of Zapotec central valley city-states. Although 8-Deer met his end as a sacrifice victim in Cuilapan, not far south of present-day Oaxaca City, in 1061, Mixtec nobles ruled on as an elite minority in Zaachila, Mitla, and other valley city-states. They preserved their dominance by the tactic of political marriage, taking daughters of the Zapotec nobility as near-hostage wives who raised Mixtec-speaking heirs.

Although virtually no Mixtec speakers remain living today in the central valley, the old Mixtec influence lives on in the Zapotec-Mixtec stylistic fusion of the architecture, pottery, jewelry, and other remains found at Zaachila, Mitla, Monte Albán, and other sites. Admire the elaborately fine *greca* mosaic frets decorating the Mitla ruins and you're enjoying the Mixtec influence; likewise, at the Santo Domingo Cultural Center museum in Oaxaca City, Mixtec craftsmanship and sophistication gleam from the golden mask of

death and the trove of gold and turquoise jewelry taken from tomb 7 at Monte Albán.

The Aztecs Invade Oaxaca

At the time the Mixtecs were consolidating their rule of the Valley of Oaxaca, the Aztecs ("People of Aztlán"), a collection of seven aggressive immigrant subtribes, had eclipsed the Toltec civilization that Quetzalcoatl-Topiltzín had founded north of present-day Mexico City. After migrating from a mysterious western land of Aztlán ("Land of the Herons") into the lake-filled valley that Mexico City now occupies, around 1250, the Aztecs' fiercest tribe, whose members called themselves the México (MAY-shee-kah), clawed its way to dominion over the Valley of Mexico. In 1325, the México founded their capital, Tenochtitlán, on an island in the middle of the valley-lake. During the next century, Tenochtitlán grew into a magnificent city, from which Aztec armies, like Roman legions, marched out and subdued kingdoms for hundreds of miles in all directions.

In 1434, the Aztecs, under Emperor Itzcóatl, conquered the northern Mixtec domains in the Tehuacán Valley; several years later his successor, Moctezuma Ilhuicamina, attacked southward, defeating Atonaltzin, the Mixtec lord of Coixtlahuaca. Besides yielding booty and a small army of captives, the victory opened the path to the entire Mixteca and the Valley of Oaxaca.

By 1456, the Aztecs were firmly fixed in the valley, having established a garrison at Huaxyacac, the site of present-day Oaxaca City. From that point, however, the Aztecs found their access to the remainder of the central valley and the coveted southern lands of Tehuantepec blocked by the strong Zapotec city-state of Zaachila. After 30 frustrating years, the Aztecs, then under Emperor Ahuizotl, bargained with Cosijoeza (koh-see-hoh-EY-zah), the king of Zaachila, for peaceful access toward Tehuantepec in the southeast. Cosijoeza soon regretted the concession. In 1494, the Aztecs broke the agreement and seized and subjugated Mitla, at the eastern end of the valley. Enraged, Cosijoeza rushed his forces southeast and fortified their Isthmus hilltop bastion at Guiengola, which blocked the Aztecs' progress to their southern capital at Tehuantepec and Chiapas beyond.

After a seven-month siege of Guiengola, the frustrated Aztecs again resorted to diplomacy. They proposed a new alliance, in the form of a marriage between King Cosijoeza and Coyollicatzin (koh-yoh-yee-KAH-tseen), the daughter of the new Aztec Emperor Moctezuma I. The Aztecs' hidden agenda: they expected Coyollicatzin to spy upon Cosijoeza; true love, however, won out as Coyollicatzin refused to play the pawn and remained loyal to her husband Cosijoeza. The Aztecs eventually made peace in return for nominal tribute. Cosijoeza turned his Tehuantepec domain to his son Cosijopí and returned home to reign over his Zapotec people at Zaachila in the central valley.

Despite a king's ransom in yearly tribute—mounds of quetzal feathers, dozens of sacks of cochineal, hundreds of pounds of gold, thousands of bolts of cloth—the Aztec's millions of Oaxacan subjects always seemed to be rebelling someplace until the Spanish conquistadores arrived and toppled the Aztecs from power in 1521.

THE CONQUEST

Although Christopher Columbus and the generation of explorers who followed him had discovered a new world in America, their dreams of riches had eluded them. In Spain's new Caribbean island colonies both gold and native workers, who had mostly died from European diseases, were scarce. A new wave of adventurers, among them Hernán Cortés, a minor nobleman from the poor Spanish province of Extremadura, turned their vision toward new fabled empires—perhaps even the elusive Cathay—beyond the setting sun. In Cuba, Cortés patched together a motley force of 550 men, an assortment of small ships, a few horses, and cannon and sailed west in early 1519. By the time they landed on Mexico's Gulf Coast on 22 April 1519, Cortés's men, torn by dissension and realizing the impossible odds against them, were near mutiny.

Cortés, however, cut his losses and exploited his opportunities with extraordinary aplomb. He won over the doubters, isolated the dissenters, and ended any thoughts of retreat to Cuba by burning his ships. Next he capitalized on the lucky coincidence that he had landed on the Mexican coastline in the Aztec year of Ce Acatl, exactly the same 52-year cyclical anniversary year in which Quetzalcoatl-Topiltzín had vowed to return from the east to reclaim his kingdom.

As he led his band of adventurers westward over the mountains toward the Aztec capital of Tenochtitlán, Cortés played Quetzalcoatl to the hilt, awing local leaders. Coaxed by Doña Marina, his wily native translator-mistress-confidante, local chiefs began to add their armies to Cortés's march against their Aztec oppressors.

Tenochtitlán, Capital of the Empire
A few months later, inside the gates of Tenochtitlán, the Venice-like island-metropolis, it was the Spaniards' turn to be awed: by gardens full of animals, gold and palaces, and a great pyramid-enclosed square where tens of thousands of people bartered goods gathered from all over the empire. Tenochtitlán, with perhaps a quarter of a million people, was the great capital of an empire as large and rich as any in Europe.

Moctezuma II, the lord of that empire, fearing that Cortés was in fact the god Quetzalcoatl incarnate, had followed Cortés's progress toward Tenochtitlán with trepidation. Wishing not to offend, Moctezuma II had sent Cortés sumptuous gifts of gold, coupled with warnings to stay away. Encouraged by the gold, Cortés demanded an early audience with the emperor, who pathetically surrendered himself to Cortés's custody and "donated" his entire empire to the Spanish crown.

Spaniards Enter Oaxaca

With his position temporarily secure, Cortés dispatched emissaries west, east, and south. To Oaxaca he sent Hernando Pizarro and Diego de Ordaz, each with small detachments, to reconnoiter for riches. Pizarro searched for gold in the Papaloapaon basin around Tuxtepec and later the Chinantla, while Ordaz passed through the Mixtec kingdoms of Yanhuitlán and Sosola on his way to the Gulf Coast.

The Aztecs Force a Spanish Retreat

Meanwhile, however, the people of Tenochtitlán were rioting against Spanish brutality. On 1 July 1520, with Moctezuma II mortally wounded by his own countrymen, Cortés and his men, forced by the sheer numbers of rebellious Mexicans, retreated, hacking a bloody path through thousands of screaming Aztec warriors to safety on the lakeshore.

Hearing the news of Cortés's defeat, Mexican garrisons in Oaxaca dealt a similar blow against the local Spanish expeditions, attacking and killing dozens of Spaniards and their indigenous allies.

Although Cortés was down, he wasn't out. In succeeding months, as his forces regathered strength in the Valley of Mexico, he pushed the conquest of the south. Alonso de Avila arrived in Oaxaca in late 1520 and accepted the ambassadors of Zapotec kings Cosijoeza and Cosijopí, who were more than willing to ally themselves against their Aztec overlords. Concurrently, other Spanish expeditions thrust into Oaxaca: Gonzalo de Sandoval successfully counterattacked against the Aztec garrisons, while Juan Cedeño obtained the submission of the Chinantecs and the northern Zapotecs.

Tenochtitlán Falls and Oaxaca Is Conquered

In late 1521, reinforced by fresh soldiers, horses, a small fleet of armed sailboats, and 100,000 Indian allies, Cortés retook Tenochtitlán. The stubborn defenders, led by Cuauhtémoc, Moctezuma's nephew, fell by the tens of thousands beneath a smoking hail of Spanish grapeshot. The Aztecs, although weakened by smallpox, refused to surrender. Cortés found, to his dismay, that he had to destroy the city in order to take it.

Soon after Cortés's triumph, the Zapotec kings Cosijoeza and Cosijopí sent ambassadors declaring their submission to him and his king, Charles V. This alarmed the Mixtecs, who, with the backing of the Chinantec king of Tuxtepec, declared war on the Zapotecs. At the request of his new Zapotec allies, Cortés dispatched Francisco de Orozco in December 1521 and Pedro de Alvarado a month later with a few hundred infantry and a handful of cavalry to pacify Oaxaca. After a few skirmishes, Orozco took possession of Huaxyacac, the site of present-day Oaxaca City, which the Aztec garrisons had occupied since 1456. A few hours later, on the same day, 25 December 1521, padre Juan Díaz celebrated the first Catholic mass in Oaxaca territory. A month later at the same spot, Alvarado, with the help of padre Bartolomé de Olmedo, helped negotiate a peace agreement between the Mixtecs and Zapotecs.

With the valley and northern Oaxaca pacified, Cortés sent Alvarado to conquer the Oaxacan Pacific Coast. On 4 March 1522, Alvarado defeated Casandoo, the Mixtec king of Tututepec, and with colonists displaced from the Valley of Oaxaca by Cortés orders, he founded the Villa Segura de la Frontera ("Secure Village of the Frontier"). He went on to pacify the whole coast, including Tonameca, Pochutla, Huatulco, and Astata, all the way east to Tehuantepec.

NEW SPAIN

With much of the former Aztec empire firmly in his grip and his lieutenants continuing to lead their forces in triumph in all directions, Cortés anticipated the grand domain that would eventually expand to more than a dozenfold the size of old Spain. He wrote his king, Charles V, ". . . the most suitable name for it would be New Spain of the Ocean Sea, and thus in the name of your Majesty I have christened it."

Even as he was building the new Mexico City atop the ruins of old Tenochtitlán, Cortés dreamed of a kingdom of his own. His first information of the fertile, spring-like Valley of Oaxaca came from his own scouts and from the ambassadors the Oaxacan kings had sent. Cortés moved quickly to carve out his Oaxaca domain, sending orders with Pedro de Alvarado to remove all Spanish settlers from the valley. When Cortés personally arrived in Oaxaca in 1523 he found to his chagrin that settlers that he had previously ordered out of the valley had returned and were squatting on the land he wanted for himself. He sent the instigators to Mexico City in chains and dispersed the settlers again.

He granted his friends and relatives, including his son Martín and his two illegitimate daughters, *encomiendas* (rights to land and native labor) at strategic points all over Oaxaca, then, in October 1524, marched off on an exhausting two-year expedition to Honduras.

By the time Cortés returned in 1526, the settlers had again returned and reestablished their village at Huaxyacac. Moreover, they had petitioned the king of Spain, Carlos I, for a charter for their settlement, which they had christened **Antequera,** in honor of the ancient Granada town of the same name. To Cortés's great displeasure, the petition was granted, by royal decree, on 14 September 1526.

Undeterred, Cortés took charge and began building his Valley of Oaxaca domain. He staked out the best bottomland, built haciendas, and set his native laborers to planting wheat and sugarcane. Cortés then traveled to Huatulco and Tehuantepec, where he built a port and ships to explore the Pacific. Concurrently, Cortés strengthened his alliance with King Cosijopí, who reciprocated by converting (along with thousands of his Tehuantepec subjects) to Christianity, taking the name Juan Cortés Cosijopí.

Hernán Cortés, Marquis of the Valley of Oaxaca

Cortés realized that his de facto kingdom needed both a queen and royal recognition, so he traveled to Spain in 1528 to get both. A year later he returned with his young noble bride, Juana de Zúñga, and the grand title of Marqués del Valle de Oaxaca, which included a singularly generous grant of land, subjects, and privileges. For many years thereafter, he and his heirs received upward of 80,000 gold pesos a year from tens of thousands of Indian subjects on three million acres of domains scattered from the Valley of Mexico through the present states of Morelos, Mexico, Guerrero, and Veracruz to Oaxaca. Cortés's Valley of Oaxaca holdings, the crown

Hernán Cortés

jewel of his domain, encompassed most of the best valley land. In a wide, 350,000-acre swath, it stretched 25 miles, including 34 villages and towns, from Etla in the north to Coyotopec in the south. Excluded, however, was the one-league square (two square miles) of the town of Antequera, which grew into the present-day Oaxaca City.

The Missionaries

While the conquistadores scoured the countryside for gold and subjugated the local people, missionaries began arriving to heal, teach, and baptize them. The Dominicans were the first and most numerous in Oaxaca. Padre Minaya built the first Oaxaca convent, dedicated to Saint Paul, in Antequera around 1530. Other Dominicans settled in Tlaxiaco, Etla, and Tehuantepec, where King Cosijopí financed a church for them in 1538. Other orders—Franciscans, Augustinians, Bethlehemites, and more—soon joined them. Missionary authorities customarily enjoyed a sympathetic ear from Charles V and his successors, who earnestly pursued Spain's Christian mission, especially when it coincided with their political and economic goals.

Besides saving souls, the missionaries introduced new plants, flowers, and vegetables, and useful European crafts, such as ironworking, glassmaking, wool processing, and pottery glazing. They learned native tongues and wrote catechisms in Zapotec, Mixtec, and other local dialects. Within a few dozen years, the fields, orchards, and vineyards dotted with dozens of churches around the Valley of Oaxaca and beyond testified to the dedication of both the missionaries and their native converts.

Unfortunately, in order to speed the process of conversion, which the missionaries viewed as a sort of divine manifest destiny, native temples, idols, and paintings were destroyed. Historical records were irretrievably lost. The Spaniards also banned native song and dance, fearing that they kept alive old beliefs.

Although the missionaries on the whole provided a kinder, gentler counterbalance to the often brutal and exploitative conquistadores and colonists, they were not entirely blameless. In their zeal to build churches, convents, and monasteries, they also demanded the backbreaking labor of the newly converted. Moreover, those resistant to conversion were dealt with harshly, sometimes beaten, tortured, or killed.

In Oaxaca, however, which was primarily a Dominican stronghold, *indígenas* were spared the worst excesses of the more zealous Franciscans. Bartolomé de las Casas, a Dominican friar, devoted his life to fighting for the rights of the native people. This champion of social justice earned the sobriquet "Apostle of the Indians."

The King Takes Control

By 1530, the crown, through the Council of the Indies, had begun to wrest power away from Cortés and his conquistador lieutenants. Cortés had granted many of them rights of *encomienda:* taxes and labor of an indigenous district. In exchange, the *encomendero,* who often enjoyed the status of feudal lord, pledged to look after the welfare and souls of his native charges.

From the king's point of view, though, tribute pesos collected by *encomenderos* translated into losses to the crown. Moreover, many *encomenderos* callously exploited their indigenous wards for quick profit, sometimes selling them as slave labor in mines and on plantations. Such abuses, coupled with European-introduced diseases, began to reduce the native population at an alarming rate.

By 1540, strongly influenced by Dominican padre Bartolomé de las Casas, the outspoken "Apostle of the Indians," the king and his councillors realized that the native Mexicans were in peril, and without their labor New Spain would vanish. They acted decisively. New laws would shift power toward the crown and limit abuses to the king's native subjects. Decreed in 1542 and enforced by a powerful *visitador* (inspector general), the **New Laws of the Indies** abolished perpetual rights of *encomienda,* outlawed slavery of native Mexicans, and limited their labor and tribute payments.

Although Oaxacan colonists protested vehemently, some native groups benefited. With the support of the new bishop of Antequera, Juan López de Zárate and the missionary padres, Zapotecs around the Valley of Oaxaca mounted a legal fight against excessive *encomienda* payments.

COLONIAL OAXACA

Congregación

Despite the Oaxaca Valley Marquesate, Spanish garrisons, a score of Spanish-run haciendas, a few mines, and the capital town Antequera, Oaxaca had a sparse population of no more than a thousand Spaniards around 1550. On the other hand, the native population, while reduced, still numbered several hundred thousand, widely dispersed over the entire territory, and largely controlled by the hereditary native nobility. The Spanish authorities, in order to break the hold of the old chiefs on the natives, began moving indigenous populations into *congregaciones:* new townships in potentially productive areas—valleys, mines, and along royal roads. Each township had its *cabercera* (head town) and *sujeto* (subject) villages. Indigenous governing councils, supervised by Spanish agents, were responsible for local order and collection of tribute.

The missionary clergy initially went along with *congregación* because it led to more converts, but after a generation of seeing the cruel reality of people displaced from their land and traditions, opposed it. In 1604, although the policy was officially abandoned and some of the people returned to their original way of life, many did not. Their descendants remain living in the original *caberceras,* which comprise a significant portion of present-day Oaxaca's 570 *municipios* or governmental townships.

The natives, in being shifted toward traditional Spanish occupations, in which they worked mines, harvested sugarcane and wheat, and tended sheep and cattle, were forced to abandon the way of life that had sustained them for millennia. In a few generations even the memory of their extensive irrigation works—diversion dams and canals that fed terraced fields—was lost.

The severe consequences of this forgotten water-conservation tradition have become acute in modern Oaxaca. Increasing population has led to lack of bottomland, forcing families to poor uplands that without irrigation cannot sustain them. Slash-and-burn dry farming, non-contour plowing, overgrazing, and overcutting of forest have turned large tracts of Oaxaca into eroded wasteland.

Population Collapse

In a real sense, European disease, rather than the conquistadores, subdued Mexico. Despite the missionary fathers' most benign efforts and the most beneficial effects of the king's New Laws, typhus, measles, smallpox, and other European plagues wiped out about 90 percent of the Mexican indigenous population within a few generations after the conquest. Although estimates vary, most experts agree that preconquest Mexico's 15–25 million native population had shrunk to a mere 1.3 million by 1650.

Oaxaca's figures reflect a similar tragedy. Of a population that archaeologists estimate at around two million in 1500, only 150,000 remained in 1650. In some cases, such as the mines of Santa Catalina Martir, in 1580, a combination of overwork and disease killed thousands; those remaining simply fled into the hills. In the southern Oaxaca valley towns, plagues reduced thriving towns such as Teitipac, Ocotlán, and Miahuatlán from populations of thousands to a few dozen inhabitants nearly overnight.

Today's Mexicans can, ironically, look forward to the year 2019, the 500th anniversary of Cortés's landing, when Mexico's native-speaking population will have recovered to its preconquest level of approximately 25 million.

The Changing Role of the Church

During the colonial era, civil and church authorities increasingly came into conflict with missionary orders, whose independent status derived directly from Papal authority, in contrast to locally administered ("secular") clergy, who answered to local bishops. Disputes usually revolved around treatment of the natives, whose welfare missionaries often outspokenly championed. The kettle, always bubbling, sometimes boiled over. In 1647, Bishop Cerda Benevente of Antequera tried to kick all Dominican fathers out of their churches; in 1749 Bishop Maldonado tried to replace 27 Dominicans with clergy under his control. The issue of power was finally settled in 1767 when the King of Spain expelled all Jesuit missionaries from his New World colonies. This chilled the liberal activist tendencies of clergy everywhere in Mexico and led to an increasingly conservative church establishment.

During Spain's Mexican colonial twilight, the church, increasingly profiting from the status quo, became fat and largely complacent. The biblical tithe—one-tenth of everything, from crops and livestock to rents and mining profits—filled church coffers. By 1800, the church owned half of Mexico. Moreover, all clergy (including the lay church officers) and the military were doubly privileged. They enjoyed right of *fuero* (exemption from civil law) and could be prosecuted by ecclesiastical or military courts only.

The Colonial Economy

In trade and commerce, New Spain existed for the benefit of the mother country. Spaniards enjoyed absolute monopolies by virtue of the complete prohibition of foreign traders and goods. Colonists, as a result, paid dearly for often shoddy Spanish manufactures. The Casa de Contratación, the royal trade regulators, always ensured the colony's yearly balance of payments would result in deficit, which would be made up by bullion shipments from New Spain mines (from which the crown raked 10 percent off the top).

If New Spain was a tradition-bound feudal domain, Oaxaca was even more so. The crown regulated nearly everything. Any kind of enterprise required a royal license, issued through a bureaucracy that required bribes as part of the cost of doing business. Wealth flowed directly from the labor of the native people. Although

Oaxaca people produced lots of corn, wheat, cattle, sheep, wool, and some silk, cochineal was by far Oaxaca's most valuable export.

Whatever native people produced, they all had to pay taxes, whether directly to the local collector or as tribute to the *encomendero* owner of the estate where they lived. For many poor native families, the problem of getting enough to eat year-round was doubly acute because of the seasonal nature of their produce. They began to rely upon *alcaldes mayores,* local royal officials, for cash advances on crops, especially cochineal. Through their official posts, *alcaldes mayores* enjoyed a monopoly, which forced local folks to sell to them for a pittance. This hated monopoly payment system, known as **repartmiento,** although officially forbidden, was rampant during the mid-1600s, when a swarm of Oaxaca uprisings led to the killing of Tehuantepec's greedy *alcalde mayor* and a number of his henchmen by an angry crowd of native cochineal producers.

Reform didn't come until the 18th century, when Spanish authorities saw the light and banned the *repartmiento* system, replacing the *alcaldes mayores* with less corruptible salaried agents known as *intendentes.*

The bustling cochineal trade led to boom times

COCHINEAL—NATURE'S RICHEST RED DYE

Cochineal *(cochinilla)* is a prized rich scarlet dye, long cultivated in Mexico before the conquest. The Spanish, immediately seeing its export value, expanded production, especially in Oaxaca, where its production became a major source of cash for native Oaxacans faced with increasing tribute demands. The rise of the textile industry in England, the Low Countries, France, and Spain further propelled demand for Oaxacan cochineal, renowned as the most brilliant, richest red dye in the world. The word spread, and, by its peak during the 17th and 18th centuries, Spain's cochineal trade extended as far as China. Although largely replaced by cheaper synthetic dyes by 1900, cochineal is still locally cultivated in the Valley of Oaxaca.

The actual source of the dye is the female of a type of scale insect, *Dactylopius coccus,* which feeds off a variety of nopal (prickly pear) cactus. Typically, families or village cooperatives own patches of nopal, from which they brush the female beetles during the fall harvest. The beetles are then dried, ground, and boiled in water. The resulting dye suspension is purified and evaporated, leaving pure crimson cochineal crystals, still preferred by many Oaxaca Valley weavers.

A demonstration farm, dedicated to the revival of cochineal, welcomes visitors to see its experimental cactus garden and small museum at Santa María Coyotepec, on the highway about four miles (six kilometers) south of the Oaxaca airport.

hanging wool out to dry after dyeing in Teotitlán del Valle

POPULATION CHANGES IN NEW SPAIN

	Early Colonial (1570)	Late Colonial (1810)
peninsulares	6,600	15,000
criollos	11,000	1,100,000
mestizos	2,400	704,000
indígenas	3,340,000	3,700,000
blacks	22,000	630,000

in colonial Oaxaca. The region, previously a backwater, neglected by Mexico City authorities, benefited from a monopoly on cochineal production after 1745. Population tripled during the 1700s, reaching 20,000 and making the city of Oaxaca (whose name was officially changed from Antequera in 1786) New Spain's third largest city by 1800.

The benefits of the new prosperity did not extend equally to all Oaxacans, however. As the administrative center for the entire region, most wealth flowed to Oaxaca City, where a rich elite, of mostly Spanish-born government and church officials and owners of large estates, raked in the lion's share of the profits. Below them, a modicum of treasure and respectability trickled down to the small locally born white and mixed-blood professional and merchant class. Finally, the great majority of mixed and pure native descent who did the hard work—the spinners, the weavers, the masons, shoemakers, bakers, farmers and laborers—plugged along as best they could at the city's least desirable margins.

Despite its faults, New Spain lasted three times longer than the Aztec empire. By most contemporary measures, both Oaxaca in particular and New Spain as a whole were prospering in 1800. The native and mixed-blood labor force was completely subjugated and increasing, and the galleon fleets were carrying home increasing tonnage of silver, gold, and cochineal worth millions. Spanish authorities, however, failed to recognize that Mexico had changed in 300 years.

Criollos, the New Mexicans
Nearly three centuries of colonial rule gave rise to a burgeoning population of more than a million criollos—Mexican-born descendants of Spanish colonists, many rich and educated—to whom

top status was denied.

High government, church, and military office had always been the preserve of a tiny but powerful minority of *peninsulares*—European-born Spaniards. Criollos (kree-OH-yohs) could only watch in disgust as unlettered, unskilled *peninsulares* (derisively called *gachupines*—wearers of spurs) were boosted to authority over them.

Although the criollos stood high above the mestizo (mixed native-Spanish), Indian (more properly *indígena*), and black (African-Mexican) underclasses, that seemed little compensation for the false smiles, the deep bows, and the costly bribes that *gachupines* demanded.

Mestizos, *Indígenas,* and *Negros*
Upper-class luxury existed by virtue of the sweat of Mexico's mestizo, *indígena,* and black laborers and servants. African slaves were imported in large numbers during the 17th century after typhus, smallpox, and measles epidemics had wiped out most of the Indian population. In Oaxaca, a small African-born black population of around 2,000 in 1650 rose gradually to approximately 10,000, both pure and mixed, by 1800. Although the African-Mexicans contributed significantly (crafts, healing arts, dance, music, drums, and marimba), they had arrived last and experienced discrimination from everyone.

INDEPENDENCE

The chance for change came during the aftermath of the French invasion of Spain in 1808, when Napoléon Bonaparte replaced King Ferdinand VII with his brother Joseph on the Spanish throne. Most *peninsulares* backed the king; most criollos, however, inspired by the example of the recent American and French revolutions, talked and dreamed of independence. One such group, urged on by a firebrand parish priest, acted.

El Grito de Dolores
"*¡Viva México! Death to the Gachupines!*" Father **Miguel Hidalgo**'s impassioned *grito* from the church balcony in the Guanajuato town of Dolores on 16 September 1810 ignited passions. A mostly *indígena,* machete-wielding army of 20,000 coalesced around Hidalgo and his compatriots, Ignacio Allende and Juan Aldama. Their ragtag mob raged out of control through the Bajío, killing hated *gachupines* and pillaging their homes.

Hidalgo advanced on Mexico City but, unnerved by stiff royalist resistance, retreated and regrouped around Guadalajara. His rebels, whose numbers had swollen to 80,000, were no match for a disciplined, 6,000-strong royalist force. Hidalgo (now "Generalisimo") fled north but was soon apprehended, defrocked, and executed. His head and those of his comrades— Aldama, Allende, and Mariano Jiménez—were hung from the walls of the Guanajuato granary (site of the slaughter of 138 *gachupines* by Hidalgo's army) for 10 years as grim reminders of the consequences of rebellion.

The 10-Year Struggle
Others carried on, however. A former mestizo student of Hidalgo, **José María Morelos,** carried the Independence struggle to Oaxaca in earnest by defeating the Oaxaca capital's royalist defenders on 25 November 1812. He set up a revolutionary government and fanned the flames with his liberationist newspaper *El Correo Americano del Sur (The American Post of the South)* until seriously defeated in Michoacán a year later. The victorious royalists retook Oaxaca City on 29 January 1814, sending defending *insurgente* commander Ramón Rayón fleeing north to Tehuacán, Puebla.

Although the royalists seriously damaged the rebel cause by capturing and executing Morelos in December 1815, Morelos's compatriot **Vicente Guerrero** continued the fight, joining forces with criollo royalist Brigadier Agustín de Iturbide. Their Plan de Iguala promised "Three Guarantees"—the renowned Trigarantes: Independence, Catholicism, and Equality—which

their army (commanded by Iturbide, of course) would enforce. On 21 September 1821, Iturbide rode triumphantly into Mexico City at the head of his army of Trigarantes. Mexico was independent at last.

But the cost of the struggle had been great, especially in Oaxaca. Ten years of war had decimated the cochineal industry and sent Oaxaca's rich Spaniards and their capital fleeing to Mexico City and Europe. The criollo professional and business class now found themselves at the top of the social ladder, but with little money for rebuilding. Everyone tightened their belts as Oaxaca industry reverted to traditional products: soap, *aguardiente* (white lightning) distillation, *pulque* (native beer), wool, leather, and pottery.

Moreover, in Mexico as a whole, Independence had resolved few grievances except to expel the *peninsulares.* With an illiterate populace and no experience in self-government, Mexicans began a tragic 40-year love affair with a fantasy: the general on the white horse, the gold-braided hero who could save them from themselves.

The Rise and Fall of Agustín I
Iturbide—crowned Emperor Agustín I by the bishop of Guadalajara on 21 July 1822—soon lost his charisma. Attempting to assert his authority, Iturbide dissolved the national Congress on 31 October, igniting a roar of protests. Among the loudest protesters was Iturbide's military governor of Oaxaca, Colonel Antonio de León. In a pattern that became sadly predictable for succeeding generations of topsy-turvy Mexican politics, ambitious commanders issued *pronunciamientos,* declarations against the government. Supporting *pronunciamientos* followed, and old revolutionary heroes Guerrero, Guadalupe Victoria, and Nicolás Bravo endorsed a "plan"—the Plan of Casa Mata (not unlike Iturbide's previous Plan de Iguala)—dethroning Iturbide in favor of a republic. Iturbide, his braid tattered and brass tarnished, abdicated in mid-February 1823.

On 1 June 1823, carried away by liberationist zeal, León set up a local provisional government that declared Oaxaca to be a "free and independent" state and wrote a state constitution. Simultaneously, delegates in Mexico City were doing the same, creating the republic of the Estados Unidos Mexicanos ("United Mexican

States"), which Oaxaca soon joined. The country overflowed with republican zeal. Oaxacans rewrote their state constitution to conform with the federal document, creating a governor, bicameral legislature, local governments, and state departments, including public instruction and the Institute of Sciences and Arts (now the Benito Juárez Autonomous University). Graduates of the institute, notably Mexico's famous pair of presidents, Benito Juárez and Porfirio Díaz, both of indigenous descent, gradually began to fill the leadership vacuum left by the departed Spanish elite.

The Disastrous Era of Santa Anna
Antonio López de Santa Anna, the eager 28-year-old military commander of Veracruz, whose *pronunciamiento* had pushed Iturbide from his white horse, maneuvered to gradually replace him. Throughout the latter 1820s the government teetered between liberal and conservative hands six times in three years. Finally, unhappy with the 1828 presidential election result, Santa Anna "pronounced" in favor of the losing candidate, old independence *insurgente* Vicente Guerrero. This put Santa Anna at odds with government commanders all over the country—especially in Oaxaca City—which he attacked, but soon found himself seriously besieged in the fortress-like convent of Santo Domingo.

But Lady Luck, as usual, intervened in favor of Santa Anna. At the height of the siege, on 20 November 1829, government agents discovered that a Spanish force was being assembled in Cuba to re-invade Mexico. Faced with the external threat, former bitter enemies soon joined hands. On 5 January 1829, Santa Anna rushed from Oaxaca City with a combined force that, a few months later, defeated an abortive Spanish invasion attempt on the Gulf at Tampico. "The Victor of Tampico," people called Santa Anna.

In 1831, a rebellious, still-powerful Vicente Guerrero was kidnapped in Acapulco and handed over to agents of conservative President Anastasio Bustamante in Huatulco. He was taken to Oaxaca City and executed at the old convent in Cuilapan on 14 of February 1831. Later, upon the initiative of young Oaxaca legislative deputy Benito Juárez, Guerrero's remains were placed in an elaborate silver urn and re-interred in six days of solemn ceremonies

at Santo Domingo convent in the city.

In late 1832, the national government was bankrupt; mobs demanded the ouster of President Bustamante in retaliation for Guerrero's execution. Santa Anna issued a *pronunciamiento* against Bustamante, which Congress soon obliged, elevating Santa Anna to "Liberator of the Republic" and "Conqueror of the Spaniards" and naming him president in March 1833. More interested in the hunt than the prize, Santa Anna quickly resigned his office to Vice President Gómez Farías.

Santa Anna would pop in and out of the presidency like a jack-in-the-box 10 more times before 1855. First, he foolishly lost Texas to rebellious Anglo settlers in 1836. He later lost his leg (which was buried with full military honors) fighting the emperor of France.

Santa Anna's greatest debacle, however, was to declare war on the United States with just 1,839 pesos in the treasury. With his forces poised to defend Mexico City against a relatively small 10,000-man American invasion force, Santa Anna inexplicably withdrew. U.S. Marines surged into the "Halls of Montezuma," Chapultepec Castle, where Mexico's six beloved Niños Héroes cadets fell in the losing cause on 13 September 1847.

In the subsequent Treaty of Guadalupe Hidalgo, Mexico lost two-fifths of its territory—the present states of New Mexico, Arizona, California, Nevada, Utah, and Colorado—to the United States. Mexicans have never forgotten; they have looked upon gringos with a combination of admiration and disgust ever since.

Despite the national debacle, Oaxaca prospered under the 1848–52 governorship of Benito Juárez. Among his first acts was to deny Santa Anna, who was fleeing from American invaders, transit across Oaxaca territory. Besides keeping the peace, Juárez opened hundreds of elementary schools, a swarm of teacher's academies, and nearly wiped out the state debt. Improved roads and new bridges attracted Italian investment in mines; new coffee production began to replace Oaxaca's lost cochineal output. English entrepreneurs built a textile and hat factory, and artisans in Atzompa, near Oaxaca City, resumed producing their renowned pottery again in earnest. Oaxaca City's population swelled by more than 25 percent, to 24,000, between 1844 and 1854.

But for Santa Anna, however, enough was not enough. Called back as president for the last and 11th time in 1853, Santa Anna, now "His Most Serene Highness," financed his war against the liberals by selling off a part of southern New Mexico and Arizona, known as the Gadsden Purchase, for $10 million.

REFORM, CIVIL WAR, AND INVASION

The Reforms

Mexican leaders finally saw the light and exiled Santa Anna forever. While conservatives fumbled, searching for a king to replace Santa Anna, liberal leaders (whom Santa Anna had exiled or kept in jail) stirred up their own successful revolution. Juárez, having triumphantly returned to the Oaxaca governorship, and others plunged ahead with three controversial reform laws: the Ley Juárez, Ley Lerdo, and Ley Iglesias. These *reformas,* integrated into a new liberal Constitution of 1857, directly attacked the privilege and power of Mexico's corporate landlords, clergy, and generals: Ley Juárez abolished *fueros,* the separate military and church courts; Ley Lerdo forbade excess corporate (read: church) landholdings, and Ley Iglesias reduced or transferred most church power to the state.

Despite their liberal authors' good intentions, some of the reform provisions resulted in negative consequences. Although Ley Lerdo (the "Law of the Divestiture of the Property of the Dead Hand") succeeded in wiping out bloated church landholdings, it also forced thousands of native communities to sell their traditional land. Such sales invariably benefited the few rich individuals who could afford to buy, at the expense of the great mass of native Mexicans who became landless as a result. The reverse consequence was equally negative. It created a new class of superlandowners: *latifundistas,* who soon ruled small kingdoms with impunity all over Mexico.

Oaxaca, fortunately, ran counter to the national trend. Lack of local capital and isolation from Mexico City led to little investment in Oaxaca land, so most communal holdings remained in indigenous hands. Moreover, of the several hundred church parcels sold in Oaxaca, one-third were, surprisingly, bought by native Mexicans.

Alarmed by the reforms, conservative generals, priests, and businessmen and their mestizo and *indígena* followers revolted. The resulting War of the Reforms (not unlike the U.S. Civil War) ravaged the countryside for three long years until the victorious liberal army paraded triumphantly in Mexico City on New Year's Day 1861. In a thumping congratulations from the electors, Juárez outdistanced all rival candidates and became president in March 1861.

Juárez and Maximilian

Benito Juárez, the leading *reformista,* had won the day. His similarity to his contemporary, Abraham Lincoln, is legend: Juárez had risen from humble Zapotec native origins to become a lawyer, a champion of justice, and the president who held his country together during a terrible civil war. Like Lincoln, Juárez's triumph didn't last long.

Imperial France invaded Mexico in January 1862. Despite a formidable French force, which eventually ballooned to 60,000, Mexican regulars and guerrillas achieved a number of victories, several under the leadership of Oaxacan colonel (later general) Porfirio Díaz. Díaz rocketed to fame as the "Victor of Puebla" whose troops routed the French on 5 May ("Cinco de Mayo") 1862. The French nevertheless managed to occupy Mexico City and several state capitals, including Oaxaca City, by summer 1864.

After two costly years pushing Juárez's liberal army into the hills, the French installed the king Mexican conservatives thought the country needed. Austrian Archduke Maximilian and his wife Carlota, the very models of modern Catholic monarchs, were crowned emperor and empress of Mexico in June 1864.

The naive Emperor Maximilian I was surprised that some of his subjects resented his presence. Meanwhile, Juárez refused to yield, stubbornly performing his constitutional duties in a somber black carriage one jump ahead of the French occupying army. After Díaz's signal victories at Carbonera and Miahuatlán in Oaxaca in late 1866, the climax came in May 1867, when liberal forces besieged and defeated Maximilian at Querétaro. Juárez, giving no quarter, sternly ordered Maximilian's execution by firing squad on 19 June.

Juárez Re-elected; Díaz Rebels

Benito Juárez's tumultuous popular approval and reelection to the presidency in October 1867 was not without its costs. His critics, notably Sebastián Lerdo de Tejada and Porfirio Díaz (who retired from active military duty to seek the presidency himself) accused Juárez of heavy-handed constitutional violations. Under Díaz's influence, a number of military commanders stirred up local uprisings. Undeterred, Juárez worked day and night at the double task of reconstruction and reform. Single-mindedly, he pushed to amend the Constitution of 1857, a course that triggered a major armed revolt, the Rebellion of La Noria, by Díaz in 1871 to "restore the purity" of the constitution against Juárez's alleged transgressions. Although his political momentum was weakened, Juárez was reelected president over both Tejada and Díaz in October 1871, but he died of a heart attack on 18 July 1872. In his honor, Oaxaca City fathers renamed their city, officially, "Oaxaca de Juárez."

The passing of Benito Juárez, the stoic partisan of reform, signaled hope to Mexico's conservatives. They soon got their wish: General Don Porfirio Díaz, the "Coming Man," was elected president in 1876.

ORDER AND PROGRESS

Pax Porfiriana

Don Porfirio is often remembered wistfully, as old Italians remember Mussolini: "He was a bit rough, but, dammit, at least he made the trains run on time."

Although Porfirio Díaz's humble Oaxaca mestizo origins were not unlike Juárez's, Díaz was not a democrat: when he was a general, his officers often took no captives; when he was president, his country police, the *rurales,* shot prisoners in the act of "trying to escape."

Order and progress, in that sequence, ruled Mexico for 34 years. Foreign investment flowed into the country; new railroads brought the products of shiny factories, mines, and farms to modernized Gulf and Pacific ports. Mexico balanced its budget, repaid foreign debt, and became a respected member of the family of nations.

Oaxaca also gained material benefits from the Porfiriata, the label Mexican historians attach to

Díaz's long rule. The Mexico City rail link, which arrived in 1892, was the high point of three decades of public works improvement: bridges, roads, ports, electricity, sewage, an elegant theater, an Isthmus rail line, a state museum, and an enlarged Institute of Arts and Sciences. Rich foreign and Mexican investors dug dozens of new mines and built several factories, producing shoes, soap, hats, matches, glassware, cigarettes, and beer. In the southern mountains, coffee farms proliferated after the government offered a rebate for planting 2,000 coffee trees or more. Oaxaca City's population doubled, to nearly 40,000, during Díaz's rule.

The human price, nevertheless, was high. The rich, who included hundreds of resident foreigners, soaked up most of the profits while Oaxaca's poor, who lacked the money to benefit directly from the new civic improvements, struggled along as best they could. And although in Oaxaca most natives were able to hold on to their land, nationally Díaz's government did not intervene to prevent more than a hundred million acres—one-fifth of Mexico's land area (including most of the arable land)— being turned over to rich Mexicans and foreigners. Poor Mexicans suffered the most. By 1910, 90 percent of Mexico's *indígenas* had lost their traditional communal land. In the spring of 1910, a smug, now-cultured, and elderly Don Porfirio anticipated with relish the centennial of Hidalgo's Grito de Dolores.

REVOLUTION AND STABILIZATION

¡No Reelección!

Porfirio Díaz himself had first campaigned on the slogan. It expressed the idea that the president should step down after one term. Although Díaz had stepped down once in 1880, for an interregnum as Oaxaca's governor, in 1884 he got himself elected president again and remained in office for 26 consecutive years. In 1910, Francisco I. Madero, a short, squeaky-voiced son of rich landowners, opposed Díaz under the same banner.

Although Díaz had jailed him before the election, Madero refused to quit campaigning. From a safe platform in the United States, he called for a revolution to begin on 20

PORFIRIO DÍAZ

Porfirio Díaz, Mexico's most controversial and longest-serving president, was born in the city of Oaxaca on 15 September 1830. His parents, José de la Cruz Díaz and Petrona Mori, were of poor Mixtec-mestizo origin. Porfirio's father died when he was three, and he spent his childhood working at odd jobs to support his mother while attending public and parochial schools. He entered seminary in Oaxaca in 1843, dropped out after three years, and resumed studies, in law, at the Institute of Arts and Sciences, where he briefly taught in 1854.

A seminal event occurred for young Porfirio in 1854, when it was publicly announced that the entire faculty of the institute unanimously supported the notorious conservative dictator Antonio López de Santa Anna. Díaz asked that his abstention be recorded, and when publicly accused of siding with the liberal cause, he declared his support for General Juan Álvarez, leader of the liberal rebellion in Guerrero. The die was thus cast: for the next 50 years, Díaz never wavered from the image of a resolute, determined liberal, who possessed the courage of his convictions.

Forced to flee, Porfirio joined a rebel guerrilla band in the northern Sierra and, later, in 1856, the Oaxaca National Guard, where he found purpose fighting for Benito Juárez's liberal side during the civil War of the Reforms. His valor and ability elevated him to the rank of brigadier general at the time of the liberal triumph in 1861.

During the imperialist French Intervention, his military reputation skyrocketed when his forces defeated the French army at Puebla on 5 May 1862, the still-celebrated Cinco de Mayo national holiday. After 25 battles and the liberation of Oaxaca, Puebla, and Mexico City, Díaz retired from the military in 1867 at the age of 37.

It turned out that Díaz's insatiable ambition was driving him toward the presidency. He opposed Juárez and Lerdo de Tejada in the 1871 election, which, with no clear winner, was thrown into Congress, where Juárez was re-elected. Díaz revolted unsuccessfully; Juárez died and Lerdo de Tejada became president. Díaz rebelled again, in 1876, promulgating the doctrine of *"No Reelección"* in his Plan of Tuxtepec. Lerdo de Tejada fled, and Porfirio Díaz finally assumed the presidency legally on 5 May 1877.

Mexico, however, remained a hotbed of revolt. Díaz found that he had to put some of his democratic principles aside to remain in office and keep the country together. He reasoned in essence that, after all, if you don't have a government, you can't have democracy. His treatment of captured local rebels— *Matalos en caliente* ("Kill them on the spot")—was typically brutal.

Díaz retained enough of his liberal idealism to follow his own *No Reelección* prescription to step down from the presidency in 1880 to become governor of Oaxaca, but after that he was re-elected consecutively and held office for 28 more years, until 1911.

November. The response in Oaxaca was typical: in the countryside, a few leaders rallied around Madero's banner, but Díaz had them rounded up and then got his nephew, Félix, installed as governor.

¡No Reelección! after all, is not much of a platform. But millions of poor Mexicans were going to bed hungry, and Díaz hadn't listened to them for years.

Villa and Zapata

In May 1910, those millions of poor Mexicans began to stir. In Oaxaca, a swarm of small rebellions broke out, then coalesced into a general revolution, which toppled Félix Díaz from the governorship. Simultaneously, up north in Chihuahua, followers of Francisco (Pancho) Villa, an erstwhile ranch hand, miner, peddler, and cattle rustler, began attacking the *rurales,* dynamiting railroads, and raiding towns. Meanwhile, in Morelos state, just north of Oaxaca, horse trader, farmer, and minor official Emiliano Zapata and his *indígena* guerrillas were terrorizing rich *hacendados* and forcibly recovering stolen ancestral village lands. Zapata's movement gained steam and by mid-May had taken the Morelos state capital, Cuernavacoa. Meanwhile, Madero crossed the Río Grande and joined with Villa's forces, who took Ciudad Juárez. Soon the *federales,* government army troops, began deserting in droves, and on 25 May 1911 Díaz submitted his resignation.

The 34-year period (1876–1910) known as the Porfiriata was marked by stability and modernization. Díaz managed stability by conciliation, negotiation, cajolery, and, if all these failed, repression. He accomplished what no other president had been able to do—control the army. Under Díaz the army quieted down, stayed in its barracks, and left politics to the politicians.

A stable Mexico attracted foreign investment. Mostly American and British entrepreneurs and engineers expanded railroads from a mere 400 miles in 1876 to 15,000 miles by 1910. New factories, mills, and mines blossomed along the railroads, which brought raw materials and took away manufactured goods to cities and modernized ports.

Díaz's industrialization plans were directed by a clique of advisers who professed to apply scientific principles to government and became known as the Científicos. Their policies, however, were decidedly elitist and ended up concentrating land, wealth, and power in foreign and upper-class hands, pushing Mexico's already poor indigenous population into even deeper poverty.

In 1908, Díaz hinted in an interview that he would retire in 1910 at the age of 80. This encouraged his growing political opposition, and when Díaz changed his mind and stood for another term in 1910, he was opposed by northern factory owner Francisco I. Madero, who campaigned on Díaz's original *"No Reelección"* slogan. Díaz had Madero jailed and won election to his eighth presidential term.

But this time, Díaz was too tired to keep the lid on; his long rule collapsed partly because of its own success. Díaz had transformed the country. In many ways it reflected his original liberal vision of a stronger, richer, and better-educated Mexico, with a democratic balance of power and a procedure for orderly succession. But Díaz's failures, driven by cynicism, complacency, and a thirst for dominance, produced a regime that, like a dinosaur, fell under its own weight on 31 May 1911.

Díaz, in exile in Paris, complaining of French food and yearning for some home-cooked Oaxacan fare, died on 2 July 1915.

Porfirio Díaz

As Madero's deputy, General Victoriano Huerta, put Díaz on his ship of exile in Veracruz, Díaz confided: "Madero has unleashed a tiger. Now let's see if he can control it."

Madero's star, nevertheless, was still rising. As he paraded triumphantly into Mexico City, revolutionary state governments were blossoming all over the country. Benito Juárez's son, Benito Juárez Maza, served briefly as Oaxaca's *maderista* governor in 1911–12 until he was killed in a local skirmish.

The Fighting Continues

Emiliano Zapata turned out to be that very tiger whom Madero had unleashed. Meeting with Madero in Mexico City, Zapata fumed over Madero's go-slow approach to the "agrarian problem," as Madero termed it. By November 1912, Zapata had denounced Madero. *"¡Tierra y Libertad!"* ("Land and Liberty") the Zapatistas cried, as Madero's support faded. The army in Mexico City rebelled; Huerta forced Madero to resign on 18 February 1913, then murdered him four days later.

The rum-swilling Huerta ruled like a Chicago mobster; general rebellion, led by the "Big Four"—Villa, Alvaro Obregón, and Venustiano Carranza in the north, and Zapata in the south—soon broke out. Pressed by the rebels and refused United States recognition, Huerta fled into exile in July 1914.

Meanwhile in Oaxaca, fighting between liberals and conservatives, much like the wars for Independence and the Reforms, laid waste to the countryside, killing commerce and sending foreign investors fleeing. But unlike the rest of the country, Oaxaca had no majority class of landless campesinos and consequently no great radical cause or leader to champion it.

Disgusted with the barbaric war of attrition ravaging the rest of the country, many Oaxaca leaders publicly repudiated the "Big Four" and declared Oaxaca a "sovereign" republic and tried to deny access to revolutionary outsiders.

Oaxacan conservatives, however, made a serious error in betraying and murdering Jésus Carranza, brother of El Primer Jefe ("First Chief") Venustiano Carranza. Soon *Carranzista* battalions invaded Oaxaca and quickly defeated local forces, sending Oaxacan leaders scurrying to Mexico City or to the mountains, where they fought on for years as guerrillas.

The Constitution of 1917

The national struggle ground on for three more years as authority seesawed between revolutionary factions. Finally Carranza, who controlled most of the country by 1917, got a convention together in Querétaro to formulate political and social goals. The resulting Constitution of 1917, while restating most ideas of the Reformistas' 1857 constitution, additionally prescribed a single four-year presidential term, labor reform, and subordinated private ownership to public interest. Every village had a right to communal *ejido* land, and subsoil wealth could never be sold away to the highest bidder.

The Constitution of 1917 was a revolutionary expression of national aspirations and, in retrospect, represented a social and political agenda for the entire 20th century. In modified form, it has lasted to the present day.

Obregón Stabilizes Mexico

On 1 December 1920, General Alvaro Obregón legally assumed the presidency of a Mexico still bleeding from 10 years of civil war. Although a seasoned revolutionary, Obregón was also a negotiator who recognized that peace was necessary to implement the goals of the revolution. In four years his government pacified local uprisings, disarmed a swarm of warlords, executed hundreds of *bandidos,* obtained U.S. diplomatic

MUSEO DE LA REVOLUCIÓN, CHIHUAHUA

Francisco Villa crying at the grave of Madero

recognition, assuaged the worst fears of the clergy and landowners, and began land reform.

With Obregón as an example, Oaxaca's new governor García Vigil went to work. Despite the irritant of remnant revolutionary guerrilla bands in the countryside, Vigil pushed a successful land reform and wrote a new constitution, which is essentially in effect today. His tax reform plans, however, ran into trouble with Oaxaca's rich landowners and came to nothing when he was assassinated in 1924.

At the national level, Obregón's success set the stage for Plutarco Elías Calles, Obregón's Secretaría de Gobernación and handpicked successor, who won the 1924 national election. Aided by peace, Mexico returned to a semblance of prosperity. Calles brought the army under civilian control, balanced the budget, and shifted Mexico's revolution into high gear. New clinics vaccinated millions against smallpox, new dams irrigated thousands of previously dry acres, and campesinos received millions of acres of redistributed land.

Simultaneously, Calles threatened foreign oil companies, demanding they exchange their titles for 50-year leases. A moderate Mexican supreme court decision over the oil issue and the skillful arbitration of U.S. Ambassador Dwight Morrow smoothed over both the oil and church troubles by the end of Calles's term.

Calles, who started out brimming with revolutionary fervor and populist zeal, became increasingly conservative and dictatorial. Although he bowed out peaceably in favor of Obregón (the constitution had been amended to allow one six-year nonsuccessive term), Obregón was assassinated two weeks after his election in 1928. Calles continued to rule for six more years through three puppet-presidents: Emilio Portes Gil (1928–30), Pascual Ortiz Rubio (1930–32), and Abelardo Rodríguez (1932–34).

Calles Forms the PRI

In 1929, President Calles united three of Mexico's major constituencies: the country poor (represented by the Confederación Nacional de Campesinos, CNC), the workers (Confederación de Trabajadore Méjicanos, CTM), and the middle classes (Confederación de Nacional de Organizaciones Populares, CNOP). Calles christened his new super political party the Partido Revolucionario Institucional (Institutional Revolutionary Party), or PRI, or, pronounced simply, the "pree."

The PRI dominated Mexican, and especially Oaxacan, politics during the 60 years after its founding. PRI presidents handpicked their PRI successors, who always got elected. Federal government contracts and salary money flowed from PRI headquarters in Mexico City to state and municipal officials, who were nearly always loyal local members of the PRI.

Oaxaca, isolated from the national economy and with no influential revolutionary ex-general to demand its fair share of national patronage, was consistently underfunded and mostly ignored by the central government. Nevertheless, despite a severe earthquake in 1931 and general economic depression, Oaxacans managed some modest public works improvements during the 1930s and early '40s. A paved road to Monte Albán led to important archaeological discoveries; other new highways branched out from the valley to the Mixteca, the Isthmus, and to Puerto Ángel. Oaxaca City residents benefited from a few improvements, such as a new water works and restoration of the opera house. But revolution and hard times had taken their toll: in 1940, Oax-

aca City's population, about 40,000, was still the same as in 1910.

Lázaro Cárdenas, President of the People

Although he had received Calles's blessing for the 1934 presidential election, ex-general Lázaro Cárdenas, the 40-year-old former governor of Michoacán, immediately set his own agenda. Cárdenas worked tirelessly to fulfill the social prescriptions of the revolution. As morning-coated diplomats and cabinet ministers fretted in his outer office, Cárdenas ushered in delegations of campesinos and factory workers and sympathetically listened to their problems.

In his six years of rule, Cárdenas moved public education and health forward on a broad front, supported strong labor unions, and redistributed 49 million acres of farmland, more than any president before or since.

Cárdenas's resolute enforcement of the constitution's Artículo 123 brought him the most renown. Under this pro-labor law, the government turned over a host of private companies to employee ownership and, on 18 March 1938, expropriated all foreign oil corporations.

In retrospect the oil corporations, most of which were British, were not blameless. They had sorely neglected the wages, health, and welfare of their workers while ruthlessly taking the law into their own hands with private police forces. Although Standard Oil cried foul, the U.S. government did not intervene. Through negotiation and due process, U.S. companies eventually were compensated with $24 million plus 3 percent interest. In the wake of the expropriation, President Cárdenas created Petróleos Mexicanos (Pemex), the national oil corporation that continues to run all Mexican oil and gas operations to the present day.

Manuel Avila Camacho

Manuel Avila Camacho, elected in 1940, was the last general to be president of Mexico. His administration ushered in a gradual shift of Mexican politics, government, and foreign policy as Mexico allied itself with the U.S. cause during WW II. Foreign tourism, initially promoted by the Cárdenas administration, ballooned. Good feelings surged as Franklin Roosevelt became the first U.S. president to officially cross the Río Grande when he met with Camacho in Monterrey in April 1943.

As World War II moved toward its 1945 conclusion, both the United States and Mexico were enjoying the benefits of four years of governmental and military cooperation and mutual trade in the form of a mountain of strategic minerals, which had moved north in exchange for a similar mountain of U.S. manufactures that moved south.

CONTEMPORARY MEXICO AND OAXACA

The Mature Revolution

During the decades after WW II, beginning with moderate President **Miguel Alemán** (1946–52), Mexican politicians gradually honed their skills of consensus and compromise as their middle-aged revolution bubbled along under liberal presidents and sputtered haltingly under conservatives. Doctrine required of all politicians, regardless of stripe, that they be "revolutionary" enough to be included beneath the banner of the PRI, Mexico's dominant political party.

Mexico's revolution hasn't been very revolutionary about women's rights, however. The PRI didn't get around to giving Mexican women, millions of whom fought and died alongside their men during the revolution, the right to vote until 1953.

Alemán's government in 1947 began construction of a huge power and irrigation dam in the Río Papaloapan watershed of northern Oaxaca. The resulting Miguel Alemán dam, completed a few years later, created a mammoth 2.3-million-acre reservoir. Although providing a large chunk of the region's growing electricity demand and an assured irrigation supply for thousands of new fruit, dairy, and vegetable farms, the project required the painful relocation of many thousands of poor Mazatec, Chinantec, and Mixe *indígena* families.

Political Trouble in Oaxaca

Meanwhile, in Oaxaca City, trouble was breaking out, triggered by unpopular actions of Governor Edmund Sánchez Cano. Merchants, who objected to his new taxes, and students, who resented the governor's interference in university affairs, got together and occupied the state government palace. Before the dust settled, federal

troops were occupying the city and Mexico's second-in-command, the Secretaría de Gobernación, had forced Governor Sánchez's resignation and taken over the state government.

Trouble erupted again in 1951. This time, the dispute had roots among coffee farmers in Oaxaca's southern Sierra. Growers, far removed from Oaxaca City, had been shipping their coffee directly from Pacific ports or by remote roads directly to Mexico City, where they had developed strong commercial and political connections. Although responsible for Oaxaca's major export, coffee growers enjoyed little influence among state officials in Oaxaca City. One of these growers, Mayoral Heredia, had become a close family friend of President Miguel Alemán, who endorsed Heredia's successful PRI candidacy for governor of Oaxaca in 1950.

Upon taking office in December 1950, Heredia replaced the local politicos with his own Mexico City cadre, then proceeded with plans to modernize Oaxaca's agriculture, with subsidies paid by new state taxes. The ensuing dispute revolved fundamentally around the question of power: Who should control Oaxaca—the city leaders as usual, or Mexico City–oriented appointees?

Soon, most townspeople—notably among them, local businesspeople and university professors and students—lined up angrily against the governor. The governor's sole supporters were the state police, who, in the heat of action, shot two protesting university students. After a one-day national student strike and weeks of daily protests, the merchant-student-professor coalition mounted a citywide general strike. Finally, President Alemán had to send in a federal regiment to restore order. Discredited, Governor Heredia was forced to replace his cabinet with city leaders. They reversed his modernization plans: they judged the present dirt roads adequate and found no need for tractors or irrigation. Oaxaca agriculture would sputter along as it had for the past hundred years. Rebuffed, Governor Heredia soon resigned in July 1952.

Political Activism of the '60s and '70s

Women, voting for the first time in a national election, kept the PRI in power by electing liberal **Adolfo López Mateos** in 1958. Resembling

Lázaro Cárdenas in social policy, López Mateos redistributed 40 million acres of farmland, forced automakers to use 60 percent domestic components, built thousands of new schools, and distributed hundreds of millions of new textbooks. *"La electricidad es nuestra"* ("Electricity is ours"), Mateos declared as he nationalized foreign power companies in 1962.

Despite his left-leaning social agenda, unions were restive under López Mateos. Protesting inflation, workers struck; the government retaliated, arresting Demetrios Vallejo, the railway union head, and renowned muralist David Siqueiros, former Communist party secretary.

Despite the troubles, López Mateos climaxed his presidency gracefully in 1964 as he opened the celebrated National Museum of Anthropology, appropriately located in Chapultepec Park, where the Aztecs had first settled 20 generations earlier.

In 1964, as several times before, the outgoing president's Secretaría de Gobernación succeeded his former chief. Dour, conservative **Gustavo Díaz Ordaz** immediately clashed with liberals, labor, and students. The pot boiled over just before the 1968 Mexico City Olympics. Reacting to a student rebellion, the army occupied the National University; shortly afterward, on 2 October, government forces opened fire with machine guns on a peaceful downtown rally crowd, killing hundreds and wounding thousands.

The Mexico City troubles re-ignited political activism in Oaxaca. Local university students, organized as the Federación Estudiantil de Oaxaca (FEO), mounted a successful campaign in support of bus drivers in 1970. In 1972, the students joined with workers and poor farmers, forming the Coalición de Obreros, Campesinos, y Estudiantes de Oaxaca (COCEO). They led off with a fight on behalf of sidewalk vendors to prevent the Saturday market being moved to the city's southern outskirts. After that, a disgruntled student splinter faction set off three small bombs: in the PRI-dominated union office, at an English-language library, and in the (empty) folk-dance amphitheater on the hill above the city. Fortunately, no one was injured. Later, in the mid-'70s, the COCEO supported and helped organize rural land invasions by villagers, organized and supported city workers'

unions, and backed hillside squatters on the city's northern edge.

The actions in the capital inspired activists in other parts of Oaxaca. In Juchitán, on the Isthmus, students united with workers and poor farmers to form the Coalición Obero, Campesino, y Estudiantil del Istmo (COCEI). Unlike its Oaxaca City counterpart, the COCEI had a strong indigenous Zapotec cultural orientation, with women exerting important, although behind-the-scenes leadership roles. Moreover, their cultural unity produced unusual militancy and political skill. Through a series of actions—strikes, boycotts, marches, and demonstrations—they opposed city hall cliques and local *caciques* (bosses) at the painful cost of 20 of their number killed or kidnapped by police, soldiers, and hired thugs. Their payment in blood, however, led to significant improvements in working and living conditions for poor people in Juchitán and other Isthmus communities. Moreover, they forced the local establishment politicos to recognize their legitimacy by winning the 1980 local elections and making Juchitán one of the few towns in Mexico without a PRI-dominated city government.

Meanwhile, back in Oaxaca City, student influence peaked, then faded in 1977 over a dispute that started with election of the university (Universidad Autonoma de Benito Juárez de Oaxaca, UABJO) rector, equivalent to a university president in the United States. Actions escalated until snipers were killing people in university buildings. As police stepped in to restore order, students protested and organized strikes. Fed up with the turmoil, merchants, property owners, and the local PRI organized their own anti-student shutdown, triggering a student-worker march upon the central plaza. State police opened fire, killing one and wounding dozens. That night the federal government clamped down. Troops took control, and Zárate Aquino, the third Oaxaca governor to be forced from office within a generation, left permanently. Soldiers patrolled the city for nine months, demonstrations were banned, and the anti-establishment COCEO coalition collapsed.

Having had to deal with a generation of Oaxacan political turmoil, the federal government began to direct more resources to Oaxaca. Federal expenditures and employment in Oaxaca City doubled during the 1970s. Improved roads linked villages to the city, electric lines extended into formerly isolated mountain villages, a host of schools and health centers proliferated, and many villages and towns got clean water systems for the first time. With the money and power flowing from Mexico City, Oaxaca's local merchant and professional old guard gradually lost their influence over state government.

New Mexican Industrialization

Despite its serious internal troubles, Mexico's relations with the United States were cordial. President Lyndon Johnson visited and unveiled a statue of Abraham Lincoln in Mexico City. Later, President Díaz Ordaz met with President Richard Nixon in Puerto Vallarta.

Meanwhile, bilateral negotiations produced the **Border Industrialization Program.** Within a 12-mile strip south of the U.S.-Mexico border, foreign companies could assemble duty-free parts into finished goods and export them without any duties on either side. Within a dozen years, a swarm of such plants, called maquiladoras, were humming as hundreds of thousands of Mexican workers assembled and exported billions of dollars worth of shiny consumer goods—electronics, clothes, furniture, pharmaceuticals, and toys—worldwide.

Concurrently, in Mexico's interior, Díaz Ordaz pushed Mexico's industrialization ahead full steam. Foreign money financed hundreds of new plants and factories. Primary among these was the giant Las Truchas steel plant at the new industrial port and town of Lázaro Cárdenas at the Pacific mouth of the Río Balsas.

Very little of Mexico's new industrial development reached Oaxaca, however. Oaxaca's sparse industry, with few exceptions, remained simple, producing raw materials or goods for local consumption only.

Oil Boom, Economic Bust

Discovery in 1974 of gigantic new oil and gas reserves along Mexico's Gulf Coast added fuel to Mexico's already rapid industrial expansion. During the late 1970s and early '80s, billions in foreign investment, lured by Mexico's oil earnings, financed other major developments—factories, hotels, power plants, roads, airports—all over the country.

A modest share of Mexico's new oil wealth

trickled to Oaxaca, in increased government jobs, infrastructure construction, and the new cross-Isthmus pipelines and Salina Cruz oil refinery, completed in 1977. Soon 3,000 Oaxacan workers were processing 800,000 barrels of Gulf crude a year into gasoline, diesel and jet fuel, and liquid propane and butane, which tank trucks, railway cars, and ocean tankers distributed all over Mexico and the Pacific Rim.

The negative side to these expensive projects was the huge dollar debt required to finance them. President **Luis Echeverría Alvarez** (1970–76), diverted by his interest in international affairs, passed Mexico's burgeoning balance of payments deficit to his successor, **José López Portillo.** As feared by some experts, a world petroleum glut during the early 1980s burst Mexico's ballooning oil bubble and plunged the country into financial crisis. When the 1982 interest came due on its foreign debt, Mexico's largest holding company couldn't pay the $2.3 billion owed. The peso plummeted more than fivefold, to 150 per U.S. dollar. At the same time, prices doubled every year.

In the mid-'80s President **Miguel de la Madrid** (1982–88) was straining to get Mexico's economic house in order. He sliced government and raised taxes, asking rich and poor alike to tighten their belts. Despite getting foreign bankers to reschedule Mexico's debt, de la Madrid couldn't stop inflation. Prices skyrocketed as the peso deflated to 2,500 per U.S. dollar, becoming one of the world's most devalued currencies by 1988.

Such economic belt-tightening invariably hits the poor hardest, and Oaxacans are among Mexico's poorest. Oaxaca's families average only about US$2,000 income per year—about one-third of the Mexican average, and less than a tenth of the U.S. average. The problem is much worse for Oaxaca's dirt-poor, who, in Oaxaca City, make up about one-third of the population. Their yearly average family income hovers somewhere around $1,000, less than $100 per month. With basic food prices not much different from in the United States, hunger, if not outright starvation, has been an everyday fact for many Oaxacans for as long as they can remember.

Salinas de Gortari, Solidaridad, and NAFTA

Public disgust led to significant opposition during the 1988 presidential election. Billionaire National Action Party candidate Michael Clothier and liberal National Democratic Front candidate Cuauhtémoc Cárdenas ran against the PRI's Harvard-educated technocrat Carlos Salinas de Gortari. The vote was split so evenly that all three candidates claimed victory. Although Salinas de Gortari eventually won the election, his showing, barely half of the vote, was the worst ever for an Institutional Revolutionary Party president.

Salinas de Gortari, however, became Mexico's "Coming Man" of the '90s. He seemed serious about democracy, sympathetic to the *indígenas* and the poor, and sensitive to women's issues. One of Salinas de Gortari's biggest domestic successes was the popular "Solidarity" (Programa Nacional de Solidaridad, PRONASOL) program, which aided poor communities in locally run self-help, cultural, sanitation, health, agricultural and other projects. Especially targeted were small, mostly indigenous Oaxaca coffee producers who, through local Solidaridad committees, received hundreds of interest-free loans.

Salinas de Gortari's major international achievement, despite significant national opposition, was the North American Free Trade Agreement (NAFTA), which he, U.S. President George Bush, and Canadian Prime Minister Brian Mulrooney negotiated in 1992 and which the Canadian, U.S., and Mexican legislatures ratified in 1993.

However, on the very day in January 1994 that NAFTA took effect, rebellion broke out in Oaxaca's neighboring state of Chiapas. A small but well-disciplined campesino force, calling itself Ejército Zapatista Liberación Nacional (Zapatista National Liberation Army, EZLN) or "Zapatistas," captured a number of provincial towns and held the former governor of Chiapas hostage. Although PRI officials minimized the uprising and President Clinton expressed confidence in the Mexican government, many thoughtful observers wondered if Mexico was ready for NAFTA.

The Zapatista revolt rattled Oaxaca. In a social trend that had been growing at least since the Isthmus Zapotec community became politicized and formed the COCEI during the '70s, indigenous communities all over the state began pushing for their rights under the Mexican constitution. Prime movers in this movement have been lib-

erationist Catholic priests and nuns, especially in remote country parishes.

Although successful clergy-led projects have sprung up around the capital, in the Mixteca, the southern Sierra, and other Oaxaca locations, the Isthmus provides the most successful examples. Under the leadership of clergy, in dozens of communities around Tehuantepec, thousands of indigenous people—Mixe, Chontal, Huave, Zapotec, and others—organize self-help, cultural, political, and communal work programs. Their moneymaking activities range from raising coffee, sheep and chickens to milling corn and producing pottery, which they sell in the Tehuantepec, Salina Cruz, and Juchitán markets.

One of the most successful actors in all this ferment has been the Unión de Comunidades de la Region del Istmo (UCIRI), headquartered in Lachaviza, north of Tehuantepec. Fed up with corrupt middlemen and discouraged by the lack of governmental help, small coffee growers banded together and now represent 3,000 growers in 50 communities. Besides working together in production, transportation, and sales, they organize cooperative self-education (especially in organic farming) and run a savings bank, clinic, and cooperative grocery, hardware, and drug stores.

The Zapatista revolt has struck the common chord—of autonomy—among virtually all of Oaxaca's indigenous social-political groups. Echoing the Zapatistas in Chiapas, their political goals usually include the right of self-rule by their own traditional means.

A National Tragedy

In mid-1994, Mexico's already tense political drama veered toward tragedy. While Salinas de Gortari's chief negotiator, Manuel Camacho Solis, was attempting to iron out a settlement with the Zapatista rebels, Luis Donaldo Colosio, Salinas's handpicked presidential candidate, was gunned down just months before the August balloting. However, instead of disintegrating, the nation united in grief; opposition candidates eulogized their fallen former opponent and later earnestly engaged his replacement, stolid technocrat Ernesto Zedillo, in Mexico's first presidential election debate.

In a closely watched election relatively unmarred by irregularities, Zedillo piled up a solid plurality against his PAN (National Action Party) and PRD (Revolutionary Democratic Party) opponents. By perpetuating the PRI's 65-year hold on the presidency, the electorate had again opted for the PRI's familiar although imperfect middle-aged revolution.

A New Economic Crisis

Zedillo, however, had little time to savor his victory. The peso, long propped up by his predecessor's fiscal policies, lost one-third of its value in the few days before Christmas 1994. A month later, the peso was trading at about six per dollar, and Mexican financial institutions, their dollar debt having nearly doubled in a month, were in danger of defaulting on their obligations to international investors. To stave off a worldwide financial panic, U.S. President Bill Clinton in February 1995 secured an unprecedented multibillion-dollar loan package for Mexico, guaranteed by United States and international institutions.

Although disaster was temporarily averted and Mexico became an overnight bargain for dollar-spending travelers, the cure for the country's ills required another painful round of inflation and belt-tightening for poor Mexicans. During 1995, national inflation soared by 52 percent, pushing already-meager wages down an additional 20 percent. More and more families became unable to purchase staple foods and basic medicines. Malnutrition soared sixfold, and third world diseases, such as cholera and dengue fever, resurged in the countryside.

The Political Cauldron Bubbles On

At the same time, Mexico's equally serious political ills seemed to defy cure. Raul Salinas de Gortari, an important PRI party official and the former president's brother, was arrested for money laundering and political assassination. As popular sentiment began to implicate Carlos Salinas de Gortari himself, the former president fled Mexico to an undisclosed location.

Meanwhile, as negotiations with the rebel Zapatistas sputtered on and off in Chiapas, popular discontent erupted in Oaxaca's western neighbor-state, Guerrero, leading to the massacre of 17 unarmed campesinos at Aguas Blancas, in the hills west of Acapulco, by state police in June 1995. One year later, at a demonstration protesting the

a call to "Stop Repression!"

massacre, a new, well-armed revolutionary group, **Ejército Popular Revolucionario** (People's Revolutionary Army, EPR) made its appearance. Scarcely two months later, on 28 August, EPR guerrillas killed more than two dozen police and soldiers at several southwest Mexico locations, including four sailors at the naval garrison in Huatulco, Oaxaca. Some guerrillas were also slain and identified, providing the government with clues. Although President Zedillo's immediate reaction was moderate, platoons of soldiers and police were soon scouring rural Guerrero, Oaxaca, Michoacán, and other states, searching homes and arresting suspected dissidents.

In September and October 1995, the army and police rounded up more than a dozen community leaders in the Oaxacan southern Sierra villages of San Agustín Loxicha and San Francisco Loxicha. Although later released, the leaders complained that they were "beaten, threatened with death, and forced to confess to membership in the EPR." A year and a half later, the former mayor of San Agustín Loxicha, Alberto

Antonio, was arrested and charged with murder. He denied government charges that he is guerrilla Comandante Francisco, a high-ranking member of EPR.

Mexican democracy got a much-needed boost when notorious Guerrero governor Ruben Figueroa, who had tried to cover up the Aguas Blancas massacre with a bogus videotape, was forced from office. At the same time, although the official negotiations with the Zapatista rebels were stalled over the issue of indigenous rights, the Zedillo government gained momentum in addressing other local grievances in Chiapas by building new rural electrification networks and refurbishing health clinics. Similar federal action seemed to be forthcoming in Oaxaca also, when, in early 1996, President Zedillo recognized that "success or failure of [his] social policy" depended on Oaxaca and announced an unprecedented $1 billion in federal expenditures in Oaxaca for the upcoming fiscal year.

Nevertheless, continued federal military presence, especially in Guerrero, Oaxaca, and Chiapas, seemed to trigger violent incidents. Worst was the massacre of 45 indigenous campesinos, including women and children, at Acteal, Chiapas, in late December 1997 by paramilitary gunmen. Federal investigators later linked the perpetrators to local PRI officials. In mid-1998, the EPR appeared in Ayutla, Guerrero, leafleting villagers and giving impromptu speeches. Government soldiers responded with repression, violent searches, and torture. Finally, federal troops cornered and killed 11 suspected EPR members in a schoolhouse 50 miles east of Acapulco.

The rough federal army and police searches, arrests, and jailings have energized a flurry of political action. Oaxacan human rights groups, already protesting against unpunished violence, have upped the pressure for reforms at the state and national level. The official Oaxaca State Human Rights Commission (Comisión Estatal de Derechos Humanos, CNDH) hears complaints and issues "nonbinding and autonomous recommendations" to relevant authorities.

Fortunately, foreign visitors in Oaxaca have been unaffected by such disputes. In Oaxaca City especially, and along well-traveled highways, in resorts, towns, and sites of touristic interest, foreign visitors are generally much safer than in their home cities in the United States, Canada, or Europe.

Economic Recovery and Political Reforms

The best news for which the government could justly claim credit was the dramatically improving national economy. By mid-1998, annual inflation had dropped below 15 percent, investment dollars were flowing back into Mexico, the peso had stabilized at about eight to the U.S. dollar, and Mexico had paid back every penny of its borrowed U.S. bailout money.

Moreover, in the political arena, although the justice system in Oaxaca and other states left much to be desired, a pair of unprecedented events signaled an increasingly open political system. In the 1997 congressional elections, voters elected a host of opposition candidates, depriving the PRI of an absolute congressional majority for the first time since 1929. A year later, in early 1998, Mexicans were participating in their country's first primary elections—in which voters, instead of political bosses, chose party candidates.

Although Zedillo's presidential ride had been rough, he entered the twilight of his 1994–2000 term able to take credit for an improved economy, some genuine political reforms, and relative peace in the countryside. The election of 2000 revealed, however, that the Mexican people were not satisfied.

End of an Era: Vicente Fox Unseats the PRI

During 1998 and 1999 the focal point of opposition to the PRI's three-generation rule had been shifting from lackluster left-of-center Cuauhtémoc Cárdenas to relative newcomer Vicente Fox, former President of Coca Cola Mexico and clean former PAN governor of Guanajuato.

Fox, who had announced his candidacy for President two years before the election, seemed an unlikely challenger. After all, the minority PAN had always been the party of wealthy businessmen and the conservative Catholic right. But blunt-talking, six-foot-five Fox, who sometimes campaigned in *vaquero* boots and a ten-gallon cowboy hat preached populist themes of coalition building and "inclusion." He backed up his talk by carrying his campaign to hardscrabble city *barrios,* dirt-poor country villages and traditional outsider groups, such as Jews.

Meanwhile, as the campaign heated up in early 2000, the PRI candidate, suave, ex-Interior Secretary and governor of the drug-plagued state of Sinaloa, sounded the usual PRI themes to gatherings of party loyalists. At the same time, dour PRD liberal Cuauhtémoc Cárdenas, having resigned from a mediocre term as mayor of Mexico City, faded to a weak third place. On the eve of the election, polls predicted a dead heat of about 40 percent of the vote each for Fox and Labastida.

In a relatively orderly and fair July 2 election, Fox decisively defeated Labastida, 42 percent to 38 percent, while Cárdenas polled a feeble 17 percent. Fox's win also swept a PAN plurality (223/209/57) into the 500-seat Chamber of Deputies lower house (although the Senate remained PRI-dominated).

Nevertheless, in pushing the PRI from the all-powerful presidency after 71 consecutive years of domination, Fox had ushered Mexico into a new, more democratic era.

Despite stinging criticism from his own ranks, President Zedillo, whom historians were already praising as the real hero behind Mexico's new democracy, made an unprecedentedly early appeal for all Mexicans to unite behind Fox.

On the eve of his 1 December 2000 inauguration, Mexicans awaited Fox's speech with hopeful anticipation. He did not disappoint them. Although acknowledging that he couldn't completely reverse 71 years of PRI entrenchment in his one six-year term, he vowed to ride the crest of reform, by revamping the tax system and reducing poverty by 30 percent, by creating a million new jobs a year through new private investment in electricity and oil production and forming a new common market with Latin America, the United States, and Canada.

He promised, moreover, to secure justice for all by a much-needed reform of police, the federal attorney general, and the army. Potentially most difficult of all, Fox called for the formation of an unprecedented congressional "Transparency Commission" to investigate a generation of past grievances, including the 1968 massacre of student demonstrators and assassinations of, among others, a Roman Catholic cardinal in 1993 and a popular presidential candidate in 1994.

Regardless of whether Vicente Fox can accomplish such an earnestly ambitious agenda during his single term, it's clear that a legion of Mexican people, including many former opponents, doubters, and cynics, are loudly cheering him on.

ECONOMY, GOVERNMENT, AND POLITICS

THE ECONOMY

Postrevolutionary National Gains

By many measures, Mexico's 20th-century revolution appears to have succeeded. Since 1910, illiteracy has plunged from 80 percent to 10 percent, life expectancy has risen from 30 years to nearly 70, infant mortality has dropped from a whopping 40 percent to about two percent, and, in terms of caloric intake, Mexicans are on average eating about twice as much as their turn-of-the-century forebears.

Decades of near-continuous economic growth account for rising Mexican living standards. The Mexican economy has rebounded from its last two (1982 and 1995) recessions due to plentiful natural resources, notably oil

and metals; diversified manufacturing, such as cars, steel, and petrochemicals; steadily increasing tourism; exports of fruits, vegetables, and cattle; and its large, willing, low-wage workforce.

Recent Mexican governments, moreover, have skillfully exploited Mexico's economic strengths. The Border Industrialization Program has led to millions of jobs in thousands of border maquiladora factories, from Tijuana to the mouth of the Río Grande. Dependency on oil exports, which led to the 1980s' peso collapse, has been reduced from 75 percent in 1982 to only 12 percent in 1994. Foreign trade, a strong source for new Mexican jobs, has burgeoned since the '80s, due to liberalized tariffs as Mexico joined General Agreement on Tariffs and Trade (GATT) in 1986 and NAFTA in 1994.

SOCIOECONOMIC STATISTICS:
OAXACA VS. MEXICO VS. THE U.S.

	Oaxaca	Mexico	U.S.
Approximate average daily income per active worker	$4.60	$8.14	$100
Corn productivity	.5 ton/acre	.5 ton/acre	1.6 ton/acre
Tractor use by farmers	20%	38%	100%
Infant mortality	1.6%	1.7%	.6%
Inhabitants per doctor	1,370	935	400
Average grade attained in school	5.4	7.2	13
Illiteracy	23%	11%	3%
Population (estimated year 2000)	3,600,000	100,940,000	270,000,000
Yearly population growth	1.9%	2.1%	.5%

Sources: Mexican government census and *World Almanac and Book of Facts,* 1998

As a result, Mexico has become a net exporter of goods and services to the United States, its largest trading partner. Although Mexico suffered a peso collapse of about 50 percent (in relation to the U.S. dollar) in 1995, the Zedillo administration acted quickly. Belt-tightening measures brought foreign investment flowing back to Mexico by 1997 and inflation, which had initially surged, cooled down to less than 15 percent per year by 1998. Although some factory and business closures led to increased unemployment in 1995, benefits from the devalued peso, such as increased tourism and burgeoning exports, have contributed to an improved economic outlook as Mexico enters the 21st century.

The Oaxacan Economy
Despite huge gains, Mexico's Revolution of 1910 is nevertheless incomplete. In Oaxaca, it remains especially so. Oaxaca lags far behind the rest of Mexico in many categories of economic success. Income, for example, hovers at about half the national average. The latest national census figures indicate that average daily earnings per active worker stood at about US$4.60 for Oaxacans and about US$8.10 for Mexicans in general. Although these figures are derived from the latest (1990) census fig-

ures, severe inflation during the recession of 1994–95 probably has held earnings constant at best since 1990. Such numbers demonstrate the difficult reality confronting the poorest Oaxacan families. When asked by 1990 census takers to categorize their incomes, one in four Oaxacan active wage earners said they received no income. The next higher category, about 14 percent—one in seven—reported income of between zero and the equivalent of about US$1 per day.

A look at more government figures provides clues as to who most of Oaxaca's poor are. According to official census figures, agriculture—overwhelmingly corn farming, but also cattle, fruit, and fish—occupies slightly more than half of Oaxaca's active workers, but accounts for only one-fifth of the value of Oaxaca's yearly economic output. The remaining four-fifths is generated by the other half of Oaxaca's workers who are, consequently, responsible for approximately four times as much production value as the farmers.

At the human level, the typical Oaxacan lives on a farm and is poor, even by Mexican standards. The typically six family members, dad José, 36, mom María, 31, three kids, 2, 6, and 11, and grandma, 56, earn next to no cash income and must subsist on what they can

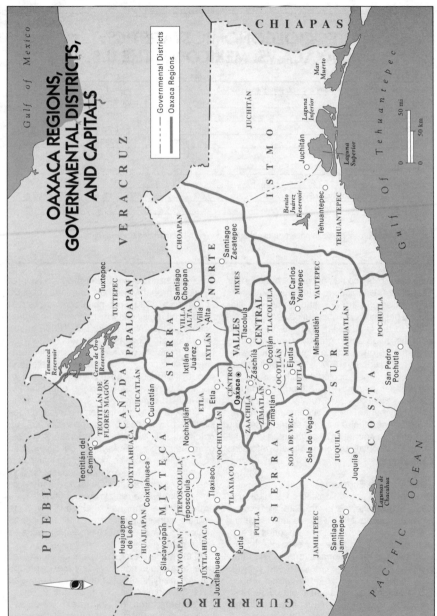

OAXACA REGIONS, GOVERNMENTAL DISTRICTS, AND CAPITALS

© AVALON TRAVEL PUBLISHING, INC.

INCOME DISTRIBUTION—REGIONAL VS. NATIONAL

Approximate percent of active workforce which earns the equivalent $US per day:

	$0	$0–1	$1–3	$3–5	$5–10	$10–20	$20–30	more than $30
Mexico	7%	14%	13%	36%	15%	10%	5%	3%
Oaxaca	25%	14%	14%	25%	9%	5%	2%	1%

Estimated from 1990 national census. Percentages do not add to 100% because some respondees declined to categorize their earnings.

produce and gather. This typically is limited to corn, squash, beans, eggs, garden vegetables, an occasional chicken or turkey, and maybe a little wild game. Staples that they don't produce must be bought or bartered for at the village market. So once a week María bundles up some tomatoes, carrots, and potatoes from her garden and maybe one of her half dozen young roosters. With her middle child in tow, she walks the six miles uphill to the village. With luck, María will return by early evening, having sold or traded everything for perhaps a liter of cooking oil, a kilo of sugar, a spool of thread, and a yard or two of bright ribbon.

While María is at the market, José pulls weeds for a few hours in his *milpa* (cornfield). Although his acreage is small, perhaps no more than two or three acres, he usually manages two harvests of corn a year. In a good season, this might amount to two tons, as long as he keeps the mice and rats away from it. Every year he stores about a ton of corn for home consumption and sells the other ton for about $100 to Conasupo, the government commodity agency. If all goes well, he reckons, in three years he'll save enough to replace his family's present stick-and-adobe, dirt-floor house with a new, sturdy two-room concrete house with interior water tap and a toilet.

Solving the Problems

Like José, many thousands of Oaxacan farmers must struggle to better their lot. The government is generally sympathetic to their efforts and recognizes that Oaxaca, with its plentiful sun and adequate (but sharply seasonal) rainfall, is a potential trove of grain, fruit, fiber, meat,

and fish for the rest of the country and maybe even for export. But the problems are manifold. Although Oaxaca has expanses of rich land, especially in the Isthmus, the Papaloapan, and the central valley, about a fifth of Oaxaca's land, especially in the Mixteca, is useless because of severe erosion. Another third is partly so. Before the conquest, much of Oaxaca's farmland was terraced and irrigated, not unlike the millet terraces of Nepal and the rice terraces of Bali. Although Oaxacans lost that precious knowledge, it could be relearned, and the old water channels and hillside terraces (which are still visible at many locations) could be restored.

Meanwhile, on the present land, productivity could be greatly increased. To raise corn production from the current half ton per acre to the U.S. level of two tons per acre would require mechanization, fertilizer, an irrigation water supply, and the know-how to make everything come together. At present, however, only about one-fifth of Oaxaca's farmers have access to a tractor (compared to 38 percent nationwide), very few have the money for fertilizer, only about 15 percent have access to irrigation water, and most have completed five years or less of schooling. Nevertheless, a focused, long-term government-to-people partnership, not unlike the Tennessee Valley Authority in the United States, could restore prosperity in the Oaxacan countryside.

One route to a better life for many Oaxacans has been to get out. Census figures indicate that about 40 percent of people born in Oaxaca are living and working in other parts of Mexico, the United States, or Canada. While Oaxacan people don't want to leave home,

ECONOMIC ACTIVITY—REGIONAL VS. NATIONAL

The following figures represent categories by percent of population engaged in the activity and percent of value of total output.

	Agriculture	Industry	Construction	Commerce	Transportation	Private Services	Government Services
MEXICO							
Population	23%	21%	7%	13%	4%	16%	13%
Value of Output (% of total)	7%	23%	5%	22%	9%	14%	20%
OAXACA							
Population	53%	12%	5%	8%	3%	8%	10%
Value of Output (% of total)	18%	13%	5%	20%	9%	15%	20%

Note: Population percentages, from census figures, do not add to 100% because some respondents declined to categorize their occupations.

lack of local jobs forces them to. Unlike northern Mexican states close to U.S. cities filled with people who want to buy Mexican-made shoes, telephones, mops, lamp fixtures, and bicycles, Oaxaca, in the far south, is surrounded by other equally disadvantaged Mexican states. Oaxaca, with few nearby markets, attracts only a dribble of new factories and consequently generates scant new jobs. If Oaxaca had resources such as oil or gold, the story would be much different.

Although emigration has slowed Oaxaca's population growth in general, Oaxaca City is an exception. Country people seeking a better life started arriving in Oaxaca City in the 1940s when the population was about 40,000, and they're still coming. Present trends project Oaxaca City's population at 350,000 at the beginning of the 21st century. All the new neighbors make life more crowded for the average Oaxaca City family—parents with two or three children—who typically must manage on about US$10 per day. The survival mode for many such city families has been enterprise: Mom takes in laundry or starts a neighborhood store on the front porch; Dad works one and a half jobs, and both Mom and Dad sell *taquitos* out front on Saturday and Sunday nights. Oaxacans, like everyone, do what they must to get by.

Tourism

Partly because of their isolation and difficult economic circumstances, Oaxaca folks are in many ways like people of yesteryear. Unlike people in some parts of Mexico and much of the United States, Canada, and Europe, most Oaxacans have yet to join the headlong race into the future. And therein lies Oaxaca's charm. The native women's bright traditional costumes, the venerable, monumental buildings, the stick-and-adobe thatched houses, the *vaqueros* on horseback, the oxcarts, all of which symbolize backwardness and poverty in some eyes, are a delight to increasing numbers of visitors, both domestic and foreign.

But as a visitor please remember the reality behind Oaxaca's charm. Please be tolerant, generous in your gratuities, and bargain gently. If you do, Oaxacans will welcome your presence and try even harder to make your visit worthwhile.

State and federal government planners years ago recognized Oaxaca tourism's potential benefits. Their strategy, formulated in the late '80s, is yielding results. While tourist visitations have quadrupled, Oaxaca City's proud old monuments have been restored, the central plaza blooms with old Mexico charm, village-run tourist accommodations have sprouted in the countryside, and the coastal Bahías de Huatulco resort continues to grow gradually while retaining its precious tropical forest hinterland.

This is all good news if Oaxaca's increasing tide of visitors doesn't ruin the charm that they came to enjoy in the first place. Instead let's hope that Oaxaca's culture and natural assets will be enriched *because* of their tourist value. If so, campesinos will preserve, rather than wipe out, the local wildlife because they realize that visitors come *because* of the wildlife. For the same reason, artisans will fashion more enticing handicrafts, people will continue to dress up and dance in their bright costumes, towns will build museums and conserve their old monuments, archaeologists will restore crumbled cities to their original glory.

GOVERNMENT AND POLITICS

The Constitution of 1917

Mexico's governmental system is rooted in the Constitution of 1917, which incorporated many of the features of its reformist predecessor of 1857. State constitutions, including Oaxaca's, must conform to the federal Constitution, which, with some amendments, remains identical to the 1917 document. Although drafted at the behest of conservative revolutionary Venustiano Carranza by his handpicked Querétaro "Constitucionalista" congress, the 1917 Constitution was greatly influenced by Alvaro Obregón and generally ignored by Carranza during his subsequent three-year presidential term.

Although many articles resemble those of its U.S. model, the Constitution of 1917 contains provisions developed directly from Mexican experience. Article 27 addresses the question of land. Private property rights are qualified by societal need; subsoil rights are public property, and foreigners and corporations are severely restricted in land ownership. Although the 1917 constitution declared *ejido* (jointly held) land inviolate, recent 1994 amendments allow, under certain circumstances, the sale or use of communal land as loan security.

Article 23 severely restricts church powers. In declaring that "places of worship are the property of the nation," it stripped churches of all title to real estate, without compensation. Article 5 and Article 130 banned religious orders, expelled foreign clergy, and denied priests and ministers all political rights, including voting, holding office, and even criticizing the government.

Article 123 establishes the rights of labor: to organize, bargain collectively, strike, work a maximum eight-hour day, and receive a minimum wage. Women are to receive equal pay for equal work and be given a month's paid leave for childbearing. Article 123 also establishes social security plans for sickness, unemployment, pensions, and death.

On paper, Mexico's constitutional government structures appear much like their U.S. prototypes: a federal presidency, a two-house congress, and a supreme court, with their counterparts in each of the 31 states. Political parties field candidates, and all citizens vote by secret ballot. In Oaxaca, local federal elections determine Oaxaca's national legislative delegation: about 20 deputies of the approximately 500-seat lower house and four senators of the 120-odd upper house seats. PRI dominance of Oaxacan elections, although not as complete as in the past, still continues, with the majority of Oaxaca's deputies and senators being PRI members.

Despite Mexico's increasingly active legislative bodies, Mexican presidents still enjoy greater powers than their U.S. counterparts. They can suspend constitutional rights under a state of siege, can initiate legislation, veto all or parts of bills, refuse to execute laws, and replace state officers. The federal government, moreover, retains nearly all taxing authority, relegating the states to a role of merely administering federal programs.

Although ideally providing for separation of powers, the Constitution of 1917 subordinates both the legislative and judicial branches, with the courts being the weakest of all. The supreme court, for example, can only, through repeated deliberations, decide upon the constitutionality of legislation. Five separate individuals must file successful petitions for writs *amparo* (protection) on a single point of law in order to effect constitutional precedent.

The President and the PRI

Mexican presidents successively built upon their potent constitutional mandate for three generations. The **Institutional Revolutionary Party**

"You're 18 and you haven't done it? Register to vote!"

(PRI), whose handpicked candidates held the presidency continuously for decades, became an extralegal parallel government, as powerful as or more so than the formal constitutional government. The PRI is organized hierarchically, in three separate labor, farmer, and "popular" (this last mostly government, business, and professional workers) columns, which send delegates from local committees to state and, ultimately, national conventions.

Past Mexican presidents, as heads of the PRI, traditionally reigned at the top of the party apparatus, sending orders through the national PRI delegates, who in turn looked after their respective state delegations. The delegates reported on the performance of the state and local PRI committees to get out the vote and carry out party mandates. If the local committee's performance was satisfactory, then federal subsidies, public works projects, election funds, and federal jobs flowed from government coffers to the state and local level through PRI organizations. In your hometown, if you were not in the PRI or didn't know someone who was, you might have found it difficult to get a small business loan, crop subsidy, government apartment, teaching job, road-repair contract, or government scholarship.

State and Local Government

Oaxaca, like all 31 Mexican states, has an elected governor and state legislature. The Oaxaca voters elect 24 deputies (one from each of 18 electoral districts and six at large) to the state congress, which holds its sessions in the Palacio de Gobierno, adjacent to Oaxaca City's central plaza. With minimal tax powers, the state government is mostly relegated to oversight of federal public works, social welfare, health, and education programs in 30 regional administrative *distritos* (districts).

Distritos vary widely in extent, from the largest, Juchitán, in the Isthmus, to tiny Zaachila, the smallest, in the central valley, not far south of Oaxaca City. Although second smallest in area, Oaxaca's most populous and economically most important district is the Centro district, which contains the capital, Oaxaca City.

Oaxaca's 30 *distritos* are in turn divided, often along ethnic lines, into a host 570 *municipios* (townships), each with its *cabercera* (head town) and subsidiary *agencias,* usually country villages, each of which oversees a scattering of surrounding *rancherias* (hamlets). Oaxaca's crazy quilt of 570 *municipios,* by far the most of any Mexican state, reflects Oaxaca's ethnic richness. Many of the *municipios* encompass a single ethnic group whose members are united by common kinship, language, and costume.

Its *municipios* are where much of Oaxaca's civic action is. If you get a traffic ticket, you'll probably be told to go to the *municipio's presidencia municipal* (like a city hall) to pay your fine and recover your driver's license. From the *presidencia municipal* reigns the *municipio's* publicly elected *presidente* (like a mayor), *alcaldes* (judges), and *regidores* (administrators) of various ranks, who oversee the *municipio*'s *policía municipal* and organize public works.

Parallel to and interlocking with this formal Spanish-derived hierarchy is the less formal indigenous *consejo de ancianos* (council of elders), members of which attain their status by a cumulative lifetime of civic service. Operating mostly by discussion and consensus, the council of elders (which sometimes includes the *presidente* and other elected officials) gets its way through discussion, persuasion, and final approval or veto of civic proposals.

Although *municipios* collect minimal monetary taxes, they often require community members to perform *tequio* (public service) in lieu of taxes. For men, such work might be repairing a local bridge or police or fire duty; women, on the other hand, might perform child care or sweep the city streets or the municipal market.

Political Reform

Reforms in Mexico's stable but top-heavy "Institutional Revolution" came only gradually. Characteristically, street protests were brutally put down at first, with officials only later working to address grievances. Dominance by the PRI led to widespread cynicism and citizen apathy. Regardless of who got elected, the typical person on the street used to tell you that office-holders were bound to retire with their pockets full.

Nevertheless, during the last dozen years of the 20th century, Mexico took significant strides toward pluralism. Minority parties increasingly were electing candidates to state and federal office. Although none captured a majority of any state legislature, the strongest non-PRI parties, such as the conservative pro-Catholic **Partido Acción Nacional**, or National Action Party (PAN), and the liberal-left **Partido Revolucionario Democratico (PRD)**, elected governors. As early as 1986, minority parties were given federal legislative seats, up to a maximum of 20, for winning a minimum of 2.5 percent of the national presidential vote. In the 1994 election, minority parties received public campaign financing, depending upon their fraction of the vote.

Following his 1994 inaugural address, in which he called loudly and clearly for more reforms, President Ernesto Zedillo quickly began to produce results. He immediately appointed a respected member of the PAN opposition party as attorney general—the first non-PRI cabinet appointment in Mexican history. Other Zedillo firsts were federal Senate confirmation of both supreme court nominees and the attorney general, multiparty participation in the Chiapas peace negotiations, and congressional approval of the 1995 financial assistance package received from the United States. Zedillo, moreover, has organized a series of precedent-setting meetings with opposition leaders which led to a written pact for political reform and the establishment of permanent working groups to discuss political and economic questions.

Of major symbolic importance was Zedillo's campaign and inaugural vow to separate both his government and himself from PRI decision-making. He kept his promise, becoming the first Mexican president in as long as anyone could remember who did not choose his successor.

A New Mexican Revolution

Finally, on 2 July 2000, like a Mexican Gorbachev, Ernesto Zedillo, the man most responsible for Mexico's recent democratic reforms, watched as PAN opposition reformer Vicente Fox swept Zedillo's PRI from the presidency after a 71- year rule. Moreover, despite severe criticism from his own party, Zedillo quickly called for the country to close ranks behind Fox. Millions of Mexicans, still dazed but buoyed by Zedillo's statesmanship and Fox's epoch-making victory, eagerly awaited Fox's inauguration address on 1 December 2000.

He promised nothing less than a new revolution for Mexico, and backed it up with concrete proposals. Reduce poverty by 30 percent with a million new jobs a year from revitalized new electricity and oil production, a Mexican Silicon Valley, and free trade between Mexico, all of Latin America, the United States, and Canada. Fox promised justice for all, through a reformed police, army, and the judiciary. He promised conciliation and an agreement with the Zapatista rebel movement in the south, including a bill of rights for Mexico's native peoples. With all of Mexico listening, Fox brought his speech to a hopeful conclusion: "If I had to summarize my message today in one sentence, I would say: Today Mexico has a future, but we have lost much time and wasted many resources. Mexico has a future, and we must build that future starting today."

PEOPLE

Let a broad wooden chopping block represent the high plain, the *altiplano* of Mexico; imagine hacking at one half of it with a sharp cleaver until it is grooved and pocked. That fractured surface resembles Mexico's central highlands, where most Mexicans have lived for millennia. The most severely shattered southern end of the Mexican landscape encompasses Oaxaca, whose rugged topography has isolated its original inhabitants behind high ridges and yawning barrancas for untold generations. In their seclusion they developed separate tongues and hierarchical societies that viewed outsiders with suspicion and hostility, as odd-speaking, barely human barbarians from across the canyon or behind the mountains. When the Spanish conquerors arrived in Oaxaca they found a region divided among hundreds of separate subtribes, speaking 16 main languages broken down into scores of mutually unintelligible dialects. The Oaxacans' own divisions, as much as Spanish horses and steel, led to their quick downfall. The Spanish merely added their own layers atop the existing divisions—of territory, language, caste, class, and wealth—that continue to shape both Mexico and Oaxaca to the present day.

Mesoamerica

Although Oaxacan native peoples are divided by their diverse languages and rugged topography, they nevertheless share many folk customs, not only with each other but with tens of millions of other native peoples in a broad belt, beginning around Mexico's Tropic of Cancer and stretching south and east to Honduras and El Salvador. Anthropologists call the entire region Mesoamerica, a single label reflecting its broad cultural unity. Anthropologists believe that this universal symphony of belief and practice flows from tenaciously held traditions handed down from Mexico's great preconquest civilizations. And nowhere are these folk practices more persistent than in Oaxaca, Mesoamerica's heartland. If you're curious about how most Americans lived before Columbus and Cortés, you needn't look any farther than the Oaxaca countryside.

POPULATION

The Spanish colonial government and the Roman Catholic religion provided the glue that over 400 years has welded Mexico's fragmented people into a nation. Mexico's population, about 100 million in 2000, is exploding at the rate of more than 20 percent per decade. Despite considerable emigration, Oaxaca's population, estimated to be about 3.6 million in the year 2000, is ballooning at nearly the same rate. This was not always so. Historians estimate that European diseases, largely measles and smallpox, probably wiped out as many as 20 million—perhaps 95 percent—of Mexico's *indígena* population within a few generations after Cortés stepped ashore in 1519. Oaxaca's population dropped correspondingly from a preconquest level of about two million to a mere 150,000 by 1650. Oaxaca's native peoples, ironically, can look forward to the year 2019, five centuries after Cortés, when their

Oaxaca city jam session on the plaza

MESOAMERICA AND OAXACA

population will have recovered approximately to its preconquest level.

By 1600, Mexico's indigenous population had dropped so low that the Spanish began to import sizable numbers of African slaves, whose numbers swelled to several tens of thousands by 1650. Although much of the African lineage has been absorbed into Mexico's general population, several thousand African-Mexicans still maintain separate small communities in the Costa Chica, the coastal region spreading both east and west from the Oaxaca-Guerrero border.

ETHNIC GROUPS

Although by 1950 the country's population numbered 25 million, it was completely transformed. The **mestizo,** a Spanish-speaking person of mixed blood, had replaced the pure native Mexican, the *indígena* (een-DEE-hay-nah) as the typical Mexican.

This trend is not as strong in Oaxaca. Although perhaps three of four Mexicans would identify themselves as mestizo, fewer than half of Oaxacans probably would. Among many native

Oaxacans, the label "mestizo" borders on the derogatory, despite the long colonial tradition that, by virtue of their part-European blood, mestizos were elevated to the level of *gente de razón*—people of "reason" or "right."

The typical mestizo family enjoys most of the benefits of the modern world. They typically own a modest concrete house in town. Their furnishings, simple by developed-world standards, will often include an electric refrigerator, washing machine, propane stove, television, and a car or truck. The children go to school every day, and the eldest son sometimes even looks forward to college.

Above the mestizos, a tiny **criollo** (Mexican-born white) minority, a few percent of the total population, inherits the privileges—wealth, education, and political power—of their colonial Spanish ancestors.

The typical *indígena* family lives in a small adobe house in a remote valley, subsisting on corn, beans, and vegetables from their small, unirrigated *milpa* (cornfield). They usually have chickens, a few pigs, and sometimes a cow, electricity, but no sewage connection. Their few hundred dollars a year cash income isn't enough

MESOAMERICAN CALENDAR

The Mixtec and Zapotec ancestors of present-day Oaxacans ordered their lives with the same calendric system as many Mesoamerican linguistic groups, including the Maya, the Aztecs, the Tarascans, and many others. Their system combined two major calendric cycles. First, they used the agricultural calendar, tied to the seasons and derived from the approximately 365-day (actually 365.2422) cycle of the sun through the background of stars and constellations.

The Mesoamerican counting system was basic to the calendar's operation. The Mesoamericans didn't count by decimals, but rather used a vigesimal (20-count) system. They logically divided their agricultural year into 18 "months" of 20 days each, with a five-day short month at the year-end. A given day, therefore, might be called, instead of 11 June or 12 June, 5-Deer or 6-Deer and so forth.

They tracked ceremonial dates, such as birthdays, with a separate ritual or divinatory calendar of 260 days that combined 20 separate named days with numbers one through 13. Succeeding days were identified as, for example, 2-Water, 3-Monkey, 4-Dog, and so on.

A given date was a unique coincidence of both calendars, which you can imagine as a pair of meshed cogwheels, turning in lockstep. As you picture the calendric cogwheels turning, at a given moment a certain cog (marked as 2-Water, for example) in the solar calendar will always be meshing with some slot (marked as 5-Flower, for example) in the ritual calendar, producing a unique combination of two numbers and two names (since the solar and the ritual calendars have different—365 vs. 260—respective totals of cogs and slots). For example, 1 June 1999 might be described as 2-House, 5-Flower; 2 June 1999 might follow, for example, as 3-House, 6-Deer, and 3 June 1999 as 4-House, 7-Monkey. (Note that the solar calendar progresses through named "months," such as "House" in the example, while the ritual calendar does not.)

In this system dates are unique, but only for a determined time period, because the entire calendric cycle repeats itself after all two number-two name combinations have occurred. This happens every 52 solar years (or, in days, 52 times 365 or 18,980 days). During this time the intermeshed ritual calendar must pass through exactly the same num-

to buy even a small tractor or refrigerator, much less a truck. The *indígenas* (or, mistakenly but commonly, Indians), by the usual measurements of income, health, or education, squat at the bottom of the social ladder. (See also Indigenous Groups, below.)

Sizable **African-Mexican** communities, or *negros,* descendants of 17th- and 18th-century African slaves, live in the Gulf states and along the Guerrero-Oaxaca coastline. Last to arrive, they experience discrimination at the hands of everyone else and are integrating very slowly into the mestizo mainstream.

SHARED OAXACAN CUSTOMS

Settlement Patterns

Oaxaca's present 570 *municipios* (townships), each with its main town and market, reflect community boundaries often dating back more than a thousand years. Although the Spanish imposed their civic pattern of church, *presidencia* (city hall),

and major stores and prominent residences all clustered around a central plaza, the native people still hold to their tradition of concentrating their homes in a number of *barrios* (neighborhoods) on the outskirts. Native peoples have sometimes stretched the Spanish pattern, reverting to their ancient "empty town" custom. Here, only the mestizo and criollo elite permanently live in town, while natives maintain empty in-town houses, which they occupy only during market and ceremonial occasions. Most of their days they spend by their country *milpas* (cornfields).

Birth, Life, and Death

Christian baptism is everyone's first major life event; it's so important that a number of communities believe that a baby is not fully human until baptized. If an unbaptized baby dies, the parents must make haste to bury the body immediately, with little ceremony. If not, the spirit of the unbaptized baby might escape and become a *nagual,* a malevolent animal that will harm people who cross its path.

ber of days. Dividing 18,980 by its number of 260 cogs, you come up with the exactly 73 revolutions that the ritual calendar must undergo in the same 52 solar years.

Besides the Mixtecs and Zapotecs, all other Mesoamerican groups probably feared that cataclysmic events might occur at the end of each 52-year period, measured from some mythical beginning. High priests and presumably the populations at large observed solemn ceremonies, performed sacrifices, and watched the sky for auspicious portents, such as a bright overhead star, a conjunction of planets, or a comet, on the eve of their 52-year cyclical "millennium."

Knowledge of the Zapotec and Mixtec calendars is gradually being accumulated. Scholars believe that they have been used since at least the early urban stage, around 500 B.C., approximately the founding of Monte Albán. Alfonso Caso, the discoverer of Monte Albán's earliest stages, associated a common but undeciphered Monte Albán glyph, of a headdress in profile, with the solar year. For Caso, this indicated that certain personages wearing such headdresses either interpreted, read,

or manipulated the calendar. The ritual calendar, called *piye* in Zapotec, was also certainly used at Monte Albán.

As in other parts of Mesoamerica, persons were named by their birth date, such as 8-Deer, 3-Dog, or 7-Monkey in the ritual calendar. Such name-dates occur as glyphs associated with personages recorded in stone or on the surviving hieroglyphic paper books, called *codices,* such as the Codex Nuttall.

The Mesoamericans, as the Europeans, had to apply corrections to keep the solar calendar in correspondence with the seasons. This will happen only if the year averages, over the millennia, 365.2422 days. The presently used Gregorian calendar (which was instituted by Pope Gregory VIII in 1582) corrects the solar year approximately to 365.2425 days (compared to the actual 365.2422) by omitting the leap year every three out of four centuries. Therefore, although the years 1700, 1800, and 1900 were not leap years (that is, they were permitted only 365 days, instead of 366), the year 2000 was permitted 366 days. The Mayas, scholars believe, did a little better than this; they corrected the solar calendar to 365.2420 days.

Baptism is also the time when the web of *compadrazgo* relationships starts to influence a person's life. This begins when parents designate their *compadres* (best friends) as *padrinos* (godparents) to their newly born. As children mature, with parental consent they designate their own *compadres.* Formal ceremonies often solemnize *padrino* and *compadrazgo* bonds, which might continue through generations of loyal *padrino* and *compadre* relationships.

With babies, nursing often lasts two or three years, or at least until the next child comes along. Preschool children experience little imposed discipline except the responsibility of watching after younger siblings. Loud or disruptive children might get spanked or shunned, however. Formal schooling is usually considered so important that families often sacrifice so that children, especially boys, may attend at least six grades of school. Although children of poorer parents experience few, if any puberty rites, richer parents often honor their children,

especially girls, with a number of Catholic ceremonies, such as first communion, confirmation, blessing of their pet animals, and *quinceana* (coming out) at age 15. Among poorer folks, a girl becomes an adult with marriage, often by age 14 or 15. A boy enters manhood through either marriage or entering *servicio* (community service). He's expected to pay community assessments and perform *tequio* (communal work) service. As a young man matures, he is expected to fulfill the duties of a series of increasingly important *cargos* (offices). If successful, at middle age he is rewarded with the rank of *principal* (elder) and admitted to the village council of elders.

Death is usually marked by 24 hours of mourning while the body lies in state at home, usually with candles, incense, and flowers. Wrapped in a *petate* (reed mat) or a coffin, the body is buried, along with the deceased's favored trinkets, and perhaps favorite food. Rituals continue periodically thereafter, especially at nine days as well as one year after burial.

Marriage, Family, and Inheritance

Traditional marriage is an alliance between families, initiated by the groom's parents, often through a go-between. Girls begin to marry as early as 14, boys at 16 or 17. The more well-to-do marry later. Often prospective grooms and brides perform services for the other's family, sometimes even taking up temporary residence (but not sleeping with their intended) while everyone gets acquainted. The contents of the couple's dreams often carry weight in the decision to marry. Polyandry, marriage of a woman to two brothers, although sanctioned in some communities, is not common. On the other hand, well-to-do husbands, while remaining married, sometimes support additional women in separate households.

Although extended families generally encompass two, three, or four generations, couples often establish their own households after the birth of their first child. Even though both the wife's and the husband's relatives enjoy equal kinship status, couples are more likely to live near the husband's relatives. Other practices are male-weighted. Boys usually inherit more land than their sisters, and family names, nearly always Spanish, are inherited from the father. Among some Mixtecs and Mazatecs, the father's first name, interestingly, becomes his children's surname. (This is not unlike the practice among some northern Europeans — "Johnson," "Svensen," and "Mendelsohn," for example).

Household Life

The basic house has a single room, a dirt floor, stick-and-adobe walls, and a thatched roof. Better houses have more rooms, adobe or concrete walls, a concrete floor, and perhaps a flush toilet. Household goods hang on pegs and nails all around the walls. Overhead, rafters support grain and other heavy storage. Beds are either on floor mats or hammocks. A small altar with saint and candle occupies one corner, with the kitchen in the other. Cooking is either over open fire or on an adobe stove. Tortillas are heated on a flat adobe *comal* (grill); beans, chilies, and stews are cooked in pottery jars *(ollas)* or metal pots over the open fire. Women grind corn by rolling with their stone *mano* on the *metate* basin. They grind chilies in their *molcajete* (mortar).

Men do all the heavier outside work: clearing, burning, farming, building, repairing, plus fishing, hunting, and tending cattle and horses. If fields are far from the homestead, men sometimes take up temporary residence there during planting and harvest. Women cook, sew, wash clothes, gather fruit, flowers, and wild herbs, and tend household animals, such as pigs, goats, chickens, and turkeys. Women do most, if not all, of the marketing. Both men and women carry heavy loads.

Dress

Verbal descriptions pale in comparison to the color and excitement of a Oaxaca town fiesta or big market day. Country people, especially in remote areas, still wear the traditional cottons that blend the Spanish and native styles. Men usually wear the Spanish-origin fiber sombrero (literally, "shade-maker") on their heads, loose white cotton shirt and pants, and leather huaraches on their feet. Women's dress is often more colorful. It can include a *huipil* (long, sleeveless dress), often embroidered in bright floral and animal motifs, or a handwoven *enredo* (wraparound skirt that identifies the wearer with a particular locality). A very common addition is the Spanish-tradition all-purpose woven shawl *(rebozo),* which can carry a baby, a bag of corn, or maybe even a chicken or two, as well as protect from the rain or sun. A *faja* (waist sash) and, in the winter, a *quechquémitl* (shoulder cape) complete the costume.

Making a Living

The great majority of Oaxacan indigenous people cultivate native corn, along with a number of other secondary crops, such as beans, squash, potatoes, chili peppers, and tomatoes. Depending upon soil and climate, they may also harvest potatoes, maguey (for alcoholic drinks), and fruits, such as mangos, papaya, cherimoya, *zapote,* and avocado. Other native crops might be cotton or henequen, for fiber, and perhaps cocoa beans, *hule* (rubber), and chicle (chewing gum) for cash. Locally cultivated introduced cash crops include wheat, bananas, coffee, sugarcane, sesame seeds, and peanuts.

Many families or sometimes entire villages specialize in pottery, cloth weaving, or bas-

Oaxacan construction workers typically earn $3–5 per day, when they can get it.

ketry. Although the appearance of cheap, machine-made cloth has weakened the tradition, many Oaxacan women still weave family garments with the ancestral backstrap loom. Treadle looms, introduced by the Spanish and operated by either men or women, are common around Oaxaca City. Potters, both women and men, practice their craft all over Oaxaca. Methods vary; they might confine themselves to the native hand-coiling or the Spanish-introduced potter's wheel, or use a combination of both. (See Arts and Crafts section in the On the Road chapter.)

Governmental and Religious Institutions

Although women exercise considerable behind-the-scenes influence, men customarily occupy the formal community leadership positions. Minor *presidencia* (city hall) positions are usually appointive; later senior positions, such as *regidor* (administrator), *alcalde* (judge), and *presidente* (mayor) are often elective. In-town native homes cluster in one or more *barrios* on the outskirts. A town *regidor* acts as an agent for one or more *barrios.*

Paralleling such formal civil institutions are the religious, which center on the *mayordomía,* the office responsible for the oft-elaborate ceremonial trappings and yearly fiesta of the barrio's patron saint. The barrio's *regidor* or one of its *cofradias* (religious fraternities) designates the *mayordomo* for a one-year *mayordomía* responsibility. If donations for the patronal fiesta are inadequate, the *mayordomo,* often a wealthy individual, is expected to add a generous contribution of his own. Although this may spell temporary poverty for the *mayordomo,* his reward is great community prestige. A lifetime of such service will often assure election to the status of elder *(principal* or *anciano)* and exalted (so exalted that elders are rarely prosecuted for wrongdoing) membership in the council of elders, upon whose resources and sage advice the community relies.

RELIGION

Although the vast majority of Oaxacan *indígenas* consider themselves Catholics, their religion blends the catechism of the missionary fathers with ancient native beliefs. Deities in their age-old Mesoamerican pantheon assume thinly disguised identities among the host of Catholic gods and saints. Besides paying obeisance at the village church altar, Oaxacan country folks also appease mountain, water, and underworld spirits with offerings and sacrifices at sacred summits, springs, and caves. Before killing a deer, for example, a hunter often asks permission of the *señor del monte* (lord, or spirit, of the mountain). Sometimes *hechiceros* (wizards) or *ancianos* lead entire communities in cornfield ceremonies for a successful harvest, with flower offerings, candles, food, and sacrificial turkeys and chickens.

Other old beliefs persist. Many folks, especially in remote areas, believe that *animas* (spirits) of the dead, besides the Catholic God and the saints, influence the living. Appeasement of *animas* peaks on 2 November, the Day of the Dead, when many families gather all night, with candles, flowers, incense, and the deceased's favorite foods, at graves of their

THE VIRGIN OF GUADALUPE

Conversion of the *indígenas* to Catholicism was sparked by the vision of Juan Diego, a poor farmer. On the hill of Tepeyac north of Mexico City in 1531, Juan Diego saw a brown-skinned Virgin Mary enclosed in a dazzling aura of light. She told him to build a shrine in her memory on that spot, where the Aztecs had long worshipped their "earth mother," Tonantzín. Juan Diego's brown Virgin told him to go to the cathedral and relay her instruction to Archbishop Zumárraga.

The archbishop, as expected, turned his nose up at Juan Diego's story. The vision returned, however, and this time Juan Diego's brown Virgin realized that a miracle was necessary. She ordered him to pick some roses at the spot where she had first appeared to him (a true miracle, since roses had been previously unknown in the vicinity) and take them to the archbishop. Juan Diego wrapped the roses in his rude fiber cape, returned to the cathedral, and placed the wrapped roses at the archbishop's feet. When he opened the offering, Zumárraga gasped: imprinted on the cape was an image of the Virgin herself—proof positive of a genuine miracle.

In the centuries since Juan Diego, the brown Virgin—La Virgen Morena, or Nuestra Señora La Virgen de Guadalupe—has blended native and Catholic elements into something uniquely Mexican. In doing so, she has become the virtual patroness of Mexico, the beloved symbol of Mexico for *indígenas,* mestizos, blacks, and criollos alike.

departed. People also appease saints for favors; however, if prayers are not answered, a person may also punish a saint by abusing its figurine. Sometimes evil dwarfs, the devil, or malevolent female spirits lure men to ruin. At birth, people acquire *tonos,* powerful guardian spirits, often in the guise of mountain lions, jaguars, and eagles who, if treated with respect, might protect them throughout life. Sickness, commonly thought to be afflicted by an evil spell, loss of soul by fright, or "bad air," is treated by the incantations of a traditional village healer.

Healers employ other remedies, such as consumption or avoidance of certain foods, sucking (to remove the mysterious object causing the illness), modern medicine, and herbs and poultices. Especially common is a steam bath in the traditional *temascal,* a permanent wood or stone structure or temporary mat-covered brush hut, which many Oaxacan households maintain individually (rather than communally).

Catholicism, spreading its doctrine of equality of all persons before God and incorporating native gods into the church rituals, eventually brought the native Mexicans into the fold. Within a hundred years, nearly all natives had accepted the new religion, which raised the universal God of all humankind over local tribal deities.

Every Mexican city, town, and village celebrates the cherished memory of their Virgin of Guadalupe on 12 December. This celebration, however joyful, is but one of the many fiestas that Mexicans, especially the *indígenas,* rejoice in. Each village holds its local fiesta in honor of its patron saint, who is often a thinly veiled sit-in for some local pre-Cortesian deity. Themes appear Spanish—Christians vs. Moors, devils vs. priests—but the native element is strong, sometimes dominant. During Semana Santa (Holy Week) at Pinotepa Nacional in coastal Oaxaca, for example, Mixtec people, costumed as Jews, shoot arrows skyward, simultaneously reciting traditional Mixtec prayers.

LANGUAGE

Oaxacan Indigenous Languages

Linguists recognize 16 separate languages spoken in Oaxaca today. Experts identify each of them with one of five language families. North American language family names are conventionally derived by combining the names of the northernmost and southernmost languages of the group. Thus, Otomanguean, Oaxaca's most widespread language family, derives its label from Otomi, spoken northwest of Mexico City, and Mangue, spoken in southeast Mexico. All of Oaxaca's native language speakers occupy pretty much the same territories that they did at the time of the conquest. The Otomanguean, by location, moving generally west to east, are: Amusgo, Chatino, Trique, Mixtec, Chocho, Ixcatec, Popoloca, Cuicatec, Mazatec, Chinantec, and Zapotec. A language pair of eastern Oaxaca, Mixe (MEE-shay) and Zoque (SOH-kay), probably distantly related to Mayan dialects, are often lumped into a second family, the Mixe-Zoque family. Three other languages are the only representatives of their respective families. Nahuatl (the language of the Aztecs) of the Uto-Aztecan family; Chontal, of the Hokan-Coahuiltecan family; and Huave, of its own family, Huave.

Understanding in Oaxaca is further complicated by a proliferation of dialects. Mixtec speakers from Jamiltepec, on the Pacific Coast, for example, do not generally comprehend the Mixtec dialect of a town, such as Tlaxiaco, across half a dozen ridges 100 miles away. The same is true for Oaxaca's other major languages: Zapotec, Mazatec, Chinantec, and Mixe, and to a lesser degree for the minor languages.

Few nonindigenous people, whether foreigners or Mexican, have made the intense effort required to speak and understand a Oaxacan native language. All of the Otomanguean languages, like the Chinese dialects, are tonal. This means that a given word takes on different meanings depending upon the pitch—low, high, rising, or falling—with which it is enunciated. Consequently, in big market towns, Spanish is often the lingua franca of buying and selling. Nevertheless, at many country markets, aware visitors notice many people, usually older folks, who speak no Spanish at all.

Please take note that the Spanish names for the Zapotec, Mixtec, Mazatec, and Chinantec languages are Zapoteco, Mixteco, Mazateco, and Chinanteco, while the respective home territories of each group are the Zapoteca, Mixteca, Mazateca, and Chinantla.

INDIGENOUS LANGUAGES

The 1990 national census figures list populations of those over five years old who speak an indigenous Oaxacan language:

Language	Population	% of Total Oaxacans	Important Centers in Oaxaca
Zapotec	402,000	15.4%	Tlacolula, Juchitán, Miahuatlán
Mixtec	387,000	14.9%	Tlaxiaco, Huajuapan de León, Jamiltepec
Mazatec	168,000	6.5%	Huatla de Jiménez, Jalapa de Díaz
Chinantec	104,000	4.0%	Valle Nacional
Mixe	95,000	3.6%	Ayutla, Zacatepec
Chatino	29,000	1.1%	Nopala, Juquila
Amusgo	28,000	1.1%	San Pedro Amusgos
Chontal	24,000	.9%	Santiago Astata
Trique	15,000	.6%	Tilapa
Cuicatec	13,000	.5%	Cuicatlán
Huave	12,000	.5%	San Mateo del Mar, San Dionisio del Mar
Nahua	10,000	.4%	Salina Cruz, Tuxtepec
Zoque	5,000	.2%	San Miguel Chimalapa, Santa María Chimalapa
Chocho	3,000	.12%	Coixtlahuaca
Ixcatec	1,000	.04%	Ixcatlán
Popoluco	1,000	.04%	Santiago Chazumba
Totals	1,297,000	49.8%	

NATIVE PEOPLES OF OAXACA

© AVALON TRAVEL PUBLISHING, INC.

INDIGENOUS GROUPS

Although anthropologists and census takers classify them according to language groups (such as Mixtec, Zapotec, or Nahua), *indígenas* typically identify themselves as residents of a particular locality rather than by language or ethnic grouping. And although as a group they are referred to as *indígenas* (native, or aboriginal), individuals are generally made uncomfortable (or may even feel insulted) by being labeled as such.

While the mestizos are the emergent self-conscious majority class, the *indígenas* remain mostly invisible, keeping to their country hamlets, except during town market days and fiestas. Typically, they are politically conservative, socially traditional, and tied to the land. On market day, the typical *indígena* family might make the trip into town. They bag up some tomatoes, squash, or peppers, and tie up a few chickens or a pig. The rickety country bus will often be full, and the mestizo driver may wave them away, giving preference to his friends, leaving the *indígenas* to trudge stoically along the road.

Their lot, nevertheless, has been slowly improving. *Indígena* families now often have access to a local school and a clinic. Improved health has led to a large increase in their population. Official census counts, however, probably run low. *Indígenas* are traditionally suspicious of government people, and census takers, however conscientious, seldom speak the local dialect.

Recent figures nevertheless indicate that about 50 percent of Oaxacans are *indígenas*—that is, they speak one of Oaxaca's 16 native languages. Of these, about a fifth speak no Spanish at all. These fractions, moreover, are changing only gradually. Many *indígenas* prefer the old ways.

Once a year, in mid-July, thousands of indigenous people, from hundreds of ethnically distinct Oaxaca communities, converge on Oaxaca City for the Guelaguetza (gay-lah-GHET-sah) folk dance festival. Dazzled by the whirling color and spectacle, visitors begin to grasp the richness and sheer magnitude of Oaxacan folk tradition. Although their diversity is staggering, the simple fact is that the majority—about three of every five—of indigenous Oaxacans speak some dialect of one of two languages, Zapotec or Mixtec. Of these, the most numerous and visible are the Zapotecs, the people whom visitors encounter first in excursions from Oaxaca City.

Zapotecs

The Spanish label "Zapoteco" comes from Aztec, rather than Zapotec tradition. The Zapotecs call themselves Ben Zaa, or "People of the Clouds." The Aztecs heard this as *Tsapotécatl*, or Zapote People, a less-than-flattering "fruit eater" label.

Zapotec speakers, who number upward of 400,000, make up about one-third of Oaxaca's native people. The Zapotecs, moreover, are the most visible for more reasons than their numbers. In contrast to the Mixtecs, the Zapotecs, led by their kings Cosijoeza and Cosijopí, allied themselves with the Spanish right from the beginning. Nearly unique among Mexican indigenous groups, Zapotecs have figured prominently in national politics. Mexico's most beloved president, Benito Juárez, was of Zapotec origins. Lately, Zapotecs, including many women, have strongly influenced politics and government in the Isthmus, through the Coalición Obero, Campesino, y Estudiantil de Istmo, or COCEI (Confederation of Workers, Farmers, and Students of the Isthmus).

Zapotec influence goes much further. Although frequented by nearly all of Oaxaca's indigenous groups, a number of Oaxaca's largest native markets, such as Oaxaca City and Tehuantepec, are run by Zapotecs. Backcountry centers, where Zapotecs own and manage most stalls and stores, are hostile to penetration by mestizo merchants.

Individual Zapotec-speaking persons usually identify themselves more strongly with region or locale than language. (You might expect this, since the several Zapotec regional dialects are virtually separate languages, differing as much as French, Spanish, Italian, and Portuguese.) Living and work patterns, likewise, depend much more on locale—tropical coast, cool mountain, or highland valley—than ethnicity. Oaxaca's four Zapotec regions (and their important market centers), moving clockwise from Oaxaca's center, are the central valley (Oaxaca, Tlacolula, Etla), northern Sierra (Ixtlán, Yalalag, Villa Alta), Isthmus (Tehuantepec, Juchitán), and southern Sierra (Miahuatlán, Pochutla).

Zapotec communities are generally skillful at resolving disputes. If informal means—neighborly discussion, arbitration, or the council of elders—fail, then the argument will nearly always be resolved in the local court. Blood feuds, common in some Oaxacan communities, are rare among the Zapotecs.

Although Zapotec speakers are gradually adopting new ways, many still remember the old gods, especially the god of rain, fertility, and lightning, known as Cocijo, in the central valley. On masks you may see him as a lizard. He controls the clouds and may even release *granizo* hail onto a wrongdoer's crops. Some southern Zapotecs conceive of the world as an island in a vast sea, watched down upon by a hierarchy of heavenly hosts.

Other old beliefs persist. Influential animals, such as the *correcamino* (roadrunner), who brings good luck, the *tecolote* (small owl), who brings bad, and the *mariposa* (butterfly), who

Oxen yokes are still an important item in Oaxaca, where only about a third of the farmers have access to a tractor.

signifies death, are important actors in Zapotec fables. Besides mysterious incantations, Zapotec traditional healers, both men and women, use a wealth of herbal cures: wild garlic for high blood pressure, cloves for toothaches, *rosa de fandango* (a type of mint) for conception, *epazote morada* (a type of basil) for worms.

Although midwives traditionally preside over birthing, fathers are expected to be present to ensure a healthy baby. Pregnant women are often exhorted not to eat honey or mamey fruit. If possible, mothers are treated royally after giving birth. They traditionally remain in bed for three weeks, get plenty of massages, take *temascal* steam baths, and eat lots of chicken, chilies, and salt.

Mixtecs

It's probably not an accident that the Mixtecs' self-label, Nyu-u Sabi, "People of the Rain" (or "Clouds") has the same meaning as the Zapotecs' name for themselves. Linguists estimate that around 3,000 years ago, they were, in fact, the same people. They're not the same today, however. Their languages, although related, are mutually unintelligible, and their homelands are on opposite sides of Oaxaca.

The Mixtecs, who number upward of 350,000, comprise about 30 percent of Oaxacan native speakers. Nearly all live in three geographic zones in western Oaxaca: the Mixteca Baja, Mixteca Alta, and Mixteca de la Costa. The **Mixteca Baja** is the dry plateau-land basin of the Río Mixteco, which runs adjacent to the Puebla-Guerrero border, about 100 miles (160 km) west by northwest of Oaxaca City. Major centers are Santiago Juxtlahuaca in the south, Huajuapan de León in the north, and San Agustín Atenango in the center. Bordering the Mixteca Baja to the southwest is the **Mixteca Alta,** a highland of pine-tufted peaks cut by lush deep canyons. Its major market centers, moving from north to south, are Teposcolula, Tlaxiaco, and Putla. Bordering the Mixteca Alta on the south is the **Mixteca de la Costa,** a roughly 50- by 50-mile (80-kilometer) region of hills and valleys abutting the Guerrero border on the west and spreading southward from the foothills to the mangrove-fringed coastline. Its major centers are Pinotepa Nacional in the center and Santiago Jamiltepec to the east.

A few thousand Mixtec speakers also occupy a pair of intriguingly isolated enclaves: Cuyamecalco (near the market town of San Juan Chiquihuitlán) in the northern Sierra, and around Mixtequilla, the "Little Mixteca" just north of Tehuantepec, in the Isthmus.

Although Mixtec-speaking people have passed down a rich heritage, as a group they are now among Oaxaca's poorest. Of the Mixteca's three regions, the people in the Costa are generally the best off. Santiago Jamiltepec, for example, where Mixtec-speakers compose 70 percent of the population, has many Mixtec shop owners, in contrast to upland Mixtec centers where mestizos often dominate commerce.

Exceptions notwithstanding, most Mixtecs are subsistence farmers. Agriculture is typically based on age-old slash-and-burn methods. Fields lie fallow for five years, then brush is burned, cleared, and the ground planted with corn, usually employing a *coa* (digging stick). Oxen, when they are used for plowing or hauling, are often rented. Irrigation, except near valley-bottom creeks, is not common. On the coast, the warmer climate allows more options for cash crops, such as bananas, mangos, *panela,* brown sugar from cane, cotton, and peanuts, although distribution is limited and local.

Another cash possibility that Mixtecs have not generally developed is coffee, which mestizo, Trique, and European immigrant growers harvest successfully on the Mixteca Alta's semitropical forested mountainsides, using Mixtec day labor.

Moreover, despite their proximity to rich ocean resources, very few coastal Mixtecs fish. Instead, they buy dried fish from the many blacks, descendants of African slaves, whose modest houses and fields dot the coastline.

The Mixtecs seem to have cornered the palm-frond weaving market. In the dry Mixteca Baja, homeland to wild forests of short palms, people gather and dry the fronds, and whenever two hands are free everyone—father, mother, children, grandmother, grandfather—weaves them into everything, from mats and hats to toys and baskets.

Lack of good roads hinders market access all over the Mixteca. A large proportion of Mixtec homesteads lie at the end of foot trails, along which produce must be hauled by hand or burro. Even if a farmer could harvest a ton of mangos (potentially worth maybe $500) from his four trees, how could he, his wife, a baby, and two children, and three neighbors haul them five miles by trail, then 20 miles by dirt road, to some market where people have the money to buy his mangos? He tells himself that maybe he and his neighbors will get together, widen the trail and buy a used truck. Yes . . . someday.

Faced with such odds, instead of saving for that someday truck, many Mixtec farmers opt to accumulate prestige by fulfilling *compadrazgo* (contributing to friends) or *mayordomía* (religious festival) obligations. Although such charitable action often leads to poverty, generosity, in the Mixtec (and Mexican) mind is, after all, much preferable to parsimony.

Coastal Mixtec women enjoy an unusual degree of autonomy. Besides often handling family purse strings and doing all the marketing, they typically keep their own family names and own property independently of their husbands. For some Mixteca Alta and Mixteca Baja men, traveling to the coast is believed to be dangerous, partly for fear that some Costa Mixteca woman, through witchcraft, might steal (or disable) their penis. So, men, watch out for them, especially around the Pinotepa Nacional market, where they often wear their best finery, which customarily includes an heirloom *pozahuanco* wraparound skirt of brilliant natural-dyed red cochineal and deep purple horizontal stripes. From afar, you'll easily recognize them, carrying themselves proudly, with their *jícara* hatlike gourd bowl tipped whimsically on their heads. Some women sell hand-loomed *pozahuancos* in the market. The authentic ones, by which coastal Mixtec women judge each other, sell for $150 or more.

Mazatecs

In contrast to the Zapotecs and Mixtecs, the Mazatec territory, the **Mazateca,** is relatively concentrated into a roughly 35- by 50-mile corner at Oaxaca's very northern tip. Mazatec villages and farms spread across two very fertile climatic zones: lush semitropical forested uplands and tropical rainforest river bottomland of the Papaloapan River basin. Major market centers are Teotitlán del Camino and Huatla de Jiménez, both in the western highlands. Important subsidiary centers, many in the highlands around

Huatla, are Cosolapa, Santa María Chilchotla, Huehuetlán, Eloxotitlán, San José Tenango, Mazatlán, Chiquihuitlán, Ayautla, and Jalapa de Díaz. The eastern lowland has no dominant Mazatec center, partly because of the displacement of thousands of families during construction of the Miguel Alemán Dam. Although the Mazatecs' homeland spills over into neighboring Puebla and Veracruz states, around 170,000, or about 90 percent, live in Oaxaca.

The Mazatecs' own name for their homeland, Ampaad, which translates as the "Place Where the People Are Born," reflects their own creation myth. Legends say that the great tropical trees of Ampaad gave birth to three types of people: giants; ordinary-size humans, who became the present Mazatecs; and smaller people, who became the monkeys. The label "Mazatec" derives from the Aztec Nahuatl language and translates as "People of the Deer."

Left largely to themselves, the Mazatecs have retained many of their own traditions. Many of these they hold in common with their Chocho-, Popoloca-, and Ixcatec-speaking neighbors, whose tongues linguists sometimes lump into a Mazatec-language subfamily. Their isolation has left Mazatec speakers among the least hispanicized of Oaxacans; as a group, as many as 40 percent speak little or no Spanish.

In 1944, government planners initiated the Papaloapan Project, which called for a huge hydroelectric works in the Mazatec heartland. The project's centerpiece, christened as the Miguel Alemán Dam and Reservoir in 1955, created a mammoth lake in the Mazatec lowland, drowning hundreds of thousands of acres of fertile Papaloapan basin forest and farmland. Although water and electric power were the projected benefits, the human cost turned out to be enormous. Mazatec society was torn by the forced removal of 22,000 poor Mazatec people to unfamiliar, often undesirable territory. Fortunately, the rest of the Mazatec population, largely in the western highlands around Huatla de Jiménez, remained undisrupted. Mexican authorities have since generally avoided such socially disruptive mega-projects.

Although most Mazatec families are subsistence corn, bean, and squash farmers, many cultivate fruits (mango, mamey, *zapote,* papaya, banana, and avocado) and coffee as cash crops on their fertile acreage. Although some farmer cooperatives have found national and international markets for their fruit and coffee, many individuals seem content to sell their produce for low local prices at Huatla de Jiménez and other Mazateca markets.

Mazatec women are renowned for their costumes and adornments. At markets and festivals especially, watch for them in their famously bright *huipiles,* horizontally striped in the middle, vertically on the sides. Beneath the *huipil* they often wear a loom-woven blue and white horizontally striped skirt. Their hair is also part of their decoration. They keep it soft and dark with a preparation called *pistle,* made from the core of the mamey fruit, and typically braid it with bright ribbons. Many women take pride in their home embroidery and hand-woven cotton, silk, and wool, which they sometimes sell at markets.

As in the past, scarcity of priests weakens Catholic influence in the Mazateca. Priestly visits are so rare that many Mazatec campesino couples have two or three children by the time they enjoy a Catholic church wedding ceremony. When a priest does arrive, rustic churches are customarily thronged with couples bringing children for baptism. For the ceremony, they buy a small lead cross, which they hang with a bright ribbon around their child's neck. In addition to Catholic baptism, Mazatec parents sometimes ask a diviner to read the ancient *tonalpohualli* 260-day ritual calendar to discover their newborn's *tona* guardian spirit.

Mazatec people often gather for non-Catholic religious rites in fields and at sacred springs, caves, or mountains. Mazatec people especially venerate El Rabón peak, which towers over Jalapa de Díaz, and whose kilometer-high vertical rock walls are said never to have been scaled. There on that lofty summit live the *dueños* (earth spirits), who must be appeased with prayers and *copal* incense for the return of lost souls. In the Mazateca lowland, *brujos* (witch doctors) carry out similar ceremonies at Cabeza de Tilpan cave near San José Tenango.

Traditional healers are very busy in the Mazateca. Among their weapons against illness, many include natural forest-gathered hallucinogens. Common are *hongos alucinantes* (hallucinogenic mushrooms), *semillas de la Virgen* (seeds of the Virgin) or *ololiuhqui,* and *hojas de la pas-* *tora* (leaves of the shepherdess). These, used by either the patient or the healer, may induce enlightening visions that will lead to a cure.

Chinantecs

Although Oaxaca's approximately 100,000 Chinantec-speaking people live on some of Mexico's best-watered land, the majority are poor. Inaccessibility, not easily tillable tropical forests, and lack of gold or silver relegated the Chinantecs to the margin during colonial times. The Chinantecs' homeland, the Chinantla, is a 70- by 40-mile region around the important market town of Valle Nacional in northeast Oaxaca. The Chinantla's natural division into eastern lowland (Chinantla Grande) and western upland (Chinantla Pichinche) was apparent to the first Spanish arrivals in the 1520s. For the Spanish conquistadores, the Chinantecs weren't pushovers. After years of seesaw skirmishes, the Spanish mounted their final push at Yetzelalag. Chinantec legend recounts that at the battle's height the Chinantec warriors invoked their gods, who opened the mountain, allowing them to escape. Nevertheless, the Chinantecs submitted to three centuries of labor on Spanish tobacco and sugarcane plantations and cattle ranches.

Although the Spanish colonial policy of *congregación* led to the abandonment of many original town sites, the upland Chinantla retained a number of important market centers. Among the most important and colorful are Sochiapan, Tlacozintepec, Usila, Quiotepec, and San Pedro Yolox in the western uplands; Valle Nacional and Ayozintepec in the center; and Petlalpa, Lalana, and Jocotepec in the southwest lowlands.

During the 19th century, new colonists introduced coffee, pineapple, and rice agriculture, which, with the Papaloapan Project, continues in modern form today. Although the project forced painful relocations on thousands of lowland Mazatec and Chinantec peoples, it ended their isolation. Government jobs, schools, clinics, electricity, sanitary and water systems changed life forever in the Chinantec lowlands. At the height of the disorder, swarms of protests erupted. Oaxacan bishops denounced government relocation efforts: "The *indígenas* continue to be the ones always exploited, those who must pay the price of any progress."

For good or bad, the Papaloapan Project lifted the native residents' health, literacy, and general standard of living at the expense of erasing most of their age-old ways of life. In contrast to the Chinantla highlands, few traditional markets function in the lower Chinantla. On the other hand, the government-planned communal and corporate plantations have greatly increased productivity. The Chinantla regularly produces the lion's share of Oaxaca's tobacco, rice, sugarcane, chilies, and pineapples. The workers, however, receive only a minimum of the benefits. Most profits flow to the government agencies, which control everything—seeds, planting, credit, harvesting, and marketing.

Nevertheless, tradition still rules in much of the upper Chinantla. In the minds of many Chinantec-speakers, the old fertility gods "Father and Mother Maize" still command the rain even though their prayers are Catholic. The cosmos is still a battleground between day, ruled by the young and vigorous sun, and night, ruled by the twinkling old stars. Some still believe that Creation's original people, who refused to bow down before the god-sun, were changed to monkeys and banished to the forest forever for their error. In some villages, *rayos,* powerful members of lightning cults, can still hurl lightning bolts against neighboring villages and know how to defend the home village against reverse attacks.

Mixes and Zoques

Their cultural and common Mayan linguistic linkages have led most experts to believe that the original Mixe and Zoque (MEE-shay and SOH-kay) people, together with the Popoluca of present Veracruz state, occupied a single territory. Invasions, first by the Zapotecs and Aztecs and then the Spanish forced the present territorial divisions. The Mixes (population around 100,000) occupy the mountainous belt that stretches about 100 miles (160 km) from the central valley's eastern edge to the most easterly Mixe center, San Juan Guichicovi, several miles short of the cross-Isthmus highway-rail line. Thirty-five miles (55 km) farther east, Zoque territory (population around 5,000), divided between two sprawling *ejido* grants, begins. From the Santa María Chimalapa-San Miguel Chimalapa line it spreads east, across the wild Chimalapas mountainous jungle to the Chiapas border. The few remaining Popoluca-speakers are limited to a few isolated villages in eastern Veracruz state.

Despite several costly campaigns, Spanish force of arms never really conquered the Mixes. If they were conquered at all, it was by 16th-century Dominican missionaries who accomplished with kindness what Spanish guns and steel could not. By the end of the colonial era, they had established nine vicarages, among them Juquila Mixes, San Miguel Quetzaltepec, Asunción Puxmecatan, Ayutla, and San Juan Guichicovi, which all remain important Mixe market towns. Ayutla, closest to the central valley, is dominant.

Anthropologists generally describe Mixe traditions as "less developed" than other Oaxacan groups. They describe a "culture unsuited to the environment," as if the Mixe ways of life first flowered in fairer, more fertile lands and never completely adjusted to the cold, marginal, mountainous regions where the Mixes fled in the face of foreign invasions. Such a speculation also explains the Mixes' well-known wariness and avoidance of outside contact. The Zoque, by contrast, adapted relatively easily to Spanish ways and share little of the Mixes' shyness.

Spanish attempts to congregate the Mixes into towns were only minimally successful. Mixe people largely moved back into the countryside, leaving little-used empty houses in town. Today most live in country hamlets clinging to mountainsides, with individual houses built on level stilt platforms.

Turbulence has marred the Mixes' recent history. In 1938, President Lázaro Cárdenas wanted to reward the Mixe people for their support of the Republic against the infamous 1865 French Intervention. He persuaded the Oaxaca legislature to award them semi-autonomous status in an all-Mixe district. However, a dispute broke out over the location of the district capital. The towns of Ayutla, Cacalotepec, and Zacatepec had their leading supporters, but Luis Rodríguez of Zacatepec was the most ruthless. While the others protested weakly, he led a four-year reign of terror—kidnapping, cattle rustling, torture, murder, and pillage—with the implicit support of Governor Vicente González. In 1943, Rodríguez cut off the feet and tongue of one prominent opponent and had another assassinated on the steps of the

TAKING PEOPLE PICTURES

Like most folks everywhere, typical Oaxacan people on the street rarely appreciate strangers taking their pictures. The easiest route to overcoming this is a local friend, guide, or even a willing interpreter-bystander) who can provide an introduction. Lacking that, you'll need to be at least semi-fluent in Spanish in order to introduce yourself or say something funny to break the ice.

A sometimes useful way to go is to offer to send them a copy of their picture. If they accept, make sure that you follow through. If somehow the picture doesn't come out, at least send them a picture of you, explaining why.

Although it's becoming less common, some people still believe that they might lose their souls if they let you take their picture. In such a case, humor again might help (or perhaps offering to let them take a picture of you first).

Markets are wonderful picture-taking places but pose challenges. Vendors are often resistant, to the point of hostility, if you try to take their picture behind their sumptuous pile of tomatoes or stack of baskets. The reasons aren't hard to understand. They're grumpy partly because sales are probably disappointing, and, since they have to stay put, they probably feel used. Buying something from them might go a long way toward soothing their feelings.

Under all circumstances, please do not offer to pay people for the privilege of taking a person's picture. It will be a shame if you do because they're going to be thinking money whenever they see tourists. Much better, turn the photo session into a person-to-person exchange by offering to send them a copy of their picture.

As for church picture-taking, remember churches are places of worship and not museums. Don't be rude by trying to take pictures of people at the altar. Moreover, churches are usually dark inside, and, unless you have a flash-suppress option or unusually high-speed film, your flash will disturb worshippers.

Government Palace in Oaxaca City. Enough was enough for Governor Sánchez Canom, who left Oaxaca City to intervene. But while he was gone, Rodríguez got him replaced. After that, Rodríguez was in complete control, murdering opponents with impunity, collecting tribute from towns and even 10 percent from religious fiestas and holding 500 prisoners in forced labor. Even after his death in 1952, his heirs tried to extend their reign until the 1970s. Despite Luis Rodríguez's notorious legacy, Zacatepec remains the Mixe district capital to the present day.

In 1972, partly in response to the trouble, Mixe people organized themselves into the grassroots social-political Federación Mixe. They soon coalesced with the already-existing local Worker's Federation of Chinantecs, Zapotecs, and Mixes and the national General Union of Workers and Farmers of Mexico (UGOCM).

Mixe and Zoque social traditions closely follow Mesoamerican patterns. Mixe religion has striking parallels to those described in the Maya sacred book, the *Popol Vuh*. Their legends say that the Mixe god Kondoy was hatched from an egg, grew rapidly, and traveled, battling Aztec armies. He returned and arranged the world in the Mixe image, then retired to the Mixe sacred mountain, Zempoatepetl, where he still lives.

Belief in the *nagual* persists among the Mixes. If an unbaptized baby dies, the parents must make haste to bury the body immediately, with little ceremony. If not, the spirit of the unbaptized baby might escape and become a *nagual,* a malevolent animal that will harm people who cross its path. Sometimes the *nagual* takes human form as a witch that can transform itself into an animal or other scary form and cause general mischief and illness by infusing some type of object into the victim's body. Traditional healers combine a number of remedies, such as *temascal* steam bathing, rubbing with herbs, prayers, sucking, and vision-inducing plants, to remove such infusions.

Chatinos
The southern Sierra country of the nearly 30,000 strong Chatinos is a 1,200-square-mile enclave surrounded by Mixtecs on the west, Zapotecs on the north and east, and mestizos and African-

Mexicans on the south coast. Their language, part of the Zapotec sub-family, resembles Sierra Zapotec. Chatino market centers, besides the central and dominant Santa Catarina Juquila, are Panixtlahuaca, San Juan Quiahije, San Pedro Juchatengo, Nopala, and Zacatepec. Besides its commercial and political influence, Santa Catarina Juquila is a major pilgrimage center, especially for the hundreds of thousands of faithful who arrive on 8 December to honor their beloved Virgin of Juquila.

Most Chatino families are subsistence farmers; Zapotec and mestizo traders dominate commerce in the market centers. In addition to the customary corn, beans, and squash, farmers also cultivate coffee, either as day laborers or on their own land, in which case they sell the surplus for cash at the market.

Amusgos

The approximately 30- by 30-mile Amusgo territory straddles the Oaxaca-Guerrero border. About a third of the 30,000 Amusgo speakers live in Oaxaca, around the small centers of Cacahuatepec and San Pedro Amusgos, while the remainder live on the Guerrero side, near the centers of Ometepec, Xochistlahuaca, and Tlacoachistlahuaca.

Linguists reckon that the Amusgo language, a member of the Mixtec language subfamily, separated from Mixtec between 2000 and 1000 B.C. Around A.D. 1000 the Amusgos came under the domination of the strong coastal Mixtec kingdom of Tututepec. In 1457 they were conquered by the Aztecs and not long after, by the Spanish in the 1520s. Decimation of the Amusgo population by disease during the 16th century led to the importation of African slave labor, whose descendants, known locally as *negros* or *costeños* live along the Guerrero-Oaxaca coastline.

Although the Amusgo population eventually recovered, many of the old colonial-era haciendas remained intact until modern times. The Amusgos, isolated from the mainstream of modern Mexican life, retain their age-old corn-bean-squash farming tradition. Moreover, they have received little attention from anthropologists or archaeologists, although several likely archaeological mounds exist near Amusgo villages.

Amusgo women are nevertheless famous for their hand-embroidered *huipiles,* whose colorful floral and animal designs fetch willing customers in Oaxaca tourist centers. Even better, Amusgo women often wear their *huipiles,* appearing as heavenly visions of spring on dusty small-town side streets.

Triques

About 50 miles farther north from the Amusgo territory, about 15,000 Trique (TREE-kay) people live in their 20- by 15-mile highland pocket of the Mixteca Alta. You'll see plenty of them in the Juxtlahuaca town market—especially Trique women—selling their brilliant red-striped wool *huipiles* in the middle of the town square. Long ago, the Trique fled into the mountain vastness, from first Mixtec, then Aztec, and finally Spanish invaders. Some of their main centers are San Isidro Chicahuaxtla, San Juan Copala, and Tilapa, all south of Juxtlahuaca and north of Putla de Guerrero.

The Trique have only grudgingly accepted outside authority. Rebellions broke out often during the colonial era and later. In 1843 Trique forces rebelled against state and federal authorities, who required five years to jail and execute the responsible leaders. Subsequently, during the later 19th and 20th centuries, coffee became a major Trique product and coffee beans became their money, which traders turned into alcohol and guns. Rebellion, which again required federal forces to suppress, broke out in Copala in 1956. The federal garrison remains in Copala to the present day.

Only at Chicahuaxtla, in the high Mixteca country (just off of Hwy. 125, about 25 miles, 40 km west of Tlaxiaco), did Christianity have much effect, due to the compassionate persuasion of Father Gonzales Lucero hundreds of years ago. Consequently, much of the Trique's folklore survives to the present day. An oft-told creation myth describes the sun and the moon, gods who once lived in a *calabaza* (calabash), but who broke out and rode a rabbit and a cat into the heavens to light the world. Around 25 March traditional *curanderos* lead services at a sacred cave near Copala, about 13 miles (20 km) along the highway south of Juxtlahuaca, to appease the old gods. They sacrifice a lamb and a goat while the gathered crowd offers incense and flowers.

Chochos, Ixcatecs, and Popolucas

Emigration and Spanish literacy are fast reducing the number of speakers of Chocho, Ixcatec, and Popoluca, three related tongues of the dry canyonlands of the northwest Oaxaca. Of the three, the Chocho people are dominant, in their extensive homeland around Coixtlahuaca and subsidiary centers of Tequixtepec and Tepelmeme. If you're going to hear any of Chocho language, it will probably be in the market at Tepelmeme, just off the Oaxaca-Puebla expressway about 15 miles (24 km) north of Coixtlahuaca.

Defeated by the Mixtecs in the 1300s and the Aztecs a hundred years later, the Chochos were again subdued by Spanish conquistadores Orozco and Alvarado in 1522 and later converted by Dominican Father Fermín Abrego. Coixtlahuaca was a thriving Chocho and Ixcatec market until around 1900, but loss of topsoil to erosion has forced many families to emigrate.

If you're going to hear any Ixcatec at all, it will be in Ixcatlán, the sole Ixcatec *municipio,* accessible by dirt road about 20 miles (32 km) northeast from Coixtlahuaca. The same is approximately true of Popoluco, whose few remaining speakers in Oaxaca live in the sliver of territory by the Puebla border, around Santiago Chazumba on Hwy. 125.

Cuicatecs

The Cuicatec language, by contrast, is holding its own, due to the isolation and richness of the homeland of the Cuicatecos ("People of Song"). About 15,000 Cuicatec people inhabit their present territory, mainly the *municipios* of Concepción Pápalo, San Juan Tepeuxila, San Pedro Teutila, and Santiago Nacaltepec in the mountains east of district capital Cuicatlán and south of the Santo Domingo River canyon.

Archaeological digs around Pápalo and other sites reveal Toltec influences, hinting that the Cuicatec lands may have been a haven for some of the refugees from the fall of Tula, the Toltec capital in the north, around A.D. 1060.

Historians believe that Cuicatec speakers numbered about 60,000 before the conquest. They were defeated by both the Aztecs, around 1456, and the Spanish, in the person of conquistador Martín Mezquita in 1526. Nevertheless, during the colonial era the Cuicatecs resisted both Catholic conversion and forced plantation labor by fleeing into the mountains, where they remain today. Although the Dominicans established a church in Pápalo in 1630 and tried to convert them, Catholic influence remains weak. The old gods, notably *já iko,* the lord of their sacred mountain, Cerro Cheve, still live on in the hearts and minds of many Cuicatec people.

Today you might hear some Cuicatec spoken at the busy market at Cuicatlán, where Cuicatec women come down from the mountains to sell their highland handicrafts: wool serapes and jackets, flower and animal-motif embroidered *huipiles,* and palm-leaf sombreros, *petates,* and *cestas* (hats, mats, and baskets).

Cuicatec people also earn cash collectively from the concession in which they allow the paper mill in Tuxtepec to harvest some of their forest trees. The money goes to finance community projects.

Huaves

The Isthmus territory of the Huave people encompasses the shoreline of the big Lagunas Superior, Inferior, and the Mar Muerto. About 12,000 Huave-speaking people live there, notably around the villages of San Mateo del Mar, Santa María del Mar, San Dionisio del Mar, and San Francisco del Mar.

The Huave language, not clearly identified with any other language family, is generally classified in a family of its own. This is further supported from studies by colonial historians, indicating that the Huave may have migrated from the Nicaraguan Pacific Coast and settled around the present-day Jalapa del Marqués on the Isthmus. The more numerous Zapotecs, invading around 1375, forced them to the edges of the lagoons, where they now live.

Generally ignored and neglected by everyone, the Huaves hold on to many preconquest beliefs. In the absence of Catholic priests, native *curanderos* practice thinly veiled pagan rites in some village churches.

Although they subsist mainly on corn, beans, chilies, vegetables, and occasional meat, Huave-speaking people earn cash from their fish catches. Men sell fresh fish to wholesalers who arrive afternoons at the shoreline villages, while women sell the surplus as dried fish at Salina Cruz, Tehuantepec, and Juchitán markets.

Nahuas

Along the coast, in a 20-mile (32-km) strip west of Salina Cruz and with the small town of Morro de Mazatán at its center, lies an enclave of Nahua (Nahuatl- or Aztec-speaking people). Besides this small region, several thousand more Nahuatl speakers live in two other small Oaxaca enclaves in the north, one around Tuxtepec and the other next to the Puebla border, wedged between Mazatec, Ixcatec, Chocho, and Popoluca territories. Such Nahuatl enclaves are probably remnants of early colonies established by the Aztec emperors after their armed expansion into Oaxaca in the 1400s.

Chontals

Finally, a few miles farther west lies the Chontal (sometimes known as "Tequistlatec") territory. The Chontals are most visible on the coast, at Santiago Astata and San Pedro Huamelula. Today, about 25,000 speakers of Chontal, a language of the Hokan language family (widespread, from the north Gulf Coast to Central America) live in their approximately 1,000-square-mile domain.

The Chontals are among the least modernized of Oaxaca indigenous groups. They have always tenaciously resisted invasion (although many in the zone due west of Tequisistlán have adopted the Zapotec language). Although many live near the coast, they do little fishing. They live mostly by corn-based subsistence farming, emigrating to the Isthmus or elsewhere for cash employment.

Relatively unaffected by Catholicism, their traditions remain strong. A popular fable is of their folk-hero King Fane Kansini, whom, legend says, an elderly couple hatched as an infant from an egg that they had found. The old couple soon discovered that the infant had supernatural powers. As he matured, Fane Kansini acquired the burning desire to save his people from the Zapotecs. He invented body armor and a wondrous new kind of arrow, which he used to defeat the Zapotec king in battle and thus save the Chontal people from annihilation. The Chontal-Zapotec mutual enmity continues to the present time.

ON THE ROAD

SPORTS AND RECREATION

ON THE BEACH

It's easy to understand why many Oaxaca vacationers stay right at the beach. And not just at the popular crystalline stretches around the Bays of Huatulco, Puerto Ángel, and Puerto Escondido. Some adventurers flee the resorts to find even more pristine strands hidden in far corners along the entire Oaxacan coast. There they discover solitude and the rich wildlife of shorelines varying from mangrove-edged lagoons and algae-decorated tidepools to shoals of pebbles and sand of a dozen colors and consistencies.

Sand makes the beach, and Oaxaca has plenty, from warm, black mica dust to cool, velvety, white coral. Some beaches drop steeply to turbulent, close-in surf fine for fishing. Others are level, with gentle, rolling breakers made for surfing and swimming.

Oaxaca's beaches yield fascinating troves of shells and treasures of flotsam and jetsam. **Beachcombing** is more rewarding during the summer storm season when big waves deposit acres of fresh shells—among them conch, scallops, clams, combs of Venus, whelks, limpets, olives, cowries, starfish, and sand dollars.

During the summer-fall rainy season, beaches near river mouths are often fantastic outdoor galleries of wind- and water-sculpted snags and giant logs deposited by the downstream flood.

Viewing Wildlife
Wildlife watchers should keep quiet and always be on the alert. Animal survival depends on them seeing you first. Occasional spectacular offshore sights, such as whales, dolphins, and manta rays, or an onshore giant constrictor, beached squid or octopus, crocodile, or even a jaguar looking for turtle eggs may reward those prepared to wait and watch for them. Don't forget your binoculars and your *Field Guide to Mexican Birds* (see the Booklist).

WATER SPORTS

Swimming, surfing, windsurfing, snorkeling, scuba diving, and kayaking are Oaxaca's water sports of choice. For details on local favorite spots, conditions, rental shops, and equipment, see the travel chapters.

Safety First

As viewed from Oaxaca beaches, the Pacific Ocean usually lives up to its name. Many protected inlets, safe for child's play, dot the coastline. Unsheltered shorelines, on the other hand, can be deceiving. Smooth water in the calm forenoon often changes to choppy in the afternoon; calm ripples lapping the shore in March can grow to hurricane-driven walls of water in November. Such storms can wash away sand, changing a wide, gently sloping beach into a steep one plagued by turbulent waves and treacherous currents.

Undertow, whirlpools, crosscurrents, and occasional oversized waves can make ocean swimming a fast-lane adventure. Getting unexpectedly swept out to sea or hammered onto the beach bottom by a surprise breaker are potential hazards.

Never attempt serious swimming when tipsy or full of food; never swim alone where someone can't see you. Always swim beyond the breakers (which come in sets of several, climaxed by a big one, which breaks highest and farthest from the beach). If you happen to get caught in the path of such a breaker, avoid it by diving under and letting it roll harmlessly over you. If you do get caught by a serious breaker, try to roll and tumble with it (as football players tumble) to avoid injury.

Poisonous sea snakes, although rare and shy, do inhabit Oaxaca waters. Much more common, especially around submerged rocks, is the moray eel. Don't stick your fingers or toes in any concealed cracks.

Now and then swimmers get a nettle-like jellyfish sting. Be careful around coral reefs and beds of sea urchins; corals can sting (like jellyfish), and you can get infections from coral cuts and sea-urchin spines. Shuffle along sandy bottoms to scare away stingrays before stepping on one. If you're unlucky, its venomous tailspines may inflict a painful wound.

First Aid: If you suffer a coral scratch or jellyfish sting, experts advise you should wash the afflicted area with ocean (not fresh) water and pour alcohol (rubbing alcohol or a liquor, such as *mescal,* tequila, or *aguardiente*), if available, over the wound, then apply hydrocortisone cream from your first-aid kit or the *farmacia.*

Injuries from sea urchin spines and stingray barbs are both painful and sometimes serious. Physicians recommend similar first aid for both: first remove the spines or barbs by hand or with tweezers, then soak the injury in hot-as-possible fresh water to weaken the toxins and provide relief. Another method is to rinse the area with an antibacterial solution—rubbing alcohol, vinegar, wine, or ammonia diluted with water. If none is available, the same effect may be achieved by rinsing with urine, either your own or someone else's in your party. Get medical help immediately.

Low-tech recreation, such as this Foosball game, is popular in Oaxaca.

FISH

A bounty of fish dart, swarm, jump, and wriggle in Oaxaca's surf, reefs, lagoons, and offshore depths. While many make delicious dinners (albacore, red snapper, pompano), others are tough (sailfish), bony (bonefish), and even poisonous (puffers). Some grow to half-ton giants (marlin, jewfish), while others are diminutive reef-grazers (parrot fish, damselfish, angelfish) whose bright colors delight snorkelers and divers. Here's a sampling of what you might find underwater or on your dinner plate.

bonito

BOB RACE

black marlin *(marlin negro):* six feet; blue-black; deep waters; good taste
blue marlin *(marlin azul):* eight feet; blue; deep waters; poor taste
bobo *(barbudo):* one foot; blue, yellow; found in surf; fair taste
bonefish *(macabi):* one foot; blue or silver; found inshore; poor taste
bonito *(bonito):* two feet; black; deep waters; good taste
butterfly fish *(muñeca):* six inches; black, yellow; reef fish*
chub *(chopa):* one foot; gray; reef fish; good taste
croaker *(corvina):* two feet; brownish; found along inshore bottoms; rare and protected
damselfish *(castañeta):* four inches; brown, blue, orange; reef fish*
dolphinfish, mahimahi *(dorado):* three feet; green, gold; deep waters; good taste

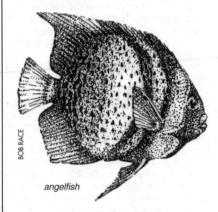

angelfish

BOB RACE

albacore *(albacora, atún):* two to four feet in size; blue; found in deep waters; excellent taste
angelfish *(ángel):* one foot; yellow, orange, blue; reef fish*
barracuda *(barracuda, picuda):* two feet; brown; deep waters; good taste

barracuda

ERIN DWYER

Snorkeling and Scuba Diving

Many exciting clear-water sites, such as the Bays of Huatulco and Playa Estacahuite at Puerto Ángel and Playa Angelito in Puerto Escondido, await both beginner and expert snorkelers and divers. Veteran divers usually arrive during the dry winter and early spring when river outflows are mere trickles, leaving offshore waters clear. In Huatulco, professional dive shops rent equipment, provide lessons and guides, and transport divers to choice sites.

While convenient, rented equipment is often less than satisfactory. To be sure, serious divers bring their own gear. This might include wetsuits in the winter, when some swimmers begin to feel cold after an unprotected half hour in the water.

Surfing, Sailing, Windsurfing, and Kayaking

Oaxaca has the Mexican Pacific's acknowledged best surfing beach, the renowned Playa Zicatela "pipeline" at Puerto Escondido. The surf everywhere is highest and most exciting during the

grouper *(garropa):* three feet; brown, rust; found offshore and in reefs; good taste

grunt *(burro):* eight inches; black, gray; found in rocks, reefs*

jack *(toro):* one to two feet; bluish-gray; offshore; good taste

mackerel *(sierra):* two feet; gray with gold spots; offshore; good taste

mullet *(lisa):* two feet; gray; found in sandy bays; good taste

needlefish *(agujón):* three feet; blue-black; deep waters; good taste

Pacific porgy *(pez de pluma):* one to two feet; tan; found along sandy shores; good taste

wahoo

parrot fish *(perico, pez loro):* one foot; green, pink, blue, orange; reef fish

pompano *(pómpano):* one foot; gray; inshore bottoms; excellent taste

puffer *(botete):* eight inches; brown; inshore; poisonous

red snapper *(huachinango, pargo):* one to two feet; reddish pink; deep waters; excellent taste

roosterfish *(pez gallo):* three feet; black, blue; deep waters; excellent taste

sailfish *(pez vela):* five feet; blue-black; deep waters; poor taste

sardine *(sardina):* eight inches; blue-black; offshore; good taste

sea bass *(cabrilla):* one to two feet; brown, ruddy; reef and rock crevices; good taste

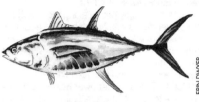

yellowfin tuna

shark *(tiburón):* 2–10 feet; black to blue; in- and offshore; good taste

snook *(robalo):* two to three feet; black-brown; found in brackish lagoons; excellent taste

spadefish *(chambo):* one foot; black-silver; found along sandy bottoms; reef fish*

swordfish *(pez espada):* five feet; black to blue; deep waters; good taste

triggerfish *(pez puerco):* one to two feet; blue, rust, brown, black; reef fish; excellent taste

wahoo *(peto, guahu):* two to five feet; green to blue; deep waters; excellent taste

yellowfin tuna *(atún amarilla):* two to five feet; blue, yellow; deep waters; excellent taste

yellowtail *(jurel):* two to four feet; blue, yellow; offshore; excellent taste

*fish that are generally too small to be considered edible

July–Nov. hurricane season, when big swells from storms far out at sea attract platoons of surfers to favored beaches.

Windsurfers, sailboaters, and kayakers—who, by contrast, require more tranquil waters—do best in the Oaxaca winter or early spring. Then they gather to enjoy the near-ideal conditions at many coves and inlets near the resorts.

While beginners can have fun with the equipment available from rental shops, serious surfers, windsurfers, sailboaters, and kayakers should pack their own gear.

POWER SPORTS

Power sports, such as water-skiing, parasailing, and jet skiing, are not widespread on Oaxaca beaches. In parasailing, a motorboat pulls while a parachute lifts you, like a soaring gull, high over the ocean. After 10 minutes they deposit you (usually gently) back on the sand. Personal watercraft are like snowmobiles except they operate on water, where, with a little practice, even beginners can quickly learn to whiz over the waves.

Although the luxury hotels at Huatulco provide experienced crews and equipment for such activities, practice while sober and with caution. Moreover, you, as the paying patron, have a right to expect that your providers and crew are themselves both cautious and sober besides being well-equipped.

Beach Buggies and ATVs

Some visitors enjoy racing along the beach and rolling over dunes with beach buggies and ATVs (all-terrain vehicles—*motos* in Mexico), balloon-tired, three-wheeled motor scooters. While certain resort rental agencies cater to the growing use of such vehicles, limits are in order. Of all the proliferating high-horsepower beach pastimes, these are the most intrusive. Noise, exhaust and gasoline pollution, injuries to operators and bystanders, scattering of wildlife and destruction of their habitats have led (and I hope will continue to lead) to the restriction of beach buggies and ATVs on beaches.

TENNIS AND GOLF

Most Oaxacans are working too hard to be playing much tennis and golf. Consequently, tennis and golf courses are nearly completely restricted to Oaxaca City and the Bays of Huatulco. If you are planning on a lot of golf and tennis, check into one of the several Huatulco hotels with easy access to these facilities. Use of hotel tennis courts is often, but not always, included in your hotel tariff. If not, fees will run about $10 per hour. Golf greens fees, which begin at about $50 for 18 holes, are usually extra.

FISHING

Experts agree that the Oaxaca coast is a world-class deep-sea and surf fishing ground. Sportspersons routinely bring in dozens of species from among the several hundred that have been identified in Oaxaca waters.

Surf Fishing

Most good fishing beaches away from the immediate resort areas will typically have only a few locals (mostly with nets) and fewer visitors.

Oaxacans do little sportfishing. Most either make their living from fishing or do none at all. Some local folks catch fish for supper with nets. Consequently, few Oaxaca shops sell fishing equipment. Plan to bring your own, including hooks, lures, line, and weights.

In any case, the cleaner the water, the more interesting your catch. On a good day, your reward might be *sierras, cabrillas,* porgies, or pompanos pulled from the Oaxaca surf.

You can't have everything, however. Foreigners cannot legally take Mexican abalone, coral, lobster, pismo clams, rock bass, sea fans, shrimp, turtles, or seashells. Neither are they supposed to buy them directly from fishermen.

Deep-Sea Fishing

Santa Cruz de Huatulco, and to a lesser extent, Salina Cruz and Puerto Ángel, are well-known jumping-off-spots for the big prize marlin and sailfish.

A deep-sea boat charter generally includes the boat and crew for a full or half day, plus equipment and bait for two to six persons, not including food or drinks. The full-day price depends upon the season. Around Christmas and New Year and before Easter (when reservations will be mandatory), a boat can run $400 at Huatulco, less during low seasons and at the other spots.

Renting an entire big boat is not the only choice. *Pangas,* outboard launches seating two to six passengers, are available for as little as $50, depending on the season. Once six of my friends hired a *panga* for $50, had a great time, and came back with a boatload of big tuna, jack, and mackerel. A restaurant cooked them up as a banquet for a dozen of us in exchange for the extra fish, and I discovered for the first time how heavenly fresh *sierra veracruzana* can taste.

Bringing Your Own Boat

If you're going to be doing lots of fishing, your own boat may be your most flexible and economical option. One big advantage is you can go to the many excellent fishing grounds the charter boats do not frequent. Keep your equipment simple, scout around, and keep your eyes peeled and ears open for local regulations and customs, plus tide, wind, and fish-edibility information.

FIESTAS

The following calendar lists national and notable Oaxacan holidays and festivals. For many more details, see the destinations cited. If you happen to be where one of these is going on, get out of your car or bus and join in!

1 January: **¡Feliz Año Nuevo!** (Happy New Year!—national holiday), especially in Santiago Jamiltepec and Teotitlán del Valle

6 January: **Día de los Reyes** (Day of the Kings), especially in Santos Reyes Nopala—traditional gift exchange; townsfolk perform favorite traditional dances

13–17 January: **Fiesta del Dulce Nombre de Jesús** (Festival of the Sweet Name of Jesus), in Santa Ana del Valle, Tlacolula and Zimatlán—troupes perform many traditional dances, including the Dance of the Feathers

17 January: **Día de San Antonio Abad**—decorating and blessing animals

20–21 January: **Fiesta de San Sebastián,** especially in San Pedro y San Pablo Tequixtepec, Pinotepa Don Luis, and Jalapa de Díaz

25 January: **Fiesta del Apóstol de San Pablo** (Festival of Apostle St. Paul), in Mitla—masses, processions, feast, fireworks, *jaripeo* (bull-roping and riding), and dancing

2 February: **Día de Candelaria,** especially in Tututepec—plants, seeds, and candles blessed; procession and bullfights

5 February: **Constitution Day** (national holiday)—commemorates the constitutions of 1857 and 1917

24 February: **Flag Day** (national holiday)

February: The four days before Ash Wednesday, usually in late February, many towns, especially San Juan Colorado, Putla, Pinotepa Don Luis, and Juxtlahuaca, celebrate **Carnaval**—Mardi Gras-style extravaganzas

February–March: Celebrations continue during Lent *(cuaresma),* especially in Santiago Jamiltepec and Pinotepa Nacional for several weeks

Second Friday of Lent (nine days after Ash Wednesday): **Fiesta del Señor del Perdón** (Festival of the Lord of Forgiveness), in San Pedro and San Pablo Tequixtepec—big pilgrimage festival

Second Friday of Lent: **Fiesta del Señor de Piedad,** in Santiago Astata

Fourth Friday of Lent (23 days after Ash Wednesday): **Fiesta del Señor de Misericordias,** in Santa María Huatulco

Fourth Friday before Easter Sunday: **Fiesta of Jesus the Nazarene,** in Huaxpaltepec

Week before Palm Sunday: **Week of Ramos,** especially in Jamiltepec

Friday before Good Friday (11 days before Easter Sunday): **Feria Comercial** (Commercial Fair), in Huatla de Jiménez—many traditional folk dances

18–19 March: **Fiesta de San José,** in Valle Nacional; on the weekend closest to 10 March in San José Mogote

21–31 March: **Juegos Florales** (Flower Games), in Oaxaca City

21 March: **Birthday of Benito Juárez,** the "Hero of the Americas" (national holiday), especially in Benito Juárez's birthplace, Guelatao—a whirl of traditional dances

April: **Semana Santa** (pre-Easter Holy Week, culminating in Domingo Santa, Easter, national holiday), in many locales, especially San Juan Colorado, Pinotepa Don Luis, and Pinotepa Nacional

Good Friday, two days before Easter Sunday: **Fiesta de la Santa Cruz de Huatulco** (Festival of the Holy Cross of Huatulco)

Saturday before Easter Sunday: **Sábado de Gloria** in San Miguel Tequixtepec—people, called *mecos,* don masks and do a kind of adult trick or treat for the occasion

First week in April: **Feria del Mango** (Mango Fair), in Tapanatepec

26–29 April: **Fiesta de San Pedro Mártir de Verona,** in San Pedro Yucunama

1 May: **Labor Day** (national holiday)

3 May: **Fiesta de la Santa Cruz** (Festival of the Holy Cross), in many places, especially Salina Cruz, Tehuantepec, and Unión Hidalgo

5 May: **Cinco de Mayo** (national holiday)—celebration of the defeat of the French at Puebla in 1862

10 May: **Mothers' Day** (national holiday)

10–12 May: **Fiesta of the Coronation of the Virgin of the Rosary**

(*continued on next page*)

FIESTAS
(continued)

11 to 16 May: **Fiesta de San Isidro Labrador** (Festival of Saint Isador the Farmer), in Ixcatlán.

15–30 May: **Velas de San Vicente Ferrer,** in Juchitán (also many more—see the special topic *Velas* of the Isthmus)

Late May-early June: **Feria Tuxtepec,** in Tuxtepec—big expo and folkloric dance festival

2–3 June: **Fiesta de San Antonio de Padua,** in Jalapa de Díaz

23–24 June: **Fiesta de San Juan Bautista** (Festival of St. John the Baptist), especially in Tuxtepec, Valle Nacional, Cuicatlán, and Coixtlahuaca

26–30 June: **Fiesta de Santa María Santísima** in Unión Hidalgo

26–30 June: **San Isidro el Labrador** (Saint Isador the Farmer) in Unión Hidalgo

25 June: **Fiesta de San Pedro,** in Santa María Huamelula; 27–30 June in San Pedro Tapanatepec; 29 June in San Pedro Amusgos; 26–30 June in Unión Hidalgo

29 June: **Fiesta de San Pablo y San Pedro** (Festival of St. Paul and St. Peter); 21–28 June in San Pedro Pochutla

1–15 July: **Fiesta of the Precious Blood of Christ,** in Teotitlán del Valle—featuring the Danza de la Pluma (Dance of the Feather)

Two Mondays following 16 July: **Lunes de Cerro** or Guelaguetza in Oaxaca City—all-Oaxaca dance extravaganza

20–24 July: **Fiesta de Santa María Magdalena** (Festival of St. Mary Magdalen), in Tequisistlán

20–30 July: **Fiesta de Santiago Apóstol** (Festival of St. James the Apostle), in Santiago Laollaga; 22–27 July in Suchilquitongo; 23–26 July in Jamiltepec and in Pinotepa Nacional; and 25 July in Juxtlahuaca

1–5 August: **Fiesta de Santo Domingo de Guzmán** in Unión Hidalgo

14 August: **Fiesta de la Virgen de la Asunción** (Festival of the Virgin of the Assumption), in Tlax-iaco; 15 August in Nochixtlán; 13–16 August in Huazolotitlán

13–18 August: **Fiesta del Barrio de Santa María Relatoca,** in Tehuantepec

26 August–2 September: **Fiesta de Santa Rosa de Lima** in Salina Cruz; 28 August in Ojitlán

25–29 August: **Fiesta de San Bartolomé,** in San Bartolomé de Quiliana; 23–24 August in San Bartolo Tuxtepec; 24–27 August in San Bartolo Coyotepec

31 August–11 September: **Fiesta Laborio,** in Tehuantepec

7–8 September: **Fiesta de la Vírgen de La Navidad,** in Huatla de Jiménez

7–9 September: **Fiesta del Señor de La Natividad** (Festival of the Lord of the Nativity) in Teotitlán del Valle

11 September: **Fiesta de la Virgen de los Remedios** in Jamiltepec

14 September: **Charro Day** (Cowboy Day), all over Mexico—rodeos

16 September: **Independence Day** (national holiday)—mayors everywhere reenact Father Hidalgo's 1810 Grito de Dolores from city hall balconies on the night of 15 September

21 September: **Fiesta of San Mateo,** in Calpulalpan

23–30 September: **Fiesta de la Preciosa Sangre de Cristo** (Festival of the Precious Blood of Christ), in Tlacochahuaya—eight days of processions, dances, fireworks, and food

27–29 September: **Fiesta de San Miguel,** in San Miguel Tequixtepec and Teotitlán del Camino—highlights include traditional dances, such as the Cristianos y Moros (Christians and Moors)

1–2 October: **Fiesta de San Miguel Arcangel,** in Puerto Ángel

First Sunday of October: **Fiesta de la Virgen del Rosario** (Festival of the Virgin of the Rosary), in San Pedro Amusgos

Fishing Licenses and Boat Permits
Anyone 16 or older who is either fishing or riding in a fishing boat in Mexico is required to have a fishing license. Although Mexican fishing licenses are obtainable from certain travel and insurance agents or at government fishing offices everywhere along the coast, save yourself time and trouble by getting both your fishing licenses and boat permits by mail ahead of time from the Mexican Department of Fisheries. Call at least a month before departure, tel. 619/233-6956, fax 619/233-0344, and ask for applications and the fees (which are reasonable, but depend upon the period of valid-

3–5 October: **Fiesta de San Francisco Asis,** in Salina Cruz

6–8 October: **Fiesta de San Dionisio,** in San Dionisio del Mar—pilgrimage

October, second Sunday: **Fiesta del Santa Cristo de Tlacolula** (Festival of the Holy Christ of Tlacolula), in Tlacolula

Second Monday in October: **Fiesta de los Lunes del Tule,** in Santa María del Tule—locals in costume celebrate with rites, folk dances, and feats of horsemanship beneath the boughs of their beloved great cypress tree

Third Sunday in October: **Fiesta de Octubre,** in Tlaxiaco—includes fireworks, basketball and *pelota mixteca* (traditional ball game) tournaments, and popular dances

12 October: **Día de la Raza** (Columbus Day)—national holiday that commemorates the union of the races

Last Sunday in October: **Día de Cristo Rey**

November: **Fiestas de Noviembre,** in Puerto Escondido—features the big folk dance festival **Fiesta Costéño**

1 November: **Día de Todos Santos** (All Saints Day)—in honor of the souls of children; the departed descend from heaven to eat sugar skeletons, skulls, and treats on family altars

2 November: **Día de los Muertos** (Day of the Dead), especially in Tuxtepec and Cacahuatepec—in honor of ancestors; families visit cemeteries and decorate graves with flowers and favorite foods of the deceased

11–16 November: **Fiesta de San Diego,** in Salina Cruz

13 November: **Fiesta de San Marcos** in San Marcos Tlapazola (tourist Yu'u town in the Valley of Oaxaca)

20 November: **Revolution Day** (national holiday)—anniversary of the revolution of 1910-17

22 November: **Fiesta de Santa Cecilia,** in Unión Hidalgo

25 November: **Fiesta de Santa Catarina,** in Santa Catarina Ixtepeji

29 November: **Fiesta de San Andrés,** in San Juan Colorado

1 December: **Inauguration Day**—national government changes hands every six years: 2000, 2006, 2012 . . . .

8 December: **Día de la Purísima Concepción** (Day of the Immaculate Conception)

8 December: **Fiesta de la Vírgen of Soledad,** in Oaxaca and Juxtlahuaca

late November–8 December: **Fiesta de la Virgen de Juquila,** in Santa Catarina Juquila—Oaxaca's biggest fiesta

8–11 December: **Fiesta de Nuestra Señora de la Concepción,** in Santa María Huatulco

12 December: **Día de Nuestra Señora de Guadalupe** (Festival of the Virgin of Guadalupe), nationwide—processions, music, and dancing honoring the patroness of Mexico

16–18 December: **Fiesta de la Virgen de Soledad,** in Oaxaca City

19–22 December: **Fiesta de Santo Tomás Apóstol,** in Ixtlán de Juárez

23 December: **Fiesta de los Rábanos** (Fiesta of the Radishes) in Oaxaca City

16–24 December: **Christmas Week**—week of *posadas* and piñatas, with midnight mass on Christmas Eve

24 December: **Nochebuena** (Christmas Eve), Oaxaca City and Yucunama

25 December: **Christmas Day** (Feliz Navidad—national holiday)—Christmas trees and gift exchange

26 December: **Vela Tehuantepec,** in Tehuantepec—everyone in town dances to the lovely melody of the *Sandunga*

31 December: **New Year's Eve**

ity and the fluctuating exchange rate). On the application, fill in the names (exactly as they appear on passports) of the persons requesting licenses. Include a cashier's check or a money order for the exact amount, along with a stamped, self-addressed envelope. Address the application to the Mexican Department of Fisheries, 2550 5th Ave., Suite 101, San Diego, CA 92103-6622.

Freshwater Fishing

Oaxaca has four large reservoirs: Yosocuta, in the Mixteca near Huajuapan de León; Cerro de Oro and Miguel Alemán, in the north near

Tuxtepec; and Benito Juárez Reservoir in the Isthmus not far from Tehuantepec. Their shorelines are scenic and easily accessible, and their waters are home to several varieties, mostly bass, plentiful enough for local folks to a make living cooking fish dinners.

FESTIVALS AND EVENTS

Mexicans love a party. Urban families watch the calendar for midweek national holidays that create a *puente* or bridge to the weekend and allow them to squeeze in a three- to five-day mini-vacation. Visitors should likewise watch the calendar. Such holidays (especially Christmas and Semana Santa, pre-Easter week) mean packed buses, roads, and hotels, especially around Oaxaca's beach resorts.

Country people, on the other hand, await their local saint's day or holy day. The name of the locality often provides the clue. For example, in Santa Cruz Papalutla, just east of Oaxaca City, expect a celebration on 3 May, El Día de la Santa Cruz (Day of the Holy Cross). People dress up in their traditional best, sell their wares and produce in a street fair, join a procession, get tipsy, and dance in the plaza.

Bullfighting

Oaxaca, unique among Mexican states, has no bullfights. Benito Juárez, as governor during the 1850s, outlawed bullfights in Oaxaca. In his honor, they remain banned.

ARTS AND CRAFTS

Oaxaca abounds with attractive, reasonably priced handicrafts. A sizable fraction of Oaxacan families still depend upon homespun items—clothing, utensils, furniture, native herbal remedies, religious offerings, adornments, toys, musical instruments. Many such traditions reach back thousands of years, to the beginnings of Mesoamerican civilization. The accumulated knowledge of manifold generations of artisans has in many instances resulted in finery so prized that whole villages devote themselves to the manufacture of a certain class of goods.

Handicrafts (*artesanías,* ar-tay-sah-NEE-ahs) shoppers who venture away from the Oaxaca City center and the coastal tourist enclaves to the source villages and towns will most likely benefit from lower prices, wider choices, and, most important, the privilege of meeting the artisans themselves. There, perhaps in a patio shop on a dusty Teotitlán del Valle side street or an Arrazola family patio, you might encounter the people and perhaps view the painstaking processes by which they fashion humble materials—clay, wool, cotton, wood, metal, straw, leaves, bark, paper, leather—into irresistible works of art.

BASKETRY AND WOVEN CRAFTS

Weaving straw, leaves, and reeds is among the oldest of Oaxacan crafts traditions. Mat- and basketweaving methods and designs 5,000 years old survive to the present day.

The drier regions of Oaxaca are sources of fronds from the dwarf palms that populate the hillsides. In the Mixteca, in places such as Huajuapan de León and Coixtlahuaca and the east side of the Valley of Oaxaca around Tlacolula, you might see people sitting on a doorstep or at a bus stop or even walking down the street while weaving a *petate* (mat) or *tenate* (basket) of creamy white palm leaf, prized for its soft, pliable texture. All over Oaxaca, nearly everyone uses *petates,* from vacationers, for stretching out on the beach, to local folks, for keeping tortillas warm and shielding babies from the sun. *Tenates* have been raised to nearly a fine art in a number of Oaxaca localities, such as San Luis Amatlán, near Ejutla in the southern Valley of Oaxaca. There, craftspersons interweave dyed fibers with the natural palm, creating attractive, sensitively executed geometric designs.

Carrizo, a bamboo-like reed that grows on stream banks all over Oaxaca Valley, is the source of stronger, more rigid baskets, usually called *canastas* when they have handles, *tenates* when they don't. Well-known Oaxaca Valley sources are San Juan Guelavía and Magdalena Teitipac on the east side and Santa Ana

Donkey saddles are but a few of the old-fashioned goods for sale at the Wednesday Etla market.

Zegache near Ocotlán in the south. Familiar variations include the prized *tenate para tortillas,* round at the top and tapering to square at the base, and *cajas para pájaros* (birdcages), sometimes fashioned in two, three, or four levels.

A third important weaving fiber in Oaxaca is *ixtle,* the dried strands from the leaves of maguey and related agave-family plants. Artisans all over Oaxaca craft *ixtle* into useful shapes, such as ropes for pulling, string bags for carrying, and hammocks for snoozing.

CLOTHING, EMBROIDERY, AND LEATHER

Although *traje* (ancestral tribal dress) has all but vanished in Oaxaca City, significant numbers of Oaxacan native women make and wear *traje,* especially in the Mazateca, Chinantla, and Zapotec Sierra in the north, the Isthmus in the southeast, the coastal Mixteca in the southwest, and the Trique in the Mixteca Alta in the west.

Most common *traje* garment is the *huipil,* a full, square-shouldered, short to mid-sleeved dress, often hand-embroidered with animal and floral designs and embellished with ribbons. Probably the most popular Oaxaca *huipiles* are the captivating designs from San Pedro de Amusgos (Amusgo tribe; white cotton embroidered with abstract colored animal and floral motifs). Others nearly as prized include the Trique styles from around San Andrés Chic-

ahuaxtla (white cotton, richly embroidered red stripes, interwoven with green, blue, and yellow, and hung with colored ribbons); Mazatec, from Huatla de Jiménez (white cotton with bright flowers embroidered in multiple panels, crossed by horizontal and vertical purple and magenta silk ribbons); and Isthmus Zapotec, from Tehuantepec (brightly colored cotton densely embroidered with either geometric designs or a field of flamboyant, multicolored flowers.

Oaxaca shops and stalls also sell other, less common types of *traje.* These include the *quechquémitl* (shoulder cape), often made of wool and worn as an overgarment in winter, and the *enredo,* a full-length skirt that wraps around the waist and legs like a Hawaiian sarong.

Mixtec women in Oaxaca's warm southwest coastal region around Pinotepa Nacional commonly wear the *enredo,* known locally as the *pozahuanco* (poh-sah-OOAHN-koh) below the waist and, when at home, go bare-breasted. When wearing their *pozahuancos* in public, they usually tie a *mandil,* a wide apron, around their front side.

Women weave the most prized *pozahuancos* using cotton thread dyed a light purple with secretions of tidepool-harvested snails, *Purpura patula pansa,* and silk dyed deep red with cochineal, an extract from the dried bodies of a locally cultivated insect, *Dactylopius coccus.* On a typical day, two or three women will be selling handmade *pozahuancos* at the Pinotepa Nacional market.

Ropa Típica

Colonial-era Spanish styles have blended with native *traje,* producing a wider class of dress, known generally as *ropa típica.* Lovely embroidered blouses *(blusas),* shawls *(rebozos),* and dresses *(vestidos)* fill shop racks and market stalls all over Oaxaca. Among the most popular is the so-called **Oaxaca wedding dress,** made of cotton with a crochet-trimmed riot of diminutive flowers hand-stitched about the neck and yoke. Some of the finest examples are made in San Antonino Castillo Velasco, just north of Ocotlán on the Valley of Oaxaca's south side.

In contrast to women, only a small fraction of Oaxacan men—members of remote groups, such as mountain Mazatec and Chinantecs in the north, the Mixes in the east, and rural Chatinos and Amusgos in the southwest—wear *traje.* Nevertheless, shops offer some fine men's *ropa típica,* such as wool jackets and serapes for highland or winter wear and *guayaberas,* hiplength, pleated tropical dress shirts.

Fine **embroidery** *(bordado)* embellishes much traditional Oaxacan clothing, tablecloths *(manteles),* and napkins *(servilletas).* As everywhere, women define the art of embroidery. Although some still work by hand at home, cheaper machine-made factory lace and needlework is more commonly available in shops.

Among the most renowned handmade example is the embroidery of Santo Tomás Jalieza, the "town of belts" *(cinturones),* in the Oaxaca central valley south of Coyotepec. Although best known for their attractive embroidered cloth and leather belts, the townsfolk have adapted their colorful designs to clothing, purses, bags, and much more.

Leather

Some Oaxaca shops offer selections of locally produced huaraches from around Miahuatlán in the south valley and Yalalag, north in the Sierra Juárez. Shops import most other leather goods from other Mexican centers, such as Guadalajara and León. For unique and custom-designed articles you'll probably have to confine your shopping to the expensive tourist resort shops. For the more usual though still attractive leather items such as purses, wallets, belts, coats, and boots, veteran shoppers go to Mercado Juárez or Mercado de Artesanías in Oaxaca City.

GLASS AND STONEWORK

Glass manufacture, unknown in pre-Columbian times, was introduced by the Spanish. Today factories scattered all over Mexico turn out mountains of **burbuja** (boor-BOO-hah) bubbled glass tumblers, goblets, plates, and pitchers, usually in blue, green, or red.

Artisans work stone, usually near sources of supply. Puebla and Tequisistlán are Mexico's main sources of decorative onyx (*onix,* OH-neeks). Factory shops turn out the galaxy of mostly roughhewn, cream-colored items, from animal charms and chess pieces to beads and desk sets, which you'll see on some Oaxaca City curio shop shelves.

Cantera, a volcanic tufa stone, occurs in pastel shades from pink to green and is quarried in several locations in the Valley of Oaxaca. Most preferred is the light jade-green *cantera* from Magdalena Etla, northwest of Oaxaca City. It has replaced the original but exhausted *cantera* source that supplied stone for most of Oaxaca City's original buildings.

For a keepsake from a truly ancient Oaxacan tradition, don't forget the hollowed-out stone *metate* (may-TAH-tay) or corn-grinding basin and the three-legged *molcajete* (mohl-kah-HAY-tay), a mortar for grinding chilies. Most examples you'll see in Oaxaca are from Teitipac, in the west valley near Tlacolula.

JEWELRY

Gold and silver were once the basis for Mexico's wealth. Her Spanish conquerors plundered a mountain of gold—ritual offerings, necklaces, pendants, rings, plates—masterfully crafted by a legion of indigenous jewelers. Unfortunately, much of that native tradition was lost as the colonial Spanish denied Mexicans access to precious metals and introduced Spanish methods. Nevertheless, a small native goldworking tradition survived the dislocations of the 1810–21 War of Independence and the 1910–17 Revolution. Meanwhile, silvercrafting, moribund during the 1800s, was revived in Taxco, Guerrero, during the 1920s, principally through the joint efforts of architect-artist William Spratling and the local community.

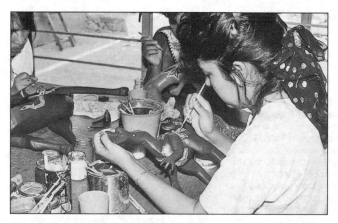

In the cottage factories of Arrazola, not far from Oaxaca City, young women paint the finish on the alebrijes *that men carve.*

Today, spurred by the tourist boom, jewelry-making is thriving in Mexico. Taxco, where guilds, families, and cooperatives produce sparkling silver and gold adornments, is the acknowledged center. Several Oaxaca shops offer Taxco-made jewelry—shimmering ornamental butterflies, birds, jaguars, serpents, turtles, and fish from the preconquest tradition. Pieces, mostly in silver, vary from humble but attractive trinkets to glittering necklaces, silver candelabras, and place settings for a dozen, sometimes embellished with precious stones.

Oaxaca also has a healthy local jewelry-making tradition. Acknowledged leader in Oaxaca City is the family firm of **Oro de Monte Albán.** Their several city and coastal resort shops offer replicas of the ancient Mixtec designs, notably of many pieces found at Monte Albán's tomb 7. Don't miss their museum shop at the Santo Domingo Cultural Center.

Tehuantepec women *(tehuanas)* have created a demand for elaborate **gold filigree jewelry,** made from fine wires and often decorated with pearls and precious stones. The finest, ranging from 10 to 18 karat (42 to 75 percent pure) gold, is more often kept in safe deposit boxes and used only on ceremonial occasions. Much more common is *chapa de oro,* gold look-alike filigree that contains no gold at all. Women sell this jewelry in Oaxaca City, at the north-central entrance of the 20 de Noviembre market and in the Isthmus, at the Juchitán and Tehuantepec markets.

WOODCARVING AND MUSICAL INSTRUMENTS

Masks

Spanish and Native Oaxacan traditions have blended to produce a multitude of masks—some strange, some lovely, some scary, some endearing, all interesting. The tradition flourishes in Oaxaca and the strongly indigenous neighboring states of Michoacán, Guerrero, and Chiapas. Here campesinos gear up all year for the village festivals—especially Semana Santa (Easter week), early December (Virgin of Guadalupe), and of the local patron, whether it be San José, San Pedro, San Pablo, Santa María, Santa Barbara, or one of a host of others. Every local fair has its favored dances, such as the Dance of the Conquest, the Christians and Moors, the Old Men, or the Tiger, in which masked villagers act out age-old allegories of fidelity, sacrifice, faith, struggle, sin, and redemption.

Although artisans craft Oaxaca masks of many materials—from stone and ebony to coconut husks and paper—wood, where available, is the medium of choice. For the entire year, carvers cut, carve, sand, and paint to ensure that each participant will be properly disguised for the festival. Although Oaxaca's larger municipalities usually have their mask maker, towns in the coastal Mixteca region, notably Santa María Huazolotitlán, are Oaxaca's busiest mask sources.

The popularity of masks has resulted in an entire made-for-tourist mask industry, which has led to mass-produced duplicates, many cleverly antiqued. Examine the goods carefully; if the price is high, don't buy unless you're convinced it's a real antique.

Alebrijes

Tourist demand has made zany wooden animals called *alebrijes* (ah-lay-BREE-hays) a Oaxaca growth industry. Virtually every family in certain Valley of Oaxaca villages—notably Arrazola and San Martin Tilcajete—runs a factory studio. There, piles of *copal* wood, which men carve and women finish and intricately paint, become whimsical giraffes, dogs, cats, iguanas, gargoyles, dragons, including most of the possible permutations in between. The farther from the source you get, the higher the *alebrije* price becomes; what costs $5 in Arrazola will probably run about $10 in Oaxaca City and $30 in the United States, Canada, or Europe.

Musical Instruments

Virtually all of Mexico's guitars are made in Paracho, Michoacán (southeast of Lake Chapala). There, scores of cottage factories turn out guitars, violins, mandolins, *viruelas,* ukuleles, and a dozen more variations every day. Products vary widely in quality, so look carefully before you buy. Make sure that the wood is well cured and dry; damp, unripe wood instruments are more susceptible to warping and cracking.

METALWORK

A score of Oaxaca City family factories turn out fine cutlery, forged ironwork, and a swarm of bright tinware mirror frames, masks, and glittering Christmas decorations.

Cutlery tradition—knives, machetes, scissors, swords and more—arrived in Oaxaca with the Spanish. Today several family shops offer their wares in town shops and market stalls, notably at the Benito Juárez market in Oaxaca City.

Traditional **ironwork,** admittedly heavy to carry home in your luggage, is made to order at a number of specialty shops in Oaxaca City. Some of the more commonly requested items, such as medieval-style lanterns and garden benches, are available on display.

Tinware *(hojalata)* (oh-hah-LAH-tah), especially the colorfully lacquered Christmas decorations—winsome angels, saints, Santas, butterflies, fruits—is Oaxaca City's most sought-after metalcraft. Running closely behind are the hosts of old-fashioned lead figures—soldiers, ballerinas, antique automobiles, angels—and fancy silvery mirror frames, metal boxes, birds, flowers, and much more. Many downtown handicrafts shops, in addition to stalls at the 20 de Noviembre market and the Mercado de Artesanías (Handicrafts Market) sell metalwork.

Moreover, be sure to ask at the same shops and stalls for *milagros,* one of Mexico's most charming forms of metalwork. Usually of brass, they are of homely shapes—a horse, dog, or baby, or an arm, head, heart, or foot. Along with a prayer, the faithful pin them to the garments of their favorite saint, whom they hope will intercede to cure an ailment or fulfill a wish.

PAPER AND PAPIER-MÂCHÉ

So popular is Tonalá, Jalisco, papier-mâché center that many Oaxaca handicrafts stores stock small flocks of birds, cats, frogs, giraffes, and other animal figurines meticulously crafted in Tonalá by building up repeated layers of glued paper. The results—sanded, brilliantly varnished, and polished—resemble fine sculptures rather than the humble newspaper from which they were fashioned.

Other paper goods you shouldn't overlook include **piñatas** (durable, inexpensive, and as Mexican as you can get), available in every town market; colorful decorative cutout banners (string overhead at your home fiesta) from San Salvador Huixcolotla, Puebla; and *amate,* wild fig tree bark paintings in animal and flower motifs, from Xalitla and Ameyaltepec, Guerrero.

POTTERY AND CERAMICS

The Valley of Oaxaca is the focus of a vibrant pottery tradition. The most renowned examples come from the village of Atzompa, a few miles west of the city. Traditionally popular for their

Already famous for their traditional green pottery, Atzompa's potters have innovated a host of fresh styles.

green-glazed clay pots, dishes, casseroles, and bowls, Atzompa potters have evolved a host of fresh styles, from graceful vases and plates blooming with painted lilies to red clay pots and bowls inscribed with artfully flowing blossoms.

San Bartolo Coyotepec village, south of the city, has acquired equal renown for its **black pottery** *(barro negro),* sold all over the world. Doña Rosa, now deceased, pioneered the crafting of big round pots without using a potter's wheel. Now made in many more shapes by Doña Rosa's descendants, the pottery's exquisite silvery black sheen is produced by the reduction (reduced air) method of firing, which removes oxygen from the clay's red (ferric) iron oxide, converting it to black (ferrous) iron oxide.

Although most latter-day Oaxacan potters are aware of the health dangers of lead pigments, some for-sale pottery may still contain lead. The hazard comes from low-fired pottery in which the lead has not been firmly melted into the glaze. Acids in foods such as lemons, vinegar, and tomatoes dissolve the lead pigments, which, when ingested, can result in lead poisoning. In general, the shiniest pottery, stoneware that has been twice fired, is the safest for dinnerware.

Although Mexican pottery tradition is as diverse as the country itself, some varieties stand out. Among the most prized is the so-called Talavera (or Majolica), the best of which is made by a few family-run shops in Puebla. The names Talavera and Majolica derive from Talavera, the Spanish town from which the tradition migrated to Mexico; prior to that it originated on the Spanish Mediterranean island of Majorca, from a combination of still older Arabic, Chinese, and African ceramic styles. Shapes include plates, bowls, jugs, and pitchers, hand-painted and hard-fired in intricate bright yellow, orange, blue, and green floral designs. So few shops make true Talavera these days that other, cheaper look-alike grades, made around Guanajuato, are more common, selling for one-half to one-third the price of the genuine article.

WOOLEN WOVEN GOODS

Mexico's finest wool weavings come from Teotitlán del Valle and the neighboring town of Santa Ana del Valle, less than an hour's drive east of Oaxaca City. Although they learned to work wool from the Spanish, the weaving tradition, continued by Zapotec-speaking families, dates back at least a thousand years before the conquest. Most families still carry on the arduous process, making everything from scratch. They gather the dyes from wild plants and the bodies of insects and sea snails. They hand-wash, card, spin, and dye the wool and even travel to remote mountain springs to gather water. The result, they say, is *vale la pena* (worth the pain): intensely colored, tightly woven carpets, rugs, and wall hangings that retain their brilliance for generations.

Although many handicrafts shops and a host of stalls in all the Oaxaca City markets sell the Teotitlán and Santa Ana weavings, a trip to Teotitlán (where Santa Ana weavers send most of their products for sale) is a "must" for Oaxaca Valley first-time visitors.

ACCOMMODATIONS

Oaxaca has lodgings to suit every style and pocketbook: world-class resorts, small beachside hotels, homey *casas de huéspedes* (guesthouses), friendly trailer parks, and miles of breezy camping beaches. The high seasons, when reservations are generally recommended, are July, late October through early November, and December in Oaxaca City; and mid-December through March, during pre-Easter week, and the month of August at the coastal resorts.

The dozens of accommodations described in this book are positive recommendations—checked out in detail—good choices from which you can pick according to your taste and purse.

Hotel Rates

The rates listed in this book are U.S. dollar equivalents of peso prices, taxes included, as quoted by the hotel management at the time of writing. Low- and high-season rates are quoted whenever possible. They are intended as a general guide only, and probably will only approximate the asking rate when you arrive. Some readers, unfortunately, try to bargain by telling desk clerks that, for example, the rate should be $30 because they read it in this book. This is unwise, because it makes hotel managers and clerks reluctant to quote rates for fear readers might hold their hotel responsible for such quotes a few years later.

In Oaxaca, hotel rates depend strongly upon inflation and season. To cancel the effect of relatively steep Mexican inflation, rates are reported in U.S. dollars. However, when settling your hotel bill, you should always insist on paying in pesos.

Websites listed in the "Internet Resources" at the end of this book might be a useful supplement to the accommodations described the destination chapters.

Saving Money

The hotel prices quoted here are rack rates: the maximum tariff, exclusive of packages and promotions, that you would pay if you walked in off the street and rented an unreserved room for one day. Savvy travelers seldom pay the maxi-

mum. Always inquire if there are any discounts or packages (*descuentos o paquetes,* pronounced "dees-koo-AYN-tohs OH pah-KAY-tays"). At any time other than the high seasons, you can generally bargain for discounts. Don't be shy; if the hotel asking price is $60, offer $30 or $40. At best, you'll get what you want; at worst, you can take your business elsewhere. Often discounts come as one or two free days for a one-week stay. Promotional packages available during slack seasons sometimes include free extras such as breakfast, a car rental, a boat tour, or a sports rental. A travel agent can be of great help in shopping around for such bargains.

You will virtually always save money if you **deal in pesos only.** Insist on both booking your lodging for an agreed price in pesos and paying the resulting hotel bill—in the same pesos, rather than dollars. The reason is that dollar rates quoted by big resorts are often based on the hotel desk exchange rate, which is customarily about 10 percent less than bank rates. For example, if the clerk tells you your hotel bill is $1,000, instead of handing over the dollars, or having him mark $1,000 on your credit card slip, ask him how much it is in pesos. Using the desk conversion rate, he might say something like 10,000 pesos (considerably less than the 11,000 pesos that the bank might give for your $1,000). Pay the 10,000 pesos or have the clerk mark 10,000 pesos on your credit card slip, and save yourself $90.

GUESTHOUSES, BED-AND-BREAKFASTS, AND HOMESTAYS

A growing fraction of Oaxaca City lodgings fall into these categories. On city residential side streets, often several blocks removed from the tourist zone, are many of the guesthouses (*casas de huéspedes*), bed-and-breakfasts, and homes where increasing numbers of families are renting rooms to visitors.

Such lodgings vary from scruffy to spic-and-span, humble to luxurious. At minimum, you can expect a plain room, a shared toilet and hot-water shower, and plenty of atmosphere for your money. In Oaxaca City and the Bays of Huatulco, rates are higher, ranging between $15 and $50, less everywhere else. Discounts are often available for long-term stays.

In addition to the guesthouse, bed-and-breakfast and homestay-style lodgings listed in the destination chapters of this book, you can also consult the many classified advertisements of the local tourist newspapers, especially in Oaxaca City.

APARTMENTS AND HOUSE RENTALS

For longer stays in Oaxaca City, many visitors prefer the convenience and economy of an apartment or house rental. Choices vary, from spartan studios to deluxe homes big enough for entire extended families. Prices depend strongly upon season and amenities, from $250 per month for the cheapest to around $1,000 for the most luxurious.

At the low end, you can expect a clean, furnished apartment with kitchen and regular maid service. Higher up the scale, houses vary from moderately luxurious homes to sky's-the-limit mansions, blooming with built-in designer luxuries, such as a swimming pool or tennis court, and including at least a gardener, cook, and maid.

Shopping Around

The Oaxaca City chapter of this book recommends several solid guesthouse, bed-and-breakfast, and apartment rentals. You can find many more through on-the-spot local contacts, such as the tourist newspapers' want ad sections, neighborhood For Rent or *Renta* signs, and local listing agents. If you prefer making rental arrangements prior to arrival, you can usually write, fax, or telephone managers—many of whom speak English—directly, using the numbers given in this book.

TOURIST YU'U

A number of rural communities, mostly on the east side of the central Valley of Oaxaca, encourage visitors to come and stay in their tourist lodges, called Yu'u in Zapotec. The government-built, spartan but comfortable, modern-standard

WHERE TO FIND TOURIST YU'U

The Oaxaca Federal-State Department of Tourism (SEDETUR) built nine tourist Yu'u in communities on the east side of the Valley of Oaxaca during the 1990s. The original nine, plus two other similar accommodations in Apoala and Huamelulpan, both in the Mixteca, total 11 built so far. For access and reservations details, see specific destinations. The following towns with tourist Yulu, in the Valley of Oaxaca, are listed moving easterly from the city.

Town	Highlights
San Sebastián Abasolo	16th-century church, 20 January San Sebastián fiesta, ruins
Santa Cruz Papalutla	16th-century church, 3 May fiesta, reed basketry, ruins
Benito Juárez	Cool, pine-scented air, camping, panoramic views
Teotitlán del Valle	Renowned weaving village, museum, historic church, hikes
Santa Ana del Valle	Master weavers' shops, museum, lake, scenic views, hikes
Tlacolula	Jewel of an old church, big, colorful Zapotec market, ruins
San Bartolomé Quialana	Picturesque hillside village, renowned colorful weaving
San Marcos Tlapazola	Famous red pottery, made by craftswomen only
Hierve El Agua	Hikes, scenic vistas, mineral springs, frozen stone cascades
These can be found in the Mixteca.	
Apoala	Idyllic village, wild canyon, cave, cascade, springs, camping
Huamelulpan	Ruined city, museum, hikes to other archaeological sites

accommodations are managed and maintained by a community-appointed *gerente* (manager). Most Yu'u have two separate one-room units that sleep up to six persons each and share a single toilet and shower bath between them. Units rent for about $5 per night per person, or $20 per family group, with towels, blankets, kitchenette, and hot water.

The tourist Yu'u offer an unique opportunity for visitors tired of the city tourist rush and who hanker for more people-to-people contact. Moreover, a number of the participating communities produce uniquely fine handicrafts and/or enjoy scenic locations.

Obtain tourist Yu'u reservations through the state-federal government tourist information office in Oaxaca City. Contact them at the central plaza's north edge, at 607 Independencia, corner G. Vigil, tel.9/516-4828, fax 9/516-0984, email: turinfo@oaxaca.gob.mx,

LOCAL HOTELS

Locally owned and operated hotels make up most of the recommendations of this book. Many veteran travelers find it hard to understand why people come to Oaxaca and spend $200 a day for a hotel room when good alternatives run as little as $25.

In Oaxaca City, many such hotels are within a block or two of the town center, with its lovely plaza, old monuments, restaurants, and shops. In the Puerto Escondido and Puerto Ángel resorts, most of them are right on the beach. Local hotels, which depend more on Mexican tourists than foreigners, generally have clean, large rooms, often with private view balconies, ceiling fans, and toilet and hot-water bath or shower. What they often lack are the plush extras—air-conditioning, cable TV, phones, tennis courts, exercise gyms, and golf courses—of the luxury resort hotels.

Booking these hotels is straightforward. All can be dialed directly for information and reservations. If your Spanish is rusty, ask for someone who speaks English: *"¿Por favor, hay alguien que habla Inglés?"* (por fah-VOR, AY ahhl-ghee-AYN KAY AV-lah een-GLAYS?) Always ask about money-saving packages and promotions when reserving.

Oaxaca City's beautifully restored Camino Real hotel was once Exconvento de Santa Catalino, the second oldest convent in New Spain.

INTERNATIONAL-CLASS RESORTS

Oaxaca has a several beautiful, well-managed international-class resort hotels in Oaxaca City and the Bays of Huatulco. Their super-deluxe amenities, moreover, need not be overly expensive. While high-season room tariffs ordinarily run $100–300, low-season packages and promotions, especially at Huatulco can cut these prices significantly. Shop around for savings through travel agents, and by calling the hotels directly through their toll-free 800 numbers (see the accompanying chart).

CAMPING, *PALAPAS,* AND TRAILER PARKS

Although Oaxaca has only a sprinkling of formally maintained places for camping, many inviting beach and inland country spots are customarily used informally.

Beach Camping

Camping at beaches is popular among middle-class Mexican families, especially during the Christmas-New Year week and during Semana Santa, the week before Easter. Other times, tenters and RV campers usually find prospective camping spots uncrowded. The best beach spots typically have a shady palm grove for camping and a *palapa* (palm-thatched) restaurant that serves drinks and fresh seafood. (Heads up for falling coconuts, especially in the wind.) Cost for parking and tenting is often minimal, typically only the price of food at the restaurant.

Beach days are often perfect for swimming, strolling, and fishing; nights are usually balmy— too warm for a sleeping bag, but fine for a hammock (which allows more air circulation than a tent). Good tents, however, keep out mosquitoes and other pesties, which may be further discouraged with good bug repellent. Tents are generally warm inside, requiring only a sheet or light blanket for cover.

As for camping on isolated beaches, opinions vary, from dire warnings of *bandidos* to bland assurances that all is peaceful along the coast. The truth is probably somewhere in between. Trouble is most likely to occur in the vicinity of resort towns, notoriously in Puerto Escondido, where a few local thugs have harassed isolated campers.

Checking Out a Beach Site: When scouting out a place to camp, a good general rule is to arrive early enough in the day to get a feel for the place. Buy a soda at the *palapa* or nearby store and take a stroll around. Say *"Buenos dias"* to the people along the way; ask if the fishing is good: *"¿Pesca buena?"* Use your common sense. If the people seem friendly, ask if it's *seguro* (safe). If so, ask permission: *"¿Es bueno acampar aca?"* ("Is it OK to camp around here?"). You'll rarely be refused.

Beach *Palapas*

Visitors can still rent *palapas* (thatched beach houses) in Puerto Escondido and Zipolite, near Puerto Ángel, and adjoining Mazunte and Ventanilla. Amenities typically include beds or hammocks, a shady thatched porch, cold running water, a kerosene stove, and shared toilets and showers, for $2–5 per day per person. You usually walk right out your front door onto the sand, where surf, shells, and seabirds will be there to entertain you.

Mountain and Backcountry Camping

Oaxaca's mountain and rural backcountry offer additional camping opportunities. Private owners and communities maintain picnic areas and informal campgrounds at choice sites, such as springs, waterfalls, caves, *sabineras* (cypress groves), and on rivers and reservoir shorelines.

Invariably, such inland sites are on private (*particular*—par-tee-koo-LAHR) or communal land. As a courtesy, you should obtain permission

---

RESORT TOLL-FREE NUMBERS AND WEBSITES

The following resort hotels and chains have branches (** = outstanding, * = recommended) at Bahías de Huatulco (HU) and Oaxaca City (OA)

Barceló, (formerly Sheraton) Website: www.barce-lo.com, HU*

Camino Real, tel. 800/ 7-CAMINO (800/722-6466), Website: www.caminoreal.com, HU**, OA**

Club Med, tel. 800/ CLUBMED (800/258-2633), Website: www.clubmed.com, HU*

Fiesta Americana, tel. 800/ FIESTA-1 (800/343-7821), Website: www.fiestaamericana.com.mx, OA

Magnihotel (formerly Holiday Inn) email: magniho-tel@huatulco.net.mx, HU*

Victoria, Website: www.hotelvictoria.com.mx, OA**

Misió de los Angeles, Website: www.misionde-losangeles.com, OA**

(More information about these and other Oaxaca hotels and chains may be accessible by visiting websites: www.mexonline.com, www.oaxaca.com, www.oaxaca4less.com, and www.baysofhuatulco.com.mx, or others. See "Internet Resources.")

TRAILER PARKS AND CAMPING

Unlike the United States, Canada, and Europe, Oaxaca has few, if any, formal camping grounds. It does, however, have a number of trailer parks and privately, communally, or governmentally managed spots that appear ripe for camping, either by "car-RV-tent" (CRVT) or "tent only" (T). Destination chapters, listed below, locate them precisely and discuss access, arrangements, and facilities, if any.

Location	Name (if any)	Comments
OAXACA CITY		
northeast side	Oaxaca Trailer Park	(CRVT)
north side (San Felipe del Agua village)		"new" trailer park (CRVT)
AROUND THE VALLEY OF OAXACA		
Teotitlán del Valle (reservoir above town)		(CRVT)
Santa Ana del Valle (reservoir above town)		(T)
San Sebastián de las Grutas		riverside camping (CRVT)
PACIFIC RESORTS AND SOUTHERN SIERRA		
Puerto Ángel (Zipolite)	Trailer Park La Palmera	east end, above the beach (CRVT)
Puerto Ángel (Zipolite)	Shambala	on the beach, west end, restaurant (T)
Chacalapa	Balneario El Paraíso	rural pocket paradise (CRVT)
San José del Pacífico	Hotel Puesta del Sol	pine-scented air, trails, and views (T)
Bays of Huatulco	Trailer Park Los Mangos	rough and ready (CRVT)
Bahía San Agustín		sand, fishing, seafood *palapas* (CRVT)
Laguna Colorada		seafood *palapas,* mangroves, beach (CRVT)
Laguna Garrapatera		wild, breezy beach (T)
Playa Cangrejo		surfing and seafood (CRVT)
Playa Brasil		(CRVT)
Puerto Escondido	Villa Relax and Trailer Park	above highway, west side (CRVT)
Laguna Manialtepec		La Alejandria lagoon, mangrove, wildlife viewing (CRVT)
Lagunas de Chacagua N.P.		Playa Cerro Hermosa; sea, sand, fishing, snorkeling (CRVT)
Charquito Atotonilco		community hot spring and sacred site (CRVT)
Playa Blanca Scenic Beach, lagoon and rustic palapa hotel		(CRVT)
Pinotepa Nacional		Río Arena, waterfall, a few miles east of town (CRVT)
Corralero (South of Pinotepa Nacional)		Uncrowded beach camping, palapa restaurants, (CRVT)
Sola de Vega		riverside camping in grand old cypress grove (CRVT)

Location	Name (if any)	Comments
THE MIXTECA		
Apoala		cave, waterfall, lodging, RV and wilderness camping (CRVT)
San Miguel Tequixtepec		small, friendly town with museum and stores (CRVT)
Tepelmeme		museum and wilderness adventure camping (T)
Yosocuta Reservoir		boating, bass fishing, and swimming (CRVT)
Tonalá Canyon		pristine river canyon (T)
Tonalá		small town; lovely cypress grove and springs (CRVT)
Juxtlahuaca		Laguna Encantada natural spring, campground (CRVT)
Yosundua		waterfall and informal campground (CRVT)
Achiutla and Río Yayata		camping by creekside cypress grove; archaeological site (CRVT)
NORTHERN OAXACA		
Benito Juárez, Cuajimoloyas	Llano de las Tarjeas and Las Vigas	pristine meadow (CRVT)
Ixtlán de Juárez vicinity	Campamento del Monte	private wooded mountainside with cabins, small campsites (CRVT)
Ixtlán de Juárez	Community Ecotours Pozuelos campsite	(CRVT)
Ixtlán de Juárez	Arco de Yagela	limestone cave (T)
Valle Nacional	Arroyo Blanco natural spring	friendly family (CRVT)
Valle Nacional	El Zuzul	community-owned natural spring (T)
Temascal Reservoir		Boating, bass fishing, and swimming (CRVT)
Ixcatlán		dozens of islands; choose one for your campsite (T)
Ixcatlán		Isla Soyaltepec, Chinantec-speaking island village (T)
THE ISTHMUS		
Tlacotepec		beautiful blue spring, picnic and camping ground (CRVT)
Laollaga		spring-fed river, picnic ground, rough trailer park (CRVT)
Unión Hidalgo		Playa Copalita; Huave fishing village (CRVT)
Zanatepec		wilderness river canyon; hot spring and lakes (T)
Rincón Juárez		Huave fishing village; seafood restaurant, quiet beach (CRVT)
Salina Cruz		Playa La Ventosa village; restaurants, beach, river (CRVT)
Santa María del Mar, east of Salina Cruz Huave		fishing embarcadero and beach, secure (CRVT)

to set up camp either from the site manager, the closest neighboring restaurant or house, or at the nearest *presidencia municipal* or *agencia*. Such permission, sometimes for a small fee, is usually granted almost automatically. Please reciprocate by keeping your campfire, if permitted, modest and under control, respecting local etiquette (don't swim or sunbathe in the nude), cleaning up thoroughly, and carrying away all your trash.

For an informative and entertaining discussion of camping in Mexico, check out *The People's Guide to Mexico*. (See the Booklist.)

Trailer Parks

Campers who prefer company to isolation usually stay in trailer parks. A few dot Oaxaca's beach resorts; Oaxaca City has two trailer parks. The most luxurious Oaxaca trailer park, in Puerto Escondido, has electricity, water, sewer hookups, and other amenities, including a swimming pool; the humblest, near Puerto Ángel, is a small lot by the beach. Prices run from a maximum of $14 per night, including enough power for air-conditioning, down to a few dollars for tent space only. Significant discounts are generally available for weekly and monthly rentals.

FOOD AND DRINK

Some travel to Mexico for the food. True Mexican food is old-fashioned, homestyle fare requiring many hours of loving preparation. Such food is short on meat and long on corn, beans, rice, tomatoes, chilies, spices, onions, eggs, and cheese.

Mexican food is the unique end-product of thousands of years of native tradition. It is based on corn—*teocentli,* the Aztec "holy food"—called *maíz* (mah-EES) by present-day Mexicans. In the past, a Mexican woman spent much of her time grinding and preparing corn: soaking the grain in limewater (which swells the kernels and removes the tough seed-coat) and grinding the bloated seeds into meal on a stone *metate.* Finally, she would pat the meal into tortillas and cook them on a hot, baked mud griddle.

Sages (men, no doubt) have wistfully imagined the gentle pat-pat-pat of women all over Mexico to be the heartbeat of Mexico, which they feared would someday cease. Fewer women these days make tortillas by hand. The gentle pat-pat-pat has been replaced by the whir and rattle of automatic tortilla-making machines in myriad *tortillerías,* where women and girls line up for their family's daily kilo-stack of tortillas.

Tortillas are to the Mexicans as rice is to the Chinese and bread to the French. A Mexican family meal, more often than not, is some mixture of sauce, meat, beans, cheese, and vegetables wrapped in a tortilla, which becomes the culinary be-all: the food, the dish, and the utensil all wrapped into one.

This most Mexican style of meal usually includes one or two of a number of specialties known by Mexicans as **antojitos** and known to everyone else as "Mexican food." These are the familiar tacos, tamales, enchiladas, quesadillas, chilies rellenos, nachos, burritos, re-fried beans, guacamole, and other combinations of corn, meat, cheese, beans, eggs, sauces, and spices that make up the menus of Mexican restaurants in the United States and Canada.

Hot or Not?

Much food served in Mexico is not "Mexican." Eating habits, as most other Mexican customs, depend upon social class. Upwardly mobile Mexicans typically shun the corn-based Indian fare in favor of the European-style food of the Spanish colonial elite: chops, steaks, cutlets, fish, clams, omelettes, soups, pasta, rice, and potatoes.

Such fare is often as bland as Des Moines on a summer Sunday afternoon. *"No picante"*— not spicy—is how the Mexicans describe bland food. *Caliente,* the Spanish adjective for "hot"

RESTAURANT PRICE KEY

In the destination chapters, restaurants that serve dinner are described as budget, moderate, expensive, or a combination thereof, at the end of each restaurant description. Budget means that the entrées cost under $7; moderate, $7-14; expensive, over $14.

vendor serving yams

weather or water, does not, in contrast to English usage, also imply spicy, or *picante.*

Vegetarian Food

Strictly vegetarian cooking is the exception in Mexico, although a few macrobiotic-vegetarian restaurants and health-food stores have opened in Oaxaca City, Puerto Escondido, and Huatulco. Meat is such a delicacy for most Oaxacans that they can't understand why people would give it up voluntarily. If vegetable-lovers can manage with corn, beans, cheese, eggs, *legumbres* (vegetables), and fruit and not be bothered by a bit of pork fat *(manteca de cerdo),* Mexican (and Oaxacan) cooking will suit them fine.

Seafood

Early chroniclers wrote that Aztec Emperor Moctezuma employed a platoon of runners to bring fresh fish 300 miles every day to his court from the sea. On the Oaxaca Pacific Coast, fresh seafood is fortunately much more available from scores of shoreline establishments, ranging from thatched beach *palapas* to five-star hotel restaurants.

Oaxaca seafood is literally there for the taking. When strolling on the beach, I have seen well-fed, middle-class local vacationers breaking and eating oysters and mussels right off the rocks. Villagers up and down the coast use small nets (or bare hands) to retrieve a few fish for supper, while communal teams haul in big netfuls of silvery, wriggling fish for sale right on the beach.

Despite the plenty, Oaxaca seafood prices reflect high worldwide demand, even at the humblest seaside *palapa.* The freshness and variety, however, make even the typical dishes seem bargains at any price.

Fruits and Juices

Squeezed vegetable and fruit juices (*jugos,* HOO-gohs) are among the widely available de-

CATCH OF THE DAY

Ceviche (say-VEE-chay): A chopped raw fish appetizer as popular on Mexican Pacific beaches as sushi is on Tokyo side streets. Although it can contain anything from conch to octopus, the best ceviche consists of diced young shark *(tiburón)* or mackerel *(sierra)* fillet and plenty of fresh tomatoes, onions, garlic, and chilies, all doused with lime juice.

Filete de pescado: Fish fillet sautéed *al mojo* (ahl-MOH-hoh) with butter and garlic.

Pescado frito (pays-KAH-doh FREE-toh): Fish, pan-fried whole; if you don't specify that it be cooked lightly *(a medio),* the fish may arrive well done, like a big, crunchy french fry.

Pescado veracruzana: A favorite everywhere. Best with red snapper *(huachinango),* smothered in a savory tomato, onion, chili, and garlic sauce. *Pargo* (snapper), *mero* (grouper), and *cabrilla* (sea bass) are also popularly used in this and other specialties.

Shellfish abound: *Ostiones* (oysters) and *almejas* (clams) by the dozen, *langosta* (lobster) and *langostina* (crayfish) *asado* (broiled), *al vapor* (steamed), or *frito* (fried). Pots of fresh-boiled *camarones* (shrimp) are sold on the street by the kilo; cafés will make them into *cóctel,* or prepare them *en gabardinas* (breaded) at your request.

A TROVE OF FRUITS AND NUTS

Besides carrying the usual temperate fruits, jugerías, and especially markets, are seasonal sources of a number of exotic (followed by an *) varieties:

avocado (*aguacate*, pronouced ah-wah-KAH-tay): Aztec aphrodisiac

banana (*platano*): many kinds—big and small, red and yellow

chirimoya* (*chirimoya*): green scales, white pulp; sometimes called an anona

coconut (*coco*): coconut "milk" is called *agua coco*

grapes (*uvas*): Aug.–Nov. season

guanabana* (*guanabana*): looks, but doesn't taste, like a green mango

guava (*guava*): delicious juice, widely available canned

lemon (*limón*, pronounced lee-MOHN): uncommon and expensive; use lime instead

lime (*lima* pronounced LEE-mah): douse salads with it

mamey* (*mamey*, pronounced mah-MAY): yellow, juicy fruit; excellent for jellies and preserves

mango (*mango*): king of fruit, in a hundred varieties June–Nov.

orange (*naranja*, pronounced nah-RAHN-ha): greenish skin but sweet and juicy

papaya (*papaya*): said to aid digestion and healing

peach (*durazno*, pronounced doo-RAHS-noh): delicious and widely available as canned juice

peanut (*cacahuate*, pronounced kah-kah-WAH-tay): home roasted and cheap

pear (*pera*): fall season

pecan (*nuez*): for a treat, try freshly ground pecan butter

piña anona* (*piña anona*): looks like an ear of corn without the husk; tastes like pineapple

pineapple (*piña*): huge, luscious, and cheap

strawberry (*fresa*, pronounced FRAY-sah): local favorite

tangerine (*mandarina*): common around Christmas

watermelon (*sandía*, pronounced sahn-DEE-ah): perfect on a hot day

zapote* (*zapote*, pronounced sah-POH-tay): yellow, fleshy fruit; said to induce sleep

zapote colorado* (*zapote colorado*): brown skin, red, puckery fruit, like persimmon; incorrectly called (*mamey*)

the exotic piña anona

lights of Oaxaca. Among the many establishments—restaurants, cafés, and *loncherías*—willing to supply you with your favorite *jugo*, the juice bars (*jugerías*) are often the most fun. Colorful fruit piles usually mark *jugerías;* if you don't immediately spot your favorite fruit, ask anyway; it might be hidden in the refrigerator.

Besides your choice of pure juice, a *jugería* will often serve *licuados*. Into the juice, they whip powdered milk, your favorite fruit, and sugar to taste for a creamy afternoon pick-me-up or evening dessert. One big favorite is a cool banana chocolate *licuado,* which comes out tasting like a milk shake minus the calories.

Alcoholic Drinks

The Aztecs usually sacrificed anyone caught drinking alcohol without permission. The later, more lenient, Spanish attitude toward getting *borracho* (soused) has led to a thriving Mexican renaissance of native alcoholic beverages: tequila, *mescal,* Kahlua, *pulque,* and *aguardiente.* *Mescal,* distilled from the fermented juice of the maguey (century) plant, originated in Oaxaca, where the best *mescales* are still made. Quality tequila and *mescal* come 76 proof (38 percent alcohol) and up. A small white worm, endemic to the maguey plant, is often added to each bottle of factory *mescal* for authenticity.

Pulque, although also made from the sap of the maguey, is locally brewed to a small alcohol content, between beer and wine. The brewing houses are sacrosanct preserves, circumscribed by traditions that exclude both women and outsiders. The brew, said to be full of nutrients, is sold to local *pulquerías* and drunk immediately. If you are ever invited into a *pulquería,* it will be an honor you cannot refuse.

Aguardiente, by contrast, is the notorious fiery Mexican "white lightning," a locally cane-distilled, dirt-cheap ticket to oblivion for poor Mexican men.

While *pulque* comes from an age-old Indian tradition, beer is the beverage of modern mestizo Mexico. Full-bodied and tastier than "light" U.S. counterparts, Mexican beer enjoys an enviable reputation.

Those visitors who indulge usually know their favorite among the many brands, from light to dark: Superior, Corona, Pacífico, Tecate (served with lime), Carta Blanca, Modelo, Dos Equis, Bohemia, Tres Equis, and Negra Modelo. Nochebuena, a flavorful dark brew, becomes available only around Christmas.

Mexicans have yet to develop much of a taste for *vino* (wine), although some domestic wines, such as the Baja California labels Monte Xanic, Domecq, and Cetto are often quite good.

Bread and Pastries

Excellent locally baked bread is a delightful surprise to many first-time visitors to Oaxaca. Small bakeries everywhere put out trays of hot, crispy-crusted *bolillos* (rolls) and sweet *pans dulces* (pastries). They range from simple cakes, muffins, cookies, and doughnuts to fancy fruit-filled turnovers and puffs. Half the fun occurs before the eating: grab a tray and tongs, peruse the goodies, and pick out the most scrumptious. With your favorite dozen finally selected, you take your tray to the cashier, who deftly bags everything up and collects a few pesos (two or three dollars) for your whole mouthwatering selection.

GETTING THERE

BY AIR

From the United States and Canada

The majority of foreign visitors reach Oaxaca by air, and a large fraction of those through Mexico City. There, travelers transfer to flights bound for either Oaxaca City, Puerto Escondido, or Bays of Huatulco-Puerto Ángel. Two exceptions are **Mexicana Airlines** and **American Airlines** flights that connect directly with Huatulco from Los Angeles and Dallas, respectively.

Most air travelers begin their Oaxaca vacations through the Mexico City gateways of San Francisco, Los Angeles, Phoenix, Denver, Dallas, Chicago, San Antonio, Houston, Atlanta, Orlando, Miami, or New York.

Although very few scheduled flights go directly to Mexico City or Oaxaca from the northern United States and Canada, charters do, especially during the winter. In locales near Vancouver, Seattle, Calgary-Edmonton, Winnipeg, Ottawa, Toronto, Montreal, Minneapolis, Detroit, Cleveland, Buffalo and Boston, consult a travel agent for charter flight options. Be aware that charter reservations, which often require fixed departure and return dates and provide minimal cancellation refunds, decrease your flexibility.

Air travelers can **save money** by shopping around, through independent ticket agents and the airlines, both by telephone and the Internet. Don't be bashful about trying for the best price. Make it clear to the airline or agent you're interested in a bargain. Ask the right questions. Are there special incentive, advance-payment, night, midweek, tour packages, or charter fares? Peruse the ads in your Sunday newspaper travel section for bargain-oriented travel agencies. An

AIRLINES SERVING OAXACA

The following scheduled airlines connect with Mexico City (MX) where connecting flights continue on to the Oaxaca destinations of Oaxaca City, Huatulco-Puerto Ángel (HU), and Puerto Escondido. American Airlines currently connects Huatulco-Puerto Ángel directly from Dallas.

Aeroméxico
tel. 800/237-6639
www.aeromexico.com

Origin	Destinations
Los Angeles	MX
Tijuana	MX
New York	MX
Miami	MX
Houston	MX
San Diego	MX
Atlanta	MX
Phoenix	MX
Dallas	MX

Mexicana
tel. 800/531-7921
www.mexicana.com.mx

Origin	Destinations
Los Angeles	MX, HU
San Francisco	MX
Tijuana	MX
Denver	MX
Miami	MX
San Antonio	MX

Delta
tel. 800/221-1212
www.delta.com

Origin	Destinations
Los Angeles	MX
Dallas	MX
Atlanta	MX
Orlando	MX
New York	MX
Miami	MX

American
tel. 800/433-7300
www.aa.com

Origin	Destinations
Dallas	HU, MX
Chicago	MX
Miami MX	

Aerocalifornia
tel. 800/237-6225

Origin	Destinations
Los Angeles	MX
Tijuana	MX

Continental
tel. 800/231-0856
www.continental.com

Origin	Destinations
Houston	MX

America West
tel. 800/363-2597
www.americawest.com

Origin	Destinations
Phoenix	MX

agent usually costs you no money, although some don't like discounted tickets because their fee often depends on a percentage of ticket price. Nevertheless, many agents will work to get you a bargain.

You may be able to also save money by booking an air/hotel package. Some airlines routinely offer Oaxaca air/hotel packages. Contact their respective package vacation agents: Mexicana, tel. 800/531-9321; Aeroméxico, tel. 800/245-8585; and Canadian World of Vacations, tel. 800/661-8881.

From Europe, Australia, Asia, and Latin America

Few airlines fly across the Atlantic or Pacific directly to Mexico. Travelers from Asia, Australia, and Europe generally transfer at New York, Chicago, Dallas, San Francisco, or Los Angeles for Oaxaca destinations.

A number of Latin American flag carriers fly directly to Mexico City. From there, easy Oaxaca connections are available via Mexicana Airlines and Aeroméxico Airlines and their respective affiliate airlines, Aerocaribe and Aeromar.

Baggage, Insurance, "Bumping," and In-Flight Meals

Tropical and temperate Oaxaca makes it easy to pack light. (See "Packing Checklist" at the end of this chapter.) Veteran tropical travelers often condense their luggage to carry-ons only. Airlines routinely allow a carry-on (not exceeding 45 inches in combined length, width, and girth) and a small book bag and purse. Thus relieved of heavy burdens, your trip will become much simpler. You'll avoid possible luggage loss and long baggage check-in lines by being able to check in directly at the boarding gate.

Even if you can't avoid having to check luggage, loss of it needn't ruin your vacation. Always carry your irreplaceable items in the cabin with you. These should include all money, credit cards, traveler's checks, keys, tickets, cameras, passport, prescription drugs, and eyeglasses.

At the X-ray security check, insist your film and cameras be hand-inspected. Regardless of what attendants claim, repeated X-ray scanning will fog any film, especially the sensitive ASA 400 and 1,000 high-speed varieties. (You can assure both protection and hand inspection for your film by packing it in the special lead-lined film bags available in any good camera store.)

Travelers packing lots of expensive baggage, or who (because of illness, for example) may have to cancel a nonrefundable flight or tour might consider buying **travel insurance.** Travel agents routinely sell packages that include baggage, trip cancellation, and default insurance. Baggage insurance covers you beyond the customary $1,250 domestic, $400 international baggage liability limits, but check with your carrier. Trip cancellation insurance pays if you must cancel your prepaid trip, while default insurance protects you if your carrier or tour agent does not perform as agreed. Travel insurance, however, can be expensive. Traveler's Insurance Company, for example, offers about $1,000 of baggage insurance per person for two weeks for about $50. Carefully weigh both your options and the cost against benefits before putting your money down.

It's wise to **reconfirm** both departure and return flight reservations, especially during the busy Christmas and Easter seasons. This is a useful strategy, as is prompt arrival at check-in, against getting "bumped" (losing your seat) because of the tendency of airlines to overbook the rush of high-season vacationers. For further protection, if possible get your **seat assignment and boarding pass** included with your ticket.

Airlines generally try hard to accommodate travelers with dietary or other special needs. When booking your flight, inform your travel agent or carrier of the necessity of a low-sodium, low-cholesterol, vegetarian, lactose-reduced meal or other requirements. (Seniors, persons with disabilities, and parents traveling with children, see also the Specialty Travel section under Other Practicalities near the end of this chapter.)

BY BUS

As air travel rules in the United States, bus travel rules in Mexico. Hundreds of sleek luxury- and first-class bus lines with names such as Elite, Estrella de Oro (Star of Gold), and Estrella Blanca (White Star) roar out daily from the border, headed south.

Since U.S. bus lines ordinarily terminate just north of the Mexican border, you must usually disembark, collect your things, and after having filled out the necessary but very simple paperwork at the immigration booth, proceed on foot across the border to Mexico, where you can bargain with a local taxis driver to drive you the few miles to the *camionera central* (central bus station). Inside the station door, handy words to have in mind are *taquilla* (ticket booth), *guardaequipajes* (baggage checkroom), *llegada* (arrival), *salida* (departure), and *sanitario* or *baño* (toilet or bathroom).

DRIVING AND BUSING
TO OAXACA

UNITED STATES

From Eastern U.S.

From Central U.S.

From Western U.S.

GUATEMALA

Gulf
of
Mexico

PACIFIC OCEAN

Sea of Cortez

Baja California

San Diego
Tijuana
Mexicali
Calexico
159/193 3:15
185/266 3:45
Tucson
Nogales
Sonoyta
262/422 6:30
Hermosillo
173/279 3:15
181/280 3:00
El Paso
Juarez
233/375 5:00
Ciudad Obregon
268/431 5:00
Chihuahua
284/457 6:30
Culiacan
139/224 2:30
Torreon
180/299 4:00
Durango
3:30
198/318 6:00
Mazatlan
182/293 4:00
Tepic
104/167 3:00
Puerto Vallarta
172/276 4:30
Manzanillo
196/314 6:15
Zacatecas
230/370 3:45
174/280 3:45
Nuevo Laredo
Laredo
McAllen
Reynosa
143/230 2:30
Monterrey
53/85 1:00
Saltillo
Ciudad Victoria
197/317 4:30
Tampico
151/243 3:15
San Luis Potosi
117/188 2:30
Guadalajara
141/227 3:00
198/318 5:45
Morelia
224/361 5:45
154/248 4:30
Queretaro
127/205 2:45
134/215 3:00
Toluca
74/119 2:15
Mexico City
Puebla
360/564 8:00
291/468 8:00
Oaxaca
293/475 5:30
Oaxaca
148/238 6:15
Puerto Ángel
291/469 8:15
259/417 6:15
Taxco
150/242 4:30
76/122 2:30
Acapulco
Playa Azul
Ixtapa-Zihuatanejo
195/311 4:30

La Paz
Cabo San Lucas

150 mi
150 km

= TOLL EXPRESSWAY

NOTE: DISTANCES ARE SHOWN AS MILES/KILOMETERS
APPROXIMATE DRIVING TIMES ARE SHOWN AS HOURS:MINUTES

© AVALON TRAVEL PUBLISHING, INC.

First- and luxury-class bus service in Mexico is generally cheaper and at least as good as in the United States. Tickets for comparable trips in Mexico cost a fraction (as little as $60 for a thousand-mile trip), compared to perhaps $150 in the United States

In Mexico, as on U.S. buses, you often have to take it as you find it. *Asientos reservados* (reserved seats), *boletos* (tickets), and information must generally be obtained in person at the bus station, and credit cards and traveler's checks are sometimes not accepted. Reserved bus tickets are typically nonrefundable, so don't miss the bus. On the other hand, plenty of buses roll south almost continuously. Two basic routes are available, either through Mexico City or down the Pacific Coast all the way.

Pacific Coast Route

The route to Oaxaca along the Pacific shore, although the longest, probably requiring three buses and three days, is the most scenic. Try to go luxury class all the way; the small additional cost is well worth it. Cross the border at Tijuana, Mexicali, or Nogales, where you can choose from at least three bus lines along the Pacific Coast route, via combined National Hwys. 15 and 200, via Mazatlán, Puerto Vallarta, Zihuatanejo, Acapulco, and finally, Puerto Escondido, in Oaxaca. At the border, get a bus as far south as you can, to at least Tepic or maybe Puerto Vallarta, where you change to a bus headed south for, most likely, Lázaro Cárdenas or Zihuatanejo, at the end of your second day. There you catch a third bus, which will take you at least to Acapulco, and at most to Puerto Escondido by the end of your third day. On the other hand, make it easy on yourself and stretch the trip to five days by resting overnight in Puerto Vallarta and Zihuatanejo along the way.

Mexico City Route

This is the quickest bus route to Oaxaca, typically about a day and a night from the south Texas border, a day longer from California or Arizona. From the western United States, cross the border at either Tijuana, Mexicali, or Nogales. From the United States Midwest, Southeast and East, cross the border at Laredo to Nuevo Laredo or McAllen to Reynosa. For most speed and com-

fort, at only a small extra cost, go by luxury-class bus to Mexico City.

Mexico City has four bus terminals—north, east, south, and west (respectively, Terminal Norte, Terminal Tapo, Terminal Sur, and Terminal Poniente). You will most likely arrive in the Terminal Norte, although a few buses from the west via Guadalajara might arrive at Terminal Poniente. In any case, if you're heading straight for Oaxaca City, from Terminal Norte, board an **Autobuses del Oriente (ADO)** or **Cristóbal Colón** bus straight to Oaxaca City, via the Puebla expressway (*autopista* or *corta*). If you're heading for the Oaxaca Pacific Coast, best board an **Estrella Blanca** affliliate or **Estrella de Oro** bus bound for Acapulco, where you can transfer to a Puerto Escondido-bound bus.

If somehow the above connections are not available at Terminal Norte (or Terminal Poniente), share a taxi (don't try it by public transit) to Terminal Sur (or Terminal Tapo for Oaxaca City via ADO) and catch an Estrella Blanca subsidiary (such as Elite, Turistar, Futura, Flecha Roja, or Transportes Cuauhtémoc) all the way to Puerto Escondido via Acapulco. If you miss the direct Puerto Escondido connection, settle for an express connection to Acapulco, where plenty of local departures head out southeast for Puerto Escondido.

Get across town to your continuing bus terminal via private taxi *(taxi particular)* or collective taxi *(colectivo)*. Although such a trip is possible by public transportation, don't try it. If you do, you're either a Mexico City veteran traveling light and know what you're getting into or willing to bear a load of frustration, pain, and the dirty looks from fellow passengers as you unwittingly poke them with your bulging backpacks and luggage in a crowded subway or local bus.

BY CAR OR RV

If you're adventurous, like going to out-of-the way places, but still want to have all the comforts of home, you may enjoy driving your RV or car to Oaxaca. On the other hand, consideration of cost, risk, wear on both you and your vehicle, and the congestion hassles in towns may change your mind.

ROAD SAFETY

Hundreds of thousands of visitors enjoy safe Mexican auto vacations every year. Their success is due in large part to their frame of mind: drive defensively, anticipate and adjust to danger before it happens, and watch everything—side roads, shoulders, the car in front, and cars far down the road. The following tips will help ensure a safe and enjoyable trip:

Don't drive at night. Range animals, unmarked sand piles, pedestrians, one-lane bridges, cars without lights, and drunk drivers are doubly hazardous at night.

Although **speed limits** are rarely enforced, *don't break them.* Mexican roads are often narrow and shoulderless. Poor markings and macho drivers who pass on curves are best faced at a speed of 40 mph (64 kph) rather than 75 (120).

Don't drive on sand. Even with four-wheel-drive, you'll eventually get stuck if you drive either often or casually on beaches. When the tide comes in, who'll pull your car out?

Slow down at the *topes* (speed bumps) at the edges of towns and for *vados* (dips), which can be dangerously bumpy and full of water.

Extending the **courtesy of the road** goes hand-in-hand with safe driving. Both courtesy and machismo are more infectious in Mexico; on the highway, it's much safer to spread the former than the latter.

Mexican Car Insurance

Mexico does not recognize foreign insurance. When you drive into Mexico, Mexican auto insurance is at least as important as your passport. At the busier crossings, you can get it at insurance "drive-ins" just north of the border. The many Mexican auto insurance companies are government-regulated; their numbers keep prices and services competitive.

Sanborn's Mexico insurance, one of the best known agencies, certainly seems to be trying hardest. It offers a number of books and services. These include a guide to RV campgrounds, road map, *Travel with Health* book, "smile-by-mile" *Travelog* guide to "every highway in Mexico," hotel discounts, and more. All of the above are available to members of Sanborn's "Sombrero" Club. You can buy insurance, sign up for membership, or order books through its toll-free number, 800/222-0158. For other queries, call 956/682-7433 or write Sanborn's Mexico, P.O. Box 310, McAllen, TX 78502.

Mexican car insurance runs from a bare-bones rate of about $5 a day to a more typical $10–15 a day for more complete coverage ($50,000/$40,000/$80,000 public liability/property damage/medical payments) including collision and theft on a vehicle worth around $15000. On the same scale, insurance for a $50,000 RV and equipment runs about $30 a day. These daily rates decrease sharply for six-month or one-year policies, which run from about $200 for the minimum to $350–1,600 for complete coverage.

If you get broken glass, personal effects, and legal expenses coverage with these rates, you're lucky. Mexican policies don't usually cover them.

You should get something for your money, however. The deductibles should be no more than $300–500, the public liability/medical payments should be about double the legal minimum (which is $50,000 total public liability, including property damage and medical payments) and you should be able to get your car fixed in the United States and receive payment in U.S. dollars for losses. If not, shop around.

Crossing the Border

Squeezing through the border traffic bottlenecks during peak holidays and rush hours can be time-consuming. Avoid crossing 7–9 A.M. and 4:30–6:30 P.M. Also, you may be able to save *mucho* time and sweat by getting all of your car-entry paperwork done at your local AAA-affiliate office prior to leaving home. Many of them will even do it for nonmembers; call for details.

The Green Angels

The Green Angels have answered many motoring tourists' prayers in Mexico. (They've rescued so many stalled drivers that next trip I think I'll carry some gifts to give whenever I see them on the road.) Bilingual teams of two, trained in auto repair and first aid, help distressed tourists along main highways. They patrol fixed stretches of road twice daily by green truck. To make sure they stop to help, pull completely off the highway and raise your hood. You may want to hail a passing trucker to call them for you (toll-free tel. 01 800/903-9200 for the tourism hot line, who might alert the Green Angels for you).

If for some reason you have to leave your vehicle on the roadside, don't leave it unattended. Hire a local teenager or adult to watch it for you. Unattended vehicles on Mexican highways are quickly stricken by a mysterious disease, the symptoms of which are rapid loss of vital parts.

A Sinaloa Note of Caution

Although *bandidos* no longer menace Mexican roads (but loose burros, horses, and cattle still do), be cautious in the infamous marijuana and opium-growing region of Sinaloa state north of Mazatlán. Best not stray from Hwy. 15 between Culiacán and Mazatlán or from Hwy. 40 between Mazatlán and Durango. Curious tourists have been assaulted in the hinterlands adjacent to these roads.

Mexican Gasoline

Pemex, short for Petróleos Mexicanos, the government oil monopoly, markets diesel fuel and two grades of gasoline: 92-octane premium and 89-octane **Magna Sin plomo** (without lead). Magna Sin (MAHG-nah seen) is good gas, yielding performance similar to that of U.S.-style regular or super-unleaded gasoline. (My car, whose manufacturer recommended 91 octane, ran well on Magna.) It cost about 55 cents per liter (or about $2 per gallon.)

On main highways, Pemex makes sure that major stations (spaced typically about 30 miles apart) stock Magna.

Gas Station Thievery

Although the problem has abated considerably in recent years, boys who hang around gas stations to wash windows are notoriously light-fingered. When stopping at the *gasolinera,* make sure that your cameras, purses, and other movable items are out of reach. Also make sure that your car has a lockable gas cap. If not, insist on pumping the gas yourself, or be super-watchful as you pull up to the gas pump. Make certain that the pump reads zero before the attendant pumps the gas.

A Healthy Car

Preventative measures spell good health for both you and your car. Get that tune-up (or long-delayed overhaul) *before,* rather than after, you leave.

Carry a stock of spare parts, which will probably be both more difficult to get and more expensive in Mexico than at home. Carry an extra tire or two, a few cans of motor oil and octane enhancer, oil and gas filters, fan belts, spark plugs, tune-up kit, points, and fuses. Carry basic tools and supplies, such as screwdrivers, pliers (including Vise-Grip), lug wrench and jack, adjustable wrenches, tire pump and patches, pressure gauge, steel wire, and electrical tape. For breakdowns and emergencies, carry a folding shovel, a husky rope or chain, a gasoline can, and flares.

Car Repairs in Mexico

The American big three—General Motors, Ford, and Chrysler—and Nissan and Volkswagen are well represented by extensive dealer networks in Mexico. Getting your car or truck serviced at such agencies is usually straightforward. While

roadside gasoline service

DETOUR INTO A CORNFIELD

Driving hazards—poorly marked roads, potholes, pedestrians, roadside horses, cattle, and burros, rattletrap cars and trucks with no lights—make rural nighttime driving in Oaxaca an iffy proposition. Add speed to the mix and you have a recipe for close calls at least and disaster at worst.

I was only doing about 30 or 35 miles per hour, and although the road was paved (something that probably lulled me into complacency) it was dark, wet, gravelly, and completely lacking either white center line or edge markings.

I blundered into a sharp left curve and in a split second found that I had to either roll my car or leave the road. I chose the latter and hurtled into someone's tall-corn *milpa*. As green stalks slapped the windshield and I bounced up and down like a Ping-Pong ball, I wondered if I was going to go over a cliff (this was hilly country), something that probably would have postponed publication of the *Oaxaca Handbook* indefinitely.

This time I was lucky. After a very long second or two, my little truck lurched to a stop, tilted at a crazy sideways angle against a big round boulder. Somehow something managed to seriously crack the front windshield and cave in both passenger-side doors, but the car didn't roll, and miraculously the motor would still run.

What does a writer on a short deadline do on such an occasion? Go get help and get rolling again if possible. The only problem was that I was way out in the country, 100 miles from the crane (Tow truck? No way!) that seemed necessary to pull my truck from where it was lodged over the boulders up the long embankment.

It turned out, I couldn't have been in a better place to get help. I climbed out of the cornfield to a nearby village, where, at 9 P.M. on Saturday night, everybody was out and about. I asked a man, named German ("Herman"), who, it seems, knew Agustín, who had a tractor. Agustín, German said, was at his girlfriend's house, where we went next.

Agustín came outside for a conference. Given his tractor, it was not a question of if the job could be done, but when.

"Can't we wait until tomorrow?" Agustín asked. "It's dark now. Best to try in the morning."

My deadline pushed me on.

"You may be right, but if possible I'd like to try now. I've got 1,500 pesos (US$150) cash. It's yours if you pull my *camioneta* out of the *milpa*."

By this time a small crowd had gathered around. Several of us piled into German's truck and headed to Agustín's place, where Agustín maneuvered a huge green John Deere tractor with seven-foot wheels out of his barn. Agustín's brother went to get a long cable and met us at the site.

With about five guys helping me, we wrapped the cable around the axle. I got behind the steering wheel, and miracle of miracles, Agustín and his tractor, like the strong right hand of God, pulled my *camioneta* straight up the rocky incline and onto the road.

Overjoyed, I immediately wanted to fulfill my promise to Agustín. I started counting out the $10 bills, one by one. When I got to eight or nine, Agustín protested.

"Stop. That's enough."

I distributed the rest of the bills to the other men and was about to leave when someone spied that the crash had flattened the right front tire. Quickly someone replaced it with my spare, and I was ready to go. I thanked everyone all round again and headed out through the Oaxaca night, shaken but unhurt and grateful to my kind rescuers.

---

parts will probably be higher, shop rates run about half U.S. prices, so repairs will generally come out cheaper than back home.

The same is not true for repairing other makes. Mexico has few, if any, Toyota or other Japanese car or truck dealers; other than Mercedes-Benz, which has some Mexican agencies, it is generally difficult to find officially certified mechanics for any British and European makes other than Volkswagen.

Many clever Mexican independent mechanics, however, can often fix any car that happens to come their way. Their humble *talleres mecánicos* (tah-YER-ays may-KAH-nee-kohs), or repair shops, dot the town and village roadsides everywhere

Although most mechanics are honest, beware of unscrupulous operators who try to collect double or triple their original estimate. If you don't speak Spanish, find someone who can assist you in negotiations. **Always** get a cost estimate, including needed parts and labor, in writing, even if you have to write it yourself. Make sure the mechanic understands, then ask him to sign it before he starts work. Although this may be a hassle, it might save you a much nastier hassle later. Shop labor at small, independent, repair shops should typically run between $15 and $25 per hour. For much more information, and entertaining anecdotes of car and RV travel in Mexico, consult Carl Franz's *The People's Guide to Mexico.* (See the Booklist.)

Highway Routes from the United States

If you've decided to drive to Oaxaca, you have your choice of four general routes. At safe highway speeds, from the Mexican border these routes require as much as five days or as little as two days, depending on your route.

The longest but most scenic route is the **Pacific route,** which starts out following Mexican National Hwy. 15 from the border at Nogales, Sonora, an hour's drive south of Tucson, Arizona. Soon you join Hwy. 15 D *cuota* (toll) expressway (or old *libre* Hwy. 15), continuing

southward smoothly, leading you through cactus-studded mountains and valleys, which turn into farms and groves and tropical coastal plain by the time you arrive in Mazatlán. Follow the peripheral bypasses *(periféricos)* that conduct traffic past the congested downtowns of Hermosillo, Guaymas, Culiacán and Mazatlán. Between these centers, you can speed along via the *cuota* Hwy. 15 D expressway virtually the entire way. If you prefer not to pay the high tolls (around $60 total for a passenger car, much more for multiple-wheeled RVs) you should stick to the old *libre* (free) Hwy. 15. Hazards, bumps, and slow going might force you to reconsider, however.

At Tepic, the Pacific route leaves Hwy. 15–15 D and continues south via Hwy. 200, winding past tobacco farms and mango orchards, through lush forest, climbing vine-hung canyons, crossing a score of rivers, past a host of palm-tufted beaches and passing the renowned vacationlands of Puerto Vallarta, Manzanillo, Ixtapa-Zihuatanejo, and Acapulco. Finally, several days after you crossed the border, you arrive at the heart of the tropical Oaxaca coast at Puerto Escondido or Puerto Ángel.

HIGHWAY ROUTES
FROM THE U.S. BORDER TO OAXACA

Route	Via	Miles/Km	Hours at The Wheel	Travel Days
Pacific	Nogales-Mazatlán Puerto Vallarta Acapulco-Puerto Ángel	1,911/3,075	46	5
Pacific-Mexico City	Nogales-Mazatlán Guadalajara-Mexico City Puebla-Oaxaca City	1,749/2,814	34	3
Central	Ciudad Juárez-Chihuahua Torreón-Zacatecas Querétaro-Mexico City Puebla-Oaxaca City	1,370/2,204	29	3
Eastern	Reynosa-Ciudad Victoria Tampico-Pachuca-Mexico City Puebla-Oaxaca City	967/1,556	22	2

A speedier variation on the Pacific route is the **Pacific-Mexico City route,** which starts out as the Pacific route but departs from the Pacific Coast, eastward, at Tepic, continuing along Hwy. 15 or 15 D, then expressway Hwy. 90 D past Guadalajara, via Toluca to Mexico City.

Across town, at the Los Reyes southeast-side suburb, pick up the Puebla-Veracruz expressway Hwy. 150D, where you continue about an hour past Puebla to a fork. Follow the south fork expressway, via Tehuacán and Nochixtlán to Oaxaca City. This nearly all-expressway route minimizes the road time from the western U.S. border to three very long, or, to be safe, four days to Oaxaca. **Note:** Be sure to arrive in Mexico City on a day of the week when **driving restrictions** (determined by the last digit of your license plate; see Special Topic, "Mexico City Driving Restrictions") do not apply to your car.

If, however, you're driving to Oaxaca from the central United States, go via the **central route,** crossing the border at El Paso to Ciudad Juárez, Chihuahua. There, National Hwy. 45, preferably via the *cuota* multilane expressway (or if not, the old *libre* two-lane highway), leads you southward past high, dry plains past the cities of Chihuahua and Jiménez (use perifécos—peripheral highways—to bypass downtowns). Continue via Hwy. 49 southwest, through Gómez Palacio and the silver colonial cities of Zacatecas and San Luis Potosí, where you connect with Hwy. 57 expressway, via Querétaro, to the northern outskirts of Mexico City.

At that point, best use the east-bound peripheral *(periférico)* expressway via Carpio and Tezcoco instead of trying to fight your way through downtown Mexico City. At Los Reyes on the southeast side of town, pick up Hwy. 150 D, the expressway east to Puebla, where you continue southeast via the toll expressway to Oaxaca (as described in the previous paragraph). To be safe, allow three daytime-only driving days for this route.

Folks heading to Oaxaca from the eastern and southeastern United States probably save the most time by crossing the border from McAllen, Texas, to Reynosa and taking the **eastern route** to Oaxaca. Continue south, via Hwy. 97 then Hwy. 101, to Ciudad Victoria, bypassing the downtown by the *periférico* (peripheral high-

way). Then connect with Hwy. 80 to Tampico. There, again bypass the downtown and pick up Hwy. 105 south headed for Tempoal de Sánchez. After a long, winding, mountain climb via Huejutla de Reyes, you reach Pachuca and continue southward via expressway Hwy. 85 to Mexico City. At Carpio in the northern suburb, take the east bypass expressway, via Tepexpan and Tezcoco, continuing to east-bound expressway 150D for Puebla. There you continue southeast to Oaxaca City (as described two paragraphs above). If you start off at dawn each morning, you could probably get to Oaxaca safely in two driving days, under the best of conditions. Best do it in three more leisurely days, including two overnights.

Bribes *(Mordidas)*

The usual meeting ground between visitors and Mexican police is in their car on the highway or downtown street. To tourists, such cases sometimes appear as mild harassment, accompanied by vague threats of having to go to the police station or having their car impounded for such-and-such a violation. The tourists often go on to say that "It was all right, though. We paid him $10 and he went away. Mexican cops sure are crooked, aren't they?"

And I suppose, if people want to go bribing their way through Mexico, that's their business. But calling the Mexican cops crooked isn't exactly fair. Police, like most everyone else in Mexico, have to scratch for a living, and they have found many tourists are willing to slip them a $10 bill for nothing. Rather than crooked, I would call them hungry and opportunistic.

BY TOUR

For travelers on a tight time budget, a pre-arranged tour package can provide a hassle-free route for sampling Oaxaca's attractions. Call a travel agent for assistance.

If, however, you prefer a self-paced vacation, or desire thrift over convenience, you should probably defer tour arrangements until after arrival. Many Oaxaca tour agencies as close as your hotel telephone or lobby-front tour desk can customize a tour for you.

Special Tours and Study Options

Oaxaca's rich archaeological and cultural heritage provides a focus for some noteworthy tour-study programs. Some of the agencies that offer such options include Elderhostel, Zapotec Tours, Horizons, Mexi-Maya Tours, Field Guides, Siemer and Hand, and Adventures into Art.

A pair of **Elderhostel** tours lead participants in Oaxaca explorations: "Oaxaca: Spanish Language and Hispanic Culture" emphasizes practice in conversational Spanish, while "Exotic Mexican Birds and Their Habitat" centers on natural history in the countryside. Both programs include visits to the archaeological sites of Monte Albán and Mitla and appreciation of indigenous tradition through visits to pottery, weaving, and wood-crafting villages and evening excursions to enjoy Oaxacan food and folkloric music and dance. Accommodations include both hotel rooms and homestays with Mexican middle-class families. For details, write or phone for the international catalog: Elderhostel, 75 Federal St., Boston, MA 02110-1941, toll-free tel. 877/426-8056, or visit website www.elderhostel.org.

Chicago-based **Zapotec Tours,** tel. 800/44-OAXAC (800/446-2922), website: www.oaxacainfo.com, leads three Oaxaca tours: a "Food of the Gods" (beginning of October) gastronomical tour, a crafts and shopping tour (mid-November), and a cultural tour, focused on the famous 1–2 November Day of the Dead festival. You may also contact Zapotec Tours by mail or fax in the United States, 4955 N. Claremont Ave., Suite B, Chicago, IL 60625, tel. 773/506-2444, fax 773/506-2445.

The **Horizons** program, on the other hand, emphasizes hands-on arts and crafts study tours. The current program, usually offered in Oaxaca during the Jan. 5–12 Day of the Kings holiday, includes elementary experience in metals, jewelry, ceramics, and paper arts. Programs customarily last about 10 days and include field trips to crafts villages and archaeological sites, and simple room and board. For more details, including an informative brochure, write **Horizons,** 108 North Main St., Sunderland, MA 01375. For

phone or fax registration by credit card only, call 413/665-0300 or fax 413/665-4141, website: www.horizons@horizons-art.org.

The **Mexi-Maya** tours feature broad cultural experiences, customarily including visits to museums, historical and archaeological sites, crafts villages, and markets. Programs often include extensions to Oaxaca's palmy coastal resorts. For more information, contact Mexi-Maya at 12South675 Knoebel Dr., Lemont, IL 60439, tel. 630/972-9393.

Birding tour operator **Field Guides** leads Oaxaca tours centering on the wildlife-rich foothill forests and lagoons of the tropical coast. Along the way, trips often include archaeological and historical sites and colorful native markets. For more information, call toll-free 800/728-4953, or fax 512/263-0117, or by Internet: email: fieldguides@fieldguides.com, or website: www.fieldguides.com.

Siemer and Hand Travel, established in San Francisco since 1959, organizes educational tours in Oaxaca for museum and university alumni groups. Tours have included "Tropical Birding," in cooperation with the National Audubon Society and "The Valley of Oaxaca: Archaeology, Arts, and Traditions," for both Bryn Mawr College and the Harvard Alumni Association. For more information, contact Siemer and Hand at 750 Battery St., Suite 300, San Francisco CA 94111,tel. 415/788-4800, fax 415/788-4133, email: robroy@siemerhand.com.

Oaxaca arts and crafts tours are the specialty of **Travel Adventures into Art,** most often in cooperation with art institutes and museums. Tours often include festivals, such as Easter, Day of the Dead (1 and 2 November) and Christmas-New Year. Other tours have focused on a special interest, such as contemporary art, textiles, or women artists. Hands-on tours emphasize actually doing art, such as painting, pottery, or photography, in a Oaxaca setting. For more information, contact President Joan LeVine Mellion, 3030 Bridgeway, Sausalito, CA 94965, tel./fax 415/331-6238, email: taia@slip.net.

GETTING AROUND

BY AIR

Travelers on tight time budgets find it useful to save a day flying, instead of driving or busing, over the Sierra between Oaxaca City and the Pacific resorts of Puerto Ángel, Bays of Huatulco, and Puerto Escondido.

Mexicana Airlines affiliate **Aerocaribe** connects Oaxaca City with Huatulco and Puerto Escondido daily (in addition to Cancún, Mérida, Villahermosa, and Tuxtla Gutiérrez). For reservations call 9/516-6088, or 9/516-0229. For flight information, call 9/511-5247.

Aerovega charter airline can connect Puerto Escondido with a number of Oaxaca destinations. Contact either a travel agent or Aerovega directly in Puerto Escondido, at 958/201-51.

Local Flying Tips

Mexican airlines have operating peculiarities that result from their tight budgets. For example, don't miss a flight—you might lose half the ticket price. Adjusting your flight date may cost 25 percent of the ticket price. Get to the airport at least an hour ahead of time. Last-minute passengers are often "bumped" in favor of early-bird waitees. Conversely, go to the airport and get in line if you must catch a flight that the airlines have claimed to be full. You might get on anyway. Keep your luggage small so you can carry it on. Lost luggage victims receive scant compensation in Mexico.

BY BUS

The bus is the king of the Oaxaca road. A host of lines connect virtually every town and most villages in Oaxaca. Three distinct levels of service—luxury or super-first class, first class, and second class—are generally available. **Luxury-class** (usually called something like Primera Plus, depending upon the line) deluxe express coaches speed between major towns, seldom stopping en route. In exchange for somewhat higher fares (about $50 Oaxaca City-Puerto

Escondido, for example, compared with $40 for first class), passengers enjoy rapid passage and airline-style amenities: plush reclining seats, air-conditioning, on-board toilet, video, and aisle attendant.

Although much less luxurious, **first-class** service costs less, is frequent, and always includes reserved seating. Additionally, passengers usually enjoy soft reclining seats and air-conditioning (if it is working). Besides their regular stops at or near most towns and villages en route, first-class bus drivers, if requested, will usually stop and let you off anywhere along the road.

Second-class bus seating is unreserved. In outlying parts of Oaxaca, there is a class of buses even beneath second class, but given the condition of many second-class buses, it usually seems as if third-class buses wouldn't run at all. Such buses are the stuff of travelers' legends: the recycled old GMC, Ford, and Dodge school buses that stop everywhere and carry everyone and everything to the smallest villages tucked away in the far mountains. As long as there is any kind of a road to it, such a bus will most likely go there.

Now and then you'll read a newspaper story of a country bus that went over a cliff somewhere in Mexico, killing the driver and a dozen unfortunate souls. The same newspapers never bother to mention the half million safe trips the same bus provided during its 15 years of service prior to the accident.

Second-class buses are not for travelers with weak knees or stomachs. You will often initially have to stand, cramped in the aisle, among a crowd of campesinos. They are warm-hearted people, but poor, so don't tempt them with open, dangling purses or wallets bulging in back pockets. Stow your money safely away. After a while, you will probably be able to sit down. Such privilege, however, comes with obligation, such as holding an old lady's bulging bag of carrots or a toddler on your lap. But if you accept your burden with humor and equanimity, who knows what favors and blessings may flow to you in return.

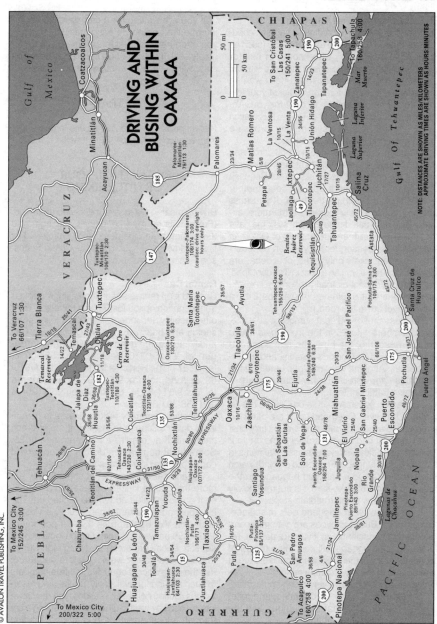

DRIVING AND BUSING WITHIN OAXACA

CHIAPAS

Gulf of Mexico

Coatzacoalcos

Minatitlán

Acayucan

VERACRUZ

To Veracruz 66/107 1:30

Tierra Blanca

Temascal 10/15 25/41

Temascal Reservoir

Jalapa de Díaz 36/58 Huautla 35/56

22/43 Tuxtepec

Temascal 14/22 27/43 Ojitlán

Tuxtepec-Teotitlán 110/180 4:30

Tuxtepec-Minatitlán 78/113 1:30

147

Tuxtepec-Minatitlán 106/170 2:30

Palomares-Minatitlán 78/113 1:30

Palomares

Matías Romero

Petapa

5/8 23/34

Tuxtepec-Pahuamares 108/174 3:00 (caution: drive daylight hours only)

Benito Juárez Reservoir

To San Cristóbal Las Casas 150/241 5:00

190

Zanatepec

200

To Tapachula 160/258 4:00

190

Unión Hidalgo 34/55

190

La Ventosa 10/15

La Venta

Tapanatepec

Mar Muerto

14/23

Ixtepec 28/45

Laollaga

49

Tlacotepec 10/15

Juchitán 11/27

Tehuantepec

Laguna Superior

Laguna Inferior

Gulf of Tehuantepec

Salina Cruz

Astata

45/72

NOTE: DISTANCES ARE SHOWN AS MILES/KILOMETERS APPROXIMATE DRIVING TIMES ARE SHOWN AS HOURS:MINUTES

Tequisistlán 30/49

Tehuantepec-Oaxaca 155/250 5:00

98/157

185

Cerro de Oro Reservoir

11/18

Tuxtepec-Teotitlán 123/198 4:00

Cuicatlán

Teotitlán-Oaxaca

Oaxaca-Tuxtepec 130/210 5:30

Santa María Totontepec

35/57

Ayutla

38/61

190

Tlacolula 21/34

6/10 Coyotepec

29/46

175 Ejutla

24/38

Pochutla-Oaxaca 149/240 6:30

San José del Pacifico 20/33

66/106

175

Pochutla-Salina Cruz 46/72

Santa Cruz de Huatulco

200

Pochutla 19/31

Puerto Ángel

Tehuacán

39/63

Teotitlán del Camino

62/100

D 135 Nochixtlán 50/80

Telixtlahuaca 22/35

135 53/86

Teotitlán-Oaxaca 143/230 2:30

31/50

EXPRESSWAY

18/29 Yucuda

Huajuapan-Oaxaca 107/172 3:00

EXPRESSWAY

Santiago Yosundua

Zaachila

8/02

10/16 Oaxaca

San Sebastián de las Grutas

Sola de Vega

131 Miahuatlán 48/78

San Gabriel Mixtepec 25/40

25/40 Nopala

El Vidrio 25/40

Puerto Escondido-Oaxaca 158/254 7:00

Juquila 30/48

San Pedro Amusgos

Río Grande

Pinotepa Nacional

Laguna de Chacahua

PACIFIC OCEAN

PUEBLA

Huajuapan de León 30/48

Tonalá 30/49

39/62

Tamazulapan

25/44

190 14/23

Teposcolula

Tlaxiaco

Putla-Pinotepa 85/137 3:00

35/65

16/26 Putla

125

20/32

4/6 36/58 21/34

Juxtlahuaca

Nochixtlán-Oaxaca 106/171 4:00

Pinotepa-Puerto Escondido 89/143 3:00

45/72

GUERRERO

Chazumba

39/63

Huajuapan-Juxtlahuaca 64/103 2:30

To Mexico City 200/322 5:00

To Acapulco 160/258 4:00

200

© AVALON TRAVEL PUBLISHING, INC.

To Mexico City 152/245 3:00

50 mi

0 50 km

Tickets, Seating, and Baggage

Oaxaca bus lines do not ordinarily publish schedules or fares. You have to ask someone (such as your hotel desk clerk) who knows, or call (or have someone call) the bus station. Few travel agents handle bus tickets. If you don't want to spend the time to get a reserved ticket yourself, hire someone trustworthy to do it for you. Another way of doing it all is to get to the bus station early enough on your traveling day to ensure you'll get a bus to your destination.

Although some lines accept credit cards and issue computer-printed tickets at their major stations, most reserved bus tickets are sold for cash and handwritten, with a specific seat number (*número de asiento*) on the back. If you miss the bus, you lose your money. Furthermore, airlines-style automated reservations systems were not yet arrived at the vast majority of Oaxacan bus stations. Consequently, you can generally buy reserved tickets only at the local departure (*salida local*) station. (An agent in Tehuantepec, for example, cannot ordinarily reserve you a ticket on a bus that originates in Oaxaca City, a day's travel down the road.)

Request a reserved seat number, if possible, from numbers 1 to 25 in the front (*delante*) to middle (*medio*) of the bus. The rear seats are often occupied by smokers, drunks, and general rowdies. At night, you will sleep better on the right side (*lado derecho*) away from the glare of oncoming traffic lights.

Baggage is generally secure on Oaxaca buses. Label it, however. Overhead racks are often too cramped to accommodate airline-size carry-ons. Carry a small bag of your crucial items on your person; pack clothes and less essential items in your checked luggage. For peace of mind, watch the handler put your checked baggage on the bus and watch to make sure it is not mistakenly taken off the bus at intermediate stops.

If, somehow, your baggage gets misplaced, remain calm. Bus employees are generally competent and conscientious; if you are patient, recovering your luggage will become a matter of honor for many of them. Baggage handlers are at the bottom of the pay scale; a tip for their mostly thankless job would be very much appreciated.

On long trips, carry food, drinks, and toilet paper. Station food may be dubious and the sanitary facilities ill-maintained.

If you are waiting for a first-class bus at an intermediate *salida de paso* (passing station), you often have to trust to luck there will be an empty seat. If not, your best option may be to ride a usually much more frequent second-class bus.

BY TRAIN

Recent privatization has put an end to passenger train service in Oaxaca. Ride the bus instead.

BY CAR, TAXI, TOUR, OR HITCHHIKING

Driving a car in Oaxaca is a decision up to you. (For details on road conditions, mileage, and driving times, see the destination chapters. For tips on driving to Mexico from the United States, see Getting There, above.)

Rental Car

Car and jeep rentals are an increasingly popular transportation option for Oaxaca travelers. They offer mobility and independence for local sightseeing and beach excursions. In Oaxaca City and Huatulco, the gang's mostly all there: **Budget,** tel. 9/515-0330, Huatulco tel. 9/587-0010, fax 9/587-0019; **Hertz,** tel.9/516-2434, fax 9/516-0009; **Avis,** tel./fax 9/511-5736; and **Alamo** tel./fax 9/514-8534, Huatulco tel. 958/190-74 and 958/701-35.

Agencies generally require drivers to have a valid driver's license, passport, a major credit card, and may require a minimum age of 25. Some local companies do not accept credit cards, but offer lower rates in return.

Oaxaca car rentals are not cheap. They run more than in the United States, with a 15 percent or more "value added" tax tacked on. The cheapest possible rental car, usually a vintage stick-shift VW Beetle, runs $30–60 per day or $200–450 per week, depending on location and season. Prices are steepest during high Christmas and pre-Easter weeks. Before departure, use the international agencies' toll-free numbers to shop around for availability, prices, and reservations. During non-peak seasons, you may save lots of pesos by waiting till arrival and renting a car through a local agency. Shop around, starting with the agent in your hotel lobby or the local yellow pages (under "Automoviles, renta de").

Car insurance that covers property damage, public liability, and medical payments *is an absolute must* with your rental car. If you get into an accident without insurance, you will be in deep trouble, probably jail. Driving in Mexico is more hazardous than back home. (For important car safety and insurance information, see Getting There, above.)

Taxis

The high prices of rental cars make taxis a viable option for local excursions. Cars are luxuries, not necessities, for most Oaxacan families. Travelers might profit from the local money-saving practice of piling everyone in a taxi for Sunday park, beach, and fishing outings. You may find that an all-day taxi and driver (who, besides re-

lieving you of driving, will become your impromptu guide) will cost less than a rental car.

The magic word for saving money by taxi is *colectivo:* a taxi that you share jointly with other travelers. Your first place to practice getting a taxi will be at the airport, where *colectivo* tickets are routinely sold from booths at the terminal door.

If, however, you want your own private taxi, ask for a *taxi especial,* which will probably run about three or four times the individual tariff for a *colectivo.*

Your airport experience will prepare you for in-town taxis, which rarely have meters. You must establish the price before getting in. Bargaining comes with the territory in Mexico, so don't shrink from it, even though it seems a hassle. If you get into a taxi without an agreed-upon price, you are letting yourself in for a more serious, poten-

STOP   RAILROAD   YIELD   SPEED BUMPS
                    CROSSING   RIGHT OF WAY

ONE WAY   TWO WAY   PARKING   NO PARKING

DIP (across arroyo)   DIP (across arroyo)   BUS STOP   KEEP TO THE RIGHT

CAR-RENTAL AGENCY
TOLL-FREE NUMBERS AND WEBSITES

Alamo, United States and Canada tel. 800/522-9696, www.alamo.com: OA, HU

Avis, United States and Canada tel. 800/831-2847, www.avis.com: OA

Budget, United States and Canada tel. 800/472-3325, www.drivebudget.com: OA, HU, PE

Hertz, United States tel. 800/654-3001, Canada tel. 476/620-9620, www.hertz.com: OA

CITY KEY
OA—Oaxaca
HU—Bahías de Huatulco
PE—Puerto Escondido
In addition to the international car rental companies, many good local agents rent cars at generally lower rates. See individual destination chapters for more information.

---

tially nasty hassle later. If your driver's price is too high, he'll probably come to his senses as soon as you hail another taxi.

After a few days, getting taxis around town will be a cinch. You'll find you don't have to take the high-ticket taxis lined up in your hotel driveway. If the price isn't right, walk toward the street and hail a regular taxi.

In town, if you can't seem to find a taxi, it may be because they are all hanging around waiting for riders at the local stand, called a taxi *sitio*. Ask someone to direct you to it: Say *"Excúseme. ¿Donde está el sitio taxi, por favor?"* ("Excuse me. Where is the taxi stand, please?").

Tours and Guides

For many Oaxaca visitors, locally arranged tours offer a hassle-free alternative to rental car or taxi sightseeing. Hotels and travel agencies, many of whom maintain front-lobby travel and tour desks, offer a bounty of sightseeing, water sports, bay cruise, fishing, and wildlife-viewing tour opportunities. (For details, see the destination chapters.)

Hitchhiking

Most everyone agrees hitchhiking is not the safest mode of transport. If you're unsure, don't do it. Hitchhiking doesn't make a healthy steady travel diet, nor should you hitchhike at night.

The recipe for trouble-free hitchhiking requires equal measures of luck, savvy, and technique. The best places to catch rides are where people are arriving and leaving anyway, such as bus stops, highway intersections, gas stations, RV parks, and on the highway out of town.

Male-female hitchhiking partnerships seem to net the most rides (although it is technically illegal for women to ride in commercial trucks). The more gear you and your partner have, the fewer rides you will get. Pickup and flatbed truck owners often pick up passengers for pay. Before hopping onto the truck bed, ask how much the ride will cost.

BOB RACE

green turtle

OTHER PRACTICALITIES

ENTRY AND EXIT REGULATIONS

Tourist Cards and Visas

For U.S. citizens, entry by air into Mexico for a few weeks could hardly be easier. Airline attendants hand out tourist cards *(tarjetas turísticas)* en route and officers make them official by glancing at passports and stamping the cards at the immigration gate. Business travel permits for 30 days or less are handled by the same simple procedures.

Entry is not entirely painless, however. The Mexican government currently charges an approximate $15 fee per person for a tourist card. For air and bus travelers, this is no problem, since the fee is automatically included in the fare. The fee can be a bit of a hassle for drivers, however. At this writing the government does not allow collection of the fee by border immigration officers. Instead, the officers issue a form that you must take to a bank, where you pay the fee, thus automatically validating your tourist card. For multiple entries this can get complicated and time-consuming.

In addition to the entry fee, Mexican immigration officials require that all entering U.S. citizens 15 years old or over must present proper identification—either a valid U.S. passport, original birth certificate, or military ID, while naturalized citizens must show naturalization papers or a valid U.S. passport. (Note: For more Mexico-entry details, visit the Mexico Tourism Board's **website: www.visitmexico.com** or dial its toll-free number **800/44-MEXICO** (800/446-3942).

Canadian citizens must show a valid passport or original birth certificate. Nationals of other countries may be subject to different regulations; check with your regional Mexico Tourism Board (see chart) or, in the United States or Canada, call toll-free, tel. 800/44-MEXICO (800/446-3942).

Nationals of other countries (especially those such as Hong Kong, which issue more than one type of passport) may be subject to additional entry regulations. For advice, consult your closest Mexico Tourism Board or consulate, or the toll-free number above. (See the chart "Mexico Tourism Boards.")

More Options

For more complicated cases, get your tourist card early enough to allow you to consider the options. Tourist cards can be issued for multiple entries and a maximum validity of 180 days; photos are often required. If you don't request multiple entry or the maximum time, your card will probably be stamped single entry, valid for some shorter period, such as 90 days. If you are not sure how long you'll stay in Mexico, request the maximum. (One hundred eighty days is the absolute maximum for a tourist card; long-term foreign residents routinely make semiannual "border runs" for new tourist cards.)

Student and Extended Business Visas

A visa is a notation stamped and signed into your passport showing the number of days and entries allowable for your trip. Apply for visas at the consulate nearest your home well in advance of your departure. One-year renewable student visas and business visas longer than the routine 30 days are available, though often with considerable red tape. Check with your local Mexican consulate for details; an ordinary 180-day tourist card may be the easiest option if you can manage it.

Your Passport

Your passport (or birth or naturalization certificate) is your positive proof of national identity; without it, your status in any foreign country is in doubt. Don't leave home without one. United States citizens may obtain passports at local post offices.

Don't Lose Your Tourist Card

If you do, be prepared with a Xeroxed copy of the original, which you should present to the nearest federal Migración (Immigration) office (on duty long hours at Oaxaca's airports) and ask for a duplicate tourist permit. Lacking this, you might present some alternate proof of your date of arrival in Mexico, such as a stamped passport or

MEXICO TOURISM BOARD OFFICES

More than a dozen Mexico Tourism Board offices and scores of Mexican government consulates operate worldwide. Consulates generally handle questions of Mexican nationals, while Mexico Tourism Boards serve travelers heading for Mexico. For simple questions and Mexico regional information brochures, dial 800/44-MEXICO (800/446-3942) from the United States or Canada or visit their website: www.visitmexico.com.

Otherwise, contact one of the North American regional or European Mexico Tourism Boards for guidance:

IN NORTH AMERICA

From Arizona, California, Colorado, Hawaii, Idaho, Montana, Nevada, New Mexico, and Utah, contact **Los Angeles:** 2401 W. 6th Street, Fifth Floor, Los Angeles, CA 90057, tel. 213/351-2069, fax 213/351-2074.

From Alaska, Washington, Oregon, Idaho, Wyoming and Montana and the Canadian Provinces of British Columbia, Alberta, Yukon, Northwest Territories, and Saskatchewan, contact **Vancouver:** 999 W. Hastings St., Suite 1110, Vancouver, BC V6C 2W2, tel. 604/669-2845, fax 604/669-3498.

From Texas, Oklahoma, and Louisiana, contact **Houston:** 4507 San Jacinto, Suite 308, Houston TX 77004, tel. 713/772-2581, fax 713/772-6058 From Alabama, Arkansas, Florida, Georgia, Mississippi, Tennessee, North Carolina and South Carolina, contact **Miami:** 1200 N.W. 78th Ave. #203, Miami FL 33126-1817, tel. 305/718-4091, fax 305/718-4098.

From Illinois, Indiana, Iowa, Kansas, Michigan, Minnesota, Missouri, Nebraska, North Dakota, Ohio, South Dakota, and Wisconsin, contact **Chicago:** 300 North Michigan Ave., 4th Floor, Chicago, IL 60601, tel. 312/606-9252, fax 312/606-9012.

From Connecticut, Delaware, Kentucky, Maine, Maryland, Massachusetts, New Hampshire, New Jersey, New York, Pennsylvania, Rhode Island, Vermont, Virginia, Washington, D.C., and West Virginia, contact **New York:** 21 E. 63rd Street, 3rd Floor, New York, NY 10021, tel. 212/821-0313, 212/821-0314 fax 212/821-3067.

From Ontario and Manitoba, contact **Toronto:** 2 Bloor St. West, Suite 1502, Toronto, Ontario M4W 3E2, tel. 416/925-2753, fax 416/925-6061.

From New Brunswick, Newfoundland, Nova Scotia, Prince Edward Island, and Quebec, contact **Montreal:** 1 Place Ville Marie, Suite 1931, Montreal, Quebec H3B2C3, tel. 514/871-1052, 514/871-1103, fax 514/871-3825.

IN EUROPE

Mexico also maintains Mexico Tourism Boards throughout Western Europe:
London: Wakefield House, 41 Trinity Square, London EC3N 4DT, England, UK, tel. 207/488-9392, fax 207/265-0704.
Frankfurt: Weisenhuttenplatz 26, 60329 Frankfurt-am-Main, Deutschland, tel. 69/25–3509, fax 69/25–3755.
Paris: 4, Rue Notre-Dame des Victoires, 75002 Paris, France, tel. 1/426-15180, fax 1/428-60580.
Madrid: Calle Velázquez 126, 28006 Madrid, España, tel. 91/561-1827, fax 91/411-0759,
Rome: Via Barbarini 3-piso 7, 00187 Roma, Italia, tel. 6/487-2182, fax 6/487-3630.

---

airline ticket. Savvy travelers carry a copy of their tourist card with them, leaving the original safe in their hotel room or hotel safe.

Car Permits

If you drive to Mexico, you need to buy a permit for your car. Upon entry to Mexico, be ready with originals and copies of your proof-of-ownership papers (state title certificate or registration, or a notarized bill of sale), current license plates, and a current driver's license. The fee is about $12, payable only by non-Mexican bank MasterCard, Visa, or American Express credit cards. The credit-card-only requirement discourages those who sell or abandon U.S.-registered cars in Mexico without paying customs duties. Credit cards must bear the same name as the vehicle proof-of-ownership papers.

The resulting car permit becomes part of the owner's tourist permit and receives the same length of validity. Vehicles registered in the name of other organizations or persons must be accompanied by a notarized affidavit authorizing the driver to use the car in Mexico for a specific time.

Border officials generally allow you to carry or tow additional motorized vehicles (motorcycle, another car, a large boat) into Mexico, but will probably require separate documentation and fee for each vehicle. If a border official desires to inspect your trailer or RV, go through it with him.

Accessories, such as a small trailer, boat less than six feet, CB radio, and outboard motor may be noted on the car permit and must leave Mexico with the car.

For many more details on motor vehicle entry and what you may bring in your baggage to Mexico, consult the AAA (American Automobile Association) *Mexico Tourbook* (see the Booklist).

Since Mexico does not recognize foreign automobile insurance, you must purchase Mexican automobile insurance. For more information on this and other details of driving in Mexico, see above.

Entry for Children

Children under 15 can be included on their parents' tourist card, but complications occur if the children (by reason of illness, for example) cannot leave Mexico with both parents. Parents can avoid such possible red tape by getting a passport and a Mexican tourist card for each of their children.

In addition to a passport or birth certificate, minors (under age 18) entering Mexico without parents or legal guardians must present a notarized letter of permission signed by both parents or legal guardians. Even if accompanied by one parent, a notarized letter from the other must be presented. Divorce or death certificates must also be presented when required. Airlines will also require the name, address, and telephone number of the person meeting unaccompanied minors upon arrival in Mexico.

Oaxaca-bound travelers should navigate all such possible delays far ahead of time in the cool calm of their local Mexican consulate rather than in the hot, hurried atmosphere of a border or airport immigration station.

Pets

A pile of red tape can stall the entry of many **dogs, cats, and other pets** into Mexico. Veterinary health and rabies certificates for each animal are required. Contact Mexico Tourism Board, tel. 800/44-MEXICO (800/446-3942), or your closest Mexico Tourism Board for advice and assistance.

Returning Home

All returning U.S. citizens are subject to U.S. customs inspection. Rules allow $400 worth of duty-free goods per returnee. This may include no more than one liter of alcoholic spirits, 200 cigarettes, and 100 cigars. A flat 10 percent duty will be applied to the first $1,000 (fair retail value, save your receipts) in excess of your $400 exemption.

You may, however, mail packages (up to $50 value each) of gifts duty-free to friends and relatives in the United States. Make sure to clearly write "unsolicited gift" and a list of the value and contents on the outside of the package. Perfumes (over $5), alcoholic beverages, and tobacco may not be included in such packages.

Improve the security of such mailed packages by sending them via special **Mexpost** class, similar to U.S. Express Mail service. Even better, send them by **DHL** or **Federal Express** international courier, both of which maintain offices in Oaxaca. (Consult the local Oaxaca yellow pages for phone numbers.)

For more information on customs regulations important to travelers abroad, write for a copy of the useful pamphlet, *Know Before You Go,* from the U.S. Customs, toll-free tel. 800/973-2867, website: www.customs.ustreas.gov.

Additional U.S. rules prohibit importation of certain fruits, vegetables, and domestic animal and endangered wildlife products. Certain live animal species, such as parrots, may be brought into the United States, subject to 30-day agricultural quarantine upon arrival, at the owner's expense. For more details on agricultural product and live animal importation, write for the free booklet, *Travelers' Tips,* by the U.S. Department of Agriculture, Washington, DC 20250. For more information on the importation of endangered wildlife products, call tel. 202/720-2791 or write the Wildlife Permit Office, U.S. Department of the Interior, Washington, DC 20240.

MONEY

The Peso: Down and Up

Overnight in early 1993, the Mexican government shifted its monetary decimal point three places and created the "new" peso which subsequently has deflated to about one-third of its initial value of three per dollar. Since the peso value sometimes changes rapidly, U.S. dollars have become a much more stable indicator of Mexican prices; for this reason they are used in this book to report prices. You should, nevertheless, use pesos to pay for everything in Mexico.

Since the introduction of the new peso, the centavo (one-hundredth of a new peso) has appeared, in coins of 10, 20, and 50 centavos. Incidentally, the dollar sign, $, also marks Mexican pesos. Peso bills in denominations of five, 10, 20, 100, and 200 pesos are common. Since banks like to exchange your traveler's checks for a few crisp large bills rather than the often-tattered smaller denominations, ask for some of your change in 20- and 50-peso notes. A 200-peso note, while common at the bank, looks awfully big to a small shopkeeper, who might be hard-pressed to change it.

Banks, ATMs, and Money Exchange Offices

Mexican banks, like their U.S. and Canadian counterparts, have lengthened their business hours. Banco Internacional (BITAL), maintains the longest hours: generally as long as Mon.–Sat. 8 A.M.–7 P.M. Banamex (Banco Nacional de Mexico), generally the most popular with local people, usually posts the best in-town dollar exchange rate in their lobbies; for example: *Tipo de cambio: venta 9.615, compra 9.720,* which means they will sell pesos to you at the rate of 9.615 per dollar, and inversely buy them back for 9.720 per dollar. All of which means you should get 961.5 pesos for each of your $100 traveler's checks.

ATMs (Auto-Teller Machines) *(Cajeros Automáticos,* kah-HAY-rohs ahoo-toh-MAH-tee-kohs) are rapidly becoming the money source of choice in Mexico. Virtually every bank has a 24-hour ATM, accessible (with proper PIN identification code) by a swarm of credit and ATM cards. **Note:** Some Mexican bank ATMs will "eat" your ATM card if you don't retrieve it within about fifteen seconds of completing your transaction. Retrieve your card *immediately* after getting your cash.

Although one-time bank charges, typically about $2 per $100, for ATM cash remain small, the money you can usually get from a single card is limited to about $200 or less per day.

Even without an ATM card, you don't have to go to the trouble waiting in long bank service lines. Opt for either a less-crowded bank, such as Bancomer, Banco Serfín, Banco Internacional, or a private money-exchange office *(casa de cambio).* Often most convenient, such offices often offer long hours and faster service for a fee (sometimes as little as $0.50 or as much as $3 per $100) more than the banks.

Keeping Your Money Safe

Traveler's checks, the traditional prescription for safe money abroad, are widely accepted in Oaxaca. Even if you plan to use your ATM card, purchase some U.S. dollar traveler's checks (a well-known brand such as American Express or Visa) at least as an emergency reserve. Canadian traveler's checks and currency are not as widely accepted as U.S. traveler's checks, European and Asian even less. Unless you like signing your name or paying lots of per-check commissions, buy denominations of $50 or more.

In Oaxaca, as everywhere, **thieves** circulate among the tourists. Keep valuables in your hotel *caja de seguridad* (security box). If you don't particularly trust the desk clerk, carry what you cannot afford to lose in a money belt. Pickpockets love crowded markets, buses, and airport terminals where they can slip a wallet out of a back pocket or dangling purse in a blink. Guard against this by carrying your wallet in your front pocket, and your purse, waist pouch, and day pack (which clever crooks can sometimes slit open) on your front side.

Don't attract thieves; don't display wads of money or flashy jewelry. Don't get sloppy drunk; if so, you may become a pushover for a determined thief.

Don't leave valuables unattended on the beach; share security duties with trustworthy-looking neighbors or leave a bag with a shopkeeper nearby.

Tipping
Without their droves of visitors, Oaxacans would be even poorer. Deflation of the peso, while it makes prices low for outsiders, makes it rough for Mexican families to get by. The help at your hotel typically get paid only a few dollars a day. They depend on tips to make the difference between dire and bearable poverty. Give the *camarista* (chambermaid) and floor attendant 20 pesos every day or two. And whenever uncertain of what to tip, it will probably mean a lot to someone, maybe a whole family, if you err on the generous side.

In restaurants and bars, Mexican tipping customs are similar to those in the United States and Europe: tip waiters, waitresses, and bartenders about 15 percent for satisfactory service.

Credit Cards
Credit cards, such as Visa, MasterCard, and to a lesser extent, American Express and Discover, are widely honored in the hotels, restaurants, crafts shops, and boutiques that cater to foreign tourists. You will generally get better bargains, however, in shops that depend on local trade and do not so readily accept credit cards. Such shops sometimes offer discounts for cash sales.

Whatever the circumstance, your travel money will usually go much farther in Oaxaca than back home. Despite the national 17 percent ("value added" IVA) sales tax, local lodging, food, and transportation prices will often seem like bargains compared to the developed world. Outside of the pricey high-rise beachfront strips, pleasant, palmy hotel room rates often run $40 or less.

SHOPPING

What to Buy
Although bargains abound in Oaxaca, savvy shoppers are selective. Steep import and luxury taxes drive up the prices of foreign-made goods, such as cameras, computers, sports equipment, and English-language books. Instead, concentrate your shopping on locally made items: leather, jewelry, cotton resort wear, Mexican-made designer clothes, and the galaxy of handicrafts for which Mexico is famous.

Handicrafts
A number of Oaxaca regional centers are renowned sources of crafts. A multitude of family shops in Oaxaca City and Valley of Oaxaca villages such as Teotitlán del Valle, Santa Ana del Valle, Arrazola, Atzompa, Coyotepec, Tilcajete, San Antonino Castillo Velasco, and Ocotlán nurture vibrant traditions with roots in the pre-Columbian past.

Bargaining
Bargaining will stretch your money even further. It comes with the territory in Mexico and needn't be a hassle. On the contrary, if done with humor and moderation, bargaining can be an enjoyable path to encountering Mexican people and gaining their respect and even friendship.

The local crafts market is where bargaining is most intense. For starters, try offering half the asking price. From there on, it's all psychology: you have to content yourself with not having to have the item. Otherwise, you're sunk; the vendor will probably sense your need and stand fast. After a few minutes of good-humored bantering, ask for *el último precio* (the final price), which, if it's close, you may have a bargain.

Buying Silver and Gold Jewelry
Silver and gold jewelry, the finest of which is crafted in Taxco, Mexico City, Guanajuato and Oaxaca, decorates a number of Oaxaca shops. One hundred percent pure silver is rarely sold because it's too soft. Silver (sent from mines all over Mexico to be worked in Taxco shops), is nearly always alloyed with 7.5 percent copper to increase its durability. Such pieces, identical in composition to sterling silver, should have ".925," together with the initials of the manufacturer, stamped on their back sides. Other, less common grades, such as "800 fine" (80 percent silver), should also be stamped.

If silver is not stamped with the degree of purity, it probably contains no silver at all and is an alloy of copper, zinc, and nickel, known by the generic label "alpaca," or "Mexican," or "German" silver. Once, after haggling over the purity and prices of his offerings, a street vendor handed me a shiny handful and said, "Go to a jeweler and have them tested. If they're not real, keep them." Calling his bluff, I took them to a jeweler, who applied a dab of hydrochloric acid to each

TIANGUIS

Most important Oaxaca towns have a public outdoor market every day but a *tianguis* only once a week. The word *tianguis* is an ancient native expression, synonymous with "awning," the colorful tarpaulins that shade the mini-mountains of fruits, vegetables, crafts, and merchandise, which native people flock to buy and sell everywhere in Oaxaca.

Although trade appears to be the prime mover, people really come to *tianguis* for human contact, not only in the buying and selling itself, but for gossip, entertainment, flirtation—all of the other diversions that make life worth living.

People gather regularly for many Oaxaca *tianguis*:

OAXACA CITY

Abastos	Saturday

VALLEY OF OAXACA

Tlacolula	Sunday
Miahuatlán	Monday
Etla	Wednesday
Zimatlán	Thursday
Zaachila	Thursday
Ejutla	Thursday
Ocotlán	Friday

PACIFIC RESORTS AND SOUTHERN MOUNTAINS

Nopala	Saturday and Sunday
Juquila	Saturday and Sunday
Santa María Huatulco	Saturday and Sunday
Cacahuatepec	Sunday
Sola de Vega	Sunday
Pochutla	Monday
Astata	Tuesday
Huamelula	Thursday
Jamiltepec	Thursday

MIXTECA

Nochixtlán	Sunday
Putla	Sunday
Huajuapan	Wednesday
Juxtlajuaca	Thursday, Friday biggest
Chalcatongo	Thursday
Tonalá	Friday
Tlaxiaco	Saturday

NORTHERN OAXACA

Yalalag	Sunday
Huatla	Sunday
Valle Nacional	Sunday
Tuxtepec	Sunday
Teotitlán del Camino	Wednesday and Sunday
Jalapa de Díaz	Thursday and Sunday
Ojitlán	Wednesday

ISTHMUS

Juchitán	every day
Tehuantepec	Wednesday and Sunday

Selling sandías *(watermelons) is profitable in Tehuantepec.*

piece. Tiny, tell-tale bubbles revealed the cheapness of the merchandise, which I returned the next day to the vendor.

Some shops price sterling silver jewelry simply by weighing, which typically translates to about $1 per gram. If you want to find out if the price is fair, ask the shopkeeper to weigh it for you.

People prize pure gold partly because, unlike silver, it does not tarnish. Gold, nevertheless, is rarely sold pure (24 karat); for durability, it is alloyed with copper. Typical purities, such as

18 karat (75 percent) or 14 karat (58 percent), should be stamped on the pieces. If not, chances are they contain no gold at all.

COMMUNICATIONS

Using Mexican Telephones

Although Mexican phone service is improving, it's still sometimes hit-or-miss. If a number doesn't get through, you may have to redial it more than once. When someone answers (usually *"Bueno"*), be especially courteous. If your Spanish is rusty, say, *"¿Por favor, habla inglés?"* (¿POR fah-VOR, AH-blah een-GLAYS?). If you want to speak to a particular person (such as María), ask, *"¿María se encuentra?"* (¿mah-REE-ah SAY ayn-koo-AYN-trah?).

Mexican phones operate more or less the same as in the U.S. and Canada. Mexican phone numbers are always in a state of flux because the system is rapidly growing, but a complete telephone number (in Oaxaca City, for example) is generally written like this: 9/516-4750. As in the U.S., the "9" denotes the telephone area code *(lada)* ("LAH-dah") and the 516-4750 is the number that you dial locally. If you want to dial this number long-distance *(larga distancia)* first dial "01" then 9/516-4750. *Ladas* may be one, two, or three digits; local phone numbers may contain anywhere from four to seven digits. As a general guideline, the largest cities have one-digit *ladas,* medium-sized towns have two-digit *ladas,* and the smallest towns have three-digit *ladas.* In this book, the *lada* is included with each phone number listed.

In Oaxaca City and the larger towns, direct long-distance dialing has become the rule—from hotels, public phone booths, and efficient private Computel telephone offices. The cheapest, often most convenient way to call is by purchasing and using a **public telephone Ladatel card.** Buy them in 20, 30, 50 and 100-peso denominations at the many outlets—mini-markets, pharmacies, liquor stores—that display the blue and yellow *Ladatel* sign.

For station-to-station **calls to the United States, dial 001** plus the area code and the local number. For calls to other countries, ask your hotel desk clerk or see the easy-to-follow directions in the local Mexican telephone directory.

To reach **Mexican long-distance numbers, dial 01,** followed by the *lada* (Mexican area code) and the local number.

Another convenient (although a more expensive) way to call home is via your personal telephone credit card. Contact your U.S. long-distance operator by dialing toll-free 001-800/462-4240 for AT&T; 001-800/674-6000 for MCI; or 001-800/877-8000 for Sprint.

Another convenient, but expensive way to call home is collect. You can do this in one of two ways. Simply dial 09 for the local English-speaking international operator; or dial the A.T.&T., MCI, or Sprint number listed in the previous paragraph.

Beware of certain private "call the U.S. with your Visa or MasterCard" telephones installed prominently in airports, tourist hotels, and shops. Tariffs on these phones can run as high as $10 a minute. If you do use such a phone, always ask the operator for the rate, and if it's too high, take your business elsewhere.

In smaller towns and villages, you must often do your long-distance phoning in the *larga distancia* (local phone office). Typically staffed by a young woman and often connected to a café, the *larga distancia* becomes an informal community social center as people pass the time waiting for their phone connections.

Post, Telegraph, and Internet Access

Mexican *correos* (post offices) operate similarly, but more slowly and less securely, than their counterparts all over the world. Mail services usually include *lista de correo* (general delivery, address letters *"a/c lista de correo,"*), *servicios filatelicas* (philatelic services), *por avión* (airmail), *giros* (postal money orders), and Mexpost secure and fast delivery service, usually from separate Mexpost offices.

Mexican ordinary mail is sadly unreliable and pathetically slow. If your mailings within Mexico must be secure, use the efficient, reformed government **Mexpost** (like U.S. Express Mail) service. For international mailings, check the local yellow pages for widely available **DHL** or **Federal Express** courier service.

Telégrafos (telegraph offices), usually near the post office, send and receive *telegramas* (telegrams) and *giros. Telecomunicaciones, (Telecom)* the new high-tech telegraph offices, add telephone, public fax, and sometimes Internet to the available services.

Internet service, including personal email access, has arrived in Oaxaca City and the larger Oaxaca towns. Internet "cafés" are becoming increasingly common, especially in the resort centers. On-line rates average about $3 per hour.

Electricity and Time

Electric power in Mexico is supplied at U.S.-standard 110-volts, 60-cycles. Plugs and sockets are generally two-pronged, nonpolar, like the old pre-1970s U.S. plugs and sockets. Bring adapters for your appliances with two-pronged polar or three-pronged plugs. (Hint: A two-pronged polar plug has different prongs, one of which is generally too large to plug into an old-fashioned nonpolar socket.)

Oaxaca operates on central time, Just like Chicago, Kansas City. Dallas, and Mexico City.

STAYING HEALTHY

In Oaxaca, as everywhere, prevention is the best remedy for illness. For those visitors who confine their travel to the beaten path, a few basic common sense precautions will ensure vacation enjoyment.

Resist the temptation to dive headlong into Mexico. It's no wonder that some people get sick—broiling in the sun, gobbling peppery food, downing beer and margaritas, then discoing half the night—all in their first 24 hours. Instead, they should give their bodies time to adjust.

Travelers often arrive tired and dehydrated from travel and heat. During the first few days, they should drink plenty of bottled water and juice and take siestas.

Traveler's Diarrhea

Traveler's diarrhea (known in Southeast Asia as "Bali belly" and in Mexico as "turista," or "Moctezuma's revenge") persists even among prudent vacationers. You can even suffer turista for a week after simply traveling from California to New York. Doctors say the familiar symptoms of runny bowels, nausea, and sour stomach result from normal local bacterial strains to which newcomers' systems need time to adjust. Unfortunately, the dehydration and fatigue

from heat and travel reduce your body's natural defenses and sometimes lead to a persistent cycle of sickness at a time when you least want it.

Time-tested protective measures can help your body either prevent or break this cycle. Many doctors and veteran travelers swear by Pepto-Bismol for soothing sore stomachs and stopping diarrhea. Acidophilus (yogurt bacteria), widely available in the United States in tablets, aids digestion. Warm chamomile *manzanilla* tea, used widely in Mexico (and by Peter Rabbit's mother), provides liquid and calms upset stomachs. Temporarily avoid coffee and alcohol, drink plenty of *manzanilla* tea, and eat bananas and rice for a few meals until your tummy can take regular food.

Although powerful antibiotics and antidiarrhea medications such as Lomotil and Imodium are readily available over *farmacia* counters, they may involve serious side effects and should not be taken in the absence of solid medical advice. If in doubt, see a doctor.

Sunburn

For sunburn protection, use a good sunscreen with a sun protection factor (SPF) rated 15 or more, which will reduce burning rays to one-fifteenth or less of direct sunlight. Better still, take a shady siesta-break from the sun during the most hazardous midday hours. If you do get burned, applying your sunburn lotion (or one of the "-caine" creams) after the fact usually decreases the pain and speeds healing.

Safe Water and Food

Although municipalities have made great strides in sanitation, food and water are still major potential sources of germs in Oaxaca. Although water is safe in virtually all towns, travelers do not generally drink Oaxacan tap water. Drink bottled water only. Hotels, whose success depends vitally on their customers' health, generally provide purified bottled water *(agua purificada)*. If for any reason water is doubtful, add a few drops of household chlorine bleach *(blanqueador)* or iodine (*yodo* from the *farmacia*) per quart. Iodine crystals or tablets are also readily available in the United States and Canada from pharmacies or outdoor recreation stores. Polarpure and Aquatabs are two popular brands.

National sanitation campaign signs remind locals and visitors alike to wash their hands before handling food and after using the bathroom.

Pure bottled water, soft drinks, beer, and pure fruit juices are so widely available that it is easy to avoid tap water, especially in restaurants. Ice and *paletas* (iced juice-on-a-stick) can be risky, especially in small towns.

Washing hands with soap before eating in a restaurant is a time-honored Mexican ritual, which visitors should religiously follow. The humblest Mexican eatery will generally provide a basin and soap for washing hands *(lavar los manos).* If it doesn't, don't eat there.

Hot, cooked food is generally safe, as are peeled fruits and vegetables. Milk and cheese these days in Mexico are generally processed under sanitary conditions and sold pasteurized (ask: *"¿pasteurizado?")* and are typically safe. Mexican ice cream used to be both bad tasting and of dubious safety, but national brands available in supermarkets are so much improved that it's no longer necessary to resist ice cream in resort towns.

In recent years, improved availability of clean water and public hygiene awareness have made salads (once shunned by Mexico travelers) generally safe to eat in tourist-frequented cafés and restaurants in Oaxaca. However, lettuce and cabbage, particularly in country villages, are more likely to be contaminated than tomatoes, carrots, cucumbers, onions, and green peppers. In any case, whenever in doubt, you can obtain some protection by dousing your salad in vinegar *(vinagre)* or the juice of sliced limes *(limas),* the acidity of which kills bacteria.

Medications and Immunizations

A good physician can recommend the proper preventatives for your Oaxaca trip. If you are going to stay pretty much in town, your doctor will probably suggest little more than updating your basic typhoid, diphtheria-tetanus, and polio immunizations.

For camping or trekking in remote tropical areas—below 4,000 feet or 1,200 meters—doctors often recommend a gamma-globulin shot against hepatitis A and a schedule of chloroquine pills against malaria. While in backcountry areas, you should probably use other measures to discourage mosquitoes—and fleas, flies, ticks, no-see-ums, "kissing bugs" (see below)—and other tropical pests from biting you in the first place. Common precautions include sleeping under mosquito netting, burning mosquito coils *(espirales mosquito),* and rubbing on plenty of pure DEET (n,n dimethyl-meta-toluamide) "jungle juice," mixed 1:1 with rubbing (70 percent isopropyl) alcohol (100 percent DEET, although super-effective, dries and irritates skin).

Chagas' Disease, Scorpions, and Snakes

Chagas' disease, spread by the "kissing" (or, more appropriately, "assassin") bug, is a potential but infrequent hazard in the rural Mexican tropics. Known locally as a *vinchuca,* the triangular-headed three-quarter inch (two centimeter) brown insect, identifiable by its yellow-striped abdomen, often drops upon its sleeping victims from the thatched ceiling of a rural

MEDICAL TAGS AND AIR EVACUATION

Travelers with special medical problems might consider wearing a medical identification tag. For a reasonable fee, **Medic Alert** (P.O. Box 1009, Turlock, CA 95381, tel. 800/344-3226) provides such tags, as well as an information hot line that will provide doctors with your vital medical background information.

For life-threatening emergencies, **Critical Air Medicine** (Montgomery Field, 4141 Kearny Villa Rd., San Diego, CA 92123, tel. 619/571-0482; from the U.S. toll-free 800/247-8326, from Mexico 24 hours toll-free 001-800/010-0268) provides high-tech jet ambulance service from any Mexican locale to the United States. For a fee averaging about $10,000, they promise to fly you to the right U.S. hospital in a hurry.

house at night. It bites the victim while frequently depositing its fecal matter. This may be followed by swelling, fever, and weakness, sometimes leading to heart failure if left untreated. Application of drugs at an early stage, however, can clear the patient of the trypanosome parasites, which infect victims' bloodstreams and vital organs. See a doctor immediately if you believe you're infected.

Also while camping or staying in a *palapa* or other rustic accommodation, watch for scorpions, especially in your shoes (whose contents you should dump out every morning.) Scorpion stings and snakebites are rarely fatal to an adult but are potentially very serious to a child. Get the victim to a doctor calmly but quickly. For precautions against snakes and other venomous reptiles, see Reptiles and Amphibians in the Introduction chapter.

Injuries from Sea Creatures
While snorkeling or surfing, you may suffer a coral scratch or jellyfish sting. Experts advise that you wash the afflicted area with ocean (not fresh) water and pour alcohol (rubbing alcohol or a liquor, such as mescal, tequila, or *aguardiente*), if available, over the wound, then apply hydrocortisone cream from your first-aid kit or the *farmacia*.

Injuries from sea urchin spines and sting-ray barbs are both painful and sometimes serious. Physicians recommend similar first aid for both: first remove the spines or barbs by hand or with tweezers, then soak the injury in hot-as-possible fresh water to weaken the toxins and provide relief. Another method is to rinse the area with an antibacterial solution—either rubbing alcohol, vinegar, wine, or ammonia diluted with water. If none is available, the same effect may be achieved by rinsing with urine, either your own or someone else's in your party. Get medical help immediately.

Poisonous sea snakes, although rare and shy, do inhabit Oaxaca waters. Much more common, especially around submerged rocks, is the moray eel. Don't stick your fingers or toes in any concealed cracks.

First-Aid Kit
In the tropics, ordinary cuts and insect bites are much more prone to infection and should receive immediate first aid. A first-aid kit (with a minimum of: aspirin; rubbing alcohol; hydrogen peroxide; Potable Aqua brand tablets; iodine, or bleach for water purification; swabs; Band-Aids; gauze; adhesive tape; an Ace bandage; chamomile; Pepto-Bismol; acidophilus tablets; antibiotic ointment; hydrocortisone cream; mosquito repellent; a knife; and tweezers) is a good precaution for any traveler and a top priority for campers.

Medical Care
You will receive generally good treatment at one of the many local hospitals in Oaxaca cities and towns. For medical advice and treatment, let your hotel (or if you're camping, the closest *farmacia*) refer you to a good doctor, clinic, or hospital. Oaxacan doctors, especially in medium-size and small towns, practice like private doctors in the United States and Canada once did before health insurance, liability, and group practice. They will come to you if you request it; they often keep their doors open even after regular hours, and charge reasonable fees.

For more useful information on health and safety in Mexico, consult Dr. William Forgey's *Traveler's Medical Alert Series: Mexico, A Guide to Health and Safety* (Merrillville, Indiana: ICS Books), or Dirk Schroeder's *Staying Healthy in*

Asia, Africa, and Latin America (Emeryville, CA: Moon Publications, Inc., 1999).

CONDUCT AND CUSTOMS

Safe Conduct

Mexico is an old-fashioned country where people value traditional ideals of honesty, fidelity, and piety. Crime rates are low; visitors are often safer in Mexico than in their home cities.

Even though four generations have elapsed since Pancho Villa raided the U.S. border, the image of a Mexico bristling with *bandidos* persists. And similarly for Mexicans: Despite the century and a half since the *yanquis* invaded Mexico City and took half their country, the communal Mexican psyche still views *gringos* (and, by association all white foreigners) with revulsion, jealousy, and wonder.

Fortunately, the Mexican love-hate affair with foreigners does not necessarily apply to individual visitors. Your friendly *"Buenos dias"* or *"por favor,"* when appropriate, is always appreciated, whether in the market, the gas station, or the hotel. The shy smile you will most likely receive in return will be your small, but not insignificant, reward.

Women

Your own behavior, despite low crime statistics, largely determines your safety in Mexico. For women traveling solo, it is important to realize the double sexual standard is alive and well in

MACHISMO

I once met an Acapulco man who wore five gold wristwatches and became angry when I quietly refused his repeated invitations to get drunk with him. Another time, on the beach near San Blas, two drunken campesinos nearly attacked me because I was helping my girlfriend cook a picnic dinner. Outside Taxco I once spent an endless hour in the seat behind a bus driver who insisted on speeding down the middle of the two-lane highway, honking aside oncoming automobiles.

Despite their wide differences (the first was a rich criollo, the campesinos were *indígenas*, and the bus driver, mestizo), the common affliction shared by all four men was machismo, a disease that seems to possess many Mexican men.

Machismo is a sometimes reckless obsession to prove one's masculinity, to show how macho one is. Men of many nationalities share the instinct to prove themselves. Japan's *bushido* samurai code is one example. Mexican men, however, often seem to try the hardest.

When confronted by a Mexican braggart, male visitors should remain careful and controlled. If your opponent is yelling, stay cool, speak softly, and withdraw as soon as possible. On the highway, be courteous and unprovocative; don't use your car to spar with a macho driver. Drinking often leads to problems. It's best to stay out of bars or cantinas unless you're prepared to deal with the macho con-

sequences. Polite refusal of a drink may be taken as a challenge. If you visit a bar with Mexican friends or acquaintances, you may be heading for a no-win choice of a drunken all-night *borrachera* (binge) or an insult to the honor of your friends by refusing.

For women, machismo requires even more cautious behavior. In Mexico, women's liberation is long in coming. Few women hold positions of power in business or politics. One woman, Rosa Luz Alegría, did attain the rank of minister of tourism during the former Portillo administration; she was the president's mistress.

Machismo requires that female visitors obey the rules or suffer the consequences. Keep a low profile; wear bathing suits and brief shorts only at the beach. Follow the example of your Mexican sisters: make a habit of going out in the company of friends or acquaintances, especially at night. Mexican men believe an unaccompanied woman wants to be picked up. Ignore such offers; any response, even refusal, might be taken as a "maybe." If, on the other hand, there is a Mexican man whom you'd genuinely like to meet, the traditional way is an arranged introduction through family or friends.

Mexican families, as a source of protection and friendship, should not be overlooked—especially on the beach or in the park, where, among the gaggle of kids, grandparents, aunts, and cousins, there's room for one more.

Mexico. Dress and behave modestly and you will most likely avoid embarrassment. Whenever possible, stay in the company of friends or acquaintances; find companions for beach, sightseeing, and shopping excursions. Ignore strange men's solicitations and overtures. A Mexican man on the prowl will invent the sappiest romantic overtures to snare a *gringa*. He will often interpret anything except silence or a firm "no" as a "maybe," and a "maybe" as a "yes."

Men
For male visitors, on the other hand, alcohol often leads to trouble. Avoid bars and cantinas, and if (given Mexico's excellent beers) you can't abstain completely, at least maintain soft-spoken self-control in the face of challenges from macho drunk.

The Law and Police
While Mexican authorities are tolerant of alcohol, they are decidedly intolerant of other substances such as marijuana, psychedelics, cocaine, and heroin. Getting caught with such drugs in Mexico usually leads to swift and severe results.

Equally swift is the punishment for nude sunbathing, which is both illegal in public and offensive to Mexicans. Confine your nudist colony to very private locations.

Although with lately decreasing frequency, traffic police in Oaxaca's resorts sometimes seem to watch foreign cars with eagle eyes. Officers sometimes appear to inhabit busy intersections and one-way streets, waiting for confused tourists to make a wrong move. If they whistle you over, stop immediately or you really will get into hot water. If guilty, say *"lo siento"* (I'm sorry), and be cooperative. Although he probably won't mention it, the officer is usually hoping that you'll cough up a $20 *mordida* (bribe) for the privilege of driving away.

Don't do it. Although he may hint at confiscating your car, calmly ask for an official *boleto* (written traffic ticket, if you're guilty) in exchange for your driver's license (have a copy), which the officer will probably keep if he writes a ticket. If no money appears after a few minutes, the officer will most likely give you back your driver's license rather than go to the trouble of writing the ticket. If not, the worst that will usually happen is you will have to go to the Presidencia Municipal (City Hall) the next morning and pay the $20 to a clerk in exchange for your driver's license.

Pedestrian and Driving Hazards
Although Oaxaca's potholed pavements and "holey" sidewalks won't land you in jail, they might send you to the hospital if you don't watch your step, especially at night. "Pedestrian beware" is doubly good advice on Mexican streets, where it is rumored that some drivers speed up rather than slow down when they spot a tourist stepping off the curb. **Falling coconuts,** especially frequent on windy days, are a truly serious hazard to unwary campers and beach goers.

Cars can get you both in and out of trouble in Mexico. Driving Mexican roads, where slow trucks and carts block lanes, campesinos stroll the shoulders, and horses, burros, and cattle wander at will is more hazardous than back home, and doubly so at night.

Socially Responsible Travel
Latter-day jet travel has brought droves of vacationing tourists to third world countries largely unprepared for the consequences. As the visitors' numbers swell, power grids black out, sewers overflow, and roads crack under the strain of accommodating more and larger hotels, restaurants, cars, buses, and airports.

Worse yet, armies of vacationers drive up local prices and local people begin to lose their long-held values and traditions. While visions of tourists as sources of fast money replace habits of hospitality, television wipes out folk entertainments, Coke and Pepsi replace fruit drinks, and prostitution and drugs flourish.

Some travelers are saying enough is enough, and are forming organizations to encourage visitors to travel with increased sensitivity to native people and customs. They have developed traveler's codes of ethics and guidelines that encourage visitors to stay at local-style accommodations, use local transportation, and seek alternative vacations and tours, such as language and cultural programs and people-to-people work projects.

SPECIALTY TRAVEL

Bringing the Kids

Children are treasured like gifts from heaven in Mexico. Traveling with kids will ensure your welcome most everywhere. On the beach, take extra precautions to make sure they are protected from the sun.

A sick child is no fun for anyone. Fortunately, clinics and good doctors are available even in small towns. When in need, ask a storekeeper or a pharmacist, *¿Dónde hay doctor, por favor?"* (DOHN-day eye doc-TOHR por fah-VOHR?). In most cases, within five minutes you will be in the waiting room of the local physician or hospital.

Children who do not favor typical Mexican fare can easily be fed with always available eggs, cheese, *hamburguesas,* milk, oatmeal, corn flakes, bananas, cakes, and cookies.

Your children will generally have more fun if they have a little previous knowledge of Mexico and a stake in the trip. For example, help them select some library picture books and magazines, so that they'll know where they're going and what to expect; or give them responsibility for packing and carrying their own small travel bag.

Be sure to mention your children's ages when making air reservations; child discounts of one-half or more are often available. Also, if you can arrange to go on an uncrowded flight, you can stretch out and rest on the empty seats.

For more details on traveling with children, check out *Adventuring With Children* by Nan Jeffries. (See the Booklist.)

Travel for the Handicapped

Mexican airlines and hotels are becoming increasingly aware of the needs of handicapped travelers. Open, street-level lobbies and large, wheelchair-accessible elevators and rooms are available in virtually all Oaxaca's larger hotels.

U.S. law forbids travel discrimination against otherwise qualified handicapped persons. As long as your handicap is stable and not liable to deteriorate during passage, you can expect to be treated like any passenger with special needs.

Make reservations far ahead of departure and ask your agent to inform your airline of your needs such as boarding wheelchair or in-flight oxygen. Be early at the gate in order to take advantage of the pre-boarding call.

For many helpful details to smooth your trip, get a copy of *Traveling Like Everyone Else: A Practical Guide for Disabled Travelers* by Jacqueline Freeman and Susan Gerstein (At this writing, it's out of print but might soon be available) at bookstores or from the publisher (Lambda Publishing, Inc., 3709 13th Ave.,

---

PACKING CHECKLIST

Necessary Items
❏ camera, film (expensive in Mexico)
❏ clothes, hat
❏ guidebook, reading books
❏ inexpensive watch, clock
❏ keys, tickets
❏ mosquito repellent
❏ passport
❏ prescription eyeglasses or
   contact lenses
❏ prescription medicines and drugs
❏ purse, waist-belt carrying pouch
❏ sunglasses
❏ sunscreen
❏ swimsuit
❏ toothbrush, toothpaste
❏ tourist card, visa
❏ traveler's checks, money
❏ windbreaker

Useful Items
❏ address book
❏ birth control
❏ checkbook, credit cards
❏ dental floss
❏ earplugs
❏ first-aid kit
❏ flashlight, batteries
❏ immersion heater
❏ lightweight binoculars
❏ portable radio/cassette player
❏ razor
❏ travel booklight
❏ vaccination certificate

PACKING CHECKLIST FOR CAMPERS

Necessary Items for Campers
❑ collapsible gallon plastic bottle
❑ dish soap
❑ first-aid kit
❑ hammock (buy in Oaxaca)
❑ insect repellent
❑ lightweight hiking shoes
❑ lightweight tent
❑ matches in waterproof case
❑ nylon cord
❑ plastic bottle, quart
❑ pot scrubber/sponge
❑ sheet or light blanket
❑ Sierra Club cup, fork and spoon
❑ single-burner stove with fuel
❑ Swiss army knife
❑ toilet paper
❑ towel, soap
❑ two nesting cooking pots
❑ water-purifying tablets or iodine

Useful Items for Campers
❑ compass
❑ dishcloths
❑ hot pad
❑ instant coffee, tea, sugar, powdered milk
❑ moleskin (Dr. Scholl's)
❑ plastic plate
❑ poncho
❑ short candles
❑ whistle

Brooklyn, NY 11218, tel. 718/972-5449.) Also useful is the book, *The Wheelchair Traveler,* by Douglas R. Annand. Yet another helpful publication is the *The Air Carrier Access Act: Make It Work for You,* by the Paralyzed Veterans of America; call toll-free 888/860-7244.

Certain organizations both encourage and provide information about handicapped travel. One with many Mexican connections is **Mobili-** ty International USA (P.O. Box 10767, Eugene, OR 97440, tel. 541/343-1284, after phone, voice/TDD, fax 503/343-6812). A $35 membership gets you a semi-annual newsletter and referrals for international exchanges and homestays. Visit their website: www.misa.org.

Similarly, **Partners of the Americas,** with chapters in 45 U.S. states, works to improve handicapped understanding and facilities in Mexico and Latin America. They maintain lists of local organizations and individuals that handicapped travelers may contact at their destinations. For more information, contact them at 1424 K St. NW, Suite 700, Washington, DC 20005, tel. 800/322-7844 or 202/628-3300.

Travel for Senior Citizens
Age, according to Mark Twain, is a question of mind over matter: If you don't mind, it doesn't matter. Mexico is a country where whole extended families, from babies to great-grandparents, live together. Elderly travelers will benefit from the respect and understanding Mexicans accord to older people. Besides these encouragements, consider the number of retirees already in havens such as Puerto Vallarta, Guadalajara, Lake Chapala, Oaxaca, and other centers.

Certain organizations support senior travel. Leading the field is **Elderhostel** (75 Federal St., 3rd Fl., Boston, MA 02110-1941, tel. 877/426-8056), which publishes detailed U.S. and international catalogs of special tours, study, homestays, and people-to-people travel programs. Visit the website at www.elderhostel.org.

A number of newsletters publicize Mexico vacation and retirement opportunities. Among the best is *Adventures in Mexico,* published six times yearly and filled with pithy hotel, restaurant, touring, and real estate information for independent travelers and retirees seeking the "real" Mexico. (For information, address Adventures in Mexico, P.O. Box 31-70, Guadalajara, Jalisco 45050, Mexico, or email: dalclewis@hotmail.com. Back issues are $2; one-year subscription $16, Canadian $19.)

Several books and newsletters publicize senior travel opportunities in general. *Mature Traveler* is a lively, professional-quality newsletter featuring money-saving tips, discounts, and tours for over-50 active senior and handicapped travelers. Individual copies are $3, a one-year subscription $31.95. Editor Adele Mallot has compiled years of past newsletters and experience into the *Book of Deals,* a 150-page travel tip and opportunity book, which sells for $7.95, plus postage and handling. (Order with a credit card by calling toll-free 800/460-6676 or 916/923-6346, or writing John Stickler Publishing, P.O. Box 15791, Sacramento, CA 95852.) Another good buy is the pamphlet *Complete Guide to Discounts for Travellers 50 and Beyond,* and the book *Special Report for Discount Travelers,* which list a plethora of hotel, travel club, cruise, air, credit card, single, and off-season discounts. (Order them for $6 and $17 respectively, from Vacation Publications, Inc., 1502 Augusta, Suite 415, Houston, TX 77057, tel. 713/974-6903, website: www.vacations-magzine.com)

WHAT TO TAKE

"Men wear pants, ladies be beautiful" was once the dress code of one of the Mexican Pacific coast's classiest hotels. Men in casual Oaxaca can get by easily without a jacket, women with simple skirts and blouses.

Loose-fitting, hand-washable, easy-to-dry clothes make for trouble-free tropical vacationing. Synthetic or cotton-synthetic-blend shirts, blouses, pants, socks, and underwear will fit the bill everywhere in the coastal resorts. In Oaxaca City, the northern Oaxaca mountains, and the Mixteca Alta, especially during the winter, add a medium-weight jacket.

In all cases, leave showy, expensive clothes and jewelry at home. Stow items you cannot afford to lose in your hotel safe or carry them with you in a sturdy zipped purse or waist pouch on your front side.

Packing

What you pack depends on how mobile you need to be. If you're staying the whole time at a self-contained resort, you can take the two suitcases and one carry-on airlines allow. If, on the other hand, you're going to be moving around a lot, best condense everything down to one easily carried bag (with wheels if possible) that doubles as luggage and a soft backpack. Experienced travelers routinely accomplish this by packing prudently and tightly, choosing items that will do double or triple duty (such as a Swiss army knife with scissors).

Campers will have to be super-careful to accomplish this. Fortunately, camping along the tropical coast requires no sleeping bag. Simply use a hammock (*hamaca,* buy it in Mexico), or if sleeping on the ground, a sleeping pad and a sheet for cover. In the winter, at most, you may have to buy a light blanket. A compact tent you and your partner can share is a must against bugs, as is mosquito repellent. Additionally, a first-aid kit is absolutely necessary.

OAXACA: THE CITY

Oaxaca de Juárez (pop. 350,000, elev. 5,110 feet, 1,778 meters), the capital city of the state of Oaxaca, occupies the strategic intersection of the three great arms of the Valley of Oaxaca. From the city, the three sub-valleys diverge south, northwest, and east, like the thumb, index finger, and middle finger of a single hand. Aztec conquerors called that crucial hub, a hilltop above the present city, Huaxyacac (oo-AHSH-yah-kahk) (Point of the Guaje) for a forest of pod-bearing trees that once carpeted its slopes. The Spanish, who founded the city downhill, shifted that name to the more-pronounceable Oaxaca (wah-HAH-kah).

HISTORY

Before Columbus

As early as perhaps 20,000 years ago, small bands of people, whose ancestors had migrated from Asia, were gathering wild grains, vegetables, and fruits and hunting wild game in the present Valley of Oaxaca. They foraged from the bounty of forest and meadow while following the great herds—bison, camels, horses, deer, and mammoths—that roamed Ice Age America.

Later, around 8000 B.C., the climate had warmed, and the animal herds were gone. The people, no longer following the vast game migrations, settled into a more sedentary life. They began to sow and cultivate the fruits, vegetables, and grains they had originally gathered. By selection over generations they created more productive varieties. The remains of their handiwork litter cave floors from Tehuacán in present-day southern Puebla to Mitla in the valley west of Oaxaca City. Archaeologists have written of those remains: early varieties of corn and squash, woven fibers of cotton and maguey, stone arrow and ax heads, and stone seed-grinding implements.

The same experts believe that a few thousand years later many of those original humble fields and gardens had become productive fields supporting permanent settlements of thatched houses, not unlike many remote Oaxacan hamlets today. Later, perhaps by 2000 B.C., some of these villages had grown into towns, with proud columned stone houses for upper classes, pyramids topped by temples, and small factories for producing jewelry, mirrors, and other specialized merchandise.

Finally, around 600 B.C., people speaking a

Zapotec mother tongue founded Monte Albán on a mountaintop above the present city of Oaxaca. Monte Albán ruled the Valley of Oaxaca for more than a millennium, climaxing as a sophisticated metropolis of as many as 40,000, controlling a large and populous area of southern Mexico and enjoying diplomatic and trade relations with distant kingdoms. But for reasons unknown, Monte Albán declined to a shadow of its former glory by around A.D. 800.

Zapotec-speaking city-states, such as Zaachila, Dainzu, Mitla, and Lambityeco in the surrounding valleys, filled the power vacuum left by the decline of Monte Albán. They ruled small valley-floor kingdoms, each controlling a small flock of satellite towns. Later, Mixtec-speaking people from the northwest invaded the Valley of Oaxaca and took over Monte Albán, using it mostly as a burial ground. Their chiefs subjugated many of the Zapotec city-states and ruled as an upper-crust nobility over much of the Valley of Oaxaca, until the Aztecs invaded during the 1440s.

In 1456, after a dozen years of struggle against combined Mixtec and Zapotec forces, the victorious Aztecs established a garrison on the hill of Huaxyacac (now called El Fortín), overlooking the present city of Oaxaca. Although Aztec settlers had established a model colony by 1500 (including districts with well-known Valley of Mexico names that still exist, such as Xochimilco), their rule was brief. On 25 December 1521, after a token skirmish, conquistador Francisco de Orozco and his soldiers replaced them on the hill of Huaxyacac scarcely five months after the Spanish tide flooded the Aztecs' Valley of Mexico homeland.

Conquest and Colonization
Spanish settlers began arriving soon after the conquistadores. Hernán Cortés, hearing of the beauty and bounty of the Valley of Oaxaca from both his lieutenants and emissaries from the Zapotec king, decided early on to stake out the Valley of Oaxaca as his personal domain. Time and again during the 1520s he ordered the settlers evacuated from Huaxyacac, only to find a year or two later that they had returned. During Cortés's absence on an expedition to Honduras, the settlers petitioned for and received a charter from King Carlos V for their

town, which they christened Antequera after the old Spanish Roman city. Determined not to be outmaneuvered, Cortés personally went to Spain to plead his case and returned triumphant with the royal title of Marqués del Valle de Oaxaca. This included a grant of hundreds of thousands of acres and rights to the labor of thousands of indigenous subjects in a grand checkerboard domain stretching from the Valley of Mexico to the Isthmus of Tehuantepec. Cortés's lands surrounded the settlers' entire town of Antequera. In desperation, the townspeople petitioned the queen of Spain for land on which to grow vegetables: they were granted a one-league square in 1532, now the core of the modern city of Oaxaca.

For hundreds of years, Cortés's descendants reigned, the townspeople prospered, the church grew fat, and the natives toiled—in corn, cattle, cane, and cochineal.

Independence, Reform, and Revolution
In contrast to its neighbors in the state of Guerrero, conservative Oaxaca was a grudging player in the (1810–21) War of Independence. But as the subsequent republican tide swept the country, local fervor produced a new state constitution, including a state legislature and governmental departments, such as public instruction and the Institute of Arts and Sciences.

By the 1850s, times had changed. Oaxacans were leading a new national struggle. Benito Juárez, a pure Zapotec native Mexican, was rallying liberal forces in the civil War of the Reforms against the oligarchy that had replaced colonial rule. Born in Guelatao, north of the valley, Juárez at age 12 was an orphan sheepherder. A Catholic priest, struck by the boy's intelligence, brought him to the city as a servant and taught him Spanish in preparation for the priesthood.

Instead, Benito became a lawyer. He hung out his shingle in Oaxaca, first as a defender of the poor, then state legislator, governor, chief justice, and finally the president of Mexico. In his honor, the city's official name was again changed—to Oaxaca de Juárez—in 1872.

In 1861, after winning the three-year civil war, Juárez's Reformista forces had their victory snatched away. France, taking advantage of the United States' preoccupation with its own

MARGARITA MAZA

C alle M. Maza, a modest two-block lane on Oacaxa's northern downtown edge, memorializes Margarita Maza, both the wife of Mexico's revered president Benito Juárez and the heroine who gave her all for love and country. Her greatness and that of her husband were inextricably intertwined by their own strong liberal ideals and their collective fate. Years before Margarita was born, Benito, of pure Zapotec blood, came to Oaxaca City seeking both his sister and his fortune. He found his sister working as cook in the household of Italian immigrant and merchant Antonio Maza and his wife, Petra Parada.

Benito also found refuge and warmth in the Maza household; through the Mazas, Benito got work and social connections that led to education and introduction into Oaxacan society. Benito was 20 years old when Margarita was born, the Mazas' youngest child. He bounced the baby on his knee and played with her like an older brother as she matured and while Benito's career as a lawyer, then Oaxaca state legislator, blossomed.

By the time Margarita was 17, their mutual affection had bloomed into love, and Benito, a successful attorney at 37, proposed marriage. They were married in the church of San Felipe de Neri, in Oaxaca, on 31 July 1843. Even today such a match would be unusual; in the Oaxaca of 1843 it was virtually unheard of. That he, a poor, dark brown Zapotec, and she, a lily-white daughter of a prominent merchant, were even able to associate, much less to marry, is testament to the Mazas' liberal views.

The same liberal views and their iron determination to do something about them scarred the last half of Benito and Margarita's 26 years of married life. From around 1854, when Benito was forced into exile in New Orleans, civil war, foreign invasion, and assassination attempts forced the family to be nearly always on the move, living in unfamiliar and trying circumstances, hounded

civil war, invaded Mexico and installed an Austrian Hapsburg prince as Emperor Maximilian of Mexico.

It took Juárez five years to prevail against Maximilian and his conservative Mexican backers. Although Maximilian and Juárez paradoxically shared many of the same liberal ideas, Juárez had Maximilian executed after his defeat and capture in 1867. Juárez bathed Mexico in enlightenment as he promulgated his "Laws of the Reform" (which remain essentially in force). Although the country rewarded him with reelection, he died of exhaustion in 1871.

Another Oaxacan of native Mexican descent, General Porfirio Díaz, vowed to carry Juárez's banner. Díaz, the hero who defeated the French in the battle of Puebla on Cinco de Mayo (5 May)

of 1862, was elected president in 1876. *"No Reelección"* was his campaign cry. He subsequently ruled Mexico for 34 years.

Under Díaz's "Order and Progress," Mexico, and to a lesser degree Oaxaca, was modernized at great human cost. As railroads, factories, and mines mushroomed, property ownership increasingly became concentrated among rich Mexicans and their foreign friends. Smashed protest marches, murdered opposition leaders, and rigged elections returned Díaz to office time and again.

But not forever. The revolt that ousted Díaz in 1910 has, in theory, never ceased. For three generations the PRI, the Institutional Revolutionary Party, has presided over a uniquely imperfect Mexican form of democracy. During that time the lives of native Oaxacans have and threatened by enemies, and continually lacking money.

One of the most dangerous episodes came in 1858, when Margarita, at the age of 32, had to move her brood of five children and entire household from Oaxaca to Veracruz, where Benito was running the liberal Mexican government-in-exile. Fearing spies and assassins, Margarita took the tortuous, roundabout route over the heart of the Sierra Madre, traveling at night, on foot beside their burro-train, disguising herself in native *huipil* and sleeping by day in farmhouses of friendly Zapotec campesinos.

Later, Benito and Margarita enjoyed two years of peace together, beginning in 1861, after the liberal triumph in the civil War of the Reforms. Their marriage, although severely tried by hardship and separation, was a supremely happy one. Twelve children resulted; seven—six girls and a boy—outlived their parents. Two boys and three girls died when still young. Their love, although profoundly deep, had few pretensions. Benito called her his "old lady." She called him "Juárez" and, when asked, replied that "he is very homely but good."

Their peace together was short-lived. The French invasion forced Benito to travel the country, managing the government in a black carriage, one jump ahead of the French army. Margarita took the family on a hopscotch path into northern Mexico and finally to New York and Washington, DC. There,

she reached the depths of despair when two of her three sons died. She wrote to Benito: "The loss of my sons is killing me. . . . I prefer death a thousand times more than life. . . . I do not blame persons who kill themselves. . . . If I had been braver I should have done it a year ago."

Eventually Margarita recovered her equilibrium, buoyed by the birth of her first grandchild, a baby girl, and the admiring attention of American society, including General Ulysses S. Grant and President Andrew Johnson.

On 19 June 1867, Juárez had the French-installed Emperor Maximilian executed. This was Margarita's signal to return home. A month later, with her party of 14, she arrived in Veracruz, showered by bouquets as she walked down the gangplank.

Reunited for three happy years with Margarita in Mexico City, Benito worked like a demon to turn his dreams for Mexico into reality. But overwork took its toll, and Benito suffered a stroke in October 1870. He recovered partially to discover that Margarita was fatally ill. She died on 2 January 1871 of cancer. Although weak, Benito strained with all of his strength and with tears in his eyes to lift her body into the coffin. All of Mexico, both friends and former enemies, joined in grief with their president for their beloved Margarita Maza, who had given as much as any heroine could for both love and country.

improved gradually. Although Indian families now go to government health centers and more of their children attend government rural schools, the price for doing so is to become less Indian and more Mexican.

Times in the Valley of Oaxaca nevertheless seem to be getting gradually better. In the late 1980s, UNESCO recognized Oaxaca as one of several world sites belonging to the "Cultural Patrimony of Mankind." The government took notice and began preparing Oaxaca for an influx of visitors. Museums were built, monuments refurbished, and the venerable buildings restored. Burgeoning tourism during the '90s has visibly improved the economic well-being of many Oaxaca families.

Increased international and national awareness seems to have contributed to other

improvements. Some long-standing grievances are being recognized. In 1995, moderate PRI governor Diodoro Carrasco Altamirano pushed through an unprecedented "Usos y Costumbres" law, which legalized Oaxacan native rights to their indigenous language and their traditional, town meeting form of government.

Nevertheless, by developed-world standards, most Oaxaca City families remain very poor. The political system, moreover, is far from perfect. But now, the victory of opposition presidential candidate Vicente Fox promises a new day for democracy in Oaxaca. Granted, Fox can't work miracles, but Oaxacans are hopeful that transgressions such as police brutality, bribes of public officials, vote buying, and murder of opposition community activists will quickly become things of the past.

SIGHTS

Getting Oriented

The streets of Oaxaca still run along the same simple north-south grid the city fathers laid out in 1529. If you stand at the center of the old *zócalo* and look out toward the *catedral* across the Av. Hidalgo, you will be looking north. Diagonally left, to the northwest, you'll see the smaller plaza, **Alameda de León,** and directly beyond, in the distance, the historic hill of Huaxyacac, now called **Cerro del Fortín.**

Along the base of that hill the Pan American Hwy. (National Hwy. 190) runs generally east-west through the northern suburbs. Turn around and you'll see the porticoed facade of the **Palacio de Gobierno,** where Oaxaca's governor tends to the state's business. Half a mile behind that (although you can't see it from the *zócalo*) the *periférico* (peripheral boulevard) loops around the town's south end. There it passes the yawning but often dry wash of the **Río Atoyac** and the sprawling **Mercado Abastos,** a market and second-class bus terminal on the southwest. Finally, if you find a clear vantage point, you'll see the hill of **Monte Albán** looming 1,000 feet (300 meters) above the southwest horizon.

AROUND THE *ZÓCALO*

The venerable restored downtown buildings and streets, some converted to traffic-free malls, make a delightful strolling ground for discovering traditional Mexico at its best. The *zócalo* itself sometimes seems to be a place of slow, leisurely motion, perfect for sitting at one of many sidewalk cafés and watching the world glide by. Officially called Jardín Juárez, the *zócalo* was laid out in 1529. Its portals, clockwise from the west side, are named Flores, Clavería, Juárez, and Mercaderes.

Palacio de Gobierno

Give the guards at the front door of the statehouse a cheery *"Buenos días"* or *"buenas tardes"* and step inside. City fathers first built a city hall on the same site in 1576. Repeated earthquakes led to reconstructions, until 1948, when the present building was finally rebuilt by updating and strengthening an original 1884 building. Straight ahead, you'll see the main mural, by Arturo Bustos, completed during the 1980s. It depicts the struggles of Oaxaca's independence, reform, and revolutionary heroes. On the right, in his trademark bandanna, is *insurgente* José María Morelos y Pavón, who published the famous *El Correo del Sur* newspaper in Oaxaca during Mexico's War of Independence. In the center is Oaxaca's favorite son and Mexico's revered *presidente,* Benito Juárez, and his wife, Margarita Maza. Below them is Juárez's *reformista* cabinet (notice the young, restive, General Porfirio Díaz with the sword on the right), which struggled through two bloody wars, finally emerging, with Juárez, triumphant in 1867. On the mural's far left, you see Oaxaca's 1910 revolutionary hero in turn-of-the-century Marxian-style spectacles, Ricardo Flores Magón. Before exiting, take a look at Bustos's other two murals, on the left and right sides of the courtyard, which respectively depict Mexico's pre-Hispanic and conquest eras.

Templo y Exconvento de San Agustín

Off-*zócalo* side streets are studded with Oaxaca's old church gems. One of the most precious and most accessible is the San Agustín church and ex-convent one block due east from the Palacio de Gobierno along Calle Guerrero. One of the few Oaxacan works of the Augustinian order, the original adobe church on this site was finished in 1596, but it was seriously damaged by subsequent earthquakes. The present church, finished in 1722, replaced the original. A generation after the Augustinians were expelled in the 1860s, Bishop Gillow of Oaxaca acquired and reactivated the church in 1893 and started the Casa de Cuna, a children's home and school, which still exists next door.

San Agustín's Baroque facade blooms with a pious pastoral sculpture of a bearded San Agustín, fifth-century Bishop of Hipona, North

Africa, above the entrance arch. Below, flanking the entrance portal, stand sculptures of Augustinian Saints Alipio, on the left, and Thomas of Valencia, on the right.

Inside, the same saints grace the grand, gilded main altarpiece, with the addition of Augustinian founding fathers San Juan Sahagún and San Fulgencio. The gilded south (right) transept altar piece displays a heavenly image of Santa Monica, mother of San Agustín. Finally, look below the pulpit for the glass capsule that contains a bone-fragment relic of San Agustín, gift from the Roman Augustinians.

Mercado Juárez

The traditional Juárez market occupies the one-block square that begins just one block south of the *zócalo*. Stroll around for fun and perhaps a bargain in the honeycomb of traditional leather, textile, and clothing stalls.

While at the market, be sure to step to the southwest corner of 20 de Noviembre and Rayón for a history lesson in art inside the **Templo y Exconvento de San Juan de Dios,** which stands on the site of Oaxaca's oldest church. The present structure, completed in 1703, replaced the former earthquake-damaged 1535 town cathedral, which itself replaced the original 1521 adobe structure. Big paintings lining the nave walls depict landmarks in Oaxaca's religious history. Inside the front door, to the left, see Bishop las Casas protecting his native charges against soldiers and settlers. Farther inside is an oil of the Santa Cruz de Huatulco; next comes Oaxaca's first mass, on the banks of the Río Atoyac, on 25 November 1521, and after that, the baptism of Cosijoeza, the last Zapotec king. Also you'll find a series of oils showing the discovery, persecution, revolt, and re-acceptance of the so-called "Idolators of Los Cajonos," whom Spaniards discovered worshipping their native gods on 14 September 1700.

Catedral de Oaxaca

Return to the *zócalo*'s opposite, north side, for a look at the present cathedral. It replaced the 1550 original, demolished by an earthquake in 1696. Finished in 1733, with appropriately burly twin bell towers, the present cathedral is distin-guished by its Greek marble main altar, where a

Don't miss Oaxaca's centuries-old cathedral on the north side of the zócalo.

polished Italian bronze Virgin of the Ascension is being drawn upward to the cloud-tipped heavenly domain of the Holy Spirit (the dove) and God (the sunburst). Flanking opposite sides of the altar, notice the glass images of noble, bearded St. Peter and St. Paul.

Of considerable historical interest is the **Santa Cruz de Huatulco** (Holy Cross of Huatulco), enshrined in a chapel at the middle, south (right) side of the nave. The cross, about two feet high, is one of four made in 1612 by Oaxaca bishop Juan Cervantes from the original mysterious cross worshipped by the natives on the southern Oaxaca coast long before the conquest. An explanation, in Spanish, gives three versions of the story of the cross, which, the natives reported to the conqueror Pedro Alvarado in 1522, was erected long before by a strange, white-robed holy man, who soon departed and never returned. Bishop Cervantes sent the three other copies of the cross, respectively, to authorities at Santa María Huatulco town, Mexico City, and Rome.

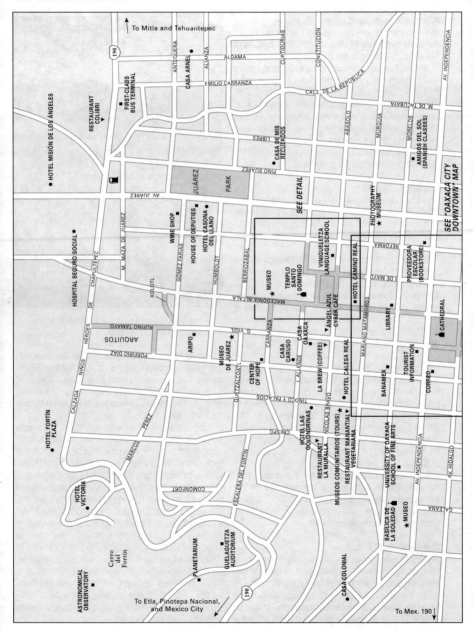

To Mitla and Tehuantepec

190

ANTEQUERA
ALDAMA
EMILIO CARRANZA
CALZ. DE LA REPÚBLICA
CURTIDURÍAS
CONSTITUCIÓN
AV. INDEPENDENCIA

CASA ARNEL
ALIANZA
M. DE TACUBAYA

RESTAURANT COLIBRÍ
FIRST-CLASS BUS TERMINAL

HOTEL MISIÓN DE LOS ANGELES

CASA DE MIS RECUERDOS
LIBRES
PINO SUÁREZ
ABASOLO
MURGUÍA
MORELOS
AMIGOS DEL SOL (SPANISH CLASSES)

JUÁREZ PARK
SEE DETAIL
SEE "OAXACA CITY DOWNTOWN" MAP

AV. JUÁREZ
WINE SHOP
HOUSE OF DEPUTIES
HOTEL CASONA DEL LLANO
PHOTOGRAPHY MUSEUM

HOSPITAL SEGURO SOCIAL
M. MAZA DE JUÁREZ
GÓMEZ FARÍAS
HUMBOLDT
BERRIOZÁBAL
VINIGUELETZA LANGUAGE SCHOOL
REFORMA
PROVEEDORA ESCOLAR (BOOKSTORE)

DE CHAPULTEPEC
XÓLOTL
MUSEO
TEMPLO SANTO DOMINGO
MACEDONIA ALCALÁ
HOTEL CAMINO REAL
5 DE MAYO

HÉROES
RUFINO TAMAYO
ARQUITOS
ARIPO
G. VIGIL
CARRANZA
ÁNGEL AZUL CYBER CAFE
CATHEDRAL

NIÑOS
PORFIRIO DÍAZ
MUSEO DE JUÁREZ
CASA CARUSO
CASA OAXACA
LIBRARY
MARIANO MATAMOROS

CALZADA
QUETZALCÓATL
CENTER OF HOPE
J. ALLENDE
LA BREW (COFFEE)
HOTEL CALESA REAL
TINOCO Y PALACIOS
BANAMEX
TOURIST INFORMATION
CORREO

PÉREZ
MARCOS
CRESPO
ESCALERA DEL FORTÍN
HOTEL LAS GOLONDRINAS
NICOLÁS BRAVO
RESTAURANT LA MURALLA
MUSEOS COMUNITARIOS (TOURS)
RESTAURANT MANANTIAL VEGETARIANA
UNIVERSITY OF OAXACA SCHOOL OF FINE ARTS
AV. INDEPENDENCIA
AV. HIDALGO

HOTEL FORTÍN PLAZA
HOTEL VICTORIA
COMONFORT
GALEANA

Cerro del Fortín
PLANETARIUM
GUELAGUETZA AUDITORIUM
BASÍLICA DE LA SOLEDAD
MUSEO

ASTRONOMICAL OBSERVATORY
190
To Etla, Pinotepa Nacional, and Mexico City
CASA COLONIAL
To Mex. 190

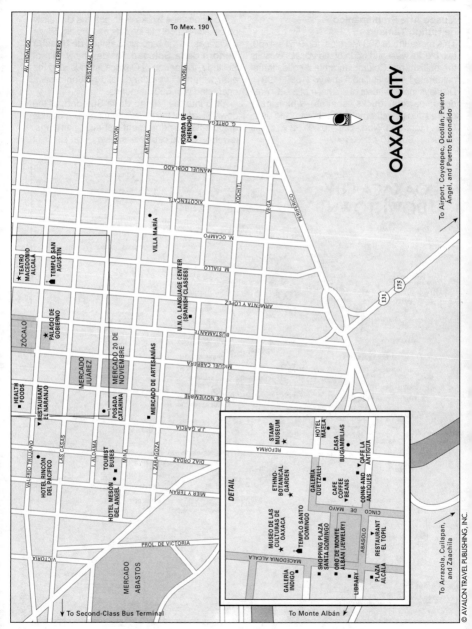

OAXACA CITY

To Mex. 190

To Airport, Coyotepec, Ocotlán, Puerto Angel, and Puerto Escondido

AV. HIDALGO
V. GUERRERO
CRISTOBAL COLON
LA NORIA
POSADA DE CHENCHO
G. ORTEGA
I.L. RAYON
ARTEAGA
MANUEL DOBLADO
XICOTENCATL
XOCHITL
VEGA
PERIFERICO

★ TEATRO MACEDONIO ALCALÁ
† TEMPLO SAN AGUSTIN
VILLA MARIA
M. OCAMPO
M. FIALLO
ARMENTA Y LÓPEZ

ZOCALO
★ PALACIO DE GOBIERNO
U.N.O. LANGUAGE CENTER (SPANISH CLASSES)
BUSTAMANTE

MERCADO JUAREZ
MERCADO 20 DE NOVIEMBRE
MIGUEL CABRERA

■ HEALTH FOODS
▼ RESTAURANT EL NARANJO
POSADA CATARINA
■ MERCADO DE ARTESANIAS
20 DE NOVIEMBRE

VALERIO TRUJANO
LAS CASAS
J.P. GARCIA
DIAZ ORDAZ
MINA
I. ZARAGOZA
L.ALDAMA

HOTEL RINCON DEL PACIFICO
TOURIST BUSES
HOTEL MESON DEL ANGEL
MIER Y TERAN

PROL. DE VICTORIA

VICTORIA
MERCADO ABASTOS

↓ To Second-Class Bus Terminal

To Arrazola, Cuilapan, and Zaachila →

© AVALON TRAVEL PUBLISHING, INC.

DETAIL

STAMP MUSEUM ★
REFORMA
HOTEL MELA
ETHNO-BOTANICAL GARDEN ★
GALERIA QUETZALLI
CASA BUGAMBILIAS
CAFE COFFEE BEANS ▼
COINS AND ANTIQUES
CAFE LA ANTIGUA ▼
CINCO DE MAYO

MUSEO DE LAS CULTURAS DE OAXACA ★
TEMPLO SANTO DOMINGO
SHOPPING PLAZA SANTA DOMINGO
ORO DE MONTE ALBÁN (JEWELRY) ■
RESTAURANT EL TOPIL ▼
ABASOLO
MACEDONIA ALCALÁ
GALERIA INDIGO ■
LIBRARY
PLAZA ALCALA ■

To Monte Albán ▶

131
175

Museo Arte Prehispánico de Rufino Tamayo

This museum, at 503 Morelos, tel. 9/516-4750, two blocks west and north of the *zócalo*, exhibits the brilliant pre-Columbian artifact collection of celebrated artist Rufino Tamayo (1899–1991). Displays include hosts of animal motifs—Colima dogs, parrots, ducks, snakes—whimsically crafted into polychrome vases, bowls, and urns. Open Mon. and Wed.–Sat. 10 A.M.–2 P.M. and 4–7 P.M., Sun. 10 A.M.–3 P.M.

Continue three blocks west, past the University of Oaxaca School of Fine Arts and the airy Plaza of Dances, to the baroque **Basilica de Nuestra Señora de la Soledad.** Inside, the Virgin of Solitude, the patron of Oaxaca, stands atop the altar with her five-pound solid golden crown, encrusted with 600 diamonds.

Step into the **Museo de la Soledad,** at the downhill side of the church, rear end. A multitude of objects of adornment—shells, paintings, jewelry—crowd cabinets, shelves, and aisles of

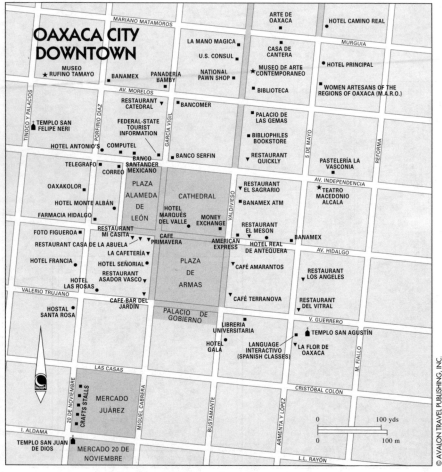

OAXACA CITY DOWNTOWN

© AVALON TRAVEL PUBLISHING, INC.

musty rooms. Large stained-glass panels tell of the images of Jesus and the Virgin that arrived miraculously in 1620, eventually becoming Oaxaca's patron symbols. Open daily 10 A.M.–2 P.M. and 4–6 P.M., tel. 9/516-5076.

ANDADOR DE MACEDONIO ALCALÁ

The tranquil Andador de Macedonio Alcalá pedestrian mall, named after the composer of the Oaxacan hymn "Dios Nunca Muere" ("God Never Dies"), leads north from the *zócalo*. Paved with Oaxaca green stone in 1985 and freed of auto traffic, the mall connects the *zócalo* with a number of distinguished Oaxaca monuments.

Teatro Alcalá
Among them is the Alcalá theater at 900 Independencia, tel. 9/516-2969 (from the back of the cathedral head right one block along Independencia to the corner of Independencia and 5 de Mayo). Christened by a 1909 opening performance of *Aida,* the Alcalá houses a treasury of Romantic-era art. Above the foyer, a sumptuous marble staircase rises to a bas-relief medallion allegorizing the triumph of art. Also take a look around the theater's gallery of paintings of Miguel Cabrera (1695-1768), a native Zapotec who rose to become New Spain's renowned Baroque painter. Also, don't miss the **Galería Nancy Canseco,** on the 5 de Mayo side, ground floor, which showcases the work of local and nationally recognized artists. Open Mon.–Sat. 10 A.M.–2 P.M. and 4–8 P.M., Sun. 4–8 P.M.

Museo de Arte Contemporaneo de Oaxaca
Continuing north along the Alcalá street mall, you soon pass the so-called **Casa de Cortés,** now the **Museo de Arte Contemporaneo de Oaxaca,** Macedonio Alcalá 202, tel. 9/514-2818, 9/514-2228, open daily except Tues. 10:30 A.M.–8 P.M. Past the bookstore (mostly Spanish but some English-language history, art, and guidebooks), exhibitions feature works of local and nationally known modern artists. Although named popularly for Hernán Cortés, the building is at least a hundred years too new for Cortés to

have lived there. The coat of arms on the facade above the door reveals it to have been the 17th-century home of a different Oaxaca family.

Exconvento de Santa Catalina
Continue uphill and, at Murguia, detour right again, to the **Ex-Convento de Santa Catalina,** the second-oldest women's convent in New Spain, founded in 1576. Although the quarters of the first novitiates were spare, the convent grew into a sprawling chapel and cloister complex decorated by fountains and flower-strewn gardens. Juárez's reforms drove the sisters out in 1862; the building has since served as city hall, school, and movie theater. Now, it stands beautifully restored as the Hotel Camino Real. Note the native-motif original murals that the renovation revealed on interior walls.

Centro Cultural de Santo Domingo
Return to the Alcalá street mall and continue another block uphill to Oaxaca's pride, the **Centro Cultural de Santo Domingo,** which contains two main parts, side by side: the **Museum of the Cultures of Oaxaca** and the **Church and Ex-convent of Santo Domingo,** both behind the broad Plaza Santo Domingo maguey garden and pedestrian square.

Inside, Santo Domingo church (open daily 7 A.M.–1 P.M. and 5–8 P.M.) glows with a wealth of art. Above the antechamber spreads the entire genealogical tree of Santo Domingo de Guzmán, starting with Mother Mary and weaving through a score of noblemen and women to the saint himself over the front door.

Continuing inside, the soaring, Sistine Chapel-like nave glitters with saints, cherubs, and Bible-story paintings. The altar climaxes in a host of cherished symbols—the Last Supper, sheaves of grain, loaves and fishes, Jesus and Peter on the Sea of Galilee—in a riot of gold leaf.

Continue next door to the museum, open daily except Mon. 10 A.M.–7:30 P.M., tel. 9/516-7672, which occupies the completely restored convent section of the Santo Domingo church. Exhibitions begin on the bottom floor in rooms adjacent to the massive convent cloister, restored in 1998 to all of its original austere beauty. A downstairs highlight is the long-neglected but now safely preserved **Library of Francisco Burgoa,** which you can walk right through and examine some of the more important works on display. The collection, 23,000 titles in all, includes its earliest work, a 1484 commentary on the works of Aristotle by Juan Versor.

A Museo sign points you upstairs via a glitteringly restored, towering domed chamber, adorned overhead with the Dominican founding fathers, presided over by Santo Domingo de Guzmán himself.

It's hard not to be impressed by the seeming miles of meticulously prepared displays divided into about a dozen long rooms covering various historical periods. One room exhibits priceless Monte Albán-era artifacts, including one of the most important of the original so-called *danzantes,* with the typically mutilated sex organs. The climax comes in the Tesoros de Tomb 7 room, where the entire gilded treasure discovered at Monte Albán Tomb 7 is on display. Besides a small mountain of gold and turquoise ornaments, notice the small but masterfully executed golden head of Ecéchatl, god of the wind, made eerie by the omission of facial skin over the jaw, to produce a nightmarishly skeletal piece of jewelry.

The museum has recently established an **ethno-botanical garden** in its big backyard. Staff customarily conduct both English and Spanish tours. Inquire at the museum front desk or tel. 9/516-7672 for schedule and access details.

A Trove of Museums

Back outside, step across Alcalá, a few doors uphill, into the rust-colored old building, now tastefully restored as the museum of the **Instituto de Artes Gráficos de Oaxaca,** tel. 9/516-6980. Inside, displays exhibit mostly contemporary etchings, wood-block prints, and paintings by artists of both national and international renown. Exhibits change approximately monthly; open daily except Tues. 9:30 A.M.–8 P.M.

Head west one block (along the Plazuela Carmen mall, off Alcalá across from the museum) to 609 Garcia Vigil and the **Casa de Juárez** museum, tel. 9/516-1860. The modest but beautifully restored house was the home of Juárez's benefactor, priest and bookbinder Father Antonio Salanueva. Rooms decorated with homey mid-19th-century furnishings realistically illustrate the life and times of a man as

revered in Mexico as is his contemporary, Abraham Lincoln, north of the border. Open daily except Mon., 10 A.M.–6 P.M.

Later, if you have time, return to the Santo Domingo church plaza and continue east past the church along Constitución to the new **Museo Philatelica de Oaxaca,** at Reforma 504, just uphill from the corner of Constitución, open daily except Mon., 9 A.M.–7 P.M., tel. 9/516-8028. Inside, showcases display the noted collection of José Cosino y Cosio, a library of international postal paraphernalia. Planners project that the museum's collection, of mostly Mexican and Oaxacan postage stamps, will grow steadily during succeeding decades.

Continue a few blocks down Reforma, turn left at Murguia, and continue half a block to the **Centro de Fotografía Alvarez Bravo,** Murguia 302, open daily except Tues., 9 A.M.–8 P.M., tel. 9/514-1933. Here, front galleries display the work of both locally prominent and internationally acclaimed photographers, while instructors in back courtyard rooms conduct photography classes for children, adult beginners, and professionals.

NORTH END

Arquitos and San Felipe del Agua Village

Long ago Oaxaca's city fathers provided for a permanent town water supply. They tapped the bountiful natural springs flowing from the mountains rising directly north of the city, topped by the towering Cerro San Felipe (elev. 10,200 feet, 3,100 meters). The aqueduct they built gave rise to the name San Felipe del Agua, the foothill village where the aqueduct begins. Although now replaced by underground steel pipes, the original 18th-century aqueduct still stands, paralleling the downhill road from San Felipe and ending in a quaint string of arches, called **Los Arquitos,** in the city neighborhood several blocks northwest of Santo Domingo church.

Starting from Plaza Santo Domingo, walk uphill four blocks north, along Alcalá; turn left at Xolotl (show-LOH-tuhl) and continue for three blocks to Tamayo, which runs uphill, paralleling the arches. The most entertaining thing about the Los Arquitos neighborhood is the way the residents have adapted to the aqueduct, ingeniously tucking their individual home and store doorways beneath the arches. Don't miss the little shrine built beneath one arch, at Tamayo 802, and also the tiny restaurant, El Pavito (The Little Peacock), beneath another. Also notice the colorfully picturesque contrast between the arches' red brick and light green *cantera* stone construction. Finally, be sure to explore some of the side lanes, such as the one opposite Tamayo 818 that heads beneath an arch and opens into a tiny plaza presided over by Archangel Gabriel. Afterward, stop for a drink or a bite to eat at the inviting Fonda de la Cruz, corner of Tamayo and Xolotl.

Next, take a taxi or a bus (catch one labeled "San Felipe," north, from the corner of Independencia and Reforma, thence uphill along Pino Suáez) or drive the few miles uphill to the source, suburban **San Felipe del Agua** village. The jumping-off point is Av. Netzahualcoyotl (naytzah-oo-wahl-coh-YOH-tuhl), which heads uphill at the big green "San Felipe" sign from its intersection with Hwy. 190 (Av. Niños Héroes), one block east of the Pemex station. Drivers, continue about two-thirds of a mile (one km), bear left at the hotel sign, then right one block, left one long block, and right again. You'll be on your way uphill, heading along Calzada San Felipe, which parallels the old stone aqueduct on your left. In a few miles the road becomes San Felipe's Calle Hidalgo, which, in turn, will lead you all the way to the bus turnaround at the foot of Cerro San Felipe.

Here the air is fresh and cool, and the view, both uphill and down, is inspiring. Below spreads the city and valley both left and right, while uphill rises the green, pine-tufted massif of Cerro San Felipe.

Continue uphill about a quarter mile to **Parque Comunal de San Felipe** trailhead and guard station. See the map at the guard station for trails that lead uphill through pine-shadowed glens and past waterfalls, all the way to the top of the mountain. It's a stiff, all-day 4,000-foot (1,200-meter) uphill hike. If clouds don't gather, and you start hiking early enough, (preferably before 9 A.M.), the stupendous mountaintop view will be your reward. Or ask for a guide at the guard station. Under any conditions, take a hat, water, lunch, and strong shoes.

Travelers who want more leisure can have it poking around the diminutive town plaza and San Felipe Apóstol church a few blocks downhill. Stop by for at least a drink at the showplace **Restaurant Las Campañas,** (patio-bar **La Ermita** in the back) on the plaza corner adjacent to the church.

chirimoya

BOB RACE

ACCOMMODATIONS

Oaxaca offers a wide range of good hotels. Air-conditioning is not particularly necessary in temperate Oaxaca, although hot-water showers (furnished by all lodgings listed below) feel especially comfy during cool winter mornings and evenings. The less expensive hotels, which generally do not accept credit cards, are mostly near the colorful, traffic-free *zócalo*. With few exceptions, Oaxaca's plush, resort-style hostelries dot the northern foothill edge of town. During holidays and festivals (Easter week, July, August, late October–early November, 15 December–4 January) many Oaxaca hotels raise their prices 20–30 percent above the numbers listed below. See the accompanying chart for hotels listed in order of price. (Note: Many of the following lodgings and much more are advertised and linked to the convenient websites: **www.Oaxaca4less.com, www.mex online.com,** and **www.oaxaca.com.)**

HOTELS

Near the *Zócalo*

Along with an enviable *zócalo* location, the **Hotel Señorial,** Portal de Flores 6, Oaxaca, Oaxaca 68000, tel. 9/516-3933, fax 9/516-3668, provides clean rooms, efficient management, a reliable restaurant, and an inviting (but unheated) swimming pool and patio. The hotel's only drawback is that a number of its interior rooms have louvered (not soundproof) communal air shaft windows and hallway transoms. This, especially during high fiesta seasons, results in noise that can't be shut out. Light sleepers should bring earplugs, especially on weekends and holidays, when the popular Señorial will be brimming with guests. The 107 rooms rent for about $34 s, $41 d, $46 t, with TV, limited wheelchair access, phones, and parking, and credit cards are accepted.

A number of good budget to moderately priced hotels cluster near the Hotel Señorial, within a block or two of the *zócalo*. Moving generally clockwise around the *zócalo*, first comes the petite **Hotel Las Rosas,** Trujano 112, Oaxaca,

Oaxaca 68000, tel. 9/514-2217, behind the Señorial and half a block from the *zócalo*. Climb a flight of stairs to the small lobby, relatively tranquil by virtue of its second-floor location. Beyond that, a double tier of rooms surrounds a homey inner patio. Adjacent to the lobby is a cheery sitting room with big, beautiful tropical aquarium and a TV, usually kept at subdued volume. The rooms themselves, although plainly furnished, are clean and tiled (except some bathrooms, which could use an extra scrubbing). Prices, at about $28 s, $35 d, $42 t, while not the bargain they once were, are relatively reasonable for such a well-located hotel. No credit cards, parking, or wheelchair access.

Although four blocks (two south, two west) from the *zócalo*, at Aldama 325, Oaxaca, Oaxaca 68000, tel./fax 9/516-4270, 9/516-5338, the **Posada Catarina,** a gem of a hotel in the market district, is worth the walk. New owners have spared little to turn this compact 30-room hostelry into an invitingly tranquil haven from the sidewalk bustle just outside the door. Rooms encircle three delightful small patios; the rear one, a petite, green grassy courtyard, is especially attractive. Rooms are no less than you would expect—immaculate, comfortable, and thoughtfully furnished with charming rustic wood furniture and old-Mexico decorations. Prices, although not a bargain, are reasonable, at $40 s, $47 d, for such a nicely appointed hotel. All rentals include modern-standard baths, fans, TV, phones, and parking. Credit cards are accepted.

Even farther out, at six blocks (three south, three west) from the *zócalo*, **Hotel Rivera del Ángel,** at Mina 518, Oaxaca, Oaxaca 68000, tel. 9/516-6666, fax 9/514-5405, offers several advantages. Downstairs, an airy, shiny, but busy lobby and restaurant area offers nothing special, but through the lobby windows, feast your eyes on the inviting big blue pool and sunny central patio. Upstairs you'll find the rooms semi-deluxe, clean, spacious, and comfortable, many with private terraces overlooking the pool patio. The hotel's main drawback, besides the questionable neighborhood (streetwalkers, low-life bars, and drunks at night), is street noise, from buses along

Mina. Ask for a *tranquilo* off-street room. Asking rates (which have risen so sharply that I may not recommend this hotel in future editions) run a steep $50 s, $62 d, low season, $65 and $70 high, with TV, fans, phones, restaurant, parking, travel agency, and tour buses to Mitla and Monte Albán. Credit cards not accepted. If you can't bargain for a better rate, especially during times of low occupancy, take your business elsewhere.

Return to the immediate *zócalo* vicinity, to the **Hóstal Santa Rosa,** a block from the *zócalo*'s southwest corner, at Trujano 201, Oaxaca, Oaxaca 68000, tel. 9/514-6714 or 9/514-6715. The streetside lobby leads past an airy restaurant to the rooms, recessed along a meandering inner passageway and courtyard. Inside, the rooms are very clean, comfortably furnished, and decorated in pastels. Rents, although raised, continue to be reasonable, usually at $30 s, $36 d, except during festivals and holidays, when they might rise as much as 40 percent. It offers TV, phones, parking, limited wheelchair access, and an in-house travel-tour agency, but no credit cards are accepted.

Continue clockwise around the *zócalo* half a block north to the longtime standby **Hotel Francia,** 20 de Noviembre 212, Oaxaca, Oaxaca 68000, tel. 9/516-4811, 9/516-4120, fax 9/516-4251, email: safer@prodigy.net.mx. Savvy new managers have brightened up the Francia with fresh white paint, a bright chandelier, potted palms, shiny lobby tile, and a new restaurant. They have also added a renovated colonial-era section (once a separate hotel next door) built around an invitingly traditional interior patio. Rooms are clean and spacious, with high ceilings and old-world dark wood furniture. Moreover, prices have risen only moderately. Rates for the 62 rooms are $28 s or d, all with baths, hot water, fans, TV, phones, and credit cards accepted, but only three parking spaces.

Walk a block and a half farther north to the restored, authentically colonial **Hotel Antonio's,** at the corner of Independencia. Here you'll be in the middle of it all, with colorful street-front ambience, a restaurant, and more than a bit of old Mexico charm within its quiet inner courtyard. It's at Independencia 601, Oaxaca, Oaxaca 68000, tel. 9/516-7227, fax 9/516-3672. The 15 thoughtfully decorated, comfortable, and clean rooms rent for about $24 s, $29 d, and $35 t;

with restaurant, but parking not included and credit cards not accepted.

Continuing counterclockwise around the zócalo, head one block east, one block south, to the southwest corner of leafy Alameda de León square in front of the cathedral and the very popular **Hotel Monte Albán,** Alameda de León 1, Oaxaca, Oaxaca 68000, tel. 9/516-2777. The hotel encloses a big patio/restaurant that hosts folk-dance shows nightly 8:30–10 P.M. During the first evening this could be understandably exciting, but after a week you might feel as if you were living in a three-ring circus. The 20 rooms, which surround the patio in two tiers, are genuinely colonial, with soaring beamed ceilings and big bedsteads. For such a nicely located hotel, rates run a relatively reasonable $27 s, $32 d, and $38 t; credit cards accepted.

For a fancier option, go to the old standby, the **Hotel Marques del Valle** on the north side of the *zócalo*, Portal Clavería, P.O. Boxes 13 and 35, Oaxaca, Oaxaca 68000, tel. 9/514-0688 or 9/516-3474, fax 9/516-9961. Guests enjoy a restored lobby, with bright chandeliers, mirrors, and shiny dark wood paneling. Upstairs, however, massive wrought-iron fixtures cast gloomy nighttime shadows through the soaring, balconied central atrium. The 96 rooms, nevertheless, retain their original 1940s polish, with handcrafted cedar furniture and marble-finished baths. Deluxe rooms have TV, carpets, and some balconies looking out on to the *zócalo*. Standard rooms rent for about $55 s or $72 d, $87 t, with restaurant/bar, limited wheelchair access, and credit cards accepted.

Conveniently situated just off the *zócalo*'s northeast corner, the newly polished up colonial-era **Hotel Real de Antequera,** Calles Hidalgo y Valdivieso, Oaxaca 68000, tel./fax 9/516-4020, 9/516-4635, offers plenty for reasonable rates. The 29 comfortable rooms around an inviting old-world-style restaurant-patio rent for $32 s, $39 d, all with bath, fans, cable TV, phones, parking, and credit cards accepted. For more information, visit the hotel's page on the website: www.oaxaca.com.

The '80s-mod **Hotel Gala,** Bustamante 103, Oaxaca, Oaxaca 68000, tel. 9/514-2251 or 9/514-1305, fax 9/516-3660, just a few doors south of the *zócalo*'s southeast corner, is for those who want comfortable, modern, deluxe

OAXACA CITY ACCOMMODATIONS BY PRICE

Accommodations (area code 9, postal code 68000 unless otherwise noted) are listed in increasing order of approximate high-season rates for two persons.

HOTELS

Hotel Villa de León, Reforma 405, tel. 516-1958, fax 516-1977, $25

Hotel Francia, 20 de Noviembre 212, tel. 516-4811, 516-4120, fax 516-4251, email: safer@prodigy.net.mx, $28

Hotel Antonio's, Independencia 601, tel. 516-7227, fax 516-3672, $29 d

Hotel Principal, 5 de Mayo 208, tel./fax 516-2535, $30

Hotel Monte Albán, Alameda de León 1, tel. 516-2777, $32

Hotel Las Rosas, Trujano 112, tel. 514-2217, $35

Hóstal Santa Rosa, Trujano 201, tel. 514-6714, 514-6715, $36

Hotel Real de Antequera, Calles Hidalgo y Valdivieso, Oaxaca 68000, tel./fax 516-4020, 516-4635, $39

Hotel Las Golondrinas, at Tinoco y Palacios 411, tel. 514-3298, tel./fax 514-2126, email: lasgolon@prodigy.net.mx, $40

Hotel Señorial, Portal de Flores 6, tel. 516-3933, fax 516-3668, $41

Hotel Gala, Bustamante 103, tel. 514-2251 or 514-1305, fax 516-3660, $45

Hotel Casona de Llano, Av. Juárez A701, tel. 514-7719, 514-7703, fax 516-2219, $47

Posada Catarina, at Aldama 325, tel./fax 516-4270, 516-5338, $47

Hotel Calesa Real, at Garcia Vigil 306, tel. 516-5544, fax 516-7232, $68.

Hotel Rivera del Ángel, Mina 518, tel. 516-6666, fax 514-5405, $70

Hotel Marques del Valle Portal Clavería, P.O. Boxes 13 and 35, tel. 514-0688, 516-3474, fax 516-9961, $72

Hotel Fortín Plaza, Av. Venus 118, Colonia Estrella, postal code 68040, tel. 515-7777, fax 515-1328, email: ortin@prodigy.net.mx, $105

Hotel Misión de Los Angeles, Calz. Porfirio Díaz 102, postal code 68050, tel. 515-00,

---

accommodations at relatively moderate prices. Rooms, although tastefully decorated and carpeted, are small. Get one of the quieter ones away from the street. The 36 rooms rent for about $40 s, $45 d, and $55 for junior suite; credit cards are accepted. With phones, TV, fans, and a restaurant, but parking is not included.

North of the Zócalo

Head two and a half blocks north, uphill, from the zócalo to the **Hotel Calesa Real,** at Garcia Vigil 306, Oaxaca, Oaxaca 68000, tel. 9/516-5544, fax 9/516-7232. Here, owners have converted an 18th-century mansion into a hotel with 70 rooms, an amazing number that you don't suspect as you enter its inviting colonial-style lobby and continue past a luscious palm-enfolded tropical pool patio. Upstairs, rooms are

1980s-standard deluxe, carpeted and pleasingly decorated in beige and pastels. They rent for about $55 s, $68 d, and $80 t, with fans, TV, phones, restaurant, small pool, and parking. Credit cards are accepted.

Location, at 5 de Mayo 208, Oaxaca, Oaxaca 68000, tel./fax 9/516-2535, right in the middle of the tranquil 5 de Mayo restaurant and shopping district, is the key for the modest, old-fashioned, **Hotel Principal,** like a slice out of the 1940s. Past the entry, the two stories of 16 rooms surround a quiet, geranium-decorated interior patio. A few sofas for sitting line the patio and upstairs corridor. The rooms are clean, high ceilinged and tile floored, with shaded bed lamps. No TV, no phones, but with hot water baths all day. Rentals of standard grade rooms run about $26 s, $30 d, $29 t.

fax 515-1680, email: hmision@oax1.prodigy.net.mx, $120

Hotel Victoria, Km 545, Carretera Panamericana, postal code 68070, tel. 515-2633, fax 515-2411, email: hvictoria@datasys.com.mx, $140

Camino Real, Calle 5 de Mayo 300, tel. 516-0611, fax 516-0732, from U.S. toll-free, 800/7-CAMINO (722-6466), $250

BED-AND-BREAKFASTS, GUESTHOUSES, AND APARTMENTS

All of the following (except for the first three—Casa Arnel, Hotel Maela, and Villa María) include breakfast for two in the lodging price:

Casa Arnel, Aldama 404, Colonia Jalatlaco, postal code 68080, tel. 515-2856, fax 513-6285, email: casa.arnel@spersaoaxaca.com.mx, $27

Hotel Maela, Constitución 206, tel. 516-6022, $28

Villa María, Arteaga 410 A, tel. 650-56, fax 425-62, $30

Casa Bugambilias,Reforma 402, tel./fax 516-1165, email bugambilias@infosel.net.mx, $58

Posada de Chencho, 4 Privado Noria 115, tel./fax 514-0043, email: pchencho@prodigy.net.mx, $60

Casa de Mis Recuerdos Pino Suárez 508, tel. 515-5645, email: misrecue@prodigy.net.mx, $64

Casa Colonial, Calle Miguel Negrete 105, tel./fax 9/516-5280, in U.S., tel. 800/758-1697, email: colonial@antequera.com, $75

Casa Caruso, Allende 11, tel. 9/516-1126; in U.S. tel. 315/696-8334, fax 315/696-5838, email: ncaruso@atsny.com, $100

Casa Oaxaca, Garcia Vigil 407, tel. 514-4173, fax 516-4412, email: casaoax@oax1.telmex.net.mx.$140

(Note: More information about many of the above lodgings is accessible via websites **www.Oaxaca4less.com, www.mexonline.com,** or **www.oaxaca.com** and other websites. See Internet Resources.)

Larger, superior rooms, $36 s or d, all with private shower baths and fans.

Oaxaca's classiest hotel, the **Camino Real,** Calle 5 de Mayo 300, Oaxaca, Oaxaca 68000, tel. 9/516-0611, or 800/7-CAMINO (800/722-6466) from the United States and Canada, fax 9/516-0732, occupies the lovingly restored former convent of Santa Catalina, four blocks north, one block east of the zócalo. Flowery secluded courtyards, massive arched portals, soaring beamed ceilings, a big blue pool, and impeccable bar and restaurant service combine to create a refined but relaxed old-world atmosphere. Rooms are large, luxurious, and exquisitely decorated with antiques and folk crafts and furnished with modern conveniences. If street noise is likely to bother you, get a room away from bustling Calles Abasolo and 5 de

Mayo. Rates run about $215 s, $250 d; with phones and TV, but parking not included; credit cards accepted.

Although a six-block walk (four north, two west) away from the zócalo, **Hotel Las Golondrinas,** at Tinoco y Palacios 411, Oaxaca, Oaxaca 68000, tel. 9/514-3298 or tel./fax 9/514-2126, email: lasgolon@prodigy.net.mx, is nearly always full. Step inside and you'll immediately see why. Rooms enfold an intimate garden, lovingly decorated with festoons of hothouse verdure. Leafy bananas, bright bougainvillea, and platoons of potted plants line pathways that meander past an intimate fountain patio in one corner and lead to an upstairs panoramic vista sundeck on the other. The care also shows in the rooms, which are immaculate and adorned with spartan-chic pastel earth-toned curtains and bedspreads and natural wood furniture. Guests additionally enjoy use of laundry facilities, a TV sitting room, a shelf of paperback books, and a breakfast restaurant 8–10 A.M. All this for only about $30 s, $40 d, and $45 t. In addition to the 27 regular rooms, two honeymoon suites rent for about $50 each.

On the other side of town, behind the Santa Domingo church, you'll find **Hotel Villa de León,** Reforma 405, Oaxaca, Oaxaca 68000, tel. 9/516-1958, fax 9/516-1977, a member of Oaxaca's endangered species of decent budget hotels. Don't be put off by the lackluster reception area; rather notice the light, airy courtyard cafeteria, encircled by an upstairs balcony of rooms. Step into one of them and you'll find it clean, carpeted, and thoughtfully decorated with rustic hand-hewn wooden beds, tables, lamps, and attractive brown bedspreads. Ask for a room away from the noisy street front. Prices run $18 s, $25 d, and $30 t, all with shower baths; credit cards accepted.

Step a few blocks farther north to the **Hotel Casona de Llano,** a favorite of visitors who enjoy the shady, untouristed ambience of Oaxaca's big Sunday park, officially Parque Paseo Juárez, but popularly **El Llano** (YAH-noh) (Plain or Flat Place). The memorable time to arrive is in the evening, when the hotel puts on its most impressive face: You enter the lobby, graced with high ceilings hung with gleaming chandeliers, continue past polished mahogany Doric columns, and enter a graceful Porfirian dining room, where guests often linger after dinner. You hear music, investigate, and find someone playing a tune on a handsomely preserved and polished upright piano in a side parlor. Your room, by contrast, is modern, comfortably furnished, and very clean. In the morning you open your door and look out upon a tranquil, grassy, inner tropical garden. The 28 rooms rent for a reasonable $37 s, $47 d, and $57 t; with fans, TV, phones, parking, and credit cards accepted. Reserve at Av. Juárez A701, Oaxaca, Oaxaca 68000, tel. 9/514-7719, 9/514-7703, fax 9/516-2219.

North Side Luxury Hotels
Three upscale suburban hostelries dot the north side of Hwy. 190. The **Hotel Victoria,** Km 545, Carretera Panamericana, Oaxaca, Oaxaca 68070, tel. 9/515-2633, fax 9/515-2411, email: hvictoria@datasys.com.mx, choicest of the three, spreads over a lush hillside garden of panoramic vistas and luxurious resort ambience. The '50s-modern lobby extends from an upstairs view bar downhill past a terrace restaurant to a flame tree and jacaranda-decorated pool patio. As for rooms, the best ones are in the newer view wing detached from the lobby building. There the junior suites are spacious, comfortable, and luxuriously appointed, with double-size bathrooms and private view balconies. The 150 rooms, bungalows, and junior suites rent for a sharply increased $140, $250, and $280 d, respectively; with TV, phones, a/c, tennis court, nightly live music, handicrafts shop, parking, and wheelchair access; credit cards accepted. For more information, visit the Victoria's website: www.hotelvictoria.com.mx.

The **Hotel Fortín Plaza,** Av. Venus 118, Colonia Estrella, Oaxaca, Oaxaca 68040, tel. 9/515-7777, fax 9/515-1328, email: fortin@prodigy.net.mx, next to the highway two blocks downhill, is hard to miss, especially at night. Its blue-lit six-story profile tops everything else in town. The hotel offers the usual modern facilities—restaurant/bar, pool, live music, disco, and parking—in a compact, attractively designed layout. Upstairs, guests enjoy deluxe, clean, and comfortable rooms with private view balconies (whose tranquillity is reduced, however, by considerable highway noise. Ask for a more *tranquilo* mountain-view room.) Room rates run about $85 s and $105 d, with phones, TV, wheelchair access, and parking; credit cards accepted. Ask for a discount or *paquete,* especially during weekdays and low occupancy months of January, May, June, and September.

Hotel Misión de Los Angeles, Calz. Porfirio Díaz 102, Oaxaca, Oaxaca 68050, tel. 9/515-1500, fax 9/515-1680, half a mile farther east (on the prolongation of Juárez), rambles like a hacienda through a spreading oak- and acacia-dotted garden-park. After a rough few days on the sightseeing circuit, it's an ideal place to kick back beside the big pool or enjoy a set or two of tennis. The rooms and suites are spacious and comfortable, with big garden-view windows or balconies. Upper rooms are quieter and more private. The 162 rooms and suites rent from about $120 d, $150 d for junior suite; with phones, parking, disco, and restaurant; credit cards accepted. For more information and reservations, email: hmision@oax1.prodigy.net.mx or visit the website: www.misiondelosangeles.com.

BED-AND-BREAKFASTS, GUESTHOUSES, AND APARTMENTS

North and East of the Zócalo

Many Oaxacans offer either lodging in their homes or apartment and house rentals. If you're a bargain hunter in Oaxaca now (or going to be in Oaxaca looking), be sure to see the classified sections of the English-language newspapers, *Oaxaca Times,* and *Oaxaca,* which usually advertise a number of economical longer-term rentals. Both papers are routinely available at hotels, shops, the federal tourist information office, north side of the *zócalo,* corner of Independencia and Hidalgo, or at the newspapers' respective offices at 307 Alcalá, tel. 9/516-3443, fax 9/516-3265, email: info@oaxacatimes.com, and Calz. P. Díaz, 321-7, Colonia Reforma, tel./fax 9/515-8764. If you want to reserve your rental early, you might ask the newspapers to fax or email you their classified pages.

Other potentially fruitful rental information sources are websites. At least two of them, **www.Oaxaca4less.com** and **www.mex online.com**, customarily advertise a number of Oaxaca long-term lodgings.

Meanwhile, read on to find out about a number of good apartments and bed-and-breakfasts sprinkled around town. Unless otherwise stated, prices given below are daily rates, usually subject to healthy discounts for long-term stays.

Starting on the north side and moving generally northeast, you'll first come to retired New York architect Nicolas Caruso's lovingly restored and decorated colonial-era mansion, **Casa Caruso,** at Allende 11, Oaxaca, Oaxaca 68000, tel. 9/516-1126, west of the corner of Garcia Vigil, four blocks north of the *zócalo.* Walk through the door and be charmed by what appears as a sultan's garden, where exotic plants fill the corners, bougainvillea spills from upper railings, and palms luxuriate in great ceramic pots. Downstairs, guests enjoy a library and tranquil courtyard for relaxing; the rooms upstairs are gorgeously furnished with antiques, handicrafts and fine art. Rates vary, from a minimum of about $100 d to a high of about $145 d, including breakfast, depending on the room, the season, and the number of people. If you can't reach Nicolas by phone in Oaxaca, try to get him in New York: tel. 315/696-8334, fax 315/696-5838, or P.O. Box 575, Tully, NY 13159, email: ncaruso@atsny.com. For more information, visit his website: www.casacaruso.com.

Equally luxurious, but a world apart, is **Casa Oaxaca,** around the east corner, uphill at Garcia Vigil 407, Oaxaca, Oaxaca 68000, tel. 9/514-4173, fax 9/516-4412, email: casaoax@oax1.telmex.net.mx. Its sky-blue colonial facade reveals nothing of its singularly unique interior. The lobby, which appears more like an art museum foyer than a lodging entrance, provides the first clue. Past that, you enter a spacious, plant-decorated courtyard, with the wall plaster artfully removed here and there to reveal the brick underlay. Continue to a rear courtyard, which centers on a blue designer pool and a *temascal* traditional native sauna. *Temascal* treatments, complete with native healer, run about $160 for four persons. All six rooms, which border the courtyards, although luxuriously and uniquely appointed with antiques, crafts, and contemporary wall art, seem austere, even to the point of coldness for some people. Rates are $140 s or d for the four smallest, yet spacious units; $180 s or d for a larger suite, and $230 for a two-story apartment above the rear courtyard. Rates include breakfast; credit cards are accepted.

Three blocks due east, behind ex-convent Santo Domingo, is **Casa Bugambilias,** a seven-room bed and breakfast artfully tucked behind a busy restaurant, at Reforma 402, Oaxaca, Oaxaca 68000, tel./fax 9/516-1165. The rooms, immaculate and thoughtfully appointed with art and handicrafts, are all different. Some open onto a lovely rear garden. Take a look at as many as possible before choosing. Rules include minimum three-night stay, children over 12 only, no pets, and no smoking. Rates run from $38 s, $50 d low season ($44 s, $58 d high) for the smallest room to $65 s, $78 d low season ($80 s, $90 d high) for the largest. All include private bath and breakfast in the attractive adjacent restaurant, La Olla. Reserve and make deposits through U.S. agent Itandewi Rodríguez, tel. 01/854-2701, email: adrian.rodriguez5@gte.net.

You can also reserve through Casa Bugambilias directly by email: bugambilias@infosel.net.mx; or find out more about them from the Oaxaca database of the general Mexico website: www.mexonline.com. Although it calls itself a hotel, the **Hotel Maela,** around the adjacent corner uphill corner at Constitución 206, Oaxaca, Oaxaca 68000, tel. 9/516-6022, feels homier than most hotels. Moreover, its prices are quite reasonable and it's on a relatively quiet street. Inside, the hall tiles shine, the ceilings are gracefully high, and the 11 rooms, mostly upstairs, are spacious, with private shower baths and attractive handmade wood dressers, beds, and end tables. Ceiling lights are bare bulbs, but nighttime reading lamps are shaded. Tariffs run about $22 s, $28 d, $32 t, with TV and parking, but breakfast not included.

Continue east a block and a half and turn north a block to the bed-and-breakfast gem **Casa de Mis Recuerdos** ("House of My Memories"), at Pino Suárez 508, Oaxaca, Oaxaca 68000, tel. 9/515-5645, email: misrecue@prodigy.net.mx. Enter the front gate and continue through a blooming, bougainvillea-festooned garden to the private home of the Valenciana family, which has been renting to students for years and now rents to foreign visitors. The rented rooms occupy rear and front sections. The four front rooms, immaculate, spacious, and lovingly decorated with folk art and furnished with handmade wooden furniture, have two bathrooms between them. They are closer to the busy street front than the five similarly furnished rear rooms, which, although they have private baths, are smaller. Guests also have the use of an airy, shaded rooftop gazebo for reading and relaxing. Breakfast, included with rentals, is served in the inviting downstairs family dining room. Rates are $32 high season, $29 low, with all linens and cleaning service included. Discounts are negotiable for long-term stays. For more information, find their page in the website: www.mexonline.com.

Farthest out (actually, under a mile) from the ócalo, **Casa Arnel,** Aldama 404, Colonia Jalatlaco, Oaxaca, Oaxaca 68080. Casa Arnel stands at the edge of downtown, so removed from the urban bustle that it feels as if it's embedded in another era. As one person explained, Jalatlaco, the formerly separate village, is "old, with stone streets . . . . [I]t's so Oaxaca." In front of Casa Arnel, the streets are indeed cobbled with stone, and across from it stands the ancient village church, San Matias Jalatlaco, beside its shady neighborhood plaza.

Casa Arnel is a family home that grew into a hotel, with about 20 rooms around a jungly garden blooming with birdcalls, flowers, and big, leafy plants. Additional amenities include a broad roof deck with umbrellas, tables, and chairs for sunning and relaxing. Old-style rooms, all with bath, are clean but bare-bulb plain. A new crop of renovated rooms is more attractive, with new bedspreads, curtains, and shiny furniture and fixtures. Prices, however, are reasonable: old-style $22 s, $27 d; new-style $27 s, $32 d; suite for four or more, $54; breakfast extra, but with restaurant, travel agency, and just three blocks from big, shady El Llano park with good restaurants and services. Bargain for a cheaper long-term rate. Reserve via tel. 9/515-2856, fax 9/513-6285, or email: casa.arnel@spersaoaxaca.com.mx; for more information visit their website: www.oaxaca.com.mx/arnel.

South and West of the *Zócalo*
Some good, long-term-style accommodations sprinkle the south and west ends of town.

Moving from east to west, start with **Posada de Chencho,** 4 Privado Noria 115, tel./fax 9/514-0043, email: pchencho@prodigy.net.mx. Part of the attraction here is the spark-plug owner, Inocencio "Chencho" Velasco, a friendly Mixtec version of Santa Claus. Such a stream of visitors from all over the world stay at his place that he seems to know someone everywhere. Moreover, very well-informed English-speaking Chencho is a treasury of information about Oaxaca, both local and statewide. His compound, 22 immaculate rooms in two stories, surrounds an inviting, green garden patio. The rooms themselves are comfortably and thoughtfully decorated, with Western-standard baths. Downstairs, guests enjoy a dining room and a big sitting room/library, besides patio nooks for reading and relaxing. Some rooms in the sun might get hot during the summer. If heat bothers you, be sure to select one in the shade, with a ceiling fan. If your room has no fan, ask Chencho to supply one. Rates run about $46 s, $60 d, including breakfast. A full-board single costs $60. Bargain for a cheaper long-term rate.

Get to Chencho's by walking east, along Guerrero, from the southeast corner of the *zócalo.* After four blocks, at Xicotencatl (shee-koh-tayn-KAH-tuhl), turn right and continue another four blocks south to Calle La Noria; 4 Privado La Noria is one of the one-block streets to your left that run south from La Noria.

Three blocks west and a block north, you'll find the attractive **Villa María,** at Arteaga 410 A, tel. 9/516-5056, fax 9/514-2562. Villa María is the labor of love of a trilingual (English, French, Spanish) owner-manager so welcoming that you immediately feel at home. Step inside her domain and you'll see the other reason for Villa María's popularity: about 15 apartments surrounding an inviting, plant-adorned inner patio, where stairways rise to rooftop sundecks furnished with comfortable chairs and shady umbrellas. The immaculate, thoughtfully decorated all one-bedroom housekeeping apartments, with themes such as "Mixteco," are completely furnished, including dishes, silverware, and maid service. Apartments vary in cost, from $30 to $60 d per night, $350–550 per month, depending on location, size, and amenities.

On the west edge of downtown, about 10 blocks due west of the *zócalo,* stands **Casa Colonial,** at Calle Miguel Negrete 105, tel./fax 9/516-5280. Personable owners Jane and Thornton Robisson, who seems to know everyone in town, call their domain the "posada with no sign," because they don't advertise and only accept guests with reservations. Upon arrival, you immediately see why Casa Colonial is such a favorite among savvy visitors. Low-rise rooms and apartments enfold a spacious, gracefully lovely inner garden. Rooms vary from high-ceilinged antique-decorated Victorians to smaller, one-person garden-side units. Besides the leisurely tropical ambience, guests enjoy the use of a spacious, refined but homey living room with a fine library and Internet connection. Room prices vary according to size and elegance from $50 s to about $95 d. Negotiate for a long-term discount. In the United States and Canada, reserve through the toll-free tel. 800/758-1697, or email: karensue@cdsnet.net. You can also reserve through Casa Colonial directly by the above tel./fax

or by emailing colonial@antequera.com. For more information, visit the website: www.mex online.com/colonial.htm.

TRAILER PARKS AND CAMPING

Oaxaca has two trailer-camping parks. First choice goes to the somewhat run-down **Oaxaca Trailer Park,** at the far northeast side of town, 900 Av. Violetas, Oaxaca, Oaxaca 68000, tel. 9/515-2796. The 100 all-hookup spaces include showers, toilets, coin laundry, recreation hall, a fence, and a night watchman. Spaces rent for about $10 per night for hookups with enough power to run light appliances but insufficient for air-conditioning, and $22 for hookups with enough power to run air conditioning; discounts for extended stays. Pets OK. Get there by turning left at Violetas, marked by the big green "Colonia Reforma" sign over the highway, several blocks east of the first-class bus terminal on Hwy. 190. Continue uphill six long blocks to the trailer park on the left.

Second choice goes to a **new trailer park** atop a panoramic valley-view knoll in foothill village San Felipe del Agua village, about three miles (five km) north of downtown. Here the American expatriate owner offers all hookups in a large country lot with lots of room for big rigs and tent space. A small clubhouse with kitchenette, shower, and toilet is also available for resident use. He asks about $5 per party for camping, $10 for RVs, including water, electricity, and drainage. For more information and reservations, write P.O. Box 252, Oaxaca, Oaxaca 68000, or call Bea Baker, tel. 9/515-6867, or 9/520-0947, or email: french@antequera.com.

This spot appears ideal for hikers and backpackers, at the jumping-off point for hiking trails (Look at the map at the community park guard station a quarter mile uphill from the San Felipe bus turnaround; see the following paragraph), past waterfalls and meadows, en route to the summit of towering, pine-tufted Cerro San Felipe (elev. 10,300 feet, 3,140 meters). The trailer park manager, who also rents horses, might serve as your guide; figure on paying him about $30 for a day's outing.

Get there by bus, taxi or car to San Felipe

del Agua village. By bus, ride "San Felipe"-marked Choferes del Sur bus from the corner of Independencia and Reforma, two blocks east of the Zócalo, thence following Pino Suárez uphill, past El Llano park. Get off at the San Felipe del Agua village plaza (see the old church on the right) and follow drivers' directions below. (Note: The end- of-the-line bus turnaround is a few blocks farther uphill from the village plaza. From there you can hike a quarter mile to the **Parque Comunal San Felipe** guard station and trailhead.)

For drivers, the jumping-off point for San Felipe del Agua is Av. Netzahualcoyotl (nay-tzah-oo-wahl-coh-YOH-tuhl), which heads uphill at the big green "San Felipe" sign from its intersection with Hwy. 190 (Av. Niños Héroes), one block east of the Pemex station. Continue uphill about two-thirds of a mile (one km), bear left at the hotel sign, then right one block and left one long block, and right again. You'll be on your way, heading uphill along Calzada San Felipe, which parallels the old stone aqueduct (on your left). In a few miles the road becomes San Felipe village's Calle Hidalgo. Just before the

San Felipe plaza, at the restaurant on the right, turn left (west) on to Calle Iturbide, then right again at the first street, Morelos, then another quick left on to the "Prolongation of Iturbide." After another long block or two downhill, at the arroyo bottom, turn right on to Chigolera; continue, winding uphill .4 mile (.6 km) to the trailer park sign and gate on left.

On the way into town from the north, RVers might check to see if the old **Rosa Isabel Trailer Park** has re-opened. At this writing, it looked abandoned. (Look along the right side of Hwy. 190, heading southeast into town, about a half mile past the big Hotel Villas Del Sol sign.) If it's functioning, it may be as I previously described in the first edition of this book: (. . . at Km 539, Carretera Nacional, Colonia Loma del Pueblo, Oaxaca, Oaxaca 68000, tel. 9/512-7210 or 9/516-0770, on Hwy. 190, on the northwest, Mexico City, side of town in the Loma del Pueblo Nuevo suburb. It features hookups, toilets, showers, and a recreation hall, with the Brenamiel tennis and sports club nearby. The 50 spaces rent for about $10 a night, with discounts for extended stays.)

FOOD

SNACKS, FOOD STALLS, AND COFFEEHOUSES

During fiestas, snack stalls along Hidalgo at the cathedral-front Alameda de León square abound in local delicacies. Choices include *tlayudas,* giant crisp tortillas loaded with avocado, tomato, onions, and cheese, and *empanadas de amarillo,* huge tacos stuffed with cheese and red salsa. For dessert, have a *buñuelo,* a crunchy, honey-soaked wheat tortilla.

At nonfiesta times, you can still fill up on the sizzling fare of taco, *torta,* hamburger, and hot dogs (eat 'em only when they are served hot) at stands that set up in the same vicinity.

For very economical, wholesome local fare, go to the acre of food stalls inside the **Mercado 20 de Noviembre,** two blocks south of the zócalo's southwest corner. Adventurous eaters will be in heaven among a wealth of succulent

chiles rellenos; piquant *moles* (moh-LAYS); fat, banana-leaf-wrapped *tamales Oaxaqueños;* and savory *sopas* and *guisados* (soups and stews). Insist, however, that your selection is served hot.

The airy, tranquil interior patio of **Hostería Alcalá** at Alcalá 307, open daily 8:30 A.M.–11 P.M., is ideal for a relaxing refreshment or lunch break from sightseeing along Alcalá mall.

For coffee and dessert, you have a number of additional downtown choices, notably **Coffee Beans,** at Cinco de Mayo 400, five blocks north of the *zócalo;* or nearby **Restaurant La Antigua,** a block east at Reforma 401, just uphill from Abasolo; or mini-café **La Brew,** two long blocks west at Alcalá 409, open Mon.–Sat. 8 A.M.–8 P.M., Sun. 8 A.M.–2 P.M., owned and operated by friendly local guide Susan McGlynn.

For baked goods by themselves, a trio of good carryout bakeries stand within a stone's throw of the *zócalo.* First, try the sweet offerings of **Tartamiel Pastelería Frances** on Trujano, half a block west from the Del Jardín café *zócalo* corner; open Mon.–Sat. 7 A.M.–8 P.M., Sun. 11:30 A.M.–7 P.M. Continue clockwise, north of the *zócalo* a block, to **Panadería Bamby,** at the northwest corner of G. Vigil and Morelos; open Mon.–Sat. 6 A.M.-9, P.M. Finally, stop by the **Pastelería La Vasconia,** a block east of the *zócalo,* at Independencia 907, between Cinco de Mayo and Reforma; open daily 7 A.M.–9 P.M.

CAFÉS AND RESTAURANTS

Around the*Zócalo*

Oaxaca visitors enjoy many good eateries right on or near the *zócalo.* In fact, you could spend your entire Oaxaca time enjoying the fare of the several *zócalo*-front sidewalk cafés. Of the seven cafés, five offer recommendable food and service. Moving counterclockwise from the northwest corner, they are Primavera, La Cafetería, Del Jardín, Terranova, and Amarantos. First place overall goes to the pricier upper-class **Terranova,** at the southeast corner, for its professionally prepared and served lunch and dinner entrées. For the best breakfasts, however, go to **Primavera,** at the diagonally opposite corner. **La Cafetería** and **Del Jardín** (with loud marimba music most nights) rate generally good for food (notably Del Jardín's tummy-warming apple strudel), but their service can be spotty. While service at **Amarantos** is usually good, its food is only fair. They all are open long hours, about 8 A.M.–midnight, and serve from very recognizable menus.

The one drawback of *zócalo*-level eating is the persistent flow of vendors, which can be unnerving. If, however, you refuse (or bargain for) their offerings gently and with humor, you might begin to accept and enjoy them as part of the entire colorful scene. (If they really get to you, best take an inside table or retreat to the one restaurant that shoos them away, the Terranova.)

Serious-eating longtimers return to **El Asador Vasco** restaurant, tel. 9/514-4755, on the second-floor balcony above the Restaurant Jardín, Portal Flores 10A. The menu specializes in hearty Basque-style country cooking: salty,

Certain Oaxacan delicacies may not appeal to everyone. Shown here: chapulines *(grasshoppers)*

spicy, and served in the decor of a medieval Iberian manor house. Favorites include fondues (bean, sausage, and mushroom), garlic soup, salads, veal tongue, oysters in hot sauce, and the *carnes asadas* (roast meats) house specialties. Open daily 1–11 P.M. Expensive; expect to pay about $20 per person.

Longtimers swear by the Oaxacan specialties at **Casa de la Abuela,** at the *zócalo*'s northwest corner, above the Primavera café. Here you can enjoy tasty, professionally prepared regional dishes and airy *zócalo* vistas from the balcony. Open daily 9 A.M.–9 P.M. Call 9/516-3544 for reservations and a good view table. Moderate.

For a tasty regional-style meal or snack, try **La Casita** around the corner, upstairs, on Hidalgo, at the plaza Alameda de León, Hidalgo 612, tel. 9/516-2917. You can order either a hearty *comida corrida* multicourse lunch or one of the tasty "mystery" offerings, such as tortilla, "cat," or "nothing" soup. Open daily 11 A.M.–7:30 P.M. Moderate.

A OAXACAN MENU

Oaxacan food adds another layer to the already rich Mexican food tradition. Oaxacan menus start off with appetizers, such as *quesillo a la plancha,* Oaxaca's famous white cheese, served melted, with guacamole and black beans. An appetizer list wouldn't be truly Oaxacan without *chapulines,* small grasshoppers grilled with minced onion in oil until crunchy.

Next come the Oaxacan *sopas* (soups), such as *sopa de guias,* a delicious stewed medley of squash flowers, tender baby squash, small corn dumplings, corn, and tender vine shoots. Other typically served soups include *caldillo de nopales,* a broth of fleshy cactus leaves, often cooked with bits of pork, chicken, or small shrimps, and *sopa de frijoles,* black bean soup, with cheese chunks and tortilla chips.

Main courses must include *moles* (MOH-lays), the most Oaxacan of all dishes. Very typical is *mole negro* (black mole), a spicy-sweet mixture of chocolate, chilies, garlic, peanuts, and a score of spices and other flavorings, cooked to a sauce, then baked with chicken or turkey. The turkey variation, called *mole de pavo,* is so *típica* that it's widely regarded as the national dish.

The mole list goes on, through *mole amarillo* (yellow mole) to *mole colorado* (red mole), a sauce of chilies, sesame seeds, almonds, raisins, bananas, tomatoes, and spices, served over chicken with rice seasoned with *chepil,* a wild local herb.

Oaxacan main-dish sauces are not necessarily chili based. Some menus feature fruit- and nut-based sauces, such as *almendrado,* an almond sauce spiced with tomatoes, green olives, and herbs and served over chicken.

Oaxacans also enjoy local variations on the usual Mexican *antojitos,* such as *chiles rellenos de picadillo.* Here the cook replaces the usual *chiles rellenos* cheese stuffing with minced, spiced pork, beef, or chicken and serves them with guacamole, grilled onion, and refried black beans.

Menu meat selections often include *cecina* (say-SEE-nah), thin slices of spicy cured pork, frequently served with bean sauce and cheese, or *tasajo,* thinly sliced grilled beef, often dished up with *chilaquiles* (tortillas cooked in chili-tomato sauce).

Finally, top off your meal with a local dessert, such as flan (egg custard), and a drink, such as *té de poleo,* a tea brewed from *poleo,* a local, mint-like herb, or *café de la olla,* a rich regional coffee sweetened with *panela,* the dark brown sugar that market vendors sell by the chunk.

For many loyal local upper-class patrons, **Restaurant Catedral,** two blocks north of the *zócalo,* at Garcia Vigil 105, corner of Morelos, tel. 9/516-3285, serves as a tranquil refuge from the street hubbub. The refined ambience—music playing softly in the background, tables set around an airy, intimate fountain patio crowned by the blue Oaxaca sky above—is half the show. The finale is the very correct service and quality food for breakfast, lunch, or supper. The Aguilar family owners are especially proud of their *moles* (MOH-lays), sauces that flavor their house specialties. These include fillets, both meat and fish, and regional dishes such as banana-leaf-wrapped *tamales Oaxaqueños.* It's open daily 8 A.M.–midnight. Moderate-expensive.

Back on Hidalgo, just past the *zócalo's* northeast corner, the spotless little *fonda* **El Mesón** specializes in a lunch buffet, at Hidalgo 805, tel. 9/516-2729. For about $3, you can select your fill of fresh fruit, salads, chili beans, and several entrées, including roast beef and pork, chicken, *moles,* tacos, tamales, and enchiladas. Open daily 8 A.M.–11:30 P.M. Budget.

More good eating, in a genteel but relaxed atmosphere, awaits you at the very popular **Restaurant El Sagrario,** around the corner behind the church at 120 Valdivieso, tel. 9/514-8059. Mostly local, youngish upper-class customers enjoy either a club/bar atmosphere (lower level), pizza parlor booths (middle level), or restaurant tables (upper level). At the restaurant level during the evening, you can best take in the whole scene around you—chattering, upbeat crowd, live guitar, flute, or jazz melodies, elegantly restored colonial details. Then, finally, comes the food, beginning, perhaps, with an appetizer, continuing with a soup or salad, then an international or regional specialty, which you top off with a light dessert and a savory espresso coffee. Open daily 8 A.M.–midnight. Music volume goes up later in the evening. Credit cards accepted. Moderate-expensive.

On the other hand, a legion of American, Canadian, and European budget travelers swear by the no-nonsense **Restaurant Quickly,** half a block farther from the *zócalo,* at 100 Alcalá, tel. 9/514-7076, on the Alcalá pedestrian mall. Once you taste the giant hamburgers, chocolate milkshakes, or pancakes (or veggies, if you prefer), you'll understand why. Open daily 8 A.M.–11 P.M. Budget.

North of the *Zócalo*

Devotees of light, vegetarian-style cuisine get what they're hungering for at **La Manantial Vegetariana,** at Tinoco y Palacios 303 (west side of street, just above Matamoros, two blocks west and three blocks north of the *zócalo).* The tranquil patio ambience sets the tone for the specialty, a set lunch *comida.* Typically they might offer soup (onion or cream of zucchini), salad (mixed greens or tomato cucumber), stew (mushroom or soya steak), bread, fruit drink, dessert and coffee or tea. About $4 until 7 P.M., $5 after that. (When they have no customers, the employees are in the habit of playing the radio loudly. However, if you ask, they'll gladly turn it off.) Open daily 9 A.M.–9:30 P.M.

Although **Restaurant La Muralla** (The Wall), tel. 9/516-2268, is a seven-block walk or taxi ride (four north, three west) from the *zócalo* to the corner of N. Bravo and Crespo, your effort will be amply rewarded. Enter the door and immediately it appears as if you've been transported to a foreign realm, perhaps somewhere in the country outside Xian or Guangzhou. Besides the standard but tastily prepared dishes (such as wonton soup, chicken chow mein, barbecued spareribs), you will be entertained by the occupants of a big, midroom tropical aquarium. Open daily 1–8 P.M.; Visa accepted. Moderate.

On the other hand, for a taste of Mexican nouveau cuisine, head for **El Laurel,** the handiwork of husband-wife owners George and Lina, so popular that they stay open only Mon.–Sat. 1:30–6 P.M. You can select from a short menu of lovingly prepared and presented appetizers, soups, salads, pastas, and meats. They're at the back of the quiet courtyard at 210 Bravo, between P. Díaz and G. Vigil, four blocks north of the *zócalo.* Moderate-expensive.

Now, moving east across town, you'll find several more good examples of the growing collection of Oaxaca's fine restaurants. Perhaps the classiest of them all is the elegantly upscale **El Che** where everything seems designed for perfection. In a luxuriously spacious and high-ceilinged dining room, tuxedoed waiters scurry with plates of delicacies, replacing your embroidered white tablecloth with another halfway through dinner, while light classical music plays in the background. The continental-style specialties—Roquefort salad, French onion soup, fillet with mushrooms and cannelloni, fine wine list—please the palates of their well-to-do clientele. Find them at 5 de Mayo 413, on the corner across the street from the south side of Santo Domingo church, open daily, about 1–11 P.M. Reservations, tel. 9/514-2122, fax 9/514-2211, are necessary. Expensive; figure a minimum of $30 per person, including wine.

Nearby and equally palate pleasing is the popular haven **Pizza Nostrana Spaghettería,** whose friendly Napoli-born owner makes certain of the correctness of her cuisine. How she manages to assemble a proper meal of, say, *prosciutto e melone, pasta boscaida al dente, zucchine dorate,* and *flan napolitane* in this corner of Mexico is a secret that I'm pleased to leave with her. Top it all with a good bottle of old-country *chianti* and a request that they play Luciano for you. She's open daily 1–11 P.M., corner of G. Vigil and and Allende, tel. 9/514-0778. Moderate.

Four blocks farther east, at Reforma 402, above Constitución, **Café La Olla** (front of Casa Bugambilias bed-and-breakfast) enjoys a loyal following of longtime North American expatriates. Here, the dark-beamed ceiling, subdued spotlighting of the art-decorated walls, quiet music, and candlelight set the refined, romantic tone. Select from a long but light menu of skillfully prepared and presented soups (Aztec soup is nearly a meal in itself), salads, Oaxacan specialties, and meats. La Olla's main drawback is street noise, which you can minimize by taking an upstairs table. Open daily except Sun., 8 A.M.–11 P.M., tel. 9/516-6668.

Right across the street, at Reforma 401, a long list of loyal patrons enjoy **Café La Antigua** for entirely different reasons. Here the main course is conversation and fine on-site roasted

"Pluma" (from the mountains above Puerto Escondido) Oaxaca coffee. Along with their savory lattes, cold cappuccinos, and mocha frappés, patrons can enjoy fresh baked goods, crepes, sandwiches, eggs, and juices. The prime mover behind all this is friendly coffee grower and owner Diego Woolrich Ramírez, who keeps La Antigua open Mon.–Sat. 9 A.M.–10 P.M., tel. 9/516-5761. Moderate.

Continue east two blocks and north two more, to the relaxing garden of **Mariscos Jorge,** standout standby of local middle and upper class patrons. Choose from a long menu of seafood (14 cocktail selections, including, shrimp, squid, and clam) salads, soups, and entrées including fish fillets, from breaded and baked to *a la diabla,* octopus, and much more. Also pleasant for breakfast. Open daily 8 A.M.–6:30 P.M., tel. 9/513-4308, on Pino Suárez, across from El Llano park. Moderate.

South of the *Zócalo*
Fewer good sit-down restaurants sprinkle the south *zócalo* neighborhoods. A trio of them, well known for Oaxacan cuisine, shouldn't be missed.

Local folks strongly recommend the no-nonsense country-style (but refined) **La Flor de Oaxaca,** at Armenta y López 311, a block east, half a block south from the *zócalo's* southeast corner, tel. 9/516-5522. Along with spotless linen and very correct service, you'll get the customary bottomless plate of warm corn tortillas to go with your entrée. The *mole*-smothered regional specialties come mostly in four styles, *con tasajo* (with a thin broiled steak), *con pollo* (chicken), *con cesina* (roast pork), or *sola* (without meat). Besides those, you can choose from an extensive menu of

equally flavorful items such as *tamales Oaxaqueños* (wrapped in banana leaves), pork chops, several soups, spaghetti, and much more. Vegetable lovers get started off right with their crisp *ensalada mixta* (sliced tomato, cucumber, onions, avocado, and lettuce with vinegar and oil dressing). Open Mon.–Sat. 7:30 A.M.–10 P.M., Sun.7:30 A.M.–3 P.M. Credit cards accepted. Moderate.

If, however, you hanker for some nouveau variations on the Oaxaca regional theme, head to **Restaurant El Naranjo** (The Orange Tree), at Trujano 203, two blocks west of the *zócalo's* southwest corner. Here the quiet, genteel patio atmosphere sets the tone, and the long, inviting menu tempts the palate. Choose among soups, salads, and Oaxaca's seven *moles,* one for each day of the week. Use them to flavor any one of a host of stuffed chilies, tamales, stewed chicken, roast pork, and much, much more. Open Mon.–Sat. 9 A.M.–9 P.M., tel. 9/514-1878. Moderate. (If you want to learn more, ask friendly owner Iliana de la Vega about her exceptional hands-on cooking classes.)

For yet another treat, try **Restaurant Los Angeles** in the Hotel Parador San Agustín, at Armenta y López 215, tel. 9/516-2022, one block east and half a block south of the *zócalo's* southeast corner. Here again the specialty is nouveau food with a Oaxacan twist. If possible, arrive with a party of three or four so you can taste as many of their delicacies as possible: squash flower stuffed with cheese with mild chili sauce; lettuce festival salad with white cheese, red bell pepper, avocado, and sesame; cream of broccoli soup; and fetuccine with spinach and cheese sauce with ham. Open daily 7 A.M.–11 P.M. Moderate to expensive.

ENTERTAINMENT AND EVENTS

Around the Zócalo

The Oaxaca *zócalo,* years ago relieved of traffic, is ideal ground for spontaneous diversions. A concert or performance seems to be going on nearly every evening. When one isn't, you can run like a kid over the plaza, bouncing a 10-foot-long *aeroglobo* into the air. (Get them from vendors in front of the cathedral.) If you're in a sitting mood, watch the world go by from a *zócalo* sidewalk café. Later, take in the folk dance performance at the Hotel Monte Albán on the adjacent Plaza Alameda de León, nightly 8:30–10 P.M., for about $3. After that, return to a *zócalo* café and enjoy the musicians who entertain most every evening until midnight.

Fiestas

There seems to be a festival somewhere in the Valley of Oaxaca every week of the year. Oaxaca's wide ethnic diversity explains much of the celebrating. Each of the groups celebrates its own traditions. Sixteen languages, in hundreds of dialects, are spoken within the state. Authorities recognize around 500 distinct regional costumes.

All of this ethnic ferment focuses in the city during the July **Lunes del Cerro** festival. Known in pre-Hispanic times as the Guelaguetza (gay-lah-GAY-tzah) (Offering), tribes reunited for rituals and dancing in honor of Centeotl, the god of corn. The ceremonies, which climaxed with the sacrifice of a virgin who had been fed hallucinogenic mushrooms, were changed to tamer mixed Christian-native rites by the Catholic Church. Lilies replaced marigolds, the flower of death, and saints sat in for the Indian gods.

For the weeks around the two Mondays following 16 July, the **Virgin of Carmen** day, Oaxaca is awash with native Mexicans in costume from all seven traditional regions of Oaxaca. The festivities, which include a crafts and agricultural fair, climax with dances and ceremonies at the Guelaguetza auditorium on the Cerro del Fortín hill northwest of the city. Entrance to the Guelaguetza dances runs about $30; bring a hat and sunglasses. Make hotel reservations months ahead of time. For more information, contact the local tourist information office, at the north edge of the *zócalo,* corner of Independencia and Garcia Vigil, tel. 9/516-4828, fax 516-0984, email: turinfo@oaxaca.gob.mx.

Note: If the first Monday after 16 July happens to fall on 18 July, the anniversary of Benito Juárez's death, the first Lunes del Cerro shifts to the next succeeding Monday, 25 July.

On the Sunday before the first Lunes del Cerro, Oaxacans celebrate their history and culture at the Plaza de Danzas adjacent to the Virgen de la Soledad church. Events include a big sound, light, and dance show and depictions in tableaux of the four periods of Oaxaca history.

Besides the usual national holidays, Oaxacans celebrate a number of other locally important

The July "Mondays on the Hill" dance performances, also known as the Guelaguetza, are a must-see Oaxacan event.

fiestas. The first day of spring, 21 March, kicks off the **Juegos Florales** (Flower Games). Festivities go on for 10 days, including crowning of a festival queen at the Teatro de Alcalá, poetry contests, and performances by renowned artists and the National Symphony.

On the second Monday in October, residents of Santa María del Tule venerate their ancient tree in the **Lunes del Tule** festival. Locals in costume celebrate with rites, folk dances, and feats of horsemanship beneath the boughs of their beloved great cypress.

Oaxacans venerate their patron, the Virgin of Solitude, 16–18 December. Festivities, which center on the Virgin's basilica (on Independencia six blocks west of the *zócalo*), include fireworks, dancing, food, and street processions of the faithful bearing the Virgin's gold-crowned image decked out in her fine silks and satins.

For the **Fiesta de los Rábanos** ("Fiesta of the Radishes") on 23 December, celebrants fill the Oaxaca *zócalo*, admiring displays of plants, flowers, and figures crafted of large radishes. Ceremonies and prizes honor the most original designs. Food stalls nearby serve traditional delicacies, including *buñuelos* (honey-soaked fried tortillas), plates of which are traditionally thrown into the air before the evening is over.

Oaxaca people culminate their *posada* week on **Nochebuena** (Christmas Eve) with candle-lit processions from their parishes, accompanied by music, fireworks, and floats. They converge on the *zócalo* in time for a midnight cathedral mass.

Folkloric Dance Shows

If you miss the Lunes del Cerro festival, some towns and villages stage smaller Guelaguetza celebrations year-round. So do a number of hotels, the most reliable of which occurs nightly at 8:30 P.M. at the Hotel Monte Albán, on Plaza Alameda de León, tel. 9/516-2777, adjacent to the *zócalo*. At other hotels, days may change, so call ahead to confirm: Hotel Camino Real, tel. 9/516-0611, Friday, $30 show with dinner, not

including drinks; Restaurant Casa de Cantera, Murguia 102, at 8:30 P.M., $8 per person, varied schedule, tel. 9/518-0666, 9/514-4603, or 9/514-7585.

Films, Theater, Music, Dance, and Art Exhibits

Many Oaxaca institutions, such as the **Museo de Arte Contemporaneo de Oaxaca**, the **Teatro Macedonio Alcalá**, the **Instituto de Artes Graficos de Oaxaca**, the **Cinema El Pochote** and others sponsor many first-rate cultural events. See the excellent monthly calendars of events in the English-language newspapers *Oaxaca Times* and *Oaxaca* for details.

Nightlife

When lacking an official fiesta, you can create your own at a number of nightspots around town.

The big hotels are reliable for live dance music and discotheques. Call to confirm programs: Camino Real, tel. 9/516-0611; San Felipe, tel. 9/513-5050; Fortín Plaza, tel. 9/515-0100; and the Victoria, tel. 9/515-2633.

Besides many of the sidewalk cafés around the *zócalo*, a number of restaurants also offer live music seasonally. Try the El Sagrario, tel. 9/514-0302, on Valdivieso behind the cathedral, evenings beginning about 9 P.M., and the Hotel Marques del Valle restaurant on the *zócalo*, tel. 9/516-3474.

Perhaps the most popular in-town nightspot is **Candela**, at Murguia 413, corner of Pino Suárez, tel. 9/514-2010, which jumps with hot salsa and African-Latin rhythms nightly from about 10 P.M. (Women, be aware that a well-known cadre of local Romeos regularly frequents this and other such downtown spots.)

A pair of other music spots you might try are in the vicinity of Santo Domingo church: **Rincón Santo Domingo**, restaurant bar, at Cinco de Mayo 411, Mexican food, live romantic music, open 8 P.M.–2 A.M. and about the same at **Cafe La Antequera**, at Reforma 401, back side of the Santo Domingo church compound.

SPORTS AND RECREATION

Jogging, Walks, and Horseback Riding

For jogging, try the public **Ciudad Deportiva** (Sports City) fields on the west side of Hwy. 190 about two miles north of the town center. Closer in, you might also jog around the big **Juárez Park** (El Llano), on Av. Juárez, three blocks east and about ten blocks north of the *zócalo.*

For an invigorating in-town walk, climb the **Cerro del Fortín** hill. Your reward will be a breezy city, valley, and mountain view. The key to getting there through the maze of city streets is to head to the **Escalera del Fortín** (staircase), which will lead you conveniently to the instep of the hill. For example, from the northeast *zócalo* corner walk north along the Alcalá mall. After five blocks, in front of the Santo Domingo church turn left onto Allende, continue four blocks to Crespo, and turn right. After three blocks, you'll see the staircase on the left. Continue uphill, past the Guelaguetza open-air auditorium, to the road (Nicolas Copernicus) heading north to the **Planetarium.** After that, enjoying the panorama, you can keep walking along the hilltop for at least another mile. Take a hat and water. The round-trip from the *zócalo* is a minimum of two miles; the hilltop rises only a few hundred feet. Allow at least a couple of hours.

Sierra Madre Horse Trails offers horseback tours (around $11/hour) in the wooded, panoramic-view foothills above San Felipe del Agua village north of town. For more information and reservations (at least one day in advance), call tel. 9/520-0947 or 9/515-6864, email: french@antequera.com.

Swimming, Tennis, and Sporting Goods

Swimmers do their thing at multi-pool **Balneario La Bamba,** tel. 9/514-0925, about 2.5 miles (four km) south of town along Hwy. 175 before the airport, on the left side, just past the big green "Experimental" sign over the highway. The pools are open daily except Mon. 10 A.M.–5 P.M.; entrance is about $3 for adults, kids $2. Serious lap swimmers should choose days and hours in order to avoid crowds, Sunday afternoon being the most crowded.

For tennis, stay at either the **Hotel Victoria** or the **Misión de los Angeles,** which have courts. Otherwise, call the **Club de Tenis Brenamiel,** next to the Hotel Villas del Sol, Km 539.5 on Hwy. 190, about three miles north of the center of town, tel. 9/512-6822, and reserve a court; about $6 an hour.

A good sporting goods and clothing selection is available at **Deportes Ziga,** on the southwest corner of Alcalá and Matamoros, next to La Mano Mágico handicrafts shop. Open Mon.–Sat. 9 A.M.–3 P.M. and 4–9 P.M..

SHOPPING

The city of Oaxaca is renowned as a handicraft shopper's paradise. Prices are moderate, quality is high, and sources—in both large traditional markets and many dozens of private stores and galleries—are manifold. In the city, however, vendors do not ordinarily make the merchandise they sell. They buy wholesale from family shops in town, the surrounding valley, and remote localities all over the state of Oaxaca and Mexico in general. If your time is severely limited, best buy from the good in-town sources, many of which are listed below.

If, on the other hand, you have the time to benefit (both because of lower prices and person-to-person contact with the artisans) by going to the villages, consult the Valley of Oaxaca chapter for sources of local village handicrafts.

Traditional Markets

The original town market, **Mercado Juárez,** covers the entire square block just one block south and one block west of the *zócalo.* Many dozens of stalls offer everything; cotton and wool items—such as dresses, *huipiles,* woven blankets, and serapes—are among the best buys. Despite the overwhelming festoons of merchandise, bargains are there for those willing to search them out.

Before diving into the Juárez market's cavernous interior, first orient yourself by looking over the lineup of stalls on the market's west side, along the block of 20 de Noviembre, between Las Casas and Trujano. Here, you'll be able to select from a reasonably priced representative assortment—black and green pottery, tinware, *huipiles,* leather goods, *alebrijes* (fanciful wooden animals), pewter, cutlery, filigree jewelry—of much that Oaxaca offers.

After your Juárez market tour, walk a block west, to J.P. Garcia, and three and a half blocks south, between Mina and Zaragoza, for a look inside the **Mercado de Artesanías** handicrafts market. Here, you'll find more of the same—a ton of textiles—*huipiles, camisas* (shirts), *blusas* (blouses), and *tapetes* (carpets)—plus *alfarería* (pottery), *alebrijes,* and some for-tourist masks.

Private Handicrafts Shops

Although pricier, the private shops generally offer the choicest merchandise. Here you can select from the very best: *huipiles* from San Pedro de Amusgos and Yalalag, richly embroidered "wedding" dresses from San Antonino Castillo Velasco, rugs and hangings from Teotitlán del Valle; pottery—black from San Bártolo Coyotepec and green from Atzompa; carved *alebrijes* animals from Arrazola; whimsical figurines by the Aguilar sisters of Ocotlán; mescal from Tlacolula; and masks from Huazolotitlán.

Most of the best individual shops lie scattered along three streets—5 de Mayo, Macedonio Alcalá, and Garcia Vigil, which run uphill, north of the *zócalo.*

A good place to get prices and selection in perspective is the crafts shop in the federal tourist information center, at 607 Independencia, off the *zócalo,* diagonally north of the cathedral. It's open Mon.–Fri. 8 A.M.–3 P.M. and 5–8 P.M., Sat. 8 A.M.–3 P.M.

Next, head north along the Alcalá mall; two blocks north of Independencia, you'll arrive at a Oaxaca favorite, the **Palacio de las Gemas,** corner of Morelos and Alcalá, tel. 9/514-4603. Although specializing in semiprecious stones and jewelry, it has much more, including a host of charming hand-painted tinware Christmas

Support local endeavors by shopping at the Mujeres Artesanías de las Regiones de Oaxaca (MARO) store. In this unique place, craftswomen demonstrate their skills and sell their quality handicrafts.

decorations, Guerrero masks, and pre-Columbian reproductions in onyx and turquoise. Open Mon.–Sat. 10 A.M.–2 P.M. and 4–8:30 P.M.

Head a block east to Cinco de Mayo, turn left (north) half a block to the big house on the right, no. 204, headquarters of MARO, **Mujeres Artesanías de las Regiones de Oaxaca.** (Craftswomen of the Regions of Oaxaca). Here a remarkable all-Oaxaca grass-roots movement of women artisans has gotten the government to stake them to a building, where they sell their goods and demonstrate their manufacturing techniques. The artisans are virtually pure native Mexicans from all parts of Oaxaca, and their offerings reflect their unique effort. Hosts of gorgeous handicrafts—wooden masks, toys, carvings; cotton *traje* native clothing, such as *huipiles, pozahuancos, quechquémitles;* wool serapes, rugs, and hangings; woven palm hats, mats, and baskets; fine steel knives, swords, and machetes; tinplate mirrors, candlesticks, and ornaments; leather saddles, briefcases, wallets, and belts—fill the shelves of several rooms. It's open daily 9 A.M.–2 P.M. and 4–8 P.M., at 204 Cinco de Mayo, Oaxaca, Oaxaca 68000, tel./fax 9/516-0670. Don't miss it; better still, do a major part of your Oaxaca shopping at this store.

Return a block west along Murguia back to Alcalá and step into **La Mano Mágico** on the west side, just below the corner of Murguia, at Alcalá 203, tel./fax 9/516-4275. The shop offers both a colorful exposition of crafts from all over Mexico and a patio workshop, where artisans work, dyeing wool and weaving examples of the lovely, museum-quality rugs and serapes that adorn the walls. Open Mon.–Sat. 10 A.M.–2:30 P.M. and 3:30–6 P.M.

Continue uphill on Alcalá, a block farther north, to the **Plaza Alcalá** complex, southwest corner of N. Bravo, which has both a tranquil courtyard restaurant and some good shops. Outstanding among them is the excellent **Libros Amate** bookstore on the on the lower level. Its extensive and expertly selected offering of English-language books about Mexico includes guides, literature, ethnography, archaeology, history, cookbooks, maps, postcards, and much more. Upstairs, Libros Amate's brother shop, **Corazón del Pueblo,** (Heart of the People) accomplishes the same with a fine, eclectic collection of Mexican handicrafts. Located at Alcalá 307, tel. 9/516-6960; open Mon.–Sat. 10:30 A.M.–2:30 P.M. and 3:30–7:30 P.M.

Half a block farther uphill, be sure to look inside **Oro de Monte Albán** jewelry store at Alcalá 403, just downhill from the Santo Domingo church front. This extraordinary family-run enterprise carries on Oaxaca's venerable goldsmithing tradition as the sole licensed manufacturer of replicas from the renowned treasure of Monte Albán tomb 7. Besides the luscious, museum-quality reproductions, Oro de Monte Albán offers a fine assortment of in-house silver and gold earrings, charm bracelets, necklaces, brooches, and much more. Open Mon.–Sat. 10 A.M.–8 P.M., Sun. noon–8 P.M., tel. 9/514-3183. You may also examine their handiwork at their companion store, part of the shop in the Santo Domingo museum across the street and uphill half a block.

Continue up Alcalá past venerable Santo Domingo church on the right and soon turn left at Carmen church and stroll a block along the street plaza, **Plazuela del Carmen.** There you can appreciate the offerings of the many local vendors, often including Zapotec and Trique women in traditional dress, weaving on their backstrap looms.

Rewards await shoppers who are willing to walk a few long blocks farther uphill, to the state-run **ARIPO** (Artesanías y Industrias Populares de Oaxaca) at 809 Garcia Vigil, tel. 9/514-4030 or 9/514-0861. You can pick from a broad, authentic, and very traditional selection of masks, *huipiles,* wedding dresses, carved animals, ceramics, tinware, and much more. Prices vary: cheap on some items and high on others. Open Mon.–Sat. 9 A.M.–7 P.M.

Fine Arts Galleries

The tourist boom has stimulated a Oaxaca fine arts revival. Several downtown galleries bloom with the sculpture and paintings of masters, such as Rufino Tamayo, Rudolfo Morales, Francisco Toledo and a host of up-and-coming local artists. Besides La Mano Mágico, listed above, a number of galleries stand out. Foremost among them is **Arte de Oaxaca,** the gallery of the Rudolfo Morales Foundation (see the Ocotlán section, in the Valley of Oaxaca chapter), at Murguia 105, between Alcalá and 5 de Mayo, open Mon.–Sat. 10 A.M.–2 P.M. and 4–8 P.M., tel. 9/514-2324 or 9/514-0910.

Also outstanding is **Galería Quetzalli,** local outlet for celebrated artist Francisco Toledo, opposite the south wall-flank of Santo Domingo church, at Constitución 104, between Reforma and 5 de Mayo, open Mon.–Sat. 10 A.M.–2 P.M. and 5–8 P.M., tel. 9/514-2606, fax 9/514-0737. Also well worth visiting is **Galeria Arte Mexicano** in the Santo Domingo shopping complex, southwest corner of Alcalá and Allende, across Alcalá from the Santo Domingo church. It's open Mon.–Sat. 10 A.M.–2 P.M. and 4–8 P.M., tel. 9/514-3815.

For something new and unusual, go to **Galería Indigo,** Allende 104, corner of Alcalá, across from Santo Domingo church. Inside, several spacious rooms contain dramatic displays of modern paintings and exquisite one-of-a-kind handicrafts, both traditional and innovative, from Mexico, Central America, and Asia. Check hours at tel./fax 9/514-3889, email: info@indigo.org.mx.

Completely different but just as interesting is

the long-time coin, antique and art store **Monedas y Antiguidades,** at Abasolo 107, between the upper end of Cinco de Mayo and Reforma. Browsers enjoy a potpourri of art, from kitsch to fine, plus a for-sale museum of dusty curious, from old silver coins and pioneer clothes irons to revolutionary photos and Porfirian-era tubas. Open Mon.–Sat. 10 A.M.–2 P.M. and 5–9 P.M., Sun. 12 noon–3 P.M., tel. 9/516-3935.

Cutlery and Metalwork Shops

Oaxaca is well known for its fine metal craft. A few families produce nearly everything, and at least three of them sell from their own shops. While in Mercado Juárez, stop by stall #5 to see the fine swords, knives, and scissors of Miguel Martínez and family, tel. 9/514-4868. Walk a few blocks west and south to see an even wider selection, plus artisans at work, at Guillermo Aragon's street-front shop at J.P. Garcia 503, open Mon.–Sat. 9 A.M.–2 P.M. and 4–8 P.M., tel. 9/626-58. Finally, to select from a charming host of old-fashioned molded and painted tin figures, from soldiers and airplanes to horses and hockey players, stop by the González family shop, at north-side Porfirio Díaz 503, #4, tel. 9/516-5432, fax 9/514-7052.

Groceries, Wine, and Natural Food

For fruits and vegetables, the cheapest and freshest are in the Juárez market, which takes up the square block immediately southwest of the *zócalo.*

For simpler, straightforward grocery shopping, stop by **Abarrotes Lonja** on the *zócalo* next to the Hotel Señorial; open daily 8 A.M.–9:30 P.M.

Lovers of fine wine needn't go without in Oaxaca any longer. Head for **La Esquina** wine and mescal shop, at the north end at Gómez Farías 212B, three blocks uphill, one block right, from the Santo Domingo church front. Find it open Mon.–Sat. 11 A.M.–3 P.M. and 5–9 P.M., tel. 9/515-2335.

Local natural food devotees get their heart's content of teas—arnica, anise, manzanilla—and ginseng, organic grains, granola, and soy burgers at **Tienda Naturista Trigo Verde,** two blocks west of the *zócalo,* at J.P. Garcia 207, open Mon.–Sat. 8:30 A.M.–9 P.M., Sun. 9 A.M.–6 P.M., tel. 9/516-2369.

Camera and Photo

Downtown has some good photo shops, most on 20 de Noviembre, a block west of the *zócalo.* Best of all is **Oaxakolor,** at 20 de Noviembre 108, tel. 9/516-3487, perhaps the best-stocked photo store in Oaxaca. It carries dozens of cameras—35 mm point-and-shoot, SLRs, professional medium format—as well as an abundance of film, including popular and professional color, slides, sheet, black and white, and a host of accessories. Open Mon.–Sat. 9 A.M.–9 P.M.

More ordinary, but still well stocked, is **Foto Figueroa** at Hidalgo 516, corner 20 de Noviembre, tel. 9/516-3766. With plenty of Kodak film and accessories, it offers quick develop-and-print service. Open Mon.–Sat. 9 A.M.–8:30 P.M.

Express Kolor, half a block farther down at 20 de Noviembre 225, tel. 9/516-1492, is better stocked, with scores of point-and-shoot cameras and many Minolta, Vivitar, and Olympus accessories. It also stocks Konica, Fuji, Kodak, and Agfa films in color and black and white, both roll and sheet. Open Mon.–Sat. 9 A.M.–8 P.M.

OTHER PRACTICALITIES

SERVICES

Money Exchange

Several banks, all with ATMs, dot the downtown area. (Note: Remove your ATM card promptly, for some local machines are known to "eat" them if left in more than about 15 seconds after the transaction is finished.) The most convenient (ATM only) is **Banamex** on one-block Valdivieso, behind the cathedral. A full-service branch serves customers just one block due east of the *zócalo,* at Hidalgo at Cinco de Mayo, tel. 9/516-5900, money exchange hours Mon.–Fri. 9 A.M.–4:30 P.M., Sat. 9 A.M.–2 P.M. If they're too crowded, go to **Banco Serfin** on the Independencia corner just north of the Cathedral, open Mon.–Fri. 9 A.M.–6 P.M., Sat. 10 A.M.–2 P.M.; U.S., Canadian, Japanese, and many European currencies and traveler's checks, tel. 9/516-1100; or Serfin's neighbor, **Banco Santander Mexicano** (Mon.–Fri. 9 A.M.–4 P.M., Sat. 10 A.M.–2 P.M.), just northwest of the cathedral, at Independencia 605, tel. 9/516-2526. Alternatively, try nearby **Bancomer** (Mon.–Fri. 8:30 A.M.–4 P.M., Sat.10 A.M.–2 P.M.), at Vigil and Morelos, a block north of the cathedral, tel. 9/512-9377.

After bank hours, go to **Casa de Cambio Internacional de Divisas,** tel. 9/516-33-99, on the Alcalá street mall just north of the *zócalo,* behind the cathedral. Although it may pay about a percent less than banks, it changes as many major currencies and traveler's checks. Open Mon.–Sat. 8:30 A.M.- 7:30 P.M., Sun. 9 A.M.–5 P.M.

Travel Agencies and Tour Services

The local **American Express** agency, Viajes Mexico Istmo y Caribe (MICSA) operates an efficient, full-service office nearby. It both sells and cashes American Express traveler's checks at the best rates in town. Located behind the cathedral, at Valdivieosio 2, tel. 9/516-2700 or 9/516-2919, fax 9/516-7475. Money service hours Mon.–Fri. 9 A.M.–2 P.M. and 4–6 P.M., Sat. 9 A.M.–1 P.M.

Although American Express does offer tours, it does not specialize in them. Among the several reliable travel agencies that do is **Oaxaca Tours,** at Alcalá 417 upstairs (four blocks uphill from the plaza), tel./fax 9/516-1005. Although Oaxaca Tours mostly arranges Oaxaca city and valley destinations, they can arrange farther-ranging excursions, through the Mixteca regions, the mountains north of Oaxaca, and the southern coast Huatulco-Puerto Escondido region.

Another reliable tour agent is longtime **Viajes Turisticos Mitla,** branch office at Hóstal Santa Rosa, Trujano 201 (a block west of the plaza's southwest corner), tel. 9/514-7800 or 9/514-7806. They offer tours, usually around the Valley of Oaxaca, including guide and transportation, for small or medium sized-groups. Their main office is at the Hotel Rivera del Ángel, at F.J. Mina 518 (two blocks south, three blocks west of the plaza), tel. 9/514-3152, fax 9/516-6175. They also provide economical bus-only tourist transportation to Oaxaca Valley sites. For more information and reservations, contact the bus departure ticket desk at the Hotel Rivera del Ángel, tel. 9/516-5357 and 9/514-3161.

More athletic travelers might enjoy the services of **Mountain Bike Tours** at J.P. Garcia 509, between Mina and Aldama, a few blocks west and south of the plaza, tel. 9/514-3144, which both rents bikes and conducts guided bike tours into the nearby countryside.

For even more extensive backcountry adventure bicycling, hiking, and camping in the mountains north of Oaxaca City (see the Northern Oaxaca chapter, first destination section), contact **Expediciones Sierra Norte,** at 406 Garcia Vigil, tel. 9/514-7775, fax 9/516-7745, email: sierranorte@oaxaca.com.

A Oaxaca regiment of private individual guides also offer tours. Among the most highly recommended is English-fluent **Juan Montes Lara,** backed up by his wife Karin Schutte. Besides cultural sensitivity and extensive local knowledge, they can also provide comfortable transportation in a GMC Suburban wagon.

Contact them at their home, at Prol. de ucaliptos 303, Colonia Reforma, Oaxaca, Oaxaca 68050, tel. 9/513-0126.

Former clients volunteer rave reviews of the tours given by American **Susan McGlynn,** who can be reached at tel. 9/518-7334, email: labrujita_oax@yahoo.com.

Another **Have Jeep Will Travel** guide service (which I haven't yet checked out) advertises back-road adventures, shopping trips, Valley of Oaxaca market-day trips, and more for four passengers. Call El Condor Jeep Service, tel. 9/516-2783; let ring eight times.

For more recommendations, go to the government tourist information office, north side of the *zócalo,* at Independencia 607, corner of G. Vigil, tel. 9/516-4828, email: turinfo@oaxaca.gob.mx.

More athletic travelers might enjoy the services of **Mountain Bike Tours** at J.P. Garcia 509, between Mina and Aldama, a few blocks west and north of the plaza, tel. 9/514-3144. Bike rentals and guided bike tours into the nearby countryside are offered.

Car Rentals
Car rentals offer another convenient road for exploring Oaxaca City and environs. Although town and valley roads present no unusual hazards, drive defensively, anticipate danger, and keep a light foot on the accelerator. Also be aware that road hazards—animals, people, potholes, barricades, rocks—are much more formidable at night.

To rent a car, all you need is a current driver's license and a credit card. However, car rentals, which by law must include adequate Mexican liability insurance, are expensive, running upward of $40 per day. Save *mucho dinero* by splitting the tariff with others.

Get your rental through either a travel agent or, before departure, through U.S. and Canadian toll-free numbers (see chart in the On the Road chapter), or in Oaxaca locally: **Budget,** tel. 9/515-0330; **Hertz,** tel. 9/516-2434, fax 9/516-0009; **Avis,** tel./fax 9/511-5736; and **Alamo,** tel./fax 9/514-8534.

Telephone, Post, and Internet
The Oaxaca *correo* (post office), tel. 9/516-2661, is across from the cathedral at the corner of the Alameda de León square and Independencia. Open Mon.–Fri. 8 A.M.–7 P.M., Sat. 9 A.M.–1 P.M.

Telecomunicaciones, tel. 9/516-4902, at the next corner of Independencia and 20 Noviembre, offers money orders, telephone, and public fax. Hours are Mon.–Fri. 9 A.M.–8 P.M. (money orders 9 A.M.–6 P.M.), Sat. 9 A.M.–4 P.M., Sun. 9 A.M.–2 P.M. (money orders 9 A.M.-noon).

For long-distance and local telephone service, buy a Ladatel phone card (widely available in stores; look for the yellow Ladatel sign) and use it in public street telephones. Lacking that, take advantage of the efficient **Computel** long-distance phone and public fax office on Independencia, across from the Plaza Alameda de León, tel. 9/514-8084, open 7 A.M.–10 P.M..

Answer your email at any one of a number of downtown spots. For example, try **Desvan,** on the *zócalo's* east side, open daily 9:30 A.M.–10 P.M.; or walk three blocks west to **Comunitel,** at 20 de Noviembre 208, open daily 7 A.M.–10 P.M.

Medical, Police, and Emergencies
If you get sick, ask your hotel desk to recommend a doctor. Otherwise, go to **Clinica Hospital Carmen,** staffed by English-speaking IAMAT Doctors Horacio Tenorio S. and Germán Tenorio V., at Abasolo 215, tel. 9/516-2512, tel./fax 9/516-0027.

For routine medicines and drugs, go to one of many pharmacies, such as the **Farmacias Ahorro** on Cinco de Mayo, near the southwest corner of Independencia, one block east of the cathedral, open daily 7 A.M.–10 P.M. After hours, call Farmacia Ahorros' 24-hour free delivery service, tel. 9/515-5000.

For police emergencies, call the **Dirección de Seguridad,** tel. 9/516-2726, at Aldama 108, just north of the *zócalo.* For fire, call the *bomberos,* tel. 9/516-2231.

Consulates and Immigration
The U.S. Consul, tel./fax 9/514-3054, holds hours Mon.–Fri. 10 A.M.–6 P.M. at Alcalá 201, three blocks north of the *zócalo.* The Canadian Consul does the same for Canadian citizens Mon.–Fri. 11 A.M.–2 P.M., at 700 Pino Suárez, local 11B, tel. 9/513-3777, fax 9/515-2147.

Other consuls customarily available in Oaxaca

are the French, at Portal B. Juárez 101, tel. 9/514-1900; British-German, at Hidalgo 817, no. 3, tel. 9/513-0865; Italian, Alcalá 400, tel. 9/516-5058; and Spanish, Porfirio Díaz 340, tel. 9/515-3525. For more information, look for consulate contact numbers in the *Oaxaca Times* or the telephone directory yellow pages, under *"Embajadas, Legaciones, y Consulados,"* or call the U.S. or Canadian Consuls above.

If you lose your tourist permit, make arrangements with **Migración** well before your departure from Mexico. Take proof of arrival date in Mexico—stamped passport, airline ticket, or copy of lost permit—to the airport Migración, tel. 9/511-5733, a day (or at least three hours) before your scheduled departure.

Language Instruction and Courses

A long list of satisfied clients attests to the competence of the **Becari Language School,** N. Bravo 210, tel./fax 9/514-6076, email: becari@antequera.com. Offerings include small group Spanish instruction, as well as cooking and dancing classes. If you desire, the school can arrange homestays with local families. Its modest midtown facility includes, besides classrooms, a social area for sitting and getting to know other students. For more information, visit the website: www.mexonline.com/becari.htm

Similarly highly recommended is the **Vinigulaza Language and Tradition** (*Vinigulaza Idioma y Tradición*) school, associated with the local English-language Cambridge Academy, at Abasolo 209 (about two blocks east, four blocks north, of the plaza), tel. 9/514-6426, email: vinigu@prodigy.net.mx. The star behind the show is the friendly and hospitable director Catherine Kumar. Offerings include instructive (and even fun) small-group Spanish instruction. Schedules are flexible, and prices, at around $35 for 10 hours per week, are very reasonable. Social activities often include no-host dinners at local restaurants and a small on-site café where students can enjoy tea, coffee, and conversation. For more info, take a look at the school's website: oaxaca.infosel.com.mx/vinigulaza.

Another with high marks is the Universidad Autonomo Benito Juárez **Centro de Idiomas** (Language Center). Find it five blocks south of the *zócalo,* on Noria, between Bustamante and Armenta y López, tel./fax 9/516-5922, email: cedio@hotmail.com.

Alternatively, try **Español Interactivo** (Interactive Spanish) language school at Armenta y López 311 B, Oaxaca, Oaxaca 68000, tel./fax 9/514-6062, email: interacc@oax1.telmex.net.mx. One block east and half a block south of the *zócalo,* by San Agustín church, the school offers three levels: regular and intensive levels with two to four students per class and private one-on-one instruction. Also offered are homestays with Oaxaca families and classes in folkloric and salsa dancing, weaving, and painting on clay and wood.

The **Instituto de Comunicación y Cultura,** in offices at 307 Alcalá, second floor, also offers Spanish courses for visitors. The minimum is one week for $100. Classes begin each Monday. The institute also arranges homestays with Mexican families. Contact director Yolanda Garcia, tel./fax 9/516-3443, website: www .iccoax.com.

Informal, minimal-fee Spanish instruction is also often available by volunteers at the **Oaxaca Lending Library,** M. Alcalá 305, corner of Murguia; open Mon.–Fri. 10 A.M.–1 P.M. and 4–7 P.M., Sat. 10 A.M.–1 P.M.

Oaxacan Cooking and Culture

Susana Trilling, Oaxaca resident and author of *My Search for the Seventh Mole* (as in MOH-lay), offers an unusual mix of Oaxacan culture, cooking, and eating, with a lodging option, at her rancho cooking school in the Etla Valley, north of the city. The simplest choice is a one-day cooking adventure, including a morning trip to a local native market to buy food, then preparing and eating later at Susana's rancho ($75). Other options are a long Thursday through Tuesday cooking and cultural adventure ($850) or an extended one-week version of the same thing ($1,595). For details, call Susana at her cellular number 9/548-3115 (or if that doesn't work, try 044-9-548-3115) or fax 9/518-7726, or email: seasons@spersaoaxaca.com.mx. For more information, visit her website: www.seasonsofmyheart.com.

Alternatively, contact Iliana de la Vega, owner of popular **Restaurant El Naranjo** about her highly recommended cooking classes. Iliana's one-day three-hour ($40) class ordinarily starts in the morning. Call 9/514-1878, or drop in at the restaurant, at 203 Trujano, two blocks west of the zócalo's southwest corner.

INFORMATION

Tourist Information

The state-federal governments maintain a good information office, that includes a handicrafts shop, at the zócalo's north edge, at 607 Independencia, corner G. Vigil, tel. 9/516-4828, fax 9/516-0984, email: turinfo@oaxaca.gob.mx, open daily 9 A.M.–8 P.M.

Publications

One of Oaxaca's best sources of new English-language books about Mexico is the **Libros Amate** store on the ground floor of Plaza Alcalá, Alcalá 307, four blocks north of the zócalo, tel. 9/516-6960; open Mon.–Sat. 10 A.M.–2:30 P.M. and 3:30–7 P.M.

Another good source is bookstore **Librería Universitaria,** at Guerrero 104, half a block east of the zócalo, tel. 9/516-4243. It has English paperbacks, both used and new, a number of indigenous language dictionaries, and guides, cookbooks, art, and history books. Open Mon.–Sat. 9:30 A.M.–2 P.M. and 4–8 P.M.

The interesting new **Librería de Bibliofiles de Oaxaca** (Bibliophiles Bookstore of Oaxaca) offers a big collection of new, mostly Spanish books, but with a good number of art, crafts, archaeology, and cultural books in English. Find them just downhill from the Santo Domingo church, at M. Alacalá 104, tel. 9/516-9901, open daily 10 A.M.–9 P.M.

Oaxaca's best general book source (nearly completely in Spanish, however) is **Proveedora Escolar,** which, as its name implies, is especially useful for those seeking a wealth of detailed, historical, geographical, touristic, cultural, and archaeological information about Oaxaca. It's a cultural experience in itself to visit the place, at Independencia 1001, open Mon.–Sat. 9 A.M. P.M. and 4–8 P.M., tel. 9/516-0489, fax 9/514-5655. The materials you'll probably most want to peruse are on the upper floors.

The daily English-language *News* of Mexico City is usually available late mornings at the stand beneath the portal at southwest corner of

mural at the Palacio de Gobierno

the zócalo. If not, try the small news shop west from the same corner at Trujano 106A, open daily 8 A.M.–9:30 P.M.

Pick up a copy of the informative tourist newspaper, the *Oaxaca Times,* at your hotel, the state or city tourist office, or at the publisher, the Instituto de Comunicación y Cultura, tel. 9/516-3443, at 307 Alcalá, second floor. For more details, visit the website: www.oaxacatimes.com.

The *Oaxaca Times* prints cultural and historical features, tourist hints, and a list of local events. Also useful is the commonly available alternative trilingual tourist newspaper *Oaxaca,* published in English, Spanish, and French, at Calz. P. Díaz, 321-7, Colonia Reforma, tel./fax 9/515-8764, email: oscarrizos@spersaoaxaca.com.mx.

Libraries

The city *biblioteca* (public library), in a lovingly restored former convent, is worth a visit, if only for its graceful, cloistered Renaissance interiors and patios. At the corner of Morelos and Alcalá, two blocks north of the zócalo, tel. 9/516-5681. Open Mon.–Fri. 9 A.M.–8:30 P.M.

Visitors starving for a good read will find satisfaction by borrowing (or buying upstairs) at least one of the thousands of volumes at the **Oaxaca Lending Library,** at M. Alcalá 305, corner of Murguia; open Mon.–Fri. 10 A.M.–1 P.M. and 4–7 P.M., Sat. 10 A.M.–1 P.M.

Volunteer Work and Donations
Local residents and visitors have bonded together to provide self-help for Oaxaca's street children and poor single-parent families. Two organizations, **Grassroots** and **Food Harvest** operate cooperatively at their headquarters, the **Center of Hope,** at 122 Jesús Carranza, at Garcia Vigil, five blocks north of the *zócalo.*

The all-volunteer organizations' efforts finds food money for schoolbooks and uniforms, housing, foster care, and much more, for homeless children and destitute single mothers and their children. They welcome donations and volunteers, and visitors are always welcome, Mon.–Fri.10 A.M.–2:30 P.M. and 5–8 P.M., Sat. 10 A.M.–2 P.M.

Outside of Oaxaca, you can send contributions to both organizations: mail checks, addressed and written to the order of "Oaxaca Street Children Grassroots," 449 Crane Ave. S, Taunton, MA 02780. Get more information from Frank Vannini, tel. 508/884-8207, email: vannini@worldnet.att.net. Also mail checks, addressed and written to the order of "Food Harvest for Oaxaca Street Children" to Mike Duffy, Treasurer, P.O. Box 96, Decatur, TX 76234, tel. 940/627-6805, email: dooner@wf.net.

GETTING THERE AND AWAY

By Air
The **Oaxaca Airport** (code-designated OAX) has several daily flights that connect with Mexico City and other Mexican destinations. Many of the Mexico City flights allow same-day connections between Oaxaca and many U.S. gateways.

Mexicana Airlines flights connect a number of times daily with Mexico City. For reservations or flight information, tel. 9/516-8414 or 9/514-7253.

Aeroméxico flights connect several times daily with Mexico City; three flights per week continue on to Tijuana. For reservations, tel. 9/516-3765 or 9/516-1066; for flight information, tel. 9/511-5055.

Mexicana Airlines affiliate **Aerocaribe** flights connect daily with Huatulco and daily with Cancún via Tuxtla Gutiérrez, Villahermosa, and Mérida. For reservations, tel. 9/516-6088 or 9/516-0229; for flight information, tel. 9/511-5247.

Aviacsa airlines connects once daily with Mexico City and once daily with Tijuana via Mexico City. For information and reservations, tel. 9/514-5123.

The Oaxaca airport provides a modicum of services, such as a good upstairs view restaurant, several shops, car rentals, a tourist information office, open daily 8 A.M.–8 P.M., tel. 9/511-5040, and an ATM.

Arrival transportation for the six-mile trip into town is easy. Fixed-fare collective taxi tickets run about $2 per person ($4 to north-side Hotels Misión de los Angeles, Fortín Plaza, and Victoria). For the same trip, a *taxi especial* (private taxi) ticket runs about $10 for four persons; larger GMC Suburbans, $16 for up to eight persons. No public buses run between the airport and town.

Car rental agents operating at the Oaxaca Airport (and some also downtown) are **Budget,** tel. 9/515-0330 ; **Hertz,** tel. 9/516-2434, fax 9/516-0009; **Avis,** tel./fax 9/511-5736; and **Alamo,** tel./fax 9/514-8534.

On **departure,** save taxi money by getting your *colectivo* airport transportation ticket ahead of time, at Transportacion Terrestres on the west side of Plaza Alameda de León, across from the cathedral, open daily 9 A.M.–2 P.M. and 5–8 P.M.

Furthermore, keep enough dollars or pesos for your $12 international departure tax (which may be collected in Mexico City) if your air ticket doesn't already cover it. If you lose your tourist permit, make arrangements with **Migración** several hours prior to departure from Mexico. Take proof of arrival date in Mexico, such as stamped passport, airline ticket, or copy of lost permit, to airport Migración, tel. 9/511-5733.

By Car or RV
Paved (but long, winding, and sometimes potholed) roads connect Oaxaca City with all regions of Oaxaca.

South to the coast via the southern Sierra, narrow **National Hwy. 175** connects along 148 winding, sometimes potholed miles (238 km) over the del Sur with its junction with Hwy. 200 at Pochutla (thence six miles to Puerto Ángel). The road climbs to more than 9,000 feet through winter-chilly pine forests and indigenous Chatino and Zapotec villages. Fill up with gas at the last-chance Pemex in Mihuatlán heading south and at Pochutla (north edge of town) heading north; carry water and blankets and be prepared for emergencies. Under dry, daylight conditions, count on about seven hours at the wheel, south from Oaxaca to Puerto Ángel, about eight hours in the opposite direction.

About the same is true for the paved **National Hwy. 131** route south from Oaxaca, which splits off of Hwy. 175 two miles (three kilometers) south of San Bártolo Coyotepec. On your way out of town, fill up with gasoline at the airport Pemex. Continue, via Zimatlán and Sola de Vega (fill again with Magna), over the pine-clad Pacific crest, a total of 158 miles (254 kilometers) to Puerto Escondido. Under dry, daylight conditions, allow about seven hours southbound, about eight hours in the opposite direction. Unleaded gasoline is regularly available midroute at the Sola de Vega Pemex only.

The 229-mile (368-km) **Hwy. 190–Hwy. 125** route connects Oaxaca southwest with coastal Pinotepa Nacional, via the Mixtec country destinations of Yanhuitlán, Teposcolula, and Tlaxiaco. Although winding most of the way, the generally uncongested road is safely drivable (subject to some potholes, however) from Oaxaca in about eight driving hours if you use the *cuota* (toll) Hwy. 190 *autopista* northwest of Oaxaca city. Add an hour for the 7,000-foot climb in the opposite direction.

The 350-mile (564-km) winding **Hwy. 190-160** from Oaxaca to Cuernavaca and Mexico City via Huajuapan de León requires a very long day, or better two, for safety. Under the best of conditions, the Mexico City-Oaxaca driving time runs 11 hours either way. Take it easy and stop overnight en route. (Make sure you arrive in Mexico City on a day when your car is permitted to drive. See the special topic Mexico City Driving Regulations.)

Alternatively, you can cut your the Mexico City-Oaxaca driving time significantly via the Mexico City-Puebla-Oaxaca *autopista,* combined 150D-131D, which, southbound, takes off from the southeast end of Mexico City's Calz. General Ignacio Zaragoza. Northbound, follow the signs on Hwy. 190 a few miles north of Oaxaca. Allow about six hours driving time at a steady 60 mph

(about 100 kph). Tolls, which are worth the increased speed and safety, run about $30 for a car, much more for a big RV.

By Bus

Luxury and First Class: Cristóbal Colón (CC) and Autobuses del Oriente (AO), Oaxaca's major luxury- and first-class carriers, operate out of the big modern terminal on Hwy. 190, Calz. Héroes de Chapultepec 1036, at Carranza, on the north side of town. Here passengers enjoy a squad of public telephones out in front, snack stands, luggage lockers, and an ATM in the drug store Farmacia Ahorros next door.

Cristóbal Colón, (CC) tel. 9/513-2424, offers service to most major points in Oaxaca. Buses connect northwest with Mixteca destinations of Nochixtlán, Tamazulapan, and Huajapan de León, continuing to Puebla and Mexico City. Westerly, they connect with the Mixteca Alta, via Teposcolula, Tlaxiaco, Juxtlahuaca, Putla de Guerrero, and Pinotepa Nacional on the coast. Southerly, they connect (often via the surer, but long Isthmus route) with Puerto Escondido, Pochutla, Puerto Ángel, and Huatulco; southeasterly, with Tehuantepec, Chiapas, and Guatemala; and northerly, with Villahermosa.

Moreover, Cristóbal Colón, operating through its agency, **Ticket Bus,** sells tickets for all first-class bus lines at both the 1036 Héroes de Chapultepec station and a convenient downtown outlet, at 20 de Noviembre 204A, tel. 9/514-6655, a block west of the *zócalo.*

Autobuses del Oriente, (ADO), also tel. 9/513-2424, offers limited Oaxaca connections, mostly along the Hwy. 190 corridor, connecting northwest with Mexico City (Tapo and Norte stations), via Nochixtlán and Huajuapan de León, and southeast with Tehuantepec and Salina Cruz. Other departures connect northwest with Veracruz, Coatzacoalcos, Villahermosa, and Mérida.

Second Class: A swarm of long-distance second-class buses runs from the *camionera central segunda clase* southwest of downtown, just north of the Abastos market. Get there by taxi, or by walking due west about eight blocks from the *zócalo* to the west end of Calle Las Casas. Cross the *periférico* (peripheral boulevard) straight across the railroad tracks;

keep walking the same direction, along the four-lane street for two more blocks, where you'll see the terminal gate on the right. Inside, you'll find an orderly array of snack stalls, a cafeteria, luggage lockers, a long-distance telephone and fax, and a squad of *taquillas* (ticket booths).

Auto Transportes Oaxaca-Pacífico, tel. 9/516-2908, and **Autobuses Estrella del Valle,** tel. 9/516-5429, travel the Hwy. 175 north-south route between Oaxaca and Pochutla-Puerto Ángel. Both lines continue, connecting along east-west coastal Hwy. 200 with Bahías de Huatulco, Puerto Escondido, and Pinotepa Nacional.

Estrella Roja del Sureste second-class and first-class buses, tel. 9/516-0694, connect directly with Puerto Escondido along newly paved Hwy. 131 north-south via Sola de Vega and Juquila. From there you can make coastal connections with Pochutla-Puerto Ángel, Bahías de Huatulco, and Pinotepa Nacional.

Fletes y Pasajes, tel. 9/622-70, offers very broad second-class service, connecting with nearly everywhere in Oaxaca: westerly, with Mixteca destinations of Nochistlán, Tamazulapan, Huajuapan, and Tlaxiaco, connecting all the way via Hwy. 125 to Pinotepa Nacional on the coast; northerly, via Teotitlán del Camino and Mazateca destinations around Huatla de Jiménez; easterly, with Mitla and Mixe destinations of Ayutla, Zacatepec, and Juquila Mixes; and southeasterly, with Isthmus destinations of Tehuantepec, Juchitán, and Salina Cruz.

Several other semi-local lines connect mostly with Oaxaca Valley points: **Choferes del Sur,** with northwest Oaxaca Valley, from San Felipe del Agua north of the city to Etla northwest. **Autobuses de Oaxaca** connects south with Cuilapan and Zaachila. **Sociedad Cooperativa Valle del Norte** connects west with Teotitlán del Valle and Tlacolula. Finally, if you want a bone-jangling (but scenic) backroads adventure, ride **Flecha de Zempoatepetl** northeast to remote Zapotec mountain native market towns of Villa Alta and Yalalag, via Tlacolula and Cuajimoloyas.

By Train

Although they're sometimes painfully slow, passenger trains still rumble along, connecting Oaxaca (via Puebla) with Mexico City, and thence with a few other Mexican destinations.

One Mexico City-bound train departs daily at 7 P.M. from the station on Calz. Madero about a mile and a half west of downtown. Service, very cheap, is by first- and second-class coach only and includes no restaurant car. Bring food, drinks, and toilet paper. Call the station, tel. 9/516-2253 or 9/516-2564, to double-check departure information and prices. Note: Due to railroad privatization, passenger train service is quickly disappearing in Mexico. By the time you read this, it may have vanished completely.

ERIN DWYER

AROUND THE VALLEY OF OAXACA

A feast of old-Mexico sights and experiences awaits travelers willing to venture outside of the city of Oaxaca. The list—colorful country markets, crafts villages, archaeological sites, venerable churches, natural wonders—goes on and on. The towns themselves help you set your itinerary. They each have their market day, when local color is at a maximum and prices are at a minimum. Moving clockwise, the prime market destinations (in addition to Oaxaca City, where the big market is the Abastos on Saturday) are Tlacolula, 45 minutes east, Sunday; Ocotlán, 45 minutes south, Friday; Ejutla, an hour south, Thursday; Miahuatlán, 90 minutes south, Monday; Zaachila, 30 minutes southwest, Thursday; Zimatlán, 45 minutes southwest, Wednesday; and Etla, 30 minutes northeast, Wednesday.

These market visits can be conveniently combined with stops at handicrafts villages and ruins. Notable handicrafts villages include Teotitlán del Valle on the east side, San Bartolo Coyotepec and Ocotlán to the south, Arrazola toward the southwest, and Atzompa on the west. Among the premier archaeological sites are Mitla and Yagul, on the east side; Zaachila, southwest;

Monte Albán, west; and Suchilquitongo and San José El Mogote, northwest.

GETTING AROUND

Rental Cars and Tourist Buses

Droves of second-class buses from the Abastos second-class terminal run everywhere in the Valley of Oaxaca. Arrive early everyday and you could cover most major valley destinations in about a week that way: two days east (Teotitláan, Tlacolula, Mitla), two days south (crafts villages, Ocotlán market), two days southwest and west (Zaachila market and archaeological site, Cuilapan, Arrazola, Monte Albán), and one day northeast (Etla market and San José Mogote). (**Get to the second-class terminal** by walking one block south from the zócalo, turn right at Las Casas, and keep walking about 10 blocks. With caution, cross the periférico boulevard. The big terminal is two blocks farther, on the right.)

More leisurely options would be to rent a car or take a tourist bus or both. Get your rental through either a travel agent or through U.S. and

Canadian toll-free car rental numbers (see chart in the On the Road chapter) or in Oaxaca locally: **Budget,** tel. 9/511-0052 airport, 515-0330 downtown, email: rentacar@antequera.com; **Hertz,** tel./fax 9/516-2434 downtown, email: hertzdirecto@iserve.net.mx; **Avis,** tel./fax 9/511-5736 airport, or Mexico toll-free 01 800/707-7700; and **Alamo** 9/514-8534.

For tourist buses, you have a number of economical choices. For example, ride one of those leaving daily from the Hotel Señorial (on the *zócalo,* tel. 9–516-3933) or from the Viajes Turísticos Mitla office, tel. 9/516-6175 (at Hotel Rivera del Ángel, at Mina 518, three blocks south, two blocks west of the *zócalo*). Other

hotels also have such bus arrangements. See your desk clerk.

Guided Tours

Alternatively, you can contact one of a number of well-informed private guides, such as English-fluent **Juan Montes Lara,** tel.9/515-7731, fax 9/515-1293, email: ftmn@hotmail.com, who guides groups of up to eight in a comfortable van. Lara's customized itineraries ordinarily include handicrafts villages, markets, archaeological sites, and more (three-hour minimum, $18 per hour for two, $25 for 3–5, $28 per hour for 6–8 persons).

Another good guide choice is the very highly

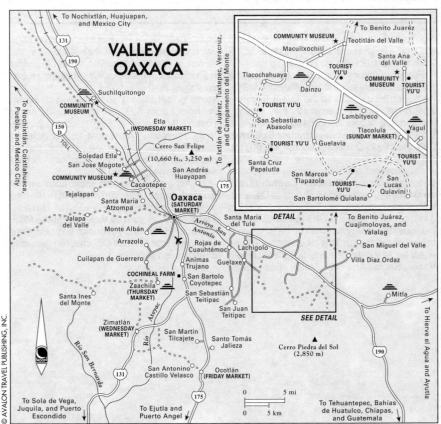

TOWN NAMES

Town names in Oaxaca (and in Mexico) generally come in two pieces: an original native name, accompanied by the name of the town's patron saint. Very typical is the case of San Jerónimo Tlacochahuaya, a sleepy but famous little place covered in this chapter. Combining both the saint's name (here, San Jerónimo) and the native name often makes for very unwieldy handles, so many towns are known only by one name, usually the native name. Thus, in the Oaxaca Valley, west side, San Jerónimo Tlacochahuaya, Santa María del Tule, Tlacolula de Matamoros, and San Pablo Villa de Mitla, for example, are commonly called Tlacochahuaya, El Tule, Tlacolula, and Mitla, respectively.

Nevertheless, sometimes a town's full name is customarily used. This is especially true when a single name—such as Etla, northwest of Oaxaca City—identifies an entire district, where many towns, such as San Agustín Etla, San Sebastián Etla, and San José Etla must necessarily be identified with their full names. In this book, although we may mention the formal name once on a map or in the text, we generally conform to local, customary usage for town names.

recommended English-speaking expatriate Susan McGlynn, who can be reached by phone, tel.9/518-7334, or email: labrujita_oax@yahoo.com.

For more recommendations, try consulting the Oaxaca state-city tourism office, tel. 9/516-4828, northwest across the street from the *zócalo* cathedral. For example, they strongly recommend federally licensed French- and English- speaking **Gabriel Sánchez Gutiérrez**, P.O. Box 987, Oaxaca, Oaxaca 68000, tel. 9/516-1991.

An excellent people-to-people tour option is to go with the **Museos Comunitarios de Oaxaca** (Community Museums of Oaxaca), with headquarters at Tinoco y Palacios 311, second floor, tel.9/516-5786, email: muscoax@prodigy.net.mx (or turismo_com unitario@umco.org). This organization acts as agent for 14 local museums, five (Teotitlán del Valle, Santa Ana del Valle, San Pablo Huixtepec, San José Mogote, and Santiago Suchilquitongo) in the Valley of Oaxaca and seven in the Mixteca. The museums offer guided tours of their localities, including ruins, churches, festivals, lakes, springs, mountain summits, and artisans' shops, with lunch thrown in, from about $25 per person. Whenever possible they furnish an English-speaking guide to the museum. Transportation, not included in the $25 price, can be via your car, taxi, or public bus. For more information, consult their website: www.umco.org

Higher up the economic scale, **commercial guided tours** also provide a hassle-free means of exploring the Valley of Oaxaca. Travel agencies such as Viajes Turisticos Mitla, Oaxaca Tours, and American Express (see Services in the Oaxaca City chapter) generally provide such services.

EAST SIDE: THE TEXTILE ROUTE

The host of colorful enticements along this path could tempt you into many days of delightful exploring. For example, on Saturday you could head out, visiting the great El Tule tree and the weavers' shops in Teotitlán del Valle and continuing east for an overnight at Mitla. Next morning, explore the Mitla ruins, then return, stopping at the hilltop Yagul archaeological site and the Sunday market at Tlacolula. In either direction, going or coming from the city, you could pause for a brief exploration at the Dainzu and Lambityeco roadside archaeological sites.

One more day would allow more time to venture past Mitla to the remarkable mountainside springs and mineral deposits at Hierve de Agua. Stay longer and have it all: a two- or three-day stay in a colorful market town such as Tlacolula or in a quiet backcountry village such as San Bartolomé Quialana or San Marcos Tlapazola. This is an option made possible by the several excellent community-run tourist Yu'u sprinkled through the valley's east side.

Santa María del Tule

El Tule is a gargantuan Mexican cypress *(ahuehuete),* probably the largest tree in Latin America. Its gnarled, house-size trunk divides into a forest of elephantine limbs that rise to bushy branches reaching 15 stories overhead. The small town of Santa María del Tule, nine miles (14 km) east of the city on Hwy. 190, seems built around the tree. A crafts market, a church, and the town plaza, where residents celebrate their El Tule with a fiesta on 7 October, all surround the beloved 2,000-year-old living giant.

Note: Eastbound, the highway funnels through traffic to a right-hand bypass before the El Tule tree itself. Stay in the left, local lane if possible. If not, park along the bypass and walk a block north to El Tule.

Tlacochahuaya

At San Jerónimo Tlacochahuaya (tlah-koh-chah-WYE-yah), about four miles (seven km) west of El Tule, stands the village's pride and joy, the venerable 16th-century **Templo y Exconvento de San Jerónimo.** Dominican padres and their native acolytes, under the guidance of Father Jordán de Santa Catalina, began its construction in 1586 and completed it a few decades later.

Tlacochahuaya is usually a quiet little town except during holidays, notably the eight days of processions, dances, fireworks, and food, climaxing on 30 September, the feast day of San Jerónimo.

The church's relatively recent 1991 restoration glows so brilliantly, especially from the white Baroque facade, that, standing beneath the spreading wild fig tree in the courtyard (or more precisely, atrium), you can feel the facade reflecting the warmth of the late afternoon sun. The atrium appears big enough to assemble a crowd of about 5,000 folks, probably the number of local *indígenas* the padres hoped to convert during the 16th century. At the atrium's corners stand the three open-air but arch-roofed chapels, or *pozas,* where the conversions took place.

Above the entrance portal, see San Jerónimo standing piously, his left hand on a skull, listening for the voice of God. Inside, glance upward at the lovely nave ceiling and appreciate the still-vital spirit of those long-dead artists who created its flowery, multicolored swirls. Look for the group of oil paintings depicting the legend of the **Virgin of Guadalupe,** with the last showing the roses miraculously tumbling from Juan Diego's cape, emblazoned with her image.

At one time, near the entrance was the pledge of the Sacerdote de Cristo (Priest of Christ), which, translated, reads

> The priest of Christ offers
> THIS MASS
> As if it were your
> FIRST MASS
> As if it were your
> ONLY MASS
> As if it were your
> LAST MASS

Get there by car, guide or by the Sociedad Cooperativa Valle del Norte local bus from the Camionera Central Segunda Clase.

El Tule, Latin America's most massive tree, is the usual first stop on valley tours east of Oaxaca City.

DAINZU AND LAMBITYECO ARCHAEOLOGICAL SITES

Among the several Oaxaca Valley buried cities, Dainzu and Lambityeco, both beside the highway, are the most accessible. Dainzu comes first, on the right about six miles (nine km) east of El Tule.

Dainzu

Dainzu (in Zapotec, "Hill of the Organ Cactus"), open daily 10 A.M.–5 P.M., spreads over an approximate half-mile square, consisting of a partly restored ceremonial center surrounded by clusters of unexcavated mounds. Beyond that, on the west side, a stream runs through fields, which at Dainzu's apex (around A.D. 300) supported a town of about 1,000 inhabitants.

The major excavation, at the foot of the hill about a hundred yards south of the parking lot, reveals more than 30 bas-reliefs of ball players draped with leather head, arm, and torso protectors. Downhill, to the west, lies the partly reconstructed complex of courtyards, platforms, and stairways. The northernmost of these was excavated to reveal a tomb, with a carved door supporting a jaguar head on the lintel and arms—note the claws—extending down along the stone doorjambs. The jaguar's face, with a pair of curious vampire teeth and curly nostrils, appears so batlike that some investigators have speculated that it may represent a composite jaguar-bat god.

A couple of hundred yards diagonally southwest you'll find the ball court running east-west in the characteristic I-shaped layout, with a pair of "scoring" niches at each end and flanked by a pair of stone-block grandstand-like seats. Actually, archaeologists know that these were not seats, because the blocks were once stuccoed over, forming a pair of smooth inclined planes that flanked the central playing area.

Lambityeco

Six miles (10 km) farther, Lambityeco, open daily 10 A.M.–5 P.M., is on the right, a few miles past the Teotitlán del Valle side road. The excavated portion, only about 100 yards square, is a small but significant part of Yegui ("Small Hill" in Zapotec), a large buried town dotted with hundreds of unexcavated mounds, covering about half a square mile. Salt making appears to have been the main occupation of Yegui people during the town's heyday, around A.D. 700. The name "Lambityeco" may derive from the Arabic-Spanish *alambique,* the equivalent of English "alembic," or distillation or evaporation apparatus. This would explain the intriguing presence of the more than 200 local mounds. It's tempting to speculate that they are the remains of *cujetes,* raised leaching beds, still used in Mexico for concentrating brine, which workers subsequently evaporate into salt.

In the present small restored zone, archaeologists have uncovered, besides the remains of the Valley of Oaxaca's earliest known *temascal* (ritual steam house), a number of fascinating ceramic sculptures. Next to the parking lot, a platform, mound 195, rises above ground level. If, after entering through the gate, you climb up its partially restored slope and look down into the excavated hollow in the adjacent east courtyard, you'll see stucco friezes of a pair of regal, lifelike faces, one male and one female, presumably of the personages who were found buried in the royal grave (Tomb 6) below. Experts believe this to be the case, because the man was depicted with the symbol of his right to rule—a human femur bone, probably taken, as was the custom, from the grave of his chieftain father.

Mound 190, sheltered beneath the adjacent large corrugated roof about 50 yards to the south, contains a restored platform decorated by pair of remarkably lifelike, nearly identical divine stucco masks. These are believed to be of Zapotec rain god Cocijo (see the water flowing from the mouths). Notice also the rays in one hand, perhaps lightning, representing power, and flowers, for fertility, in the other.

TEOTITLÁN DEL VALLE

Teotitlán del Valle, pop. 5,000, nine miles east of El Tule, at the foot of the Sierra, means "Place of the Gods" in Nahuatl; before that it was known, appropriately, as Xa Quire (shah KEE-ray) or "Foot of the Mountain," by the Zapotecs who settled it, archaeologists estimate, at least 2,000 years ago. From the age of artifacts uncovered beneath both the present town and at nearby sites, experts estimate that approximately 1,000 people were living in Teotitlán in A.D. 400.

Teotitlán people are relatively well off, not only from sales of their renowned *tapetes* (woven wool carpets), but from their rich communal landholdings. Besides a sizable swath of valley-bottom farmland and pasture, which every Teotitlán family is entitled to use, the community owns a dam and reservoir and a small kingdom of approximately 100,000 acres of pristine mountain forest and meadow, spreading for about 20 miles (32 km) along the Valley of Oaxaca's lush northeastern foothills.

Getting Oriented
Teotitlán del Valle has two principal streets: Juárez, the entrance road, runs northerly about 2.5 miles (four km) from the highway, and Hidalgo intersects it at the center of town. Turn right at Hidalgo (where the pavement becomes cobbled) and you'll be looking east, toward the town plaza and, behind it, the 17th-century town church.

Textile Shops
Nearly every Teotitlán house is a mini-factory where people card, spin, and color wool, often using hand-gathered natural dyes. Each step of wool preparation is laborious; pure water is even a chore—families typically spend two days a week collecting it from mountain springs. The weaving, on traditional hand looms, is the final, satisfying part of the process.

Visiting the factory stores should be first on your itinerary. Be sure not to miss the shops of renowned master Isaac Vasquez, at Hidalgo 30, open daily 9 A.M.–6 P.M., tel. 951/441-22. Also, be

Master weaver Isaac Vásquez demonstrates his technique on the spinning wheel in his Teotitlán del Valle shop.

certain to look inside the humbler but excellent Cooperativa Mujeres Tejedoras (Women Weavers' Cooperative) at Hidalgo 37. The best weaving is generally the densest, typically packing in about 45 strands per inch (18 strands per centimeter); ordinary weaving incorporates about half that. Please don't bargain too hard. Even the highest prices typically bring the weavers less than a dollar an hour for their labor.

Community Museum

Reserve enough time to visit the community museum, **Balaa Xtee Guech Gulal,** whose name translates from the local Zapotec as "Shadow of the Old Town." It's on the north side of Hidalgo, about a block east of Juárez. Step inside (open daily except Mon. 10 A.M.–6 P.M.) and enjoy the excellent exhibits that illustrate local history, industry, and customs. One display shows the wool-weaving tradition, introduced by the Dominican padres, including sources of some natural dyes—red cochineal *(cochinilla),* yellow moss and lichens *(musgo),* dark blue indigo *(anil),* and black *quizache* bean. Another exhibit shows the local practice of service to the bride's parents by a prospective groom, with a house mock-up showing the prospective bride making tortillas for him. Be sure to get a copy of the good English-language explanatory pamphlet.

A Walk around Town

If you arrange ahead of time, a community museum volunteer will lead you on a walking tour of the town and environs. Highlights often include visits to weavers' homes, the church, a traditional *temascal* (ritual steam house), the recently reconstructed foundation stones of the ancient town, the dam and lake, and the hike to Picacho, the peak above the town's west side. Lacking an appointment, you still might be able to arrange for a guide on the spot, or simply stroll out on your own self-guided tour.

Head east on Hidalgo. If you haven't already, take a look around the plaza-front textile stalls, then continue to the church, **Templo de la Preciosa Sangre de Cristo** (Church of the Precious Blood of Christ). Here, community adoration focuses during both the 1–15 July patronal festival and the 7–9 September Fiesta del Señor de La Natividad (Festival of the Lord of the Nativity), which include processions, fireworks, and the spectacular Danza de las Plumas (Dance of the Feathers).

The church itself, built over an earlier Zapotec temple, contains many interesting pre-Columbian stones, which the Dominican friars allowed to be incorporated into its walls. Notice the corn motif carved into the front doorway arch, similar in style to the monolith built into the outside wall at the right of the church entrance steps. Inside, admire the nave's flowery overhead decorations and the colorful Bible-story paintings. Continue from the nave into the intimate cloister *(claustro)* and see the Zapotec god of the wind, with stone curls carved to represent the wind (in the southwest corner, to the right as you enter from the nave).

Outside, behind the church, continue to the reconstructed foundation corner of the original **Zapotec temple.** Notice the uniquely Zapotec stone fretwork, similar to the famous *greca* remains at Mitla, 20 miles farther east.

If you have time, or have decided to stay the night, you can venture even farther afield. One option is to walk or drive along the bumpy but passable uphill gravel continuation of main street Calle Juárez about a mile to the town dam. After the summer rains, the reservoir fills and forms a scenic lake, good for swimming, picnicking, and even possibly camping, along its pastoral mountain-view shoreline. If you plan to camp at the Teotitlán reservoir, first ask for permission at the museum or the *presidencia municipal.*

Travelers can extend their Teotitlán adventure all the way into the mountains. From the Teotitlán reservoir, hike (be prepared with water, good shoes, and a hat), hitchhike, or drive about 10 more miles (and 5,000 feet, 1,500 meters) uphill along the good, gravel road to pine-shadowed **Benito Juárez** and **Cuajimoloyas** mountain hamlets. (See the Northern Oaxaca chapter for details.)

Back at the Teotitlán reservoir, you can also adventure up the slope of **Picacho,** the steep, peaked hill a mile west of the town. The usual route from town is along Calle 2 de Abril, which heads west, bridging the west-side arroyo. Continue uphill, bearing right at the fork at the base of the hill. First you pass some houses, then continue, curving left around the hillside. Eventually, before the summit you pass some caves *(cuevitas)*, a holy site where local folks have been gathering for sacred ceremonies each New Year's Day since before anyone can remember.

Accommodations and Food

The Teotitlán Yu'u, although easily accessible, is isolated on the entrance road by Hwy. 190, a long two-mile (three-km) walk to town. Reserve a spot through the state-federal tourist information office in Oaxaca City, at 607 Independencia, Oaxaca, Oaxaca 68000, tel. 9/516-4828, fax 9/516-0984, email: turinfo@oaxaca.gob.mx.

For **food**, sample Teotitlán's best, at the charmingly traditional **Tlamanalli** restaurant. Their menu of made-to-order Zapotec specialties, such as *sopa de calabaza* (squash soup) and *guisado de pollo* (chicken stew) is limited, but highly recommended by Oaxaca city chefs. Open daily 1–4 P.M., longer hours when more people stop by.

Getting There

You can go by car, tour, taxi, or bus. Drivers, simply turn left from Hwy. 190 at the signed Teotitlán del Valle side road, nine miles (14 km) east of El Tule. By bus, ride a Sociedad Cooperativa Valle del Norte red and yellow Tlacolula- or Mitla-bound bus from the second-class bus station *(camionera central segunda clase)* by the Abastos market at the end of Las Casas, past the *periférico* west of downtown. Get off at the signed bus stop, and walk, taxi, or hitchhike the 2.5 miles (four km) into town.

SANTA ANA DEL VALLE

This is a smaller, sleepier version of Teotitlán, where virtually every family speaks the Zapotec tongue at home and earns at least part of its living through weaving. Many older folks understand Spanish only with difficulty. Santa Ana del Valle, like Teotitlán, has thousands of acres of communal lands in the valley bottom and mountains surrounding the town. Nearly all households tend plots of corn, beans, and vegetables. Most also graze cattle, sheep, and goats in specified communal areas. These lands have been traditionally held by the town since before the conquest. Families may buy or sell

shares of their allotted land, but only within the Santa Ana del Valle community.

Your first stop should be the excellent community museum, **Shan Dany,** on the town plaza, opposite the *presidencia municipal*, open Mon.–Sat. 10 A.M.–2 P.M. and 3–6 P.M. The exhibits include an archaeological section with preconquest remains found during a recent plaza-front construction project. Also notice the ponderous monolith, brought from the mountain above town, carved with the visage of Cocijo, the god of lightning and rain. Another museum section details 1910–17 revolutionary history, when townsfolk had to flee to the hills and wage a guerrilla war against rampaging forces of "Primer Jefe" General Venustiano Carranza. Toward the rear of the museum, a pair of excellent displays illustrate more community lore: one shows many of the naturally occurring dyes, including avocado seeds, *guaje* bark, and *copal* bark, that local weavers gather and use; the other explains the Danza del la Pluma (Dance of the Feathers), in which a dozen young men dance and brighten the town plaza with their huge, round feathered hats. This dance takes place during the 26 July and 14–16 August split-date festival in honor of Santa Ana.

If you've arranged an appointment through the Museos Comunitarios in Oaxaca City, Tinoco y Palacios 311, second floor, tel.9/516-5786, email: muscoax@prodigy.net.mx (or turismo_comunitario@umco.org), the museum volunteer staff will be prepared to lead you on a two- or three-hour *recorrido* (tour) around town, including the *presa* (dam and small reservoir) and a creek (where you can cool off during the summer rainy season—bring your bathing suit), a breezy *mirador* (viewpoint) for a spectacular valley vista, and an old gold, silver, and copper mine. During the walk, staff members enjoy identifying and explaining the uses of the many medicinal plants along the path. Be sure to ask them to point out the poisonous *mala mujer* (bad woman) bush to you. Finally, they'll take you to shops of outstanding local weavers for demonstrations and possible purchases of their work.

If you arrive without an appointment, a staff volunteer may still be available, or may find someone who will lead you (offer to pay) for a small tour. If not, you can still do most of the walk on your own. The path to the dam takes off from Calle Plan de Ayala, on the east, uphill side of town. It's only about half a mile; bear left, around the hill. If you get confused, ask a younger person (most likely to understand Spanish) *"¿Donde está la presa"* (PRAY-sah), *"por favor?"* The viewpoint, the big moss-mottled rock about halfway up the steep, left-hand slope, sticks out of the hillside to the left and above the path to the dam.

Shopping
Although Santa Ana weavers sell much of their work through shops in Teotitlán del Valle and Oaxaca, they also sell directly in town, from both the **Mercado de Artesanías** on the town plaza and their home workshops. For suggestions of whom to visit, ask at the museum, or go directly to **Casa Martínez**, the house of personable master weaver Ernesto Martínez, at Matamoros 3, corner of V. Carranza, tel. 956/203-66, around the corner a few doors downhill from the town plaza. You'll also be welcome at the home shop of the friendly weaving family of Alberto Sánchez Garcia, at Sor Juanes Inés de la Cruz 1, a few blocks from the town plaza, tel. 956/206-55 or 956/204-99.

Accommodations
The comfortable Santa Ana tourist Yu'u is on the entrance road to town. It is well situated for exploring, being just a few blocks from the center of town. Reserve a spot here through the state-federal tourist information office in Oaxaca City, at 607 Independencia, Oaxaca, Oaxaca 68000, tel. 9/516-4828, fax 9/516-0984, email: turinfo@oaxaca.gob.mx.

Getting There
You can go by car, tour, taxi, or bus. Drivers, turn left at the fork across Hwy. 190 from the Tlacolula Pemex *gasolinera* (24 miles, 38 km) east of Oaxaca City. After half a mile, turn left again at the signed Santa Ana del Valle side road. Continue another few minutes; pass the tourist Yu'u, on the right, and arrive at the town plaza a few blocks farther. By bus, you can ride a Tlacolula- or Mitla-bound bus from the second-class bus station by the Abastos market, end of Las Casas, west of downtown. Get off at the Tlacolula stop on Hwy. 190 by the Pemex station. Cross to the side road on the other side of the highway and either take a taxi, ride the white Transportes Municipal del Santa Ana del Valle local bus, or hike the four miles from the highway—walk the side road half a mile to a signed Santa Ana fork; go left and continue for two more miles, passing the tourist Yu'u on the right, and then on to the town plaza a few blocks farther.

TLACOLULA

The Zapotec people who founded Tlacolula (pop. 15,000; 24 miles, 38 km east from Oaxaca) around A.D. 1250 called it Guichiibaa (Place between Heaven and Earth). Besides its beloved church and chapel and famous Sunday market, Tlacolula is also renowned for *mescal*. Get a good free sample at friendly **Pensamiento** shop, on main street Juárez no. 9, as you head from the highway toward the market. Besides many hand-embroidered Amusgo *huipiles* and Teotitlán weavings, Pensamiento offers *mescal* in 24 flavors, 17 for women and seven for men.

Just before the market, take a look inside the main town church, the 1531 **Parroquia de la Virgen de la Asunción.** Although its interior is distinguished enough, the real gem is its attached chapel, **Capilla del Señor de Tlacolula,** which you enter from the nave of the church. Every inch of the chapel's interior gleams with sculptures of angels and saints, paintings, and gold scrollwork. Notice the pair of floating angels, each holding a great pendulous solid silver censer, on opposite sides of the altar; also, admire the solid silver fence in front of the altar. Saints seem to live on in every corner of the chapel. Especially graphic are the martyrs, who reveal the way they died, such as a sorrowful San Sebastián, his body shot full of arrows, and a decapitated San Pablo, his head on the ground.

Ordinarily tranquil, the church grounds seem to nearly burst with faithful during the five-day **Fiesta del Santa Cristo de Tlacolula,** climaxing on the second Sunday of October, when the plaza is awash with merrymakers. It is then that folks enjoy their favorites, the **Danza de los Jardineros** (Dance of the Gardeners) and the spectacular **Danza de las Plumas** (Dance of the Feathers) along with a *pelota mixteca* (traditional Mixtec ball game) tournament.

The big gate bordering the church grounds leads you to the Tlacolula market. One of Oaxaca's biggest and oldest, the Tlacolula market draws tens of thousands from all over the Valley of Oaxaca every Sunday. Wander around and soak it all in—the diverse crowd of buyers and sellers, and the equally manifold galaxy of merchandise. What about a hand-hewn yoke for your oxen or a new stone *mano* and *metate* for your kitchen? If not, perhaps some live (or ground) *chapulines* (grasshoppers), maybe a live turkey for dinner tomorrow, or a hunk of sugarcane to chew on while you stroll along?

For **accommodations,** try the basic but clean homey downtown Tlacolula lodging, the **Hotel and Restaurant Regis,** at Juárez 33, tel. 956/203-32, for about $10 d. Rooms vary; look at more than one before moving in. Another good option would be the **Tourist Yu'u Tlacolula,** on Hwy. 190, less than a mile east of town. Although on the road, it's located on the pine-shaded grounds of a reforestation seedling nursery. All tourist Yu'u sleep up to six and have kitchenettes. For facilities and reservations details, contact the state-federal tourist information office in Oaxaca City, at 607 Independencia, Oaxaca, Oaxaca 68000, tel. 9/516-4828, fax 9/516-0984, email: turinfo@oaxaca.gob.mx.

YAGUL ARCHAEOLOGICAL ZONE

The remains of Yagul (Zapotec for "Old Tree"), open daily 10 A.M.–5 P.M., stand regally on their volcanic hilltop, 28 miles (45 km) east of Oaxaca City. Although only six miles from Mitla and sharing architectural details, such as Mitla's famous *greca* fretwork, the size and complexity of its buildings suggest that Yagul was an independent city-state in its own right. Local folks call the present ruin the Pueblo Viejo (Old Town) and remember it as the forerunner of the present town of Tlacolula. Archaeological evidence, which indicates that Yagul was occupied for about a thousand years, at least until around A.D. 1100 or 1200, bears them out.

One of Yagul's major claims to fame is its **Palace of Six Patios,** actually three nearly identical but separate complexes of two patios

each. In each patio, rooms surround a central courtyard. The northerly patio of each complex is more private and probably was the residence, while the other, more open, patio served administrative functions.

South of the palace sprawls Yagul's huge **ball court,** the second largest in Mesoamerica, shaped in the characteristic Oaxaca I configuration. Southeast of the ball court is Patio 4, of four mounds surrounding a courtyard. A boulder sculpted in the form of a frog lies at the base of the east mound. At the courtyard's center, a tomb was excavated; descend and explore its three *greca*-style fretwork-decorated chambers.

If it's not too hot, gather your energy and climb to the hilltop above the parking lot for a fine view of the ruin and the entire Valley of Oaxaca. The name for this prominence, the Citadel, probably was accurately descriptive, for Yagul's defenders long ago added rock walls to enhance the hilltop's security.

The airy *palapa* **Restaurant Centeotl,** tel./fax 9/516-6186, 512-0289, on the Yagul archaeological zone entrance road is worth a stop all by itself. Some experienced in Oaxacan cuisine consider Centeotl one of Oaxaca's finest restaurants. You can quickly double your Mexican food vocabulary by sampling such regional delights as *coloradito* (savory red *mole* chicken or beef stew), *verde de espinazo* (similar ingredients, but stewed in green *mole*), *sopa de guias* (corn and squash soup), and *estofado* (tasty chili, tomato, and pork stew). Open daily 11 A.M.–7 P.M.

Besides its gastronomical significance, Centeotl (sayn-tay-OH-tl) is an earnest cultural-ecological endeavor of the friendly elderly owner, who articulately explains his purpose in prose and verse. Ask for his pamphlet—*folleto* (foh-YAY-toh)—about Centeotl.

As you leave, take a look at the pre-Columbian ball game ring mounted by the restaurant entrance. Although the ring is interesting all by itself, the cannonball-size stone sphere perched atop the ring doubles the intrigue, since (if it's authentic, as the owner claims) a stone ball is in variance with general archaeological opinion that the pre-Columbian ball game was played with a rubber, rather than a rock ball. (Pity the pre-Columbian ball players who had to bat such a hard, heavy missile around with their arms, shoulders, and torsos.)

SAN BARTOLOMÉ QUIALANA AND SAN MARCOS TLAPAZOLA

Modern, professionally built, and well-maintained housekeeping accommodations at their respective tourist Yu'u make this pair of scenic hillside villages near Tlacolula good home bases for days of country exploring. Besides all the east valley attractions themselves, these little places (which, on foot, are about two miles apart) have their own set of enticements. Tlapazola women (no men) make attractive red pottery *(barra rojo)*. Locally handcrafted textiles include characteristic black-and-white wool blankets *(cobijos)* and multicolored embroidered dresses and blouses. Other available handicrafts are reed baskets and *ixtle* (maguey fiber) nets. Sights include Calvario, an unexcavated hilltop pyramid, and venerable village churches. The sylvan, oak-studded canyons of towering Cerro Piedra del Sol (elev. 9,600 feet, 2,850 meters) offer hikes to a waterfall and springs. Ask, and the tourist Yu'u manager will guide you (or find you a guide) for a nominal fee to these and other local sights.

Moreover, if you schedule your visit right, you'll get in on the country color and merrymaking of Quialana's **Fiesta de San Bartolomé** (four days around 27 August) or Tlapazola's **Fiesta de San Marcos** (13 November).

Guests at both the Quialana and Tlapazola Tourist Yu'u enjoy breezy hillside cornfield locations. The best time to stay is during the summer rains, when it's not too hot. The green corn rustles in the breeze, dogs bark faintly in the distance, clouds billow up over the lush valley and somber dark green mountains, and now and then a truck (or a loaded burro or oxcart) passes by. For facilities and reservation details, contact the tourist information office in Oaxaca City, at 607 Independencia, Oaxaca, Oaxaca 68000, 9/516-4828, fax 9/516-0984, email: turinfo@oaxaca.gob.mx.

Get to Quialana (pop. 2,500) by car, taxi, or bus and to Tlapazola (pop. 1,500) by either car, taxi, or passenger truck, all via Tlacolula, which bus passengers can reach by second-class bus from the *camionera central segunda clase,* west side of downtown. The route is via Calle Matamoros, which heads south from the middle of Tlacolula to both Quialana and Tlapazola. For Quialana, catch a taxi or the green-and-white Transportes Municipal Quialana bus; for Tlapazola, catch the green-and-white Servicios Mixto de Pasaje y Cargo small truck. If you catch the truck, be prepared to stand with the rest of the folks. For more comfort, splurge (maybe $3 or $4) with a taxi.

Drivers, turn into Tlacolula from Hwy. 190 at the Pemex gas station. Continue south, probably having to detour around the market. You will eventually reach the railroad tracks. Find Calle Matamoros, which crosses the tracks near the west end of town. Mark your odometer as you cross the tracks. Continue south for two miles (three km) to a crossroads. For Quialana, continue straight ahead almost another mile (1.4 km) to the Quialana Tourist Yu'u. The town church and plaza are just short of a mile ahead uphill. For Tlapazola, turn right at the dirt crossroads at mile two and continue another 2.8 miles (4.5 km) to the Tlapazola Tourist Yu'u, and another half mile past that to the town church and plaza.

MITLA

The ruins at Mitla, open daily 10 A.M.–5 P.M., about 31 miles (50 km) from Oaxaca City, are a "must" for Valley of Oaxaca sightseers. Mitla ("Liobaa" in Zapotec, the Place of the Dead) flowered late, reaching a population of perhaps 10,000 during its apex around A.D. 1350. It remained occupied and in use for generations after the conquest.

During Mitla's heyday, several feudalistic, fortified city-states vied for power in the Valley of Oaxaca. Concurrently, Mixtec-speaking people arrived from the north, perhaps under pressure from Aztecs and others in central Mexico. Evidence suggests that these Mixtec groups, interacting with the resident Zapotecs, created the unique architectural styles of late cities such as Yagul and Mitla. Archaeologists believe, for example, that the striking *greca* (Greek-like) frets that honeycomb Mitla facades result from the Mixtec influence.

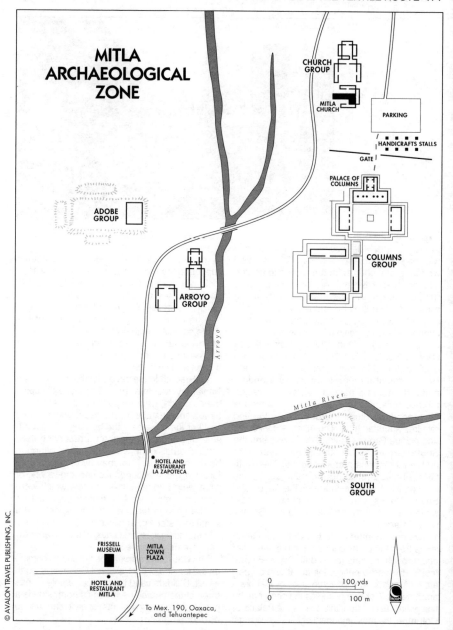

MITLA ARCHAEOLOGICAL ZONE

CHURCH GROUP

MITLA CHURCH

PARKING

HANDICRAFTS STALLS

GATE

PALACE OF COLUMNS

ADOBE GROUP

COLUMNS GROUP

ARROYO GROUP

Arroyo

Mitla River

HOTEL AND RESTAURANT LA ZAPOTECA

SOUTH GROUP

FRISSELL MUSEUM

MITLA TOWN PLAZA

HOTEL AND RESTAURANT MITLA

0   100 yds
0   100 m

To Mex. 190, Oaxaca, and Tehuantepec

© AVALON TRAVEL PUBLISHING, INC.

ruins at Mitla

Exploring the Site

In a real sense, Mitla lives on. The ruins coincide with the present town of San Pablo Villa de Mitla, whose main church actually occupies the northernmost of five main groups of monumental ruins. Virtually anywhere archaeologists dig within the town they hit remains of the myriad ancient dwellings, plazas, and tombs that connected the still-visible landmarks.

Get there by forking left from main Oaxaca Hwy. 190 onto Hwy. 176. Continue about two miles to the Mitla town entrance, on the left. Head straight through town, cross a bridge, and after about a mile, arrive at the site. Of the five ruins clusters, the best preserved is the fenced-in Columns Group. Its exploration requires about an hour. The others—the Arroyo and Adobe Groups beyond an arroyo and the South Group across the Mitla River—are rubbled, unreconstructed mounds. The North Group has suffered due to past use by the local parish. Evidence indicates the Adobe and South Groups were ceremonial compounds, while the Arroyo, North, and Columns Groups were palaces.

The public entrance to the Columns Group leads from the parking lot past a tourist market and through the gate (open daily 9 A.M.–5 P.M.). Inside, two large patios, joined at one corner, are each surrounded on three sides by elaborate apartments. A shrine occupies the center of the first patio. Just north of this stands the **Palace of Columns,** the most important of Mitla's buildings.

It sits atop a staircase inaccurately reconstructed in 1901.

Inside, a file of six monolithic columns supported the roof. A narrow "escape" passage exits out the right rear side to a large patio enclosed by a continuous narrow room. The purely decorative *greca* facades, which required around 100,000 cut stones for the entire complex, embellish the walls. Remnants of the original red and white stucco that lustrously covered the entire complex hide in niches and corners.

Walk south to the second patio, which has a similar layout. Here the main palace occupies the east side, where a passage descends to a tomb beneath the front staircase. Both this and another tomb beneath the building at the north side of the patio are intact, preserving their original crucifix shapes. (The guard, although he is not supposed to, may try to collect a tip for letting you descend.) No one knows who or what were buried in these tombs, which were open and empty at the time of the conquest.

The second tomb is similar, except that it contains a stone pillar called the Column of Life; by embracing it, legend says, you will learn how many years you have left.

The **Church Group** (notice the church domes) on the far side of the Palace of Columns is worth a visit. Builders used the original temple stones to erect the church here. On its north side is a patio leading to another interior patio surrounded by another *greca* palace.

The Frissell Museum

The University of the Americas (Mexico City) houses an exceptionally fine Oaxaca artifact collection at its **Frissell Museum,** tel. 956/801-94, just west of the Mitla town plaza. Displays include a host of finely preserved ceramic figurines, yet-to-be-deciphered Zapotec glyphs, and a Zapotec marriage certificate in stone. Open daily except Wednesdays and holidays 10 A.M.–5 P.M. A restaurant in the museum serves regional dishes from 10 A.M. until about 4 P.M.

Besides its collection, the museum's historic venerable hacienda-style home is notable in its own right. From the mid-19th century, as the **Posada La Sorpresa,** it served as a lodging, owned and operated by the longtime local Quero family. In 1950, they sold out to American artifact collector Ervin R. Frissell, who turned the hotel into both his home and a repository for his growing collection and that of his friend, Howard Leigh, noted scholar of Mixtec language and culture. Upon their deaths, the entire building and artifact collection passed to the University of the Americas.

Fiesta Principal del Apóstol de San Pablo

Mitla (pop. 11,000) although famous, is a quiet town where tranquillity is disturbed only by occasional tourist buses along its dusty, sun-drenched main street. A major exception occurs during Mitla's major Fiesta Principal del Apóstol de San Pablo, which centers on the town's venerable 16th-century church, dedicated to San Pablo Apóstol (St. Paul the Apostle). If you plan your visit during the eight days climaxing around 25 January (or also around 29 June, the day of San Pablo and San Pedro), you can join with the townsfolk as they celebrate their *patrón* with masses, processions, a feast, fireworks, *jaripeo* (bull roping and riding), and dancing.

Shopping

Instead of making handicrafts, Mitla people concentrate on selling them, mostly at the big **handicrafts market** adjacent to the archaeological zone parking lot. Here you can sample from a concentrated all-Oaxaca assortment, especially textiles: cotton *huipiles,* wool hangings and rugs, onyx animals and chess sets, fanciful *alebrijes,* and leather huaraches, purses, belts, and wallets.

Accommodations and Food

Directly across the street from the Frissell Museum, stop for a refreshment at the homey **Hotel and Restaurant Mitla,** domain of the sparkplug mother-daughter team of Teresa and Gloria González de Quero, at Benito Juárez 6, Mitla, Oaxaca 70430, tel. 956/801-12. Here you can enjoy Mexico as old-timers remember it, in a charmingly ramshackle hacienda-style farmhouse, where roosters crow, dogs snooze, and where guests can have their seasonal fill of bananas, avocados, mandarins, and papayas

greca *(fret) decorations on a palace wall at Mitla*

from a shady backyard *huerta* (orchard). Their 16 rooms vary. The upstairs tier—plain but clean, with the essentials, including hot water—is acceptably rustic. Overnight rates run about $8 s, $15 d, with parking.

Alternatively, about five blocks north, closer to the archaeological zone, try the also family-run **Hotel and Restaurant La Zapoteca**, 5 de Febrero 12, Mitla, Oaxaca 70430, tel. 956/800-26, open daily 7:30 A.M.–7 P.M., on the right just before the Mitla River bridge. The spic-and-span restaurant (praised by locals for "the best *chiles rellenos* in Oaxaca") is excellent for meals, and the 20 clean, reasonably priced rooms are fine for an overnight. Rentals run about $14 s, $18 d, $20 t, with hot water and parking.

Bus travelers can **get to Mitla** from Oaxaca by Fletes y Pasajes bus from the *camionera central segunda clase*.

HIERVE EL AGUA MINERAL SPRINGS

Although the name of this place translates as "boiling" water, the springs that seep from the side of the limestone mountain less than an hour's drive east of Mitla aren't hot. Instead, they are loaded with minerals. These minerals over time have built up into rock-hard deposits, forming great algae-painted slabs in level spots and, on steep slopes, accumulating into what appear to be grand frozen waterfalls.

The Springs

Although the springs may be crowded on weekends and holidays, you'll probably have Hierve el Agua nearly to yourself on weekdays. The first thing you'll see after passing the entrance gate is a lineup of snack and curio stalls at the cliffside parking lot. A trail leads downhill to the main spring, which bubbles from the mountainside and trickles into a huge basin that the operators have dammed as a swimming pool. Bring your bathing suit.

Part of Hierve el Agua's appeal is the panoramic view of mountain and valley. On a clear day, you can see the tremendous massif of Zempoatepetl, the grand holy mountain range of the Mixe people, rising above the eastern horizon.

From the ridge-top park, agile walkers can

hike farther down the hill, following deposits curiously accumulated in the shape of limestone minidikes that trace the mineral water's downhill path. Soon you'll glimpse a towering limestone formation, like a giant petrified waterfall, appearing to ooze from the cliff on the right.

Back uphill by the parking lot, operators have augmented the natural springs with a resort-style swimming pool where, along with everyone else, you can frolic to your heart's content.

Hikers can also enjoy following a major new **sendero peatonal** (footpath) that encircles the entire zone. Start your walk, either from the trailhead beyond the bungalows past the pool or at the other end, at the cliff edge between the parking lot and the entrance gate. Your reward will be an approximately one-hour, self-guided tour, looping downhill past the springs and the great frozen rock cascades and featuring grand vistas of the gorgeous mountain and canyon scenery along the way.

The semi-arid Hierve de Agua zone and surrounding country is habitat for a dry-country **palm** you'll probably see plenty of while strolling around. Lack of moisture usually keeps the palms small, sometimes clustering in great gardens, appearing like regiments of desert dwarfs. Local people gather and weave their fronds into *canastas* (baskets), *petates* (mats), *escobas* (brooms), and more, which they sometimes sell in the stalls by the parking lot.

Accommodations, Food and Getting There

The Hierve el Agua **Tourist Yu'u** lodging provides the key for a restful one- or two-night stay. The several clean and well-maintained housekeeping bungalows, with shower baths and hot water, rent for about $7 per person, or around $40 for up to six in a bungalow, with refrigerator, stove, and utensils. Make reservations through the tourism office in Oaxaca City, 607 Independencia, Oaxaca, Oaxaca 68000, tel. 9/516-4828, fax 9/516-0984, email: turinfo@oaxaca.gob.mx.

For food, you can bring and cook your own in your bungalow or rely upon the strictly local-style tacos, tamales, *carne asada* (roast meat), beans, and tortillas offered by the parking-lot food stalls. In any case, fruit and vegetable lovers should bring their own from Oaxaca or Mitla. Produce selection in local San Lorenzo village stores will most likely be minimal.

Get there by riding a Fletes y Pasajes San Lorenzo- or Hierve de Agua-marked bus east out of either Oaxaca City (second-class terminal) or Mitla on Hwy. 179 just south of town. Drivers, head east from Mitla along Hwy. 179, the road that branches east from Hwy. 190, two miles before Mitla town. After another approximately 11 miles (18 km), follow the signed gravel road that branches right, another five miles (eight km), through San Lorenzo village to Hierve el Agua. **Warning:** Until they get around to paving it, the clay roadbed through San Lorenzo village and beyond is **extremely slippery** when soaking wet. Under such conditions, unless you're driving a good-traction four-wheel-drive vehicle, park your car in the village and walk the final quarter mile, which steeply descends to the Hierve de Agua entrance.

SOUTH AND SOUTHWEST OF OAXACA CITY

Travelers who venture into the Valley of Oaxaca's long, south-pointing fingers, sometimes known as the Valleys of Zimatlán and Ocotlán, can discover a wealth of crafts, history, and architectural and scenic wonders. These are all accessible by day trips from the city by car or combinations of bus and taxi. Most reachable are the famous crafts villages of Coyotepec, Tilcajete, Jalieza, and others along Hwy. 175, between the city and the colorful market town of Ocotlán (best to plan a visit to all on Friday, Ocotlán's market day). Another day you can either continue farther south to soak in the nontouristed feast of sights at the big market in Ejutla or fork southwest, via Hwy. 131 through Zimatlán, to the idyllic groves, crystal springs, and limestone caves hidden around San Sebastián de las Grutas.

San Bartolo Coyotepec

San Bartolo Coyotepec (Hill of the Coyote), on Hwy. 175 14 miles (23 km) south of the city, is famous for its pottery and its 24–27 August festival. During the Fiesta de San Bartolomé, masked villagers costumed as half-man, half-woman in tiaras, blond wigs, tin crowns, and velvet cloaks dance in honor of their patron.

The town's black pottery, the renowned *barro negro* sold all over Mexico, is available at the signed pottery Mercado on the right and at a number of cottage factory shops (watch for signs) off the highway, scattered along (east side) Juárez Street. **Doña Rosa,** who passed away in 1980, pioneered the technique of crafting lovely, big, round jars without a potter's wheel. With their local clay, Doña Rosa's descendants and neighbor families regularly turn out acres of glistening black plates, pots, bowls, trees of life, and fetching animals for very reasonable prices. (Figure on about $20 for a pearly, three-gallon vase, and perhaps $2 for a cute little black rabbit.)

Cochineal Farm

On your way either to or from Coyotepec and Ocotlán, you might want to stop at the small demonstration cochineal farm and museum, just off the highway at San Bartolo Coyotepec, a few miles south of the Oaxaca airport. The farm, officially the **Centro de Difusión del Conocimiento de la Grana Cochinilla Tlapanochestli,** is the labor of love of retired chemical engineer Ignacio J. del Río Dueñas. Señor Dueñas graciously welcomes all visitors— schoolchildren, visiting scholars, neighbors, tourists—to his rancho for the purpose of breathing life into the ancient Oaxaca tradition of cochineal dye, the source of the bright reds in many of the Oaxaca weavings. (See the special topic Cochineal in the Introduction.)

Others besides Señor Dueñas believe in cochineal, produced from the bodies of the scale insect, *Dactylopius coccus,* which thrives on the thick leaves of the nopal (prickly pear) cactus, found all over Mexico and much of the western United States. Precisely *because* cochineal is a natural (as opposed to synthetic) product, it is gaining favor as a natural food and cosmetic (lipstick) coloring. The small amount of cochineal that Señor Dueñas produces sells for about $200 per kilogram (compared with silver, at about $100).

He'll be happy to show you around his acre of cactus, demonstrate how the insects are harvested, and explain his several interesting museum exhibits, which demonstrate the history and uses of cochineal. For more information, contact Señor Dueñas at Rancho La Nopalera, Km 10.5 Carretera Oaxaca-Puerto Ángel, Santa María Coyotepec, Oaxaca, tel./fax 955/100-53, email: tlapanochestili@infosel.net.mx.

Get there by bus from the *camionera segunda clase,* via regional buses Estrella del Valle, Oaxaca Pacifico, or Estrella Roja del Sureste, or more local Choferes del Sur buses.

By car turn right, southbound, at the small red roadside sign Grana Cochineal Tlapanochestli at the southern edge of Santa María Coyotepec village, on Hwy. 175 4.7 miles (7.5 km) south of the Oaxaca airport. After a few hundred yards westbound on a dirt road, another sign directs you left to the rancho.

Crafts Villages on the Road to Ocotlán

Each of the three little crafts villages not far north of Ocotlán has something unique to offer. In order to visit all of them, plus Coyotepec and Ocotlán, on Friday, you'll need to get an early start. If you're inclined to linger, it's best to allow two days for your visit. Under any circumstances, visit **San Antonino Castillo Velasco** on the same Friday that you visit Ocotlán, because it also has its *tianguis* on Friday. Two things to look for are the wonderful **breads,** fresh and yummy, as you come into town, and the famous *vestidos de San Antonino,* sometimes known as Oaxacan wedding dresses, marked by their elaborately fancy and colorful animal and floral embroidery. On Friday a few women sell them in the regular market (turn left at the first block after the bread stalls). If you arrive and no one seems to be selling any dresses, mention *"vestidos de San Antonino,"* and someone will lead you to a woman who makes them. Alternatively, ask for friendly Rosa Canseco Godines (go-DEE-nays) (address Calle Guerrero 33), one of the local *maestras* of the craft, and if she's home, she'll gladly show you examples of her beautiful work.

Bus passengers, take a taxi or walk the mile from Ocotlán. Drivers, turn west (left, northbound) at the San Antonino sign just at the northern (Oaxaca) edge of Ocotlán.

San Martín Tilcajete, about 21 miles (37 km) south of Oaxaca (not far north of the Hwy. 131 fork), and **Santo Tomás Jalieza** (south of the Hwy. 131 fork) a mile or two farther south, can be visited as a pair on any day. San Martín is one of the sources (besides Arrazola) of the *alebrijes,* fanciful wooden animals occupying the shelves of crafts stores the world over. About a dozen family stores on the town's one street are happy to show you what they have and demonstrate how they make them. Look at more than one store, because they have lots more than funny animals. They've branched out to plants, such as purple palm trees and yellow cactus. Some items, such as imaginatively painted jewel boxes and picture frames, are practical, while others, such as miniature sets of tables and chairs, are for kids three to 90.

Jalieza, on the other hand, is known as the town of *cinturones* (belts). Townsfolk, virtually all of whom practice the craft, concentrate all of their selling in a single many-stalled market in the middle of town. Step inside and you'll be tempted, not only by hundreds of hand-embroidered leather belts, but by a wealth of lovely hand-loomed and embroidered purses, shawls, small backpacks, and much more. Furthermore, asking prices are very reasonable. Open daily about 10 A.M.–6 P.M.

OCOTLÁN

Your first stop in district capital Ocotlán (pop. 20,000; 26 miles, 42 km south of Oaxaca) should probably be the interesting trio of shops run by the Aguilar sisters, Irene, Guillerma, and Josefina. Watch for their signs, on the right, on the outskirts, about a quarter mile on the Oaxaca side from the town plaza. Their creations include a host of fanciful figures in clay: vendors with big ripe strawberries, green and red cactus, goats in skirts, and bikini-clad blondes.

The main Ocotlán attraction (unless you're lucky enough to arrive for the big fiesta on the third Sunday of May) is the huge Friday market. Beneath a riot of colored awnings, hordes of merchandise—much modern stuff, but also

pottery for sale at Ocotlán

plenty of old-fashioned goodies—load a host of tables and street-laid mats. How about a handmade wooden yoke for your oxen or a saddle for your donkey? If not that, why not four or five turkeys, a goat, or perhaps half a dozen bags of hard-to-get wild medicinal plants? And be sure to pick up a kilo or two of *cal* (lime) to soak your corn. If you're looking for lots of native costumes, you'll have to head for the mountains, because few women (except for their ribbon-decorated braids) and virtually no men wear *traje*. You'll hear plenty of Zapotec, however. About half the local people are native speakers.

Since markets are best in the morning, best make Ocotlán your *first* Friday stop. Drivers could get there by heading out straight south from the city, arriving in Ocotlán by mid-morning. Spend a few hours, then begin your return in the early afternoon, stopping at the several crafts villages (see above) along the road back to Oaxaca. Gasoline is available at the Pemex *gasolinera,* on the highway, north edge of town. **Bus travelers** could do something similar, by riding an early Autobuses Estrella del Valle or Autotransportes Oaxaca-Pacífico from the second-class Abastos terminal, then returning, in steps, by taxi, stopping at the crafts villages along the way.

Casa de Cultura Rudolfo Morales
Lately, Ocotlán has come upon good times, partly due to Rudolfo Morales, the internationally celebrated but locally born artist, who has dedicated his fortune to improving his hometown. For several years, the Rudolfo Morales Foundation has been restoring churches and other public buildings, reforesting mountainsides, and funding self-help and educational projects all over Ocotlán and its surrounding district. The bright colors of the plaza-front *presidencia municipal* and the big church nearby result from the good works of Rudolfo Morales.

Morales's local efforts center at the Casa de Cultura Rudolfo Morales, in the yellow-painted mansion at Morelos 108, three doors north from the Ocotlán plaza's northwest corner. In the Casa Cultura's graceful, patrician interior Morales's family and staff manage their foundation's affairs, teach art and computer classes, and sponsor community events. They also welcome all visitors, every Friday, approximately 10 A.M.–2 P.M. and 4–6 P.M. For more information, contact the foundation's headquarters in Oaxaca City, at Murguia 105, Oaxaca, Oaxaca 68000, tel. 9/514-1532, fax 9/514-0910, email: artedeoaxaca@spersaoaxaca.com.mx.

Templo de Santo Domingo
Local people celebrate Rudolfo Morales's brilliant restoration of their beloved 16th-century Templo de Santo Domingo. Gold and silver from the infamous mines at Santa Catarina Minas, in the mountains east of Ocotlán, financed the church's initial construction. When overwork and disease tragically decimated the local native population around 1600, the mines had to be abandoned, and work on the church stopped. Although eventually completed over the succeeding three centuries, it had slipped into serious disrepair by the 1980s.

Fortunately, the Templo de Santo Domingo is now completely rebuilt, from its bright blue, yellow, and white facade to the Baroque gold glitter of its nave ceiling. Inside on the right side,

BUILDING CHURCHES

Although European architects designed nearly all of Mexico's colonial-era churches, embellishing them with old-world Gothic, Renaissance, Baroque, and Moorish decorations, native artists blended their own geometric, floral, and animal motifs. The result was a blend that manifested in intriguing variations all over Mexico. This was especially true in Oaxaca, where droves of faithful worship before gilded altars and flowery ceilings built and decorated by their long-gone ancestors. Local materials further distinguish Oaxacan churches from others in Mexico. The spectrum of soft pastels of local *cantera* volcanic stone, from yellow through gray, including green in Oaxaca City, marks Oaxacan walls and facades.

Sometimes the native influence led to poor ("provincial") versions of European designs; other times (notably, the Templo y Exconvento de Santo Domingo in Oaxaca City) artists merged brilliant native decorations with the best of European-style vaults, arches, and columns.

The Layout

Mexican church design followed the Egypto-Greco-Roman tradition of its European models. Basically, architects designed their churches beginning with the main space of the **nave,** in the shape of a box, lined with high lateral windows. Depending on their origin and function, builders constructed three basic types of churches—the monk's **monastery or convent** *(convento),* the bishop's **cathedral** *(catedral),* and the priest's parish church *(templo, parroquia).* Most Oaxacan monastic churches (nearly all now ex-convents) were begun during the 16th and 17th centuries by the missionary orders—a handful by the Franciscans, Jesuits, and Augustinians, and the overwhelming remainder by the Dominicans.

In Oaxaca, faced with the constant threat of earthquake, the Dominican padres built massively thick walls supported on the exterior with ponderous buttresses. Key elements were naves, with or without **transepts** *(cruceros),* cross spaces separating the nave from the altar, making the church plan resemble a Christian cross. They placed the **choir** *(coro)* above and just inside the inside the entrance arch.

At the opposite, usually the east, or sunrise end of the church, builders sometimes extended the nave beyond the transept to include a **presbytery** *(presbiterio),* which was often lined with seats where church officials presided. The building ended past that the at the **apse** *(ábside),* the space behind the altar, frequently in semi-circular or half-octagonal form. Within the apse rose the gilded **retable** *(retablo)* adorned with sacred images, attended by choirs of angels and cherubs.

Larger churches usually incorporated side altars presided over by images of locally popular saints, nearly always including the Virgin of Guadalupe.

The Facade

Outside, in front, rises the facade *(fachada),* sometimes in a uniform style, but just as often a mixture of Renaissance, Gothic, and baroque, with some Moorish *(mujedar)* worked into the mix. A proliferation of columns nearly always decorates Oaxacan church facades, from the classic Etruscan, Doric, Ionic, and Corinthian *(Toscano, Dórico, Jónico, Corintio)* pillars to spiraled Solomonic *(Salomónico)* barber's poles and bizarre *estipites.* *Estipite* columns, a baroque feature of Plateresque facades (so-named for their resemblance to elaborate silverware designs), usually begin with a classical capital (base) but rise, curiously, like an inverted obelisk, widening to a pair or trio of elaborately carved prismatic blocks and narrowing quickly again to an identical capital at the top.

Convents

The monastery (or convent) style churches, besides all of the above, included living and working quarters for the members of the order, typically built around a columned patio called the **cloister** *(claustro).* A corridor through an arched porch *(portería)* adjacent to the nave usually leads to the cloister, from which monks and nuns could quickly reach the dining hall, or **refectory** *(refectorio),* and their private rooms, or cells *(celdas).*

The Oaxacan missionary fathers always designed their churches with an eye to handling the masses of natives whom they hoped to convert. For them, padres included an **atrium** *(atrio),* a large exterior courtyard in front of the facade. For the partly initiated natives, they often built an open chapel *(capilla abierta)* on one side of the atrium. Conversions also occurred at smaller open chapels *(pozas),* built at the corners of the atrium.

Oaxaca Standouts

Outstanding examples (nearly all Dominican) of Oaxacan church architecture are scattered throughout the state, notably, in the following locations:

OAXACA CITY

Church and Ex-convent of Santo Domingo
Church and Ex-convent of San Agustín
Church of San Felipe Neri
Cathedral of Oaxaca
Basilica and Ex-convent of Nuestra Señora de la Soledad

VALLEY OF OAXACA

Cuilapan
Tlacochahuaya
Tlacolula
Ocotlán

MIXTECA

Teotongo
Tamazulapan
Tejupan
Coixtlahuaca
Teposcolula
San Juan Teposcolula
Tlaxiaco
Nduayaco
Yanhuitlán

NORTHERN OAXACA

Ixtlán
Calpulalpan
Ixtepeji

ISTHMUS

Tehuantepec
Juchitán

you'll pass a pious Saint John the Baptist, with Mary Magdalen at his feet. Up front, above the main altar, a white-haired, bearded Creator reigns, resembling an indigenous Father Sun, with a halo of golden rays bursting from behind his head. Below him, Jesus hangs limply on the cross, flanked below by Mother Mary with a knife in her breast and St. John the Baptist lamenting at Jesus' feet.

Walk to the nave's south, right, side, to a gilded chapel, dedicated the Lord of the Sacristy, the image above the altar. Also notice the adjacent oil painting of the Virgin of the Rosary, singular for her mestizo facial features. The Lord of the Sacristy (Señor de la Sacristía) is the object of community adoration in a **festival** of food, fireworks, processions, high masses, and dances climaxing on the third Sunday in May.

EJUTLA

Tour buses usually skip Ejutla de Crespo (pop. 20,000) because of its distance, about 36 miles (59 km) from Oaxaca City. This is a pity, because Ejutla hides some surprises, not the least of which is its huge **Thursday market.** Folks troop in from country villages all over the huge Ejutla governmental district and farther, to haggle over everything from *hamacas* and huaraches to radios and refrigerators.

Sights

Take a walk around Ejutla's shady plaza to get your bearings. The porticoed *presidencia municipal* stands on the plaza's south side, the market is on the north, and the big, proud **Templo de la Natividad** stands on the west. Sometime around 1750, the present church replaced the 16th century original (which itself replaced a big preconquest Zapotec pyramid). Over the years, earthquakes took their toll; it was extensively restored around 1900.

Several large hieroglyph-decorated stones built into the church's walls attest to the fact that the entire town remains an unexplored archaeological zone. You can find more evidence of this about two blocks north and two blocks east of the church, near the corner of Calles Altimirano and 16 de Septiembre. A big house compound encloses what appears to be a small hill, which is actually a buried temple mound. Look for the several hieroglyph-decorated preconquest stones that have been incorporated into modern walls.

Since the church is usually open, you might as well step into the cool interior and contemplate the town's patron, the **Virgin of the Nativity,** presiding above the altar in what at first glance appears to be a bridal gown. In the lovely transept chapel on the right of the nave, you'll see another image of the same patron. Local people celebrate both, with a big fiesta centering around 8 December.

For something else interesting, step over to the *presidencia* and look on the wall for Ejutla's official *escudo* (coat of arms), which incorporates no arms at all. It's a portrait in tile of a bean vine, encircling a view of the sun rising from behind Cerro El Labrador, the town's symbolic mountain, to the east. A poem, in praise of the "SUN, which rises here earlier than other lands . . . the source of life . . . without which there would be nothing" is included at the base of the *escudo*.

Practicalities

Hotel 6: Another of Ejutla's surprises is the Hotel 6, "probably the best in North America," claims the owner-operator, friendly former Olympic wrestler and civil engineer Mario E. Corres. A sign, which strikingly resembles "Motel 6" signs all over the United States and Canada, draws you into the parking lot at Km 61.5 Carretera Oaxaca-Puerto Ángel, Ejutla de Crespo, Oaxaca, tel. 957/303-50. You know you're in for something unique when you pull up to a portaled, old hacienda as big as a baseball field, with a jungle on one side, complete with tree house and a swinging rope walkway.

Inside, you'll find everything completely in order, from three spreading courtyards, a pool, and two big function rooms to a huge living room, a dining room, and a spotless, shining, old-fashioned kitchen. The climax to all this is Señor Corres's museum, complete with Señor Corres's family tree, which he gladly explains to visitors.

The 14 rooms, which after everything else seem an afterthought, are plain but clean. Some are more inviting than others. Take a look at two or three, small and large, before choosing. If the weather's warm, you'll need a fan, which some rooms have. For all this, rates are only $10 s, $11

d, with parking, toilet and shower baths, hot water, pool, and dining room. If you want three meals included with your room, the tariff runs about $15 per person.

You'll encounter most of Ejutla's services during your stroll around town—most of the available stores and services are right on or near the plaza. Starting at the *presidencia municipal*, on the south and moving clockwise, first comes *Telecomunicaciones*, which offers telegraph, money order service, and fax, under the portal just west of the *presidencia*.

On the southwest plaza corner is the town's best, **Restaurant Mary**, where a squad of hardworking teenage girls serve hearty country food daily 8 A.M.–7 P.M.

From there, down the street south, at the first corner away from the plaza, is the **bus station** where first- and second-class Autotransportes Oaxaca-Pacífico and Autobuses Estrella del Valle will take you anywhere along Hwy. 175 between Puerto Ángel and the City of Oaxaca. On the same street, a short block west from the bus station is the *correo* (post office). Switch back to the Restaurant Mary and walk west away from the plaza to **Farmacia San Antonio and Clínica Urgencias** with Dr. Lorenzo Antonio Elorza. Go to the northwest plaza corner and you'll see the Casa Altamirano **grocery store** *(abarrotería)* and half a block east of that, the open-air **market,** where you can get the fresh items that the grocery store doesn't have. Continuing north, at the street corner, is the *huarachería* **La Principal,** with a huge assortment of down-home footwear, nearly all made on-site by the owner's daughter. One short block behind (north) that is the **Clínica San Gabriel,** with a gynecologist and a general practitioner-surgeon on call 24 hours, tel. 957/302-44. If you need another *farmacia* (pharmacy) you have your choice of the Santa Fe, on the northeast side, and the Liliana, east of the plaza, next to the church. **Gasoline** is available at the highway Pemex *gasolinera* at the north edge of town.

DOWN HIGHWAY 131

Zimatlán

Travelers who head far enough along Hwy. 131, which branches west about 22 miles (35 km) south of the city through the Oaxaca Valley's southwest side, are in for more than just one treat. They pass some of Oaxaca's most productive farmland: lush fields and pastures that in summer and fall appear like a verdant carpet reaching to the foot of pine- and oak-studded mountains.

Zimatlán (pop. about 25,000), the capital of all this, appears simply as a workaday agricultural town, with a modicum of strictly local-style services. Zimatlán's pace quickens, however, on Wednesday, when the town market overflows with a flood of Zapotec buyers and sellers from the surrounding mountains. Excitement peaks during the eight days around 15 January, when folks celebrate the unique **Fiesta del Dulce Nombre de Jesús.** Keeping by their traditional ways, townspeople enjoy old-fashioned events, including processions, a big everyone-invited barbecue, *jaripeo* (bull mounting), and the Danza de la Pluma (Feathers) and Danza de los Jardineros (Gardeners), plus a *pelota mixteca* preconquest ball game tournament.

San Sebastián de Las Grutas

It's hard not to fall in love with this idyllic hidden corner of the Valley of Oaxaca. Don't be put off by the scruffy, tourist-*comedor*-cluttered Hwy. 131 turnoff intersection, 45 miles (73 km) south of Oaxaca City. After a quarter mile toward the *grutas* (caves), the road becomes a gently winding, sylvan creekside drive. The jade-green brook (sometimes muddy in wet season) gurgles downhill over little rocks and giant boulders, pausing here and there in picture-perfect swimming holes. Meanwhile, from overhead, a regal host of towering, gnarled *sabinos* (*tules* or *ahuehuetes*) shades the creek, appearing every bit as ancient and grand as their northern cousins, the California redwoods. Now and then you pass by the rustic wooden homes and the cornfields of the local farm families. Or you might glimpse the big cylindrical fermentation vats of a rough and ready roadside *mescal* factory.

About eight miles (13 km) past San Sebastián de las Grutas town (pop. 2,000) you reach the caves. The creek emerges clear and pristine, as if by magic, from beneath a big rock at the foot of a mountain. There are modern-standard tourist Yu'u cabins.

A hundred yards uphill up are the caves, which

you can tour for a fee of about $1. A guide with a pair of strong flashlights will lead you on an easy, mostly level walk through the cave's several chambers, which vary from about 20 feet (six meters) to over 200 feet (60 meters) in height. He's used to getting a tip of about $1 per person.

The cave you will see is only one of the several partly explored caves honeycombing the mountain, Cerro Cruz del Lado. Its five or six main chambers stretch about 500 yards (about .5 km) into the mountain. Inside, the formations, which include many towering stalagmites and plenty of bulging stalactites, initially appear, in the semi-darkness of the flickering flashlights, to be gargantuan mounds and columns of half-melted vanilla-chocolate-swirl ice cream. However, when your eyes get accustomed to the darkness, most of the formations, more than any cave I've ever seen, take on fanciful shapes. Bring your own flashlight and have fun dreaming up your own interpretations instead of merely seeing the guide's camel, turtle, shark, alligator (which looked like a seal to me), or tiger.

Practicalities: One could spend several enjoyable days hiking, bird-watching, swimming in the creek, sitting in the town plaza, and getting to know the local people. They're generally friendly, having seen enough visitors so that they're not afraid and don't think you're too strange. The shady streamside, moreover, appears ripe for camping, either in your tent or (self-contained) RV. Get permission first from the tourist Yu'u manager or the municipal authorities at the *presidencia* in San Sebastián de las Grutas, a mile downstream from the cave parking lot.

Alternatively, you can stay in one of the three clean, six-person tourist Yu'u units, for about $6 per person per night, with beds, blankets, showers, hot water, and furnished kitchenette. Bring your own towels, soap, and food from Oaxaca City or Zimatlán. Local supplies may be severely limited. Although reservations are not generally necessary, best reserve anyway, through the state-federal tourist information office in Oaxaca City, at 607 Independencia, Oaxaca, Oaxaca 68000, tel. 9/516-4828, fax 9/516-0984, email: turinfo@oaxaca.gob.mx.

A number of downscale eating stands near the caves sell basic local meals, which, if hot, should be wholesome. Water, drinkable directly from the pristine spring source by the caves, is not a problem here.

Get there by bus via the Solteca or Estrella Rojo del Sureste bus from the *camionera central segunda clase* (second-class bus terminal) next to the Abastos market on the southwest side of Oaxaca City. The Solteca buses, some of which go right to the caves, leave several times a day, beginning around 6 A.M. The Estrella Rojo del Sureste drops you at the intersection, eight miles from the caves. Walk or take a taxi from there. Drivers, follow Hwy. 131, a total of 53 miles (76 km) south of Oaxaca City. Allow about two hours' driving time. In the reverse, north direction, the *grutas* are 119 miles (190 km) north of Puerto Escondido. For safety, under the best of conditions, allow about four hours of daylight driving time.

Sola de Vega
San Miguel Sola de Vega (pop. 13,000), diminutive capital of the remote, sprawling governmental district of the same name, is the main service stop on Oaxaca-Puerto Escondido Hwy. 131. The town, 59 miles (95 km) south of Oaxaca (99 miles, 159 km, north of Puerto Escondido), presides over a lush mountain valley checkerboard of corn, cane, and cattle. The lovely *sabino*-shaded Sola de Vega river ripples right past the town, crossed by quaint but practical suspension footbridges. It looks as if the people have plenty of fun, spending about half their time in the water. Camping by tent or RV appears promising in shady spots by the river. Get permission from authorities at the *presidencia municipal* at the town plaza, about three blocks north from the highway.

If you arrive on Sunday, Sola de Vega's traditional market day, be sure to visit the local *tianguis* (native market) around the town plaza.

Practicalities: A few stores near the plaza can supply basic groceries. For cooked food, try one of the many country *comedores* by the highway or, if you prefer, the dining room of the plain but clean **Hotel Aguirre**, on the highway. Its 15 rooms, in three floors, rent for about $11 s or d, $16 t, with hot-water showers. Although you will not generally need a reservation, you can contact the hotel by tel. 957/400-46, 957/400-47, and 957/400-96.

Drivers, **fill up with gasoline** at the Pemex station on the north side of town, since gasoline is likely to be scarce between Puerto Escondido and Oaxaca. For other essential services, you have the *correo* and *telégrafo* by the plaza, a *centro de salud* on Independencia, off the plaza, and a private physician, Dr. Vicente Mendoza Martinez, also on Independencia. For nonprescription medicines and phone calls, go to the *farmacia-caseta larga distancia* San Miguel, right on the highway at the south (Puerto Escondido), end of town, tel. 957/400-34. Also on the highway you'll find the Solteca and Estrella Roja del Sureste bus stations.

SOUTHWEST SIDE

Cuilapan de Guerrero and Arrazola
Southwest of the city, Cuilapan de Guerrero is famous for its elaborate but unfinished **Exconvento de Santiago,** or Saint James (visible from the highway), where President Guerrero was infamously executed in 1831. Although begun in 1535, the cost of the basilica and associated monastery began to balloon. In 1550, King Philip demanded humility and moderation of the builders, whose work was finally ended by a 1570 court ruling. The extravagances—the soaring, roofless basilica, magnificent baptismal font, splendid Gothic cloister, and elaborate frescoes—remain as national treasures.

Arrazola, a few miles farther north, is one of the sources of the intricately painted ***alebrijes*** (ah-lee-BREE-hays)—fanciful wooden creatures that decorate the shelves of handicrafts shops all over Mexico and foreign countries. Bus travelers, get there by tourist bus from the city. Drivers, turn west (left) onto signed Hwy. 145 a few miles north of Cuilapan or, traveling south, 3.2 miles (5.1 km) south of the Atoyac River Bridge in Oaxaca City. Pass through San Javier village and continue from the turnoff a total of three miles (five km) to the Arrazola town plaza. Turn right immediately before the plaza onto Calle E. Zapata and turn left after one block, at Independencia. After one more block you will be at Calle Obregón, where everyone seems to be making *alebrijes*. Although every family along the street seems to craft its own variations,

Pepe Santiago and his Santa's workshop of craftspersons seem to have the edge. Inside the Santiago compound (on the right, just below the hilltop), men saw and carve away while a cadre of young women painstakingly add riots of painted brocade to everything from whimsical dragons and gargoyles to armadillos, giraffes, and rabbits.

Zaachila

About 10 miles south of Oaxaca, Zaachila (pop. 30,000), like Mitla, overlies the ruins of its ancient namesake city, which rose to prominence after the decline of Monte Albán. Although excavations have uncovered many Mixtec-style remains, historical records nevertheless list a number of Zapotec kings who ruled Zaachila as a virtual Zapotec capital. On the eve of the conquest, it was a Mixtec noble minority who dominated the Zapotec-speaking inhabitants, whose leaders the Mixtec warriors had sent fleeing for their lives to Tehuantepec.

The big forested hill that rises north of the market plaza is topped by a large, mostly unexplored pyramid. Several unexcavated mounds and courtyards dot the hill's north and south flanks. The site parking lot and entrance gate are adjacent to the colonial church just north of the plaza.

In 1962, archaeologist Roberto Gallegos (guarded from hostile residents by armed soldiers) uncovered a pair of unopened tombs beneath the summit of the Zaachila pyramid. They yielded a trove of polychrome pottery, gold jewelry (including a ring still on a left hand), and jade fan handles. Tomb 1, which is open for public inspection, descends via a steep staircase to an entrance decorated with a pair of cat-motif heads. On the antechamber walls a few steps farther on are depictions of owls and a pair of personages (perhaps former occupants) inscribed respectively with the name-dates 5-Flower and 9-Flower. Do not miss the bas-reliefs on the tomb's back wall (take a flashlight), which depict a man whose torso is covered with a turtle shell and another whose head is emerging from a serpent body.

You can reach Zaachila by tourist bus or by car from Oaxaca City. Head toward Monte Albán (look for the big road sign) west over the Atoyac River from the *periférico* at the south edge of town. Just after crossing the bridge, fork left (south) from the Monte Albán road onto the Zaachila road.

Hint: The narrow tomb staircase is negotiable by only a few persons at a time and often requires an hour for a tour bus crowd to inspect it. Rather than waste your market time standing in line, go downhill, stroll around the market, and return when the line is smaller. If driving, arrive early, around 9 A.M. on Thursday, to avoid tour bus crowds.

great blue heron

BOB RACE

WEST AND NORTHWEST OF THE CITY: THE ARCHAEOLOGICAL ROUTE

Although all of these interesting destinations are readily reachable from Oaxaca City, they are far too rich to be visited in a single day. As a minimum be sure to visit "unmissable" Monte Albán, which can be conveniently combined with a side trip to Atzompa. On another day, preferably a Wednesday, visit the Etla market, with stops at the community museums and key archaeological sites at El Mogote and Suchilquitongo nearby.

MONTE ALBÁN

Monte Albán ranks among Mesoamerica's most regal and spectacular ruined cities. The original Zapotec name was Danni Dipaa. "Monte Albán" was probably coined by a local Spaniard because of its resemblance to a similarly named Italian hill town.

Monte Albán's people cultivated corn, beans, squash, chilies, and fruits on the hillsides and adjacent valleys, occasionally feasting on meat from deer, small game, and perhaps (as did other ancient Mexicans) domesticated dogs. Tribute from surrounding communities directly enriched Monte Albán's ruling classes, and, by extension, its artisans and farmers.

The great city on the hill reigned for at least 1,200 years, between 500 B.C. and A.D. 750, as the capital of the Zapotecs and the dominant force between Teotihuacán in the Valley of Mexico and the Maya empires of the south. Archaeologists have organized the Valley of Oaxaca's history from 500 B.C. to the conquest into five periods, known as Monte Albán I through V. Over those centuries, the hilltop city was repeatedly reconstructed with new walls, plazas, and staircases, which, like layers of an onion, now overlie earlier construction.

Remains from Monte Albán Period I (500 B.C.–A.D. 1) reveal an already advanced culture, with gods, permanent temples, a priesthood, writing, numerals, and a calendar. Sharply contrasting house styles indicate a differentiated, multilayered society. Monte Albán I ruins abound

in graceful polychrome ceramics of uniquely Zapotec style.

Concurrent Olmec influences have also been found, notably in the buildings known as the **Danzantes** (Dancers), decorated with unique bas-reliefs similar to those unearthed along the Veracruz and Tabasco coasts.

Monte Albán II people (A.D. 1–300), by contrast, came under heavy influence from Chiapas and Guatemala in the south. They built strange, ship-shaped buildings, such as Monte Albán's Building J, and left unique remains of their religion, such as the striking jade bat-god now on display in the Anthropology Museum in Mexico City.

Monte Albán reached its apex during Period III (A.D. 300–800), attaining a population of perhaps 40,000 in an urban zone of about three square miles, which spread along hilltops (including the El Gallo and Atzompa archaeological sites) west of the present city of Oaxaca.

Vigorous Period III leaders rebuilt the main hilltop complex as we see it today. Heavily influenced by the grand style of the Teotihuacán structures in the Valley of Mexico, the buildings were finished with handsome sloping staircases, corniced walls, monumental carvings, ball courts, and hieroglyph-inscribed stelae depicting gods, kings, and heroic scenes of battle.

By A.D. 750 few foreign influences were continuing to enrich Monte Albán's uniquely Zapotec pottery styles. Quality declined until they seemed like mere factory copies. Concurrently, the Zapotec pantheon expanded to a horde of gods, as if mere numbers could protect the increasingly isolated Valley of Oaxaca from the outside world.

In A.D. 800, Monte Albán, mysteriously cut off from the rest of Mesoamerica, was declining in population and power. By A.D. 1000, the city was nearly abandoned. The reasons—whether drought, disease, or revolt—and the consequent loss of the necessarily imported water, wood, salt, and food supplies remain an enigma.

During Periods IV and V, Mixtec peoples from the north invaded the Valley of Oaxaca. They warred with valley Zapotecs and despite their relatively small numbers, became a ruling class in a number of valley city-states. The blend of Mixtec and Zapotec art and architecture sometimes led to new forms, especially visible at the west valley sites of Yagul and Mitla.

Monte Albán, meanwhile, although abandoned, was not forgotten. It became both a refuge and a venerated burial place. In times of siege, local people retreated within the walls of a fortress built around Monte Albán's South Platform. At other times, Mixtec nobles opened tombs and reused them as burial vaults right up until the eve of the conquest.

Exploring the Ruins

Visitors to Monte Albán enjoy a panoramic view of green mountains rising above the checkerboard of the Valley of Oaxaca. Monte Albán is fun for a picnic; alternatively, it is an auspicious place to perch atop a pyramid above the grand Main Plaza, etched by lengthening afternoon shadows, and contemplate the ages.

As you enter past the visitor center, north is on your right, marked by the grand **North Platform,** topped by clusters of temples. The **Ball Court** will soon appear below on your left. Twenty-foot-high walkways circumscribe the sunken I-shaped playing field. To ensure true bounces, builders spread smooth stucco over all surfaces, including the slopes on opposite sides (which, contrary to appearances, did not seat spectators). This, like all Oaxacan ball courts, had no stone ring (for supposed goals), but rather four mysterious niches at the court's I-end corners.

The **Main Plaza,** 1,000 feet long and exactly two-thirds that wide, is aligned along a precise north-south axis. Probably serving as a market and civic/ceremonial ground, the monumentally harmonious Main Plaza was the Zapotec "navel" of the world.

Monte Albán's oldest construction, the **Danzantes** building (surmounted by newer Building L, on the west side of the plaza between Buildings M and IV), dates from Period I. Its walls are graced with a host of personages, known commonly as the *danzantes* (dancers) from their oft-contorted postures—probably chiefs vanquished by Monte Albán's armies. Their headdresses, earplugs, bracelets, and necklaces mark them among the nobility, while

glyphs around their heads identify each individual.

Building J (circa A.D. 1), one of the most remarkable in Mesoamerica, stands nearby in midplaza at the foot of the South Platform. Speculation has raged since excavators unearthed its arrow-shaped base generations ago. It is not surprising that Alfonso Caso, Monte Albán's principal excavator, theorized it was an astronomical observatory. In the mind's eye, it seems like some fantastic ocean (or space?) vessel, being navigated to some mysteriously singular southwest destination by a ghostly crew oblivious of its worldly, earthbound brother monuments.

The **South Platform,** especially during the late afternoon, affords Monte Albán's best vantage point. Starting on the right-hand, Palace complex side, **Building II** has a peculiar tunnel on its near side, covertly used by priests for privacy or perhaps some kind of magical effect. To the south stands Building P, an undistinguished, albeit multiroom palace.

The South Platform itself is only marginally explored. Looters have riddled the mounds on its top side. Its bottom four corners were embellished by fine bas-reliefs, two of which had their engraving intentionally buried from view. You can admire the fine sculpture and yet-undeciphered Zapotec hieroglyphs on one of them, along with others, at the South Platform's plaza-edge west side.

Still atop the South Platform, turn southward, where you can see the 7-Deer complex, a few hundred yards away, labeled for the name-date inscribed on its great lintel.

Turning northward again, look just beyond Building J to Buildings G, H, and I at plaza center, erected mostly to cover a rocky mound impossible to remove without the then-unavailable dynamite. Between these buildings and the palace complex on the right stands the small chapel where the remarkable bat-god jade sculpture was found.

On Monte Albán's northern periphery stand a number of tombs that, when excavated, yielded a trove of artifacts, now mostly housed in museums. Walking west from the Northern Platform's northeast base corner, you will pass Mound X on the right. A few hundred yards farther comes the **Tomb 104** mound, presided

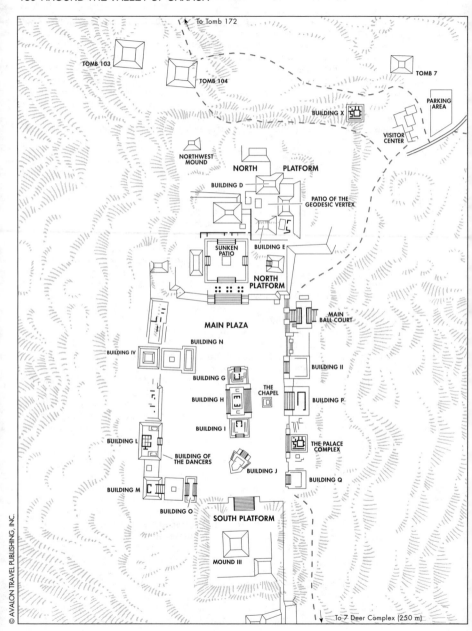

To Tomb 172

TOMB 103

TOMB 104

TOMB 7

PARKING AREA

BUILDING X

VISITOR CENTER

NORTHWEST MOUND

NORTH PLATFORM

BUILDING D

PATIO OF THE GEODESIC VERTEX

SUNKEN PATIO

BUILDING E

NORTH PLATFORM

MAIN PLAZA

MAIN BALL COURT

BUILDING N

BUILDING IV

BUILDING II

BUILDING G

THE CHAPEL

BUILDING P

BUILDING H

BUILDING I

BUILDING L

BUILDING OF THE DANCERS

THE PALACE COMPLEX

BUILDING J

BUILDING Q

BUILDING M

BUILDING O

SOUTH PLATFORM

MOUND III

To 7 Deer Complex (250 m)

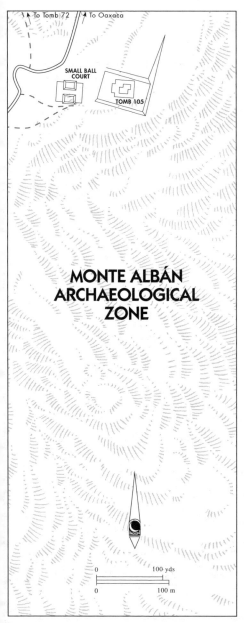

MONTE ALBÁN
ARCHAEOLOGICAL
ZONE

To Tomb 72   To Oaxaca

SMALL BALL
COURT

TOMB 105

0   100 yds

0   100 m

over by an elaborate ceramic urn representing Cojico, the Zapotec god of rain. Just north of this is **Tomb 172,** with the skeletons and offerings left intact.

Heading back along the northernmost of the two paths from Tomb 104, you will arrive at **Tomb 7** a few hundred feet behind the visitor center. Here, around 1450, Mixtec nobles removed the original 8th-century contents and reused the tomb, burying a deceased dignitary and two servants for the netherworld. Along with the bodies they left a fabulous treasure in gold, silver, jade, alabaster, and turquoise, now visible at the museum at the Centro Cultural de Santo Domingo in Oaxaca City.

A few hundred feet toward town on the opposite side of the road from the parking lot is a trail leading past a small ball court to the Cerro de Plumaje (Hill of Plumage), site of **Tomb 105.** A magnificent entrance door lintel, reminiscent of those at Mitla, welcomes you inside. Past the patio, descend to the mural-decorated tomb antechamber. Inside the cruciform tomb itself, four figures walk in pairs toward a great glyph, flanked by a god and goddess, identified by their name-dates.

Monte Albán is open daily from 10 A.M., closing promptly at 5 P.M.

Visitor Center

The Monte Albán Visitor Center, open daily 10 A.M.–5 P.M., tel. 9/516-1215, has an excellent museum, café, information counter, and good store, with many books—guides, histories, art, folklore—on Mesoamerica. First, take a look inside the museum, which displays a number of Monte Albán's famous finds. Most notable are several of the original *danzantes* monolith reliefs, recognizable by their mutilated genitals.

In the bookstore, one of the most useful archaeological guides is Ignacio Bernal's *Official Guide of the Oaxaca Valley,* which includes Monte Albán, Cuilapan, Zaachila, Dainzu, Lambityeco, Yagul, and Mitla. Also covering the same territory, but in more depth, is *Oaxaca, the Archaeological Record,* by archaeologist Marcus Winter.

Getting There

To get to Monte Albán by driving, follow the big Monte Albán sign on the *periférico* over the

Río Atoyac bridge, bear right, and continue about four miles (six km), bearing uphill, to the summit. Alternatively, go by tourist bus departing from your hotel or downtown Hotel Señorial, tel. 9/516-3933, or the Viajes Turísticos Mitla at Hotel Rivera del Ángel, tel. 9/516-6175. Several buses leave daily. A third option is to ride one of the very frequent Monte Albán buses from the Abastos terminal on the *periférico* end of Trujano.

SANTA MARÍA ATZOMPA

The modern town of Santa María Atzompa (pop. 5,000) spreads over the western end of the greater Monte Albán archaeological complex, overlying hundreds of acres of unexplored ancient remains. The majority of modern Atzompans, however, have little time for the past. They are busy producing their distinctive pottery creations—fetching emerald green-glazed cooking pots, bowls, baking dishes, plates, and more—famous all over Mexico and the world.

Now, however, they make much more than these, having developed a host of new styles. These include multicolored vases, some with artfully cut holes for placing dried or fresh flowers. Other styles include a whole range of floral designs, such as lily-adorned crosses, vases, and plates, or red pottery, inscribed with artful floral motifs.

Atzompa's artists, moreover, make it very easy to select from their wares, with an inviting Mercado de Artesanías (Handicrafts Market) and restaurant on the entrance road, right side, at the edge of town. Many artists will make custom pieces. Each of the *mercado* displays contains the name and address of the artist, whom you can contact in town nearby. (Note: Recently, some artists have been trying harder,

THE STORY OF DONAJI

The fabled marriage of King Cosijoeza of the Zapotecs to Coyollicatzin, daughter of Emperor Moctezuma II of the Aztecs, around 1490 was a happy one. It resulted in five children, the youngest of whom was a charming little girl.

The king asked his soothsayers what their divinations told of his little daughter's future. They replied that her life would be filled with tragic events and that she would finally sacrifice herself for her people. The king, saddened by the news, but happy that she would turn out to be so selfless, named her "Donaji" (Great Soul).

Earlier, Cosijoeza (koh-see-ho-AY-zah), who ruled the Zapotec Isthmus domains from his capital at present-day Tehuantepec, had been an uneasy ally of his old enemy, King Dzahuindanda (zah-ween-DAHN-dah) of the Mixtecs. In 1520, with the Aztec threat diminished by the Spanish invasion, Cosijoeza recklessly attacked the fierce Mixtecs, losing the initial battle and then nearly his life as the Mixtecs pressed their advantage.

However, the Spanish, in the person of Hernán Cortés's lieutenant, Francisco Orozco, soon imposed a Mixtec-Zapotec treaty in which Dzahuindanda received Princess Donaji as a hostage to guarantee the peace.

Having Donaji as a prisoner at Monte Albán (known as Danni Dipaa in those days) was not exactly an advantage to Dzahuindanda, for he suspected that she was as much a spy as a hostage. His guess was right. Donaji gleaned intelligence vital to the Zapotec counterattack her father Cosijoeza was planning. At the moment Dzahuindanda's forces were most vulnerable, she sent her father a secret message to attack, which he did, with complete success, except for one thing.

With the treaty broken, the outraged Mixtecs decided to do away with Donaji. They decapitated her and buried her body before her father could rescue her. Later, some Zapotecs found Donaji's remains on the bank of the Atoyac river. They were surprised to see a lovely violet wild iris blossoming from her blood. Even more surprising, they found the flower's roots growing around her head, which was without any sign of decomposition.

Three hundred years later, the Oaxaca government decided to honor the heroine who sacrificed herself for her people by adding an image of Donaji's head to the Oaxacan coat of arms, where it remains to the present day.

Monte Albán ball court

building individual stores on the road before the official Handicrafts Market. For the best selection however, pass these and go straight to the official market.)

Get to Atzompa by driving or by bus, from the Abastos second-class bus terminal. Drivers head northwest out of town, along the *periférico* in the direction of Mexico City. After about a mile, follow the Monte Albán sign, bearing left around the traffic circle, which heads you momentarily back toward town. Immediately turn right, cross the Atoyac River bridge, and continue for about half a mile, turning right at an intersection toward Atzompa. Continue another 2.5 miles (four km) to the Mercado de Artesanías and restaurant on the right.

SAN JOSÉ EL MOGOTE

Finds uncovered at San José El Mogote have shed considerable light on Valley of Oaxaca prehistory, especially during the thousand-year period preceding the founding of Monte Albán, around 500 B.C. Remains reveal that El Mogote was founded around 1500 B.C. and developed into a sophisticated center, with factory workshops supervised by elite merchants, which manufactured mica mirrors and jewelry for local and regional trade.

Modern San José El Mogote lives on, literally, in the backyards of its present Zapotec residents. The people had forgotten what was buried in

the seven or eight *mogotes* (mounds) dotting their village. From the pottery shards littering their fields, however, they suspected something was buried beneath the mounds. Archaeologists came and dug up the treasures now displayed in the community museum, the restored **Hacienda del Cacique.**

Museum and Exploring the Site

El Mogote people take justifiable pride in their museum, housed in a gorgeously restored old hacienda, the former rancho home of a local founding *cacique* (boss) family. Its intriguing displays include shell jewelry, ceramic and stone burial offerings, a reconstructed tomb, a pre-Columbian adobe wall, a photo of a *danzante* monolith (still situated in the ruins) like those found at Monte Albán, and exquisite ceramic sculptures. Outstanding among these is the amazing *diablo enchilado,* with a scowling, devilish grin, exactly like a scary red Halloween demon. **Note:** If you arrive unannounced and find the museum closed, ask across the street at the house of husband-wife jewelers, personable Hector Joel Cruz and Victoria Jiménez Jiménez.

Outside, explore the site, consisting in all of eight mounds that extend over a local half-mile square. Only one of them, the biggest, immediately behind the museum, has been extensively investigated. Climb its reconstructed stone staircase to a broad courtyard. On the courtyard's north side is an excavated shaft, customarily locked, with the *danzante* monolith at

After two thousand years, the ball court at San José El Mogote still waits to be excavated and perhaps someday reconstructed.

its bottom. Climb the regal, stair-stepped pyramid adjoining the courtyard. At the summit, you can glimpse the other mounds, scattered near and far. Most notable among these is a partly excavated ball court, a five-minute walk to the northwest, once used for the *pelota mixteca* ball game, still played locally.

Farther afield, a 10-minute walk to the southwest side of the zone past a modern but now unused stone *era* (threshing circle), local people can lead you to a corrugated iron roof that shelters the stone foundation of what archaeologists believe to be an elite family house.

While exploring the site, you may see a scattering of tiny yellow daisies. Local folks call this *yerba de conejo,* the "herb of the rabbit." They take it as a tea, or mixed with beans, for *comida,* especially before siestas. Some say that its effect is more potent than Viagra.

Festival of San José

Arrive during the third week in March and join in the fun of the patronal festival of San José, which climaxes on the weekend closest to March 19. Festivities include processions, fireworks, dances of giant figures (called *monos* or *marmotas*), and a *pelota mixteca* tournament. While at the museum, ask the volunteers to show you the *hule* (natural rubber) ball and the leather mitts currently used to play the game.

Getting There

You can reach El Mogote a number of ways.

Easiest is to arrange a tour via the Community Museums (Museos Comunitarios) headquarters in downtown Oaxaca at Tinoco y Palacios 311, second floor, tel.9/516-5786, email: muscoax@prodigy.net.mx (or muscoax@turismo_comunitario@umco.org.) You can also go solo by second-class bus from the *camionera central segunda clase,* just north of Abastos market. Catch a Nazarena bus, run by the Choferes del Sur Cooperative. Alternatively, you can catch a *colectivo* (collective microbus taxi) on the prolongation of V. Trujano, which runs along the north side of the bus station.

Drivers, head north along Hwy. 190 out of town. About 7.5 miles (12 km) from downtown, at the fork to the new *cuota* (toll) expressway, stay on the *libre* (free) old route. After less than a mile, turn left (west) at the San José Mogote side road (marked by the pyramid archaeological symbol sign). Pass over the railroad tracks, continue about half a mile, and at the bus stop shelter, turn left. Continue to the museum just past the water towers on the left.

ETLA

Although Etla's Wednesday market invariably has stalls overflowing with its famous white cheese, vendors offer various other old-fashioned merchandise. How would you like, for example, some fresh sheepskins, burro pack frames, green Atzompa pottery, or red Oaxaca tamales?

The market's main attraction, however, is the battalion of native country women offering mounds of onions, carrots, nopal cactus leaves, forest-gathered herbs, and much more.

Get to Etla much as you would get to Mogote, above. By bus, ride a Choferes del Sur Etla-marked bus from the second-class bus station. By car, head north along old *(libre)* Hwy. 190 about nine miles (15 km) from the city center and turn left at the big green Etla highway sign. The market is the prominent stone building on the right before the rail station, about a quarter mile from the highway. A couple of good restaurants, such as Chefy, on the left as you enter town, serve wholesome, home-style breakfasts and lunches. Preferably arrive at the market by about 10 A.M. to allow time for visits to El Mogote and/or Suchilquitongo later.

SUCHILQUITONGO AND CERRO DE LA CAMPANA ARCHAEOLOGICAL ZONE

Suchilquitongo

Before heading uphill to investigate the important Cerro de la Campana archaeological zone, look around the nearby Suchilquitongo town plaza. Suchilquitongo ("Place of Flowers" in the Mixtec language; pop. about 5,000) is the seat of the surrounding Suchilquitongo *municipio,* a rich domain of hills and mountains enclosing the emerald vale of the upper Río Atoyac. Using irrigation, bottomland farmers routinely bring in three crops per year, achieving some of Mexico's highest yields per acre in corn, beans, alfalfa, and squash. If only the rest of Oaxaca were so productive. Although virtually all of the bottomland is privately owned, much of the surrounding hills and mountains is undeveloped town communal property.

The Suchilquitongo **Museo Comunitario** (open daily 10 A.M.–2 P.M. and 5–7 P.M.), on the town plaza, is one of the network of more than a dozen sprinkled around the state. They're glad to provide guided tours if you reserve with the head office in the city, Tinoco y Palacios 311, second floor, tel.9/516-5786, email: muscoax@prodigy.net.mx (or muscoax@turismo_comunitario@umco.org.

The museum displays artifacts, repro-ductions, and a model of the famous Tomb 5,

discovered in the Cerro de la Campana (formerly Huijazoo) archaeological zone in 1985. A glance at the archaeological displays reveals why it's considered the most important Zapotec city-state tomb uncovered to date. It was literally a house of the dead, with the remains of at least 20 noble personages of at least three generations, with calendric birth-names, such as 5-Earth, 5-Serpent, and 12-Monkey. Before the excavation, they lay at rest in a massively built three-room, 15-foot-deep crypt complex among piles of jewelry, supplied with elaborate goods for the afterlife and surrounded by bright murals of ceremonial scenes, including a grand procession of feathered and helmeted ball players.

Another museum room illustrates the Spanish-Mexican custom of **mayordomía,** as acted out by Suchilquitongo people for their major fiesta, the 22–27 July fiesta of Santiago (St. James). Everyone participates—cooking food, making costumes, rehearsing for the dancing, setting up *ramadas* for shade, spiffing up the church, donating money—especially the *mayordomo,* the man or woman nominated by the *presidente municipal* and approved by a grand church meeting of the entire community to head all this up. The *mayordomo,* nearly always a person of means, usually ends up his or her term of office poorer, but rich with community affection and prestige.

Before you leave Suchilquitongo, you might want to see one of the town's **basket weavers** at work. For a small fee, maybe the equivalent of a couple of dollars, the person at the museum desk may be able to guide you to one of their workshops.

Suchilquitongo's other significant craft is **stonemasonry.** Local quarries mine three types—pink *(morada),* white (*blanco,* actually a pale green), and pale yellow *(amarillo)*—of the soft *cantera* (volcanic tufa) for which Oaxaca is famous. As you exit at the highway, go left a few hundred yards, and on the right you'll see the covered workshop of master stonemason **Cenobio Ausencio Pinelo Martínez,** who's teaching his sons his disappearing craft.

Exploring Cerro de la Campana

From the town plaza you can see the Cerro de la Campana cluster of hilltops above the northern horizon. The site is about a two-mile (three-km) 500-foot (150-meter) climb. If it's hot, hire a taxi. If not, be sure to wear a hat, sturdy shoes, and take water. Atop the hill, you'll find Tomb 5 (hopefully open to the public after years of restoration), a ball court, three courtyards, and three partly restored pyramids.

After you arrive atop the hill, look closely at the knolls in the immediate vicinity and you'll see that they too are topped by pyramids, approximately 20 in all. Also, as you walk next to a road-cut section of hillside, look carefully and you'll be able to spot and examine 1,500-year old pottery shards.

Climb to the highest—the cross-topped—pyramid, and your reward will be a breezy view of the entire Etla Valley and mountain panorama. Notice the Monte Albán ridge, dark, far to the southeast, to the right of distant Oaxaca City (below the Cerro San Felipe massif on the left). You can immediately see Cerro de la Campana's advantages: direct signal-fire communication with its contemporary, Monte Albán; a strong defensive position; and fertile riverbank fields. Why it was abandoned, like Monte Albán and many other Oaxacan cities around A.D. 800,

remains a puzzle for future generations of archaeologists to decipher from the bones, stones, and the mute, mysterious glyphs Cerro de la Campana's builders have left behind.

Getting There
Get there by bus via one of the frequent Suchilquitongo-marked buses, driven by Choferes del Sur, which leave from the second-class bus terminal just north of the Abastos market, west of the *periférico*. Drivers, head out of town along Hwy. 190, Mexico City direction, northwest. Bear right onto Hwy. 190 *libre* (free) at the *cuota* (toll) expressway entrance, about 7.5 miles (12 km) from the city center. Continue another several miles; pass an industrial park entrance on the left and, within a few minutes, turn left 17 miles (27 km) from the city center at the Suchilquitongo sign on the right. Continue over to the railroad tracks. On the right just before the tracks, notice Calle Rosario, which heads uphill, passing the church, about 1.5 miles (2.5 km), to the Cerro de la Campana archaeological zone. Continue another half mile to the town plaza. Climb the plaza stairway on the right to the museum.

jaguar god, Monte Albán

PACIFIC RESORTS AND SOUTHERN SIERRA

Historically, Oaxaca's southern coastal residents have both earned their livelihoods and sought their connections with the outside world by the Mar del Sur, the Southern Sea, the traditional Mexican name for the Pacific Ocean. Before roads were built, the Oaxaca coast slumbered, every bit like an isolated South Seas island, dependent upon occasional ships for trade and news from the exterior world.

The major cause of the isolation was the towering, cloud-capped wall of the Sierra Madre del Sur (Mother Range of the South). Oaxaca's high southern Sierra, always remote and mysterious, was finally unveiled in its majesty only in the 1980s, when satellite photo measurements revealed that Cerro Quiexobra, at 12,300 feet (3,750 meters), was by far Oaxaca's tallest mountain massif, a scarce 50 miles due north of the Bays of Huatulco.

From such high, cool, pine-crested summits along its entire 200-mile rampart, the Sierra Madre del Sur plunges precipitously downward more than two miles, through lush vine-hung canyon and foothill forest to the Pacific shore, an acacia-tufted expanse of endless summer.

There, as if forced southward by the weight of the high mountains, the coastline bulges to Oaxaca's (and nearly the entire country's) most southerly point, near the petite bay and resort of Puerto Ángel. From there the Oaxaca coastline bends northerly—on its east side, northeast toward the Isthmus, and on its west side, northwest toward the Mixtec Coast, often called the Costa Chica (Little Coast) in southern Mexico.

During the 1970s and '80s paved highways and airlines ended the Oaxaca coast's isolation and brought a trickle of Mexican and foreign visitors. The government recognized the area's potential and began developing a new, ecologically correct vacationland at the Bays of Huatulco. Meanwhile, visitors were discovering the South Seas village resorts of Puerto Ángel and Puerto Escondido.

Now the steady stream of vacationers can choose from a growing menu of outdoor diversions, from strolling the sand and snorkeling in hidden coves to rescuing sea turtle eggs, splashing in upland waterfalls, and lodging comfortably overnight at rustic jungle coffee farms.

PUERTO ÁNGEL AND VICINITY

During his three presidencies, Oaxaca-born Benito Juárez shaped many dreams into reality. One such dream was to better the lot of his native brethren in the isolated south of Oaxaca by developing a port for shipping the lumber and coffee they could harvest in the lush Pacific-slope jungles of the Sierra Madre del Sur. The small bay of Puerto Ángel, directly south of the state capital, was chosen, and by 1870 it had become Oaxaca's busiest port.

Unfortunately, Benito Juárez died two years later. New priorities and Puerto Ángel's isolation soon wilted Juárez's plan and Puerto Ángel lapsed into a generations-long slumber.

In the 1960s, Puerto Ángel was still a sleepy little spot connected by a single frail link—a tortuous cross-Sierra dirt road—to the rest of the country. Adventure travelers saw it at the far south of the map and dreamed of a South Seas paradise. They came and were not disappointed. Although that first tourist trickle has grown steadily, it's only enough to support

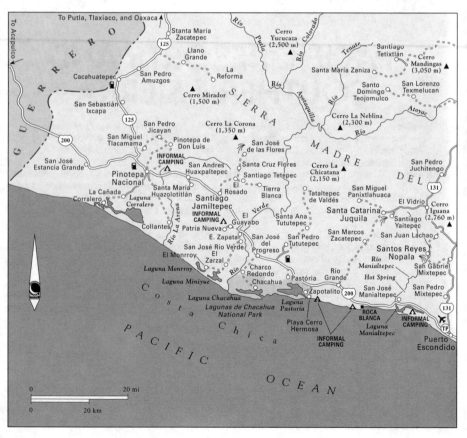

the sprinkling of modest lodgings and restaurants that now dot the beaches and hillsides around Puerto Ángel's tranquil, little blue bay.

BEACHES AND SIGHTS

Getting Oriented

Puerto Ángel is at the southern terminus of Hwy. 175 from Oaxaca, about six miles (nine km) downhill from its intersection with Hwy. 200. It's a small place, where nearly everything is within walking distance along the beach, which a rocky bay-front hill divides into two parts: Playa Principal, the main town beach, and sheltered west-side Playa Panteón, the tourist favorite. A scenic boulder-decorated shoreline *andador* (scenic walkway) connects the two beaches. (Watch out for gaps and holes in the concrete.)

A paved road winds west from Puerto Ángel along the coastline a couple of miles to Playa Zipolite, lined by a colony of hammock-and-bamboo beachfront cabañas, popular with an international cadre of budget-minded seekers of heaven on earth. Continuing west, the road passes the former turtle-processing village beaches of Playa San Agustinillo and Playa Mazunte. From there it goes on another four miles, joining with Hwy. 200 (and thence Puerto Escondido) at San Antonio village at Km 198.

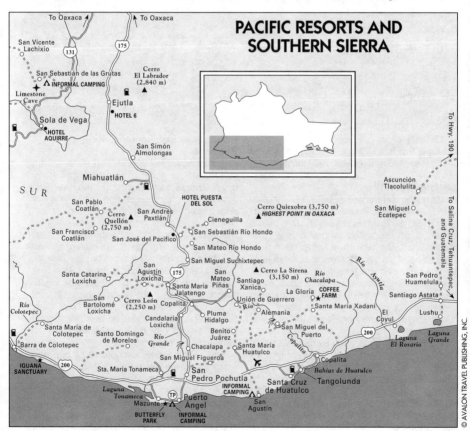

PACIFIC RESORTS AND SOUTHERN SIERRA

© AVALON TRAVEL PUBLISHING, INC.

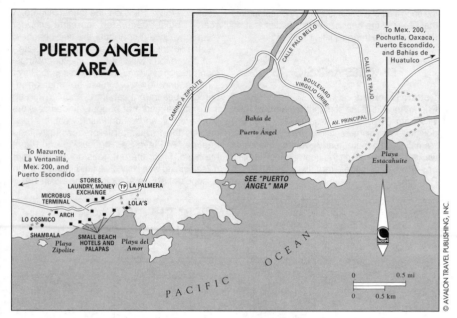

PUERTO ÁNGEL
AREA

To Mazunte,
La Ventanilla,
Mex. 200, and
Puerto Escondido

STORES,
LAUNDRY, MONEY TP LA PALMERA
MICROBUS EXCHANGE
TERMINAL
LO COSMICO ARCH LOLA'S
SHAMBALA
Playa SMALL BEACH Playa del
Zipolite HOTELS AND Amor
PALAPAS

CALLE PALO BELLO
To Mex. 200,
Pochutla, Oaxaca,
Puerto Escondido,
and Bahías de
Huatulco

BOULEVARD
VIRGILIO URIBE

CALLE DE TRAJO

Bahía de
Puerto Ángel

AV. PRINCIPAL

Playa
Estacahuite

SEE "PUERTO
ÁNGEL" MAP

PACIFIC OCEAN

CAMINO A ZIPOLITE

0   0.5 mi
0   0.5 km

© AVALON TRAVEL PUBLISHING, INC.

The major local service and transportation center is **Pochutla** (pop. 35,000), a mile north along Hwy. 175 from its Hwy. 200 junction.

Getting Around
Local buses run frequently between Pochutla and Puerto Ángel 7 A.M.–9 P.M., stopping at the Hwy. 200 intersection. Some buses continue on to Zipolite and Mazunte from Boulevard Uribe, Puerto Ángel's main bay-front street. Also from Boulevard Uribe, a local shuttle bus connects frequently with Zipolite, San Agustinillo, Mazunte and back about every half hour during daylight hours, stopping everywhere en route. Taxis also routinely make runs between Puerto Ángel and either Zipolite or Pochutla for $2–3.

You can also get around by boat. Captains routinely take parties of up to eight for sightseeing, snorkeling, and picnicking to a number of nearby beaches. Bargain at the Puerto Ángel pier (rate should run about $15/hour), or contact the local travel agent, **Agencia de Viajes Gambusino**, tel. 958/430-80 or 958/430-38.

Playas Principal, Panteón, and Estacahuite
Playa Principal's 400 yards of wide golden sand decorate most of Puerto Ángel's bay front. Waves can be strong near the pier, where they often surge vigorously onto the beach and recede with some undertow. Swimming is more tranquil at the sheltered west end toward Playa Panteón. The clear waters are good for casual snorkeling around the rocks on both sides of the bay.

Sheltered Playa Panteón (Cemetery Beach) is Puerto Ángel's sunning beach, lined with squadrons of beach chairs and umbrellas in front of beachside restaurants. **Playa Oso** (Bear Beach) is a little dab of sand beside a rugged rock sea stack beyond Playa Panteón, fun to swim to from Playa Panteón.

Playa Estacahuite, just outside the opposite (east) side of the bay, is actually two beaches in one: a pair of luscious coral-sand nooks teeming with fish grazing the living reef just offshore. (Don't put your hands in crevices; a moray eel may mistake your finger for a fish and bite.) A pair of *palapa* restaurants perched picturesquely above the beaches provide food and drinks. Get there in less than a mile by taxi or on foot via the dirt road that forks right off the highway, about 400 yards uphill from beachfront Boulevard Uribe.

Playa Zipolite

Playa Zipolite is a wide, mile-long strand of yellow-white sand enfolded by headlands and backed by palm groves. It stretches from the intimate little cove and beach of **Playa del Amor** tucked on its east side to towering sea cliffs rising behind the new-age Shambala retreat on the west end. The Playa Zipolite surf, although usually tranquil in the morning (but always with significant undertow), can turn thunderous by the afternoon, especially when offshore storms magnify both the swells and the undertow. Experienced surfers love these times when everyone but experts should stay out.

Good surfing notwithstanding, Zipolite's renown stems from its status as one of the very few nude beaches in Mexico. Bathing au naturel, practiced nearly entirely by visitors and a few local young men, is tolerated only grudgingly by local people, many of whose livelihoods depend on the nudists. If you're discreet and take off your clothes at the more isolated west end (behind the big rock), no one will appear to mind (and women will avoid voyeuristic attentions of Mexican boys and men).

Visitors' nude sunbathing habits may have something to do with the gruffness of some local people. Many of them probably prefer their former occupations in turtle fishing rather than serving tourists, who often seem to be in short supply compared to the battalion of beachfront *palapas* competing for their business.

Most Zipolite visitors stay in the palm-shaded east-end trailer park or in one of the score of hammock-equipped stick-and-thatch beachfront cabaña hotels. Often with fans and outside cold-water showers and privies, cabañas rent for $5-$10 d per night, depending upon amenities. Although many are indifferently managed, some, such as Lola's, Lo Cósmico, and Shambala (below), are unique.

Playas San Agustinillo and Mazunte

About a mile west of Zipolite, a wide, mile-long, yellow-sand beach curves past the village of San Agustinillo. On the open ocean but partly protected by offshore rocks, its surf is much like that of Zipolite, varying from gentle to rough, depending mostly upon wind and offshore swells. Small village groceries and beachside *palapa* restaurants supply food and drinks to the occasional Zipolite overflow and local families on weekends and holidays. Fishing is excellent, either in the surf, from nearby rocks, by rented *panga,* or your own boat launched from the beach. Beach camping is customary, especially at the rustic, hammock-hung roadside *ramadas,* **Palapa Lucy, Palapa Kaly,** and **Palapa Sol Mar** at the east (Zipolite) end of the beach.

Remnants of the local turtle industry can be found at the rusting former processing factories on Playa San Agustinillo (west end) and Playa Mazunte two miles farther west.

Continue a mile or two west from Mazunte and you'll come family owned *mariposario* (butterfly park) of José Enrique Sivori, an Argentine expatriate and his family who used to live in Patagonia, but moved to the Oaxaca coast to get away from the cold. His daughter, who was in charge, said that the family started the mariposario for the fun of it. Now it's a budding enterprise, on eight acres, with a visitor center and a number of screened-in enclosures. The stars of the show, besides the butter-flies (*mariposas*) are the frogs (*ranas*) mostly cute little green guys that like staying on the small trees and feasting on unsuspecting flies and gnats that happen to come along. Visiting hours are daily 9:30 A.M.–4 P.M., admission $2. For more information, contact them through fax 958/430-70, email: aquetzali@ptoescondido.com.mx.

The half-mile-long, yellow-sand Mazunte Beach, like San Agustinillo, is semisheltered and varies from tranquil to rough. Fishing is likewise good, beach camping is customary (as a courtesy, ask if it's OK), and local stores and seafood *palapa* restaurants sell basic supplies and food.

Mazunte people have also been renovating their houses and building **cabañas** to accommodate an increasing number of visitors. Some have even begun to advertise on the Internet. Signs along the road and at the beach advertise their homespun lodgings and restaurants, such as Cabañas La Huerta with

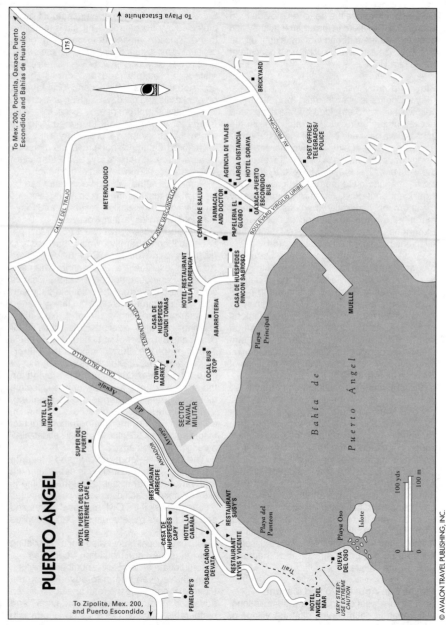

PUERTO ÁNGEL

To Mex. 200, Pochutla, Oaxaca, Puerto Escondido, and Bahías de Huatulco

To Playa Estacahuite

175

To Zipolite, Mex. 200, and Puerto Escondido

METEROLOGICO

CALLE DEL TRAJO

CALLE JOSÉ VASCONCELOS

CALLE TENIENTE AZUETA

CALLE PALO BELLO

Arroyo

Arroyo ANDADOR

Arroyo del

HOTEL LA BUENA VISTA

SUPER DEL PUERTO

HOTEL PUESTA DEL SOL AND INTERNET CAFE

CASA DE HUESPEDES CAPY

HOTEL LA CABAÑA

RESTAURANT ARRECIFE

POSADA CAÑON DEVATA

RESTAURANT SUSY'S

RESTAURANT LEYVIS Y VICENTE

PENELOPE'S

CASA DE HUÉSPEDES GUNDI TOMAS

TOWN MARKET

HOTEL-RESTAURANT VILLA FLORENCIA

ABARROTERIA

LOCAL BUS STOP

CENTRO DE SALUD

FARMACIA AND DOCTOR

PAPELERIA EL GLOBO

AGENCIA DE VIAJES

LARGA DISTANCIA

HOTEL SORAYA

OAXACA-PUERTO ESCONDIDO BUS

CASA DE HUÉSPEDES RINCON SABROSO

BOULEVARD VIRGILIO URIBE

AV. PRINCIPAL

BRICKYARD

POST OFFICE/ TELEGRAFOS/ POLICE

SECTOR NAVAL MILITAR

Playa Principal

MUELLE

Bahía de Puerto Ángel

Playa del Panteon

Playa Oso

Islote

CUEVA DEL OSO

HOTEL ANGEL DEL MAR

VERY STEEP, USE EXTREME CAUTION

Trail

0   100 yds
0   100 m

© AVALON TRAVEL PUBLISHING, INC.

its shady orchard or *huerta*, Posada Lolo, Casa de Huéspedes Los Arcos, and Restaurant La Dolce Vita, which has good lasagna.

Turtle Museum and Cosmetics Factory and Store

The former turtle processing plant at Mazunte lives on as a **turtle museum,** including aquarium, study center, and turtle hatchery. Here you can peruse displays illustrating the ongoing turtle research and conservation program and see members of most of Mexico's turtle species paddling in tanks overlooking the beach where their ancestors once swarmed. The center, on the main road at the east end of the village, is open Tuesday–Saturday 10A.M.–4:30 P.M., Sunday 10 A.M.–2:30 P.M. For more information contact Centro Mexicano de la Tortuga, P.O. Box 16, Puerto Ángel, Oaxaca 70902, tel. 958/401-22.

About a mile farther west along the main road through Mazunte village, stop by the store and works of the **Fábrica Ecología de Cosmeticos Naturales de Mazunte.** Initially funded mostly by the Body Shop Foundation, spearheaded by the local chapter of **Ec Solar** (see the Puerto Escondido section), and supported by an international government-university consortium, local workers make and sell all-natural shampoo, skin cream, hair conditioner, and more. Staff are working hard to assure that the effort catches on so that locally grown products, such as coconut, corn, and avocado oils, and natural aromatics will form the basis for a thriving cottage cosmetics industry.

Playa La Ventanilla

Continue about a mile and a half west along the main road over the low hill west of Mazunte and turn left at the signed dirt road to pristine wildlife haven Playa and Laguna la Ventanilla. Now protected by local residents, swarms of birds, including pelicans, cormorants, and herons, nest there, and a population of wild *cocodrilos* and *lagartos* is making a comeback in a bushy mangrove wetland. Boatmen headquartered at the *palapa* beach village at road's end guide visitors on a two-hour eco-tour ($10 per boat, $3 per adult, kids half price), which includes a stop for refreshment at a little lagoon island. The boatmen are known for their

wildlife-sensitivity and allow no motor vehicles within a hundred yards of their communally owned lagoon sanctuary.

The Playa La Ventanilla community has also taken responsibility for protecting the turtles that arrive on their beach against poachers. During both February and June through October, hundreds of sea turtles come ashore to lay eggs. If necessary, community volunteers help the exhausted turtles up the steep beach, where they lay their eggs. Volunteers then gather the eggs and rebury them in a secure spot. After the hatchlings emerge about a month and a half later, volunteers nurture them for about three months and release them safely back into the ocean.

Moreover, the La Ventanilla ejido invites visitors to stay in their rough-and-ready rustic but sturdy concrete concrete-floored cabanas with beds. (Bring your own mosquito net.)

ACCOMMODATIONS

Puerto Ángel Hotels and Guesthouses

Although none of Puerto Ángel's dozen or so lodgings is directly on the beach, most of them are within a stone's throw of it. The successful lodgings have given their legion of savvy repeat customers what they want: clean, basic, cool-water accommodations in tranquil, television-free settings where Puerto Ángel's natural isolation and tropical charm set the tone for long, restful holidays.

Moving west around the bay from the pier, first comes the 1960s motel-style **Hotel Soraya,** perched on the bluff above Playa Principal, Priv. José Vasconcelos 2A, Puerto Ángel, Oaxaca 70902, tel./fax 958/430-09. Well managed by personable owner Hortencia Tanus, the hotel includes a restaurant with an airy bay view, fine for bright morning breakfasts and sunset-glow dinners. Two tiers of spartan but light and comfortable rooms enclose a parking patio. Although some rooms have a/c, the fan-only ones are generally better. Rent on the upper tier for more privacy. The 32 rooms rent for about $22 s, $27 d, and $32 t low season, $33, $38, $45 high.

Although recent hurricane damage temporarily put it out of operation, the splendidly isolated

Casa de Huéspedes Rincón Sabroso, Puerto Ángel, Oaxaca 70902, tel. 958/430-95, atop the adjacent bay-vista hill has been restored to better than original condition: here guests enjoy lodgings that open onto a hammock-hung view breezeway adorned by luscious tropical greenery. Inside, rooms are very clean (but dark), with white walls, tile floors, shiny bathrooms, and natural wood furnishings. Guests have the additional option of good food and each other's company in an airy café, perched above a heavenly bay and sunset panorama. Rates for the eight rooms run about $14 s, $16 d, $19 t low season, $22, $25 and $28 high, with fans. Owners have added a pair of more private, deluxe rooms (nos. 9 and 10), for $28 d low season, $32 high.

Travelers who enjoy being right in the middle of the Puerto Ángel beachfront street scene choose the worthy **Hotel Villa Florencia,** Blv. Virgilio Uribe s/n, Puerto Ángel, Oaxaca 70902, tel./fax 958/430-44. In the shady interior lobby-patio, past the excellent street-front restaurant, tranquillity reigns as soft classic songs and instrumental music play in the background while guests read and relax on comfortable chairs and couches. Upstairs, the approximately 15 rooms are immaculate and thoughtfully decorated with local art and handicrafts. Rates run about $25 s, $30 d, and $37 t year-round; with bath, add $3 for a/c.

Equally exceptional nearby is **Casa de Huéspedes Gundi y Tomás,** the life project of friendly German expatriate Gundi López; address simply Puerto Ángel, Oaxaca 70902, tel. 958/430-68, email: gundtoma@hotmail.com. Her homey, rustic-aesthetic complex rambles up a leafy hillside to a breezy bay-view *palapa* where patrons relax, socialize, and enjoy food and drink from Gundi's kitchen. Just above that, guests enjoy a double row of several clean, simply furnished (although dark) rooms, shaded by a hammock-hung communal view porch. Besides all this, Gundi is happy to volunteer information about local sights and activities and arrange excursions for her guests. Another plus on the premises is the gallery-studio of Gundi's brother-in-law, accomplished oil painter Mateo López. Rooms with shared showers and toilets cost about $14 d low season, $17 high; larger rooms with private shower and toilet run about $17 d low season, $20 high, all with fans. Get there by walking uphill along the little alley adjacent to the town market and just opposite the beachfront naval compound.

Another Puerto Ángel gem is **Hotel La Buena Vista,** P.O. Box 48, Puerto Ángel, Oaxaca 70902, tel./fax 958/431-04, tucked on the hillside just west of the Arroyo del Aguaje. The hotel's four tiers stair-step artfully up the jungly slope. First- and second-level rooms open to shady hammock-hung view porches. On the third level, a luxuriously airy restaurant *palapa* opens to a picture-perfect bay vista. The climax is a pair of large onyx-tile-floored fourth-floor rooms that share an entire private view patio with hammocks. All rooms are immaculate, light, and simply but tastefully furnished, with spotless bathrooms. Low-season rates for the approximately 20 rooms run about $22 s or d for standard, $30 s or d for room with private balcony, and $35 for the top-floor room with double-size onyx bathtub; high season, the same go for about $30, $34, and $40, all with fans, and the deluxe rooms have hot water.

Heading around the curve of the bay to the Playa Panteón neighborhood, you'll find one of Puerto Ángel's better cheaper lodgings, **Casa de Huéspedes Capy,** Playa Panteón, P.O. Box 44, Puerto Ángel, Oaxaca 70902, tel./fax 958/430-02, sitting on the bay-view hillside by the road fork to Zipolite. Rooms, in two tiers with views toward Playa Panteón, are basic but clean with fans and cool-water private baths. Good family management is the Capy's strong suit. This shows in the shady view restaurant, Arcely, where good food in a friendly atmosphere encourages guests to linger, reading or talking, for hours. The family also watches the community TV at night; if it bothers you, ask them to turn it down. The 10 rooms rent for about $10 s, $15 d low season, $12 and $13 high. Rooms with two beds go for $18 d, $19 t low season, $19 and $20 high.

Nearby, about 100 yards along the road to Zipolite (watch for the sign at the hilltop driveway on the left), take a look at the guesthouse **Penelope's** (of Homeric legend), with only a few rooms, but a breezy, quiet hilltop setting, at P.O. Box 49, Puerto Ángel, Oaxaca 70902, tel. 958/430-73. Here owner Patricia enjoys sharing her home with guests. Also, if you indulge, be sure to try one of her uniquely delicious margaritas. Rooms come comfortably furnished with hot water showers and porches with hammocks and fans. Rentals run about $11 s, $16–22 d. Add about $4 per person for breakfast, $7 for dinner.

Downhill, on Playa Panteón, the nicely located **Hotel La Cabaña,** Calle Pedro Sainz de Barada, P.O. Box 22, Puerto Ángel, Oaxaca 70902, tel. 958/431-05, is just a few steps from Playa Panteón. Past the lobby is a verdant, plant-decorated patio, while upstairs, guests enjoy chairs and shady tables on a breezy bay-vista sundeck. Marble embellishes the baths and the floors of the 23 comfortable rooms, some with private view balconies. (During the past several years, however, two separate readers have complained about this place. One of them wrote that he was burglarized and the owner refused to report the incident to the police; take your valuables with you when you go out.) If you do decide to stay, several beachfront restaurants are conveniently nearby. Rooms rent for about $13 s, $15 d, and $19 t low season, and $16, $20, and $25 high, with fans and hot water.

Note: Sadly, the family-operated Puerto Ángel gem, Hotel Cañon Devata, was closed at this writing. Hopefully, either some of the family members or new operators will restore its operation to the excellent level that I reported in previous editions.

Hidden in the leafy canyon a hundred yards uphill from the beach is **Posada Cañon Devata,** life project of the ecological pioneer López family, P.O. Box 10, Puerto Ángel, Oaxaca 70902, tel./fax 958/430-48, email lopezk@spin.com.mx. Artists Mateo and Suzanne López—he's Mexican, she's American—became an example to local people, reforesting their originally denuded canyon property over a period of several years. They gradually added on land, so their now-lush arroyo encompasses an entire watershed-ecosystem. Although Suzanne and Mateo have now retired, their daughter Cali and son Darshave carry on the day-to-day management every bit as skillfully as their parents did.

(Their accommodations, a multiroom lodge and several luxury/rustic detached cabins, dot the slopes of their sylvan tropical forest retreat. All are comfortably furnished and thoughtfully decorated with handicrafts and Mateo's expressive primitivist oil paintings. Lodge rooms rent for about $20 d, cabins $30 d low season, $30 and $50 high, with fans and parking.

(Their restaurant serves all-organic fruits and vegetables and whole-wheat homemade bread and tortillas, while their gift shop, Sueños de Amusgo, offers one-of-a-kind handicrafts, including many Amusgo indigenous *huipiles* and a gallery of Mateo's paintings.)

Atop the hill via the adjacent steep road, the **Hotel Ángel del Mar,** Puerto Ángel, Oaxaca 70902, tel. 958/430-08, fax 958/430-14, offers a sharply contrasting style of lodging. Rates for the 42 rooms run about $27 d low season, $31 high; credit cards accepted (but you'll save lots of *pesos* if you pay cash). Guests enjoy a big, open-air dining room, swimming pool, and large light rooms with private balconies looking down upon a panoramic bay vista. Mornings, guests can enjoy sunrise over the bay and evening sunsets over the ocean. Revitalized management has recently brightened the place up with new paint everywhere and new bedspreads and lampshades to go with the venerable polished wood furniture in the rooms.

Vacationers hankering for splendid isolation can have it at **Bahía de la Luna,** on the coast about three small bays east of Puerto Ángel, at P.O. Box 90, Pochutla, Oaxaca 70900, fax 958/430-74. New owner Ivan Wastenko shares his paradise with visitors. His approximately 15 rustic-chic adobe, palm-thatched cabañas cluster on a lovely isolated crescent of golden sand. No phones, TV, or traffic; simply sun, sea, sand, and home-cooked food. Rooms, thoughtfully and comfortably furnished, rent for about $25 s, $32 d low season, $40 and $50 including three meals, with fans, but room-temperature-only water.

Get there by the rugged jeep road, signed La Boquilla, which forks east about four miles uphill from Puerto Ángel.

Zipolite Accommodations

Zipolite's line of rustic (bring your own towel and soap) lodgings starts at **Lola's,** tel. 958/432-01, 958/432-03, 958/431-62, on the east end of the beach, Playa Zipolite, Puerto Ángel, Oaxaca 70902. The friendly, elderly owner continues her decades-long good management

A TURTLE ARRIVES AT PLAYA LA VENTANILLA

It was raining, and the wind, although not cold, was driving the surf high on Playa La Ventanilla. On the rocky headland above the beach, a small hole, like a round window, appeared to have been carved in the rock. Our guide, Pedro, who had just rowed us through the community wetland-ecological preserve, explained.

"That's why we call this La Ventanilla. Because of that hole that the sea and wind have carved out."

"It's like a little window, a *ventanilla.*"

"Yes, that's right."

He then went on to tell us something we didn't expect.

"We are waiting for the turtles to arrive. They come this time of year, especially when the wind blows toward shore like this. Yesterday afternoon and night nearly 80 turtles came and laid about 8,000 eggs."

It seemed too many.

"Eight thousand? Are you sure?"

"Yes . . . and they're buried right here."

He pointed to a fenced-off area in the sand, laid out in a grid of several dozen stakes.

"Each turtle lays about 100 eggs, and we buried each one's eggs separately under each of these stakes."

Before I could answer, a lookout atop the headland yelled something.

"A turtle has come ashore."

We scanned the beach. A black, pointed silhouette showed at the edge of the sand.

"There it is."

Two or three young male villagers raced toward the beach. They stopped several steps short of the turtle, however.

"We don't want to interfere with its egg-laying."

For several minutes, we watched the turtle, not large, perhaps 50 pounds and two feet long, struggle to climb one last small sand ridge before reaching the flat part of the beach. We asked what kind of turtle it was.

"It's a *golfina* turtle, Pedro explained. "Two other kinds arrive here. The *laut,* and the *sacasillo*. The *laut* can be big . . . maybe as much as a ton. They arrive in February."

After watching the turtle struggle for a few minutes longer, Pedro decided to help. He picked it up by the shell and placed it on level sand a dozen feet farther inland. He sympathized with the turtle's plight.

"The turtle seems very tired. It's small and weak."

(although her equally personable daughter now does most of the day-to-day work) of her thatch-shaded restaurant and beach cabañas. For customers who hanker for a bit better lodging, Lola has broken new ground with Zipolite's first modern-standard units, eight new rooms with hot water and ceiling fans. The best are two front top-floor units overlooking the gorgeous beach and sunset vista.

The scene at Lola's resembles a miniresort, with the restaurant right on the beach, where guests enjoy late breakfasts, stroll out for swims, read thick novels, and kick back and enjoy convivial conversation with their mostly North American and European fellow vacationers. Although the last hurricane wiped out the rustic wood cabañas, they've been rebuilt with modern-standard stucco units that rent for about $13 s, $17 d, or $20 t, year-round, with fan and private shower baths.

The **Lo Cósmico** cabañas nestle on a cactus-dotted rocky knoll at the opposite end of the beach, Playa Zipolite, P.O. Box 36, Pochutla, Oaxaca 70900. White spheres perched on their thatched roof peaks lend a mystical Hindu-Buddhist accent to the cabañas' already picturesque appearance. In the restaurant atop the knoll, you're likely to find Regula and Antonio Nadurille, Lo Cósmico's European-Mexican owners. Regula manages the restaurant, specializing in a dozen varieties of tasty crepes, while Antonio supervises the hotel. Their hillside and beach-level cabañas are clean, candle-lit, and equipped with hammocks and concrete floors, for about $12–$17 d, with outside showers and toilets. Recently, Antonio has built a number of sturdy, rock-walled, hurricane-proof designer rooms on his view hillside. Figure about $25 d for these, including private baths.

Shambala, on the adjacent forested hillside, is as it sounds—a tranquil Buddhist-style retreat, at Puerto Ángel, P.O. Box 68, Pochutla, Oaxaca, 70900, fax 958/431-51, 958/431-52. Shambala's driving force is the friendly

The boost seemed to encourage the turtle. It immediately began digging with its flippers. After 10 minutes it began depositing its eggs in a foot-deep hole. Pedro promptly removed the eggs and placed them in a bucket. After a few minutes, the seemingly near-exhausted turtle was finished. Pedro had kept count.

"Seventy-five eggs. Not many."

"But it's better than nothing."

Pedro nodded his head in agreement.

He let the turtle cover up the empty hole. After doing so, it packed down the sand over where it had deposited the eggs, rocking its body back and forth with its flippers. Then it turned and headed back toward the waves. Pedro gently lifted it up and placed it near the water. Soon the turtle was gone, beneath the surf.

Pedro took the bucket of 75 eggs and buried them beneath a new marker alongside the other 80 markers.

"You are the turtle papa," we said. He laughed.

"Soon these eggs will hatch into thousands of little turtles, which we will return to the sea."

"And maybe many of them will return here."

"Yes, we hope so."

A turtle is helped back to sea.

owner/community leader Gloria Esperanza Johnson, who arrived in Zipolite by accident in 1970 and decided to stay, eventually adopting Mexican citizenship. She built the place from the ground up, gradually adding on until now there are about five primitive "monks' cells" and about 10 small rustic cabañas, an excellent **macrobiotic panoramic vista restaurant,** and a spiritual center. Shambala is a quiet, alcohol-free haven for lovers of reading, sunbathing, hiking, yoga, and meditation. It sits atop an enviable few acres at the edge of a sylvan hinterland. Adjacent cactus-studded cliffs plummet spectacularly to surf-splashed rocks below, while trails fan out through lush tropical deciduous forest. The very simple candle-lit thatched concrete-floored cabañas with hammocks rent for about $7 per person (for hammock space only, including hammock, $3). Toilets and showers are shared. Work exchange for room and board is negotiable.

Gloria also welcomes lovers of the outdoors to camp (about $3 per person per day) in Shambala's get-away-from-it-all jungle El Encanto retreat, in a pristine mountain river valley about an hour away by car or local bus. For more information and directions, ask Gloria or her staff assistants.

Get to both Shambala and Lo Cósmico by turning from the main road onto the dirt driveway just west of the arch at Zipolite's west end. Bear right at the first fork, then left at the next for Lo Cósmico, right for Shambala.

Posada Rancho Cerro Largo

Outstandingly innovative Posada Rancho Cerro Largo is the creation of eco-activist Mario Corella, descendant of a longtime Hermosillo, Sonora, hotel family. After knocking around in the hospitality trade for several years, Mario decided to create his own version of utopia. Mario says that he wanted to "be in contact with nature and live among the community with as little impact as possible. I would welcome guests as friends, to share the dinner table with me and the hotel staff."

He's done it, with a reception-restaurant and a number of rustically charming tile-floored, stick-and-adobe cabañas, furnished with hand-loomed bedspreads and opening to hammock-hung ocean-view verandas. The entire complex nestles in a cactus-dotted leafy hillside forest, linked by a path that meanders between panoramic ocean viewpoints to a gorgeously isolated, wave-washed sandy beach below. Rates run a reasonable $65 for two, *including* full breakfast and dinner. For reservations (mandatory in winter, highly recommended anytime), write the Posada Rancho Cerro Largo, P.O. Box 121, Pochutla, Oaxaca 70900, or fax 958/430-63. Look for the signed driveway on the Puerto Ángel-Mazunte road, four miles (6.4 km) from the Puerto Ángel bus stop.

Trailer Parks and Camping

The rustic **Trailer Park La Palmera** and café has about 20 parking (big rigs possible) or camping spaces beneath a shady, tufted grove by the road at the east end of Playa Zipolite. Reserve by writing friendly owner Fernando Torres at Carretera Playa Zipolite-Puerto Ángel, Oaxaca 70902. A spirit of camaraderie often blooms among the tents and assorted RVs of travelers from as far away as the Klondike, Kalispell, and Khabarovsk. About $6 for small RV, $10 large, gets you a space for two persons, including electricity, shared, dump station, shower and toilets, and satellite dish (if you have your own hookup). Tent spaces cost $6 for two persons.

When I arrived, friendly owner (and former engineer) Fernando was hard at work, adding a **café** and some rooms with bath (figure about $20 d) that promise to embellish his already-pleasant little haven.

One of Zipolite's best tenting spots is on the beach below Shambala. The friendly owner, Gloria Johnson, will probably allow you to use Shambala's showers and toilets for a small fee. Ask at the Shambala office (or tel./fax 958/431-51, 958/431-52) first for permission to camp.

FOOD

For a country place, Puerto Ángel has surprisingly good food, starting with the **Hotel** **Villa Florencia,** right on the main beachfront street. Lulu, the wife of the late Italian-born owner/chef, carries on his tradition, specializing in antipasti, salads, and meat and seafood pastas. Like a good country Italian restaurant, service is crisp and presentations are attractive. The modest wine list has in the past included some good old-country imports, and the pastas *al dente* and cappuccino are, of course, among the best on the coast. Open daily 8 A.M.–11 P.M. Moderate. (If you're in need of lodging, ask at the hotel desk in the rear to see some of clean, comfortable rooms. See the description of Hotel Villa Florencia a few paragraphs above.)

The unpretentiously elegant view *palapa* restaurant at the **Hotel La Buena Vista,** tel. 958/431-04, is the best spot in town for a leisurely, intimate dinner. The prodigious effort that owner/managers Lourdes and Carrie Díaz have invested in their kitchen and staff comes together beautifully. The servers, fetchingly attired in colorful Oaxaca *huipiles,* glide gracefully between kitchen and tables with a bounty of crisp salads, savory soups, tender pastas, and fresh broiled fish and meats. It's open 7:30–11 A.M. for breakfast, closed afternoons, then open for supper 6–10 P.M. Moderate.

Four or five restaurants line Playa Panteón. Here the main attraction is the beach scene rather than the food. **Susy's** and **Leyvis y Vicente** seem to be the best of the bunch. Fish will generally be the best choice; make sure it's fresh. Open seasonally about 8 A.M.–9 P.M. Moderate.

For a spectacular view with late lunch or early dinner (or even just a drink), go to the family-run **Restaurant Arrecife** that clings to the west-side headland overlooking the bay. (Follow the *andador*, pathway, toward the beach from the beachfront Av. Uribe bridge, just west of the naval compound. At the Arrecife sign, follow the stairway up the rocky headland.) The star of the Restaurant Arrecife show (of the husband-wife-daughter team) is the wife, who crafts a short but hearty menu of soups, salads, pastas, seafood and meats. Open daily 4–10 P.M.

Zipolite also has some good eating places. For hearty macrobiotic fare and a breezy beach view, go to the restaurant at **Shambala** at the west end of Playa Zipolite. Personable owner

Gloria Johnson runs a very tidy kitchen, which serves good breakfasts, soups, salads, and sandwiches. Open daily 8 A.M.–8 P.M. No alcohol. Budget-moderate.

Regula, the European co-owner of **Lo Cósmico** on the knoll just east of Shambala, cooks from a similar macrobiotic menu, although she specializes in several variations of crepes, including egg, meat, cheese, and vegetable. Open daily in high season 8 A.M.–7 P.M. Shorter hours and closed Monday during the low season.

For rustic elegance, continue past Zipolite to the view restaurant at **Posada Rancho Cerro Largo.** Friendly eco-activist owner Mario Corella invites guests to share a meal with him and the hotel staff. Don't show up unannounced; fax 958/430-63 (or stop by) a few days ahead of time and ask for a reservation.

ENTERTAINMENT AND SPORTS

Puerto Ángel's entertainments are mostly spontaneous. If anything exciting is going to happen, it will most likely be on the beachfront Boulevard Uribe where people tend to congregate during the late afternoon and evenings. A small crowd may accumulate in the adjacent restaurant Villa Florencia for coffee, talk, or something from the bar.

The town's major scheduled event is the big **Fiesta de San Miguel Arcangel** on 1 and 2 October. Then the *mascaritas* (masked children) dancers romp, carnival games and rides light up the main street, and a regatta of fishing boats parades around the bay.

Sunsets
Sunset-watchers get their best chance from the unobstructed hilltop perch of the Hotel Ángel del Mar, or Lola's, on the beach in Zipolite, where the bar and restaurant at each place can provide something to enliven the occasion even if clouds happen to block the view.

Hotel Ángel del Mar sometimes provides music for dancing during the highest seasons, most likely between Christmas and New Year and the week before Easter.

For additional diversions, head west to Puerto Escondido or east to Bahías de Huatulco, each

about an hour by car, for more and livelier entertainments.

Jogging
Potholed streets, rocky roads, and lack of grass sharply curtail Puerto Ángel jogging prospects. The highway, however, which runs gradually uphill from near the pier, does provide a continuous, more-or-less smooth surface. Confine your jogging to early morning or late afternoon, and take water along.

Swimming and Surfing
Swimming provides more local exercise opportunities, especially in the sheltered waters off Playa Panteón. Bodysurfing, boogie boarding, and surfing can be rewarding off Playa Zipolite, depending on wind and swells. **Be super-careful of undertow,** which is always a threat, even on calm days at Zipolite. If you're inexperienced, don't go out alone. Novice and even experienced swimmers sometimes drown at Zipolite. If you get caught in a current pulling you out to sea, don't panic. Experts advise that you simply float and paddle parallel to the beach a hundred yards or so to a spot where the offshore current is not so severe (or may even push you back toward the beach). On rough days, unless you're an expert, forget it. Alcohol and surf, moreover, don't mix. Bring your own board; few, if any, rentals are available.

Sailing and Windsurfing
If you have your own portable boat or windsurfing gear, sheltered **Playa Panteón** would be a good place to put it into the water, although the neighboring headland may decrease the available wind. Calm mornings at **Playas Zipolite, San Agustinillo,** or **Mazunte** (see at Beaches and Sights, preceding), with more wind but rougher waves, might also be fruitful.

Snorkeling and Scuba Diving
Rocky shoals at the edges of Puerto Ángel Bay, especially just off **Playa Panteón,** are excellent for casual snorkeling. **Playa Estacahuite,** on the open ocean just beyond the bay's east headland, is even better. Best bring your own equipment. If you don't, you can rent a snorkel and mask from Vicente, at his restaurant, Leyvis y Vicente, on Playa Panteón, for about $3 an hour.

Although Puerto Ángel has no professional dive shop, beginners can contact the well-equipped and certified dive instructors of **Buceos Triton** dive shop, tel./fax 958/708-44, at the Santa Cruz de Huatulco marina. Alternatively, try **Action Sports** tel. 958/100-55, ext. 842, at the Hotel Barceló, or the **Buceo Sotovento,** tel./fax 958/100-51, across from the Hotel Barceó, a 45-minute drive east, in Santa Cruz de Huatulco. (See the Bays of Huatulco section, below.)

Fishing

The bay-front pier is the best place to bargain for a boat and captain to take you and your friends out on a fishing excursion. Prices depend on season, but you can figure on paying about $20 an hour for a boat for four or five persons with bait and two or three good rods and reels. During a three-hour outing a few miles offshore, a competently captained boat will typically bring in three or four big, good-eating *robalo* (snook), *huachinango* (snapper), *atún* (tuna), or pompano. If you're uncertain about what's biting, go down to the dock around 2 or 3 P.M. in the afternoon and see what the boats are bringing in.

Vicente, of Leyvis y Vicente restaurant on Playa Panteón, takes out fishing parties of up to six persons for around $20 an hour, bait and tackle included. You can also arrange fishing trips through the **Gambusino Travel Agency,** tel. 958/430-80, 958/430-38, open Mon.–Sat. 9 A.M.–2 P.M. and 4–8 P.M., in the office across the street from the doctor and pharmacy on Av. Teniente Vasconcelos, just uphill from Uribe.

SHOPPING

Market

The biggest local market is the Monday *tianguis,* which spreads along the Pochutla main street, Hwy. 175, about seven miles from Puerto Ángel, one mile inland from the Hwy. 200 junction. Mostly a place for looking rather than buying, throngs of vendors from the hills line the sidewalks, even crowding into the streets, to sell their piles of onions, mangoes, forest herbs, carrots, cilantro, and jícama.

On other days, vendors confine their displays to the permanent Mercado 5 de Octubre, east side of the main street, between Calles 1 and 2 Sur.

Groceries

The best-stocked Puerto Ángel local store is the **Super Del Puerto** at the west end of beachfront street Uribe, uphill past the arroyo bridge. Also, a few little-bit-of-everything stores in Zipolite and on Uribe in the middle of Puerto Ángel sell cheese, milk, bread, some vegetables, and other essentials.

Handicrafts

For fine custom-made hammocks, visit local craftsman Gabino Silva at his country shop, off a jungly stretch of the road between Zipolite and San Agustín. He also rents a cabaña. Watch for the little sign labeled Hamacas and Cabaña on the beach side of the road, 4.2 miles (6.7 km) from the Puerto Ángel bus stop.

Some unique handicrafts are available in Pochutla. **Foto Garcia,** on main street Lázaro Cárdenas 76, west side, offers many whimsical coconut carvings by a local craftsman. It's open Monday–Saturday 8 A.M.–2 P.M. and 4–8 P.M., tel. 958/407-35.

Additionally, the *larga distancia,* **Caseta Cybeltel,** open daily 7 A.M.–10 P.M., between Calles 1 and 2 Norte (across the street from the Hotel Izola) offers a varied collection of mostly Guatemalan hand-embroidered purses, *huipiles,* shirts, vests, and 1960s-style tie-dyed apparel.

SERVICES AND INFORMATION

Money Exchange

The only regular local money exchange in Puerto Ángel is the Gambusino Travel Agency, on Vasconcelos, the street that runs from the Puerto Ángel pier uphill. Otherwise, go to **Banco Internacional** (Bital) on the Pochutla main street, Lázaro Cárdenas, tel. 958/406-98, open Mon.–Fri. 8 A.M.–7 P.M., Sat. 8 A.M.–3 P.M. Alternatively, try **Bancomer,** corner of Lázaro Cárdenas and Av. 3A Norte, tel. 958/402-59, open Mon.–Fri. 8 A.M.–5 P.M., Sat. 9 A.M.–1 P.M. Another option is **Bancrecer,** next door to Bancomer, tel. 958/407-63, open Mon.–Fri. 9

A.M.- 5 P.M., Sat. 10 A.M.–2 P.M. Call to confirm money-changing hours.

Communications and Travel Agent

The Puerto Ángel *correo* and *telecomunicaciones* stand side by side with the Agencia Municipal at the foot of Hwy. 175. Both are open Monday–Friday 9 A.M.–3 P.M.

The Puerto Ángel *larga distancia* telephone, fax office and **Internet** access is on Calle José Vasconcelos, just uphill from main street Uribe, tel. 958/430-46 or 958/430-54, fax 958/430-70, email: shenalo@hotmail.com. Hours are daily 7 A.M.–10 P.M. (Internet access is also available at Hotel Puesta del Sol and Cyber café, about half a block west of the Blv. Uribe bridge; and at Caseta Cybeltel, in Pochutla, main street, across from the Hotel Izola. They also maintain a *lista de email,* of mail messages, like *lista de correo.*

Puerto Ángel's travel agent, friendly Mati Velasco (who also runs the *larga distancia* and Internet access) of **Agencia de Viajes Gambusino,** tel. 958/430-80, 958/430-38, arranges tours and fishing trips and sells reserved air and bus tickets at her small office on Vasconcelos next door, uphill from the *larga distancia.*

Medical and Police

Puerto Ángel's friendly and respected private **doctor,** Dr. Constancio Aparicio Juárez, holds consultation hours (Mon.–Sat. 7 A.M.–2 P.M. and 5–9 P.M.) and also runs the **pharmacy,** tel. 958/430-58, on Av. Vasconcelos, across from the *larga distancia.* For serious illness requiring diagnostic specialists, Dr. Juárez recommends you go to the government Hospital Regional in Pochutla, tel. 9/584-0204, or the Seguro Social in Crucecita, tel. 9/587-01-24 or 9/587-0264.

Another option is to go to the small government **Centro del Salud** health clinic, which concentrates on preventive, rather than diagnostic medicine, on the hill behind the church. Go up Vasconcelos a long curving block, go left at the first corner, and continue another block to the health center.

For police emergencies, see the local police at the agencia municipal, end of Blv. Uribe, or call the *policía preventiva* at the Presidencia Municipal in Pochutla, on the town plaza one block east of the main north-south thoroughfare; tel. 958/431-01.

Ecological Projects

Ecological activism has spread to Mazunte, where the **Asociación de Comuneros de Mazunte** has picked up the green banner. Led by their earnest activist-president Ermilo López Bustamante, the association is building an ecologically correct time-share development and encouraging waste composting and water and forest conservation. Partly as a result of their efforts, cutting trees around Zipolite, San Agustín, and Mazunte has become a definite community no-no. Consequently, the tropical deciduous forest zone between Zipolite and Mazunte is rapidly becoming a luxuriantly healthy eco-preserve.

In a parallel but separate action, **Ec Solar,** the private ecological "Peace Corps," works hard and effectively with local campesinos to build environmentally appropriate solutions to village sewage, water, health, and agricultural problems. Its local headquarters is in Puerto Escondido, tel. 958/209-50, in the west-side Bachoco suburb, corner of Calles Huajuapan de León and Tehuantepec.

GETTING THERE AND AWAY

By Air

Scheduled flights to Mexican destinations connect daily with airports at **Huatulco,** 19 miles (30 km) east, or **Puerto Escondido,** 44 miles (71 km) west, by road from Puerto Ángel. For details see the Puerto Escondido and Bays of Huatulco sections of this chapter.

By Car or RV

Good roads connect Puerto Ángel with Puerto Escondido and Acapulco to the west, with Oaxaca to the north, and with Bahías de Huatulco and the Isthmus of Tehuantepec to the east.

Highway 200 connects westward with Puerto Escondido in an easy 44 miles (71 km), continuing to Pinotepa Nacional (135 miles, 217 km, three hours) and Acapulco in a total of seven hours (291 miles, 469 km) of driving. In the opposite direction, Bahías de Huatulco (actually

Crucecita town) is a quick 45 minutes, or 22 miles (35 km). The continuation to Salina Cruz stretches another 92 miles (148 km), or around 2.5 additional hours of driving time.

North to Oaxaca, paved but narrow and winding National Hwy. 175 connects 148 miles (238 km) over the Sierra Madre del Sur from its junction with Hwy. 200 at Pochutla. The road climbs to around 9,000 feet through cool (chilly in winter) pine forests and hardscrabble Chatino and Zapotec native villages. Fill up with gas in Pochutla. Unleaded gasoline is available at the Pochutla Pemex stations, both on Hwy. 175, one about 300 yards toward town from Hwy. 200 and the other on the north, uphill, edge of town. Carry water and blankets, and be prepared for emergencies. The next gas station is at Miahuatlán, 90 miles north. Allow about seven driving hours from Puerto Ángel to Oaxaca, about six in the opposite direction.

By Bus

One long-distance bus line, second-class Estrella del Valle, connects Puerto Ángel directly to Oaxaca via Pochutla (where travelers may connect to many long-distance destinations). Buses depart from the main-street corner of Uribe and Vasconcelos; the Pochutla bus departs hourly during daylight hours, the Oaxaca bus once nightly at 10 P.M. The adjacent Papelería El Globo serves as the information and ticket office.

Many other long-distance buses connect with points west, east, and north from Pochutla. The three separate stations cluster less than a mile from the Hwy. 200 junction along Av. Lázaro Cárdenas, the Hwy. 175 main street into Pochutla (before the town center near the taxi stand).

Many first-class **Estrella Blanca** subsidiary-line buses (such as first-class Elite, luxury-class Turistar, Flecha Roja, and Autotransportes Cuauhtémoc) depart from the station at L. Cárdenas 94, in Pochutla, tel. 958/403-80. They connect west daily with Puerto Escondido, continuing to Acapulco and Lázaro Cárdenas in Michoacán, then continuing along the Pacific Coast all the way to the U.S. border. They also connect east (many per day) with Bahías de Huatulco destinations of Crucecita and Santa Cruz de Huatulco and Salina Cruz on the

Isthmus. A few "plus" (say "ploos") luxury-class buses connect daily, all the way to Mexico City.

All first-class **Cristóbal Colón** buses (L. Cárdenas 84, tel. 958/402-74) connect east with Crucecita (several per day). Some also continue east, connecting with Salina Cruz and Tehuantepec, continuing to Chiapas destinations of Tuxtla Gutiérrez San Cristóbal and Tapachula, at the Guatemala border. A few buses connect north with Oaxaca via the long, level, Isthmus route, via Salina Cruz and Tehuantepec. During the dry season, buses also connect via the trans-Sierra but shorter Hwy. 175. One bus connects daily with Puebla and Mexico City. A few buses also connect daily west with Puerto Escondido.

Frequent second-class and some first-class service is offered by cooperating lines (tel. 958/401-38 or 958/403-49) **Autobuses Estrella del Valle, Autobuses Oaxaca Pacífico,** and **Fletes y Pasajes.** They connect west with Puerto Escondido and Pinotepa Nacional, north with Oaxaca and Mexico City, and east with Huatulco, Salina Cruz, and the Chiapas border.

UPLAND EXCURSIONS FROM PUERTO ÁNGEL

Highway 175 curves its way from Puerto Ángel north, rising from the coast, continuing past a scattering of villages set in luxuriant forests, and finally climbing to cool, pine-tufted heights, where on a clear day the shining blue Pacific far below seems half a world away.

Travelers who hurry along this route find little; many of those who linger discover pleasant surprises along the way.

San Pedro Pochutla

The capital of the Pochutla governmental district was founded around 1600. One look along the busy, cluttered main street of Pochutla (pop. about 30,000) reveals that it's a market town. This is most apparent on Monday, when the side streets off the main street (Hwy. 175, locally known as Av. Lázaro Cárdenas) bloom with colorful awnings *(tianguis)* of vendors offering a collective mountain of merchandise.

On other days, vendors confine their piles to the formal indoor market, the **Mercado 5 de Octubre,** between Calles 1 and 2 Sur (South

1st and 2nd Streets) at the downtown center, on the east side of Lázaro Cárdenas.

Although most people come to Pochutla for business or to catch a bus, this town offers more than the merely perfunctory. A closer look reveals that Pochutla is really two towns rolled into one—the busy main street and the spacious, completely automobile-free central plaza and mall just one block downhill to the east.

The perfect perch for taking it all in is the upstairs plaza-view **Restaurant San Ángel** on the plaza's west side, open daily 9 A.M.–11 P.M. You can start off the day with a good breakfast or enjoy a fresh seafood lunch or dinner while being entertained by the plaza scene below. Directly east, across the plaza, spreads the *presidencia municipal,* and to the right (south) rise the Baroque domes of the town church, the **Templo de San Pedro.**

On the west side of the plaza the townsfolk have planted a living reminder of Pochutla, whose name comes from the Aztec-language label Pochtlán (Land of the Pochotes) for the locally plentiful *pochote* tree. You'll see a young specimen with small green leaves, five to a bunch, and spines on the trunk. People say that the *pochote* tree's edible roots sustained many starving families during times of drought and war.

Excitement mounts in Pochutla during the 21–28 June **Fiesta de San Pedro y San Pablo.** Celebrations begin with early morning masses and religious processions, then carnival rides and games, food, and fireworks. Finally a parade of floats carries a gaggle of mysterious masked characters who climax the festivities with a traditional dance.

Even during non-festival times the nighttime plaza, illuminated with Porfirian-era streetlight globes, is doubly interesting, so much so that you may decide to stay overnight. If so, Pochutla can accommodate you with the invitingly traditional **Hotel Pochutla,** at Madero 102, Pochutla, Oaxaca 70900, tel./fax 958/400-33, at the plaza's northwest corner. Owners offer 34 rooms arranged around an intimate, plant-decorated inner patio. Although many downstairs rooms are musty, upstairs they are invitingly quaint, with old-world louvered tropical-style doors, some of which open to balconies overlooking the colorful plaza scene. Rates run

about $11 s, $12 d, $15 t, with fan and private hot water shower bath.

Chacalapa

About nine miles (14 km) uphill from Pochutla along Hwy. 175, the village of San José Chacalapa nestles in the tropical foothill forest. The village's most inviting roadside attraction is **Restaurant Los Reyes,** a *palapa* on the west side, open daily 7 A.M.–10 P.M. Here you can pick from a long menu of soups, seafood (cocktails, fish fillets, shrimp, snails), meat, tacos, quesadillas, guacamole, baked potato *(papa del horno),* and sandwiches (hamburger, tuna, chicken, and ham and cheese). After that, relax in the big, blue pool or stroll out into the surrounding forest.

For an extended exploration, ask the friendly family owners for a guide to the nearby waterfall *(cascada)* and curative sulfur-water lagoon. If you're lucky, they may introduce you to very knowledgeable local resident Isidro Reyes Guzmán. Along the way he will help you spot, besides the locally abundant squirrels, hawks, and eagles *(ardillas, halcones, aguilas),* some woodpeckers, toucans, parrots, ocelots, and coatimundis *(carpinteros, tucanetas, péricos, tigrillos, coatis).* He can identify medicinal plants *(plantas medicinales)* in addition to the great forest trees, such as *ceiba, guanacastle, caoba,* and *macuil.*

The Restaurant Los Reyes also displays attractive for-sale furniture, crafted from big, dried *bejuco* vines by local craftsman Abel Hernand.

You may be so charmed by Chacalapa's natural delights that you want to stay overnight. If so, nearby mini-paradise **Balneario El Paraíso** can accommodate you. Get there from the Chacalapa village center, a few hundred yards north of the restaurant. At the *presidencia,* fork right, off the highway. Within a block, turn right again, at the Eco-turismo 1.5 Km sign. After exactly one mile (1.6 km) along a dirt road, turn right onto the ranch gate. Here in addition to a big 10-foot deep, spring-fed swimming pool, a kiddie pool, swings, slides, and a shaded *palapa* for picnics, are two clean, tile-floored cabañas for rent for about $12 d, with hot water shower baths.

Although impressive, Balneario Paraíso's man-made amenities are only part of the attraction. Friendly owner Octavio Ramos and his wife will provide meals and are happy to show you around their forested ranch, dotted with mango and orange trees and cinnamon and other spices. Later, explore the surrounding luxuriant stream valley and forest for rewarding views of animals and birds in their natural surroundings.

While you're at Balneario Paraíso, be sure to visit **Rancho Alegre** (on the road, just before the Balneario). Rancho Alegre, sometimes know as Tom's Garden, is the haven of German expatriate jewelry maker Tom Bachmeier and his Colombian wife Nehier. If you're lucky, one of them will show you around their tropical mini-Eden, lush with bromeliads, orchids, ginger, and a wealth of zapote, cacao, coffee, and mango trees.

San José del Pacífico

This is a little mountaintop town with a tremendous view, so high that the Pacific Ocean is clearly visible far below. The climate is brisk and dry, and pine-clad mountains rise all around,

an ideal setting for a few days away from the tropics. What's just as good, the village has a pair of pretty fair restaurants and an invitingly rustic hotel.

Little was spared to create the **Hotel Puesta Del Sol,** whose gardens lead downhill past the view restaurant to knotty-pine cabañas. Stay in the clean, cozy mountain cabañas for $13 s or d, $20 t, with fireplace and private hot-water shower baths. Reserve directly by telephone or mail through the hotel, address San José del Pacífico, Oaxaca 70861, tel. 957/201-11.

Food is available, either at the hotel's Restaurant Esther, or the restaurant Rayito del Sol (Little Sunbeam) in the village nearby.

The main local diversions are natural, such as basking in the sun, hiking mountain trails to panoramic viewpoints, viewing wildlife, watching spectacular sunsets, and resting or reading evenings by the fireplace.

Get to San José del Pacífico by bus or car via Hwy. 175, either 65 miles (105 km) north of Pochutla or 81 miles (130 km) south of Oaxaca.

BAYS OF HUATULCO AND VICINITY

The nine azure Bahías de Huatulco decorate a couple dozen miles of acacia-plumed rocky coastline east of Puerto Ángel. Between the bays, the ocean joins in battle with jutting, rocky headlands, while in their inner reaches, the ocean calms, caressing diminutive crescents of coral sand. Inland, a thick hardwood forest seems to stretch in a continuous carpet to the Sierra.

Environmentalists shuddered when they heard that these bays were going to be developed. Fonatur, the government tourism development agency, says, however, it has a plan. Relatively few (but all upscale) hotels will occupy the beaches; other development will be confined to a few inland centers. The remaining 70 percent of the land will be kept as pristine ecological zones and study areas.

Although this story sounds sadly familiar, Fonatur, which developed Ixtapa and Cancún, seems to have learned from its experience. Up-to-date sewage treatment has been installed *ahead of time;* logging and homesteading have been halted, and soldiers patrol the beaches, stopping turtle poachers. If all goes according to the plan, the nine Bahías de Huatulco and their 100,000-acre forest hinterland will be both a tourist and ecological paradise, in addition to employing thousands of local people when

complete in 2020. If this Huatulco dream ends as well as it has started, Mexico should take pride while the rest of the world should take heed.

HISTORY

Long before Columbus, the Huatulco area was well-known to the Aztecs and their predecessors. The name itself, from Aztec words meaning "Land where a Tree (or Wood) Is Worshipped," reflects one of Mexico's most intriguing legends—of the Holy Cross of Huatulco.

When the Spanish arrived on the Huatulco coast, the local native people showed them a huge cross they worshipped at the edge of the sea. A contemporary chronicler, Ignacio Burgoa, conjectured that the cross had been left by an ancient saint—maybe even the Apostle Thomas—some 15 centuries earlier. Such speculation notwithstanding, the cross remained as the Spanish colonized the area and established headquarters and a port, which they named San Agustín, at the westernmost of the Bays of Huatulco.

Spanish ports and their treasure-laden galleons from the Orient attracted foreign corsairs—Francis Drake in 1579 and Thomas Cavendish in 1587. Cavendish arrived at the

Huatulco's Bahía Maguey provides the essentials—sun, fresh seafood, soft sand, calm, clear water—for a relaxing day at the beach.

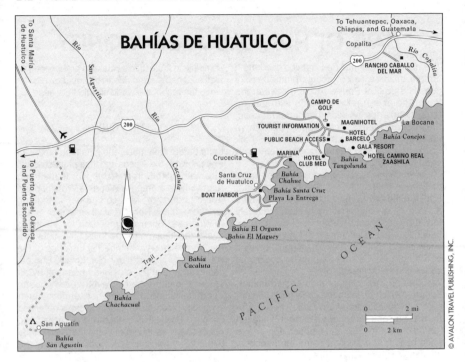

BAHÍAS DE HUATULCO

© AVALON TRAVEL PUBLISHING, INC.

bay now called Bahía Santa Cruz, where he saw the cross the Indians were worshipping. Believing it was the work of the devil, Cavendish and his men tried to chop, saw, and burn it down. Failing at all of these, Cavendish looped his ship's mooring ropes around the cross and with sails unfurled tried using the force of the wind to pull it down. Frustrated, he finally sailed away, leaving the cross of Huatulco still standing beside the shore.

By 1600, a steady trail of pilgrims were chipping pieces from the cross; so much so that in 1612, Bishop Juan de Cervantes had to rescue it. He brought the cross to Oaxaca, where he made four smaller two-foot crosses of it. He sent three specimens to church authorities in Mexico City, Rome, and Santa María de Huatulco, head town of the Huatulco *municipio.* Cervantes kept the fourth copy in the cathedral in Oaxaca, where it has remained, venerated and visible in a side chapel, to the present day.

SIGHTS

Getting Oriented

With no road to the outside world, the Bahías de Huatulco remained virtually uninhabited and undeveloped until 1982, about the time that coastal Hwy. 200 was pushed through. A few years later, Huatulco's planned initial kernel of infrastructure was complete, centering on the brand-new residential service town, Crucecita (pop. 10,000), and nearby Santa Cruz de Huatulco boat harbor and hotel village on Bahía Santa Cruz.

The Bays of Huatulco decorate the coastline both east and west of Santa Cruz. To the east, a paved road links Bahías Chahue, Tangolunda, and Conejos. To the west lie Bahías El Organo, El Maguey, and Cacaluta, all accessible by very rough roads from Santa Cruz. Isolated farther west are Bahías Chachacual and San Agustín, with no road from Santa Cruz (although a good dirt road runs to San Agustín from Hwy. 200 near the airport).

Besides Bahía Santa Cruz, the only other bay that has been extensively developed is Tangolunda, five miles east. Its golf course, small restaurant/shopping complex, and five resort hotels (Club Med, Barceó, Club Gala Resort, Magnihotel, and Zaashila) have all been fully operational since the early 1990s.

Getting Around

Frequent public **minibuses** connect Crucecita and Bahías Santa Cruz, Chahue, and Tangolunda. Taxis make the same trips for about $2 by day, $3 at night. No public transportation is available to the other bays. If the roads are passable, taxi drivers might take you for a picnic to west-side bays El Organo, El Maguey, and Cacaluta for about $25 round-trip from Crucecita or Tangolunda, perhaps $5 to Bahía Conejos.

For an extended day trip to all road-accessible bays, figure on $40–50 for either a taxi or a rental car. Call Fast Auto Rent, in Tangolunda, at tel./fax 9/581-0002, ext. 787; Alamo in Santa Cruz (at Hotel Castillo), tel. 9/587-0135 or 9/581-9074; or Budget in Crucecita at Octillo and Jazmín, tel. 9/587-0010, fax 9/587-0019.

Another option is to go by boat. The local boat cooperative (Sociedad Cooperativa Turístico Tangolunda) runs a daily excursion—around 10:30 A.M., $15 per person, kids half price—to all nine bays. Included are open bar, bilingual guide, and snacks; snorkeling is $4 extra. Reserve directly through the dock office, tel. 9/587-0081, or through a travel agent such as Paraiso Huatulco, tel. 9/581-0055, at the Hotel Barceló, ext. 784 or Servicios Turísticos del Sur, at the Hotel Castillo, tel./fax 9/587-1211; or Paraíso Huatulco, in Crucecita, tel. 9/587-0181, fax 9/587-0190.

The same cooperative also rents entire boats for up to 10 people for about $100 per day. They also do drop-off runs to the nearest beach, Playa Entrega, for about $10 per boat, round-trip; drop-off runs to more remote beaches cost around $20–30.

Local travel agents offer other tour options: several hours of sunning, swimming, picnicking, and snorkeling at a couple of Bahías de Huatulco beaches runs around $20 per person. Tours to Puerto Ángel, Puerto Escondido, and wildlife-rich lagoons go for $30–50 per person. For reservations, call Paraíso Huatulco, at the Hotel Barceló, tel. 9/581-0055, ext. 784; Servicios Turísticos del Sur, at the Hotel Castillo, tel./fax 9/587-1211; or Paraíso Huatulco, in Crucecita, tel. 9/587-0181, fax 9/587-0190.

Crucecita and Santa Cruz

Despite its newness, Crucecita (Little Cross), pop. 10,000, resembles a traditional Mexican town, with life revolving around a central plaza and market nearby. Crucecita is where the people who work in the Huatulco hotels, businesses, and government offices live. Although pleasant enough for a walk around the square and a meal in a restaurant, it's nothing special—mostly a place whose modest hotels and restaurants accommodate business travelers and weekenders who can't afford the plush hotels near the beach.

While in Crucecita, be sure to step into the church on the plaza's west side to admire the heavenly **ceiling mural** of Mexico's patron, the Virgin of Guadalupe. The mural, the largest of Guadalupe in Mexico, is the work of local artists José Ángel del Signo and Marco Antonio Contreras, whose for-sale art is on display locally. Besides the heavenly Virgin overhead, the muralists have decorated the space above the altar with the miraculous story of Don Diego and the **Virgin of Guadalupe.**

The four deluxe hotels and the few travel-oriented businesses of Santa Cruz de Huatulco (on Bahía Santa Cruz about two miles from Crucecita) cluster near the boat harbor. Fishing and tour boats come and go, vacationers sun themselves on the tranquil yellow-sand Playa Santa Cruz (beyond the restaurants adjacent to the boat harbor), while T-shirt and fruit vendors and boatmen hang around the quay watching for prospective customers. After the sun goes down, tourists quit the beach for their hotels and workers return to their homes in Crucecita, leaving the harbor and streets empty and dark.

Exploring the Bays of Huatulco

Isolation has left the Huatulco waters blue and unpolluted, the beaches white and clean. Generally, the bays are all similar: tropical deciduous (green July–Jan.) forested rocky

CRUCECITA

To Mex. 200, Airport, and Puerto Ángel

CALLE CARRIZAL

CALLE JAZMÍN

CALLE SIBALI

OAXACA PACIFICO AND ESTRELLA DEL VALLE

CALLE POCHOTE

COMEDOR JUQUILA

POSADA PRIMAVERA

POSADA MICHELLE

CALLE PALO VERDE

ESTRELLA BLANCA

BANCO INTERNACIONAL

CALLE OCOTILLO

CRISTÓBAL COLÓN

CALLE GARDENIA

CALLE BUGAMBILIAS

CALLE CARRIZAL

PUBLICACIONES HUATULCO

BAR LA CREMA

HOTEL FLAMBOYAN

DISCO MR. DON

CALLE GUANACAXTLE

FRUTERÍA ANGELITA

PLAZA

MERCADO

SEE DETAIL

CALLE GUAMACHIL

TEMPLO DE GUADALUPE

PLAZA OAXACA

CALLE FLAMBOYAN

CALLE CHACAH

PARADA DE MICROBUS (BUS STOP)

AV. OAXACA

HOTEL AMAKAL

SUPER FUENTE (GROCERIES)

POST OFFICE, TELEGRAPH, AND POLICE

TANGOLUNDA

BLVD.

0   200 yds
0   200 m

HOSPITAL SEGURO SOCIAL

To Santa Cruz de Huatulco and Bahías Organo, Maguey, and Cacaluta

To Bahías Chahue, Tangolunda, and Conejos

DETAIL

PLAZA

MERCADO

TACOS LOS PORTALES

CALLE GUAMACHIL

HOTEL GRIFER

HOTEL LAS PALMAS

MONEY EXCHANGE

PLAZA CONEJO

HOTEL POSADA DEL PARQUE

CALLE BUGAMBILIAS

CAFE OASIS

LONG DISTANCE TELEPHONE

RESTAURANT EL SABOR DE OAXACA

CENTRO DE SALUD

CACTUS BAR AND GRILL

CALLE FLAMBOYAN

CENTRA MÉDICA

FARMACIA DEL CENTRO

HANDICRAFTS MUSEUM

LAUNDRY ESTRELLA

RESTAURANT EL GIARDINO DEL PAPA

CALLE CARRIZAL

SUITES BEGONIAS

© AVALON TRAVEL PUBLISHING, INC.

headlands enclosing yellow-white coral sand crescents. The water is clear and good for snorkeling, scuba diving, sailing, kayaking, and windsurfing during the often-calm weather. Beaches, however, are typically steep, causing waves to break quickly near the sand, unsuitable for bodysurfing, boogie boarding, or surfing.

The six undeveloped Huatulco bays have neither drinking water nor much shade, and since they're so pristine, coconut palms haven't even gotten around to sprouting there. When exploring, bring food, drinks, hats, sunscreen, and mosquito repellent. When camping (which is permitted everywhere except Tangolunda), bring everything.

East Side
Bahía Chahue, about a mile from both Crucecita and Santa Cruz, is wide, blue, and forest-tufted, with a steep yellow dune stretching to the marina jetty at the east end. Chahue is uncrowded even on weekends and holidays and nearly empty the rest of the time.

About four miles farther east is the breezy and broad **Bahía Tangolunda.** Although hotels front much of the beach, a signed Playa Pública public access road borders the western edge of the golf course (turn right just past the creek bridge). Except for its east end, the Tangolunda beach is steep and the waves break quickly right at the sand. *Palapa* restaurants at the beach serve food and drinks; or, if you prefer, stroll a quarter mile for refreshments at the luxurious poolside beach clubs of the Barceó and Club Gala Resort resorts.

Over the headland about two miles farther east, **Punta Arena** (Sand Point), a forested thumb of land, juts out into wide **Bahía Conejos.** Three separate steep beaches spread along the inner shoreline. The main entrance road arrives at high-duned Playa Punta Arena. Playa Tejoncito (Little Wild Pig) is beyond the rocks far to the right; Playa Conejos (Rabbits) is to the left on the other side of Punta Arena. A few palm-frond *ramadas* for shade and a saltwater flush toilet lavatory occupy the Playa Punta Arena dune. Trees behind the dunes provide a few shady spots for RV or tent campers.

Beyond **La Bocana,** near the mouth of the Río Copalita, less than a mile farther on, a long, broad beach with powerful surfing rollers (novices

beware) stretches for at least a mile east. Beach *palapas* serve drinks and very fresh seafood. A lagoon above the beach (bring your kayak) appears ripe for wildlife viewing.

After La Bocana, the road bends inland, paralleling the **Río Copalita wildlife sanctuary,** perfect for adventurous exploring. Several operators guide visitors on river eco-tours: José Aussenac, owner of Posada Michelle, tel. 9/587-0535, organizes and guides outdoor adventure-tours. Options include bird- and animal-watching walks along riverine forest trails, kayaking river rapids, rafting, and mud baths at a riverside ranch. Very well-equipped **Huatulco Outfitters,** tel. 9/581-0315, offers several river-rafting excursions, from beginning ($25) to advanced ($75) levels.

West Side
Playa Entrega is a little dab of sand slipped into the west side of Bahía Santa Cruz. It is the infamous spot where, on 20 January 1831, Vicente Guerrero, president and independence hero, was brought ashore in custody of arch-villain Francisco Picaluga and sent to be murdered in Oaxaca a few months later.

Quarter-mile-long Playa Entrega is the ideal Sunday beach, with calm, clear water and clean yellow sand. Swimming, kayaking, and often snorkeling, sailing, and windsurfing possibilities are excellent. Some trees provide shady spots for tenting and RV camping. No facilities exist except for seasonal and holiday food and drink stands.

Get there via the main street, Boulevard Santa Cruz, which passes the Santa Cruz boat harbor. Continue west a few hundred yards to the Y (by the Hotel Binneguenda on the right). Mark your odometer. Bear left at the Y. After a few hundred yards, the road bends left and winds uphill, past panoramic viewpoints of Bahía Santa Cruz. Follow the signs and you'll soon be at Playa Entrega.

If instead of curving left to La Entrega, you continue straight ahead on the highway, you'll be headed for the Bahías El Organo, El Maguey, and Cacaluta. The roads to some of these bays have only been partly completed in recent years. Until authorities get around to finishing them, land access to the Bays of El Organo, Cacaluta, and remote Chacual will only be achievable by

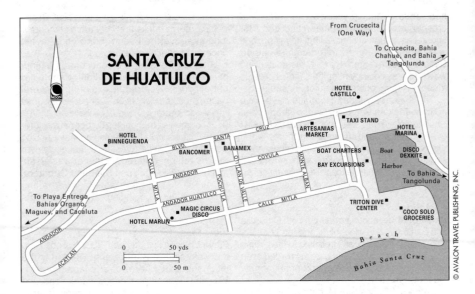

SANTA CRUZ DE HUATULCO

From Crucecita (One Way)

To Crucecita, Bahía Chahue, and Bahía Tangolunda

HOTEL CASTILLO

TAXI STAND

HOTEL MARINA

HOTEL BINNEGUENDA

BLVD. SANTA CRUZ

BANCOMER

BANAMEX

ARTESANIAS MARKET

BOAT CHARTERS

Boat Harbor

DISCO DEXKITE

BAY EXCURSIONS

COYULA

OTTLAN DE VALLE

MONTE ALBAN

POCHUTLA

ANDADOR

CALLE MITLA

To Bahía Tangolunda

To Playa Entrega, Bahías Organo, Maguey, and Cacaluta

ANDADOR HUATULCO

MAGIC CIRCUS DISCO

TRITON DIVE CENTER

COCO SOLO GROCERIES

HOTEL MARLIN

CALLE MITLA

ANDADOR

ACATLAN

0   50 yds
0   50 m

Beach

Bahía Santa Cruz

experienced drivers in off-road vehicles who know the myriad dirt tracks that wind through the tropical deciduous forest west of Santa Cruz. If in doubt, hire a taxi or take a boat tour.

Bahía El Organo is closest. About half a mile along the highway, look for a rough dirt track angling sharply left(inquire locally if you can't find it). The beach is isolated, intimate, and enfolded by rocky shoals on both sides. Some trees behind the dune provide shade.

Continuing straight ahead, the paved highway forks again (about 1.3 miles from the hotel). Continue straight ahead downhill to El Maguey or fork right to Cacaluta. The sandy crescent of **Bahía El Maguey** is bordered by tide pools tucked beneath forested headlands. Facing a protected fjordlike channel, the Maguey beach is usually calm, nearly waveless and fine for swimming, snorkeling, diving, and sailing. It would be a snap to launch a kayak or a rubber boat here for fishing in the bay. Beach access at present is on foot only. A clutter of semi-permanent seafood *palapas* line the beach. During weekends and holidays, picnickers arrive, and banana towboats and *aguamotos* (mini-motorboats) buzz the beach and bay. Although

camping is allowed, room is limited. You should bring everything essential. Beach *palapas* might be able to supply a few extras.

This trip, I found that the paved road that forks right toward **Bahía Cacaluta** ended about a mile farther, at an unsigned dirt jeep track that bumped ahead, winding past several likewise unmarked forks another mile to Bahía Cacaluta (bring a guide or try to find someone local for directions). There the bay spreads along a mile-long, heart-shaped beach, beckoningly close to a cactus-studded offshore islet. Swimmers beware, for waves break powerfully, surging upward and receding with strong undertow. Many shells—limpets and purple- and brown-daubed clams—speckle the beach. Surf fishing prospects, either from the beach itself or from rocks on either end, appear excellent. Although the sand directly behind the beach is too soft for vehicles, space exists farther back for RV parking and camping. Tenters could have their pick anywhere along the dune.

Bahía Chachacual, past the Río Cacaluta about four miles farther west, is a sand-edged azure nook accessible only with a guide, via forest tracks.

Bahía San Agustín, by contrast, is well

known and easily reachable by Pochutla-bound bus, then by the good dirt road (one-way taxi $5) just across the highway from the fork to Santa María Huatulco (at Km 236, a mile west of the airport). After about seven miles along a firm track, accessible by all but the bulkiest RVs, bear right to the modest village of *palapas* at the bay's sheltered west end. From there the beach stretches eastward along a mile of forest-backed dune. Besides good swimming, sailing, windsurfing, shell collecting, and fishing prospects, San Agustín has a number of behind-the-dune spots (follow the left fork shortly before the road's end) for RV and tent camping. Beachside *palapas* can, at least, supply seafood and drinks and maybe some water and basic groceries.

ACCOMMODATIONS

In Huatulco, as in other resorts, hotels on the beach are the most expensive. Crucecita's hotels are cheapest, Tangolunda's are most expensive, and the Santa Cruz hotels fall in between. All Huatulco lodgings have private baths with hot water.

Crucecita Accommodations

Most of the Crucecita lodgings are near the central plaza. The **Hotel Grifer,** at Guamuchil and Carrizal, a block east of the plaza, would be nothing special in most Mexican resorts, but in hotel-poor Huatulco, it is often full; reserve by writing the hotel at P.O. Box 159, Crucecita, Oaxaca 70980, tel./fax 9/587-0048. Three stories of nondescript modern rooms enclose a TV-dominated atrium; a passable street-level restaurant is convenient for breakfast. The 16 rooms rent for about $32 s or d, $36 t, with ceiling fans; no credit cards. Prices higher Christmas and Easter holidays.

Across Guamuchil, half a block back toward the plaza, the **Hotel Las Palmas,** Calle Guamuchil 206, Crucecita, Oaxaca 70980, tel. 9/587-0060, fax 587-0057, offers small, plain but clean a/c rooms on the two floors above its good street-level restaurant. The eight rooms rent for about $12 s, $27 d low season, $30 and $32 high; credit cards are accepted.

The **Hotel Suites Begonias,** at the south-

east plaza corner, offers a more deluxe, family-run alternative, Bugambilias 503, Crucecita, Oaxaca 70980, tel./fax 9/587-1390. The rooms, although clean and comfortable, have motel-style walkways passing their windows, decreasing privacy. Rates for the 13 rooms run about $22 s or d, $27 t, with fan and TV; credit cards are accepted.

Half a block away, you might consider taking one of the attractive rooms on the very top floor of the **Hotel Posada del Parque,** Flamboyan 306, Crucecita, Oaxaca 70980, tel./fax 9/587-0219, on the south side of the plaza. Although not especially large, the top-floor rooms have high rustic beamed ceilings, window views, and surround a cheery inner balcony-atrium. An airy sidewalk café downstairs serves breakfast, lunch, and dinner. All 14 rooms rent for about $22 s or d low season, with fan, $27 with a/c; $30 high season, with fan; $38 with a/c. All with TV; credit cards not accepted.

About three blocks east of the Crucecita plaza hubbub, the **Hotel Amakal** offers semideluxe, modern-standard rooms at reasonable prices. A stairway from the small, spartan lobby leads upstairs to about a dozen clean, light, white-tile-floored, tastefully decorated rooms with modern-standard baths. Rates are $22 s or d low season, with fan and $35 s, $40 d high; $32 d, low season, with a/c, $54 high. Credit cards are accepted. Street parking only. Reserve in writing at Av. Oaxaca 1, Crucecita, Bahías de Huatulco, Oaxaca 790897, or tel. 9/587-1500 or 9/587-1515, fax 9/587-0011.

A pair of simple but attractive *posadas* near the bus stations on Gardenia, four blocks north of the plaza, offer other options. The **Hotel Posada Michelle,** Gardenia 8, Crucecita, Oaxaca 70980, tel./fax 9/587-0535, run by friendly eco-tour guide José Aussenac, has about a dozen smallish but clean and comfortable rooms with big beds, baths, and good satellite TV. Some of the rooms are airy and light; others, although dark because of their half-mirrored windows (for privacy), do have white walls and open to a light, breezy second-story walkway that leads to a pleasant, hammock-hung and shady view porch. Rates for a/c rooms run about $27 d, low season, $37 high; rooms with fans only cost $22 low season and $32 high.

Posada Primavera, just around the corner at Palo Verde 5, Crucecita, Oaxaca 70980, tel. 9/587-1167, fax 9/587-0630, offers six simply furnished but clean, light, high-ceilinged upstairs rooms with bath. Windows look out onto the palmy, bougainvillea-adorned surrounding neighborhood. Rates are about $16 s or d low season, $27 high, with fans.

Santa Cruz Hotels

Three blocks from the beach in Santa Cruz, first choice goes to the **Hotel Meigas Binneguenda,** Blv. Santa Cruz 201, Santa Cruz de Huatulco, Oaxaca 70989, tel. 9/587-0077, fax 9/587-0284, email: binniguenda@huatulco.net.mx. Neo-colonial arches, pastel stucco walls, and copper and ceramics handicrafts decorate the interiors, while in the adjacent leafy patio, guests sun themselves around the elaborate cascade pool. In the restaurant, the customers seem as well fed and satisfied as the waiters are well trained and attentive. Upstairs, the colonial/modern-decor rooms are spacious, comfortable, and equipped with phones, TV, and a/c. Rates for the 75 rooms run about $65 d low season, $80 high, with parking and credit cards accepted. Bargain for a discount, especially during times of low occupancy.

Hotel Castillo Huatulco, Blv. Santa Cruz 303, P.O. Box 354, Santa Cruz de Huatulco 70989, tel. 9/587-0135 or 9/587-0144, fax 9/587-0131, east along the street three blocks, amounts to a weak second choice, unless you can get in for prices substantially less than the Binneguenda. Loosely managed, with recorded electronic rock or salsa music often thumping away in the bar, its 106 rooms, although comfortable, are crowded into a smaller space than the Binneguenda's 75. They are nevertheless popular with families on weekends and holidays but nearly empty (and perhaps bargainable) during quieter seasons. Low-season asking rates run about $100 s or d, $120 high. Bargain for a discount, especially during times of low occupancy. Phones, TV, a/c, pool, and parking; credit cards accepted. For reservations while in Mexico, dial toll-free 01–800/903-4900.

Smaller, recently renovated **Hotel Marlin,** two blocks from the beach, at Paseo Mitla 107, Santa Cruz de Huatulco, Oaxaca 70989, tel. 9/587-0055 or 9/587-1331, fax 9/587-0546, email: hmarlin@huatulco.net.mex, is only two blocks from the beach. From street level, the small lobby leads to an appealingly intimate coral-hued inner pool patio and restaurant, enfolded by three stories of rooms. Upstairs, the three dozen rooms are thoughtfully decorated with coral bedspreads, floor-length drapes, attractive, rustic tile floors, and deluxe '90s-standard bathrooms. Rates run $55 s or d low season, $90 high, with a/c, cable TV, phones and fourth night free. One possible drawback (or advantage) to all this is the hotel's adjoining discotheque—popular Friday and Saturday low season, nightly high—which the management swears cannot be heard in the rooms, even at full volume.

Tangolunda Luxury Resorts

Five luxury resort hotels spread along the Tangolunda shoreline. The Club Med dominates the sheltered western side bay, with four stack-like towers that make the place appear as a big ocean liner. The smaller Barceó (formerly Sheraton) and Hotel Gala Resort (formerly Club Royal Maeva) stand side by side on the bay's inner recess next to the golf course. The Hotel Zaashila spreads gracefully to its east-end cove, while the gleaming white Magnihotel (formerly Crown Pacific) stair-steps up the hillside, away from the beach.

The emphasis of all five resorts is on facilities, such as multiple pools, bars, and restaurants, full wheelchair access, live music, discos, shows, and sports such as tennis, golf, sailing, kayaking, windsurfing, snorkeling, diving, and swimming. Other amenities may include shops, baby-sitting, children's clubs, and arts and crafts instruction.

In contrast to the Barceó and the Zaashila, which operate in usual hotel style, the rates at the Gala Resort, Club Med, and Magnihotel are all-inclusive—including all food, sports, lessons, and entertainment. Their cuisine, although tasty and bountiful, is not fancy. The atmosphere resembles a big upscale summer camp, with hosts of options even for those who want to do nothing.

The **Barceó Huatulco** is a generic (but worthy) member of the worldwide chain, Paseo Benito Juárez, Bahía Tangolunda, Oaxaca 70989, tel. 9/581-0055, 9/581-0005, or 581-

0039, fax 9/581-0113. Rooms are comfortable, deluxe, and decorated in soothing pastels, with private bay-view balconies, phones, cable TV, and a/c. Rates for its 360 rooms and suites begin at about $100 s or d low season, about $200 high. For more information, visit the Barcelé website: www.barcelo.com.

If the **Hotel Zaashila Resort,** Bahía de Tangolunda, Huatulco, Oaxaca 70989, tel. 9/581-0460, fax 9/581-0461, tel. 800/7-CAMINO (800/722-6466) from the United States and Canada, hasn't yet gotten an architectural award, it should soon. Builders have succeeded in creating a modern luxury hotel that has an intimate feel. This begins right at the reception, a plush round *palapa,* where arriving guests are graciously invited to sit in soft chairs while being attended to by personable clerks, who are also seated, behind rustic, designer desks. You walk outside to your room through manicured tropical gardens, replete with gurgling fountains, splashing brooks, and cascading, green lawn terraces.

If the Zaashila has a drawback, it's in some of the 120 rooms, which, although luxurious and comfortable, are entirely tile-floored and could use more color and warmth. However, the arrangement of separate units, nested like a giant child's building blocks, resembles a space-age Hopi pueblo, each unit being uniquely perched among the whole, affording much privacy and light, especially in upper-floor units. Outside, a few steps downhill past the big, meandering blue pool, comes the superb beachfront: acres of luscious, billow-washed yellow sand, intimately enclosed between wave-sculpted rocks on one side and a jungly headland on the other. Low-season rentals begin at about $150, or about $250 if you must have your own little private pool. Corresponding high-season rates are around $210 and $350, with access to water sports, tennis, golf, three restaurants, and nightly live music.

If you're activity-oriented, you'll likely get more for your money at either the Club Med or the Magnihotel. The 300-room Gala Resort is very well managed and smaller; consequently, it's likely to be more personalized than both the sprawling 554-room Club Med or the Magnihotel (which, although it has relatively few rooms,

rambles up the hillside in 10 separate buildings, accessible from below via either shuttle or a funicular elevator).

Of the three hotels, the **Magnihotel** has the largest rooms. Perhaps this is meant to compensate for the drawback that it's not actually on the beach: guests must either walk or shuttle a couple of blocks to the beach club.

The biggest plus of the Magnihotel is the price, which, low season, runs only about $85 per person, double occupancy, including all meals, drinks, sports, kid's mini-club, and in-house entertainment. No fans, all air-conditioned. During high season, the same costs about $170 per person. Reserve directly at Magnihotel, Boulevard Benito Juárez 8, Bahía Tangolunda, Bahías de Huatulco, Oaxaca 70989, tel. 9/581-0044 or fax 9/581-0221, email: magnihotel@ huatulco.net.mx.

All-inclusive packages at the **Club Med** vary according to season, but run around $1,000 for two, per week low-season, plus around $100 in membership fees. Child (6–11 years) rates run about half adult prices. High season rates are considerably higher. Call 800/CLUBMED (800/258-2633) for information and reservations in the United States and Canada, or check the website: www.clubmed.com.

The **Gala Resort** all-inclusive rates run about $125 per person, low season, $165 high; kids six years or under, with parents, go free, while kids 7–11 years are about $50 low season, $60 high; 12–15 about $70 low, $100 high. Reserve directly at Gala Resort Huatulco, P.O. Box 227, Bahías de Huatulco, Oaxaca 70989, tel. 9/581-0000, fax 9/581-0220. For information and reservations in the United States and Canada, call 800/888-4252.

Camping
Although the downscale former Trailer Park Mangos in Santa Cruz has been closed, authorities generally permit **camping** at all of the Bahías de Huatulco except Tangolunda. You might save time by checking with the government tourist information office for any access changes or recommendations. Find them in the Tangolunda hotel zone on the far inland side, west edge of the hotel-shopping complex, tel. 9/581-0176, open high season Mon.–Fri. 9 A.M.–5 P.M., Sat. 9 A.M.–2 P.M.

A couple of scenic (but not very private) potential tenting spots are the popular **Playa Entrega** and **Playa Maguey.** For those craving seclusion, **Playa El Organo** may be better; it's about a one-mile forest walk from the pavement. (For more details, see West Side under Exploring the Bays of Huatulco, above.)

The soldiers who guard the beaches against turtle poachers and squatters also make camping much more secure. They usually welcome a kind word and maybe a cool drink as a break from their lonely and tedious vigil.

FOOD

Aside from the Tangolunda hotels, nearly all good Huatulco eateries are near the Crucecita plaza.

Breakfast and Snacks

For inexpensive homestyle cooking, try the *fondas* at the Crucecita Mercado (Market), between Guamuchil and Guanacastle, half a block off the plaza.

The Mercado stalls are good for fresh fruit during daylight hours, as is the **Frutería Angelita,** open daily 7 A.M.–9 P.M., just across Guanacastle.

Also nearby, the **Panadería San Alejandro,** at the southeast plaza corner of Flamboyan and Bugambilias, tel. 9/587-0317, open 6 A.M.–10 P.M., offers mounds of scrumptious baked goodies.

The crowds will lead you to Crucecita's best-bet snack shop, **Los Portales Taco and Grill,** corner of Guamuchil and Bugambilias, right on the plaza, tel. 9/587-0070. Breakfasts, a dozen styles of tacos, Texas chili (or, as in Mexico, *frijoles charros*—"cowboy beans"), and barbecued ribs are their specialties. Beer is less than a dollar. Open daily 6–2 A.M.

For a relaxing drink or a sandwich in Santa Cruz, go to the **Cafe Huatulco,** tel. 9/587-1228, at the bandstand in the shady Santa Cruz town plaza, a block west of the marina *embarcadero.* The friendly husband-wife team's mission is to promote the already well-deserved popularity of Huatulco's mountain-grown coffee, which they grind fresh daily for their good capuccinos and café lattes. For

information about Huatulco coffee, email them at cafeplumahua@huatulco.net.mx.

Restaurants

The refined sidewalk atmosphere of **Cafe Oasis** has made it Crucecita's plaza-front restaurant of choice. Beneath cooling ceiling fans, customers watch the passing plaza scene while enjoying a full bar and a professionally prepared and served menu of breakfast, good espresso, fruit, salads, hamburgers, Mexican and international specialties, and much more. At the southeast plaza corner (Bugambilias and Flamboyan), open daily 8 A.M.-midnight, tel. 9/587-0045.

Nearly as successful is **Restaurante Sabor de Oaxaca,** on the bottom floor of the Hotel Las Palmas on Guamuchil, half a block from the plaza, tel. 9/587-0060. Wall art, folk crafts, and quiet conversation set the tone, while tasty country specialties fill the tables. Try their Oaxacan-style tamales or *botanas Oaxaqueños*—cheese, sausage, pork, beef, and guacamole snacks. Open daily 8 A.M.– 11 P.M.

Lovers of fine Italian cuisine can't miss enjoying a meal at Crucecita's class-act restaurant, **El Giardino del Papa** (The Pope's Garden), brainchild of owner Rossana Pandolfini of Amalfitano, and chef Mario Saggese of Salerno. Mario, who was once the Pope's bodyguard, immigrated to Mexico to follow his passion for cooking. Rossana asked Mario to come to Huatulco because she craved pasta *al dente* the way it's "supposed to be" in the old country. Although the Mario's suggestions include *calamari criollo, scampi al brandy, insalata Mediterrenea,* and *spaghetti a la Mario,* what ever you get will be tasty. Call for reservations, tel. 9/587-4763, especially during the winter. Find the restaurant one block west of the plaza's southwest corner, at Flamboyan 204, open daily 2 P.M.-midnight. Expensive.

Travelers weary of the plaza tourist scene can find authentic Mexican cooking at **Comedor Juquila,** which does quite well on nearly exclusively local patronage. Tasty regional specialties—*moles, pansita, chiles rellenos,* tamales—are its key to success. Open daily 7 A.M.–10 P.M., off of Gardenia, five blocks north of the plaza, corner of Palo Verde.

ENTERTAINMENT

Hangouts and Dancing

Huatulco entertainments center on the Crucecita plaza. Although the hubbub cools down weekdays and low seasons (and hot clubs seem to change as often as the Huatulco breeze), many spots heat up significantly during the high winter season.

The **Cactus Bar and Grill**, tel. 9/587-0648, on the Flamboyan side of the plaza, sometimes livens up with videos and music. On the other hand, you can get swept up nightly by the seasonal salsa and Latin rock repertoire of the band at the **Sports Bar Iguana** next to Tacos Los Portales, Bugambilias side of the plaza. Open about 11 A.M.–2 A.M., in season.

You need only follow your ears to the source at **Mr. Don** bar, at the diagonally opposite plaza corner of Gardenia and Guanacastle, upstairs. Here, live Latin rock is featured nightly in season and on weekends 8 P.M.–2 A.M.

In Santa Cruz, lights flash, fogs descend, and customers gyrate to the boom-boom at **Magic Circus** disco in the Marlin Hotel on Calle Mitla, two blocks behind Banamex off the main boulevard. Admission (from around 10 P.M.) runs about $10. Call 9/587-0055 to confirm.

Nearby, continue your party at **Dexkite** disco, which offers continuous recorded reggae, salsa, and Latin rock from about 9:30 P.M. At the Marina Hotel and Resort, in Santa Cruz, Calle Tehuantepec 112; call for confirmation, tel. 9/587-0965.

Sunset Cruise and Piano Bar

Lovers of quieter diversions might enjoy going on a wine and soft-music sunset cruise on the sailboat *Luna Azul.* For more information, tel. 9/587-0945.

For tranquil piano-bar atmosphere, go to **Ven Aca** (Come Here), in Santa Cruz, west end, past the park, next to Banamex, nightly from about 8 P.M., tel. 9/587-1651.

The **Hotel Barceó** in Tangolunda is one of the most reliable sources of hotel nightlife. Live music often plays before dinner (about 6–8 P.M.) in the lobby bar, and "Fiesta Mexicana" tourist shows rev up (usually Friday, more often high season) year-round. Contact a travel agent

or call the hotel direct at 9/581-0055 for details and reservations (about $37 per person, including buffet and all drinks.) Other hotels, such as the Magnihotel, Gala Resort, and Zaashila may also offer similar entertainments, in season.

SPORTS AND RECREATION

Walking, Jogging, Tennis, and Golf

Huatulco's open spaces and smooth roads and sidewalks afford plenty of walking and jogging opportunities. One of the most serene spots is along the Tangolunda Golf Course morning or evening. Also, an interesting sea-view forest trail takes off from Bahía Conejos.

If you're planning on playing lots of tennis, best stay at one of the Tangolunda luxury resorts. Otherwise, the Barceó, tel. 9/581-0055, 9/581-0005, and the Tangolunda Golf Course, tel. 9/581-0037, fax 9/581-0059, rent tennis courts for about $8 per hour. Call for rental information and reservations.

The breezy green **Tangolunda Golf Course,** tel. 9/581-0037, fax 9/581-0059, designed by the late architect Mario Chegnan Danto, stretches for 6,851 yards down Tangolunda Valley to the bay. The course starts from a low building complex (watch for bridge entrance) off the Hwy. 200-Tangolunda Highway across from the sanitary plant. Greens fee runs about $50, cart $16, club rental $13, caddy $15. The tennis courts, maintained by the same government corporation that owns the golf course, are next to the clubhouse on the knoll at the east side of the golf course.

Horseback Riding, Bicycle Rentals, and Tours

Rancho Caballo del Mar on the road (east past Tangolunda) to Copalita, about a mile south of Hwy. 200, guides horseback trips along the ocean-view forest trail that stretches from their corral to the eco-preserve zone by the Río Copalita. The four-mile tour, which costs about $25 per person at the ranch (more if through an agent), returns via Bocana shoreline vista point for lunch. For more information and reservations, contact a travel agent, such as Turismo Conejo in Crucecita, tel. 9/587-0009.

Adventurers can also walk the same four-mile round-trip in around three hours. Take a hat, water, and a bathing suit, and start early (around 8 A.M.) or late (around 3 P.M.) to avoid the midday heat.

Mountain Biking and Adventure Tours

Discover Tours Huatulco, also known as Rent-a-Bike, hires out mountain bikes and leads bicycle tours, ranging from leisurely half-day jaunts for $10 to challenging all-day jungle trail adventures for about $25 per person. Contact them in Tangolunda at Plaza Las Conchas, across from Hotel Barceó, tel. 9/581-0002, tel./fax 9/587-0678.

For an even more challenging menu, contact **Aventuras Huatulco.** Besides mountain biking, they also offer jungle hikes, horseback riding, kayaking, wildlife-viewing, rock-climbing and rapelling at three different backcountry locations: Punta Celeste, Piedra de Moros, and Copalitilla.

Please **resist the temptation** to go on a widely-advertised rip-roaring "jungle tour" by four-wheel *moto* all-terrain vehicle (ATV) motorcycle. The vehicles are noisy, hazardous to the rider, polluting to the environment, and tear up forest trails and scare away animals. It would be healthier for both you and the Huatulco ecosystem to ask the provider to guide you along the same trip by much less intrusive mountain bike, or, even better, on foot.

Río Copalita Eco-Touring and Rafting

José Aussenac, owner of Posada Michelle, organizes and guides outdoor adventure-tours in the east-side Río Copalita wildlife sanctuary. Options include bird- and animal-watching walks along riverine forest trails, kayaking river rapids, and mud baths at a riverside ranch. Call him, tel. 9/587-0535, for more information and reservations.

Very well-equipped **Huatulco Outfitters,** tel. 9/581-0315, at the first shopping complex on the left as you enter Tangolunda, offers several river-rafting excursion, from beginning ($25) to advanced ($75) levels.

Upland Jungle Eco-Touring and Coffee Farms

Local tour operators guide hiking and bird-watching tours to waterfalls, springs, archaeo-logical zones, pilgrimage and sacred sites, and coffee farms in the jungly foothill hinterland north of Huatulco. One of the most experienced and environmentally sensitive operators is **Turismo Conejo** in Crucecita, at Plaza Conejo, on Guamuchil, half a block east of the town plaza, tel. 9/587-0009, fax 9/587-0054, email: tonino@caramail.com. Turismo Conejo offers a range of options, from one-day walks along the Copalita River (ruins, bird-watching by canoe, mud bath) and jungle jeep safaris and lunch at La Gloria coffee plantation to jungle overnights (waterfalls, rock hieroglyphic paintings) to complete five-day excursions from Oaxaca City, including all of the above. Other agents may also offer similar tours; contact your hotel tour desk.

Swimming, Surfing, Snorkeling, and Scuba Diving

Swimming is ideal in the calm corners of the Bahías de Huatulco. Especially good swimming beaches are at **Playa Entrega** in Bahía Santa Cruz and **Bahía El Maguey.** A few spots are also good for surfing. **Huatulco Outfitters,** tel. 9/581-0315, at the first shopping complex on the left as you enter Tangolunda, offers completely equipped surfing excursions.

Generally clear water makes for rewarding snorkeling off the rocky shoals of all of the Bays of Huatulco. Local currents and conditions, however, can be hazardous. Novice snorkelers should go on trips accompanied by strong, experienced swimmers or professional guides. Bring your own equipment; gear purchased locally will be expensive at best and unusable at worst.

Huatulco scuba divers enjoy the services of well-equipped and professional **Buceos Triton** dive shop in Santa Cruz de Huatulco, in the small complex between Santa Cruz main beach and boat harbor, tel./fax 9/587-0844. Owner and certified instructor Enrique La Clette has had extensive training in France, the United States, and Mexico City. He starts novices out with a pool mini-course, followed by a three-hour ($60) trip in a nearby bay. Snorkelers go for about $30, with good equipment furnished. Open Mon.–Sat. 9 A.M.–2 P.M. and 5–7 P.M.

Buceos Triton's PADI open-water certification course takes about five days and runs about $350, complete. After that, you are qualified for more advanced tours, which include local shipwrecks, night dives, and marine flora, fauna, and ecology tours.

La Clette, a marine biologist by training, is a leader in the local ecological association that watchdogs Fonatur's Huatulco development work.

If Buceos Triton is all booked up, try **Action Sports,** at the Barceó Hotel, tel. 9/581-0055, ext. 842; email: charlie_diver@hotmail.com, or **Buceo Sotovento** across from the Hotel Barceó, inside the Hotel Club Plaza Huatulco, tel./fax 9/581-0051, or on the Crucecita plaza, south side, tel. 9/587-1309, email: scubahector@huatulco.net.mx.

Fishing and Boat Launching

The local boat cooperative **Sociedad Servicios Turísticos Bahía Tangolunda** takes visitors out for fishing excursions from the Santa Cruz boat quay. For a launch with two lines and bait, figure on paying about $40 minimum for a three-hour excursion. For big-game fishing, rent a big 40-foot boat, with lines for several persons, for about $400. More reasonable prices might be obtainable by asking around among the fishermen at the Santa Cruz boat harbor or the village at San Agustín.

On the other hand, you can leave the negotiations up to a travel agent, who will arrange a fishing trip for you and your friends. You can stop afterward at a beachside *palapa,* which will cook up a feast with your catch. Save money by bringing your own tackle. Rates for an approximately three-hour trip for three run about $60 if you supply your own tackle, $120 if you don't. Contact the agent at your hotel travel desk, or an outside agent, such as **Paraíso Huatulco** in the Hotel Flamboyan, on the Crucecita plaza, tel. 9/587-0181, fax 9/587-0190, or **Turismo Conejo,** also in Crucecita, tel. 9/587-0009.

Some of the Huatulco bays offer easy boat-launching prospects, especially at sites at easily reachable Bahía Chahue marina and Bahía Santa Cruz's Playa la Entrega. Easy launching is also possible at more remote spots, especially at the protected beaches, where you can drive to the water's edge, such as at Playa Entrega and Bahía San Agustín.

SHOPPING

Market and Handicrafts

Crucecita has a small traditional market (officially the Mercado 3 de Mayo) east of the plaza, between Guanacastle and Guamuchil. Although produce, meats, and clothing occupy most of the stalls, a few offer Oaxaca handicrafts. Items include black *Obarra* pottery, hand-crocheted Mixtec and Amusgo *huipiles,* wool weavings from Teotitlán del Valle, and whimsical duck-motif wooden bowls carved by an elderly, but sharp-bargaining, local gentleman.

Steep rents and lack of business force many local silver, leather, art, and other handicrafts shops to hibernate until tourists arrive in December. The few healthy shops with good selections cluster either around the Crucecita plaza, the Santa Cruz boat quay, or in the Punta Tangolunda shopping complex adjacent to the Barceó (or shops in the hotel itself).

vendor with his duck-motif woodcrafts in Crucecita

In Crucecita, one of the most reliable crafts stores is **Plata de Taxco,** open daily, 9 A.M.–9 P.M., tel. 9/587-0818, (next to Hotel Suites Begonias, a few doors south of the plaza's southwest corner). Here you can select from an all-Mexican assortment—shiny *barro negro* (black pottery) from the Valley of Oaxaca, pottery moon and sun faces from Tonalá, Jalisco, *talavera* ware from Puebla, crazy wooden animals *(alebrijes)* from Arrazola, near Oaxaca, an lots of glistening silver jewelry from Taxco.

Also, with a similar assortment, the private handicrafts museum—Museo de Artesanías Oaxaqueñas—next to the Cafe Oasis, east side of the plaza, deserves a look.

Supermarket, Laundry, and Photo Supplies

The supermarket **La Fuente** in Crucecita on east-side Av. Oaxaca offers a large stock of groceries, an ice machine, and a little bit of everything else, a block east of the Pemex station, tel. 9/587-0222. Open daily 8 A.M.–10 P.M.

Take your washing to the **Lavandería Estrella,** tel. 9/587-0585, open Mon.–Sat. 8 A.M.–9 P.M. Find it a block east of the Crucecita plaza, on Flamboyan, corner of Carrizal.

For film and quick develop and print, go to **Foto Conejo,** tel. 9/587-0054, just off the Crucecita plaza, across Guamuchil from the market. Besides a photo portfolio of the Bays of Huatulco, the friendly owner stocks supplies, point-and-shoot cameras, and Kodak, Fuji, and Konica slide and print film. Open daily 9 A.M.–8 P.M.

SERVICES

Money Exchange

For cash, you may either use the ATMs at all of Huatulco's banks or go inside. In Crucecita, try long-hours **Banco Internacional** (Bital), open Mon.–Fri. 8 A.M.–7 P.M., Sat. 9 A.M.–3 P.M., at 1204 Gardenia, corner of Palma Real, five short blocks north of the town plaza. Other banks are in Santa Cruz. **Banamex,** on the main street Av. Santa Cruz, corner of Pochutla, tel. 9/587-0322, exchanges both U.S. and Canadian traveler's checks Mon.–Fri. 9 A.M.–3 P.M., Sat. 9 A.M.–2 P.M. **Bancomer** across the street, tel.

9/587-0003, does about the same Mon.–Fri. 8:30 A.M.–2 P.M. and Sat. 9 A.M.–2 P.M. Call to check money-changing hours.

After bank hours, go to the hole-in-the-wall Money Exchange booth on Guamuchil, near the corner at the east side of the Crucecita plaza, tel. 9/587-1309, open Mon.–Sat. 7A.M.–9 P.M.

Post and Telecommunications

The Huatulco *correo* and *telecomunicaciones* stand side by side, across from the Pemex gas station on east-side Blv. Tangolunda. Post office, tel. 9/587-0551, hours are Mon.–Fri. 8 A.M.–7:30 P.M., Sat. 9 A.M.–12:30 P.M. *Telecom,* tel. 9/587-0894, is open Mon.–Fri. 8 A.M.–7:30 P.M. and Sat.–Sun. 9 A.M.–noon.

For telephone, buy a *Ladatel* telephone card and use it at public telephone, or go to one of the *larga distancias* on Carrizal, near the Hotel Grifer, such as **Caseta Telefónica Gemenis,** tel. 9/587-0735 or 9/587-0736, open daily 8 A.M.–9:30 P.M.

Internet connection is available at the PC Internet store on Plaza Galería, behind Hotel Amakal, past the gas station, about four blocks east of the Crucecita plaza.

Immigration and Customs

Both Migración and the Aduana are at the Huatulco airport. If you lose your tourist permit, try to avoid trouble or a fine at departure by presenting Migración with proof of your date of arrival—stamped passport, an airline ticket, or preferably a copy of your lost tourist permit—a day (or at least a couple of hours) before your scheduled departure.

Medical and Police

Among the better of Huatulco private clinics is **Central Médica,** half a block east of the Crucecita plaza, at Flamboyan 205. For consultations, call tel. 9/587-0104 or 9/587-0435.

For an English-speaking, U.S.-trained doctor, go to IAMAT (International Association for Medical Assistance to Tourists) member and general practitioner Dr. Andrés González Ayvar, tel. 9/587-0687, cellular 044 9/587-6065. His regular consultation hours are Mon.–Sat. 10 A.M.–2 P.M. and 6–9 P.M.

Alternatively, go around the corner to the 24-hour government **Centro de Salud** clinic, tel.

9/587-1421, on Carrizal, a block east of the Crucecita plaza, or the big **Seguro Social** hospital, tel. 9/587-1182, 9/587-1183, or 9/587-1185, in Crucecita, on the boulevard to Tangolunda, a quarter mile south of the Pemex gas station.

For routine medications, Crucecita has many pharmacies, such as **Farmacia del Centro,** plaza corner of Flamboyan and Bugambilias, tel. 9/587-0232, open Mon.–Sat. 8 A.M.–10 P.M., Sun. 9 A.M.–2 P.M. and 5–10 P.M., at street level, below the Hotel Begonias.

For police emergencies, call the Crucecita *policía,* tel. 9/587-0210, in the Agencia Municipal behind the post office, across the Tangolunda boulevard from the Pemex *gasolinera.*

INFORMATION

Tourist Information Offices
The Huatulco office of the Oaxaca Secretary of Tourism is in the Tangolunda hotel zone, inland side, west edge of the hotel-shopping complex., tel./fax 9/581-0176, open high season, Mon.–Fri. 9 A.M.–5 P.M., Sat. 9 A.M.–2 P.M.

Newspapers, Books, and Magazines
The bookshop in Tangolunda at the Barceó, tel. 9/581-0055, stocks English-language paperback novels, Mexico art and guidebooks, newspapers such as *USA Today,* and many magazines.

In Crucecita, the small **Publicaciones Huatulco** newsstand sells the English-language *News* of Mexico City (which arrives around noon), at the corner of Gardenia and Macuil, three blocks north of the plaza; open daily 6 A.M.–9 P.M. Reserve your copy by paying in advance.

Pick up a copy of *Huatulco Magazine* the handy commercial tourist booklet, at your hotel or a store or travel agent or at their office, tel. 9/587-0342 at Cerrada de tlacolula no. 3, in Santa Cruz.

Ecology Association
Local ecologists and community leaders monitor Huatulco's development through their **Asociación Pro Desarrollo Sociocultural y Ecologíos de Bahías de Huatulco.** Association president marine biologist Enrique

La Clette and his associates are working earnestly to assure the government's plan— that 70 percent of Huatulco will remain undeveloped—continues in force as development proceeds. One of their initial victories was to dissuade Club Med from dumping its raw sewage into Tangolunda Bay. Enrique, who is friendly and fluent in English, enjoys talking to fellow nature lovers. Drop into his dive shop, Buceos Triton, in Santa Cruz de Huatulco, in the complex between the boat harbor and the beach, tel./fax 9/587-0844.

GETTING THERE AND AWAY

By Air
The **Huatulco airport** (officially the Aeropuerto Internacional Bahías de Huatulco, code-designated HUX) is just off Hwy. 200, eight miles (13 km) west of Crucecita and 19 miles (31 km) east of Puerto Ángel. The terminal is small, with only check-in booths, a few snack bars, and handicrafts and trinket shops (but fortunately, with a Banco Internacional ATM for arrival cash.)

A few reliable carriers connect with U.S. and Mexican destinations:

American Airlines connects with Dallas during the winter-spring high season. For reservations, call a travel agent, such as Paraíso Huatulco, tel. 9/587-0181, fax 9/587-0190.

Mexicana Airlines flights connect daily with Mexico City. For reservations, call Mexicana's office on Plaza Chahue shopping center, tel. 9/587-0223 or 9/587-0243, or toll-free in Mexico 01 800/502-2000.

Aerocaribe connects with Oaxaca and Puerto Escondido. For reservations, call a travel agent.

United Airlines, American Airlines, and **Canada 3000** offer seasonal, mostly winter **charter-flight** connections with U.S. and Canadian destinations. For reservations, call a travel agent.

Huatulco **air arrival** is usually simple. Since the terminal has no hotel booking agency or money-exchange counter (although there is an ATM), come with a hotel reservation and sufficient pesos to last until you can get to the bank in Santa Cruz or Crucecita. After the typically quick immigrations and customs checks, arrivees have a choice of efficient ground transportation to town. Agents sell tickets for collective GMC Suburbans to Crucecita or Santa Cruz or Tangolunda (about $7). A private *taxi especial* for three, possibly four passengers, runs about $8. Prices to Puerto Ángel are about double these.

Mobile travelers on a budget can walk the couple of blocks from the terminal to Hwy. 200 and catch one of the frequent public **minibuses** headed either way to Crucecita (east, left) or the Pochutla (Puerto Ángel) junction (west, right).

Car rental agents are usually on duty for flight arrivals. If they're not, make a reservation ahead of time and they will meet your flight: **Budget** in Crucecita, tel. 9/587-0010, fax 9/587-0019; **Alamo** in Santa Cruz, tel. 9/581-9074 or 9/587-0135; or local agent **Fast Auto Rent** in Tangolunda (which offers, among others, jeep-like Trackers), opposite the Hotel Barceó, tel./fax 9/581-0002, email: fastrent@hotmail.com, Mexico toll-free number 01 800/210-8167. During the winter especially, make reservations in the United States and Canada prior to departure.

By Car or RV
Paved highways connect Huatulco east with the Isthmus of Tehuantepec, west with Puerto Ángel and Puerto Escondido, and north with Oaxaca.

Highway 200, the east-west route, runs an easy 100 miles (161 km) to Tehuantepec, where it connects with Hwy. 190. From there it continues northwest to Oaxaca or east to Chiapas and the Guatemala border. In the opposite direction, the Hwy. 200 route is equally smooth, connecting with Pochutla (Puerto Ángel), 22 miles (35 km) west, and Puerto Escondido, 66 miles (106 km), continuing to Acapulco in a long 322 miles (519 km). Allow about three hours to Tehuantepec, an hour and a half to Puerto Escondido, and to Acapulco, a full nine hours' driving time, either direction.

Highway 175, the cross-Sierra connection north with the city of Oaxaca, although paved, is narrow, winding, and frequently potholed, with few services in the 80-mile high Sierra stretch between its junction with Hwy. 200 at Pochutla (22 miles west of Crucecita) and Miahuatlán in the Valley of Oaxaca. The road climbs to 9,000 feet into pine-tufted, winter-chilly Chatino and

Zapotec country. Be prepared for emergencies. Allow eight hours northbound, seven hours southbound, for the entire 175-mile (282-km) Huatulco-Oaxaca trip.

By Bus
Several long-distance bus lines connect Huatulco with destinations east, west, and north. They depart from small separate terminals in Crucecita, scattered mostly along Calle Gardenia north of the plaza.

Many daily **Cristóbal Colón** first-class buses, terminal located on Gardenia, four blocks north of the plaza, tel. 9/587-0261, connect west with Pochutla (Puerto Ángel) and Puerto Escondido. Buses also connect east with the Salina Cruz and Tehuantepec on the Isthmus, continuing either east to San Cristóbal las Casas and Tapachula in Chiapas, or northwest to Mexico City via Oaxaca and Puebla.

A few **Estrella Blanca** buses, from their terminal five blocks north of the Crucecita plaza, corner of Palo Verde, tel. 9/587-0103, connect west with Pinotepa Nacional and Acapulco via Pochutla and Puerto Escondido, and east with Salina Cruz.

A few second- and first-class **Estrella del Valle** and **Autobuses Oaxaca-Pacífico** buses connect daily with Oaxaca via Pochutla, from Jazmin, corner Sabali, nine blocks north of the plaza, tel. 9/587-0193.

UPLAND EXCURSIONS FROM THE BAYS OF HUATULCO: COFFEE COUNTRY

A century before the Bays of Huatulco development even got on the drawing board, the cooler, greener Huatulco uplands were home to a community of farmers and fruit and coffee ranchers. Bypassed by the new Hwy. 200 and the coastal resort development, the foothill region above the Bays of Huatulco is a treasury of traditional Oaxaca life and natural diversions—wildlife to view, springs and waterfalls to splash in, and jungle coffee ranches to visit and explore.

The foothill destinations of Santa María Xadani and La Gloria Coffee Farm make an enjoyable day trip by car or tour. By bus, allow two days, including an overnight at the coffee farm. Along the way, nature lovers will enjoy the leafy foothill country, laced with springs and cascades gurgling through leafy, vine-hung woodland, rich with birds, mammals, and fluttering butterflies.

Santa María Huatulco

Colonial-era Santa María Huatulco (pop. 9,000) is the head town of the sprawling Huatulco *municipio,* which encompasses the entire Bahías de Huatulco development. Although living at the center of a mountain, jungle, and seashore domain, Santa María Huatulco people have traditionally looked toward the emerald Sierra rising precipitously on their northern horizon. Those mountains and their foothills are the main source of Huatulco's wealth—the aromatic produce that a host of coffee farms *(fincas cafetaleras)* produce.

Taste Huatulco coffee in one of the cafés, such as the inviting, family-run **Las Flores** on the town plaza, east side. While you're on the plaza, take a stroll around; inspect the unique *ollas* (jars) made into fountains, an inviting part of the plaza decoration. Also take a look around the former market, uniquely built on pillars in the middle of the plaza.

Finally, step inside the old town church, the **Templo de Nuestra Señora de la Concepción.** Inside above the altar you'll find the Señora, and in the transept chapels a pair of mysterious, venerated objects. In the left chapel stands the **Señor de Misericordias,** an image that turned up strangely in Santa Cruz de Huatulco in the 17th century, and which people have worshipped ever since. Additionally, in the right chapel is one of the four copies of the **Santa Cruz (Holy Cross) de Huatulco,** fashioned by the Bishop of Oaxaca, Juan de Cervantes, from the enigmatic ancient seashore cross. It was sent here in 1612.

Huatulco's plaza front is generally sleepy (and especially tranquil during the cool of the evening) except during fiestas and market days. The town celebrates three main fiestas. The first is on the fourth Friday of Lent (23 days after Ash Wednesday, usually in March), when folks celebrate the Señor de Misericordias. Good Friday, two days before Easter Sunday, is the Fiesta de la Santa Cruz de Huatulco. The 8–11 December fiesta honors Nuestra Señora de la Concepción. The weekly **market days** are Saturday and Sunday, when vendors' *tianguis*

decorate the center of town, about three blocks south of the plaza.

Get to Santa María Huatulco by local minibus from Crucecita (bus stop a block east of the Crucecita plaza) or the Pochutla Hwy. 200 crossing. If necessary, transfer to a second bus at the side road to Santa María Huatulco, at Km 238, about a mile west of the Huatulco airport or about 17 miles (27 km) east of the Pochutla crossing.

Santa María Xadani

This is a gently sloping hillside village (pop. 1,000) tucked in a luxuriantly forested valley (about 13 miles, 21 km from Hwy. 200), with at least four separate social orders: people, dogs, pigs, and chickens. The town pride (at the village's upper end) is the **church,** dedicated to village patron the Virgen de la Concepclón, whom townsfolk, joined by many outsiders, celebrate in a big fiesta climaxing on 15 August.

Nearby sights include a *cascada* (waterfall) and a spring *(ojo de agua),* **Encanto,** warm on one side and cool on the other. Farther afield, one-day tours by taxi or your own car could include the **Pozo de Santa Cruz** (Well of the Holy Cross) spring and the spectacular **Cascada del Diablo** (Devil's Waterfall).

For a guide (Spanish-only), contact friendly local resident **Gregorio Cruz Cruz,** preferably at least a day or two ahead of time. Write him, Gregorio Cruz Cruz, Domocilio Conocido, Santa María Xadani, Pochutla, Oaxaca 70999, or better, leave a message at the town telephone, 958/404-10. Expect to pay (negotiate ahead of time) about $20 per day for his service.

If you're tempted to linger, Xadani (shah-DAH-nee) offers basic services, including a pharmacy, private doctor, and a *centro de salud* (health clinic).

If you can, time your arrival on Sunday to coincide with the town market *tianguis.*

La Gloria Coffee Farm

About five miles (eight km) past Xadani, you'll arrive at El Llano (YAH-noh), the site of La Gloria, a little German farm in the jungle. The parents of La Gloria's owner-operator Gustav Sherenberg arrived from the wreckage of World War II, seeking a new life in Mexico. The dream that they carved out remains with Gustav (now Gustavo), who continues to improve on it.

The centerpiece, a Saxony-style whitewashed farmhouse and its antique furnishings—polished oak wall telephone, heirloom old-world sideboard, 1940s-vintage shortwave radio—endure for guests to admire and enjoy.

The buildup is a tour around the farm, which you should do not long after arrival. Along the path, you'll see acre after acre of green shiny-leafed coffee bushes beneath a canopy of great giants of the forest—*ceiba, caoba* and Juan Diego trees. At the far point of the walk, the farm's sustaining source, a crystalline spring, wells up from a rocky bed. On the way back, the path winds beneath both wild and cultivated trees hung with exotic fruits—brown *mamey,* green *zapote,* and the otherworldly *piña anona.* Near the farmhouse, don't miss the **herb garden,** with familiar cilantro, *yerba buena, yerba santa,* and half a dozen others you probably have never heard of. The fun of all this climaxes at breakfast or dinner with the family around the great hardwood dinner table, big enough for a dozen.

The Sherenberg (actually Sherenberg-Noyola) family invites you to enjoy their farm with them, either for a day, including lunch, or overnight, including comfortable, cozy jungle cabaña lodging with lunch, breakfast, and dinner included. Expect to pay about $50 per person for an overnight with food, $20 for lunch and tour only.

Reserve by writing Familia Sherenberg-Noyola, Apdo. Postal 220, Bahías de Huatulco, Oaxaca 70989, or calling 958/706-97.

Xadani and La Gloria are off the signed side road on the north side of Hwy. 200, seven miles (11.4 km) miles west of Copalita village, river, and bridge (41 miles, 66 km east of Pochutla; 74 miles, 119 km west of Salina Cruz). If arriving by car, set your odometer as you turn off the highway. Continue immediately through a village (which has a store with unleaded gasoline) along a good gravel road through Xadani to the church (12.7 miles, 20.4 km). Proceed, bearing left around the rear side of the church, then straight ahead another 5.4 miles (8.7 km) to La Gloria coffee farm.

Local minibuses from Pochutla and Crucecita can take you at least to Copalita or even the highway turnoff. From there you can catch a taxi or thumb a ride to Xadani.

EAST TOWARD THE ISTHMUS: CHONTAL COUNTRY

The approximately 90-mile (145-km) Hwy. 200 stretching east from Huatulco to Salina Cruz is easy to travel, and consequently can pass swiftly without a pause. This, however, would be a pity, for you'd miss a whole swath of interesting and beautiful country—curving, sandy beaches, wildlife-rich lagoons, and colorful Chontal villages and markets—along the way.

Santiago Astata

Astata (pop. 7,000) is near the midpoint (about 47 miles, 76 km) between Huatulco and Salina Cruz. This village is the closest thing to a metropolis along this part of the coast. The townsfolk proudly display their Chontal heritage with a big announcement *"Nañoje faá loj pijeda"* ("Welcome to Santiago Astata") over the town entrance road.

By far the best time to arrive is during the Tuesday *tianguis,* when the townspeople are so busy buying and selling that they are less likely to notice a few camera-toting visitors.

Folks will be even less self-conscious (and so distracted that they might not mind having their pictures taken) during the big local **Fiesta del Señor de Piedad** on the second Friday of Lent (second Friday after Ash Wednesday), usually in late February or March.

Even if you don't arrive during any fiesta, you should still take a look inside the church, where you'll find both of the town patrons, Santiago (on horseback, with sword in hand) and the Señor de Piedad.

Another favorite town diversion is the **community spring,** where you can splash like everyone else. It's at the roadside a block or two west of the town entrance. Afterward, enjoy a snack at one of the several *comedores* by the town highway crossing.

For those in need of basic **services,** Astata has doctors (Dr. Bernardo Herrera J. and Dr. María Garcia L.), a pharmacy, and a public telephone, 958/406-23, all near the church and plaza.

San Pedro Huamelula

If you missed Astata's Tuesday market, you can get in on Huamelula's market on Thursday by following the signed inland side road from Hwy. 200, just a fraction of a mile east of Astata. After about three miles, as you enter Huamelula town, you pass a number of new schools, including Alma Chontal (Chontal Soul) primary school, a secondary school, and Colegio de Bachilleres del Estado de Oaxaca (Oaxaca State Junior College).

Go through town (stores, a few *comedores,* pharmacy, doctor) to the old but restored bright birthday-cake yellow-and-blue church, **Templo de San Pedro.** Inside, the same bright yellow and blue continues, right up to the altar, presided over by a very antique Saint Peter. In the right transept chapel, pay your respects to an even older Santa Lucia in the glass case.

Here, the usually serene atmosphere shifts to raucous and jubilant during the 25 and 26 June **Fiesta de San Pedro.** Processions, fireworks, food, and carnival rides and games climax in traditional dances, including the popular Los Turcos (The Turks).

East to Salina Cruz

The sights along the eastern stretch past Astata are mostly natural, including mangrove-tufted lagoons, palmy beaches, and breezy viewpoints. What follows is a summary of some ripe possibilities to anticipate along the way. Measure mileage east from Astata or west from the Hwy. 200 and Trans-Isthmus Highway intersection at the north edge of downtown Salina Cruz.

Moving east from Astata, arrive at the **Laguna Colorada** dirt side road (from Astata east seven miles or 11 km; west 41 miles or 66 km). The dirt road leads a few miles along the west edge of a glassy, wildlife-rich mangrove lagoon to a beach.

Another several miles along (east 19 miles, 31 km or west 29 miles, 47 km), another wildlife-rich mangrove lagoon, **Laguna Garrapatera,** is visible from the highway, at Km 348. A wave-washed white sandspit borders the lagoon on the ocean side. The lagoon looks fine for kayaking or rubber rafting, and the beach could be great for camping if you can get to it.

At Km 349, Hwy. 200 rises to a viewpoint overlooking the idyllic green **Río Bamba Valley** (east 20 miles, 32 km, or west 28 miles, 45 km). Several miles farther (east 31 miles, 50 km, or west 17 miles, 27 km) arrive at the dirt road turnoff to surfing and seafood *palapa* restaurant beach **Playa Cangrejo** (Crab Beach).

Next, pass **Morro Mazatán** town (east 36 miles, 57 km, or west 13 miles, 21 km). Finally, arrive at the signed dirt side road to **Playa Brasil,** which has a great oceanfront breeze-blown sand hill on its west end (east 41 miles, 65 km, or west eight miles, 13 km).

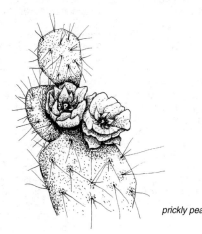

prickly pear

LOUISE FOOTE

PUERTO ESCONDIDO AND VICINITY

Decorated by intimate coves and sandy beaches and washed by jade-tinted surf, Puerto Escondido enjoys its well-deserved popularity. Despite construction of a jet airport in the 1980s, Puerto Escondido remains a place where everything is within walking distance, no high-rise blocks anyone's sunset view, and moderately priced accommodations and good food remain the rule.

Puerto Escondido (Hidden Port) got its name from the rocky Punta Escondida, which shelters its intimate half-moon cove that perhaps would have remained hidden if local farmers had not discovered that coffee thrives beneath the cool forest canopy of the lush seaward slopes of the Sierra Madre del Sur. They began bringing their precious beans for shipment when the port of Escondido was established in 1928.

When the coast highway was pushed through during the 1970s, Puerto Escondido's then-dwindling coffee trade was replaced by a growing trickle of vacationers attracted by the splendid isolation, low prices, and high waves. With some of the best surfing breaks in North America, a permanent surfing colony soon got established. This led to more nonsurfing visitors, who were arriving in droves by the 1990s to enjoy the comfort and food of a string of small hotels and restaurants lining Puerto Escondido's still-beautiful but no longer hidden cove.

AROUND TOWN

Getting Oriented
Puerto Escondido (pop. 35,000) seems like two small towns separated by Hwy. 200, which runs along the bluff above the beach. The upper town is where most of the local folks live and go about their business, while in the town below the highway, most of the restaurants, hotels, and shops spread along a single, touristy, beachfront street mall, **Av. Pérez Gasga.**

Avenida Pérez Gasga runs east-west, mainly as a pedestrian mall, where motor traffic is allowed only before noon. Afternoons, the *cadenas* (chains) go up, blocking cars at either end.

Beyond the west-end *cadena*, Pérez Gasga leaves the beach, winding uphill to the highway, where it enters the upper town at the *crucero,* Puerto Escondido's only signaled intersection. From there, Pérez Gasga continues into the upper town as Av. Oaxaca, National Hwy. 131.

Getting Around
In town, walk or take a taxi, which should run no more than $2 to anywhere. For longer local excursions, such as Lagunas Manialtepec and Chacahua (westbound), and as far as Pochutla (near Puerto Ángel) eastbound, ride one of the very frequent *urbano* minibuses that stop at the *crucero.*

BEACHES AND ACTIVITIES

Puerto Escondido's bay front begins at the sheltered rocky cove beneath the wave-washed lighthouse point, Punta Escondida. The shoreline continues easterly along Playa Principal, the main beach, curving southward at Playa Marineros, and finally straightening into long, open-ocean Playa Zicatela. The sand and surf change drastically from narrow sand and calm ripples at Playa Principal to a wide beach pounded by gigantic rollers at Zicatela.

Playa Principal
The best place to appreciate Puerto Escondido is not from the cluttered Pérez Gasga mall, but from one of the shady restaurants that front Playa Principal, the main beach. It's here that Mexican families love to frolic on Sunday and holidays and sun-starved winter vacationers doze in their chairs and hammocks beneath the palms. The sheltered west side is very popular with local people who arrive afternoons with nets and haul in small catches of silvery fish. The water is great for wading and swimming, clear enough for casual snorkeling, but generally too calm for anything else in the cove. However, a few hundred yards east around the bay, the waves are generally fine for bodysurfing and boogie boarding, with a minimum of undertow.

Although not a particularly windy location, windsurfers do occasionally bring their own equipment and practice their sport here. Fishing is fine off the rocks or by small boat, easily launched from the beach. Shells, generally scarce on Playa Principal, are more common on less-crowded Playa Zicatela.

Playa Marinero

As the beach curves toward the south, it increasingly faces the open ocean. Playa Marineros begins about 100 yards from the Marineros, the east-side rocky outcroppings in front of the Hotel Santa Fe. The jutting forms supposedly resemble visages of grizzled old sailors. The waves can be rough here. Swimmers beware; appearances can be deceiving. Intermediate surfers practice here, as do daring boogie boarders and body surfers.

Turn around and gaze inland at the giant Mexican flag waving in the breeze on the hill above the east-side beach. At dawn every rainless day, soldiers of the 54th Infantry Battalion raise the colossal banner, which measures about 82 by 59 feet (18 by 25 meters) and is so heavy that it takes 25 of them to do it.

Playa Zicatela

Past the Marineros rocks you enter the hallowed ground of surfing, Playa Zicatela. The wide beach of fine golden-white sand stretches south for miles to a distant cliff and point. The powerful Pacific swells arrive unimpeded, crashing to the sand with thunderous power. Surfers and nonsurfers alike congregate year-round, waiting for the renowned "Escondido pipeline," where grand waves curl into whirling liquid tunnels, which expert surfers skim through like trains in a subway. At such times the watchers on the beach outnumber the surfers by as many as 10 or 20 to one. Don't try surfing or swimming at Zicatela unless you're expert at both.

West-Side Beaches: Playas Puerto Angelito, Carrizalillo, and Bachoco

About a mile west of town, the picture-postcard little blue bays of Puerto Angelito and Carrizalillo nestle beneath the sea cliff. Their sheltered gold-and-coral sands are perfect for tranquil picnicking, sunbathing, and swimming. Snorkeling and scuba diving are tops, among shoals of bright fish grazing and darting among the close-in coral shelves and submerged rocky outcroppings. Get there by launch from Playa Principal or by taxi. On foot (take a sun hat and water) follow the street that angles from Pérez Gasga uphill across from the Hotel Nayar. Continue a few hundred yards and angle left again at Camino a Puerto Angelito (Road to Puerto Angelito) and follow the trail down the cliff. Carrizalillo is another quarter mile west.

Playa Bachoco, a mile farther west, down the bluff from the Hotel Posada Real, is a long, scenic strip of breeze-swept sand, with thunderous waves and correspondingly menacing undertow. Swimming is much safer in the inviting pool of the adjacent Hotel Posada Real beach club.

If you're strong, experienced, and can get past the breaking waves, snorkeling is said to be

Galo Sánchez (left) and his family and friends are returning thousands of baby turtles to the wild from their turtle rescue sanctuary at Barra de Colotepec, a few miles east of Puerto Escondido.

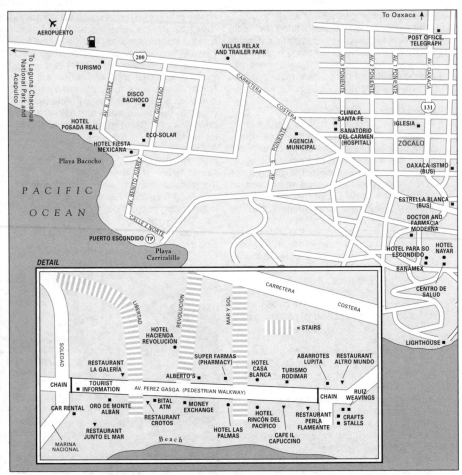

good around the little surf-dashed islet a hundred yards offshore.

Although Playa Bachoco's rock-sheltered nooks appear inviting for camping, local people don't recommend it because of occasional *rateros* (thugs and drunks) who roam Puerto Escondido beaches at night.

Trouble in Paradise

Occasional knifepoint robberies and muggings have marred the once-peaceful Puerto Escondido nighttime beach scene. Walk alone and you invite trouble, especially along Playa Bachoco and the unlit stretch of Playa Principal between the east end of Pérez Gasga and the Hotel Santa Fe. If you have dinner alone at the Hotel Santa Fe, avoid the beach by returning by taxi or walking along the highway to Pérez Gasga back to your hotel.

Fortunately, such problems seem to be confined to the beach. Visitors are quite safe on the Puerto Escondido streets themselves, often more so than on their city streets back home.

Beach Walking

The ***andador*** concrete walkway, which circles the lighthouse point, provides a pleasant, breezy afternoon (or sunset) diversion. From the west chain, follow the street that heads toward the lighthouse. Soon, on the left, stairs head left down on to the beach cove, where, in front of the Capitania del Puerto building, the *andador* heads left along the rocks. It continues above the spectacularly splashing surf for about half a mile. Return by the same route or loop back through side streets to Pérez Gasga.

For a longer walk, you can stroll as far out of town along on Playa Zicatela as you want, in outings ranging from an hour to a whole day. Best avoid the heat of midday and bring along a sun hat, shirt, drinks, and snacks (and perhaps sunglasses) if you plan on walking more than a mile past the last restaurant down the beach. Your reward will be the acrobatics of surfers challenging the waves, swarms of shorebirds, and occasional finds of driftwood and shells. After about three miles you will reach a cliff and a sea arch, which you can scamper through at

LAGUNA MANIALTEPEC

To Río Grande and Pinotepa Nacional

TROPICAL

DECIDUOUS

FOREST

Río Manialtepec

El Zacatal

El Corozal

El Carnero

Laguna Manialtepec

Las Negras

Isla El Gallo

La Alejandria

Las Hamacas

La Salina

TROPICAL

DECIDUOUS

FOREST

TROPICAL

DECIDUOUS

FOREST

To Puerto Escondido

PACIFIC OCEAN

Sandy Beach

0   1 mi

0   1 km

© AVALON TRAVEL PUBLISHING, INC.

low tide to **Playa Barra de Colotepec,** the beach on the other side.

Playa Barra de Colotepec's surf is as thunderous as Zicatela's and the beach even more pristine, being a nesting site for sea turtles. The beach continues for another mile to the jungle-fringed lagoon of the Río Colotepec where, during the dry winter season, a host of birds and wildlife, both common and rare, paddle and preen in the clear, fresh water.

You could break this eight-mile round-trip into a pair of more leisurely options. Hike A could cover Zicatela only; on Hike B you could explore Barra de Zicatela and the Laguna de Colotepec by driving, taxiing, or busing straight to La Barra, the beach village just west of the Río Colotepec. Access is via the signed side road just before (west of) the Río Colotepec bridge.

Boat Tours
Travel agencies and the local boat cooperative, **Sociedad Cooperativa Punta Escondida,** offer trips for parties of several passengers to beautiful local bays, including Carrizalillo and Puerto Angelito, plus Manzanillo, Puesta del Sol, and Coral. The minimum one-hour trip takes you to a number of sandy little coves east of town, including Carrizalillo (Little Reed), Manzanillo

(Little Apple), Puerto Angelito, Coral, and Puesto del Sol (Sunset). Take drinks, hats, sunscreen, perhaps sunglasses, and don't go unless your boat has a sunroof. Trips can be extended (about $15 per additional hour) to your heart's content of beach picnicking, snoozing, and snorkeling.

SIGHTS OUT OF TOWN

Whether you go escorted or independently, outings away from the Puerto Escondido resort can reveal rewarding glimpses of flora and fauna, local cultures, and idyllic beaches seemingly half a world removed from the Pérez Gasga tourist hubbub.

Farthest afield, to the west of Puerto Escondido, are the festivals, markets, and handicrafts of Mixtec towns and villages around Jamiltepec and Pinotepa Nacional, the mini-paradise of Roca Blanca, and the crystalline beaches and wildlife-rich mangrove reaches of the Lagunas de Chacahua National Park. To the east lie the hidden beaches of **Mazunte, Zipolite,** and the picture-book **Bay of Puerto Ángel,** with their turtle museum, au naturel sunbathing, and very accessible off-beach snorkeling, respectively. A bit farther are the nine breezy Bays of Huatulco, ripe for swimming, wildlife viewing, biking, and river rafting. (For details, see the relevant previous and succeeding sections.)

Nearby Excursions, West and East Side
Closer at hand, on the west side, especially for wildlife lovers and beach goers, are the jungly lagoons and pristine strands of the **Laguna de Manialtepec** and the nearby hot springs and Chatino sacred site of Atotonilco.

Atotonilco Hot Springs
The **Aguas Termales Atotonilco** hot springs, a Chatino sacred site, provide an interesting focus for a day's outing. The jumping-off point is the village of San José Manialtepec, about half an hour by bus or car west of Puerto Escondido.

At the village, you should hire someone to show you the way up the semi-wild canyon of the Río Manialtepec. The trail winds along cornfields, beneath forest canopies and past Chatino Indian villages. Finally you arrive at the hot spring, where a rock basin bubbles with very hot (bearable to the brave), clear, sulfur-smelling water. **Get there** by driving or busing to the Hwy. 200 turnoff for San José Manialtepec, around Km 116, just east of the Río Manialtepec bridge. Village stables provide horses and guides to the hot springs. It's a very easy two-mile walk, except in times of high water on the river, which the trail crosses several times.

A pair of **grassroots conservation projects** on Puerto Escondido's east side are well worth a visit. First, just a few miles from Puerto Escondido, in Barra de Colotepec, visit the **turtle sanctuary** of Galo Sánchez, that he's named Producción Ecoturístico Colotepec. Galo, his wife, family, and neighbors started with a beachfront turtle rescue effort that now includes crocodiles and iguanas. Their aim is to return all of the endangered creatures that they are nursing to the wild. They're happy to receive visitors daily, 8 A.M.–5 P.M., and ask a nominal donation of about $1 per person; if you can afford more, give it. Get there either by car or mini-bus from the Puerto Escondido highway crossing. About four miles east of town, just before the big Río Colotepec bridge, turn right on to the side road to the village. Continue about a mile until the road forks. Galo's house is on the left side.

A more mature but equally laudable effort has been mounted by Marcelino López Reyes, at his **Iguana Nursery** about half an hour by car or bus east of Puerto Escondido. Marcelino, a veterinarian, has been working for about 15 years at the nearby government turtle hatching station at Escobillo, helping to hatch and return about 900,000 leatherback *(laut)*, olive ridley *(golfina)*, and hawksbill *(carey)* turtles to the wild.

For about the last 10 years friendly Marcellino has also devoted himself to his personal mission: to restore local populations of iguanas and land turtles. Although the last hurricane demolished his operation, he's got it back up and running, with dozens of healthy reptilian residents in a big outside enclosure. Besides the green *iguana verde (Iguana iguana)*, and black *iguana prieta (Ctenosaura pectinata)*, he's also restoring two local species of endangered land turtles, the *tortuga del monte (Rinoclemys pulcherrima)*, and the *tortuga sabanera (Rinoclemys Ruvida)*. Don't miss visiting him (watch for the *criadero iguana* sign), at the east side of the Río Coazoaltepec bridge about 21 miles (34 km) east of Puerto Escondido, or 23 miles (37 km) west of Puerto Ángel-Pochutla. The best time to find him there is around 5 P.M., after work on weekdays. If he's not there, one of his young assistants will probably be on hand to show you around. He appreciates a donation of about $1 or more if you have it.

Tours
Puerto Escondido agencies conduct many of the above outings and more. Among the very best are the **Hidden Voyages Ecotours** of the Canadian husband-wife team of Michael Malone and Joan Walker. Working through the competent Viajes Dimar travel agency, Av. Pérez Gasga 906, P.O. Box 22, Puerto Escondido, Oaxaca 71980, tel./fax 958/207-34 and 958/207-37, ornithologist Michael and artist/ecologist Joan lead unusually informative beach, lagoon, and mountain tours seasonally, mid-December–Easter. In addition, they also offer a sunset lagoon wildlife and beach excursion, plus a two-day trip to Nopala, center of Chatino Indian culture, including a coffee plantation in the cool Sierra Madre del Sur mountain jungle. Their trips ordinarily run $55 per day, per person.

Other Dimar tours include a full-day jaunt east

to the turtle museum at Playa Mazunte, continuing to Playa Zipolite, where you can stop for lunch and an afternoon of snorkeling around Puerto Ángel. The cost runs about $27 per person. Additionally, they offer an all-day hiking, picnic, and swimming excursion at a luxuriously cool mountain river and cascade in the sylvan Sierra Madre foothill jungle above Pochutla for about $55 per person (minimum four persons).

Alternatively, try one of the tours guided by **Ana Marquez,** a highly recommended government-certified tour guide and native of Puerto Escondido. Her itineraries cover the coast from the renowned blowhole at Huatulco's Maguey Bay to the crocodile nursery at Chacahua National Park. Contact her at home at Futuro Mzna 7 no. 214, Fracc. Costa Chica, Puerto Escondido, Oaxaca 71984, tel. 958/220-01, or at her Tigre Azul cyber café, beachside near the west end chain, or email: ana@anasec-otours.com. For more information, visit her website: www.anasecotours.com.

ACCOMMODATIONS

Hotels and Bungalows

The successful hotels in Puerto Escondido are appropriate to the town itself: small, reasonably priced, and near the water. They dot the beachfront from Playa Zicatela around the bay and continue up Av. Pérez Gasga to the highway. Most are either on the beach or within a stone's throw of it, which makes sense, because it seems a shame to come all the way to Puerto Escondido and not stay where you can soak up all the scenery.

Downhill along Pérez Gasga from the *crucero* is the **Hotel Paraíso Escondido** on a short side street to the left, Calle Union 1, Puerto Escondido, Oaxaca 71980, tel. 958/204-44. A tranquil colonial-chic refuge, the hotel abounds in unique artistic touches—Mixtec stone glyphs, tiny corner chapels, stained glass, and old-world antiques—blended into the lobby, corridors, and patios. The two levels of rooms nestle around a lovely view pool and restaurant patio. The rooms themselves are large, with view balconies and designer tile bathrooms, wrought-iron fixtures, and handcrafted wooden furniture. It is very popular with North American and German winter

vacationers; get reservations early. The 24 rooms rent for about $50 s, $58 d low season, $75 and $85 high, with a/c, pool, kiddie pool, and parking, but *no* credit cards are accepted.

Just downhill is the 1950s' genre **Hotel Nayar,** Pérez Gasga 407, Puerto Escondido, Oaxaca 71980, tel. 958/201-13, fax 958/203-19, spreading from its inviting pool patio past the reception to a viewpoint restaurant. Its spacious, spartan, but comfortable, air-conditioned rooms have private balconies, many with sea views. Improved management has recently cleaned up this nicely located hotel. The Nayar's 36 rooms run about $22 s, $27 d, $32 t, low season, $27, $32, $37 high, add $6 for a/c.

The popular **Hotel Loren,** Av. Pérez Gasga 507, Puerto Escondido, Oaxaca 71980, tel. 9/582-0057, fax 9/582-0591, downhill half a block farther, is as good as it first appears, from its leafy pool patio and its private balcony view rooms to its rooftop sundeck. Intelligent clerks staff the desk while *camaristas* scrub the rooms spotless every day. (They also assiduously spray with DDT; tell them "no DDT" if you'd prefer they didn't.) The rooms spread through two three-story buildings; the front building rooms have better views. Reserve a *cuarto con vista* if you want a view room. Reservations are often necessary, especially in the winter. The 24 basic but comfortable rooms rent for about $20 s or d, $25 t low season, $32 s or d, $38 t high, with parking, fans, and some a/c (add $10); credit cards accepted.

Right on the beach amid the tourist-mall hullabaloo is the longtime favorite, **Hotel Las Palmas,** Av. Pérez Gasga s/n, Puerto Escondido, Oaxaca 71980, tel. 958/202-30, fax 958/203-03. Its main plus is the palmy, vine-strewn patio where you can sit for breakfast every morning, enjoy the breeze, and watch the boats, the birds, and families frolicking in the billows. The big drawback, besides sleepy management and no pool, is lack of privacy. Exterior walkways pass the room windows, which anyone can see through. Closing the curtains unfortunately makes the (fan-only) rooms very dark and hot. This doesn't bother the legions of return customers, however, since they spend little time in their rooms anyway. Tariffs for the 40 smallish rooms run about $16 s or d, $19 t low season,

$17, $23, $27 high, with phones, restaurant, but no parking; credit cards accepted.

The **Hotel Rincón del Pacífico,** next door to the Hotel Las Palmas, offers about the same, at Av. Pérez Gasga 900, Puerto Escondido, Oaxaca 71980, tel. 958/200-56 or 958/201-93, fax 958/201-01. The two tiers of clean, comfortable rooms enfold a shady patio that looks out onto the lively beachfront. As at the Hotel Las Palmas, a stay in one of the glass-front rooms sometimes feels like life in a fishbowl. This is nevertheless a very popular hotel. Reserve early. Rates for the 28 rooms run about $18 s or d, $22 t low season, $24 s, $28 d, $33 t high. Four suites with TV and a/c rent for about $30 s or d low season, $50 high; with a restaurant, but no parking or pool; credit cards accepted (but not American Express).

Although it's not right on the beach like its neighbors across the street, the rooms of the **Hotel Casa Blanca,** Av. Pérez Gasga 905, Puerto Escondido, Oaxaca 71980, tel. 958/201-68, fax 958/207-37, are larger, cooler, and much more private. Some rooms even have private balconies, fine for people-watching on the street below. Guests report noise is not a problem since cars and trucks are banned on Gasga noon–7 A.M. Other amenities include hot water, a shelf of used paperback books, and beyond the graceful arches that border the lobby, a petite, inviting pool patio. The 21 clean, comfortable rooms rent for about $19 s, $28 d, and $32 t all year, with fans. Visa and Mastercard accepted, but no parking.

Puerto Escondido's class-act hostelry is the newish **Hotel Santa Fe,** Av. del Morro, Playa Marinero, Puerto Escondido, P.O. Box 96, Puerto Escondido, Oaxaca 71980, tel. 958/201-70 or 958/202-66, fax 958/202-60, built in graceful neocolonial style appealing to both Mexican and foreign vacationers. With curving staircases, palm-shaded pool patios, and flower-decorated walkways, the Santa Fe achieves an ambience both intimate and luxuriously private. Its restaurant is outstanding. The rooms are spacious, comfortable, and thoughtfully appointed with hand-painted tile, rustic wood furniture, and regional handicrafts. Moreover, the big new room tier that owners added lately has enhanced the hotel's ambience, with an airy, elevated pool patio connecting the new tier

with the original section. The 50 rooms rent for about $60 s or d low season, $90 high; with TV, a/c, phones, and parking; credit cards accepted.

A few hundred yards south along the beach is the **Casas de Playa Acali,** Av. del Morro, P.O. Box 11, Puerto Escondido 71980, tel. 958/202-78 or 958/207-54, a colony of rustic cabañas clustered around a blue pool in a banana, palm, and mango mini-jungle. The cabañas themselves, like a vision out of a romantic South Seas tale, are built with walls made of sticks (non-see-through) and sturdy plank floors, raised above ground level. Units are clean and equipped with fans, mosquito nets, and good bathrooms. Rentals run about $16 s, $22 d, and $25 t low season; $27, $32, $38 high, with fan, hot water shower, small refrigerator, and parking. Additionally, they offer a few rustic sunset-view bungalows perched on their bamboo and mango-decorated hillside. Rentals cost about $25 low season, $40 high, for one to four, with kitchens, and beach-view hammock-hung front porches. Credit cards are accepted.

Farther south on Av. del Morro, which runs along Playa Zicatela, rises the three-story **Hotel Arco Iris,** Av. del Morro s/n, Colonia Marinero, Puerto Escondido, Oaxaca 71980, tel. 958/223-44, fax 958/204-32, email: arcoiris@ptoescondido.com.mx. A flowery, shady green garden surrounds the hotel, leading to an attractive pool patio. For those who love sunsets, sand, and waves (and don't mind their sometimes insistent pounding), one of the spacious, simply furnished top-floor view rooms might be just the ticket. The Arco Iris's proximity to the famous "Puerto Escondido pipeline" draws both surfers and surf-watchers to the third-floor restaurant La Galera, which seems equally ideal for wave-watching at breakfast and sky-watching at sunset. Low-season rates for the 26 rooms run about $26 s or d, $30 t; suites with kitchen, about $30 s or d, $32 t (add about 15 percent high season); with fans and parking.

Next comes **Beach Hotel Inés,** Av. del Morro, P.O. Box 44, Playa Zicatela, Puerto Escondido, Oaxaca 71980, tel. 958/207-92, fax 958/223-44, email: pedrovoss@yahoo.com, website: www.hotel-ines.com, the life project of German expatriate Peter Voss and his daughter, Inés. Their 35 units occupy the palmy periphery of a lush, pool-café-garden layout, which climaxes with an attractive, stuccoed, two-story complex of rooms at the back side. At the poolside tables, longtime repeat guests linger for coffee and conversation after late-morning breakfasts, stroll the beach in the afternoon, and return for a balmy sunset happy hour. Other days they sunbathe au naturel or relax in the petite but luxurious health club, which provides massage and hot tub.

Most of the rentals are hotel-style rooms, in deluxe and super-deluxe grades, with clean, light interiors, comfortable furnishings, and well-maintained bathrooms. Additionally, they rent six downscale second floor (popular with surfers) shared-bath cabañas, and a pair of bungalows with outdoor kitchens, sleeping four to six. Deluxe rooms go for about $30 s or d low season, $43 high; super-deluxe, about $60 low season, $80 high, cabañas, about $20 d, and the bungalows, about $40 low, $56 high, all with discounts negotiable for long-term rentals.

Farther along Playa Zicatela is the very tidy **Rockaway,** Av. del Morro, Playa Zicatela, Puerto Escondido, Oaxaca 71980, tel. 958/206-68, a fenced-in cluster of about 15 clean, concrete-floored bamboo-and-thatch cabañas. Spacious and fan-equipped, they sleep about four and have private showers and toilets, mosquito nets, and shady, hammock-hung front porches. An inviting, leafy pool patio occupies the center, while the manager's cabaña, offering water-sport rentals and supplies, stands to one side. Cabaña rentals run about $8 per person low season, $23 per cabaña for up to four; $10 and $40 high season. Weekly or monthly discounts are negotiable, with parking and adjacent pizzeria.

Trailer Park and Camping
Occasional muggings and robberies on the beach have eliminated virtually all camping on Puerto Escondido beaches (with the possible exception of Easter week, when such large crowds flock into town that they spill onto the beaches). Moreover, the long-time Puerto Escondido Trailer Park has been recently sold to developers and is no longer functioning.

However, a smaller new park, **Trailer Park and Villa Relax,** has brightened the prospects of finding camping and RV space, although not on the beach. Ready for occupancy beneath the shade of a west-side mango grove (eat all you want in-season, March–April) and managed by friendly on-site owner Sylvia Gómez Aragon, the park offers about a dozen spaces, with all connections, a lovely oval pool, hot showers, tennis court, and a snack bar. She charges $10 for small trailers and RVs, $12 for large. She also rents 10 new, clean, and airy rooms with TV, private balconies, and fans for about $20 for two, $27 for four. For reservations, call her at 958/208-09. Find the park on the north side of the highway, between the west-side (airport) gas station and town.

FOOD

Breakfast and Snacks
Mornings you can smell the luscious aroma around **Panadería Carmen** along Playa Marinero, on the little street that heads toward Playa Marinero from Hwy. 200, just past the bridge. Follow the fragrance to the source, a small homey shop with a few tables for savoring the goodies. These days, however, co-owner Carmen Arizmendi usually spends her mornings at her new venture, Cafecito (see below). Afternoons, you might see her swimming in the bay, beyond the waves. Open Mon.–Sat. 7 A.M.–8 P.M.

Now, Carmen's devotees have a second spot to enjoy her pastries: **Cafecito,** right on Zicatela beach (next to Bungalows Acuario). Here you can savor a cappuccino and one of her goodies as you watch the surfers conquering the waves.

Right in the middle of the Av. Pérez Gasga bustle, **Cafe Capuchino** serves as a gathering place for tourists and local folks who enjoy good desserts and coffee with their conversation. Furthermore, the best homesickness remedy in town is the apple pie, a slice of which enables you to endure a minimum of one more hard week on the local beaches. Open daily 8 A.M.–11 P.M.

Also fun for breakfast are the shady, scenic beach-view restaurants **Junto del Mar** and **Restaurant Crotos.** (See below.)

Restaurants
Most of Puerto Escondido's reliable restaurants line Av. Pérez Gasga. Beginning just outside the west-end chain, first comes the street-side patio of **Restaurant Sardina de la Plata,** Av.

fishing for dinner

Pérez Gasga 512, tel. 958/203-28, the brainchild of Barcelona-born owner/chef Fernando de Abascal López. His life mission is orchestrating his unique seafood repertoire, such as the Catalan specialty Txanguro de Jaiva (snails, shrimp, and octopus in a white sauce) or Mero a la Sol (a sea bass feast for a party of 4–10). Besides such exotica, he also serves good pasta, steaks, lobster, Mexican plates, and breakfasts. Open daily 7:30 A.M.–11 P.M.; credit cards accepted. Moderate.

Just inside the chain, on the inland side of Pérez Gasga, **Restaurant La Galería** usually has customers even when most other local eateries are empty. The reason is the excellent Italian fare—crusty, hot pizzas, rich pastas and lasagna, bountiful salads, and satisfying soups—which the European-expatriate owner puts out for her growing battalion of loyal customers. Open daily 8 A.M.-midnight. Moderate.

Across the street, the local rage is the excellent, airy **Restaurant Junto del Mar** (By the Ocean), which offers class-act breakfasts—rich coffee, fresh fruit, hotcakes, eggs—and

many delectable lunch and dinner options. Specialties include shrimp-stuffed fillets, octopus cooked with garlic, and lobster and shrimp brochettes. Mornings are brightened by the always changing beach scene; evenings the setting turns romantic, with soft candlelight and strumming guitars. Open daily 8 A.M.–11 P.M., tel./fax 958/212-72. Moderate. Credit cards are accepted.

A block farther east, breakfast patrons at beachfront **Restaurant Crotos,** at shady view tables, enjoy the fascinating morning beachside scene. Later, at lunch and dinner, back beneath the luxuriously breezy, palm-fringed *palapa,* the house specialties—jumbo shrimp, broiled lobster, and super-fresh pompano, attractively presented, competently served, and delicious—seem like a welcome bonus. Open daily 8 A.M.–11 P.M. Moderate.

Near the east end of the Pérez Gasga mall, the **Restaurant Perla Flameante** offers good food, incense, new-age jazz, and a beach view from beneath a big, cool *palapa.* The friendly, conscientious staff take pride that they make everything in-house, from the mayonnaise to the potato chips that come with their big fishburger. Seafood fillets rule the menu. The varieties, such as sierra, tuna, yellowtail, and mahimahi, are exceeded only by the number of styles—Cajun, teriyaki, wine, and herbs, pepper-mustard, butter and garlic, orange—in which they are served. Open daily 7 A.M.–11 P.M.; credit cards accepted.

Devotees of authentic Italian food find paradise at **Restaurant Altro Mundo,** just half a block outside of the east-end chain. White tablecloths and wine glasses set the stage. Start off, perhaps, with Crema Altro Mundo, continue with an Ensalata Mista, share a plate of Lasagna di Calamari, and climax with Fettuccine Flameante and Filete di Dorado. Open for dinner only, daily 6 P.M.–midnight, tel. 958/214-55.

If you have dinner at the restaurant of the **Hotel Santa Fe,** on Av. del Morro, east side of the bay, tel. 958/201-70, you may never go anywhere else. Savory food, impeccably served beneath a luxurious *palapa* and accompanied by softly strumming guitars, brings travelers from all over the world. Although everything on the menu is good, they are proudest of their Mexican favorites, such as rich tortilla soup, bountiful plates of *chiles rellenos,* and succulent snapper, Veracruz style. Open daily 7:30 A.M.–11 P.M. Moderate-expensive.

Farther south along Zicatela beach, **Restaurant Cafecito** (formerly Bruno's) is headquarters for a loyal platoon of local surfers and Canadian and U.S. visitors. Breakfasts, hamburgers, and fresh seafood plates are bountiful, tasty, and won't cost you a bundle. Open daily, about 8 A.M.–10 P.M. Budget-moderate.

At the far end of Av. del Morro on Zicatela Beach is friendly **Art and Harry's Surf Inn,** named after the Canadian expatriate owners' grandfathers, open daily noon till about 10 P.M. The restaurant, a big, airy upper-floor *palapa,* is best around sunset when patrons enjoy Frisbee golf and more unobstructed sunsets per year than any other *palapa* in Puerto Escondido. Personable co-owner Patty Mikus keeps customers coming with her fresh salads, soups, and tasty (honey, garlic, teriyaki, Hawaiian, or marinera) fish plates.

ENTERTAINMENT AND EVENTS

Sunsets and Happy Hours
Many bars have sunset happy hours, but not all of them have good sunset views. Since the Oaxaca coast faces south (and the sun sets in the west), bars along east-side Zicatela Beach, such as the Hotel Santa Fe, Hotel Arco Iris, Restaurant Cafecito's, and Art and Harry's, are the only ones that can offer unobstructed sunset horizons.

If, on the other hand, you prefer solitude, stroll the bay-front *andador* walkway to near the lighthouse. Start on the Playa Principal (main beach), west side, past the Capitán del Puerto office. From breezy perches above the waves, you'll enjoy an equally panoramic sunset.

Strolling Pérez Gasga
Strolling the Pérez Gasga mall is Puerto Escondido's prime after-dinner entertainment. By around 9 P.M., however, people get weary of walking and since there are few benches, begin sitting on the curb and sipping bottles of beer near the west-end chain. Unfortunately, city officials lately have been frowning upon such

apparently dissolute behavior and have had a few of the curb-sitters arrested. Meanwhile, people hope that some amiable compromise will be reached.

The main attraction of curb-sitting is watching other people sitting on the curb, while listening to the music blasting nightly from the tiny open-air bars of **Bar Fly, Tubo,** and **Wipe Out,** 50 feet away. The music is so loud little can be gained by actually taking a seat in the bars themselves except hearing impairment.

On the other hand, lower-volume music lovers might enjoy the Latin live music club, **El Son y la Rumba,** beach side, basement level, near the west-end chain

Those who prefer to dance go to some of the town's discos. On Pérez Gasga, try **Revancha de Moctezuma** (Montezuma's Revenge), across from the Hotel Las Palmas. Alternatively, try the old standby, **Disco Bachoco** on Av. Gueletao, in the west-side Bachoco suburb.

Festivals
Puerto Escondido pumps up with a series of fiestas during the low-season (but excellent for vacationing) month of November. Scheduled *Fiestas de Noviembre* events invariably include surfing and usually sportfishing, cooking, and beauty contests, and, notably, the dance festival, **Fiesta Costeño,** when a flock of troupes—from Pochutla, Pinotepa Nacional, Jamiltepec, Tehuantepec and more—perform regional folk dances.

Visitors who hanker for the old-fashioned color of a traditional fiesta should arrive in Puerto Escondido by 18 December, when seemingly the whole town takes part in the fiesta of the **Virgen de Soledad.** Besides being the patron saint of the state of Oaxaca, the Virgen de Soledad is also protectress of fishermen. To honor her, the whole town accompanies the Virgin's image by boat out to the bay's far reach, and then returns with her to the church plaza for dancing, fireworks, and bullfights.

If you can't be in Puerto Escondido in time to honor the Virgin in December, perhaps you may be able to take a day trip one hour west of Puerto Escondido to enjoy a fiesta at one of the small towns around Pinotepa Nacional or to celebrate the Virgin of Juquila with the mountain Chatino folks.

SPORTS AND RECREATION

Walking, Jogging, and Horseback Riding

Playa Zicatela is Puerto Escondido's most interesting walking course. Early morning, before the heat and crowds, is good for jogging along the level section of Av. Pérez Gasga. Avenida del Morro (which parallels) Playa Zicatela is good for jogging anytime it isn't too hot. For more walking details, see Beach Walking, in this chapter, above.

Ease your hiking by riding horseback along Zicatela beach. Rentals are available on the beach in front of Hotel Santa Fe.

Gym and Tennis

The **Acuario Gym** on Playa Zicatela at the Hotel Acuario has a roomful of standard exercise equipment. Single visits run about $2, one-month passes about $20.

One of the only night-lit tennis courts in town available for public rental ($6 per hour) is at the **Hotel Fiesta Mexicana.** Call the hotel at 958/200-72 for a reservation.

Surfing, Snorkeling, and Scuba Diving

Although surfing is de rigueur for the skilled in Puerto Escondido, beginners often learn by bodysurfing and boogie boarding first. Boogie boards and surfboards are for sale and rent ($7 per day) at a number of shops along Pérez Gasga, such as **100 Hamacas** (next to Hotel Rincón del Pacífico) and at **Central Surf** (by Cafecito and on Pérez Gasga) on Playa Zicatela (open daily 9 A.M.–2 P.M. and 4–7 P.M.). **Rockaway,** a few hundred yards farther south along the beach, rents surfboards ($7 per day) and boogie boards ($7 per day) and sells related supplies.

Beginners practice on the gentler billows of **Playa Principal** and adjacent **Playa Marinero** while advanced surfers go for the powerful waves of **Playa Zicatela,** which regularly slam foolhardy inexperienced surfers onto the sand with backbreaking force.

Clear blue-green waters, coral reefs, and droves of multicolored fish make for good local snorkeling and diving, especially in little **Puerto Angelito** and **Carrizalillo** bays just west of town. A number of Av. Pérez Gasga stores sell serviceable amateur-grade snorkeling equipment.

A professional dive shop, **Aventura Submarina,** has recently gained a foothold in Puerto Escondido. It's run by friendly veteran PADI instructor Jorge Pérez Bravo, at Pérez Gasga 601 A, a few doors inside the west-end chain, tel. 958/223-53, email: asubmarina@ptoescondido.com.mx. Introductory lesson, including one offshore dive, runs about $60, including equipment. For certified open water divers (bring your certificate), a one-tank night dive costs about $45, a two-tank day dive, about $60.

Alternately, a number of divers operate out of Huatulco, an hour and a half drive east. Contact the very professional **Buceos Triton** shop in Santa Cruz de Huatulco, tel./fax 9/587-08-44, or **Action Sports,** in Tangolunda, at the Barceó Hotel, tel. 958/100-55, ext. 842, fax 9/587-05-37, or Leeward Dive Center, inside the Hotel Club Plaza Huatulco, tel./fax 958/100-51. (For more details, see the Bays of Huatulco section.)

Sportfishing

Puerto Escondido's offshore waters abound with fish. Launches go out mornings from Playa Principal and routinely return with an assortment including big tuna, mackerel, snapper, sea bass, and snook. The sheltered west side of the beach is calm enough to easily launch a mobile boat with the help of usually willing beach hands.

The local **Sociedad Cooperativa Nueva Punta Escondida,** which parks its boats right on Playa Principal, regularly takes fishing parties of three or four out for about $20 an hour, including bait and tackle. Check with boatmen right on the beach. Additionally, travel agencies, such as Viajes Dimar, Av. Pérez Gasga 905, tel. 958/207-34, 958/202-37, arrange such trips at about the same prices.

SHOPPING

Market and Handicrafts

As in most Mexican towns, the place to begin your Puerto Escondido shopping is the local **Mercado,** on Av. 10 Norte one long block west of the electric station on upper Av. Oaxaca. Although produce occupies most of the space, a number of stalls at the south end offer authentic handicrafts. These might include Guerrero painted pottery animals; San Bártolo Coyotepec black pottery; masks from Guerrero and Oaxaca with jaguar, devil, and scary human-animal motifs; the endearing multicolored pottery animals from Iguala and Zitlala in Guerrero; and beautiful crocheted *huipiles* from San Pedro Amusgos and Pinotepa Nacional.

Back downhill on Av. Pérez Gasga, the prices increase along with the selection. Perhaps the most fruitful time and place for handicraft shopping is during the cooler evenings, within the illuminated cluster of crafts stalls just beyond the Gasga east chain.

One shop at that spot, the **Ruiz** textile stand, with genuine handmade rugs and serapes from Teotitlán del Valle near Oaxaca City, stands out. Fine-quality rugs are the most tightly woven—typically about 20 strands per centimeter (50 per inch).

Another good, authentic shop is **Creaciones Alberto,** tel. 958/202-84, named for the elderly master craftsman of Puerto Vallarta, whose sons and daughters sell his fine handiwork (and that of associated craftspersons) in a number of Pacific Mexico centers. Find them on Peréz Gasga, west of the mall, north side. Open Mon.–Sat. 9 A.M.–2 P.M. and 5–10 P.M. For jewelry purchasing hints, see the Shopping section of the On the Road chapter.

Oaxaca's venerable jewelry tradition is well represented at the very professional **Oro de Monte Albán,** on Pérez Gasga, oceanside, by the west chain. Here are authentic museum-grade replicas of the celebrated Mixtec-style trove discovered in Monte Albán's tomb 7. Find them open Mon.–Sat. 10 A.M.–2 P.M. and 6:30–10:30 P.M., closed Sun. low season, tel. 958/205-30.

The Uribe silversmithing family well represents Taxco tradition at their **Platería Taxco,** open Mon.–Sat. 9 A.M.–2 P.M. and 5–10 P.M., Sun. 7–10 P.M., tel. 958/216-72, a few doors east. Choose from a host of fetching floral, animal, and abstract designs, in silver and turquoise, garnet, jade, and other semiprecious stones.

For unique women's resort wear, look for **Bambaleo,** a gem among the T-shirt clutter,

on the beach side, toward the Pérez Gasga east end, open 10 A.M.–10 P.M. Here, locally crafted from lovely hand-painted cloth from Indonesia, a riot of skirts and tops festoon walls and a host of racks.

During the day, if the sun gets too hot for comfort, duck into the shade of the small shopping Plaza del Conquistador, just east of Pharmacy Courtés. Several stalls offer attractively varied, all-Mexico handicrafts, including masks, *huipiles,* lacquerware, papier-mâché, baskets, black pottery, and much more.

Groceries and Photography

Abarrotes Lupita, a fairly well-stocked grocery, offers meats, milk, ice, and vegetables. In addition, it stocks a few English-language publications, such as the *News* of Mexico City and magazines such as *Time, Life,* and *Newsweek,* on the inland side of Gasga, outside of the east-end chain. Open daily 10 A.M.–11 P.M.

Out on Playa Zicatela, where stores are not nearly so common, the friendly **Abarrotes Merlin** offers a small grocery selection; open daily 9 A.M.–10 P.M., tel. 958/211-30.

Foto Express Figueroa, tel. 958/205-26, on Gasga next to Viajes Dimar, offers fast photofinishing services, Kodak color print and slide film, and a moderate stock of accessories, including point-and-shoot cameras. Open daily 9:30 A.M.–2 P.M. and 4:30–8 P.M.

For a better camera selection, visit **Foto Discuento,** west end of the Pérez Gasga mall, open Mon.–Sat. 9 A.M.–9 P.M., Sun. 9 A.M.–4 P.M., tel. 958/203-54.

SERVICES

Money Exchange

Banamex, at Pérez Gasga 314, with ATM, uphill from the Hotel Nayar, tel. 958/206-26, changes U.S. and Canadian cash and traveler's checks Mon.–Fri. 9 A.M.–3 P.M., Sat. 9 A.M.–2 P.M. You can also use the Banco Internacional 24-hour ATM, around the midpoint of the on Pérez Gasga mall, next to the Hotel Las Palmas.

After hours, the small *casa de cambio* (money exchange) office on Pérez Gasga, a few doors west of Hotel Las Palmas, changes a larger range of foreign currencies for a correspondingly larger fee. Open Mon.–Sat. 9 A.M.–9 P.M., Sun. 10 A.M.–5 P.M., tel. 958/582-2800. A second *casa de cambio* offers similar services, on Playa Zicatela, by Cafecito, tel. 958/205-92, open daily 9 A.M.–7 P.M.

Communications

The *correo* and *telégrafo* are side by side on Av. 7 Norte, corner Av. Oaxaca, seven blocks into town from the *crucero*. The post office, tel. 958/209-59, is open Mon.–Fri. 8 A.M.–4 P.M., Sat. 9 A.M.–1 P.M.; the *telégrafo*, which has public fax (tel. 958/202-32), is open Mon.–Fri. 9 A.M.–7:30 P.M., Sat. 9 A.M.-noon (Mon.–Fri. 9 A.M.–1 P.M. and 3–5 P.M. for money orders).

For local and long-distance telephone, purchase a *Ladatel* public telephone card at one of many Pérez Gasga stores and use it in street telephones. First dial 001 for calls to the United States and Canada, and 01 for long-distance calls within Mexico.

More conveniently located on Pérez Gasga, a *larga distancia* offers both telephone and fax service, daily 8 A.M.–10:30 P.M., tel./fax 958/204-48, across from Restaurant La Galería. On Playa Zicatela, use the public long-distance telephone at the desk of the Hotel Acuario.

Beware certain prominently located "Call Home With Your Credit Card" telephones. Tariffs on these phones can run $5 or more per minute. Ask the operator for the rate; if it's too high, take your business elsewhere.

Internet access, daily, until around 9 P.M., is available at cyber café **Tigre Azul,** run by eco-activist Ramon Acebo and his wife, Ana Marquez, beach side, about a block inside the west-end Pérez Gasga chain, tel. 958/215-33, 958/218-71, or 958/210-23, email: econdido@oax1.telmex.net.mx.

Travel Agent and Car Rentals

The best travel agent in town is the Viajes Dimar agency, at the middle of the tourist mall, at Av. Pérez Gasga 906, P.O. Box 22, Puerto Escondido, Oaxaca 71980, tel./fax 958/207-34, 958/202-37.

Rent a car at **Budget Rent a Car** on Calle Juárez in the Bachoco suburb, by the airport, tel. 958/203-12.

Hospital, Police, and Emergencies

For medical emergencies, go to the 24-hour **Hospital Santa Fe,** tel. 9/582-0541, which has an internist, pediatrician, gynecologist, and a dental surgeon on call. For more routine consultations, office hours are Mon.–Fri. 9 A.M.–2 P.M. and 4–8 P.M., Saturday 9 A.M.–2 P.M. Find the hospital three blocks west of the *crucero,* uphill from the highway on Calle 3 Poniente between Calles 2 and 3 Norte.

Alternatively, go next door, to the **Sanatorio del Carmen,** 958/218-76, or 958/201-74, with a number of female doctors on call.

You could also consult with English-speaking general practitioner Dr. Francisco Serrano, above the highway, at Calle 1 Norte 205, two blocks west of the main street, across Calle 1 Norte from Bancomer.

You may also go to the 24-hour government health clinic, **Centro de Salud,** no telephone, on Av. Pérez Gasga, just uphill from the Hotel Loren.

Get over-the-counter remedies and prescriptions at either of the two good tourist-zone pharmacies: the 24-hour **Farmacia La Moderna,** of Dr. José Luis Esparzar, tel. 958/205-49, on Gasga a block below the *crucero,* or **Super Farmacia,** open 8 A.M.–2 P.M. and 5–10 P.M., tel. 958/201-12, on the Pérez Gasga mall.

For police emergencies, call the **municipal police** at 958/204-98, or go to the headquarters in the Agencia Municipal on Hwy. 200, about four blocks west of the Pérez Gasga *crucero.*

Meditation and Massage

Healing is the mission of partners Patricia Heuze and Alejandro Villanuevo, who operate **Villa Temazcalli** meditation and massage center, west end of town, on Av. Infragante, two blocks uphill from the highway. Facilities include rustic hot baths, an indigenous-style *temazcalli* hot room, and massage room in an invitingly tranquil tropical garden setting. Prices run about $15 each for massage and the hot tub, and about $11 for one, $13 for two, and $16 for three, for the *temazcalli.* For more information and appointments, call 958/210-22 or 958/210-23.

Laundry

Get your laundry done, Mon.–Sat. 8 A.M.–8 P.M.,

Sun. 8 A.M.–5 P.M., at the **Lavamatico del Centro,** two doors downhill from Banamex, on Pérez Gasga, about two blocks uphill from the west-end chain.

INFORMATION

Tourist Information Office
Most months of the year, Oaxaca tourism staffs a small **information office** on Pérez Gasga, just inside the west-end chain. Otherwise, you can consult the friendly, well-informed *oficina de turismo* staff, tel./fax 958/201-75, email: gina@inpuerto@yahoo.com, who distribute a map of Oaxaca. They're available Mon.–Fri. 9 A.M.–3 P.M. and 6–8 P.M., just off of Hwy. 200, in the little office on the beach side of the highway, a couple of blocks east of the airport Pemex gas station.

Ecology Organizations and Projects
Ec Solar, the private Mexican ecological "Peace Corps," maintains its local low-profile headquarters in a house in Puerto Escondido, tel. 958/209-50, in the west side suburb of Bachoco, at the corner of Huajuapan de León and Tehuantepec. They work quietly with local communities on environmentally appropriate self-help drainage, water, manufacturing, and agricultural projects. For more information, contact either Ec Solar (in Spanish) or the national director, Hector Marchelli, in Mexico City, tel. 5/434-431, at Av. Eugenia 1510, Colonia Narvarte, Mexico City, D.F.

Much more accessible is the local ecological effort, **Eco Escondido,** coordinated by Ramón Acebo, owner of the Restaurant Tigre Azul, beach side, about a block inside the west-end Pérez Gasga chain, tel. 958/215-33, 958/218-71, or 958/210-23, email: econdido @oax1.telmex.net.mx. The major project is the recycling plant at the Hotel Acuario on Playa Zicatela.

Another nearby eco-project is the **turtle sanctuary** at Playa Escobilla, about 20 miles (30 km) east of Puerto Escondido. There, a cadre of SEMARNAT (Secretariat of Marine Natural Resources) professionals and volunteers is rescuing, hatching, and returning tens of thousands of baby turtles to the sea annually.

Publications
One of the few outlets of any English-language newspaper is the Abarrotes Lupita, on Pérez Gasga, just outside the east-end chain. The *News* from Mexico City usually arrives around 3:30 P.M. Prepay to assure yourself a copy. Sometimes there may be a few copies of popular magazines, such as *Time, Newsweek,* and *People.*

The best source of English-language (and French and German) books in town is the **Book Exchange,** at the Cafe Casa Babylon, next to the Hotel Acuario on Playa Zicatela.

GETTING THERE AND AWAY

By Air
The small jetport, officially the **Aeropuerto Puerto Escondido** (code-designated PXM), is just off the highway a mile west of town. Only a plain waiting room with check-in desks, the airport has no services save a small snack bar. *Colectivos* to hotels in town run $2 per person. Arrivees with a minimum of luggage, however, can walk a block to the highway and flag down one of the many eastbound local minibuses, which all stop at the main town highway crossing. Arrive with a hotel in mind (better yet a hotel reservation in hand), unless you prefer letting your taxi driver choose one, where he will probably collect a commission for depositing you there.

Although **car rental agents** may not routinely meet flights, they will meet you if you have a reservation. Call **Budget** car rental, tel. 958/203-12 or 958/203-15.

Be prepared to pay the $12 international **departure tax** or its Mexican peso equivalent if your ticket doesn't already include it. If you lose your tourist card, avoid trouble or a fine by taking your passport and some proof of your arrival date (such as a stamped passport, a copy of your lost tourist card, or an air ticket) to *Migracion* at the airport for help *before* your day of departure.

A few regularly scheduled flights connect Puerto Escondido with other Mexican destinations:

Aerocaribe Airlines flights connect daily with Mexico City and daily with Oaxaca and Huatulco.

For reservations or flight information, call 958/220-24 or 958/220-23.

If the above flights cannot take you where you want to go fast, try **Aerovega,** the dependable local air-taxi service. Telephone 958/201-51 or Viajes Dimar, on Gasga, tel. 958/207-34 or 958/207-37, for information and reservations.

Puerto Escondido is also accessible via the Puerto Ángel-Huatulco airport, one hour away by road. See the Bays of Huatulco chapter.

By Car or RV

National Hwy. 200, although sometimes winding, is generally smooth and uncongested between Puerto Escondido and Pinotepa Nacional (89 miles, 143 km, two and a half hours) to the west. From there, continue another 160 miles (258 km, 4.5 hours) to Acapulco. Fill up at Puerto Escondido before you leave, although gasoline is available at several points along the routes.

Traffic sails between Puerto Escondido and Puerto Ángel, 44 miles (71 km) apart, in an easy hour. Actually, Pochutla is immediately on the highway; Puerto Ángel is six miles downhill from the junction, or alternatively accessible via the very scenic paved shortcut at San Antonio village, Km 198. Santa Cruz de Huatulco is an easy 22 miles (35 km) farther east.

To or from Oaxaca, all-paved but sometimes roughly potholed National Hwy. 131 connects directly north, along main street Av. Oaxaca, via its winding but spectacular 158-mile (254-km) route over the pine-clad Sierra Madre del Sur. The route, which rises 9,000 feet through Chatino foothill and mountain country, can be chilly in the winter, and has few services along the lonely 100-mile middle stretch between San Gabriel Mixtepec and Sola de Vega. Take water and blankets and be prepared for emergencies. Allow about nine hours at the wheel, from Puerto Escondido, eight hours the other way, from Oaxaca. Fill up with gasoline at the airport Pemex stations on either end before heading out. Unleaded gasoline is only consistently available at the Sola de Vega Pemex *gasolinera* en route.

By Bus

Several long-distance bus lines serve Puerto Escondido; several offer first-class service.

Estrella Blanca subsidiary lines (luxury and first-class Elite and Futura and others), from the station on Av. Oaxaca just uphill from the *crucero,* tel. 958/204-27, travel the Hwy. 200 Acapulco-Isthmus route. More than two dozen daily *salidas de paso* come through en route both ways between Acapulco and Pochutla and Huatulco (Crucecita) and Salina Cruz. Other additional buses pass through, connecting with either Ixtapa-Zihuatanejo or Mexico City via Acapulco.

Cristóbal Colón, the other major first-class bus line, is on Av. 1 Norte between Av. 2 Oriente and Av. 1 Oriente, about three blocks uphill, one block east from the Pérez Gasga highway crossing, tel. 958/210-73. They serve the Oaxaca coast, beginning in Puerto Escondido, connecting all the way to San Cristóbal las Casas in Chiapas and Tapachula, at the Guatemala border. Intermediate destinations include Pochutla, Huatulco (Crucecita), and Salina Cruz. At Pochutla, passengers can transfer to Cristobal Colón Oaxaca-bound buses. One of these continues via Puebla to Mexico City.

Cooperativa Oaxaca-Istmo, on Hidalgo, one block east of Av. Oaxaca, corner of 1 Oriente, tel. 958/203-92, offers mainly second-class but some first-class service. Several daily local departures connect Puerto Escondido east, with Oaxaca via Tehuantepec. Intermediate destinations include Pochutla (Puerto Ángel,) and Huatulco (Crucecita). Additionally, first-class Transol bus departures connect with Oaxaca via Hwy. 131.

Cooperating lines **Autobuses Estrella del Valle** and **Autotransportes Oaxaca Pacífico** on Hidalgo, corner of 3 Oriente, tel. 958/200-50, provide both first- and second-class connections east with Pochutla, Bahías de Huatulco (Crucecita). Also, both first- and second-class buses connect with Oaxaca, via both Hwy. 175 through Pochutla and Hwy. 131, directly from Puerto Escondido.

Other minor mostly second-class bus lines offer departures from the gravel lot, at Calle 10 Norte and main street Hwy. 131 (also known as Av. Oaxaca). From there and also at a small storefront station on Hidalgo between 1 Oriente and 2 Oriente **Autobuses Estrella Roja del Sureste** and **Transol** buses , tel. 958/206-03 connect (via pilgrimage town Juquila) along Hwy. 131 with Oaxaca.

UPLAND EXCURSION INTO CHATINO COUNTRY

Head north from Puerto Escondido along Hwy. 131 and you enter the homeland of the Chatino people, who have lived quietly in their remote mountain hamlets longer than anyone can remember. Long neglected and little studied by historians and anthropologists, the Chatinos are now increasingly learning of their distinguished past and appreciating the value of their traditional language and customs.

In the old days, the only reason most outsiders ever came to Chatino country was the miraculous Virgin of Juquila, celebrated every December by adoring crowds who overflow Juquila's dozen-odd hotels and bed down in doorways, cars, buses, and the surrounding mountain forest, just to push their way to within 50 feet of the tiny, frail, beloved figurine.

Nopala people tell another story altogether. Theirs is the former domain of the great Chatino kings, whose history is just beginning to be uncovered by scholars. Nopala is also an important center of coffee production, surrounded by dozens of *fincas cafetaleras* (coffee farms), which in February and March harvest and roast a trove of fragrant beans for local, national, and international consumption.

An important consequence of the *fincas cafetaleras* is that they've sparked a renaissance of ecological awareness throughout Oaxaca's entire southern Sierra. Many growers have found markets for their produce from environmentally aware European and North American buyers, who prefer to buy coffee organically grown, without pesticides and herbicides, just exactly as the local growers have done since coffee was first introduced among Chatino people during the late 19th century.

Encouraged by their contacts with outside eco-activists, certain coffee farm owners and other ecologically aware local entrepreneurs have begun to offer tours, food, and lodging to visitors, who are trickling into Nopala in ever-increasing numbers.

SANTOS REYES NOPALA

Nopala (pop. 6,000, elev. 2,000 feet, 600 meters) is tucked into the upper valley of the Río Manialtepec, the heartland of Chatino country. Archaeologists reckon that the Chatino people have been living there for at least two thousand years. Stelae found at the nearby Cerro La Iglesia archaeological site resemble the famous Olmec-style *danzantes* of Monte Albán and are generally believed to date from the same period, around 500 B.C.

Nopala's townspeople nevertheless live very much in the present, enjoying a bit of the profits from their home-grown coffee. The government, moreover, has provided them with a generous sprinkling of schools: *primarias,* a *secundaria,* and, for the university-bound, a *preparatoria,* unusual for such a small, out-of-the way town. Afternoons in town you can immediately see the positive effect of all this: hundreds of smartly dressed, bright-eyed schoolchildren trooping home after their classes are done.

Part and parcel with the increased emphasis in education, Oaxaca's unique new Usos y Costumbres law is having a significant local effect. No political parties, hubbub, or vote payoffs are necessary. A simple town-hall vote of the assembled citizenry is now sufficient to place Nopala's *presidente municipal* in office.

Sights

Nopala, "Land of the Nopales" in the Aztec language (which translates to La B'ya in Chatino), is a pretty little place, perched on a hill surrounded by green mountains. You can best appreciate all this by climbing the stairs (as a formality, ask the policeman on the porch if it's OK) to the top floor of the *palacio municipal,* just uphill from the main-plaza market. On the south (sunny side) rises **Cerro de Atole,** with the cross on top, where everyone climbs on 3 May, the Día de la Cruz, and feasts upon the view, including the blue Pacific.

The name of the mountain, from *atole,* a universal Mexican drink made from corn, comes from the time when every house in town was a *jacal,* or thatched hut. In those days, building a new house was a community affair, when all the neighbors would climb the Cerro de Atole to gather the *pasto* (grass) for the new house's roof. When the work was all done, the owner would reward his friends with a party, which would include plenty of *atole.*

On the opposite side, toward the northwest, notice the apparent gash below the mountain summit, which rises perhaps three miles beyond the town limits. That's the big waterfall **Cascada de San Juan Lachao,** a locally popular place for cooling off on a hot day. To the right of that, approximately due north, rises **Cerro La Iglesia,** named for the ruined fortified city, an important archaeological site, halfway down its flank. A bit farther to the right (east) of that, also halfway down yet another jungle-clad mountain, you can just make out some of the buildings of **Finca Costoche,** a locally prominent coffee farm, named for the jaguarundi, a wildcat and ferocious chicken eater common in these parts.

In the northeast foreground, to the right behind the plaza-front buildings, you may be able to make out the mossy, colonial-style facade of the venerable **Templo de Los Reyes Santo Magos** (Church of the Holy Magi Kings), now replaced by the new church on its left. From here, townsfolk hold their yearly patronal festival for three days centering on El Día de Los Reyes, 6 January. Invariably, townsfolk will enjoy a big party, including fireworks, a *calenda* (procession) carrying the images of their patron kings, and the town's favorite dances. These include the Guajalote (offering of the turkey) and Las Chilenas, a courtship dance not unlike the renowned Jarabe Tapatía, the so-called Mexican Hat Dance of Guadalajara.

Also in the foreground, to the east, you can see the red-brick decor of the one-of-a-kind **Hotel Palacio Chatino,** the town's most prominent hotel, labor of love of Dr. Elfego Zurita.

As you make your way down from atop the *palacio municipal,* be sure to take a close look at the several stelae embedded into the upper-floor and stairwell walls. Archaeologists, who dug them up at Cerro La Iglesia, believe them to represent Chatino high priests or kings, dating from about 500 B.C. If you look carefully around the bases, you'll see some yet-to-be deciphered name-dates, presumably of the personages represented. Notice that the upstairs figures have their arms folded over their chests, as in a burial, while the one in the middle of the stairwell is a priest in the act of human sacrifice, holding an obsidian knife in his right hand and a (gulp!) human heart in his left. (Note: Plans are afoot in Nopala to open a new museum to display their artifacts; by the time you read this, the above-mentioned stelae may have been moved to the new museum.)

Accommodations

Nopala is ready for visitors, with a pair of good country-style hotels and at least three acceptable *comedor* restaurants. The best of the bunch is **Hotel Palacio del Chatino,** whose bright red-and-white brick decor you probably already saw from atop the *palacio municipal.* The friendly physician-owner has polished his little six-room hotel (three on top and three on the bottom, all around an interior garden) into a first-rate establishment. Rooms are clean and comfortably furnished with hot water, fans, and big double beds. The upper ones especially have plenty of air and light and look out on valley and mountain views on two sides. They're hard to beat, especially this far out in the country, for $8 s, $11 d. Reserve in writing through the owner, Dr. Elfego Zurita, at 55 Hidalgo, Nopala, Oaxaca 71960, or by phone, tel./fax 958/600-00.

The other lodging is the **Posada Nopala** of American expatriate Pablo (Paul) Nunn Cleaver, also owner of Tabachín Apartments on Zicatela Beach in Puerto Escondido. Posada Nopala's hacienda garden-style layout consists of four luxuriously built rooms, complete with charming Baroque architectural details, including carved solid hardwood doors. These rooms share one elaborately luxurious onyx and tile bathroom. Another larger house, which includes the dining room and the owner's quarters, has two similarly elaborately decorated rooms with their own baths. During high winter season, expect to pay some bucks (probably around $50 per person for two, including dinner and breakfast) for lodging here. Amenities include a big orchard in the back with all the mandarin oranges and mangos you can eat (in season). Reserve through the owner,

Pablo Nunn Cleaver, in Puerto Escondido, at Apartmentos Tabachín del Puerto, Av. del Morro s/n, Colonia Marinero, Puerto Escondido, Oaxaca 71980, tel. 958/211-79 or 958/216-64, or in Nopala, at Posada Nopala, Prolongación Calle Hidalgo s/n, Santo Reyes Nopala, Oaxaca 71960, tel. 958/600-32.

Food
Nopala can supply you with plenty of local-style food. If you want, start at the big **market,** which operates every day but is even bigger on *tianguis* days, Saturday and Sunday. The hundreds of native Chatino women flood into town in bright *traje* (native dress) with their loads of *calabazas* (gourds), *cal* (limestone), *camote* (candied root, like sweet potato), *guajalotes* (turkeys), and much more.

If you'd rather not prepare your own dinner, pick out the goodies you want at the clean *fondas* (foodstalls) on the street adjacent, below the main market. Or if you'd rather, go to one of the more formal *comedores,* such as the **Sarita,** on Hidalgo, about two blocks downhill from the market.

Services and Information
Nopala's key service establishments are clustered right around the inviting, shady central plaza. Adjacent uphill, to the left of the *palacio municipal,* is the **correo** (post office), open Mon.–Fri. 9 A.M.–1 P.M. and 3–6 P.M., and the *telégrafos* stacked above it, open Mon.–Fri. 9 A.M.–3 P.M.

At the end of the alley adjacent to the post office is Dr. Zurita's **Farmacia "Willey,"** open daily 6 A.M.–10 P.M.. The larga distancia (long-distance) telephone office, tel./fax 958/600-00, is at the hotel Palacio del Chatino reception, behind the pharmacy.

While in town, be sure to contact personable, well-informed local photographer **Frédy Zárate,** who likes to show people around town. Farther afield, he can take you on excursions to local sights, such as the San Juan Lachao waterfall, the Cerro La Iglesia archaeological site, a coffee farm, and more. Expect to pay about $20 per day for his services. Write or call him (in Spanish) ahead of time at his house, at Esquina Zaragoza y Iturbide, Nopala, Oaxaca 71960, tel. 958/600-43.

Getting There and Away
Get to **Nopala** from Oaxaca by second-class buses **Estrella Rojo del Sureste** or **Solteca (or Transol)** from the *camionera central segunda clase* at the Mercado Abastos (take a taxi) on Oaxaca's south side. From Puerto Escondido, go by the same bus lines from the parking lot at the upper, northern, end of town, at Calle 9 Norte and Av. Oaxaca, across from the electric station.

By car or RV from Oaxaca, drive the paved but often potholed Hwy. 131 south 120 miles (194 km, figure around six hours for safety) to San Gabriel Mixtepec. In the middle of town, where the road cuts sharply left, continue straight onto the paved side street. Continue another seven miles (12 km) along a good but curvy sand and gravel road (go slow to retain traction) to Nopala. Allow about five hours for this up and down, winding trip.

In the opposite direction, from Puerto Escondido, drive 27 curving, sometimes rough, uphill miles (44 km) north along Hwy. 131 to San Gabriel Mixtepec. In the middle of town, when the road makes a sharp turn right, go left at the paved side street. Continue another seven miles (12 km) along a good but winding sand and gravel road to Nopala (go slow for traction). Allow about two hours for safety.

SANTA CATARINA JUQUILA: SHRINE FOR ALL SEASONS

Much of the life in the Chatino mountain town of Juquila (hoo-KEE-lah, pop. 15,000) revolves around its renowned patron, the Virgin of Juquila, the object of adoration for multitudes who begin converging on the town around the first of December.

The reason for all the hubbub is a small, frail figurine scarcely more than a foot tall, which was donated to Juquila by a priest, Father Jordán de Santa Catalina, of the neighboring town of Amialtepec in 1713. Father Jordán feared that the image, which was already locally adored, deserved a more secure home than his rude *jacal.*

The love the faithful show for the Virgin of Juquila has grown over the centuries. Somehow she strikes chords of sympathy in the hearts of Mexicans, perhaps partly because

TROUBLE IN CHATINO COUNTRY

Juquila's bustle appears so focused by the constant flow of faithful that you might think that the Virgin is all that Juquila is about. Beneath the busy surface, however, lies a complex network of personal relationships held together by political, business, kinship, and *compadrazgo* ties.

In the recent past, this tight social system, fueled by a communal forest property boundary dispute between Juquila and the rival town of Yaitepec, led to a local war that in some years resulted in hundreds of shootings, knifings, and machete slashings. Scores of Juquila and Yaitepec men bear scars of such violent encounters.

Fortunately, however, peace seems to have come to Chatino country, with the shaking of hands over a government-brokered pact in late 1998, fixing the boundary between Juquila and Yaitepec. For a fascinating in-depth look into Chatino social relationships and this dispute, check out James Greenberg's book, *Blood Ties: Life and Violence in Rural Mexico*. Details are contained in the Suggested Reading section.

of her frailty and also because she's a simple figurine of a native woman, not unlike a preconquest goddess idol.

She was first revered by the Chatino people of Amialtepec during the 16th century when she resided in the town church. But in 1633 the entire town of Amialtepec burned down, and one of the sole remembrances left intact was the Virgin, who from that point forward became a symbol of hope for Chatino people.

Sights

The Juquila town plaza, half a block uphill from the terminus of Av. Antonio Valdez, the entrance drive into town, is *the* place to appreciate Juquila. If you're driving, park your car in the lot of the Hotel del Carmen (on the right-hand side of Valdez, half a block before the plaza) and either check in at the desk or order breakfast or lunch. If busing, walk or ride a taxi from the Juquila station about a mile ahead along Valdez to the plaza.

The Baroque shrine-church, the **Santuario de Nuestra Señora de Juquila,** faces approximately east (unusual for Mexico, where most churches face west). If you face west, toward the church, the *palacio municipal* stands on your left, on the plaza's south side. On your right (north), sloping below the plaza level, stands the town market. Main plaza-front business street Calle Benito Juárez runs south to your immediate left, while on your immediate right, the same thoroughfare continues north as Calle Revolución, where *tianguis* awnings spread on Saturday and Sunday.

Step inside the church, where the tiny Virgin stands above the main altar, surrounded by flowers and encircled by a halo of blue fluorescent light. Multiple copies of the Virgin rest to one side of the main altar, while in a right-hand chapel other copies, hung with *milagros* (wish medals), preside above a host of flickering candles.

Back in the nave, the faithful continuously arrive and quietly seat themselves in the pews, while others kneel before the altar, gazing at the Virgin. The diminutive figure is decorated with a pearl-garnished silk cape. Her face is of brown complexion, and upon her head rests a regal, native-style headdress. In front of the altar stand boxes for donations and personal letters to the Virgin.

La Capilla del Pedimento

Despite the supernumerary virgins in the plaza church itself, another nearby hilltop shrine, locally known as the Capilla del Pedimento, also draws multitudes of pilgrims. You'll find it near the clutter of roadside stalls about three miles back, east along the highway, out of town.

At the stalls you can purchase nearly everything from food, drinks, and religious pictures and reproductions of the Virgin to *milagros,* candles, and flower gifts for her. Collect your offerings and follow the human flow north of the highway about a quarter mile to the small summit chapel.

There you'll see a larger ceramic reproduction of the Virgin in a pink silken robe, heavily hung with *milagro* medals. For an appreciation of the annual mountain of adoration that the Virgin receives, stroll around behind the chapel and marvel at the pile upon pile of offerings, far too

offerings to the Virgin piled up at the La Capilla del Pedimento

numerous to count or save, left by untold thousands of pilgrims.

Other commonly visited sights not far away from Juquila include the old Chatino center of **Amialtepec** and the spectacular 165-foot (50-meter) waterfall, **Cascada Chorro Conejos.** Ask at your hotel desk for a guide to show you the way.

Accommodations

Juquila's probable best-bet hotel is the **Hotel del Carmen,** at the town center at Antonio Valdez s/n, Juquila, Oaxaca 71900, tel./fax 952/400-04 (in Oaxaca City, tel. 9/515-8872, 9/515-8556). With an entrance driveway leading to a big rear parking lot, this is an especially convenient option for drivers in congested Juquila. The approximately 40 rooms, clean and mostly semi-deluxe, rent for about $17 s, $21 d, $25 t year-round, with hot water shower baths, TV, good restaurant, and parking. Some rooms are better than others. Check the mattress before moving in. Some may feel as if they're stuffed with rocks.

(The management claims to be solving this problem.)

Other cheaper options are available around the plaza half a block uphill. The best of these is probably the homey, family-run **Posada los Ángeles,** at the plaza's southeast corner, at Calle Benito Juárez 2, Barrio Grande, Juquila, Oaxaca 71900, tel. 952/400-73. The approximately 20 rooms are clean, simply furnished, and well-maintained, with shaded (as opposed to bare-bulb) lamps. Rooms vary; if possible, get one with a balcony plaza-front view. Rooms with one double bed rent for $13 s or d; with two double beds, $16 for three persons, $21 for four.

If the Ángel is full, try the **Hotel Juquila Plaza** on the plaza, right in front of the church at Av. Revolución 4, Juquila, Oaxaca 71900, tel. 952/400-66. Rooms, although clean enough, aren't as thoughtfully furnished or as well-maintained as the Posada del Ángel. Some, however, have plaza-front views. They rent for about $15 s or d, $18 t year-round, with hot-water shower baths and parking.

If the rush of pilgrims has filled all the above accommodations, you can try others in the downtown, among them the **Hotel San Nicolas,** Calle Antonio Valdes s/n, tel. 952/401-20, and the **Hotel La Conchita,** below and behind (southwest) of the church, at Calle Hidalgo s/n, tel. 952/400-15.

Food

Several sources around the plaza offer things to eat. For fruits and vegetables, go to the **market** on the plaza's north side. A convenient grocery source is **Abarrotes El Centro,** tel. 952/400-60, on the plaza's northeast corner, across Revolución from the market. Hearty country-style food, always wholesome if hot, is available at *fondas* (permanent foodstalls) in the market.

The few good restaurants are mostly confined to the hotels. Fanciest in town is the restaurant in the **Hotel del Carmen,** on Antonio Valdez, half a block north of the church, with a good standard menu of soups, sandwiches, meats, poultry, and Mexican specialties. Open daily about 7:30 A.M.–10 P.M., tel. 952/400-04.

For a homier option, go to the restaurant **La Angelita,** in the Hotel Posada los Ángeles, opposite the church on the plaza's northeast corner, tel. 952/400-73. Here, the friendly female hotel owner supplies patrons with tasty local-style *desayunos, comidas,* and *cenas* (breakfasts, lunches, and suppers) daily, approximately 7 A.M.–10 P.M.

Entertainment and Events

The big Saturday and Sunday *tianguis* (spreading from the northeast corner of the plaza) is Juquila's main regular event. It swells to a 15-day marathon blowout during the December **Fiesta de la Virgen de Juquila.** The celebration begins quietly in late November with early morning masses and religious processions; builds with a street carnival, floats, and fireworks; and climaxes around 8 December with traditional and modern dances, tapering off after the 12 December Virgin of Guadalupe festival.

Shopping

Stalls on Revolución past the plaza's northeast corner offer a variety of local handicrafts and food delicacies. Handicrafts include embroidered *huipiles,* belts *(cinturones),* tablecloths *(manteles),* and napkins *(servilletas).* Foods include coffee, coconut candy, and *panela* brown sugar.

Stands near the church offer a wealth of old-time religious souvenirs. The Hotel del Carmen sells attractive replicas of the Virgin of Juquila.

Services

Juquila, the capital of the big southern Sierra Juquila governmental district, offers some basic services (but unfortunately no bank at this writing). The ***correo*** (post office), and the ***telecomunicaciones*** (public fax and money orders), tel. 952/400-23, are in the rebuilt *palacio municipal,* south side of the plaza. A public telephone office, **Caseta Lidia,** offers long-distance and public fax service inside, rear, of the market, tel. 952/400-92.

For routine medicines and drugs, try the plaza-front **Farmacia Dolores,** opposite the church. If you get sick, follow the recommendation of your hotel desk, or hire a taxi to take you to the local **Hospital Civil.** Alternatively, near the plaza, consult with general practitioner **Dr. José Luis Zavaleta,** on Revolución, uphill side, a few doors beyond the plaza's northeast corner, or above Abarrotes Zavaleta, directly across the plaza from the church.

Getting There and Away

Juquila is accessible from the coast, north via paved but sometimes potholed, Hwy. 131, the main north-south street through Puerto Escondido. Fill up with gasoline, then follow the winding 55-mile (88-km) route, climbing to the cool, 8,000-foot summit to El Vidrio crossing (gas station and rough, truck-stop *comedores).* There, drivers fork left and continue another 19 miles (30 km) west to Juquila. For safety, allow about 3.5 hours for the entire curvy, uphill trip.

The same is approximately true heading south from Oaxaca City. Fill up with gasoline at the airport Pemex station south of town and continue to about two miles (three km) south of Coyotepec, where you fork right on Hwy. 131. Continue, winding uphill and down, past Sola de Vega (roadside hotel, restaurant, and unleaded gasoline) to the El Vidrio summit crossing (103 miles, 166 km). Turn right at the fork and continue the remaining mostly paved, but sometimes bumpy 19 miles (30 km) west to Juquila.

A pair of long-distance second-class bus lines serve Juquila from both Oaxaca and Puerto Escondido. From the Oaxaca second-class bus terminal near the west-side Abastos market, ride either **Solteca (Transol)** or **Estrella Roja del Sureste** to Juquila. The same lines connect with Juquila from Puerto Escondido. They depart from the bus lot at the corner of Av. 9 Norte and main street Av. Oaxaca, across from the electric station at the north end of town.

WEST TO THE MIXTEC COAST

In reality, the Costa Chica (Little Coast), which includes the Oaxacan Pacific Coast west of Puerto Escondido and the adjoining state of Guerrero coast all the way to Acapulco, isn't very little. Hwy. 200, heading out of Puerto Escondido, requires approximately 300 miles to traverse it.

From Puerto Escondido you head northwest, first passing settlements such as San José Manialtepec, on the southern fringe of Chatino-speaking country. Next you pass the wildlife refuges of Laguna Manialtepec and Lagunas de Chacagua National Park and continue into the Mixtec coast (Mixteca de la Costa) past its main towns of Tututepec, Jamiltepec, and Pinotepa Nacional.

To many native people of Oaxaca's Costa Chica, Spanish is a foreign language. A large fraction of the *indígenas*—Chatino, Mixtec, and Amusgo—live in remote valleys and foothill villages, subsisting as they always have now on corn and beans, without sewers, electricity, or paved roads. Those who live near towns often speak the Spanish they have learned by coming to market. In the Costa Chica town markets you will brush shoulders with them—men, sometimes in pure-white cottons, and women in colorful embroidered *huipiles* over wrapped hand-woven skirts.

Besides the native Mexicans, you will often see **African-Mexicans**—*morenos,* brown ones—known as *costeños* because their isolated settlements are near the coast. Descendants of African slaves imported hundreds of years ago, the *costeños* subsist on the produce from their village gardens and the fish they catch.

Costa Chica *costeños* and *indígenas* have a reputation for being unfriendly and suspicious. If true in the past (although it's certainly less so in the present), they have had good reason to be suspicious of outsiders, who in their view have been trying to take away their land, gods, and lives for 300 years.

Communication is nevertheless possible. Your arrival might be the event of the day for the residents of a little foothill or shoreline end-of-road village. People are going to wonder why you came. Smile and say hello. Buy a soda at the store or *palapa*. If kids gather around, don't be shy. Draw a picture in your notebook. If a child offers to do likewise, you've succeeded.

LAGUNAS DE CHACAHUA NATIONAL PARK AND VICINITY

The Lagunas de Chacahua National Park spreads for about 20 miles of open-ocean beach shoreline and islet-studded jungly lagoons midway between Pinotepa Nacional and Puerto Escondido. Tens of thousands of birds typical of a host of Mexican species nest in the mangroves of the two main lagoons, Laguna Pastoría on the east side and Laguna Chacahua on the west, and fish the waters.

The fish and wildlife of the lagoons, overfished and overhunted during recent years by local people, are now recovering. Commercial fishing is now strictly licensed. A platoon of Marines patrols access roads, shorelines, and the waters, making sure catches are within legal limits. Crocodiles were hunted out during the 1970s, but the government is restoring them with a hatchery on Laguna Chacahua.

For most visitors, mainly Mexican families on Sunday outings, access is by boat, except for one rugged road. From east-side Zapotalito village, the local fishing cooperative offers full- and half-day boat excursions to the beaches, Playa Hermosa on the east side and Playa Chacahua on the west.

Exploring Lagunas de Chacahua

Zapotalito, on the eastern shore of Laguna Pastoría, is the sole easy access point to the Lagunas de Chacahua. Get there from the Zapotalito turnoff at Km 82, 51 miles from Pinotepa and 41 miles from Puerto Escondido. (Local buses run from Río Grande all the way to Zapotalito on the lagoon, while second-class buses from Puerto Escondido and Pinotepa Nacional will drop you on the highway.)

From the Zapotalito landings, the fishing cooperative, Sociedad Cooperativa Turística

Escondida, enjoys a monopoly for transporting visitors on the lagoons. The boatmen used to make their livings fishing; now they mostly ferry tourists. Having specialized in fishing, they are generally neither wildlife-sensitive nor wildlife-knowledgeable. Canopied powerboats, seating about 10, make long, full-day trips for about $70 per boat. Cheaper (about $30) half-day excursions take visitors to nearby **Playa Cerro Hermosa** at the mouth of Laguna Pastoría for a couple of hours' beach play and snorkeling—if you bring your own snorkeling gear. (If you don't like these prices, continue about 200 yards along the road to the landing of the smaller Sociedad Cooperativa Marea Roja and bargain for a cheaper rate.) On the other hand, you can save yourself $30 and drive or walk the approximately two miles along the shoreline dirt road from Zapotalito to Playa Cerro Hermosa. Here you'll find a lovely open-ocean beach good for surf-fishing and beach sports, camping, a wildlife-rich lagoon mangrove wetland, and several *palapa* restaurants.

The full-day destination, Playa Chacahua, about 14 miles distant, unfortunately seems to necessitate a fast trip across the lagoon. It's difficult to get these powerboats to slow down. They roar across broad Laguna Pastoría, scattering flocks of birds ahead of them. They wind among the islands, with names such as *Escorpión* (Scorpion), *Venados* (Deer), or *Pinuelas* (Little Pines), sometimes slowing for viewing multitudes of nesting pelicans, herons, and cormorants. They pick up speed again in the narrow jungle channel between the lagoons, roaring past idyllic, somnolent El Corral village, and break into open water again on Laguna Chacahua.

The **crocodile hatchery** is at Chacahua village on the west side of the lagoon, home to about two dozen local *costeño* families, a shabby hotel, and a pair of lagoonside *palapa* restaurants. Past the rickety crocodile caretaker's quarters are a few enclosures housing about a hundred crocodiles segregated according to size, from hatchlings to six-foot-long toothy green adults.

The tour climaxes at the west half of

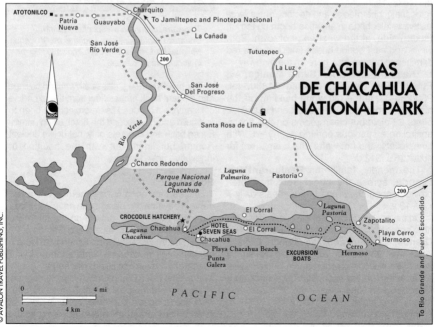

Chacahua village across the estuary. Palms line the placid lagoon, shading the **Hotel Siete Mares** (Seven Seas) bamboo tourist cabañas. The hotel, a quiet, rustic tropical resort, offers a small restaurant, showers and toilets, a few cabins (rent negotiable from about $10, depending upon season), and a beautiful beach a short walk away.

Playa Chacahua is lovely *because* of its isolation. The unlittered golden-white sand, washed by gently rolling waves, seems perfect for all beach activities. You can snorkel off the rocks nearby, fish in the breakers, and surf the intermediate breaks that angle in on the west side. A few *palapas* provide food and drinks, and for beachcombers, wildlife viewers, and backpackers (who bring their own water), the breezy, jungle-backed beach spreads for 10 miles both ways.

Río Grande

Río Grande (pop. 10,000), five miles east of the Lagunas de Chacahua-Zapotalito access road, is a transportation, supply, and service point for the region. Right on the highway are *abarroterías* (groceries), pharmacies and doctors, and a *larga distancia* telephone in an office-booth on the left (south) side, at the west edge of town. Both west- and east-bound buses (including the red Jamiltepec buses) stop here on the highway.

The downscale **Hotel Santa Monica,** Av. Puebla, Río Grande, Oaxaca 71830, tel. 958/260-33, is the big white building off the highway's north side, at the west end of town. It offers 22 plain but clean rooms on two floors, encircling a spacious parking courtyard. With fans, toilets, and hot water, the rooms rent for about $6 s, $12 d.

The friendly, family-run **Restaurant Río Grande,** across the street from the hotel, provides good cheer and hearty meals daily 7 A.M.–10 P.M.

On the east edge of town, the once inviting but now somewhat neglected **Hotel Paraíso Río Grande,** Carretera 200, Río Grande, Oaxaca 71830, tel. 958/261-96, offers a big swimming pool (if it's in working order) and a kiddie pool in a spreading, grassy patio, plus large brick-and-tile rooms with either fans or a/c. The 20 rooms (check for mildew) rent for about $8 s or $16 d, and $25 t with a/c and TV.

The warm, sulfurous waters of the spring Charquito Atotonilco, near Lagunas de Chacahua National Park, have long been known locally for their curative properties.

The hotel's soaring, classically vaulted ceilings and elegant brick arches flow from the expertise of its architect builder. His life project has been to first build and now extend the hotel, using unreinforced brick and concrete only, not unlike ancient Roman buildings, but with the addition of innovative new designs.

Roca Blanca

Travelers hankering for an afternoon or a few tranquil days on the beach, can have it at Roca Blanca (White Rock), tucked on the shoreline about six miles (10 km) east of Río Grande or 22 miles (36 km) west of Puerto Escondido. Here a rustic palapa restaurant fronts a long curving beach of yellow-white sand, washed by gentle rollers. Islet Roca Blanca perches picturesquely offshore, softening the Pacific swells. On the west side, a lagoon, backed by a scenic jungle of rocky outcroppings, provides shelter for kiddie play and often some impromptu palapas that await restoration by new occupants.

If you want to stay, but arrive unequipped for camping, check out the adjacent **cabañas.** Here $8 gets you a petite, round, thatched wooden house with a bed for two, with showers and toilets in an adjacent concrete building. There are also a lot for parking self-contained RVs and a lagoon-side beach good for setting up a tent and kayaking or rubber-boating either in the ocean or the lagoon. Be prepared with bug repellent, especially around sunset. For more information, check with the owner, Andres López Solano, tel. 958/263-28, in Río Grande.

SAN PEDRO TUTUTEPEC

Tututepec (pop. 10,000) is a hill town that perches on the breeze-cooled view heights about five miles inland from Hwy. 200. Get there by turning right, or north, at the signed side road at Santa Rosa de Lima, 45 miles (72 km) west of Puerto Escondido (or 44 miles, 71 km east of Pinotepa Nacional). After about two miles from the highway, turn left at the fork, which leads a few more miles uphill to Tututepec and ends at the town plaza.

Few local residents appear aware of their town's proud tradition as the only Oaxaca kingdom that withstood the 15th-century Aztec invasion and remained independent at the time of the conquest in 1522. Today's residences are built perfunctorily on the same hilltops where Tututepec's kings raised their pyramids and temples.

Nevertheless, a few excavated remains give clues to Tututepec's past splendor. Climb the concrete stairs leading uphill from the west side of the town plaza to a hilltop mini-park and church. On the right side, a roof shelters a number of monoliths—of a high priest, a pair of Quetzalcoatl-like serpents, and a headless jaguar—carved in styles reminiscent of Teotihuacán and Tula (Land of the Toltecs).

While you're atop the hill, take a look inside the town church. On the altar is the image of St. Peter, the town patron (who, however, is not the object of the main local festival, which is the Fiesta de Candelaria, around 2 February).

While you're in Tututepec, you can avail yourself of a number of services located in the vicinity of the town plaza. These include *abarroterías* (grocery stores), a *correo* (post office), a *telecomunicaciones* (money orders and public fax), tel. 954/100-81, and a *centro de salud* (health center), tel. 954/100-39. Gasoline is available at the Pemex station on Hwy. 200, not far east of the Tututepec turnoff.

CHARQUITO ATOTONILCO HOT SPRINGS

About 10 miles (16 km) west of the Tututepec side road, Hwy. 200 passes over the **Río Verde,** Oaxaca's longest river, which funnels the entire runoff from Oaxaca's central valley into the Pacific a few miles downstream. West of the river, near the Km 48 marker, just over a half mile (one km) west of Charquito village, turn left at the Guayabo-labeled side road for Atotonilco hot springs and sacred site.

If driving, set your odometer at the turnoff. Continue through Guayabo (2.1 miles, 3.4 km), Patria Nueva (2.8 miles, 4.5 km), and a shallow river bed (about a foot and a half deep during the rainy season) to the hot spring at 4.2 miles (6.8 km).

This source of warm, sulfury, curative water has been used and revered by untold generations of local people. Folks have built a small chapel on the hill above the pair of springs: the first is to the right, below the road, beneath an immense, spreading *guanacastle* tree, and the second is marked by a wide, waist-deep riverbank bathing pool.

A continuous stream of mostly local people bathe here, especially on Sundays and holidays. If you've got extra time, this might be an interesting place to set up a tent or park your RV for a few days (at a respectful distance from the springs themselves; as a courtesy, ask if it's OK to camp). Unless you're under three, *do not bathe nude.* Please respect local custom by wearing at least a modest bathing suit while using the hot springs.

On the slope above the springs, pay your respects inside the small chapel, dedicated to the **Virgen de los Remedios.** Here, at the altar, people give "thanks to the virgin for the hot waters that have been provided."

SANTIAGO JAMILTEPEC

About 68 miles (109 km) west of Puerto Escondido or 18 miles (at Km 30) east of Pinotepa Nacional is the hilltop town of Jamiltepec (hah-meel-teh-PAYK). Two-thirds of its 20,000 inhabitants are Mixtec, who preserve a still-vibrant indigenous culture. A grieving Mixtec king named the town in memory of his infant son, Jamily, who was carried off by an eagle from this very hilltop.

Around Town

The central plaza, about a mile from the highway (follow the signed side road north—right, westbound), stands at the heart of the town. You can't miss it, because of the proud town plaza-front clock (and sundials) and market, always big, but even bigger and more colorful on Thursday, the day of the traditional native *tianguis.*

Moreover, several big festivals are instrumental in preserving local folkways. They start off on New Year's Day and resume during the weeks of Lent *(cuaresma),* usually during February and March. Favorite dances, such as the Los Tejerones (Weavers), Los Chareos, Los Moros (The Moors), and Las Chilenas act out age-old events, stories, and fables. Los Tejerones, for example, through a cast of animal-costumed characters, pokes fun at ridiculous Spanish colonial rules and customs.

Soon after, Jamiltepec people celebrate their renowned pre-Easter (week of Ramos) festival, featuring neighborhood candlelight processions accompanied by antique 18th-century music. Hundreds of the faithful bear elaborate wreaths and palm decorations to the foot of their church altars on Domingo de Ramos (Palm Sunday).

Later, merrymaking peaks again, between 23 and 26 July during the Fiesta de Santiago Apóstol (Festival of St. James the Apostle) and on 11 September with a festival honoring the Virgen de los Remedios. All this celebrating centers on the town church, the **Templo de Santiago Apóstol,** destroyed by a 1928 earthquake but brilliantly restored from 1992 to 1999. Dominican padres supervised the original construction of mortar moistened with egg yolks during the 16th century. Take a look inside, where the town patron St. James (sword in hand) and the Virgen de Los Remedios (Virgin of the Remedies) preside above the altar.

Regardless of the festivals, Jamiltepec at midday is a feast of traditional sights and sounds, accessible by simply strolling around the market and side streets. For an interesting side excursion, take a stroll to some of the local *ojos de agua,* community springwater sources. From the plaza's northeast side, head east, downhill, along Calle 20 de Noviembre. After about a block you'll arrive at a covered basin *(pileta)* built into the hillside rocks on the left, where folks fill bottles and jars with drinking water. Continue downhill another couple of blocks to *ojo de agua* **El Aguacate,** where another covered basin, on the left, supplies drinking water, while a cluster of folks wash clothes and bathe in a natural spring beneath an adjacent shady roof.

If you're interested in a more spectacular water diversion, follow the gravel road by local minibus or car north out of town about 15 miles (25 km) to the *cascada* (waterfall) in the foothill country near San José de las Flores village.

Handicraft Shopping

Jamiltepec is well worth a stop if only to visit its market handicrafts shops, such as **Yu-uku Cha-kuaa** (Hill of Darkness) of Santiago de la Cruz Velasco. Personable Santiago runs his shop at the Jamiltepec plaza market, because the government cluster of shops (Centro Artesanal de la Costa, on the highway) was closed down, victim of a dispute over control. The local Mixtec artisans wanted to manage their own handicrafts sales, while the regional branch of the INI (Instituto Nacional Indigenista) preferred to manage instead. The Mixtecs stuck together and refused to bring their handicrafts, closing the government operation.

Some of those crafts—masks, *huipiles,* carvings, hats—occupy the shelves and racks in Santiago's shop by the market's northeast entrance (ask for Santiago by name), open until about 4 P.M. His home (where he also sells handicrafts) is located on main street Av. Principal at Francisco Madero, by *seguro social,* the government health clinic (turn off at the highway sign). If you don't want to miss him, write Santiago at Av. Principal, Esquina Fco. Madero, Barrio Grande, Sec. 5, Jamiltepec, Oaxaca 71700.

Practicalities

Jamiltepec, capital of the Jamiltepec governmental district, has a number of basic hotels, restaurants, and services (but not yet a bank) near the town plaza. For an overnight, take a look at the **Hotel Díaz,** at the northeast plaza corner at Hidalgo 4, Jamiltepec, Oaxaca 71700, tel. 958/280-50. It offers a dozen clean, basic rooms around an airy upstairs patio for about $6 s, $8 d, with fan and private bath (but room temperature water only). If it's full, take a look at **Hotel Maris,** tel. 958/280-42, and **Hotel Pérez,** tel. 958/288-29 or 958/282-49, both on Calle Josefina O. Domínguez nearby.

For medicines and drugs, go to **Farmacia del Perpetua Socorro** (Pharmacy of Perpetual Relief), Hidalgo 2 at the plaza's northeast corner, run by a team of friendly sisters. If you need a doctor, they recommend either **Dr. Manuel Moto,** on Hwy. 200, in town *barrio* Sección 4, or the *seguro social* **Hospital de la Madre,** with 24-hour emergency service, in town *barrio* Las Flores.

WEST OF JAMILTEPEC

San Andres Huaxpaltepec

For 20 miles west of Jamiltepec, Hwy. 200 stretches through the coastal Mixtec heartland, intriguing to explore, especially during festival times. The population of Huaxpaltepec (oo-wash-pahl-tay-PAYK), about nine miles (14 km) west of Jamiltepec, 12 miles (20 km) east of Pinotepa Nacional, sometimes swells from 4,000 to 20,000 or more during the three or four days before the day of Jesus the Nazarene (the fourth Friday before Good Friday). The entire town becomes a spreading warren of shady stalls, offering everything from TVs to stone *metates.* Purchase of a corn-grinding *metate,* which, including stone *mano* (roller), sells for about $20, is as important to many a Mixtec family as a refrigerator is to an American. Mixtec husband and wife usually examine several of the concave stones, deliberating the pros and cons of each before deciding.

The Huaxpaltepec Nazarene fair is typical of the larger Oaxaca country expositions. Even the highway becomes a lineup of stalls; entire native clans camp under the trees, and mules, cows, and horses wait patiently around the edges of a grassy trading lot as men discuss prices. (The fun begins when a sale is made and the new owner tries to rope and harness his bargain steed.)

Even sex is for sale within a quarter of very tightly woven no-see-through grass houses, patrolled by armed guards. Walking through, you may notice that instead of the usual women, one of the houses might be offering men dressed in low-cut gowns, lipstick, and high-heeled shoes.

Santa María Huazolotitlán

At nearby Huazolotitlán (ooah-shoh-loh-teet-LAN, pop. 3,000) several resident woodcarvers craft excellent **masks.** Local favorites are jaguars, lions, rabbits, bulls, and human faces. Given a photograph (or a sitting), one of them, if asked, might even carve your likeness for a reasonable fee. (Figure perhaps $40–60.) Near the town plaza, ask for José Luna, Lázaro Gómez, or the master Idineo Gómez (who are all related and live in the town *barrio* Ñii Yucagua).

Textiles are also locally important. Look for the colorfully embroidered animal- and floral-motif *huipiles, manteles,* and *servilletas* (native smocks, tablecloths, and napkins). You might also be able to bargain for a genuine heirloom *pozahuanco* (handwoven wraparound skirt) for a reasonable price. (See the special topic *Pozahuancos* in the Pinotepa Nacional section, following.)

Besides all the handicrafts, Huazolotitlán people celebrate the important local **Fiesta de la Virgen de la Asunción** 13–16 August. The celebrations climax on 14 and 15 August, with a number of favorite traditional dances in which you can see why masks are locally important, especially in the dance of the Tiger and the Turtle on 14 August. The finale comes on 15 August, with the ritual dance of the Chareos, dedicated to the Virgin.

Huazolotitlán is about two miles via the paved road that forks south uphill from Hwy. 200 in Huaxpaltepec. Get there by driving, hitchhiking (with caution), riding the local bus, or hiring a taxi for about $2.

PINOTEPA NACIONAL AND VICINITY

Pinotepa Nacional (pop. about 45,000; 157 miles, 253 km, east of Acapulco; 90 miles, 145 km, west of Puerto Escondido) and its neighboring communities represent an important indigenous region. Mixtec, Amusgo, Chatino, and other peoples stream into town for markets and fiestas in their traditional dress, ready to combine business with pleasure. They sell their produce and crafts—pottery, masks, handmade clothes—at the market, then later get tipsy, flirt, and dance.

The Name

So many people have asked the meaning of their city's name that the town fathers wrote the explanation on a wall next to Hwy. 200 on the west side of town. Pinotepa comes from the Aztec-language words *pinolli* (crumbling) and *tepetl* (mountain); thus "Crumbling Mountain." The second part of the name came about because, during colonial times, the town was called Pinotepa Real (Royal). This wouldn't do after independence, so the name became Pinotepa Nacional, reflecting the national consciousness that emerged during the 1810–21 struggle for liberation.

The Mixtecs, the dominant regional group, disagree with all this, however. To them, Pinotepa has always been Ñií Yo-oko (Little Place). Only within the town limits do the Mexicans (mestizos), who own most of the town businesses, outnumber the Mixtecs. The farther from town you get, the more likely you are to hear people conversing in the Mixtec language, a complex tongue that uses a number of subtle intonations to make meanings clear.

Market

Highway 200, called Av. Porfirio Díaz on the west side (B. Juárez on the east) of town, is Pinotepa's one main business street. It passes a block north of the main market, by the big, fenced-in secondary school on the west side, and continues about a mile to the central plaza.

Despite the Pinotepa market's exotic goods—snakes, iguanas, wild mountain fruits, forest herbs and spices—its people, nearly entirely Mixtec, are its main attraction, especially on the big Wednesday and Sunday market days. Men wear pure-white loose cottons, topped by woven palm-leaf hats. Women wrap themselves in their lovely striped purple, violet, red, and navy blue *pozahuanco* sarong-like horizontally striped skirts. Many women carry a polished tan *jicara* gourd bowl atop their heads, which, although it's not supposed to, looks like a whimsical hat. Older women (and younger ones with babies at their breasts) go bare-breasted with only their white *huipil* draped over their chests as a concession to mestizo custom. Others wear an easily removable *mandil*, a light cotton apron-halter above their *pozahuanco*. A few women can ordinarily be found selling beautiful handmade *pozahuancos*.

Festivals

Although the Pinotepa market days are big, they don't compare to the week before Easter (Semana Santa). People get ready for the finale with processions, carrying the dead Christ through town to the church each of the seven Fridays before Easter. The climax comes on Good Friday (Viernes Santa), when a platoon of young Mixtec men paint their bodies white to portray Jews, and while intoning ancient Mixtec chants shoot arrows at Christ on the cross. On Saturday, the people mournfully take the Savior down from the cross and bury him and on Sunday gleefully celebrate his resurrection with a riot of fireworks, food, and folk dancing.

Although not as spectacular as Semana Santa, there's plenty of merrymaking, food, dancing, and processions around the Pinotepa *zócalo* church on 25 July, the day of Pinotepa's patron, Santiago (St. James).

Accommodations and Food

The motel-style **Hotel Carmona,** Av. Porfirio Díaz 127, Pinotepa Nacional, Oaxaca 71600, tel. 954/322-22, fax 954/323-22, on Hwy. 200 about three blocks west of the central plaza, offers three stories of clean, not fancy, but thoughtfully decorated rooms, a big backyard garden with pool and sundeck, and a passable restaurant. For festival dates, make reservations. The 50 rooms run about $16 s, $22 d, $28 t, fan only; $24, $30, and $36 for a/c.

If the Carmona is full, check the two high-profile newer hotels, **Pepe's** and **Las Gaviotas,** tel. 954/328-38, fax 954/320-56, $10 d with fan, beside the highway on the west side of town. Of the two, Pepe's, at Carretera Pinotepa Nacional-Acapulco Km 1, Pinotepa Nacional, Oaxaca 71600, tel. 954/343-47, fax 954/336-42, is the much better choice, with 35 spacious, semideluxe rooms for a reasonable $10 s, $13 d fan only; $17 and $23 with a/c; with good TV, hot water, restaurant, and parking

Third choice goes to clean **Hotel Marisa,** downtown on the highway, Av. Juárez 134, north side of street, tel. 954/321-01, fax 954/326-96, $8 d with fan and parking.

Campers enjoy a tranquil spot (best during the dry late fall-winter-spring season) on the **Río Arena** about two miles east of Pinotepa. Eastbound, turn left just after the big river bridge. Continue a few hundred yards, past a pumphouse on the left, to a track that forks down to the riverbank. Notice the waterfall cascading down the rocky cliff across the river. You will sometimes find neighbors-campers in RVs or tents and poor but friendly sand collectors—set up on the riverside beneath the abandoned Restaurant La Roca (now just a rock-wall ruin), a few hundred yards up the smooth stream, excellent for kayaking (if you have some way of returning back upstream.)

For food, Pinotepa has a number of recommendable restaurants. First choice goes to **Marcelina's Big Burger,** on the side street across Díaz from Bancomer. The hardworking, friendly owner-manager offers a bountiful menu, featuring genuinely giant and delicious hamburgers, several styles of juicy *tortas,* fruit salad with honey and granola, and more. Good for breakfast. Open daily 8:30 A.M.–10 P.M.

For a light lunch or supper, try the very clean and friendly family-run **Burger Bonny,** at the southeast corner of the main plaza, open daily 11 A.M.–10 P.M. Besides six varieties of good hamburgers, Burger Bonny offers *tortas,* tacos, french fries, hot dogs, microwave popcorn, fruit juices, and *refrescos,* at very reasonable prices.

Also very worthy is traditional **Fonda Toñita,** a block north of the church-front, at the corner of Aguirre Palancares. Local folks flock here for the hearty afternoon *comida* (pick the entrée, and you get rice and tortillas thrown in free); also good for breakfast, Mon.–Sat. 7 A.M.–9 P.M.

Services

Exchange money over the counter or use the ATM at all Pinotepa banks. Try **Bancomer** (U.S. traveler's checks and cash, open for money exchange Mon.–Fri. 8:30 A.M.–5:30 P.M., Sat. 10 A.M.–2 P.M., tel. 954/323-40, 954/322-27, corner of Díz and Progreso, two blocks west of the plaza, or **Banamex** across the street, open Mon.–Fri. 9 A.M.–5 P.M., Sat. 9 A.M.–2 P.M. Alternatively, try the long-hours (open Mon.–Fri. approximately 8 A.M.–7 P.M., Sat. 8 A.M.–3 P.M.) **Banco Internacional,** tel. 954/339-49 or 954/339-79, also on Av. Progreso, but across Porfirio Díaz and uphill block from Bancomer.

The *correo* (post office), tel. 954/322-64, is open Mon.–Fri. 8 A.M.–7 P.M., Sat. 9 A.M.–1 P.M., by the bus station, about two blocks west and across the street from Bancomer. The *teleco-municaciones* (money orders, public telephone and fax) is two blocks north of the Presidencia Municipal (along Av. Lic. Alfonso Pérez Gasga) and open Mon.–Sat. 8 A.M.–8 P.M., Sat. 9 A.M.-

---

POZAHUANCOS

To a coastal Mixtec woman her *pozahuanco* (wraparound skirt) is a lifetime investment symbolizing her maturity and social status, something that she expects to pass on to her daughters. Heirloom *pozahuancos* are of hand-spun thread, dyed in several shades. Women dye them by hand, always including a pair of necessary colors: a light purple *(morada)* from secretions of tidepool-harvested snails, *Purpura patula pansa,* and silk dyed scarlet red with cochineal, a dye extracted from the beetle *Dactylopius coccus,* cultivated in the Valley of Oaxaca. Increasingly, women are weaving *pozahuancos* with synthetic thread, which has a slippery feel compared to the hand-spun cotton. Consider yourself lucky if you can get a traditionally made *pozahuanco* for as little as $100. If someone offers you a look-alike for $20, you know it's an imitation.

noon. ***Larga distancia*** Lada Central telephone and fax office, on the plaza, south side, is open longer, evening hours.

For a doctor, go to the **Clínica Rodriguez** at 503 Aguirre Palancares, tel. 954/323-30, one block north, two blocks west of the central plaza church-front. Get routine medications at one of several town pharmacies, such as the 24-hour **Super Farmacia,** on Díaz, a block west of the central plaza church-front.

Getting There and Away

By **car or RV,** Hwy. 200 connects west to Acapulco (160 miles, 258 km) in an easy 4.5 hours driving time. The 89-mile (143-km) connection to Puerto Escondido can be done safely in about 2.5 hours. Additionally, the 239-mile (385-km) Hwy. 125–Hwy. 190 route connects Pinotepa Nacional to Oaxaca, via Putla de Guerrero and (Tlaxiaco, 136 miles, 219 km). Although winding most of the way and potholed at times, the road is generally uncongested. It's safely drivable in a passenger car with caution, from Pinotepa to Oaxaca (follow the toll *autopista* near Oaxaca) in about eight hours (under dry conditions) at the wheel from Pinotepa, and seven hours in the reverse, downhill, direction from Oaxaca.

Several long-distance **bus** lines connect Pinotepa Nacional with destinations north, northwest, east, and west. **Estrella Blanca** and subsidiaries Elite, Gacela, and Flecha Roja, tel. 954/322-54, offer several daily first- and second-class *salidas de paso* (buses passing through) departures west to Acapulco, Zihuatanejo, and Mexico City, and east to Puerto Escondido, Pochutla (Puerto Ángel), Bahías de Huatulco, and Salina Cruz, from their station on Porfirio Díaz about three blocks west of the *zócalo.*

Smaller, mostly second-class lines **Fletes y Pasajes, Estrella del Valle,** and **Oaxaca Pacífico** operate out of a pair of small stations one block north of the central plaza church-front, on side street Aguirre Palancares. Fletes y Pasajes, tel. 954/321-63, connects daily with Oaxaca via Putla, Tlaxiaco and Nochixtlán, by Highways 125 and 190. Estrella del Valle and Oaxaca Pacífico buses, tel. 954/326-97, also connect with Oaxaca, but in the opposite direction: first east, either to Puerto Escondido to

church near Pinotepa

Pochutla (Puerto Ángel), then continuing north over the Sierra to Oaxaca via either Hwy. 131 or 175, respectively.

First-class **Cristóbal Colón** also operates out of a small station on the same street, about one block farther west. A few daily departures connect, via Highways 175 and 190 northeast through Putla and Tlaxciaco, with Oaxaca (by the fast *autopista* via Nochixtlán), and northwest with Mexico City (via Puebla). Other departures connect east with Puerto Escondido.

EXCURSIONS NORTH OF PINOTEPA

The local patronal festival year begins early, on 20 January, at **Pinotepa Don Luis** (pop. 5,000), about 15 miles by back roads northeast of Pinotepa Nacional, with the uniquely Mixtec festival of San Sebastián. Village bands blare, fireworks pop and hiss, and penitents crawl, until the finale, when dancers whirl the local favorite dance, Las Chilenas.

Yet another exciting time around Pinotepa Nacional is during **Carnaval,** when nearby communities put on big extravaganzas. Pinotepa Don Luis, sometimes known as Pinotepa Chica (Little Pinotepa), is famous for wooden masks the people make for their big Carnaval festival. The celebration usually climaxes on the Sunday before Ash Wednesday, when everyone seems to be in costume and a corps of performers gyrates in the traditional dances: Paloma (Dove), Tigre (Jaguar), Culebra (Snake), and Tejón (Badger).

Pinotepa Don Luis bubbles over again with excitement during Semana Santa, when the faithful carry fruit- and flower-decorated trees to the church on Good Friday, explode Judas effigies on Saturday, and celebrate by dancing most of Easter Sunday

San Juan Colorado, a few miles north of Pinotepa Don Luis, usually appears as just another dusty little town until Carnaval, when its festival rivals that of its neighbors. Subsequently, on 29 November, droves of Mixtec people come into town to honor their patron, San Andres. After the serious part at the church, they celebrate with a cast of favorite dancing characters such as Malinche, Jaguar, Turtle, and Charros (Cowboys).

Amusgo Country

Cacahuatepec (pop. about 5,000; on Hwy. 125 about 25 miles north of Pinotepa Nacional) and its neighboring community San Pedro Amusgos are important centers of the Amusgo people. Approximately 20,000 Amusgos live in a roughly 30-mile-square region straddling the Guerrero-Oaxaca state border. Their homeland includes, besides Cacahuatepec and San Pedro Amusgos, Xochistlahuaca, Zacoalpán, and Tlacoachistlahuaca on the Guerrero side.

The Amusgo language is linguistically related to Mixtec, although it's unintelligible to Mixtec speakers. Before the conquest, the Amusgos were subject to the numerically superior Mixtec kingdoms until the Amusgos were conquered by the Aztecs in 1457, and later by the Spanish.

Now, most Amusgos live on as subsistence farmers, supplementing their diet with occasional fowl or small game. Amusgos are best known to the outside world for the lovely animal-, plant-, and human-motif *huipiles,* which Amusgo women

always seem to be hand-embroidering on their doorsteps.

Although **Cacahuatepec** enjoys a big market each Sunday, that doesn't diminish the importance of its big Easter weekend festival, the day of Todos Santos (All Saints), and Day of the Dead, 2 November, when, at the cemetery, people welcome their ancestors' return to rejoin the family.

San Pedro Amusgos celebrations are among the most popular regional fiestas. On 29 June, the day of San Pedro, people participate in religious processions, and costumed participants dressed as Moors and Christians, bulls, jaguars, and mules dance before crowds of men in traditional whites and women in beautiful heirloom *huipiles.* Later, on the first Sunday of October, folks crowd into town to enjoy the traditional processions, dances, and sweet treats of the fiesta of the Virgen de la Rosario (Virgin of the Rosary).

Even if you miss the festivals, San Pedro Amusgos is worth a visit to buy *huipiles* alone. Three or four shops sell them along the main street through town. Look for the sign of **Trajes Regionales Elia,** the little store run by Elia Guzmán, tel. 958/286-97. Besides dozens of beautiful embroidered garments, she stocks a few Amusgo books and offers friendly words of advice and local information.

EXCURSION SOUTH OF PINOTEPA

If you hanker for a little sea breeze and the murmur of the waves, spend a day or a week at **Playa Corralero,** about 18 miles (28 km) south

zapote

by a paved but potholed, finally sandy but smooth road. Get there by car or the passenger trucks (*camionetas*) that head south on the street one block west from the Hotel Carmona. Along the way, in the beginning, you'll pass rolling tropical forest country, partially tamed to corn and cattle.

About twelve miles (19 km) from Pinotepa, the road forks. The left, paved branch continues to Laguna Corralero village, a pleasant small town (pop. about 2,000) of fisherfolk on the tidal estuary-lagoon. Hikers could probably bargain with a boatman at the village to ferry them across the lagoon to the open ocean channel and beach (say "*Ramada Guelaguetza, por el mar*").

Otherwise, hikers should get off the truck at the fork and walk or hitchhike the right-fork road the additional six miles to the beach *ramadas*. Drivers should likewise turn right at the fork. Along the way, you pass through a thick prickly pear cactus mini-forest along the beach. Finally you arrive at the beachfront *ramada* restaurants beside a jetty and broad channel which a dredge keeps open for fishing boats.

The beach itself is of coarse to medium yellow-white sand, rather steep, with the consequent undertow. Waves, which don't appear good for surfing, break strongly and quickly close to shore. The same conditions, however, make the beach perfect for **surf fishing.** If you prefer solitude and don't mind a few cows for company, you can set up camp along the wide, grassy dune and camp most anywhere for four miles before the *ramadas*. (Caution: On the sand, use four-wheel drive with caution; if not, be very careful to avoid getting stuck—which might happen even with four-wheel drive anyway.)

On the other hand, if you prefer company, park or tent near the road's end *ramadas*. The *ramada* **Guelaguetza,** nearest the beach, run by the friendly López Herrera family, will provide you with plenty of economical fish dinners and *refrescos,* plus shade for your vehicle and/or tent.

ERIN DWYER

THE MIXTECA

The Mixteca, the homeland of the Mixtecs, Oaxaca's "People of the Clouds," spreads over an immense domain encompassing the state's entire northwest, stretching northward from the tropical Pacific Coast over the high, cool pine-tufted Sierra to the warm, dry "Land of the Sun" along Oaxaca's northern border. The Mixteca's vastness and diversity have led Oaxacans to visualize it as three distinct sub-regions: the Mixteca Alta, Mixteca Baja, and Mixteca de la Costa. These labels reflect the geographical realities of the Mixteca's *alta* (high) and *baja* (low) mountains and the tropical Pacific *costa* (coastal plain).

The Mixteca Alta comprises the Mixteca's highest, greenest country—the governmental districts of Nochixtlán, Teposcolula, Tlaxiaco, and Juxtlahuaca. The Mixteca Baja includes, on the other hand, the warm, dry districts of Coixtlahuaca, Huajuapan, Silacayoapan, and Juxtlahuaca along Oaxaca's northern frontier. The Mixteca de la Costa lies south of all this, encompassing the tropical coastal districts of Putla and Jamiltepec on Oaxaca's southwest border.

This chapter traces a counterclockwise circle route through the Mixteca, northwest from Oaxaca City. First, we arrive in Nochixtlán, scarcely an hour from Oaxaca City, and use it as a base for exploring the southern Mixteca Alta. Next the route continues north through country renowned for its exquisite and monumental Dominican churches, then on to the warm, sunny Mixteca Baja country around Huajuapan de León. There our journey curves through the scenic back door to the Mixteca Alta—the cool, verdant, roof of Oaxaca.

NORTHWEST FROM OAXACA CITY

NOCHIXTLÁN

Nochixtlán (noh-chees-TLAN, pop. 13,000), busy capital of the governmental district of Nochixtlán, is interesting mostly for its colorful market and services and as a jumping-off point for exploring the wonders of the idyllic mountain valley of Apoala and the remains of the ancient Mixtec cities at Tilantongo and Yucuita.

Sights

Nochixtlán town itself spreads out from its plaza, which is directly accessible from Hwy. 190, from the Oaxaca side by north-south street Calle Progreso and, from the adjacent, Tamazulapan side, by east-west Calle Porfirio Díaz. The streets intersect at the northwest corner of the central plaza. From there you can see the 19th-century twin-towered **Templo de La Asunción** rising on the plaza's opposite side. Adjacent, to the right of the church, the *presidencia municipal* spreads for a block along Calle Hidalgo. At the plaza's northeast side is the big market, which expands into a much larger *tianguis* (Aztec word for "awning") on Sunday, when native folks from all over northwest Oaxaca crowd in to peruse, haggle, and choose from a mountain of merchandise.

The major patronal **fiesta,** celebrating Santa María de La Asunción, climaxes around 15 August and includes *calendas* (religious processions), *marmotas* (giant dancing effigies), *mascaritas* (dancing men dressed as women), nearly continuous fireworks, a blastingly loud public dance, and a carnival of food, games, and rides that brightens the entire central plaza.

Accommodations and Food

Nearly everything you'll need is on or near the plaza except for the town's two recommendable hotels, the **Hotel Santillan,** on the highway's west (Tamazulapan) side half a block west of the Colón-Sur bus station, at Porfirio Díaz 88, Nochixtlán, Oaxaca 69600, tel./fax 952/203-51.

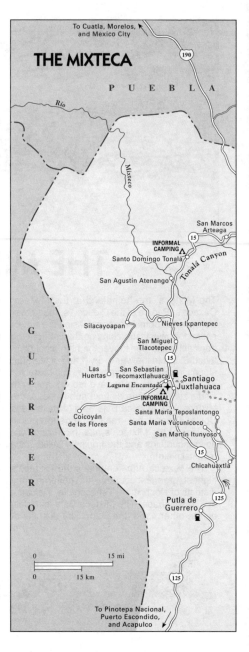

THE MIXTECA

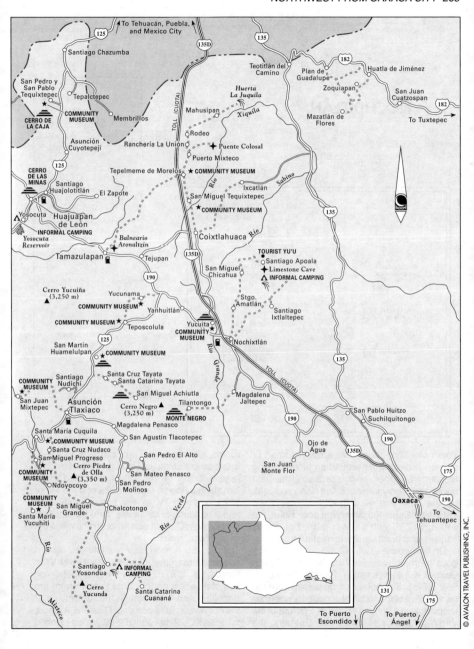

To Tehuacán, Puebla, and Mexico City

Santiago Chazumba

Teotitlán del Camino

Plan de Guadalupe

Huatla de Jiménez

Zoquiapan

San Juan Cuatzospan

San Pedro y San Pablo Tequixtepec

Tepalctepec

COMMUNITY MUSEUM

Membrillos

Mahusipan

Huerta La Juquila

Xiquila

Mazatlán de Flores

To Tuxtepec

CERRO DE LA CAJA

Asunción Cuyotepeji

Rancheria La Unión

Rodeo

Puente Colosal

Puerto Mixteco

CERRO DE LAS MINAS

Santiago Huajolotitlán

Tepelmeme de Morelos

El Zapote

COMMUNITY MUSEUM

San Miguel Tequixtepec

COMMUNITY MUSEUM

Ixcatlán

Río

Sabino

Yosocuta

INFORMAL CAMPING

Yosocuta Reservoir

Huajuapan de León

Balneario Atonaltzin

Coixtlahuaca

Río

Tamazulapan

Tejupan

TOURIST YU'U

Santiago Apoala

Limestone Cave

INFORMAL CAMPING

San Miguel Chicahua

Cerro Yucuiña (3,250 m)

Yucunama

COMMUNITY MUSEUM

Yanhuitlán

Stgo. Amatlán

Santiago Ixtlaltepec

COMMUNITY MUSEUM

Teposcolula

Yucuita

COMMUNITY MUSEUM

Nochixtlán

San Martín Huamelulpan

COMMUNITY MUSEUM

Río Grande

TOLL (CUOTA)

COMMUNITY MUSEUM

Santiago Nudichi

Santa Cruz Tayata

Santa Catarina Tayata

San Miguel Achiutla

San Pablo Huitzo

Suchilquitongo

COMMUNITY MUSEUM

San Juan Mixtepec

Asunción Tlaxiaco

Cerro Negro (3,250 m)

Tilantongo

MONTE NEGRO

Magdalena Jaltepec

Santa María Cuquila

COMMUNITY MUSEUM

Magdalena Penasco

San Agustín Tlacotepec

Ojo de Agua

Santa Cruz Nudaco

San Miguel Progreso

San Pedro El Alto

Cerro Piedra de Olla (3,350 m)

COMMUNITY MUSEUM

Ndoyocoyo

San Mateo Penasco

San Pedro Molinos

San Juan Monte Flor

Oaxaca

COMMUNITY MUSEUM

Santa María Yucuhiti

San Miguel Grande

Chalcotongo

Río Verde

To Tehuantepec

Río Mixteco

Santiago Yosondua

INFORMAL CAMPING

Cerro Yucunda

Santa Catarina Cuananá

To Puerto Escondido

To Puerto Ángel

© AVALON TRAVEL PUBLISHING, INC.

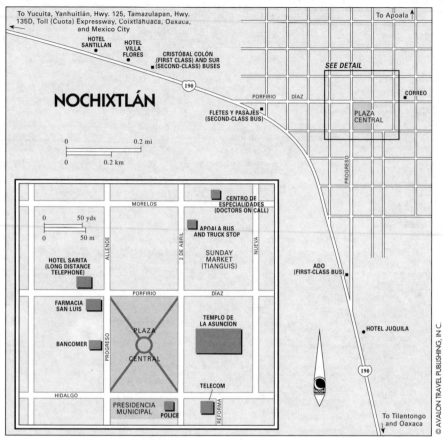

To Yucuita, Yanhuitlán, Hwy. 125, Tamazulapan, Hwy. 135D, Toll (Cuota) Expressway, Coixtlahuaca, Oaxaca, and Mexico City

To Apoala ↑

HOTEL SANTILLAN
HOTEL VILLA FLORES
CRISTÓBAL COLÓN (FIRST CLASS) AND SUR (SECOND-CLASS) BUSES

SEE DETAIL

NOCHIXTLÁN

190

PORFIRIO   DÍAZ

CORREO

FLETES Y PASAJES (SECOND-CLASS BUS)

PLAZA CENTRAL

0   0.2 mi
0   0.2 km

PROGRESO

ADO (FIRST-CLASS BUS)

CENTRO DE ESPECIALIDADES (DOCTORS ON CALL)

MORELOS

APOALA BUS AND TRUCK STOP

0   50 yds
0   50 m

SUNDAY MARKET (TIANGUIS)

ALLENDE

2 DE ABRIL

NUEVA

HOTEL SARITA (LONG DISTANCE TELEPHONE)

HOTEL JUQUILA

PORFIRIO   DÍAZ

FARMACIA SAN LUIS

BANCOMER

PROGRESO

PLAZA CENTRAL

TEMPLO DE LA ASUNCIÓN

190

HIDALGO

TELECOM

PRESIDENCIA MUNICIPAL   POLICE

REFORMA

To Tilantongo and Oaxaca

© AVALON TRAVEL PUBLISHING, IN C.

The motel-style rooms are arranged in an L-shaped two-story tier around an inner parking lot garden. Upper rooms, probably the best choice are plainly furnished, but clean and light. By the time you read this, they may have installed the planned swimming pool. Rates are $10 s, $17 d, with shower bath, hot water, parking, and good family-run restaurant.

On the opposite side of town, second choice goes to the new **Hotel Juquila**, at Carretera Oaxaca Km 1, Nochixtlán, Oaxaca 69600, tel. 952/205-81. The hotel's name comes from the owner's love of the Virgin of Juquila, for whom he keeps a candle burning in front of a picture of the Virgin on the hotel front desk. Upstairs, the rooms, although new, are sparely decorated, with bare-bulb fixtures. Perhaps by the time you read this the owner will have added more furnishings. Rooms rent for $22 s or d, no TV, or $27 s or d with TV, all with hot water showers and a restaurant downstairs. Find the hotel on the highway, Oaxaca side, about half a mile from the center of town.

If the above two hotels are full, you have a couple of marginal choices, the **Hotel Villa Flores,** tel. 952/202-58, by the Cristóbal Colón bus station few doors closer to town from the Santillan, and the **Hotel Sarita,** downtown at the northwest plaza corner of Díaz and Allende, tel. 952/200-22, fax 952/202-02. When I looked for a second time, the Sarita's rooms, most with baths, still needed a good scrubbing.

As for restaurants, the **Roma,** Morelos 34, tel. 952/203-14, gets three stars for food and service. Genteel owner Marcela Santiago Alvarado's short but carefully prepared selection of eggs, chicken, beef, pork, and Oaxacan specialties and the refined, air-conditioned atmosphere afford a relaxing respite from Nochixtlán's street hubbub. Find the Roma one block north (along Allende) and half a block west (on Morelos, north side) from the plaza's northwest corner.

Second choice goes to **Restaurant Claudia,** one of the better family-style eateries on Díaz, along the block just west of the plaza. It's open daily 8 A.M.–8 P.M. for *desayuno* (breakfast), *comida* (dinner), and *cena* (supper), when you can stay up and watch the late-night movie with the family owners.

Services

You can get nearly anything you want on or near the Nochixtlán plaza. Moving clockwise from the northwest corner, for economical *fonda* (fixed stall) food, fruits, vegetables, and groceries, go to the **market** on the plaza's north side. A block farther east along Díaz, north side, you'll find the *correo* (post office), open Mon.–Fri. 9 A.M.–3 P.M. Skip across the plaza to the south side of the church to *teleco-municaciones* (public telephone, money orders, and fax) at the corner of Hidalgo and Reforma, tel. 952/200-53. Next, find the **police station** *(preventiva)* at the west end of the *presidencia municipal,* corner of Hidalgo and Progreso. For money changing, go to **Bancomer,** open Mon.–Fri. 9 A.M.–3 P.M., tel. 952/201-54, smack in the middle of the plaza's west side. A few doors farther, go to **Farmacia San Luis,** tel./fax 952/204-84, at the plaza's northwest corner, across Díaz from the Hotel Sarita, where you can use the **long-distance telephone** and fax, 952/202-02.

A bit farther afield, you'll find a good **bakery,** on Díaz, a block and a half west of the plaza, and a travel agent, **Viajes Gran Via,** tel. 952/204-14, at Díaz 62, across the street. For **doctors,** go to the Centro de Especialidades, with general practitioners, a pediatrician, gynecologist, and internist on call, at Morelos 18 (a block north of

the plaza's and a block and a half east of the plaza's northwest corner), tel. 952/204-94.

Getting There and Away

At least four long-distance bus lines serve Nochixtlán. First-class **Cristóbal Colón** and **Sur,** operating jointly out of their west-side station on Díaz (Hwy. 190), tel. 952/203-87, provide broad service southeast with Oaxaca, northwest with the Mixteca Baja (Tamazulapan, Coixtlahuaca, Huajuapan), continuing to Puebla and Mexico City, and west with the Mixteca Alta and the coast (Teposcolula, Tlaxiaco, Juxtlahuaca, Putla, and Pinotepa Nacional) and intermediate points.

Fletes y Pasajes, on Díaz, one block east of the highway A, tel. 952/205-85, covers approximately the same destinations, but with both first- and second-class service. **Autobuses del Oriente** (ADO), operating out of a Oaxaca-side station, about half a mile from the town center, at the corner of Hwy. 190 and Calle Progreso, provides first-class connections southeast with Oaxaca and northwest with Puebla, Veracruz, and Mexico City.

Drivers can cover the 50 miles (80 km) from Oaxaca in an easy hour via the *cuota autopista* (toll expressway). If you want to save the approximately \$6 car toll (big RVs and trailers more), figure about two hours via the winding old Hwy. 190 *libre* route.

FORGOTTEN KINGDOMS

Yucuita

Yucuita (pop. 500) was once far more important than it is today. It started as a village around 1400 B.C., then grew into a town of 3,000 inhabitants around 200 B.C., about the same time that early Monte Albán was flourishing. Later, by A.D. 200, it lost population and became a center secondary to Yucuñudahui, several miles north.

The claim to fame of drowsy, present-day Yucuita, about five miles (eight km) northwest of Nochixtlán, is that it sits atop the old Yucuita, one of the Mixteca's largest and most important archaeological zones. City officials received donations of so many artifacts that they had to organize a small **community museum** to hold them. Kindly museum keeper Jesús Ramírez, who lives just uphill from the town-plaza museum, offers, when possible, to open it up for any interested visitor. (If he can't open the museum on a given day, he'll most likely try to do it the next.)

Inside, Jesús points out (in Spanish) interesting aspects of the collection (mostly pottery): 2,000-year-old turkey eggs, human-effigy censers and bowls, *manos* and *metates,* just like those used today, and a platoon of small, toy-like figurines. The most intriguing piece in the museum is a carved stone relief of a seated figure, appearing Olmec-influenced, holding what looks like a bunch of flowers. Maybe this is related to the meaning of Yucuita, which in Mixtec means "Hill of Flowers."

Get started exploring the **Yucuita archaeological zone** by climbing the reconstructed steps (fast becoming part of the ruins themselves) next to the paved through-town highway, about a mile south of the town plaza. If you're slim and

The adventurous can enter Yucuita Archaeological Zone via tunnel.

adventurous, you can enter the site via a dry **tunnel** that runs about a hundred feet from the entrance steps to a big opening and then continues another hundred feet to a final opening, where you can lift yourself out. (Warning: Carry a flashlight to spot pesties, such as scorpions and rattlesnakes, in time to back out. If this scares you, don't try the tunnel.)

Aboveground, what you mostly see is an expansive bean field littered with the stones from the walls and foundations of ancient Yucuita. Pottery shards are common—the colored ones especially stand out. A couple hundred feet to the south of the tunnel opening, inspect the partly reconstructed temple mound with an unfinished stairway and four belowground chambers. Archaeologists say that the entire site, elongated along a north-south axis, is riddled with buried structures, whose remains extend beyond the high hill (the original Hill of Flowers) to the north.

Getting There: Reach Yucuita via minibus from Calle Porfirio Díaz, in front of the Nochixtlán market, or on Hwy. 190, northwest side of town. Drivers, head northwest on Hwy. 190 from Nochixtlán. Continue straight ahead along the old highway, *not* the *cuota* expressway, toward Huajuapan. Pass the gas station and continue for about two miles until you'll see a signed right turnoff to Yucuita. Southbound drivers, watch for the signed left turnoff to Yucuita before Nochixtlán. If you reach the Pemex *gasolinera,* before the *cuota* toll expressway, you have gone too far. Turn around and look for the signed Yucuita right turnoff.

Tilantongo and Monte Negro Archaeological Zones

The Tilantongo archaeological zone is the town itself (pop. 4,000), which sits smack on top of storied ancient Tilantongo. In the old days, around A.D. 1050, Tilantongo was the virtual capital of the Mixteca, ruled by the ruthless but renowned Mixtec king **8-Deer of the Tiger Claws.** Carved stones built into the Tilantongo town church wall attest to Tilantongo's former glory.

The town government commissioned a mural, now on the wall inside the present *presidencia municipal,* which dramatically portrays the legendary Mixtec Flechador del Sol (Bowman of the Sun) and copies of pages from the Codex Nutall, a preconquest document in blazing color that records glorious events in Mixtec preconquest history. See if you can identify 8-Deer on one of the pages reproduced in the mural.

At least as important and more rewarding to explore is the much older Monte Negro archaeological zone atop the towering, oak-studded **Black Mountain** (Monte Negro) visible high above Tilantongo. A rough road, difficult for passenger cars but easier for high-clearance trucks or jeep-like vehicles, allows access to the top in about an hour. If you have no wheels, you may be able to get a taxi driver to take you up there. If not, perhaps someone with a truck might accept the job. Fit hikers should allow about three hours for the uphill climb, two hours for lunch and exploring the site, and two hours for the return. Take plenty of water, wear a hat and strong shoes, and use a good sunscreen. You must obtain permission from authorities at the *presidencia,* who require that a local guide (whom they will furnish) accompany you.

Monte Negro flourished about the same time as early Monte Albán, from about 500 to 0 B.C. The 150-acre hilltop zone is replete with ruined columned temples, raised residences of the elite (complete with inner patios), ceremonial plazas, and a ball court, all aligned along a single avenue. Monte Negro's long, north-south orientation is reminiscent of Monte Albán, although its structures are not as grand. For reasons unknown, Monte Negro, as Monte Albán, was abandoned during the Late Urban Stage, around A.D. 800. All that remains are the old city's stone remnants, while its descendants still husband the land you see in all directions from the breezy hilltop. Some of what surrounds you is thick oak forest; other parts are fertile, terraced corn and bean fields, while much, in mute testimony to the passage of time, is tragically eroded.

Getting There: Bus passengers can go by the white Tilantongo-Nochixtlán bus, which makes the trip about three times a day from Calle Porfirio Díaz, in front of the Nochixtlán market. Drivers, follow Hwy. 190 (old *libre* route) to the Jaltepec turnoff about eight miles (13 km) southeast (Oaxaca direction) from Nochixtlán. Mark your odometer at the turnoff. The road is paved to the Jaltepec plaza (5.8 miles, 9.3 km), where you turn right. The road is dirt and gravel,

often rough, after that. Follow the signs. Turn left at a church (11 miles, 18 km) and right after a bridge (15.2 miles, 24.5 km). You'll pull up to Tilantongo plaza after 18 miles (29 km) and about an hour of steady, bumpy driving.

OAXACA'S SHANGRI-LA: THE VALE OF APOALA

It's hard to describe the valley of Apoala, tucked in the mountains north of Nochixtlán, with anything less than superlatives. A fertile, terraced, green vale nestles beneath towering cliffs far from the noise, smoke, and clutter of city life. Apoala is no less than a Oaxacan Shangri-La—a farming community replete with charming country sights and sounds: log-cabin houses, men plowing the field with oxen, women sitting and chatting as they weave palm-leaf sombreros, dogs barking, and burros braying faintly in the warm dusk. The spring-fed river assures good crops; people, consequently, are relatively well off and content to remain on the land. They have few cars, almost no TVs, and absolutely no telephones.

What's more, the local folks are ready for visitors. I arrived at a string stretched curiously across the narrow gravel entrance road, where I realized that there must be a good reason for this, so I stopped instead of just barging in. The explanation is that the local folks want to tell you about the wonders of their sylvan valley. The entrance fee is about $5 per group, including guide, who is an absolute "must."

Exploring Apoala

The tour, which takes about two hours, begins at the **Cave of Serpent,** translated from the local Mixtec dialect, which all townsfolk speak. Just before the cave, you pass a crystalline spring welling up from the base of a towering cliff. This spring supplies a large part of the Apoala River flow, which ripples and meanders down the valley and which folks use to keep their fields green. Another major part of its flow wells up from beneath a huge rock across the creek, below the cave entrance.

Entering the cave, be careful not to bump your head as you descend the tight, downhill entrance hollow. Immediately you see why your guide is so important. He carries a large battery and light to illuminate the way. In the first of the cave's two galleries, bats flutter overhead as your guide reveals various stalactites and then flashes on the subterranean river gurgling from an underground dark lagoon, unknown in extent. What *is* known, however, is that the water from the lagoon arrives at the springs at Tamazulapan, more than 30 miles (50 km) away. Someone long ago dropped some oranges into the cave lagoon in Apoala, and they bobbed to the surface later in Tamazulapan.

In the other cave gallery (careful, the access is steep and slippery), the light focuses on a towering stalagmite capped by a bishop's visage, complete with clerical miter and long beard. On the other side you see a stalactite shaped exactly like a human leg.

After the cave, you'll probably head up-valley between a pair of cliffs that tower vertically at least 500 feet. If you speak Spanish or have someone to interpret, be sure to ask the guide to explain the names and uses of **medicinal plants** *(plantas medicinales)* along the path. Every plant, even the notorious *mala mujer* (bad woman), which your guide can point out, seems to have some use.

Soon, above and to your left, you'll see the towering, yellowish 2,000-foot rampart, **La Peña Donde Murió El Aguila con Dos Cabezas** (The Rock Where the Eagle with Two Heads Died). No kidding. It seems that, once upon a time, a huge eagle that actually had two heads lived in one of the many caves in the rock face. The problem was, it was killing too many calves, so one day one of the villagers shot it. The Eagle with Two Heads, however, lives on in the imaginations of Apoalans.

Finally, after about 20 minutes of walking and wondering at the natural monuments towering around you, the climax arrives: a narrow, river-cut breach in the canyon, like some antediluvian giant had cut a thin slice through a mountain of butter. The slice remains, between a pair of vertical rock walls, called **Las Dos Peñas Colosales** (The Two Colossal Rocks).

The grand finale, down-valley about a mile, is the waterfall **Cola del Serpiente** (The Serpent's Tail). You walk down a steep forested trail that looks out on a gorgeous mountain and valley panorama. At the bottom, the Apoala River,

having already tumbled hundreds of feet, pausing for spells in several pools, finally plummeting nearly 300 feet (90 m) in a graceful arc to an emerald green pool surrounded by a misty, natural stone amphitheater.

Accommodations and Food

Camping, by self-contained RV or tent, would be superb here. The community has set aside a choice, grassy riverside spot across the river from the cave at the upper end of town, heavenly for a few days of camping. The tariff, payable at the tourist Yu'u (see below) is about $3 per day. Clear, pristine spring water, perfect for drinking, wells up at the foot of the cliff at road's end nearby. Wilderness campers can choose among more isolated spots upstream, ripe for swimming and wildlife viewing. (Always swim with a bathing suit, however; skinny-dipping is locally disapproved.)

Noncampers shouldn't miss staying in Apoala's superb **Tourist Yu'u,** the place where you first met your guide. This Yu'u is a model of Oaxaca's improved second-generation tourist accommodation. Besides three very clean, spacious, and comfortable modern-standard rooms with either one or two double beds, it features a light, spacious solarium-sitting room-snack café, serving water, beer, sodas, and light breakfast, lunch, and early supper. Guests can also eat their own food there. If you do, bring everything with you, as Apoala has no well-stocked stores. The lodging price, about $5 a person in the middle of paradise, is hard to beat. Reservations are recommended; contact the state-federal tourist information office in Oaxaca City, 607 Independencia, Oaxaca, Oaxaca 68000, tel. 9/516-4828, fax 9/609-84, email: turinfo@oaxaca.gob.mx.

Guide Service

If you'd like a guide for more local exploring, contact very knowledgeable and personable **Leopoldo Guzman Alvarado,** who, if he can't guide you himself, will find someone who can.

Getting There

Like Shangri-La, Apoala isn't easy to get to. Bus passengers have it easiest. The Apoala community provides a white Apoala-marked minibus, which leaves from Calle 2 de Abril near the corner of Morelos (a block north of the plaza's northeast corner), five days a week (Friday, Saturday, Sunday, Monday, and Wednesday) at around 3 P.M., arriving in Apoala at around 5 P.M. It departs Apoala for Nochixtlán on the same days at around 8 A.M. Check locally for the Apoala bus schedule with stores or bus or truck drivers parked along 2 de Abril. Otherwise, passenger trucks make the same trip hourly until about 5 P.M. from the same spot.

For drivers, the 26-mile rough dirt and gravel road is a challenge, especially in an ordinary passenger car. The route heads north from downtown Nochixtlán; turn left from Calle Porfirio Díaz (the street that runs past the north side of the plaza) two blocks past the market. Follow the road signs all the way.

Trucks, vans, and VW Beetles carry nearly all the traffic to Apoala, although a careful driver in an ordinary car can usually complete the trip with minimal damage. The ideal vehicle, of course, would be a high-clearance truck or sport-utility vehicle, such as a Jeep, with strong tires. Four-wheel drive, not necessary under dry conditions, would be mandatory in heavy rain. Lighter, maneuverable campers could make it; very large rigs probably not, because of the narrow, steep, and winding descent into Apoala Canyon.

DOMINICAN ROUTE SOUTH

Of the four missionary orders—Franciscans, Jesuits, Augustinians, and Dominicans—who established an important presence in New Spain, the Dominicans were dominant in Oaxaca. Hernán Cortés had barely begun to resurrect Mexico City from the rubble of old Tenochtitlán when a stream of Dominican padres was heading southeast to Oaxaca. For the next three centuries, until republican reforms forced many of them from Mexico during the latter 1800s, the padres earnestly pursued the spiritual thrust of Spain's two-pronged "God and Gold" mission in the New World. The Dominicans converted, educated, protected, and advocated for Oaxaca's native peoples, often in conflict with brutal and greedy Spanish soldiers and colonists.

The Dominicans' legacy remains vibrant to this day. More than 90 percent of Oaxacans consider themselves Catholics, and lovely old Dominican ex-convent/churches decorate the Oaxacan countryside. Some of these outstanding venerable monuments—notably at Yanhuitlán, Teposcolula, and Coixtlahuaca—grace the Mixteca Alta, not far from the modern town of Tamazulapan, making it a natural base for extended exploration of what has become known as Oaxaca's Dominican route. The Dominican route's more isolated northern section—north and west of Tamazulapan—is usually explored via Coixtlahuaca, from Nochixtlán and Oaxaca City (for details, see the Dominican Route North section).

TAMAZULAPAN AND VICINITY

Tamazulapan (tah-mah-soo-LAH-pahn, pop. about 20,000), partly by virtue of its crossroads position on the National Highway 190, has outgrown its more venerable, but isolated, neighbor towns and become the major service and business center for the Teposcolula district. You know you're in Tamazulapan immediately as you pass its town plaza, which proudly displays a semicircular columned monument right by the highway in honor of Benito Juárez, "Benemérito de las Américas." Upon reflection, nothing seems more appropriate directly on the Pan-American Highway.

Sights
As you stand on the edge of the highway (locally known as Carretera Cristóbal Colón) looking at the Benito Juárez monument, you'll be facing approximately north. The noble, portaled *presidencia municipal* will appear straight ahead, behind the square, the **Plaza Constitución.** To your right beyond the storefronts along plaza-front Calle Independencia rise the ruddy cupolas of the eighteenth-century Dominican **Templo de la Natividad.** Bordering the plaza on your left are the stores and services along Calle Juárez.

Step into the cool calm of the venerable Dominican church which, although large and harmoniously decorated, is not architecturally comparable to the masterpieces at Coixtlahuaca, Yanhuitlán, and Teposcolula. What is unique, however, are the two images on the altar, both brightly illuminated. The bottom figure is an unusual reclining figure of Jesus in what appears to be a transparent casket. This figure is locally paraded and celebrated, along with food, games, dancing, and a basketball tournament, in a festival culminating on 3 May, **El Día de la Cruz.**

Above the figure of Jesus is the petite town patron, **La Virgen de la Natividad** (The Virgin of the Nativity), whom townsfolk celebrate in a fiesta culminating on 8 September. As you retrace your steps, exiting through the church garden, you pass the old Dominican convent on the left, in a state of advanced decay.

Sights Nearby

Tamazulapan townsfolk love their **Balneario Atonaltzin.** You'll see why if you drive, taxi, or walk the 1.5 mile (2.5 km) north along the road to Tepelmeme (plaza-front Calle Independencia). Soon after a bridge, you'll see the *balneario* on the right. This spot would be a merely typical Sunday family bathing resort if it were not for its crystalline, naturally disinfected sulfurous springs. The waters gurgle up, cool and clear, from a pair of sources in the rocky cliff behind the Olympic double-size pool—a lap swimmer's delight (except on Sundays and holidays, when it's filled with frolicking families). It's open daily 9 A.M.–6 P.M., admission about $1. Besides the big main pool, there are a pair of kiddy pools, a

local-style restaurant, volleyball, dressing areas, and a few picnic tables.

Two lesser known but nevertheless interesting spots are the nearby ***ojo de agua*** swimming hole and the **Xatachio archaeological zone.** The *ojo de agua* (literally, eye of water), a general term for a natural spring or source of water, is about 100 yards back from the *balneario* toward town, on the right, below the creek bridge. Step toward the ruined building on the right, and you'll see the creek cascading into a big blue pool. Before the Balneario Atonaltzin was built, this was a popular swimming hole. Today, because the water, although invitingly blue, is probably much less than pure, it's mostly used by women for washing clothes. Although the tall, steep riverbank near the bridge is nonnegotiable, you can get down to the water via a path to the right around the ruined building, through the brush, up some stone steps, and down again to the creek.

The unexcavated Xatachio (shah-TAH-cheeoh) archaeological zone is accessible via the dirt side road on the left just past the Balneario Atonaltzin. You'll first spot the zone as a brush-covered hill, about half a mile away on the left. **Note:** Do not try to explore the site on your own, however. The site lies on communal land, and people are rightly suspicious of possible artifact looters. Go to the *presidencia municipal* on the plaza and ask for permission (preferably through a local spokesperson, such as the owner or manager of your hotel); offer to pay someone (approximately $10) to act as a guide for a couple of hours. Any artifacts you

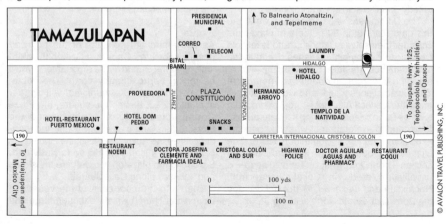

might stumble upon are legally the joint property of the INAH (National Institute of Archaeology and History) and the local community.

Tejupan

If you have time, stop for a few minutes for a look inside the relatively humble, but nevertheless worthy, Dominican church and ex-convent at Tejupan, in the Tamazulapan valley north of Yanhuitlán. Tejupan is a sleepy farming town, basking in its past glory, visibly represented by its noble, multiportaled *palacio municipal* and the distinguished 17th-century Dominican **Templo y Exconvento de Santiago Apóstol,** across the street. Memorable inside the church is the pretty, pink transept chapel, left side, dedicated to the Virgin of Guadalupe. The ex-convent section, in severe need of repair, stands to the right of the church front entrance.

Get to Tejupan by bus or car via the signed side road off Hwy. 190 about seven miles (11 km) southeast of Tamazulapan, or about eight miles (13 km) northwest of the Hwy. 190–Hwy. 125 junction northwest of Yanhuitlán.

Accommodations

Of Tamazulapan's four basic but acceptable hotels, most prominent is the four-story **Hotel Dom Pedro,** a few doors north of the plaza at Cristóbal Colón 24, Tamazulapan, Oaxaca 70280, tel./fax 953/300-19. The 25 plain but clean upstairs rooms (no elevator) run about $11 s or d, with toilets and hot water showers, basic restaurant downstairs, and parking, but no TV or phones. Credit cards are not accepted.

Although **Hotel Puerto Mexico** a few doors farther north at Cristóbal Colón 12, Tamazulapan, Oaxaca 70280, tel. 953/300-44, appears humdrum from the outside, guests enjoy an inviting tropical patio blooming with green banana trees. Rooms are clean and carpeted but have the almost universal Mexican small-town bare bulb hanging from the middle of the ceiling. Bring your own clip-on lampshade. Rates are about $13 s, $16 d, $23 t, with hot water showers, parking, and TV, but no phones. Credit cards not accepted.

With approximately the same room price and basic amenities as the Dom Pedro is the newish high-rise **Hotel Gilda** (HEEL-dah), 16 Madero, Tamazulapan, Oaxaca 70280, tel. 953/301-53.

Find it about two blocks along the street running uphill across the highway from the north end of the plaza.

The only hotel in town with any old-Mexico charm is the downscale **Hotel Hidalgo,** Hidalgo 7, Tamazulapan, Oaxaca 70280, tel. 953/300-91. It offers a quiet, off-highway location one block east along the street that runs in front of the *presidencia municipal.* The 12 basic but clean rooms around a parking patio rent for about $5 s, $9 d, with bath.

Food

You can buy groceries and some fruits and vegetables at one of the plaza-front *abarroterías,* such as **Proveedora** (Supplier) de Abarrotes, tel. 953/300-89, Juárez 4, west side, or **Hermanos Arroyo,** Independencia 5, tel. 953/302-30, on the plaza's opposite side.

For inexpensive prepared food, try the nighttime taco stands or one of the several sit-down snack bars along the highway-front blocks across the highway from the plaza.

As for restaurants, although the Hotels Dom Pedro and Puerto Mexico offer breakfast, lunch, and dinner, you'll do better by walking a few steps to **Restaurant Noemi,** Cristóbal Colón 12, tel. 953/300-47, between the two hotels. The grandmotherly owners put out Mexican home-style breakfasts, lunches, and suppers, including savory *café de la olla* (pot-brewed coffee), at very reasonable prices.

You'll probably do nearly as well at the clean, highway-front **Restaurant Coqui** (KOH-kee), Cristóbal Colón 57, tel. 953/301-09, open daily 7 A.M.–10 P.M., a block and a half east from the plaza. Although she'll cook nearly anything you want, the friendly owner is best at Oaxacan country delicacies, such as *chiles rellenos, enchiladas tasajos* (beef enchiladas), and Oaxacan tamales, all covered with plenty of *mole.*

Services

Tamazulapan provides a number of basic services along the highway-front blocks on or near the plaza. The town **bank,** Bital, with ATM, in the *presidencia municipal* portal is open Mon.–Fri. 8 A.M.–7 P.M., Sat. 8 A.M.–3 P.M., near the plaza's northwest corner. The *correo* (post office) is next door east, open Mon.–Fri. 9 A.M.–1 P.M. and 3–6 P.M. A few doors east of the post office, **Telecom** offers public telephone, money order, and fax, 953/301-13; hours are Mon.–Fri. 9 A.M.–3:30 P.M. For after-hour long-distance calls, go to the Hotel Dom Pedro desk, on the highway.

Two doctors offer consultations and medicines at their highway-front pharmacies. Choose either **Dr. Josefina Clemente,** at her Farmacia Ideal, on the highway directly opposite the plaza, or **Dr. Aguilar Aguas,** a block and a half east at Cristóbal Colón 43, consultation hours Mon.–Fri. 2–8 P.M., Sat. 8 A.M.–2 P.M. and 4–8 P.M., tel. 953/300-84.

For a **police** emergency, call 953/302-13 or go to the Delegación de Transito highway police, on duty 24 hours, half a block east and across the highway from the plaza.

Getting There and Away

Bus lines **Cristóbal Colón** and **Sur** operate jointly out of their highway-front station, tel. 953/301-16, across from the plaza. Their buses connect southeast with Oaxaca via Nochixtlán, west with Coixtlahuaca, northwest via Huajuapan with Puebla and Mexico City, and southwest with Teposcolula and Tlaxiaco, where you can transfer to a bus headed for Pinotepa Nacional on the Pacific Coast.

For drivers, via Hwy. 190, Tamazulapan is approximately 84 miles (133 km) or two hours northwest of Oaxaca, and 25 miles (41 km) or 45 minutes southeast of Huajuapan. By paved secondary road via Tejupan, Tamazulapan is 22 miles (34 km) or 45 minutes west of Coixtlahuaca; via paved Hwy. 190–Hwy. 125, it is 22 miles (36 km) or 45 minutes north of Teposcolula.

TEPOSCOLULA

Although smaller in population than Tamazulapan, Teposcolula (pop. 5,000) continues to outrank it as district capital, a distinction it gained back in 1740. Its history, however, reaches back much farther. When the Spanish arrived in the 1520s, they found well-established Mixtec towns on the hillsides above a beautiful lake-filled valley. They drained the lake for farmland and moved the population down to Teposcolula's present location. Abiding by common practice, the Spanish kept the Mixtec name, Teposcolula (Place Surrounded by Springs), tacking on the Catholic patronal title San Pedro y San Pablo. This produced a name so long that practically no one refers to the official San Pedro y San Pablo Teposcolula. People, however, still remember the old preconquest settlements on the hillsides. The old palace and temple foundations still stand, at El Fortín (The Fort) on the uphill slope behind the town and Pueblo Viejo (Old Town) on the pine-clad hilltop across the valley.

Get yourself oriented by standing (or imagining you're standing) on the sidewalk on the through-town highway, facing the tree-shaded town plaza. North will be straight ahead, toward the cartoon-bright, repainted *presidencia municipal* on the far side of the plaza. The main streets are 20 de Noviembre (the highway), Madero (along the plaza's left, west side), and Iturbide (along the plaza's right, east side). Diagonally on your left stands the renowned church and ex-convent Templo y Exconvento de San Pedro y San Pablo.

Templo y Exconvento de San Pedro y San Pablo

Most visitors head right over to the old 1538 Dominican church and ex-convent, one of Oaxaca's most important, not only for its historical significance, but also for its monumental architecture, much of which you can view from the exterior by walking around to church's back (west) side. Here rises the famous recently restored **Capilla Abierta** (Open Chapel), with massive, soaring arches and gigantic buttresses. Visitors often wonder why such a huge outdoor chapel was needed right next to an equally massive indoor church. The adjacent grassy expanse provides the reason. It's the **atrium,** the extension of the outdoor chapel, the largest in Mexico, where the Dominican builders imagined 10,000 native faithful (who were not allowed inside) gathering for mass. Although their vision was fulfilled for a span of perhaps a generation after the conquest, the native Mixtec population collapsed by 1600, leaving the huge expanse, equal to three football fields, forever empty.

(Note: The Teposcolula church was seriously damaged by the 1999 earthquake; by the time you read this, it may have been restored to the glory that I originally described): Walk inside the

Teposcolula's famous Templo y Exconvento de San Pedro y San Pablo

church and you'll see the original towering gilded **retablo,** which was removed from behind the altar and placed on the left side of the nave. Straight ahead, replacing it in the apse, behind the altar, rises a cheerier, simpler collection of saints and angels, surrounding Teposcolula's diminutive god-hero, the **Señor de Vidrieras** (Lord of Glass), above the altar. Local people celebrate him in a big eight-day festival climaxing on the first Friday of Lent. Events include traffic-stopping processions, pilgrimages, a flower parade, plenty of fireworks, crowning of a queen, floats, bull-roping and riding, and a big community dance.

Find the side door to the **ex-convent** (open daily 10 A.M.–6 P.M.) on the right of the nave; it serves mostly as a museum of paintings by noted 16th-century artists Andrés de la Concha and Simón Pereyns. As you walk, see if you can recognize the functions—refectory (dining), kitchen, chapel, cloister, monks' cells (upstairs)—of the various rooms that you pass by or through. (See special topic, Building Churches in the chapter Around the Valley of Oaxaca.)

During your visit, be sure to notice one fresh, very recognizable modern or restored painting of Jesus with wounds, at the right hand of a very youthful God the Father, with the Holy Spirit (in the form of a radiant dove) above them. In the middle of the dining hall (refectory) notice the interesting painting of St. Michael the Arcangel, dangling a fish. Also, around the cloister, note the paintings that depict the baptism, school days, mission, and dreams of Santo Domingo.

Community Museum and the House of the Chiefess
In the lot across the street from the church stands the Teposcolula **Museum and Cultural Center.** Volunteers display a dusty collection of odds and ends, including dozens of charming little clay animal, human, and divine figurines. Another room contains an intriguing assortment of local carpentry and wood sculpture, including a uniquely inventive, nude female *Flechadora del Sol* (Archer of the Sun), a name given by her creator, personable local sculptor and museum president Manuel Ramírez Pérez.

If the museum happens to be closed, ask at the *larga distancia* telephone office, on the plaza's northeast corner, for Señor Ramírez Pérez (Spanish only) or his friend, equally friendly Señor Amancio Odriozola. If possible, they'll open the museum for you and also they can suggest guides to lead you to the local archaeological sites, **El Fortín** and **Pueblo Viejo**. Note: Don't try to go to these sites without permission from the museum, because local folks are rightly suspicious of strangers poking around their archaeological zones.

A close-in site that you can visit without permission is the **Casa de la Cacica** (kah-SEE-kah, House of the Chiefess). Step west about three blocks, along the street heading due west from the middle of the church's huge grassy atrium. The street ends at a school, and on the right is the Casa de la Cacica.

The building is unique, for it is one of the few remaining stone structures built by the Spanish specifically for indigenous nobles. The Spaniards' motivation was probably to concentrate and thus more easily control the local Mixtec population, who were living in dispersed hillside settlements when the Spanish arrived. They built a house and evidently persuaded the local *cacica* to live there, hoping that her people would follow her.

Step inside and you'll see that although the building is roofless, its relatively good condition makes it a prime candidate for restoration. Inside on the right, notice the upper-level *tapanco* (grain-storage room) floored with ancient wooden beams. In an opposite left-side corner, see the small "escape" door.

Practicalities

Teposcolula's first hotel (at least in recent times), the **Hotel Juvi,** Teposcolula, Oaxaca 69500, tel. 951/820-64, now makes an overnight stay possible. When I looked it over, its layout was unique—12 rooms around a parking courtyard containing the ancient, crumbling family homestead. It will be a pity, but by the time you arrive, they may have torn down the old house.

Anyway, children of the original ancestors have built a brand-new, sparely furnished (but clean) lodging, with bare, correctly country Mexican fluorescent bulbs to go with the shiny new bathroom fixtures.

You can buy basic food supplies at plaza-front groceries or treat yourself to a hearty afternoon *comida* at the town's good **Restaurant Eunice,** open daily 8 A.M.–8 P.M. on a block behind the east side of the presidencia municipal. If, however, you're sick, consult the **doctor** in his **Farmacia Nelly** on the plaza-front east side, by the highway. To mail a letter, make a phone call, or use a fax, go to the **correo** or **telégrafo,** which stand side by side on Madero, the half a block north of the plaza's northwest corner. After-hours, go to the *larga distancia* (long-distance telephone) office at the plaza's northeast corner.

Bus transportation to/from Teposcolula is easy and frequent. Bus passengers arrive at and depart from the bus station (Autobuses Sur, Cristóbal Colón, and Fletes y Pasajes) on Hwy. 125, half a block east from the plaza. Buses connect southeast with Oaxaca, north with Tamazulapan, Huajuapan, and Mexico City, and south with Tlaxiaco and the Pacific Coast.

For drivers, Hwy. 125 runs right past Teposcolula's town plaza, about eight miles (13 km) southwest of its junction with the Oaxaca-Mexico City Hwy. 190. Using the Nochixtlán *cuota* (toll) expressway, drivers should allow around two hours to safely cover the approximately 78-mile (125-km) Oaxaca-Teposcolula distance; add at least another hour if going by the old *libre* route. From Tamazulapan in the north, allow about 45 minutes for the 22 miles (36 km) via Hwy. 190–Hwy. 125 and about an hour for the 29 miles (47 kilometers) along Hwy. 125 from Tlaxiaco in the south.

YUCUNAMA

Teposcolula's petite neighbor, Yucunama (pop. 600), is attractive partly *because* of its small size. Imagine taking a seat on a stone bench one bright, blue summer morning in Yucunama's flower-decorated town plaza. Birds flit in the bushes and perch, singing, in the trees. Now and then someone crosses the square and returns your *"Buenos dias."* You admire the proud, whitewashed bandstand at the plaza center; behind it rises the old church facade, patriotically decorated like a birthday cake in red, white, and green. From the plaza, cobbled streets pass rustic stone houses and continue downhill to verdant fields which, in the distance, give way to lush oak and pine-tufted woodlands.

Although it sounds too good to be true, it is. Yucunama's beauty is probably one reason that Mixtec people have been living there for at least 4,000 years. Its name, which means "Hill of Soap," perhaps reflects the town's spic-and-span plaza, clean-swept streets, and newly painted public buildings. It's a pure Mixtec town, for although Yucunama is part of the Teposcolula district, Spanish settlers never lived there. In fact, in 1585 the all-Mixtec townsfolk declared themselves an independent republic. Nothing came of that, but Yucunama's people nevertheless retain their independent spirit.

Sights

Make the community museum, **Bee Nu'u** (House of the People), on the plaza opposite the dignified, porticoed *presidencia municipal,* your first stop. If it's not open, walk across to the *presidencia municipal* and ask if someone might open it. Say (or show them) this: *"¿Puede alguién mostrar el museo para nosotros?"* ("Can someone show us the museum?") If you're lucky, you'll get introduced to Maestro Antonio Martínez Sánchez, the museum's guiding light.

He articulately explains (in Spanish) the museum's several very interesting exhibits. These include the original of the *Lienzo Yucunama,* an *amate* (wild fig bark paper) document from the 1300s that details the 35 tribute payments of a Yucunama Mixtec noblewoman with the name-date 5-Eagle, and her first and second husbands, 12-Flower and 10-Eagle, to her father, who lived in a nearby town. In the cabinet below the *lienzo* stands a copy of the famous **Codex Nutall** (folded like an accordion), which details, in full color, the exploits of the renowned Mixtec lord 8-Deer. Maestro Antonio will provide some details (including odysseys to Coatzacoalcos on the Gulf Coast, and perhaps as far as Panama) of 8-Deer's adventures. If you don't understand Spanish, Maestro Antonio (whose many talents include teaching and leading local dance groups) is worth your bringing a friend to translate for you.

Another fascinating exhibit displays the complete remains of a robust 70-year-old noblewoman (notice her very husky leg bones) and the trove of goods recovered from her grave, one of a score of burials retrieved by archaeologists locally.

Yucunama's richness as an archaeological zone is further evidenced by the two 1996 INAH (National Institute of Archaeology and History) survey maps of the buried remains of a pair of classic period (300 B.C.–A.D. 300) towns nearby. If you're strongly interested, ask and you may be able to get permission and a guide. Expect to pay $20 for a full-day guided trip; transportation is extra.

On the other hand, you can step outside the museum and guide yourself on a short stroll to a pair of nearby local sights. Walk down Calle Independencia (from the museum, follow the left side of the plaza, past the *presidencia*) about three long blocks east to the picture-perfect **town fountain,** fed by the old town aqueduct. You may see women doing the day's laundry in the adjacent arched, public washhouse basins. A block south and a couple more blocks downhill east, at the end of Calle Libertad, you can marvel at Yucunama's oldest resident, the gigantic 1,000-year-old (at least that old, Maestro Antonio says) **El Tule,** or *ahuehuete* cypress tree *(Taxodium mucronatum),* a distant cousin of the California redwood. If you get lost, you can identify El Tule by its tall, bushy green silhouette, or mention El Tule (TOO-lay) to anyone.

Food and Accommodation
Maestro Antonio invites visitors to his **Cafe and Posada El Danzante,** across the street from the north portal of the *presidencia municipal,* open daily 8 A.M.–10 P.M. He and his wife take pride in their home-cooked Oaxaca *moles,* mild *chiles rellenos,* and giant *tlayudas* (flour tortillas) and their pre-Columbian specialties.

Antonio and his wife also invite visitors to stay with them, in several of the rooms they've prepared in their refined, art-decorated house. Rates run about $11 per person. Reserve by writing Maestro Antonio Martínez Sánchez, Hotel Posada El Danzante, Yucunama, Oaxaca 69556, or calling them, in Spanish, tel. 954/550-58.

Fiestas
You'll have even more fun if you arrive during one of Yucunama's festivals. The biggest is the patronal **Fiesta de San Pedro Mártir de Verona,** which culminates on 29 April. Festivities begin on the 26 April with a *calenda* (procession) and plenty of *mescal, aguardiente,* and *pulque* for those so inclined. Sometimes town men dress up like women and perform the dance of the *mascaritas.* The fun continues with more processions, plenty of flowers, food, fireworks, masses, and a dance on 29 April.

Other especially festive times in Yucunama include the fiesta of the Virgen del Rosario (first Sunday in October), the Day of the Dead (1 and 2 November), and the Christmas Eve procession, where everyone in town accompanies the infant Jesus to the church, then watches (or does) the traditional dance of the Pastor y Pastorela (Shepherd and Shepherdess).

Getting There and Away
Yucunama is about six miles (nine km) northwest of the Hwy. 125–Hwy. 190 intersection. Drivers, follow the signed graded gravel road that takes off from the north corner of the intersection. By bus, ride a Cristóbal Colón, Sur, or Fletes y Pasajes bus to the Hwy. 125–Hwy. 190 intersection, then hike the six miles or take a *colectivo* (collective taxi) from there. A number of snack stands and small stores at the intersection can provide water and food. Unless prepared

to camp, hikers should arrive early; Yucunama has no hotel.

YANHUITLÁN

It sometimes seems a miracle that the Dominican padres, against heavy odds and isolated as they were in the far province of Oaxaca, were able to build such masterpieces as their convent and church in Yanhuitlán. Upon reflection, however, their accomplishments seem less miraculous when you realize the mountain of help the padres received. When Father Domingo de la Cruz began the present church, in 1541, Yanhuitlán retained the prosperity and the large skilled population that it had when it was a reigning Mixtec kingdom prior to the arrival of the Spanish. For a workforce, de la Cruz used the labor of thousands of Mixtec workers and artisans, who deserve much of the credit for the masterfully refined monuments which they erected.

And monuments, indeed, they still are. Approaching Yanhuitlán from the northwest, the road reaches a point where the entire Yanhuitlán Valley spreads far below. In the bright afternoon sun, a single white-shining, colossal building—the Yanhuitlán church—dwarfs everything else in sight.

Up close you see why. Its exquisitely sculptured Renaissance facade towers overhead, making those standing on the front steps appear like ants. A graceful semicircular arch frames the entrance, while in the niche to the left stands the robed St. Francis of Assisi. In the right niche, Santa Margarita de Alacoque occupies the position customarily reserved in Dominican church facades for Santo Domingo de Guzmán, the Dominican order's revered founder. Santo Domingo is nevertheless present. Directly above the front portal, a masterful relief of Holy Mother Mary shelters a diminutive Santo Domingo and Santa Catarina de Siena, like small children, beneath her cape.

The church, officially the **Templo y Exconvento de Santo Domingo de Guzmán,** is as much a museum of national treasures as it is a place of worship. In fact, it is divided so: the ex-convent, which you enter on the right, has been converted to a museum. Inside, you begin to appreciate the gigantic proportions of the place as you circle the cloister, passing beneath ponderous but delicately designed arches that appear to sprout and spread from stone cloister columns like branches from giant trees. On the stairway leading upstairs at the cloister's corner, don't miss the mural of Jesus dressed like a 16th-century dandy except for his bare feet and the little angel perched on his shoulder.

The nave (which will probably be beautifully restored by the time you read this) glows with golden decorations. Overhead, stone rib arches support the ceiling completely, without the need of columns, creating a single soaring, heavenly space. Up front, above the altar, Santo Domingo presides, gazing piously toward heaven, his forehead decorated by a medallion that appears remarkably like a Hindu *thika*. Before you exit, take a look by the front door for the dramatic painting of Jesus, whip in hand, driving the money changers from the temple.

Get to Yanhuitlán, on Hwy. 190, by Sur, Fletes y Pasajes, or Cristóbal Colón bus. By car, head 12 miles (19 km) north along Hwy. 190 from Nochixtlán or 23 miles (37 km) south from Tamazulapan.

DOMINICAN ROUTE NORTH

COIXTLAHUACA

Coixtlahuaca (pop. about 3,000), although the capital of an entire governmental district encompassing a significant fraction of the Mixteca Baja's *municipios,* is a small town even by Oaxaca standards. Before the conquest, it was a powerful Chocho-speaking (Chocholteco) chiefdom, so strong that in the 1400s the Coixtlahuaca warriors stopped the invading Aztecs, forcing them to detour through Tlaxiaco. During colonial times and through the 19th century, Coixtlahuaca (koh-eeks-tlah-OOAH-kah) continued to be an important Chocholteco market center. But depopulation by emigration and increased education and literacy in Spanish have reduced the number of Chocho speakers to a handful of elderly folks in the surrounding countryside.

Most visitors enter Coixtlahuaca from the toll *autopista* from Oaxaca. Just inside the edge of town, a big sign on the left marks the road north to San Miguel Tequixtepec. Straight ahead a couple of more blocks, most drivers turn right on Independencia, the main town street. Nearly all stores and services are spread along Independencia, which continues several blocks past the plaza then the church, both above and to the left of the street. Bus passengers will arrive at the Auto buses Sur bus station, one block along Independencia.

Sights

Coixtlahuaca's past importance is reflected in its grand church, the **Templo y Exconvento de San Juan Bautista,** one of Oaxaca's largest. Inside, its nave stretches to the proportions of a grand European cathedral, its vault soaring overhead, supported by a delicate network of brilliantly painted colored stone arches. Dominican friar Francisco Marín, Coixtlahuaca's first vicar, was the moving force behind all this grandeur, initiating construction in 1546. Although the Reforms forced closure of the convent in 1856, the Dominicans continued to run it as a church until 1906, when locally based "secular" clergy took over.

In addition to its grand proportions, the church has much of interest. As you enter, notice the dark-complexioned image of African padre San Martín de Porres, in a friar's robe, on the right. Farther into the nave, gaze overhead and admire the whirling, rainbow-hued floral designs, lovingly executed by long-dead native artists. All are original, although time and recent replastering have erased much that you don't see. On the right, take a look at the unusually large side altar to the Virgin of Guadalupe and continue to the main altar, where St. John the Baptist, Coixtlahuaca's patron saint, presides at the foot of the towering, gilded *retablo* (altarpiece).

The town is mostly quiet, except for fiestas, which include the patronal festival of San Juan Bautista, around 24 June, and the festival of the Señor del Calvario (Lord of Calvary), during the last half of May. The fiestas include processions, carnival games, traditional food, the hazardous *jaripeo* bull roping and riding, and the Jarabe Chocholteco traditional Coixtlahuaca courtship dance.

Practicalities

One of the few hotels, if not the only one, along the expressway between Nochixtlán and Tehuacán, Puebla, is the local **Hotel Marina Sol,** Calle Independencia s/n, Coixtlahuaca, Oaxaca, no telephone. Although the rooms are of the basic bare-bulb variety, they're clean and spacious, with shower bath and hot water. Summer humidity, however, might cause rooms to accumulate mildew. Beds may need fresh linens; don't hesitate to request them before moving in. Guests additionally enjoy a tranquil garden setting, decorated with statuesque, green Roman pines, and a countryside view deck behind the reception. Prices run an economical $9 d. Reservations are rarely necessary.

Coixtlahuaca has two or three restaurants and taco shops on Independencia, plus a pharmacy, La Lupita, and a couple of stores where you can buy the renowned Coixtlahuaca rolls—big, brown, and not too sweet, sprinkled with a bit of sesame—perfect with coffee or tea.

Around the town plaza, other services include a *caseta larga distancia* (long-distance telephone office) on the southwest corner by the church, a post office above and to the right of the *presidencia municipal,* and the pharmacy San Rafael.

Bus passengers can get to Coixtlahuaca via Nochixtlán. From the Oaxaca first-class terminal, take a **Sur** or **Cristóbal Colón** bus to Nochixtlán. Continue via Sur to Coixtlahuaca. From Tamazulapan, get to Coixtlahuaca by the Sur bus line via the paved road through Tejupan.

Drivers from Oaxaca simply follow the toll *(cuota) autopista* north approximately 80 miles (129 km), 90 minutes, to Coixtlahuaca. From Tamazulapan, Yanhuitlán, or Teposcolula, drivers get to Coixtlahuaca via the paved road east from the Hwy. 190 junction at Tejupan, south of Tamazulapan, continuing an easy 15 miles (24 km) to Coixtlahuaca.

SAN MIGUEL TEQUIXTEPEC

Tequixtepec (Hill of the Conch) is the Aztec translation of the town's original Chocho name, Jna Niingui. Local legend says that Tequixtepec was the site of a now-lost temple dedicated to the god of the conch.

The local region comprises the *municipio* of San Miguel Tequixtepec; once rich, fertile, and thickly populated, it has fallen on hard times. Overgrazing, tree cutting, and selling the stones from the old irrigation terraces have degraded the Tequixtepec region into a semi-desert. Many hills are half-eroded bare stone. Some good land exists at the stream bottoms, but many people are discouraged by such hardscrabble farming. Most residents leave to work for a year in Oaxaca, Mexico City, or the United States, then come back and live for three or four years on their earnings. The population has dwindled from 3,000 around 1900 to perhaps 600 now.

It turns out, however, that San Miguel Tequixtepec is a village with grit. It shows in the people and their efforts to reverse their fortunes. A major moving force behind the local folks' determination is personable community leader Juan Cruz Reyes, who spearheaded the remodeling of a ruined schoolhouse into a working museum, now a focus for showing off Tequixtepec's valuable touristic assets: a graceful 1809 *presidencia municipal,* a dignified 17th-century church, woven-palm handicrafts, and, in the vicinity, a colonial-era fossil bridge and prehistoric rock paintings.

Sights

If you arrive heading north along the Coixtlahuaca road, after about five miles (eight km) you cross a creek bridge, where you can gaze upon an adjacent crumbling colonial-era stone-arched bridge. It's a remnant of Tequixtepec's glory days, when merchants marketed small fortunes of locally grown silk and red cochineal dye. Tequixtepec tradition says that one such merchant, Don Diego de San Miguel, built the bridge around 1590 to easily transport his products to the formerly big market in Coixtlahuaca. (Although still crossable on foot at this writing, the old bridge, in sore need of restoration, will probably soon fall victim to one of Oaxaca's frequent earthquakes.)

At the town plaza two miles (three km) farther north, make your first stop at the **community museum.** If available, a volunteer will show you the exhibits of local historical lore, fossils (notably, a huge mammoth tusk), local archaeological finds, and handicrafts. (If the museum is closed, ask around to see if someone might be available to open it up for you.)

If you've made a prior appointment (see Guides, following), volunteers will be available to show you around the town, probably starting at the town church, the **Parroquia de San Miguel Arcángel,** built of locally quarried rose *cantera* stone. The vases you see topping the churchyard fence are from Atzompa, near Oaxaca, and are always ready to be filled with flowers during the town's festivals. Foremost is the big 27–29 September town patronal fiesta in honor of San Miguel. Highlights include traditional dances, such as the Cristianos y Moros (Christians and Moors), each of the festival days. Other important fiestas are celebrated on Palm Sunday (Domingo de Ramos) and Sábado de Gloria (the Saturday before Easter Sunday), when people, for the occasion called *mecos,* don masks and do a kind of adult trick or treat. They go from store

The antique bridge just south of San Miguel Tequixtepec, still standing after more than 400 years, is nevertheless in need of repair.

to store, asking for something to drink and dancing with whoever is present. Yet another important day in Tequixtepec is Sunday, when, before 3 and 4 P.M., teams face off for a game of *pelota mixteca,* the local version of the ancient Mesoamerican ball game.

As you walk around town, be sure to ask your guide to take you to someone who is weaving palm leaves. This won't be difficult, since everyone appears to be doing it during most of their waking hours. Townsfolk gather and sun-dry the leaves of the little local wild palms, which they craft into a number of useful items, notably mats, grain bags, rope, and sombreros. Although their reward (about a quarter of a dollar for a sombrero) is pathetically small, at least the raw materials are free and everyone seems to have plenty of time on their hands. This is especially true during the hot (Feb.–June) dry season, when people do their weaving in cool, backyard *cuevas* (caves), most often in the company of others, when work becomes a party.

Something else you shouldn't miss during your around-town walk is a traditional *temascal* ritual hot room. Many local traditional curers have built *temezcales* of stone in their back yards for healing, especially for women after childbirth.

Finally, if the season is right, don't miss sampling a tuna (cactus apple). Simply pluck one from the leaf-tip of the many neighborhood nopal (prickly pear) cactuses. If it's red and ripe, you'll be in for a sweet, delicious treat.

Hieroglyphic Rock Painting Excursion

Farther afield, but well worth a day's time for travelers interested in antiquities and the great outdoors, are the local **pinturas rupestres** (rock paintings), which adorn the walls of a nearby river canyon. The jumping-off point, for which you certainly will need a guide, is Rancho La Barrete, a few miles from town, where a rocky but easy trail heads down into a shallow canyon, the Arroyo Palo Solo Arroyo, of the local Río Grande.

As you descend, keep quiet and keep your eyes peeled for coyote, deer, fox, skunk, armadillo, wild turkeys, or any of a host of bird species. Your immediate destination is the **Cueva de la Iglesia**—a sacred site where children used to be baptized on a large flat rock below the cave. In the cave above you can see an eagle's nest; nearby is a prehistoric painting dubbed the "alligator man."

Farther down the canyon, climb over a low ridge and cross an often dry tributary, the Río Seca. Soon you pass Peña Pirul and Peña Amarillo, a pair of painting-decorated cliff faces pocked with caves, and, above, ancient walls and irrigation terraces. Finally, after passing through a forest of moss-draped trees, comes the climax, the **Peña de los Guerreros** (Rock of the Warriors), adorned with plumed figures carrying shields and feathered lances.

Guides

It is best to have made an appointment before arriving at the Tequixtepec museum. This is very easy to do through the Community Museums in Oaxaca, headquarters at Tinoco y Palacios 311, second floor, Oaxaca, tel. 951/657-86, email: muscoax@antequera.com. Lacking an appointment, you might try contacting the museum directly. Telephone (in Spanish) the Tequixtepec long-distance number, tel. 953/301-93, and leave a message (or a fax if they have a machine by then; ask for *"tono fax, por favor."*) telling your arrival time. Either Juan Cruz Reyes, the museum president, or one of his committee members should reply. You can also contact them by writing to the Museo Comunitario, Juan Cruz Reyes, Presidente, Domocilio Conocido, San Miguel Tequixtepec, Oaxaca 79360.

Even if you arrive unannounced (but by noon) you still might be able to hire a guide (Spanish-speaking only) to lead you to the rock paintings for a modest fee, perhaps $10. Jacobo Cruz Gúzman and Joventino Cruz Cruz, the competent local men who guided me, said they'd be glad to do the same for others if possible.

Practicalities
Although when I was there, no one offered comfortable lodging in Tequixtepec, this may change soon. Otherwise, stay at the hotel in Coixtlahuaca seven miles away, or camp by tent or self-contained RV, for which it would be no problem to obtain permission from the generally hospitable townsfolk. Ask Juan Cruz Reyes or one of the other museum volunteers for permission.

Basic groceries are available at a pair of stores, one of which also runs the long-distance telephone. One is on the corner across the main street, half a block south from the museum, and the other, a block north, is run by the friendly sisters Elvia and Cari Córdoba Reyes. Given half a day's notice, the sisters will also cook hearty, wholesome, reasonably priced meals for you.

From Oaxaca, get to Tequixtepec by bus via Nochixtlán and Coixtlahuaca. From the Oaxaca first-class terminal, ride a bus, such as **Sur** or **Cristóbal Colón,** to Nochixtlán. Continue via Sur, to Coixtlahuaca, where you can catch a *colectivo* (collective taxi) north the seven miles to Tequixtepec.

Bus passengers can also get to Coixtlahuaca, thence Tequixtepec, from Tamazulapan, by the Sur bus line, via the paved road through Tejupan.

For drivers, access to Tequixtepec is also best through Coixtlahuaca. From Oaxaca, simply follow the *cuota autopista* north approximately 80 miles (129 km), 90 minutes, to Coixtlahuaca, and continue another seven miles (11 km) north via the gravel road to Tequixtepec.

From Tamazulapan, Teposcolula, or Yanhuitlán, access is best via the paved (but intermittently potholed) road that intersects Hwy. 190 at Tejupan, from which Coixtlahuaca is an easy 15-mile (24-km) half-hour drive.

TEPELMEME DE MORELOS

Tepelmeme de Morelos (pop. 1,600), eight miles north of Tequixtepec, has enjoyed a rich history. Before the conquest it was a semi-independent chiefdom, a tributary of Nochixtlán, at times allied with neighboring Mixtec and Ixcatec chiefdoms. The Mixtec connection was so strong that anthropologists sometimes speak of preconquest Tepelmeme as a fused Mixtec-Chochotec culture. Tepelmeme's earliest Christian church, founded by the Dominican missionaries not long after the conquest, was built over an earlier Mixtec-style temple at the same spot where the present church stands on the town plaza.

Despite Spanish dominance, Tepelmeme's Chocho-speaking rulers retained influence over their people into the 18th century. At that time, during the 80 years until 1743, their dynasty was united with the Ixcatec kingdom of Ixcatlán, to the northwest. The great majority of Tepelmeme people continued to speak Chocho until around 1900, when improved education and Spanish literacy began to reduce the number of Chocho speakers to the small group of elderly folks who still speak it.

The present town appears to be the rival metropolis of the Coixtlahuaca district, sometimes overshadowing the district capital in hustle and bustle. One sign of Tepelmeme's vitality is its market, which sometimes sprawls over the center of town. The source of Tepelmeme's prosperity is its relatively fertile valley soil, not nearly as eroded as many other Mixteca Baja communities. Some farmers, consequently, have money for wells, pumps, and electricity for irrigation. A number are prosperous enough to even own tractors.

Sights

Tepelmeme, laid out along a north-south axis, has two town plazas. The more formal of the two, a *jardín* with grass and a promenade-encircled bandstand, borders the church on its east side and the *presidencia municipal* on the south. Farther south, behind the *presidencia,* is the town's real heart—the scruffy but busy **market plaza.**

Your first stop should be at the community museum, **Niace** (nee-AH-say), which in Chocho means "Mountain of Honey." The museum is behind the *presidencia* at the market plaza's northeast corner. It's best to arrive by appointment, made through the Community Museums in Oaxaca City, Tinoco y Palacios 311, second floor, Oaxaca, tel. 951/657-86, email: muscoax@antequera.com; otherwise the museum will probably be closed.

The museum's collection, mainly artifacts, includes a huge ceremonial conch shell uncovered from one of region's several excavated archaeological sites. Most prominent are the copies of the ancient but sophisticated glyphs painted on the cliff face at the awesome Puente Colosal natural bridge. (See below.)

Townsfolk built the *jardín*-front church, the newly restored **Templo de Santo Domingo de Gúzman,** in 1769 to replace an earlier, conquest-era church. Community adoration climaxes here during the major 1–4 August festival in celebration of Santo Domingo. Folks mark his memory with pilgrimages, processions, baptisms, confirmations, fireworks, and a big carnival.

Inside, don't miss the right transept chapel, dedicated to the Sacred Heart of Jesus. Here you'll find five intriguing banners, one for each of the town's *mayordomías,* the community organizations separately responsible for Tepelmeme's 10 yearly religious festivals. The pervasive influence of the *mayordomías* is visible, both separately during the individual festivals that they each organize, and collectively, on the first Friday morning of each month, when their dozens of members, representing virtually all the town's families, gather to parade their five respective banners around the *jardín.*

Excursions: Puente Colosal and Huerta de Juquila

With a prior appointment, a museum guide will be available to escort you (13 miles, 21 km) to the point of departure for the two-mile, two-hour round-trip hike down a forested boulder-strewn creek bottom to Puente Colosal. Here it appears as if a glacier-era lake once filled a deep limestone box canyon. Over eons, the water gradually dissolved the limestone, finally scooping out a yawning, 200-foot-high tunnel through a towering mountain ridge. The result is spectacular Puente Colosal, probably the world's tallest natural stone bridge.

Puente Colosal has most certainly inspired awe in human visitors for thousands of years. Some inscribed their presence, in both primitive rock paintings and refined (probably city-state stage A.D. 1000–1500) Mixtec glyphs, graphically painted on Puente Colosal's stone face. Someday, when archaeologists finally crack the ancient Mixtec code, humanity will know what Puente Colosal inspired them to record for posterity on its stark bedrock walls.

Get there, by permission only through the Tepelmeme museum or municipal authorities, accompanied by a local guide. A rugged, high-clearance vehicle is necessary for the last few miles of this route: mark your odometer at the Tepelmeme town center. Head north through town to the expressway entrance (1.2 miles, two km). Continue north to the expressway bridge, Puente La Unión (six miles, 9.6 km). With caution, just before the bridge, exit left at the unofficial dirt driveway. Cross back over the expressway via the bridge, then, after a fraction of a mile, turn right (6.3 miles, 10 km) at the T at Ranchería La Unión. At mile 8.3 (13.4 km) turn left at another T, at Ranchería Puerto Mixteco. Continue down a mountain-rimmed farm valley past a hillside spring and small dam at Rosario (10.4 miles, 16.7 km). Continue down-canyon via the increasingly rough track to road's end (13.5 miles, 21.7 km). Puente Colosal is at the downstream end of the canyon. Scramble downhill via a steep trail to the shady stream bottom, then boulder-hop the remaining mile and a half. Although the stream bottom is usually dry, **beware of possible flash flooding** from upstream thunderstorms. Take a hat, binoculars, camera, strong shoes, and drinking water.

Well-equipped wilderness backpackers might enjoy spending an overnight or two beneath Puente Colosal's grand, sheltering rock ceiling.

The environs are ripe for wildlife viewing, expert-grade vertical rock climbing, and exploring past Puente Colosal's downstream portal, where the stream bottom continues into a lush, semitropical mountain-walled wild valley.

Even more remote is the locally famous and idyllic **Huerta de Juquila** grove and waterfall. Access, strictly by museum or municipally approved guide only, is also north of Tepelmeme via the expressway to Puente La Unión. In this case, however, you turn left at the T (see Puente Colosal directions) at Ranchería La Unión. The route continues another 18 miles (29 km) into the mountainous backcountry on foot or by horseback. The key intermediate destination is Mahusipan village (at 13 miles, 21 km), where you continue approximately another five miles (eight km) to Huerta de Juquila.

Practicalities

Around the market plaza you'll find sources of both food and basic services. Get groceries, fruits, and vegetables at market stalls. Wholesome cooked food—tamales, tacos, chicken, soups and stews—is available from market-front *fondas*. For stamps and letter-mailing, go to the *correo* (post office), by the museum on the market plaza's north side. If you're ill, go to the **Centro de Salud** health clinic, at the *jardín* southeast corner, between the *presidencia* and the church. You can also make long-distance phone calls at the little *larga distancia* three blocks north of the jardín, past the bridge, along the street by the west side of the of the *presidencia municipal*.

Bus passengers, get to Tepelmeme via Tequixtepec, where you should continue via *colectivo* the eight more miles north to Tepelmeme. Drivers, from Oaxaca drive north two hours, approximately 95 miles (153 km), via the *cuota* expressway to the Tepelmeme exit. From Tamazulapan, drivers head along Calle Independencia, which becomes the gravel road leading directly to Tepelmeme (via Teotongo and Ihuitlán). Figure about an hour and a half of relatively easy but sometimes bumpy driving for the 27-mile (43-km) trip.

LAND OF THE SUN: THE MIXTECA BAJA

HUAJUAPAN DE LEÓN AND VICINITY

Huajuapan de León (pop. 50,000), with good hotels, restaurants and many services, makes a comfortable base for enjoying the intriguing corners of the northern Mixteca Baja. Day trips north, via the Tehuacán road, open the fertile, green vale of the Río Mixteca with its colorful hamlets, venerable churches, and archaeological sites. Similarly, excursions south, along the high road to the Mixteca Alta, reveal a wealth of hiking, camping, boating, and fishing opportunities.

What's even better is that the town itself has much to offer. For first-time arrivees, untouristed Huajuapan de León is a pleasant surprise. The town center—plaza, church, and *presidencia municipal*—is removed a few blocks south of the Hwy. 190 clutter and bustle. Although the present town dates only from colonial times, the surrounding region, which city hall boosters call Tierra del Sol (Land of the Sun), has been inhabited for many millennia. The extensive Cerro de Las Minas (Hill of the Mines) archaeological zone, just a mile north of the present town, was a ceremonial, market, and governmental center for thousands of inhabitants during its apex, around A.D. 500. It was excavated during the late 1980s.

Huajuapan (a tongue twister; say oo-ah-WAH-pahn) put itself on the map during Mexico's War of Independence. After two years of seesaw rebellion, national attention focused on Huajuapan, where *insurgente* Valerio Trujano was leading local forces in blocking the advance of a well-disciplined royalist force. Inspired by faith in their patron saint, **El Señor de los Corazones** (The Lord of the Hearts), the Huajuapan fighters resisted a royalist siege of 111 days, until relieved by Independence hero General José María Morelos on 23 June 1812.

Later, in the early 1820s, Huajuapan's favorite son, Antonio de León (thus, Huajuapan de León) played a crucial role in securing Mexican Independence. He was among the first leaders in conservative Oaxaca to support Agustín de Iturbide's Plan de Iguala, which finally freed Mexico from Spain. Later, León headed the fight against Iturbide when he proclaimed himself emperor, then dissolved Congress. León (by then a general at the age of 29) and Nicolas Bravo captured Oaxaca City for republican forces on 9 June 1823.

Sights

The town's choice people-watching spot is the tranquil, old-fashioned town plaza, **Plaza Central Antonio de León,** bordered by the *presidencia municipal* on its west side. On the plaza's north side stands a distinguished bronze statue of General Antonio de León (1794–1847). Also on the north side, across the street from the plaza, rise the twin spires of the late-19th-century **Catedral de la Virgen de Guadalupe.** A major plaza-front thoroughfare is Antonio de León, on the west side, which becomes Valerio Trujano as it continues north to its highway crossing. On the plaza's east side runs Av. Porfirio Díaz, which jogs around the back side of the cathedral, becoming Av. Nuyoo (noo-YOH-oh) as it heads north to the highway.

The plaza's major source of early evening entertainment is the army of birds, mostly black grackles, who around sunset head from all directions straight for the big, bushy plaza trees. For about an hour they flutter, cackle, and squabble for perches until they finally settle down for the night.

Stroll over for a look inside the cathedral. For Mexico, this is a very new church. Earthquakes repeatedly damaged the previous structures occupying the site since colonial times. The present church, built new in the late 1800s, was so severely damaged by earthquakes that it had to be extensively rebuilt and earthquake-proofed in the 1960s. But for the people of Huajuapan it's not the building but what it contains that counts.

Inside, a brilliantly illuminated Virgin of Guadalupe occupies the main front altar, while in the right-side chapel, the **Capilla del Sagrario del Señor de los Corazones,** a painted celebration of baroque glitter climaxes in the beloved, dark-complexioned Señor hanging limply above the altar. On auspicious days the faithful arrive in a near-continuous stream to pay their respects. As you leave, on the wall in the small sub-chapel on the left, just outside the door, look for the heart festooned with little metal *milagros* wish offerings, which beseeching pilgrims have left for the Señor.

Huajuapan Market

If it's Wednesday, the day of Huajuapan's big *tianguis* market, walk to Colón, which borders the church's north side. Turn right; after about a block, follow Zaragoza, the street heading diagonally northeast, two long blocks to the market on the right. Besides doing your grocery shopping from stalls in the covered section, wander beneath the shady *tianguis* (awnings) for your pick of the best, from mounds of luscious bananas, tomatoes, cucumbers, and squashes. During the summer and fall you'll also see plenty of pears, peaches, guavas, and grapes. Also admire the piles of deep red chilies and bright yellow *flor de calabaza* (squash flower) used for flavoring soups and stews. Here and there you'll glimpse piles of old-fashioned items, such as corn husks (for wrapping tamales), *cal* (limestone) for soaking corn, red *jamaica* (hah-MAHEE-kah) petals for delicious drinks, nopal cactus leaves, *tamarindo* and *guaje* pods, yellow *manzanilla* (chamomile) flowers, and hunks of *panela* (brown sugar). Throughout your walk, take note that the women vendors are definitely in charge, although few wear *traje* (native dress).

You'll also find some **handicrafts.** Locally made items include red- and black-streaked **pottery,** in practical shapes, such as *ollas* (pots), bowls, and *comales* (griddles); and **stone,** carved into *manos, metates* and *molcajetes* for grinding corn and chilies. Local folks also sell plenty of items woven from **palm.** These include sombreros, *bolsas* (purses), *petates* (mats), and *cestas* (baskets). Another, off-market source of woven palm handicrafts is the little **Artesanías de Palma** store downtown at Nuyoo 13, half a block uphill from the cathedral.

Although few if any local people make textiles, they do import and sell, mostly *huipiles,* from other parts of Oaxaca. You'll probably find some on Wednesday, if you look around the covered section.

Museum and Cerro de las Minas Archaeological Zone

Be sure to spend at least an hour investigating

HUAJUAPAN DE LEÓN

To Mexico City

0   0.25 mi

0   0.25 km

Colonia Río Balsas

Colonia El Calvario

190

CARRETERA INTERNACIONAL

2 DE ABRIL

NUYO

5 DE FEBRERO

Colonia Tepeyac

16 DE SEPTIEMBRE

FRAY DE LAS CASAS

CRISTÓBAL COLÓN AND ADO

AVILA CAMACHO

SUR

Colonia Los Presidentes

VALERIO TRUJANO

NUYO

REFORMA

CONSTITUCIÓN

MORELOS

MINA

CATHEDRAL

PALACIO MUNICIPAL

PLAZA CENTRAL

ANTONIO DE LEÓN

Colonia Centro

JIMÉNEZ

Colonia La Providencia

CORREO

SEE DETAIL

MINA

15

To Tonalá, Juxtlahuaca, and the Pacific Coast

RÍO MIXTECO

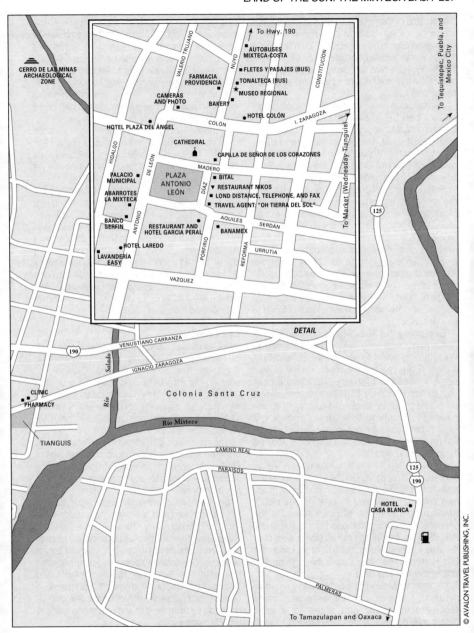

CERRO DE LAS MINAS
ARCHAEOLOGICAL
ZONE

To Hwy. 190

AUTOBUSES
MIXTECA-COSTA

FLETES Y PASAJES (BUS)

FARMACIA
PROVIDENCIA

TONALTECA (BUS)

MUSEO REGIONAL

CAMERAS
AND PHOTO

BAKERY

HOTEL COLÓN

VALERIO TRUJANO

NUYO

CONSTITUCIÓN

HOTEL PLAZA DEL ÁNGEL

COLÓN

I. ZARAGOZA

CATHEDRAL

CAPILLA DE SEÑOR DE LOS CORAZONES

HIDALGO

DE LEÓN

MADERO

PLAZA
ANTONIO
LEÓN

DÍAZ

BITAL

RESTAURANT NIKOS

PALACIO
MUNICIPAL

ABARROTES
LA MIXTECA

LONG DISTANCE, TELEPHONE, AND FAX

TRAVEL AGENT: "OH TIERRA DEL SOL"

BANCO
SERFIN

ANTONIO

AQUILES

SERDÁN

RESTAURANT AND
HOTEL GARCIA PERAL

BANAMEX

PORFIRIO

REFORMA

HOTEL LAREDO

URRUTIA

LAVANDERÍA
EASY

VAZQUEZ

To Market (Wednesday Tianguis)

125

DETAIL

To Tequistepec, Puebla, and Mexico City

190

VENUSTIANO CARRANZA

Salado

IGNACIO ZARAGOZA

CLINIC

PHARMACY

Colonia Santa Cruz

Río

Río Mixteco

TIANGUIS

CAMINO REAL

PARAISOS

125

190

HOTEL
CASA BLANCA

PALMERAS

To Tamazulapan and Oaxaca

© AVALON TRAVEL PUBLISHING, INC.

the remains of Cerro de las Minas, a major urban stage (A.D. 300–800) Mixtec town. Artifacts uncovered on this hill just north of town during the 1980s demonstrate characteristics of so-called Ñuiñe glyphs, which archaeologists recognize as one of the five unique writing systems of ancient Mesoamerica.

Similar finds unearthed at contemporaneous Mixteca Baja ruined cities, such as Tequixtepec, Chazumba, Miltepec, Suchitepec, Lunatitlán, and Mixtlahuaca, led archaeologists to name the style by the Mixtec label, Ñuiñe (nyoo-EE-nyay), for the "Hot Country," the Mixteca Baja, where they have been found.

Before charging up the hill, however, first visit the new municipal **museum,** at Nuyoo 15, half a block uphill from the church. open daily except Monday, 9 A.M.–2 P.M. and 4–8 P.M. Professionally prepared exhibits on the bottom floor give an overview and explanations of the exquisite finds at Cerro de las Minas. Upstairs is a library and beautifully displayed life-sized mock-ups—community, work, economics, fiestas, religion, costumes of present Mixteca Baja people. Another room exhibits local colonial to modern history.

Exploring the Site: After the museum, get to the ruins by driving, hiking, or hailing a taxi. Wear sturdy walking shoes, a hat, and take water. From the town center, follow Nuyoo north across the highway and three blocks past the uphill church. Continue straight ahead, up a steep, rocky track and turn right to the parking lot, marked by a Zona Arqueología sign. From there, on foot, scramble uphill past the retaining wall to the highest point, **Mound 1,** on the east side.

From the top, the entire Huajuapan Valley spreads all directions. On the south side, in the distance, rise the downtown cathedral's ruddy twin towers. Far behind them stand the cloud-draped heights of the Mixteca Alta. On the opposite, north side, flat-topped Cerro Yucunitza, the site of another hilltop ruined city, towers over the valley. Below Yucunitza's right shoulder, the Río Mixteca meanders below the high brushy hills of the Mixteca Baja.

Unrestored Mound 1, most certainly a former pyramid, slopes downhill past some reconstructed walls and stairs to a wide ceremonial courtyard. Descend Mound 1 to the courtyard. On its north side are the previously excavated Tombs 4 and 5. On the south side, a staircase descends to a smaller courtyard complex of what appear to be residential walls and patios. Continue west to **Mound 2,** a partly reconstructed ceremonial pyramid. Looking south toward town from its summit, you can view the clear outlines of a partially excavated **ball court** about a hundred yards down the slope.

Continue west, descending the regal, restored ritual staircase, down the west side of Mound 2 to a grand 100-yard-square courtyard. Ahead rises **Mound 3,** a brushy hill that probably conceals yet another staircase and pyramid summit.

The visible hilltop remains of Cerro de las Minas around you were the ceremonial hub of a small city that, at its apex around A.D. 500, was home to perhaps 4,000 people whose hundreds of homes extended over scores of surrounding hillside acres. Like Monte Albán, archaeologists do not know the city's original name. What they do know, however, is that, like Monte Albán and several other of Oaxaca's ancient cities, the inhabitants of Cerro de las Minas mysteriously abandoned it around A.D. 800.

Las Campanas

Las Campanas park, a lovely streamside stroll on Huajuapan's northwest outskirts, is worth at least an hour's visit. At Las Campanas, community efforts have preserved a unique natural desert-like spring and habitat, decorated with rock outcroppings and ferny shady nooks. Tables beneath streamside willows make for perfect picnicking.

The name Las Campanas (The Bells) derives from the stalactites hanging from the ceilings of shallow, streamside caves. If struck just right, a stalactite will vibrate and ring with a soft, bell-like monotone.

Las Campanas, although readily accessible, is not well marked and is easy to miss. Follow the road to Mexico City about a mile west of Huajuapan town center. Las Campanas nestles in a shallow arroyo on the left, marked by an old Hotel Crystal sign about a block or two after the entrance driveway to the Universidad Tecnología de la Mixteca. If you pass a government nursery *(vivero)* on the left, you've gone too far; turn around and return one block to Las Campanas.

Accommodations

Of Huajuapan's several acceptable hotels, two stand out. Visitors who enjoy soaking up Mexico should choose the immaculate **Hotel Garcia Peral,** by the central plaza at Porfirio Díaz 1, Huajuapan de León, Oaxaca 69000, tel. 953/207-77 or 953/207-42, fax 953/220-00. The 37 rooms in three levels surround an inviting pool patio blooming with tropical plants and birdsong. Rooms are comfortably furnished with beige bed covers, reading lamps, attractively rustic tile floors and modern-standard bathrooms. Rates run about $29 s, $32 d, with fans, good restaurant-bar, pool, and sauna; credit cards accepted.

Second choice goes to suburban **Hotel Casa Blanca,** on Hwy. 190, Oaxaca side, about a mile from town at Amatista 1, Colonia Sta. Teresa, Huajuapan de León, Oaxaca 69000, tel. 953/207-79, fax 953/209-79. This is a good option for drivers anxious to avoid downtown traffic. The Casa Blanca's 80 semi-deluxe rooms, in two-story tiers scattered through a spacious garden complex, are carpeted and comfortable. Make sure, however, that everything is working before moving in. Tariffs are about $23 s, $23 d, $34 t, with baths, TV, fans, pool patio, good restaurant, parking, no phones, but credit cards are accepted.

Back downtown you'll find some downscale, but acceptable, choices. Take a look at **Hotel Laredo,** just a block south of the plaza, at Antonio de León 13, Colonia Centro, Huajuapan de León, Oaxaca 69000, tel. 953/204-02, 953/207-99. The 26 rooms, stacked in three levels around a parking courtyard, are plain and less than immaculate. If not acceptable, ask them to clean up what's wrong before paying. Rates, however, are right, at about $12 s or d, with bath, fan, parking, restaurant; credit cards not accepted.

On the opposite, north side of the plaza, you might also consider **Hotel Plaza del Ángel,** Valerio Trujano 22, Huajuapan de León, Oaxaca 69000, tel. 953/208-51. Although not much to look at from the outside, the Ángel has carpeted, and therefore quiet, hallways. Rooms, plain but clean, have baths. Rates run about $10 s, $13 d, with TV, fans, parking, but no phones; credit cards not accepted.

Other, very cheap, rough hotel choices dot Nuyoo and Colón near the second-class bus stations. Try the Hotel Rivera Amador, at Nuyoo 13, tel. 953/209-62, or Hotel Colón, at Colón 10, tel. 953/208-17 or 953/218-60.

Food

Huajuapan's best grocery, vegetable, and fruit source is the town **market,** about four blocks west of the plaza. For a few basic items and a cultural experience ("we buy and sell corn, calabash seeds, and aluminum"), visit the Porfirian-era general store **Abarrotes La Mixteca** for your cooking oil, mayonnaise, rope, and shovels. Find it at Antonio de León 7, half a block south of the plaza, by the Banco Serfin. Satisfy your hankering for cake, pie, and cookies, at the **bakery,** the Espiga de Oro, at Nuyoo 9, half a block uphill from the cathedral.

Across the street from the bakery, you can do plenty of wholesome local-style eating at the **Restaurant El Dorado,** a few steps uphill from the corner of Colón.

On the other hand, for refined plaza-front dining, try the open-air restaurant at the **Hotel Garcia Peral.** Pick from the long menu of a little bit of everything, from cream of asparagus soup and hamburgers to shrimp salad, filet mignon, or *cabrito al pastor* (baby goat, shepherd style). Open daily 8 A.M.–10:30 P.M., tel. 953/215-32. Moderate.

For relaxing courtyard ambience, quiet music, and genteel conversation, go to **Restaurant Nikos,** on the plaza's east side, on Díaz next to Banco Internacional. Here you can choose from a list of tasty American-style hamburgers or a number of hearty Oaxacan-style specialties. Also open for good breakfasts, daily except Monday, 8 A.M.–10:30 P.M., tel. 953/218-71. Moderate.

Services and Information

A number of **banks** around the plaza, all with ATMs, change money. Best for its long hours is **Banco Internacional** (Bital) on Díaz, at the plaza's northeast corner, open Mon.–Sat. 8:30 A.M.–6:30 P.M., tel. 953/201-69.

If somehow Bital isn't satisfactory, step over to **Banco Nacional de Mexico** (Banamex), a block south, corner of Serdán and Díaz, open Mon.–Fri. 9 A.M.–5 P.M., Sat. 9 A.M.–2 P.M., tel. 953/212-82 or 953/234-04; or **Banco Serfin,** open Mon.–Fri. 9 A.M.–4 P.M., Sat. 10 A.M.–2 P.M., another block south, corner of León and Galindo, tel. 953/204-24.

For stamps, letters, and postal money orders, go to the *correo* (post office), open Mon.–Fri. 8 A.M.–6 P.M., Sat. 9 A.M.–1 P.M., tel. 953/206-92, at 5 de Febrero 16, on the south side. (From the plaza's southwest corner, walk south on León three blocks to 5 de Febrero; turn right and continue another two blocks to the post office on the left side of the street.)

Long-distance telephone and fax are readily available at **Caseta del Centro,** tel. 953/219-15, fax 953/203-50, on Díaz, east side of the plaza. It's open Mon.–Sat. 8 A.M.–9 P.M.

If you're sick, one of the best places to go for a doctor is the **Centro de Especialidades de la Mixteca,** Zaragoza 24, tel. 953/213-55, across from the town market three blocks west of the plaza. It has about 15 specialists on call, from gynecologists and pediatricians to internists and a cardiologist.

For medicines and drugs, go next door from the aforementioned doctors' office to the **Farmacia de Descuento,** open Mon.–Sat. 8 A.M.–10 P.M., tel. 953/213-55. Alternatively, closer to the plaza, try **Farmacia La Providencia,** at Nuyoo 18, half a block north from the church.

Although Huajuapan has a city *turismo* office on the upper floor of the *presidencia municipal* at the west side of the plaza, you might get more good information by consulting friendly José Flores Cubas, owner of the **Turismo "Oh Tierra del Sol,"** at the plaza's southeast corner. He's open Mon.–Sat. approximately 9 A.M.–2 P.M. and 4–7 P.M., tel. 953/245-55, fax 953/226-56.

Get your wash done at **Lavandería Easy,** tel. 953/213-76, on Hidalgo, one block west, one block south from the plaza's southwest corner

Getting There and Away

Several first- and second-class bus lines operate out of various terminals, providing direct connections with many Oaxacan and national destinations. The busy first-class terminal, tel. 953/228-48, six blocks north of the plaza at the Hwy. 190 intersection with Nuyoo, is the center for **Cristóbal Colón, Autobuses del Oriente (ADO), and Autobuses Unidos (AU)** ticket sales, arrivals, and departures. Principal connections, including many intermediate

destinations, are southeast with Nochixtlán and Oaxaca; south via Hwy. 15 and Tonalá with Juxtlahuaca, where you can transfer on to Tlaxiaco, Putla, and Pinotepa Nacional; and northwest with Puebla and Mexico City.

The four second-class bus stations are on Nuyoo, along the block north of the cathedral. **Sur,** tel. 953/214-21, at the corner of Bravo and Nuyoo, offers second-class connections southeast, including a swarm of intermediate destinations, with Tamazulapan, Nochixtlán, and Oaxaca; south with Juxtlahuaca, Putla, and Tlaxiaco; north with Puebla; and northwest with Cuautla, Morelos. **Fletes y Pasajes,** tel. 953/200-51, at Nuyoo 13, half a block uphill from the cathedral, offers approximately the same connections as Sur. A third, smaller line, **Tonalteca,** tel. 953/232-82, operating out of a storefront terminal at Nuyoo 9, a few doors downhill from Fletes y Pasajes, offers connections along the north-south Tonalá-Juxtlahuaca-Putla route all the way to Pinotepa Nacional, on Oaxaca's Pacific Coast. Similar service is offered by the small competing line, Autobuses Mixteca-Costa, at Nuyoo 19, tel. 953/213-12.

Drivers have their pick of four major paved highways radiating from Huajuapan. Northwest, Hwy. 190 connects—196 miles (316 km) via Cuautla, Morelos—with Mexico City. Two winding lanes and numerous big trucks along the way slow traffic along this route. Figure about seven hours under good conditions, either way. A much quicker alternative is to first head northeast via Hwy. 125, 74 miles (118 km), two hours, to Tehuacán, Puebla. There, connect with the *cuota* expressway, which will whisk you in another four hours, via Puebla, to Mexico City.

For Oaxaca City, follow Hwy. 190 for 70 miles (113 km), two hours, southeast to Asunción Nochixtlán. Continue via the toll expressway to Oaxaca, another 50 miles (80 km), about one additional hour.

Drivers can also head south, via Tonalá, along the paved, lightly trafficked secondary road, which takes two hours to Juxtlahuaca (62 miles, 100 km). South of Juxtlahuaca 25 miles (40 km, one hour), at the Hwy. 125 junction, either head left (east) along the Hwy. 125 another 21 miles (34 km) and one hour to Tlaxiaco, or go right, south along Hwy. 125 via Putla to Pinotepa

Nacional on the Pacific Coast (a total, from Huajuapan, of 206 miles or 332 km). Allow six hours' driving time south to the coast, seven hours east to Tlaxiaco.

NORTH OF HUAJUAPAN: INTO THE ÑUIÑE REGION

National Highway 125 winds north along the rural, the tree-shaded valley of the Río Mixteco, passing a sprinkling of little towns, sleepy except during fiestas, when they liven up with days of processions, barbecues, and carnivals. Along this route, interest climaxes at San Pedro y San Pablo Tequixtepec, where townsfolk welcome visitors to visit their community museum. There, you can view the Ñuiñe engraved monoliths, whose cryptic inscriptions have convinced archaeologists that they represent a unique written language.

By car, starting early, you could enjoy this 75-mile (121-km) total round-trip excursion in a day, allowing time for a picnic in Tequixtepec (22 miles, 35 km from Huajuapan) around the midpoint. Bus travelers, head out by ADO, Sur, or AU bus straight from Huajuapan, for Tequixtepec. At the entrance road, catch the town colectivo van and ride the three miles (five km) to town. Afterward, either continue north or return to Huajuapan stopping along the way, if time allows.

Santiago Huajolotitlán

This small town four miles north of Huajuapan is well known, both for its annual patronal festival and as the place where the Virgin of Guadalupe appeared in 1978. First, stop at the town church, the **Templo de Santiago Apóstol,** built between 1835 and 1840. Inside, to the right as you enter, notice the popular San Isidro Labrador, the patron of farmers, animals, and children, with his customary yunta (yoked pair) of oxen and a child. Folks celebrate his memory on 15 May, when children bring their animals to church to be blessed.

Also, don't miss the uniquely quaint town patron, **Santiago Caballerito** (Little Saint), mounted on a small horse, waving a big sword. His festival, celebrated 26–29 July, usually includes plenty of fireworks, flowers,

music, marches, and mañanitas (early morning masses).

Also, on the slope of Cerro del Chilar, northwest of town, is the **Capilla de la Virgen de Guadalupe,** built over the spot where a shepherd saw the Virgin in December 1978. Thousands of believers subsequently flocked to the site, now relatively unfrequented, where the chapel stands.

Río Mixteco Valley and Asunción Cuyotepeji

North of Huajolotitlán, the river valley, especially lush during the cooler summer rainy season, when it's abloom with fields of vegetables, tall green corn, and waving wheat. The natural charm climaxes at the riverbank itself, decorated by groves of stately ahuehuetes or sabinos (Mexican cypresses). Here and there, where the highway nears or crosses the river, pause for a stroll along the river and enjoy a spell in the company of the old shady giants.

During mid-August you also might enjoy getting in on the fun of the **Fiesta de Santa María de la Asunción,** at Cuyotepeji, about 12 miles north of Huajuapan. At least take a look inside the church, known for its gilded Baroque main retablo (altarpiece), which is adorned by the Holy Mother ascending to heaven guided by a choir of adoring cherubs.

San Pedro y San Pablo Tequixtepec

You could easily spend your entire day at Tequixtepec (formally, San Pedro y San Pablo Tequixtepec), pop. 1,400, the head town of the municipio of the same name. Make your first stop at the community museum, **Memorias de Yucundaayee** (yoo-koon-dah-ah-YAY-ay), named with the town's original Mixtec label (Hill of the Standing Conch), which the Aztecs translated to Tequixtepec.

The museum, adjacent to the town presidencia municipal, is regularly open Mon.–Thurs. about 10 A.M.–2 P.M. and 4–7 P.M. The professionally prepared exhibits display the intriguing, glyph-carved monoliths, with Spanish language explanations of their Ñuiñe writing style. Despite a generation of study and excavations, archaeologists still can say little about the people depicted. Although their feathered visages remain mute to us, maybe someday experts will decipher the Ñuiñe glyphs and understand their messages.

If you have arranged an appointment, a museum volunteer can take you on an extensive tour, including a three-hour round-trip hike to **Cerro de La Caja** (Mountain of the Box), a regal hilltop ruined town. There among other things, you'll be able to inspect a ponderous box-like monolith, inscribed with a number of graphic Ñuiñe reliefs, one of which includes a personage devouring a captive. Make an appointment with Museos Comunitarios de Oaxaca (headquarters at Tinoco y Palacios 311, second floor, tel. 951-657-86, email: muscoax@prodigy.net.mx, website: www.umco.org) or by leaving a message with the town telephone office, tel. 953/207-09, for the *museo comunitario* or museum *presidente* Abigail Moran Morales.

Back in town, be sure to visit the church, dedicated to the **Señor del Perdón** (Lord of Forgiveness), who is celebrated in a big regional fiesta and pilgrimage climaxing on the second Friday of Lent. At that time, 20,000 people crowd into little Tequixtepec, sleeping in the plaza, the town pilgrimage shelter, and in scores of buses parked along the road to town. The object of all is to ask forgiveness from the Señor del Perdón, who presides above church's front altar.

Before you leave, ask your guide for a demonstration of **palm weaving,** which many townsfolk do during their spare moments. Both individual weavers and the museum sell examples of woven sombreros, *petates,* and *cestas* (hats, mats, and baskets) and more. Additionally, be sure to step 100 years into the past into the Porfirian-era store of grandfatherly **"Tino" Moran Castillo.** Here you might say a good word, make a small purchase, and enjoy a sip of his zingy homemade brandy, which Faustino claims is "very good for your health."

Santiago Chazumba

The main yearly attractions here, at dusty Chazumba, about 37 miles (60 km) north from Huajuapan, are its two major festivals, in honor of **Santiago** (24–26 July) and the **Señor de Esperanza** ("Lord of Hope"—the 15 days beginning Good Friday).

The town's permanent jewel is its church, dedicated to Santiago Apóstol (St. James the Apostle). Although it seems a small miracle that such a monumental building and refined works of art can be found in such an isolated little place, it is the Chazumba townsfolk's intense devotion, rather than divine intervention, that has produced the monumentally resplendent results over centuries of effort. While inside, among all the glitter, don't miss the baptismal chapel to the right of the front door, the Señor de Esperanza in the transept chapel, and Santiago above the front altar.

The Chazumba bus station supports a few highway-side eateries. Best seems to be the **Restaurant Los Arcos,** where you might be able to enjoy house specialties such as *mole de guajalote* (turkey with mole sauce), *tamales de frijol* (bean tamales), and *barbacoa* (barbecued beef, pork, or chicken).

Besides food, Restaurant Los Arcos also provides a **long-distance telephone and fax,** tel. 952/500-83. Moreover, in town, across the highway, you'll find a *correo* (post office) open Mon.–Fri. 9 A.M.–1 P.M. and 3–6 P.M., and a *telégrafos* for money orders and fax, open Mon.–Fri. 9 A.M.–3 P.M.

ADO and **Sur** buses, which depart from the Restaurant Los Arcos, connect several times a day north with Tehuacán, Puebla and Mexico City, and south with Huajuapan, Nochixtlán, Oaxaca, and intermediate points.

SOUTH OF HUAJUAPAN: ALONG THE HIGH ROAD TO THE MIXTECA ALTA

This lightly traveled but all-paved route, Oaxaca State Highway 15, branches south from Huajuapan, opening a scenic back door to Oaxaca's cool, green, and culturally rich Mixteca Alta. Along the way you'll cross rushing mountain rivers, wind through fertile, mountain farm valleys, and climb to high ridges where you can gaze back down upon it all.

Pleasant surprises along the way include boating, fishing, camping, and lakeside cabins at Yosocuta Reservoir and riverside hiking and wilderness camping in spectacular Tonalá Canyon. A few miles farther, at colonial-era Tonalá town, you can enjoy a cool, shady walk, a picnic, and camping in the town's great old *sabino* grove. Finally, at the route's end, at

Temescals, traditional hot rooms for healing, are common throughout the Mixteca.

Juxtlahuaca, enjoy a relaxing stroll and a restful overnight camping in the pine grove beside the crystalline, emerald-green Laguna Encantada.

Yosocuta Reservoir

This big artificial lake, eight miles (13 km) south of Huajuapan, confined by the government-built Yosocuta dam on the Río Mixteco, rises and falls with the seasons. From February through July, the reservoir drains, nourishing irrigated crops. Its level consequently falls, leaving an ugly bathtub-like lakeshore ring. However, by October the lake usually refills, rising to its brim, gently lapping the shoreline at **Parador Yosocuta,** the major lakeside access point.

Here you have several choices. Lake-view restaurants offer snacks, drinks, and fresh black bass dinners. A concession, owned by the Yosocuta town fishing cooperative and managed by friendly English-speaking Samuel Martínez, offers lake tours by boat ($7–12 per party), fishing excursions ($12 an hour), boat rentals, bait, and fishing poles (from about $40); launching fee for your own motorboat runs about $4.

If you decide to stay overnight, Samuel will let you set up your tent on the lakeshore or park your self-contained RV overnight in the parking lot free. He also rents out a few attractive lakeshore four-person cabins, with their own hot water baths and porch-front hammock hooks, for about $9 nightly.

Tonalá Canyon

South, past a high, pine-studded ridge and pass, Oaxaca Hwy. 15 winds down to the Tonalá valley. There, 27 miles (43 km) south of Huajuapan, beneath the foot of **Puente Morelos,** a steel-arch highway bridge, the Río Mixteco issues through the deep defile of Cañon de Tonalá.

A trail cut into the canyon wall leads to a diversion dam about a mile upstream. The trail begins at some stairs not far from the bridge's north footing. It continues spectacularly, above the river along the diversion canal, winding beneath towering 1,000-foot moss-mottled cliffs, green-tufted like a classical Chinese painting. At one point, a great boulder overhangs the trail; at another, a mass of ferns appears to cascade from the vertical rock wall.

At the dam, the trail ends at a small park and commemorative plaque that records that President Gustavo Díaz Ordaz came here during the late '60s to dedicate the dam, a part of the federal Río Balsas Basin Development Project. A rough, informal trail continues past the dam. After 50 downhill yards it leads to a flat spot on the right, with a bit of shade, safely above the river for camping.

For equipped and prepared wilderness adventurers, the river farther upstream, which runs about 10 miles through a wild, deep gorge, might be heaven. Overhead, vultures and eagles soar; coyotes, foxes, and wildcats hunt along the shore; and butterflies flutter among streamside trees and wildflowers. The river, rushing and often muddy during the summer rainy season, slows to a clear, tranquil creek during the dry winter and spring. **Warning:** Although the Yosocuta Dam upstream probably minimizes the hazard, hikers should be aware of possible flash flooding from upstream thunderstorms.

Santo Domingo Tonalá

The sleepy little farm community of Santo Domingo Tonalá (pop. 3,000) owns a pair of gems: its 16th-century Dominican-founded church and ex-convent, the **Templo de Santo Domingo,** and the lovely sylvan *sabinera* (cypress grove) behind the church. First, take a look inside the church, behind its front garden, a block north of the town plaza. Just past the entrance hangs an intriguing portrait of Angel Gabriel holding the scales of justice, deciding which of a cluster of beseeching souls will be admitted to Paradise. Farther on stands an image of the beloved African Dominican padre San Martín de Porres. The treasures climax in the right-side chapel, in a glittering, gorgeous small *retablo,* appearing as intricate as filigree and dedicated to the Holy Sacrament. Continue outside to the church's right, east side and enjoy a turn through the garden within the old convent cloister.

Tonalá's annual **festivals** revolve around the church. Arrive between 1 May and 4 May and get in on the fun (dancing, cockfights, and bull roping and riding) of the **Fiesta de la Santa Cruz.** A few months later, around 4 August, Tonalá folk rev up again for more of the same during the **Fiesta de Santo Domingo.**

You'll find the *sabinera* two blocks behind the church. Stroll around and soak in the cathedral-like loveliness beneath the old trees. Perhaps you will agree that the magnificent, gnarled old veteran *sabinos,* or *ahuehuetes,* are in their own way as magnificent as stately old-growth groves of their cousins, the California redwoods. They certainly approach the size of redwoods. At the grove's far west (left as you enter) end, find the gnarled old grandparent of them all, 15 feet in diameter and 50 feet around. During your walk, you probably will notice the several small, clear rivulets running through the grove. This is no coincidence; local folks believe

sabinos to be the most intelligent of trees; they always grow where the water flows.

Accommodations and Food: Best of all, the grassy tree-bordered lot at the *sabinera's* east end (highway side) seems fine for **tent camping.** Before setting up, however, obtain permission from the town police or other authorities at the *presidencia municipal* on the plaza. Although the natural spring water running beneath the trees is probably pure for drinking, stay on the safe side by buying bottled water in one of the stores on the plaza, or by using your filter or adding a water purifying tablet to the spring water.

Alternatively, consider Tonalá's downscale hotel, **Los Mangos,** Lázaro Cárdenas 27, Santo Domingo Tonalá, Oaxaca, tel. 953/100-23, marked by a tall mango tree, on the entrance road from the highway. The grandmotherly owner offers 10 rooms; check them over before moving in. Mildew can be a problem here, so ask for fresh linens if necessary. All rooms have baths, with hot water 6–9 A.M., she says. Rentals run about $5 s, $7 d, with all the mangos you can eat, in season.

For cooked food, the Los Mangos' owner runs an inviting restaurant on the premises. Alternatively, for some tacos, tortas, or a hamburger, you can try the *lonchería* across the street from her restaurant. A store or two on or near the plaza can supply basic groceries. The plaza-front **market,** biggest on Friday, is the best local source of fruits and vegetables.

Services

If you're sick, go to the **centro de salud,** on Lázaro Cárdenas, the main entrance thoroughfare, downhill past the church. For routine medications and drugs, try the **Farmacia Santa Cruz** a block uphill from the hotel. For **long-distance telephone and fax** go to the *larga distancia* across the street from the Hotel Los Mangos.

Getting There

Bus passengers can reach Yosocuta, Tonalá Canyon, and Tonalá town by second-class **Fletes y Pasajes, Tonalteca,** or **Sur** buses, either south from Huajuapan or north from Juxtlahuaca.

From Huajuapan drivers should first head

west along Hwy. 190 to a signed Juxtlahuaca or Tonalá left turnoff, about a mile west of the city center. After another mile (1.5 km) turn right at the main street, Av. Mina; continue another eight miles (13 km) to Yosocuta. Continue a total of 27 miles (43 km) to Tonalá Canyon, 30 miles (50 km) to Tonalá town, and 62 miles (100 km) to Juxtlahuaca. North from Juxtlahuaca, the distances are approximately 32 miles (51 km) to Tonalá, 35 miles (56 km) to Tonalá Canyon, and 54 miles (87 km) to Yosocuta. Figure about two hours at the wheel, either direction.

SANTIAGO JUXTLAHUACA AND VICINITY

Santiago Juxtlahuaca (pop. about 30,000) is the largest town and major service and governmental center for the Juxtlahuaca district. It's clear why the town has prospered. It nestles in a deep, fertile valley between a pair of towering oak- and pine-studded mountain ranges. Main roads branch south, west, and north, connecting Juxtlahuaca with the outside world.

A second glance at the surrounding mountains reveals sinuous trails so steep that it's a wonder how anyone could climb them. But people do—the Mixtec and Trique-speaking mountain people, for whom Juxtlahuaca's big *tianguis* is the focus of their week. They rise long before dawn and bundle up their merchandise—perhaps a basket packed with flowers, potatoes, or carrots; maybe they pile on a few hand-loomed bright red-striped *huipiles.* Husband and wife sling the loads on their backs, adjust the tumplines on their foreheads, and begin the steep trek downhill, with hope that this will be a good *tianguis,* and they won't have to haul everything back uphill tomorrow night.

Orientation and Sights
Orient yourself by the tall, straitlaced bell tower of the town church, the **Templo de Santiago Apóstol,** visible from all over town. The church faces west, downhill, toward the adjacent town plaza. If you stand looking at the church, south will be on your right, north on your left. The uphill direction, toward the rear of the church, is east. Main east-west streets are Libertad, which runs along the church's north side; Porfirio Díaz, along

the church's south side by the plaza; and Benito Juárez, along the plaza's south side. Important north-south streets are Lázaro Cárdenas, a block behind the church, and Independencia, a block farther east, uphill.

If at all possible, schedule your Juxtlahuaca visit to coincide with its two-day *tianguis,* big on Thursday but among Oaxaca's biggest on Friday. Vendors' awnings (known in the Aztec language as *tianguis*) stretch from curb to curb, beginning at the town plaza just downhill from the church, and overflow, filling half of Juxtlahuaca's south-side streets.

The star actors of the *tianguis* are the **Trique women,** who proudly wear their horizontally striped bright red wool *huipiles* over their black woolen skirts. (If you wonder why in sunny Mexico they wear wool, it's because afternoons are often cloudy and cool in Juxtlahuaca, especially during the summer and fall rainy season, and doubly so in the Triques' mountaintop villages.)

A number of Trique women congregate in the town plaza's center, selling their home-spun textiles: *huipiles,* black *enredos* (skirts), and blouses. They don't like having their pictures taken, but several remedies exist for curing camera shyness. (See the special topic Taking People Pictures in the Introduction.)

From the plaza, plunge into the hubbub of stalls on the south-side street, Benito Juárez. Along your meandering path you'll find loads of lovely fruit—many exotic tropical varieties—*anonas, pitahayas, guanabanas, zapotes*—but also plums, apples, pears, grapes, and peaches in the summer. You'll also see a fair amount of pottery, especially along Calle Lázaro Cárdenas, the north-south street that runs behind the church. Varieties include flower-painted hard-glazed bowls, cups, and plates from Santa Rosa in the Valley of Oaxaca; green ware from Atzompa, also in the Valley of Oaxaca; and red and black jugs, plates, and bowls from Puebla. A few stalls also sell woven palm baskets, mats, and sombreros from around Huajuapan de León.

If you're in the market for **masks,** go to the shop of master craftsman Alejandro Jesús Vera Guzman, at Lázaro Cárdenas 301 Sur, corner of Melchor Ocampo, tel. 955/400-60, two blocks west of the uphill side of the church. His store is

Juxtlahuaca is a regional center for the Mixtecs' pelota mixteca traditional ball game.

in the left-hand side of the southwest corner grocery. He got started creating masks (devils seem to be his specialty) for local fiesta dances; now he sells to the public. His prices aren't cheap; expect to pay $40 and up. From him, however, you're getting the genuine article. If you lend him your photo, he'll even create a mask of you, for around $150.

While you're wandering around, you might take a look inside the **church.** Just as you enter the door, look into the small alcove on the right and you'll see the town patron, **Santiago** (St. James), sword in hand, on his usual white horse, but this time with a cowboy hat atop his head. Up front, above the altar, you'll see Santiago in more traditional dress. Step left, into the left transept chapel, and see the **Virgen de Soledad** presiding above the altar.

Festivals and Events

Local townsfolk celebrate both Santiago and the Virgen de Soledad in big festivals. Santiago's culminates around 25 July, with a number of traditional dances: the Christians and Moors (a variation of the Dance of the Conquest; the Moors are the bad guys); the Chilolos (masked men, posing as women, in bells and skirts); and the town favorite, the Diablos (Devils). Much the same thing goes on during the 8 December Virgen de Soledad festival. In addition, **Carnaval** is big in Juxtlahuaca. On the four days before Ash Wednesday, the beginning of Lent, townsfolk whoop it up with the masked dance

Rubios (Blondes), a parody of the Spanish conquistadores, and the Machos dance.

Juxtlahuaca, moreover, is a center of *pelota mixteca,* the Mixtec version of the ancient Mesoamerican ball game. Although commonly played with a *hule* (natural rubber) ball, the local variation is to use a leather ball. Players wrap their hands in thick cloth and bat the ball in a court, not unlike tennis. Local teams get ready for the yearly November tournament nearly every afternoon in the long sandy court marked out just below the church.

Laguna Encantada

Yet another good reason for coming to Juxtlahuaca is Laguna Encantada (Enchanted Lagoon), a deep crystalline emerald-green lake beside the Huajuapan highway about two miles north of town. Laguna Encantada, set like a jewel at the foot of a towering mountain, is a precious asset that besides supplying irrigation water, supplies the adjacent communal swimming pool and picnic and camping ground. Even if you don't camp there, you should at least go for a stroll around its shoreline, made picture-perfect by the family of gnarled old *ahuehuete* cypresses inhabiting its banks.

Both tent and RV **camping** prospects at Laguna Encantada could hardly be better. A broad cypress-shaded campground on the lake's north side provides plenty of grassy space to spread out. As a courtesy, ask the caretaker, friendly Natalia Ramos de Morales, who runs the snack stand, if camping is OK. It always will be both allowed and free, especially if you buy a few tacos and drinks from her.

She recommends that visitors hike up to the top of the hill, Mogote de la Tialeja, just north of the campground. Natalia (a definite local booster) says that the Mogote, a former Mixtec settlement, is full of artifacts (which must remain in place; Mexican law forbids their removal). Artifacts or not, your reward for the 750-foot (250-meter) summit climb will be an airy, panoramic valley and mountain view.

Accommodations and Food

Juxtlahuaca has several hotels, of which at least two are recommendable. Nicest is the family-run **Hotel Mixteco,** Independencia 200, Juxtlahuaca, Oaxaca 69700, tel. 955/400-25, near the corner of Libertad, two blocks behind the church. The 13 plainly furnished but clean rooms encircle a homey mango and lemon tree-decorated patio. Rooms rent for about $8 s, $ 13 d, and $18 t, with hot water shower baths and parking; credit cards not accepted.

Alternatively, try the **Hotel Diana,** at Porfirio Díaz 300, Juxtlahuaca, Oaxaca 69700, tel. 955/400-76, a block downhill from the plaza. The 30 basic but clean rooms with hot water baths begin at about $11 s, $15 d, and $26 t, with TV, hot water showers and parking; credit cards not accepted. Larger-size rooms with two beds run about $22 d.

Plaza-front taco stands and market *fondas* (permanent stalls) provide plenty of very inexpensive local-style food. Remember: If it's hot, it's wholesome. Market vegetable and fruit selection is super, especially during the summer. To e on the safe side, peel, cook, or scrub with soap and water any fruit or vegetable you eat. Stores such as **Estrada Fería,** on Lázaro Cárdenas, half a block south of Díaz, a block uphill from the plaza, supply basic groceries.

Juxtlahuaca people are prosperous enough to support a few restaurants. Always busy is the **Comedor Tere,** behind the church on Lázaro Cárdenas, a block uphill from the plaza, open daily 7 A.M.–11 P.M. The specialty here is a hearty afternoon four-course *comida,* typically soup, rice, stew, and dessert, for about $3.

Other restaurant choices are *taquería* **Rebe** and the excellent, family-run **López Pizza**

(pizza, spaghetti, calzone, hamburgers, and lettuce and tomato salad if you ask for it.) Find them both near the corner of Lázaro Cárdenas and Libertad.

Services

Change money at the air-conditioned **Banco Internacional** (Bital), tel. 955/404-27 or 955/404-28, on Lázaro Cárdenas behind and a block south of the church. Its long money-changing hours are Mon.–Fri. 8 A.M.–7 P.M., Sat. 8 A.M.–3 P.M. If they're closed, use their ATM. If Bital doesn't suit you, go to Juxtlahuaca's **Banamex,** tel. 955/404-17 or 955/404-18, also with an ATM, open Mon.–Fri. 9 A.M.–5 P.M., Sat. 9 A.M.–2 P.M., one block directly south of the plaza. After bank hours, try **Casa de Cambio Intermex** on the plaza, tel. 955/403-42.

Juxtlahuaca's *corrco* (post office), open Mon.–Fri. 9 A.M.–1 P.M. and 3–6 P.M., Sat. 9 A.M.–noon, is downhill from the church, at the northwest plaza corner. *Telecomunicaciones,* providing public fax, 955/400-44, and money orders, is open Mon.–Fri. 9 A.M.–3 P.M. and Sat. 9 A.M.–noon, on Díaz, half a block downhill from the plaza. For after-hours long-distance phone and fax, go to either of the two private *larga distancias* on the plaza's south side.

For travel services, go to **Micsa Agencia de Viajes,** tel. 955/404-46 or 955/402-32, 300 Lázaro Cárdenas Sur, corner of Melchor Ocampo, three blocks south of the church.

A number of doctor-owned pharmacies on Lázaro Cárdenas, such as the **Farmacia Diana Luz** of Doctor Amadeo T. Chaves, tel. 955/400-14, are open until 9 P.M. for consultation, prescriptions and sales right on the spot. For hospital or emergency medical service, Juxtlahuaca has a **general hospital** about a mile north of town on the Huajuapan highway, tel. 955/403-07, 955/403-08, or 955/403-09.

For gynecological consultation, see **Doctora Iralda Budar Villavicenzio,** at her house at 104 Independencia Norte, or her office, on Lázaro Cárdenas, a block and a half south of Díaz, tel. 955/401-84. Her hours are Mon.–Fri. 8 A.M.–2 P.M. and 4–8 P.M., on call 24 hours in emergency.

Getting There and Away

Several long-distance bus lines connect Juxtlahuaca with various Oaxaca and national destinations. Stations are on the highway. First-class **Sur** and **Cristóbal Colón** buses connect north with Huajuapan, Puebla, and Mexico City; northeast with Tlaxiaco, Teposcolula, and Tamazulapan; southeast with Nochixtlán and Oaxaca; and south with Putla and Pinotepa Nacional. **Fletes y Pasajes** second-class buses connect north with Tonalá, Huajuapan, Cuautla (Morelos), and Mexico City, and east and southeast with Tlaxiaco, Teposcolula, Nochixtlán, and Oaxaca. **Tonalteca** and **Autobuses Mixteca-Costa** second-class buses connect south with Putla and Pinotepa

Nacional and north with Tonalá and Huajuapan.

For drivers, paved (but sometimes potholed) mountain roads connect Juxtlahuaca with Oaxaca destinations: north with Huajuapan de León, 62 miles (100 km), two hours; south with Putla de Guerrero, via Oaxaca Hwy. 15 (20 miles, 32 km), thence via National Hwy. 125 (17 miles, 28 km), a total of 37 miles (60 km), in about an hour; or east, with Tlaxiaco, via Oaxaca Hwy. 15 (20 miles, 32 km), then via National Hwy. 125 (30 miles, 48 km), a total of 50 miles (80 km), in about two hours.

ROOF OF OAXACA: THE MIXTECA ALTA

The Mixteca Alta, Oaxaca's temperate Mixtec highland, is a land poor in gold but rich in scenic and cultural assets: airy mountain vistas, colorful village markets, pine-scented breezes, beloved old churches, tumbling waterfalls, ancient ruins, and crystalline springs await the traveler who ventures into the Mixteca Alta.

Moreover, travel within the Mixteca Alta is not difficult. Tlaxiaco, with its hotels, restaurants, bus connections, and services, is a good base for exploring the Mixteca Alta. From Tlaxiaco, roads lead out east past cool, green mountain vistas to the enigmatic ruins at Huamelulpan and Achiutla, south over the airy Chalcatongo plateau to the Cascada Esmeralda at Yosundua, and west to the friendly little Mixtec-speaking museum towns of Cuquila and San Miguel Progreso.

ASUNCIÓN TLAXIACO

Tlaxiaco (tlah-shee-AH-koh) is far more important than its population of about 30,000 would imply. It's the economic capital of the entire Mixteca Alta, a magnet for thousands of vendors from all over central and southern Mexico and thousands more native folks who swarm into town for the **Saturday** *tianguis* (native market), second only to the big Saturday market in Oaxaca City.

The town, also capital of the Tlaxiaco governmental district, was even more important in times past. During the "Order and Progress" of President Porfirio Díaz (1876–1910), Tlaxiaco's

significance perhaps eclipsed even Oaxaca City. Its key position on the trade route between Puebla and Veracruz and the southern Pacific Coast, as well as its large hinterland population, made Tlaxiaco the trading and supply center for much of southwest Mexico. Rich merchants and entrepreneurs, both Mexican and foreign, together with wealthy landed *hacendados,* constituted a local upper crust who, for a generation, earned Tlaxiaco the unofficial title of "Little Paris."

The Dominican friars certainly understood Tlaxiaco's importance as early as 1550, when Friar Francisco Marín began building the monumental town church, the Templo de la Asunción. Scholars have identified details in the church's decorations that resemble those of the main church in the city of Caceres, Spain. This link has added a piece to one of the puzzles of Oaxaca's great Dominican churches: where did the Dominican clerics, presumably isolated in the Oaxaca hinterlands, acquire the skill to create the masterpiece churches of Yanhuitlán, Teposcolula, Coixtlahuaca, and Tlaxiaco? The answer may lie in a previously unknown connection between the Dominican friars and the noted Rodrigo Gil de Montañon, master of Spanish Gothic-Plateresque architecture and builder of the Caceres church. (See the special topic Building Churches in the chapter Around the Valley of Oaxaca)

Sights
Let **Plaza Constitución,** the hub of the Tlaxiaco

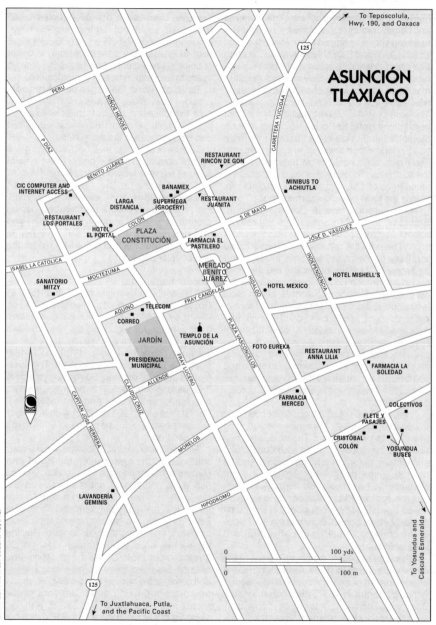

To Teposcolula,
Hwy. 190, and Oaxaca

125

PERU

NINOS HEROES

CARRETERA VUCUDAA

ASUNCIÓN
TLAXIACO

P DIAZ

BENITO JUAREZ

RESTAURANT
RINCÓN DE GON

MINIBUS TO
ACHIUTLA

CIC COMPUTER AND
INTERNET ACCESS

BANAMEX

LARGA
DISTANCIA

SUPERMEGA
(GROCERY)

RESTAURANT
JUANITA

S DE MAYO

RESTAURANT
LOS PORTALES

HOTEL
EL PORTAL

COLÓN

PLAZA
CONSTITUCIÓN

FARMACIA EL
PASTILERO

JOSÉ D. VÁSQUEZ

ISABEL LA CATOLICA

MOCTEZUMA

MERCADO
BENITO
JUÁREZ

INDEPENDENCIA

HOTEL MISHELL'S

SANATORIO
MITZY

FRAY CANDELAS

HIDALGO

HOTEL MEXICO

AQUINO

TELECOM

CORREO

JARDÍN

TEMPLO DE LA
ASUNCIÓN

PLAZA VASCONCELOS

FOTO EUREKA

RESTAURANT
ANNA LILIA

FARMACIA LA
SOLEDAD

PRESIDENCIA
MUNICIPAL

ALLENDE

FRAY LUCERO

COLECTIVOS

CAPITAN JOSE HERRERA

CLAUDIO CRUZ

FARMACIA
MERCED

FLETE Y
PASAJES

MORELOS

CRISTÓBAL
COLÓN

YOSUNDUA
BUSES

MOON

LAVANDERÍA
GEMINIS

HIPODROMO

0   100 yds

0   100 m

To Yosundua and
Cascada Esmeralda

© AVALON TRAVEL PUBLISHING, INC.

125

To Juxtlahuaca, Putla,
and the Pacific Coast

market, a few blocks uphill from the cluttered and bumpy through-town highway, be your key to finding your way around town. Main east-west streets Colón and 5 de Mayo run along the north and south sides, respectively, of Plaza Constitución. East of the plaza, they intersect the other main town streets, Independencia and Hidalgo, which both run north, uphill from the highway. The perfect spot to visualize all this is the front porch of the **Hotel El Portal,** which perches on the uphill (north) side of the plaza. From there you'll see the bell tower of the town church, Templo de la Asunción, a few hundred yards to the southwest. To the right of the church, behind some trees on the west side of a shady *jardín,* stands the town *presidencia municipal.*

Make sure to arrive in Tlaxiaco by noon, Saturday, in time to soak in its spreading, colorful, Saturday *tianguis.* It's fun to just wander around beneath the rainbow of awnings shading a galaxy of merchandise, both modern and traditional. Especially interesting are the time-tested handmade goods: *calabazas* (gourds) cut and carved into bowls, utensils, and musical instruments; extensive assortments of forest-gathered roots, seeds, bark, dried flowers, and nuts, ready to brew into teas to cure dozens of illnesses; traditional clothes—hand-embroidered *huipiles* and *blusas* from all over Oaxaca; *canastas, petates,* (baskets, mats) and sombreros woven from palm; and leather *cinturones, bolsas,* and *billeteras* (belts, purses, and billfolds).

The added plus of all the bustle, of course, is the people, especially the native women, who really run the whole show. The men, who help transport the goods, usually stand back (and sometimes, unfortunately, get drunk) and let their spouses do the buying and selling. Perhaps the best two spots for native action are the narrow **Plaza Vasconcelos,** which heads downhill for a block from the southeast corner of Plaza Constitución, and the front steps of the church, a hubbub of native fruit and vegetable sellers.

While you're people-watching in front of the church, the **Templo de la Asunción,** take a break and step into its cool, calm interior. Although begun in 1550, the church, once a Dominican convent, has been continually modified and strengthened since that time.

Towering overhead, a network of unreinforced (no steel: all stone) Gothic arches have, amazingly, supported the entire ceiling for more than 400 years, freeing the nave from the clutter of columns and creating an heavenly, soaring space for worship, rest, and contemplation.

Tlaxiaco's patron, the **Virgen de la Asunción,** presides from above the altar. High above her, note the all-seeing eye (which looks every bit like its counterparts painted on many Buddhist and Hindu stupas in India and Nepal.)

Townsfolk celebrate their beloved patron in a pair of annual **fiestas.** The first, the official patronal religious festival, kicks off on 14 August and continues for two more days with processions, food, and fireworks. The second, the secular town **Fiesta de Octubre,** occurs around the third Sunday of October and includes fireworks, basketball and *pelota mixteca* (traditional ball game) tournaments, and popular dances.

Accommodations

Of Tlaxiaco's sprinkling of hotels, the **Hotel El Portal,** Constitución 2, Tlaxiaco, Oaxaca 69800, tel. 955/201-54, affords a superb plaza-front vantage for exploring the colorful town center. Inside past the reception, you enter an elegantly restored grand patio, softly illuminated by an overhead skylight. The three stories of approximately 50 rooms encircle a back parking courtyard. The rooms are spartan, but clean, comfortable, and well-maintained. Rentals run about $20 s, $23 d, with hot water shower baths and parking; credit cards not accepted.

Although less favorably located a few blocks southeast of the town center, the **Hotel San Mishell's,** Independencia 11, Tlaxiaco, Oaxaca 69800, tel. 955/200-64, offers attentive on-site family management. The dozen superior-grade rooms in a two-story tier surround an inviting inner garden patio. Inside, rooms are clean, carpeted, and thoughtfully decorated. Outside the rooms, on a shady garden-view porch, guests enjoy soft chairs for reading and relaxing. Standard grade rooms, although clean and comfortable occupy a two-story tier beside an adjacent parking patio. Superior grade rooms rent for about $17 s, $28 d, with TV; standard grade run about $10 s, $16 d, without

TV. All rooms have hot water shower baths and parking, credit cards not accepted.

Nearby, a block and a half west of Plaza Constitución, stands the downscale old standby, the family-run **Hotel Mexico,** at Hidalgo 13, Tlaxiaco, Oaxaca 69800, tel. 955/200-86. Rooms, in "new" (private bath) and "old" (shared bath) sections, surround a rambling inside patio. All of the 20-odd rooms are clean; the "old" rooms are plainly furnished, while the "new" are thoughtfully decorated with wood furnishings, attractive bedspreads, and drapes. Rates for "old" rooms run about $6 s, $7 d, $12 t; the "new," $12 s, $14 d, $22 t, all with hot water available only in the morning until 11 A.M.; credit cards not accepted.

Food
Taco stands and *fondas* (food stalls) at the covered **Mercado Benito Juárez** (walk one block south of the Plaza Constitución's southeast corner.) are your best source of economical meals and snacks. Basic groceries are available at plaza-front *abarroterías,* notably at **Super Mega,** at plaza's northeast side, a block east of Hotel El Portal, next to Banamex. Baked goods are also sold at several stalls at the Mercado Benito Juárez.

A few **restaurants** cater to the handful of Tlaxiaco residents who can afford to eat out. Fortunately, Tlaxiaco diners enjoy what is perhaps the Mixteca Alta's best restaurant, the highly-recommended old-Mexico rustic style **Restaurant Los Portales,** on Porfirio Díaz (the north-south street just west of the Hotel Portal), a block north of the plaza. Here, you can choose from a long menu professionally prepared and served soups, salads, meats, seafood and poultry. Although they suggest several house specialties, no matter, everything they serve is good. Open daily 7 A.M.–10 P.M.; moderate.

Also very popular is the refined **Rincón de Gon** at Colón 11, a block east of the plaza. You can start with a choice of breakfasts, including *huevos con jamón* (ham and eggs), omelettes, fruit, granola, and hotcakes. For lunch or supper, choose from several salads, and among entrées of fish, meat, poultry, and Mexican specialties. Some evenings, beginning around 9, patrons enjoy relaxing guitar music. Open daily 7 A.M.–11 P.M. moderate.

Third choice goes to **Restaurant Juanita,** with a menu long on local fare, with plenty of eggs *al gusto* (any style), *pollo frito* (fried chicken), *chuleta de puerco* (pork chop), and *enchiladas de mole,* accompanied by all the tortillas you can eat and all the TV you can watch. For dessert, you can have *duraznos* (canned peaches) or *platanos fritos con miel* (fried bananas with honey). Open daily except Sun. 8 A.M.–9 P.M. Budget.

Services and Information
Change money at Tlaxiaco's bank, **Banamex,** at Colón 1, open Mon.–Fri. 9 A.M.–3 P.M., Sat. 9 A.M.–1 P.M., tel. 955/201-33 and 955/200-98. After hours, use its up-front **ATM** for cash.

Buy stamps or send letters at the *correo* (post office) on the north side of the *jardín* in front of the church, open Mon.–Fri. 9 A.M.–2 P.M., Sat. 9 A.M.–1 P.M. Next door, at *telecomunicaciones,* you can send or receive a fax or money order; open Mon.–Fri. 8 A.M.–7 P.M., Sat. 9 A.M.–noon, tel. 955/204-65.

Telephone long distance or send a fax at the *caseta larga distancia,* tel. 955/203-13, 955/203-14, or 955/201-47, open daily 7 A.M.–11 P.M., at the northeast plaza corner next to the Hotel El Portal.

Answer your email and access the **Internet** at CIC computer store, at 5 Porfirio Díaz (a block north of the plaza's northwest corner), corner of Juárez.

If you need a doctor, ask for a recommendation at your hotel desk, or go to Dr. Javier Noé Alavez Cervantes, tel./fax 955/200-28, at **Sanatorio Mitzy,** Moctezuma 4, a block and a half west from the plaza.

Otherwise, consult highly recommended general practitioner Doctor Manuel López Hernádez, at the ISSTE (Seguro Social) clinic, tel. 955/207-50, on Hwy. 125, Oaxaca direction, about a mile east of town.

For nonprescription medicines and drugs, try **Farmacia La Soledad,** tel. 955/201-59, at Morelos 5, corner of Independencia, or **Farmacia La Merced,** open Mon.–Sat. 8 A.M.–9 P.M., Sun. 10 A.M.–2 P.M. one block west at the corner of Morelos and Hidalgo, or **Farmacia El Pastillero** (Pill Seller), half a block east of the plaza's southeast corner; open Mon.–Sat. 9 A.M.–9 P.M.

For film, development, and some point-and-shoot cameras and photographic supplies, go to Tlaxiaco's Fuji film dealer, **Foto Eureka,** on Hidalgo, two blocks south, one block east of the plaza, tel. 955/202-49, open Mon.–Sat. 8 A.M.–9 P.M., closed Sunday.

Tlaxiaco's laundry, **Lavandería Geminis,** is open Mon.–Sat. 8 A.M.–4 P.M. and 5–8 P.M., at Capitán José Herrera 20, two blocks west, three blocks south of the plaza.

For travel information and services, try the **Agencia de Viajes Mícsa** travel agent, tel. 955/202-85, at Hidalgo 9, a block east, half a block south of the plaza.

Getting There and Away

A welter of taxis, local buses and minivans, and long-distance buses deposit and pick up a small army of passengers daily downhill on Hwy. 125, locally called Av. Hipodromo.

Long-distance service includes **Sur** and **Cristóbal Colón,** from their station at Hipodromo 24 B, tel. 955/201-82, between Independencia and Hidalgo. Buses connect east and southeast, with Teposcolula, Yanhuitlán, Nochixtlán, and Oaxaca; north with Tamazulapan, Huajuapan, Puebla, Cuautla (Morelos), and Mexico City; and south with Putla and Pinotepa Nacional on the Pacific Coast.

Also, second-class **Fletes y Pasajes** long-distance buses, tel. 955/204-32, connect east and southeast with Teposcolula, Yanhuitlán, Nochixtlán, and Oaxaca, and south with Putla and Pinotepa Nacional.

SOUTH OF TLAXIACO

Although the glorious Cascada Esmeralda (Emerald Waterfall) at the end of the road is reason enough to venture out on this 106-mile (171-km) round-trip excursion, the sights along the way make the journey doubly enjoyable. You'll gaze at a succession of mighty pine- and oak-studded mountains, mile upon mile of green, terraced fields, and, oddly in contrast, one of the most spectacularly eroded landscapes in Oaxaca. Moreover, you'll pass more log cabins than a trip through all of Montana and Wyoming. And if you go on Sunday, you'll get a chance to visit a pair of busy country markets. Finally, self-contained

RV or tent campers can enjoy a superbly scenic natural camping site at the dramatic top of Cascada Esmeralda. The all-paved route climbs to the top of the Mixteca Alta—the 9,000-foot (2,700-meter) cool, fertile, Chalcatongo plateau—before descending to Yosundua and the subtropical Esmeralda valley, where on a clear day, folks say, you can glimpse the blue Pacific.

The Road to Chalcatongo

Drivers, start out by at least 10 A.M., because in the Mixteca (Land of the Clouds), especially in the summer-fall rainy season, sunny mornings often turn gray, drizzly, and cool by the midafternoon. By bus, go earlier, just south of the corner of Hwy. 125 (Tlaxiaco's Calle Hipodromo) and Independencia. Look for either the yellow, orange, and white **Unión de Transportistas Ñundeya,** minibuses, or the orange, yellow, blue, and white **Auto Transportes Yosundua** buses which head south about every half hour 6 A.M.–6 P.M. Drivers, take the same route and mark your odometer at the Hwy. 125 crossing as you start south. Best fill up with gasoline in town (gas on east, Oaxaca, side only) beforehand. There is only one gas station en route, at Chalcatongo (although stores along the way do sell Magna). If you want to eat well along the way, best take your own picnic, especially during he winter, when upcountry fresh fruit and veggie supplies are at low ebb.

At mile 10 (km 16) the road reaches an overlook where you can gaze down upon the **Magdalena Peñasco** valley, with erosion so dramatic that, like the scenic Badlands of Dakota, it's a sight in itself. The reason isn't so difficult to figure. Long ago the people cut the trees for fuel and houses, then farmed the hills without contour terracing. They let sheep and goats overgraze the meadows, and when downpours began forming gullies it was too late. Today the entire valley looks like a red, rutted devil's playground.

As you continue downhill, you'll see folks along the road weaving palm leaves, especially on Sunday, as they walk toward the weekly Magdalena Peñasco *tianguis* (country market). Passing the town square and market, at around mile 12 (km 19) notice one of Magdalena's major public buildings—a turquoise-blue log house—on the right.

Around mile 21 (km 34), continuing through **San Mateo Peñasco,** it's difficult not to be awed by the towering, stone-faced mountain on the right. In times past (or maybe even in times present) this awesomely rugged rampart, which local people call simply La Peña (The Rock), must have been a sacred mountain, with its own *Señor del Monte* (Lord of the Mountain).

Today, a cross stands partway up the slope, where the villagers climb on 3 May, the Día de la Santa Cruz (Day of the Holy Cross). Although arduous, the climb to the summit appears do-able with effort by in-shape people wearing hats and sturdy shoes and carrying drinking water. Don't attempt it, however, without permission from the San Mateo Peñasco municipal authorities, who can probably suggest a guide whom you can hire to show the way.

In contrast to the eroded Magdalena valley, the surroundings of **San Pedro Molinos,** at mile 28 (km 45), appear the model of progressive farming practice. Lush valley-bottom fields give way to terraced, mid-slope gardens, which lead to a crown of thick, summit forests. Molinos town is marked by its spiffy, portaled *presidencia municipal.*

Farther on, at **Santa Catarina Ticúa** at around mile 31 (km 50), note the uniquely picturesque three-story log house, on the right just as you arrive at the town plaza and church. Next, step across the plaza and take a look inside the brilliantly painted 18th-century church, dedicated to martyr Saint Catherine. If you're lucky, you'll arrive on 24 or 25 November, when local people are celebrating Santa Catarina with processions, fireworks, sports contests, and dances. If not, at least, you can admire the Mixtec pre-Columbian floral designs on the church's walls and ceiling, and maybe afterwards, if its a warm day, you might pause for dip in the **community swimming pool** outside next to the church. Finally, after working up an appetite, stop for a break at the local restaurant **La Mixteca,** on the left of the highway (southbound) behind the water tower-clock on the way out of town.

Chalcatongo

At around mile 37 (km 60) you reach high and cool, sometimes even chilly, Chalcatongo (pop. 2,000). Chalcatongo has two plazas, the first one bordered by the distinguished church, the **Templo de la Natividad,** whose patron is the Virgen de la Natividad. Townsfolk celebrate her with a fiesta on 8 September. Take a look inside, which was undergoing renovation and should be quite handsome by the time you read this. Chalcatongo is quiet except for Thursday, when thousands of local folks and vendors from as far as Mexico City crowd in for a big country *tianguis.*

At the second plaza, one block ahead, one block left, stands the *presidencia municipal.* Although both plazas have a sprinkling of taco shops, only a couple places in town appear to qualify as restaurants. One is the **Restaurant Tres Coronas** (at the hotel, below) and **Restaurant El Calvario,** which you'll see at the corner of Guerrero and Insurgentes, second floor, as you continue south out of town. Both of these places have no menu and customarily offer only one entráe—usually a tasty, wholesome beef or chicken stew, usually served with rice and tortillas. If you order à la carte, you'll probably have to settle for something basic, such as eggs *rancheros* or *a la Mexicana,* chicken tacos, or maybe a hamburger. For salad, you usually can count on tomatoes *jitomate* and avocado.

Chalcatongo also has the **Hotel Cliserio,** owned and operated by friendly English-speaking Señor Eliseo Cliserio Nicolas Valdez. His hotel stands across the plaza from the church. Unfortunately, the rooms, which rent for about $7 s, $13 d, with bath and hot water (when the heater's working), are plain to the point of drabness and could use a good scrubbing. But they'll provide a roof over your head and a blanket or two, if you need them. Look at several rooms and choose the best.

Yosundua and Cascada Esmeralda

Drivers lucky enough to arrive in Yosundua (at mile 51, km 82) on Sunday will probably find the way to the waterfall blocked by the big, colorful *tianguis.* Stroll around for a while, then detour downhill, then ahead, via the street that runs in front of the big church, **Templo Santiago Apóstol.** The church is dedicated to Saint James

Cascada Esmeralda

equipped, is to set up their tent or park their self-contained RV in the informal meadow **campground** at the top of the Cascada Esmeralda, at mile 53 (km 85). There, the blue-green (a bit murky during the summer rains, however) Río Esmeralda (Emerald River) pauses a while in an inviting pool (safe only at low water) before it plunges over the cliff. The road winds another few hundred yards down a steep grade; continue on foot down a steep short path to the foot of the falls, where you're surrounded by natural beauty. On one side, the waterfall, split into a lacy network of petite cascades, cools you with gentle spray, while on the other, far below, a grand, sun-dappled verdant valley of field and forest nestles beneath a host of sharp, soaring peaks.

EAST OF TLAXIACO

The country east of Tlaxiaco undulates over small, fertile vales and green, pine-forested hilltops, many crowned with the ruins of ancient buried towns and cities. Two of the largest and most interesting of those ruins are at Achiutla and Huamelulpan, not far from Tlaxiaco.

San Miguel Achiutla

The archaeological site at Achiutla (ah-shee-YOO-tlah, pop. 1,000) is among Oaxaca's histor-ically most intriguing, partly because it contains both pre- and postconquest ruins. These include the remains of the earthquake-collapsed original Dominican church and a grand preconquest ruined complex, once the site of a renowned Mixtec oracle.

Getting There: The gorgeous pine-forested mountains and lush (summer-fall rainy season) valleys you pass along the way are part of the fun of Achiutla. Bus travelers go most conveniently by the minibuses that leave from the corner of Calle Cinco de Mayo and Hwy. 125 (Av. Independencia) at the northeast corner of downtown. Alternatively, bargain for a taxi to take you to the Achiutla turnoff (signed Santa Catarina Tayata) about nine miles east of town, then catch a truck from there. If so, find out the price—ask, *"¿Cuanto cuesta a Achiutla?"* ("How much to Achiutla?")—before getting on.

the Apostle, whom townsfolk celebrate 23–26 July. Bus passengers should either hire a taxi or hike straight ahead from the Yosundua bus stop about 2.5 miles (four km) and 1,000 feet downhill to the Cascada Esmeralda.

If you're hungry, stop by the clean, family run, home-style **Restaurant Manantial** (Restaurant Spring), named for the town's crystal-clear water source, nearby. It's open daily 8 A.M.–9 P.M., at the far, southeast edge of town, where the gravel road heads south to the Cascada Esmeralda.

If you miss the last bus back, you can stay at very rough and ready **Hotel California,** whose owner returned from California with a wad of cash and decided to build himself a hotel. He now has 31 mostly empty, extremely basic concrete-floored rooms that he rents for $8 s, $12 d, with bath and (maybe) hot water. You can't miss the place, because it's purple and green, and, except for the church, is the biggest building in town.

A better overnight option, for people who are

The road, although gravel, is easily passable by experienced drivers in ordinary cars. Set your odometer at the Santa Catarina Tayata turnoff. After 1.2 miles (1.9 km), turn left at the fork. Continue through Santa Catarina Tayata (5.2 miles, 8.4 km) and follow the left fork (5.4 miles, 8.7 km). At 6.4 miles (10.3 km) pass over Río Yayata bridge and by the lovely creekside grove of ancient *ahuehuete* trees. Some of the gnarled giants, 10 feet in diameter, must be at least a thousand years old. The adjacent creekside meadows provide good **camping** spots. (Bring water.) First, however, get permission (usually no problem) from the municipal authorities at Santa Catarina Tayata.

At mile 10.5 (km 17) you get the first glimpse of the old San Miguel Achiutla church on the hill straight ahead. Take a left at the T (10.8 miles, 17.4 km), then right (11.2 miles, 18 km) and continue straight ahead for the old church on the right, ruins on left (12.6 miles, 20.3 km), and San Miguel Achiutla town at 14 miles (22.5 km).

Exploring the Site: The area of historical and archaeological interest lies on an airy, scenic hilltop, west of the modern town. The present church, the antique **Templo y Exconvento de San Miguel Achiutla,** stands on the rise to the south of the road. It supplanted an even older church, now in ruins, on the other side of the road, probably built atop the preconquest oracle temple. Beyond that rises a cemetery occupying what appear to be three preconquest ceremonial courtyards cut, like grand stair steps, into a mountainside that rises another mile to a high, breezy summit.

First, however, walk south across the broad atrium that leads to the present church. On your way, take a look at the pair of ponderous bronze bells, dated 1848, hanging from a rustic, ground-level *campanario*. The Dominicans built the church probably during the 1600s, several decades after the original building was begun in 1558 across the road. The new church, dedicated to Archangel St. Michael, grew into a prosperous vicarage, surrounded by a cluster of dependent congregations. Times changed, however. The previously new church is now crumbling and nearly abandoned. Its doors open regularly only for Sunday mass at 10 A.M., after which folks lock up and return downhill for an 11 A.M. mass at the church in town.

A major exception occurs during festivals, celebrating the Sacred Heart of Jesus (19 June), **Carnaval** (Sunday, Monday, and Tuesday before Ash Wednesday), and especially the **Fiesta de San Miguel,** 21–29 September, when masses fill the old church every day.

The old place is well worth a look around inside. Try finding the *sacristan* (church-keeper), who's often nearby. If you're sufficiently persuasive, he might open the door for you.

You'll find the inside completely unrestored except for the gilded, baroque main altarpiece, recently refurbished after it collapsed under its own weight. In addition to the native artists' colorful floral designs, the nave walls hold a gallery of precious 16th-century paintings. Don't miss the one showing the angel St. Michael enticing a mortal into heaven. Up front, bats flit and flutter out of the baptismal chapel on the left. On the opposite side, note the unusual screened platform high on the south wall, said to have accommodated cloistered nuns who nevertheless wanted to view mass in the nave. The door on the nave's right front leads to an open courtyard, which in turn leads to the ex-convent's former working and living quarters.

Outside, across the road, the ruin of the original church probably stands atop the renowned Achiutla oracle temple. This spot abounds with legends. A Mixtec codex records that one Tilantongo queen was born from a tree in Achiutla. So powerful was Achiutla's magic that people came, believing it to be the home of an all-seeing spirit, an oracle, known then as the **Corazón del Pueblo** (Heart of the People), who, acting through the local priests, could portend future events. No less than the Emperor Moctezuma, when Cortés threatened his capital, sent emissaries to Achiutla. They asked that proper sacrifices be made to the oracle in return for a divination of the result of Cortés's threat. The answer was that Moctezuma's grand empire would be destroyed.

Past the ruined church, climb along paths through the ancient retaining walls, built by long-dead Mixtec masons, to the cemetery's upper levels. Gaze out toward the fertile Achiutla valley far below, encircled by a verdant crown of pine-capped mountains.

Nearby, scattered around you, the cemetery's oldest legible tombstones date from around

1900; many others, unreadably weathered and crumbling, appear much older. Buried beneath those—no one yet knows how deep or old—lie the relics of Achiutla's past.

Achiutla Services: Drowsy little Achiutla town downhill has a basic grocery store, a *centro de salud* (health clinic), police (at the *presidencia municipal*), and gasoline, at a store at the west edge of town.

San Martín Huamelulpan

The community museum at Huamelulpan (oo-wah-may-LOOL-pahn), about a mile off Hwy. 125, three miles east of the Achiutla turnoff, was built partly to display the artifacts uncovered at the town's important archaeological zone. The National Archaeology and History Institute (INAH) installed the museum's archaeological exhibits in 1978. Later, the local community took over and did its own oral history project during the late 1980s, which resulted in the museum's traditional medicine displays.

Note the sign on the post on the right as you reach the town plaza. It reads, roughly: "Please stop and register at the community museum and get a guide to show you the ruins." If you arrive when the museum is closed, ask around for someone to guide you.

The museum, officially the **Museo Comunitario Ihitalulu** (ee-ee-tah-LOO-loo), is open regularly Wed.–Sun. 10 A.M.–5 P.M. You'll pass the archaeological section first, with its especially notable monolith of Dzahui, the Mixtec god of rain, lightning, and thunder (akin to the Zapotec god Cocijo). Also fascinating are burial remains, including a complete skeleton and bowls for portions of water, food, and pulque for the afterlife. Next comes the equally intriguing **traditional medicine** exhibit, detailing methods that *curanderos* (curers), *yerberas* (herbal healers), and *parteras* (midwives) use to treat their clients. Conditions commonly treated include *el parto* (childbirth), *el empacho* (stomach infections), *mal de aire* (shivering, and head and body aches; compare: malaria), and *el espanto* (soul loss, accompanied by severe anxiety). Displays illustrate many remedies, from herbal teas and *temascal* hot baths to doses of chicken blood and incantations beseeching forgiveness from earth spirits.

Exploring the Archaeological Zone: Leave time for a stroll around the archaeological zone. It was first visited in 1933 by Alfonso Caso of Monte Albán fame, and it has been intensively excavated and partly reconstructed by several others since the 1950s. Finds reveal that Huamelulpan was a small city occupied between 400 B.C. and A.D. 600, approximately the same epoch as Monte Albán.

The zone rambles extensively over many hundreds of acres, running north of town along an approximate east-west line. The most westerly discovered remains lie on the high west-side **Cerro Volado** hilltop. The most intensively reconstructed portion is the so-called Church Group, near the church, a few hundred yards east beyond the town plaza and museum. Start at the church itself, which has what appears to be a grinning preconquest god of death skeleton-monolith built into its right (south) wall. If you continue walking south along the road in front of the church, you will be passing the partly reconstructed **ball court,** reachable by ascending the rise to the left (east) of the road. Note, at the ball court's south end, the reconstructed half of its I-shaped layout. Continue east, up the second embankment, to a regal **ceremonial courtyard** climaxed on its east side with an elegant staircase and retaining walls. Climb those stairs to another level and yet another courtyard crowned by an equally elegant but smaller **ceremonial platform.**

Huamelulpan community museum volunteers lead visitors on tours of their archaeological zone, including Cerro Volado, for a fee of about $20. Arrive early and you may be able to arrange such a tour on the spot. Guides and also lodging at Huamelulpan's **tourist house** can also be arranged through the Oaxaca Community Museum Headquarters in Oaxaca City, Tinoco y Palacios 311, second floor, tel. 951/657-86, email: muscoax@prodigy.net.mx, website: www.umco.org.

Get to Huamelulpan by Tlaxiaco-bound second-class Fletes y Pasajes bus from either Oaxaca, Nochixtlán, Tamazulapan, or Teposcolula. Get off at the Huamelulpan turnoff on Hwy. 125, about half an hour (13 miles, 21 km) past Teposcolula. In the reverse direction, ride a Fletes y Pasajes bus from Tlaxiaco about half an hour and get off at the Huamelulpan turnoff. Walk about a mile to the museum on the town plaza.

WEST OF TLAXIACO

This is high, cool country, of pine-brushed mountains, villages and cornfields. The people are reserved but quick to return your wave and smile. They see so few outsiders, that although they try to avoid it, they can't help staring as you pass, wondering why you've come. For at least two of these communities, Santa María Cuquila and San Miguel Progreso, visitors have an immediate reason for coming: to see their community museum.

Santa María Cuquila

The Aztecs, to whom the Cuquila (koo-KEE-lah) people were tributaries at the time of the conquest, coined the name Cuquila, which roughly translates to "Snakes in the Brush." The Mixtec-speaking local people, however, previously called their village Ñu Kuiñe, which means "Town of the Tiger" in the local tongue.

Now, Cuquila (pop. 1,000) is organizing a museum with a number of rare artifacts, including hieroglyph-inscribed stones found in the big archaeological zone nearby, and documents from the 1580s, such as a map of the town and several decaying pages recording a plethora of information—town borders, officials' names, events, and perhaps even a little gossip—of early colonial days in Cuquila.

The museum also displays examples of locally made present-day pottery and hand-woven *huipiles*. If you ask to see the *artesanos*—potters and weavers—at work, they would be happy to oblige if at all possible.

The museum committee presently consists of museum president Severino Ayala; local *primaria* school teacher Nicolas Ayala; his nephew, Eduardo Escobar; and Maximiliano Ilario Santiago. All are qualified to take you on a tour (about two miles and two hours round-trip) to their "old town" archaeological site on a hill nearby. Archaeologists estimate that the site was occupied for about 1,300 years, from 400 B.C. to A.D. 900. The ceremonial area, consisting of the remains of a pair of royal residences, a main plaza, two tombs, and a ball court, spreads over about two and a half acres. Expect to pay about $10 for a two-hour guided tour on foot. The Cuquila museum is open by appointment through the Oaxaca Community Museums head office in Oaxaca City, Tinoco y Palacios 311, second floor, tel. 951/657-86, email: muscoax@prodigy.net.mx, website: www.umco.org. Locally, please call, or better yet, have your hotel desk clerk call, 955/201-77, the town long-distance telephone, to make an appointment.

Get to Cuquila by local minivan, or Fletes y Pasajes or Cristóbal Colón bus from Juxtlahuaca, Tlaxiaco, or Putla. By car, Cuquila is right on Hwy. 125, 12 miles (19 km) west of Tlaxiaco, 35 miles (56 km) east of Juxtlahuaca, or 32 miles (51 km) northeast of Putla.

San Miguel Progreso

Two miles (three km) from the signed turnoff from Hwy. 125, San Miguel Progreso (pop. 3,000) welcomes visitors to its museum. The museum committee has arranged the museum displays in four different sections. First are the historic papers, such as a 1780 document defining the town limits and a copy of a 1580 *lienzo* that maps the location of buildings, roads, rivers, and town boundaries. Next comes an excellent exposition of the local wool-weaving craft, then a mock-up of a typical indigenous dwelling. An archaeological section demonstrates finds, such as stone ax blades, ceramic vases, lance points, and human burial remains, including grave offerings. A final display models the preconquest method of terraced agriculture.

The local area contains a number of interesting sites, enough for a whole day of exploring. These include three unexcavated archaeological zones: Lomatutaya (Where the People Rest), Tuxau (Fifteen Words), and Panteón de los Angelitos (Cemetery of the Little Angels). Also nearby are two sacred caves, where masses are celebrated on 3 May, El Día de la Santa Cruz (The Day of the Holy Cross).

Time your arrival on the locally important festival dates, 29 September (Fiesta de San Miguel) or the fifth Friday of Lent (Fiesta de las Tres Caidas de Jesús), when you can get in on the fun of fireworks, food, dancing, processions, music, flowers, and carnival diversions.

To make sure that one of the museum committee members is available, contact them through the Museos Comunitarios de Oaxaca headquarters at Tinoco y Palacios 311, second floor, tel. 951/657-86, email: muscoax@prodigy.net.mx, website: www .umco.org.

Get to San Miguel Progreso by bus or car as described for Cuquila above, except that the signed side road (off of Hwy. 125) to San Miguel is about four miles (six km) past Cuquila (from Tlaxiaco) and a corresponding distance closer to Juxtlahuaca and Putla. Continue about two miles along the side road to San Miguel.

PUTLA DE GUERRERO: LAND OF WATER

After a week traveling in the cool high, Mixteca Alta, the rush of warm, moist tropical air you enjoy when entering the upland valley of Putla de Guerrero (pop. 30,000) feels like another country. Banana trees overhang the road; mangos, in season, sell for a dime apiece; the aroma of roasting coffee scents the air; and people fill their afternoons by splashing in a host of local swimming holes.

You might want to linger a day or two and bask in the warmth. If so, Putla's colorful market and its modicum of hotels, restaurants, and services can help make your visit interesting and comfortable.

Orientation and Sights
The town centers on a leafy *jardín,* about four blocks west, downhill from Hwy. 125. The *jardín,* bordered by the *presidencia municipal* on the south, a line of shops on the north, and the church, at its northwest corner, focuses community activity.

The bustling market, busiest on Sunday, is a block behind the *presidencia.* Here you'll find stalls offering the handmade textiles—*huipiles, rebozos* (shawls), *blusas,* and *enredos* (wraparound skirts)—for which Putla is well known. Materials vary from wool, homespun and woven by highland Trique women, to cottons, hand-embroidered by coastal Mixtecs.

Entertainment and Events
Ordinarily quiet Putla livens up during its regionally important fiestas. **Carnaval Putleco,** celebrated the Sunday, Monday and Tuesday before *miércoles ceniza* (Ash Wednesday), is rich in traditional dances. Local favorites, nearly always performed, are Los Viejos (The Old Ones), El Macho, and Los Copala.

Later in the year, folks crowd the church-front atrium for the **Fiesta de la Natividad,** which kicks off on 6 September with a grand *calenda* (procession) and flower-decorated floats, continues with a feast of fireworks on 7 September, and climaxes on the following day with *peleas de gallo* (cockfights), *jaripeo* (bull roping and riding), and a big community dance.

Other times, Putla people cool off from the heat, frolicking in the mountain streams that flow past the town. You can join the fun on a hot afternoon by asking a taxi driver to take you to a *balneario* (bathing spot); one of the best is about two miles along the highway uphill from town.

Accommodations
Putla's best hotel is the comfortable **Hotel Beyafrey,** about three blocks south and two blocks west of the plaza, at Guerrero 9, Putla de Guerrero, Oaxaca 71000, tel. 955/302-94. The approximately 30 high-ceilinged, clean rooms rent for about $11 s, $14 d, and $17 t, with toilets and hot water showers, fan, TV, restaurant, big pool and patio around in back, and parking.

Nearby, but not nearly as attractive, is the cheaper **Hotel Nieto 1,** corner Sonora and Guerrero, Putla de Guerrero, Oaxaca 71000, tel. 955/303-31, about three blocks south and one block west of the plaza. The 20 rooms are stacked in three stories. Plain but clean, they rent for about $9 s, $13 d, and $16 t, with bath, hot water, TV, and parking. Get an upper room for more light and privacy; look at more than one before moving in.

Food
You can find plenty of luscious fruits and vegetables and many inexpensive, local-variety meals in *fondas* in and around the market. For basic groceries, try the **Abarrotería Mary Carmen,** at the southwest plaza corner across the street from the *presidencia municipal.*

For a tasty pastry or pizza snack, go to the refined, TV-free coffee nook **C and S Café** on Guerrero, across the street from the Hotel Beyafrey. Friendly owners Cristina and Silvio, who make all their pastries and roast their own coffee, say that they prefer the soft music that emanates from their speakers to television.

As for restaurants, the most visible town-center eatery seems to be the family-style **Comedor Familiar Gonzales,** open daily 8 A.M.–8 P.M., on the corner at the north side of the basketball court, a block north of the jardí. If you want something fancier, go a few doors farther uphill, to **Restaurant Don Memo** open Mon.–Sat. noon–9 P.M.

Other restaurant choices are near the hotels. For breakfast or lunch, try **Restaurant Albert,** open Mon.–Sat. 8 A.M.–9 P.M., tel. 955/303-28, corner of Guerrero, across from Hotel Nieto 1, or hc restaurant at the **Hotel Beyafrey,** a block west at Guerrero 9.

A couple of other good restaurant choices are on the edges of town. For supper, go to **Sammy's Place,** on the west side (turn left just past the Hotel Beyafrey; after two blocks, turn right); open daily, 6 P.M.–midnight. Alternatively, on the highway try **Restaurant Tito's,** decorated with a gallery of paintings, showing sentimental Putla scenes in times past. You also might say a good word to the friendly travel agent-owner, Tito Chaves, who's proud of his

BOB RACE

eclectic menu of soups, salads, and seafood, beef, chicken, and pork entrées. On the highway, next to the Cristóbal Colón bus station; open daily 2–10 P.M.

Services
You'll find many of Putla's basic services near the town jardín. Change money or use the ATM at **Bancomer,** tel. 955/300-28, open for money changing Mon.–Fri. 9 A.M.–4 P.M., Sat. 9 A.M.–4 P.M., a block north from the jardín's west side, across from the basketball court. Alternatively, go to **Banamex,** tel. 955/306-10 or 306-11, on the highway. After bank hours, change money at **Casa de Cambio Intermex,** tel. 955/305-90, half a block east of the Presidencia, at Morelos 10.

The Putla *correo* (post office), open Mon.–Fri. 8 A.M.–3 P.M., is just west, next to the *presidencia municipal,* south side of the plaza. **Long-distance phone** and fax 955/300-30 are available at the *caseta* on the *jardín's* north side.

For routine nonprescription medicines and drugs, go to the **Pastillería de Descuento,** open daily 7 A.M.–10 P.M., on the *jardín's* west side. If you're ill, however, ask for advice at your hotel desk or go to see **Doctora. Silvia Zarate** at her *Farmacia Popular,* tel. 955/302-52, open daily 7 A.M.–2 P.M. and 4–8 P.M., at the *jardín's* northeast corner. Medical consultations are also available at the **General Hospital,** a block north of the *jardín's* east side, across the street from the basketball court.

Getting There and Away
Five long-distance bus lines operating from stations on or near the highway connect Putla with many Oaxaca destinations. First-class **Cristóbal Colón,** tel. 955/301-63, on the highway, connects south with Pinotepa Nacional; northeast with Oaxaca via Tlaxiaco and Nochixtlán; and north with Mexico City via Juxtlahuaca, Huajuapan, and Puebla. Second-class **Sur,** at Sonora 34A, tel. 955/303-50, by the Hotel Nieto, offers approximately the same connections as Cristóbal Colón. **Fletes y Pasajes** second-class buses, tel. 955/300-47, on the highway next to Cristóbal Colón, connect south with Pinotepa Nacional; northeast with Oaxaca via Tlaxiaco and Nochixtlán; and north with Mexico City via Juxtlahuaca, Huajuapan,

and Cuautla (Morelos). Additionally, second-class **Tonalteca** and **Autobuses Mixteca-Costa** buses connect south with Pinotepa Nacional and north with Juxtlahuaca, Tonalá, and Huajuapan.

For drivers, paved Hwy. 125 connects Putla south with Pinotepa Nacional, on the Pacific Coast via 80 miles (128 km) of winding, sometimes potholed, mountain road. Allow three hours for safety. In the opposite direction Hwy. 125 and Oaxaca Hwy. 15 connect Putla north with Juxtlahuaca in about 37 miles (59 km). Winding and sometimes steep grades require slow going. Allow two hours uphill, an hour and a half downhill. About the same is true for the 48-mile (77-km) connection northeast, along Hwy. 125, with Tlaxiaco, which, for safety, requires about two and a half hours uphill, two hours down.

NORTHERN OAXACA

The vast, extravagantly diverse northern Oaxaca landscape encompasses three of Oaxaca's traditional geo-cultural regions: the pine-tufted northern Sierra, the fertile, tropical Papaloapan basin, and the oases of the desert-like Cañada canyon land. Here travelers ready to venture north of the Valley of Oaxaca can find their heart's content of high mountains for camping, hiking, and climbing; tropical rivers and grand, glassy lakes for fishing, swimming, and boating; crystalline springs welling from the base of emerald mountains; and country markets where people wear colorful age-old village costumes and speak ancient traditional dialects.

This chapter is organized as a grand circle tour, initially exploring the cool mountain country villages Benito Juárez and Cuajimoloyas, which

perch at the first high crest north of Oaxaca City. From there, deep into the mountains, visitors will encounter the lushly forested, wildlife-rich country around the beloved president Juárez's northern Sierra birthplace. The route continues north again, down into the luxuriantly fertile Papaloapan basin. Using the tropical river town Tuxtepec as a base, we explore the cultural and natural riches of the Chinantec and Mazatec ancestral homelands. The road heads west, into the high Mazateca, to Huautla de Jiménez, a mountain town made internationally famous by the hallucinogenic mushrooms of renowned *curandera* María Sabina. Finally, south to Oaxaca City, travelers experience the warm, irrigated grove and orchard country of Teotitlán del Camino and Cuicatlán.

NORTHERN SIERRA

UP FROM THE VALLEY: BENITO JUÁREZ AND CUAJIMOLOYAS

This pair of little mountain towns perch nearly a mile above the Valley of Oaxaca at the first towering crest of the cool, pine-tufted Sierra Juárez. The attraction here is not the towns themselves, but their gorgeous mountain environs and all that implies: great billowing clouds, summer wildflowers, cool crystalline spring water, and the scent of pine.

Furthermore, the communities and the Oaxaca government, in their effort to develop the outdoor touristic resources of the northern Sierra, have built a tourist Yu'u accommodation and a new community-run *comedor* (dining room) at Benito Juárez.

Sights

The village of Benito Juárez (pop. approx. 1,000) runs along a single east-west ridge-crest road. The tourist Yu'u and the community center, **Casa del Pueblo,** with the *comedor* and a cozy fireplace, are at the east end, uphill. At that point, signs direct you toward a number of possible diversions: You can stroll among the springs trickling downhill through the adjacent pine-shaded **Parque Recreational,** or follow the sign marked Mirador, walking along the road (follow each uphill fork) about 1.5 miles (2.5 km) north to the *mirador* (viewpoint) tower atop a craggy 10,000-foot (3,000-meter) high perch. Here the view seems limitless. On the south side, steeply beneath you, spreads the central valley's verdant checkerboard of meadow, field, and pasture. On the north side, a succession of dark green mountain ridges stretch northward until they merge and become a deep purple silhouette on the horizon. On another day, walk or get a ride about eight miles (12 km) east, past the little settlement of Los Llanos, to another viewpoint, the famous **Peña Larga,** a gigantic, 50-foot tall rock where you can perch to your heart's content.

Another possibility is to follow the six-mile (10-km) *sendero peaton* (pedestrian trail) by

mountain bike or on foot. The tourist Yu'u manager rents the bikes and furnishes you with a guide. For more extensive trips, see Mountain Guides, below.

Alternatively, you can simply wander around and enjoy yourself. Plenty of folks, Zapotec people (most of whom speak Spanish), are out tending their terraced cornfields, watching their cattle, and doing household chores.

Cuajimoloyas (kooah-hee-moh-LOY-ahs, pop. 1,000), four miles (six km) east along the ridge road from Benito Juárez, is the metropolis of this part of the mountains. A sign as you enter town translates that Cuajimoloyas has "churches, a pharmacy, health center, telephone, and restaurant." It has all of these, plus a few small stores and an eatery or two.

Accommodations and Food

Cuajimoloyas has a downscale four-room hotel, the **Yacautzi,** right on the road as you enter the south side of town from Benito Juárez. The door was locked when I went by, so I didn't get to look inside. At least it will be a roof over your head if you arrive in the rain.

The best local accommodation is the Benito Juárez **Tourist Yu'u,** with three guest rooms, without bath, that open to a large common hall. The toilets and showers (with hot water) are shared. Although a bit run-down at this writing, the Benito Juárez Yu'u is still a relatively cozy place, with a big fireplace, plenty of wool blankets, and a basic kitchen with refrigerator available for guest use. Bring your own soap and towel and all your food, except water, which is crystal pure on this mountaintop. Reserve a spot through the state-federal tourist information office in Oaxaca City, at 607 Independencia, Oaxaca, Oaxaca 68000, tel. 9/516-4828, fax 9/516-0984, email: turinfo@oaxaca.gob.mx. (For more lodging possibilities, see Mountain Guides below.)

Alternatively, the area is ripe for tent or self-contained RV **camping.** The community identifies at least two spots, both meadows, with good spring water. The closest is called **Llano de las Tarjeas,** a total of about eight

NORTHERN OAXACA

To Tehuacán, Puebla, and Mexico City

To Córdoba and Veracruz

Tierra Blanca

V E R A C R U Z

Parque
Natural
Laguna
de
Temascal

Temascal
Reservoir

To Loma Bonita and Minatitlán

Naranja Titla

P U E B L A

Río
Papaloapan

145

Cerro Palma

Santa
Elena

Río
Lodo

INFORMAL
CAMPING

Santa María
Chilchotla

Buenos Aires

Temascal

San Francisco
Huehuetlán

Limestone
Cave

INFORMAL
CAMPING

Isla
Soyaltepec

MIGUEL ALEMÁN
DAM

Sierra Mazateca

135

182

Eloxochitlan

Huatla de Jiménez

HOTEL
NANGUINA

Río
Papaloapan

Tonto

San Francisco
Salsipuedes

San Antonio
Nanahuatipan

Plan de
Guadalupe

Cerro Rabón
(2,350 m)

San Pedro
Ixcatlán

Tuxtepec

182

Zoquiapan

Santa María
Ascunción

San Juan
Cuatzospan

Jalapa de Díaz

Teotitlán
del
Camino

San Juan
de los Cues

Santo
Domingo

182

San Lucas
Ojitlán

MIGUEL DE LA MADRID DAM

Río
Xiquila

Mazatlán
de Flores

Chiquihuitlán

Santo
Domingo

Flor Batavia

Cerro de Oro
Reservoir

Paso
Canoa

HOTEL POSADA
CHINANTECO

147

Santa María
Tecomavaca

Río
Santo

Cuyamecalco

Santa María
Tlalixtac

San Felipe
Usila

San José
Chiltepec

Río
Valle
Nacional

Río
El
Obispo

To Juchitán, Tehuantepec, and Salina Cruz

Santiago
Quiotepec

San Miguel
Santa Flor

Río
Piedras

Santa María
Jacatepec

INFORMAL
CAMPING

Cuicatlán

Río

Santa María Pápalo

Valle
Nacional

Zuzul

Arroyo Blanco

Cerro Cheve
(3,255 m)

Río
Perfume

San Juan Tepeuxila

Santiago

Sierra

INFORMAL
CAMPING

San José del Chilar

Santiago
Dominguillo

Río
Las
Nueltas

San Juan
Quiotepec

San
Pedro
Yolóx

Río La Nopalera

175

Madre

Río

de

135

Santiago Comaltepec

Cerro Analco
(3,100 m)

Oaxaca

Santiago Nacaltepec

San Pablo
Macuiltianguis

Grande

Cajones

La Carbonera

INFORMAL
CAMPING

Santa María
Zoogochi

Lachichina

Camotlán

Cerro
Zempoaltepetl
(2,750 m)

San Juan
Yaé

Yuquila

Vijanos

Villa Alta

San Francisco
Telixtlahuaca

Ixtlán de Juárez

Limestone
Cave

Calpulalpan

Las
Delicias

San Pablo
Huitzo

Güelatao

Amatlán

Santa María Yalina

Zoogocho

190

Santa Catarina Ixtepeji

Lachatao

Santa María
Yavesia

135D

Cerro
San Felipe
(3,250 m)

CAMPAMENTO
DEL MONTE

Latuvi

Las
Vigas

INFORMAL
CAMPING

Yalalag

190

San Andrés
Huayapan

INFORMAL
CAMPING

San Miguel
Cajonos

San Pablo Yaganiza

175

Parque
Nacional
Benito
Juárez

Cuajimoloyas

Llano
Grande

Benito Juárez

PUEBLOS
MANCOMUNADOS

To Nochixtlán, Huajuapan, and Mexico City

TOLL (CUOTA)

MooN

Oaxaca

Teotitlán del Valle

Díaz Ordaz

0   20 mi

0   20 km

Tlacolula

175

135

190

© AVALON TRAVEL PUBLISHING, INC.

miles (13 km) east of Benito Juárez, past Cuajimoloyas. During the summer and fall, this meandering meadow bordered by a multitude of pines is decorated with a galaxy of wildflowers—lavender buttercups, red lilies, baby blue eyes, white and yellow daisies, and many more. Water comes from a pristine brook, home to some little darting fish. (Foresters have set up a small fish hatchery here, evidently in an attempt to breed more of the little critters.) **Las Vigas** (The Timbers), a similar meadow also good for camping, is about four miles (six km) farther east.

To camp at either Llano de las Tarjeas or Las Vigas, get permission from the manager *(gerente)* of the tourist Yu'u or a town official at the Casa del Pueblo. Then drive, taxi, or hike four miles east along the ridgeline through Cuajimoloyas. Continue another three miles (five km) to a Las Tarjeas sign on the left. Follow similar signs another 1.8 miles (three km) to Llano de las Tarjeas. (The road is narrow, rough, and only marginally negotiable by passenger cars. Big RVs won't make it; smaller campers could.) For Las Vigas, back on the road, continue another mile or two past the Las Trejeas sign; turn left (north) at the road to Lavasia and Lachatao. Continue a few more miles to the Las Vigas turnoff on the right.

Eating out doesn't appear to be an important activity in either Benito Juárez or Cuajimoloyas. The choices are limited to one or two local-style restaurants, such as **La Montaña**, in Cuajimoloyas, and the **Casa del Pueblo** community *comedor* in Benito Juárez.

Getting There and Away

By bus, the best option is to ride the "Turismo de Benito Juárez" bus that leaves from behind the *camionera central segunda clase* (second-class bus terminal) on the prolongation of Calle Las Casas on the west side of Oaxaca City. Otherwise, ride a Tlacolula-bound **Fletes y Pasajes** (or other) bus from the second-class bus terminal, and get off at the Tlacolula Pemex gas station and wait across the street at the side road that heads north. There, catch a blue **Sociedad Cooperativa Flecha de Zempoatepetl** bus headed for Cuajimoloyas. (They go several places, so ask *"¿A Cuajimoloyas?"* before getting on.) For Benito

Juárez, get off at the mountain crest, at the junction where the Benito Juárez road splits left (west). Walk or catch a ride the four miles (six km) to the Benito Juárez Tourist Yu'u and Casa del Pueblo. **Note:** Fit backpackers could, alternatively, hike the car-RV route, described below, by bus and foot via Teotitlán del Valle.

By car or RV, drive to Benito Juárez via Teotitlán del Valle. Turn left at the signed Teotitlán del Valle Hwy. 190 turnoff about 18 miles, (30 km) east of Oaxaca City. Continue straight through town, uphill on an initially bumpy road. A mile or two later, past a dam, the gravel and graded road gets better. Ordinary cars and most RVs could negotiate it readily under dry conditions, although it's marginal when wet. Four-wheel-drive vehicles could do it anytime. At the town, at the top of the ridge, follow the Cabañas signs right (east) about half a mile to the tourist Yu'u and the town center, Casa del Pueblo (turn left half a block uphill past the Yu'u).

Mountain Guides

Another option is to go with well-equipped **Empresa Ecoturística Comunitaria** (Community Ecotouristic Enterprise) (formerly Expediciones Sierra Norte), run by friendly, English-speaking Adriana Guzmán. She and her staff work in cooperation with a network of about a dozen Sierra Norte communities, called **Pueblos Mancomunados,** that include, besides Benito Juáez and Cuajimoloyas, Yavesia, Latuvi, Amatlán, and Lachatao. Jointly they have established a 60-mile (100-km) signposted hiking and mountain biking trail network and offer accommodation in rustic village cabins and tourist Yu'u.

Adriana and her staff make reservations in the cabins, help obtain access and camping permits and outfit and guide parties for camping, hiking, and biking outings into the mountains north of Oaxaca City, beginning in the area around Benito Juárez and Cuajimoloyas and extending north toward the other villages. They can furnish camping gear, mountain bikes, transportation and more. Contact them in Oaxaca City at 406 Garcia Vigil, Oaxaca 68000, tel. 9/514-8271 fax 9/516-7745, email: SierraNorte@oaxaca.com, website: www.sierranorte.org

ALONG THE ROAD TO IXTLÁN

The high road to northern Oaxaca winds far uphill, climbing over lush, pine-clad crests and descending into deep river canyons to the Sierra Juárez, the mountainous birth-land of Benito Juárez, Oaxaca's beloved favorite son. Besides its historical and sentimental significance, the Sierra Juárez's pristine, thickly forested ridges and shadowed stream valleys are a natural garden-of springs, meadows, caves, and waterfalls-a de facto wilderness refuge for dozens of endangered species, including all of Mexico's wild cats.

The best hub for exploring the Sierra Juárez is the small town of Ixtlán de Juárez, easily reachable by bus or car, about 37 miles (60 km) north from Oaxaca City via Hwy. 175.

Although Ixtlán de Juárez is a worthy destination, journeys are sometimes equally memorable for the bright moments en route. The road to Ixtlán is no exception. You might uncover some pleasant surprises while lingering along the way, such as the invitingly rustic mountain restaurant and refuge Campamento del Monte, or San Andrés Huayapan and Ixtepeji, a pair of little towns with nevertheless big gems of churches.

By bus, ride a Cuenca (koo-AYN-kah) bus bound for Ixtlán (or Valle Nacional or Tuxtepec) from Oaxaca's ADO-Cristóbal Colón first-class station, on Hwy. 190 at the north side of town. Drivers, set your odometer and head out from the junction where Hwy. 175 splits north from Hwy. 190, about three miles east of the Oaxaca City center.

San Andrés Huayapan Church and Reservoir

If you have time, detour into San Andrés Huayapan (left turnoff from Hwy. 175), approximately 2.5 miles (four km) uphill from Hwy. 190. First of all, take a look inside the town's jewel-the distinguished, double-towered 17th-century **Templo de San Andrés.** Past the front door, admire the mural of the Last Supper in the nave and the colorful sculpture of San Andrés in the main altarpiece's central niche.

Afterward, taxi or drive to the **Presas de Huayapan** (Dams of Huayapan) a mile or two

southeast of town. The pair of dams, although built for irrigation, have created a popular, scenic recreation reservoir (prettiest during late-summer high water, when no ugly bathtub-like ring scars the lakeshore), forming petite bays in the folds of the surrounding forested hillsides. Restaurants serve food, and concessionaires rent boats. Swimming, however, is not recommended, due to the lakeshore's steep incline.

Campamento del Monte

About 17 miles (27 km) north, you arrive at an attractive view restaurant perched on the right, or east, side of Hwy. 175. Although the restaurant is worth a stop all by itself, the Campamento del Monte, a small resort of a few rustic cabins sprinkled in the pine-oak forest above the highway, offers even more. The family Pérez Chaves, who first built the restaurant, then the cabins, has named them individually: Toro de Silviero, Laguna Azul, Colmilla Blanco, and Luna de Octubre. Like their names, each is uniquely inviting, built with rustic wood, tile, and brick, with plenty of light, tree-framed mountain and forest vistas, a fireplace with lots of wood, an outdoor grill, hot water shower bath, stove, and refrigerator (although you have to furnish your own towels, bedding, and pots, pans, dishes, and utensils). All this for about $15 per night.

Rentals are popular, so they warn you to be sure to reserve, including a 50 percent deposit, at least 10 days ahead. Call 9/511-1335 Mon.–Fri. 3–9 P.M. or write Campamento del Monte, Km 27, Carretera Oaxaca-Guelatao, Oaxaca. Although their literature insists on prior reservations, they do rent to drop-ins between 3 and 9 P.M. if they have a cabin available, which is likely Sunday through Thursday. Bring mosquito repellent, especially necessary early evenings during the summer wet season.

In addition to cabin rentals, the managers also welcome day visitors for about $7 per car. Diversions include picnicking, bird- and animal-viewing, and rambling through the gorgeous pine- and oak-studded hillside to local view summits.

Santa Catarina Ixtepeji

Drivers, probably much more so than bus travelers, will find this detour convenient. Follow the signed turnoff at about 21 miles (34 km) from Hwy. 190. Continue for about four miles (six km) downhill to the **Templo de Santa Catarina,** by far the biggest building in sleepy Ixtepeji (eeks-tay-PAY-hee). Here (unless you plan your visit to coincide with three days of the Fiesta of Santa Catarina, around 25 November), the main attraction is the church's towering, exquisite Renaissance facade. Prominent are the eight exquisitely spiraled Solomonic columns, four above and four below. Notice also the facade's empty niches, which once sheltered St. John the Evangelist, St. Nicolas, and St. Michael, now shattered and ignominiously deposited on the ground beneath the facade, where they were probably toppled by an earthquake. Nevertheless, St. Peter remains, with Bible, flag, and staff, on the left, as does St. Catherine, high above, with flowing robe and sword.

AT THE SUMMIT: IXTLÁN DE JUÁREZ AND VICINITY

If a Mexican person told you that he lived in Ixtlán, you still wouldn't know where that was, for there are many Ixtláns in Mexico. The reason is twofold. The maguey plant is widespread in Mexico, and the Aztecs were so dominant at the time of the conquest that their names for local towns are still used today. The prefix *ix* refers to *ixtle,* the Aztec word for the fibers of the maguey plant. The suffix *-tlan* means "land," or "place of." So the many Ixtláns are all places the Aztecs named "Land of the Maguey." Oaxaca Ixtlán people gave their town a unique name, honoring President Benito Juárez, by calling their town Ixtlán de Juárez.

People don't grow much maguey around Ixtlán de Juárez anymore, nor do they grow any cochineal, cultivation of which created a number of millionaires in the vicinity. Their money built the ornate old Churrigueresque churches in Ixtlán and the neighboring town of Calpulalpan.

What Ixtlán people do grow a lot of is wood, in the thick forests coating this part of the northern Sierra. Wisely, they don't cut too much timber, so their forests remain rich habitats for many wild creatures, notably, all species of Mexican native cats (especially the jaguar and mountain lion), spider monkeys, and tapirs, many of which have disappeared in other parts of southern Mexico. The diversity of species is so rich in Ixtlán's woodlands that a panel of experts convened by the World Wildlife Fund has rated the local forest as one of the world's 17 outstandingly biodiverse ecosystems. What's great for visitors is that the Ixtlán de Juárez community invites them to come see and appreciate their wild treasures through a special community-run ecotourism company.

Sights

Ixtlán de Juárez (pop. 8,000), despite being the capital of its own sprawling governmental district, feels like a village, where the main evening activity is to either watch or join the kids playing basketball on the courts in the central plaza, then get *cena* (supper) before the mom-and-pop *comedores* close around 8:30 P.M. Walk three blocks in any direction and you're in the woods. But don't worry, you won't get lost. Just let the faithful chime of the plaza tower clock lead you.

The *presidencia municipal,* on the plaza's north side, is a major landmark. Main streets are Sidencio Hernández on the plaza's west side, 16 Septiembre on the east side, and Revolución, which runs north-south behind the *presidencia municipal.*

Ixtlán's main in-town sight is its treasured 17th-century **Templo de Santo Tomás Apóstol,** just northwest of the town plaza, behind the faithful, very proper plaza clock. The present *templo,* started by Dominican fathers about 1640, replaced an earlier all-adobe church. Construction was completed about a century later, in 1734. The first thing to notice about old Santo Tomás is that it's made of the same light green *cantera* that you see so much of in the Oaxaca City's public buildings. Ixtlán's source, however, is local.

Decorating the baroque facade's summit is a bas-relief showing the dramatic confrontation of doubting Thomas with the risen Jesus. Inside, instead of the usual one golden *retablo* behind the altar, several more decorate the nave walls, with gilded saints, angels, and masterfully pious 16th- and 17th-century oil paintings. The main *retablo,* behind the altar, shows the kneeling St. Thomas touching the chest of the risen Jesus, the act that, according to the Gospels, removed all doubt of the resurrection's reality. Finally, before you leave, glimpse inside the baptistery, on the right side of the nave, where Benito Juárez was baptized in 1806.

If you're lucky enough to arrive between 19 and 22 December, you can join the local folks in the patronal **Fiesta de Santo Tomás Apóstol.** Festivities include tying up traffic on the highway with *calendas* (processions) while bombs are blasting overhead, *mañanitas* (5 A.M. masses), *jaripeo* (bull roping and riding), and the Betaza traditional courtship dance.

Ecotour

Most of the natural sights around Ixtlán are on communal land, so you must make arrangements for a guide from the community-run Ixtlán ecotour agency, **Viajes Ecoturísticos Schiaa Rua Via** (Mountain Where the Clouds Are Born) to accompany you. Tours include bird- and animal-watching, cloud forest hikes, cave exploring, wilderness camping, and more, leaving from the agency's headquarters at the northeast corner of the town plaza. Guides are competent and well-trained by the agency's guiding lights and founders, biologists Norma Angélica Montes Rodríguez and Gustavo Ramírez Santiago. Expect to pay about $25 per person per day, excluding transportation. Contact their office at Ixtlán de Juárez, Oaxaca 68725, open Mon.–Sat.9 A.M.–2 P.M. and 4–8 P.M., Sun. 9 A.M.–2 P.M., tel./fax 955/360-75, email: eco_ixt@hotmail.com.

You can reach the natural sights described below by bus or by passenger car via Hwy. 175 north and the road southeast to Calpulalpan. What follows is a summary of the guided ecotour that, in the capable hands of Viajes Ecoturísticos, I enjoyed in a single day, driving my car. (Using local bus transportation, together with about 15 miles of hiking, fit travelers, accompanied by a guide, could cover the same ground in two days.)

First, follow Hwy. 175 north 18.6 miles (30 km) and turn right onto a gravel road at the red cross, labeled Zoogochi. Set your odometer. On the gravel road, follow the right fork at 1.5 miles; continue a total of 4.2 miles (6.7 km) from the highway to a summer wildflower-carpeted grassy meadow on the left, known locally as **Latziruetze** (Meadow of the Thistles), with good spring water and possible wilderness tenting spots.

Continue along the same route (bear right at the first fork and left at the next two) another 2.2

miles (3.5 km) from the highway, a total of 6.4 miles (10.3 km) to **Los Pozuelos** shelter, cozy for camping (no tent needed; the sturdy roof shelters against rain). From there you can walk the rough jeep track a quarter mile uphill to the *mirador* tower, where on a clear day you can see 18,700-foot (5,700-meter) Volcán de Orizaba, Mexico's highest mountain, jutting above the northern horizon.

Also from the Los Pozuelos shelter, walk the trail signed Camino Real, and you will be following the route of long-vanished Aztec, Zapotec, and Mixtec traders, who trekked between the Gulf Coast and the Valley of Oaxaca. A few hundred yards along the trail downhill (actually about 320 paces from the shelter) you'll see a big, standing tree trunk on the left; at the end of a rough path about 200 feet downhill is a permanent spring, fine for drinking.

Around the spring, you can't help but notice the long clumps of moss hanging eerily from the trees. This is a sure sign that you're in the **cloud forest,** a remnant island of Ice Age flora, with many species, such as wild begonias (look for clusters of their small-blossomed magenta flowers), ferns, dwarf bamboo, liquidambar, and many others, in common with the mountains in the southeastern United States. Here in the Sierra Norte of Oaxaca, the cloud forest covers the humid Gulf-facing northern slopes at altitudes between 6,500 and 10,000 feet (2,000 and 3,000 meters).

Next, return to Ixtlán and head out to explore a hidden cave, spring, and waterfall all in one. Go by the road to Calpulalpan from the southeast edge of Ixtlán. About four blocks east of Hwy. 175, follow the paved road past the lumber mill for 3.2 miles (5.1 km), where you turn left onto a gravel road. Follow about a mile, or as far as you can, by car. Continue walking downhill. Before the creek, go left at the rough trail, uphill into the woods. After about 100 yards, you'll be at **Arco de Yagela,** a cave that you approach via a yawning, stalactite-walled rock amphitheater (thus *arco,* or arc). Just inside the cave's mouth, a waterfall splashes into springs welling up from the beneath the rocks. The cave itself, whose dark cavity beckons a few feet behind the waterfall, can be accessed only with an expert guide and equipment. It has not been completely explored. A small party could camp on the small, level dry space in the arc to the left of the cave mouth, or a larger party could spread out in a big open spot across the creek.

Calpulalpan

Little Calpulalpan (pop. 3,000) perches on its hillside about six miles (9.6 km) east along the road from Ixtlán. The town's pride is its church, the **Templo de San Mateo,** completed by the Dominicans in 1718. Ordinarily serene, the church grounds overflow with merrymakers during the **Fiesta de San Mateo,** which climaxes yearly on 21 September.

The church's renovated interior soars to a magnificent wooden ceiling. Charmingly naive designs painted by early native artisans decorate the front, below the choir, while a pair of angels, following Jesus' exhortation to become "fishers of men," dangle fish from opposite sides of the front altar. Lining both side walls, several elaborate baroque *retablos* display a gallery of colorful saints and pious 18th-century oil paintings.

Uphill a few blocks from the church, the town *centro de salud* has a unique twin, the **Centro de Medicinas Tradicionales** (Center of Traditional Medicine), across a connecting patio. An herb-drying apparatus out front gives hints of the treatments practiced by the traditional healers (hours Mon.–Fri. 9 A.M.–2 P.M. and 4–7 P.M.) inside the conventional-appearing modern white stucco building.

BENITO JUÁREZ

Mexico's memory of Benito Juárez, its most revered president, is draped in legend. What's certain is that he was born on 21 March 1806 in the northern Oaxacan *municipio* of San Pablo Guelatao, at the hamlet of Santo Tomás Ixtlán. When his parents of pure Zapotec origin, Marcelino Juárez and Brigida Garcia, died tragically when Benito was three, his uncle took him in. After a quiet childhood, mostly spent shepherding his uncle's flocks in the surrounding hills, Benito left for Oaxaca City in December 1818 to live with his sister, María Josefa.

For Benito, this was a lucky stroke. He became part of the Maza household, where María Josefa lived and worked as a cook. In the genteel, well-to-do Maza family surroundings, young Benito gained exposure to music, books, politics, and people—not possible for a poor boy in the country. Moreover, he met Margarita Maza, who, with the blessing of her parents, later became his wife.

While living with the Mazas, Benito immediately gained the attention of priest and bookbinder Antonio Salanueva, who, recognizing his exceptional qualities, took Benito under his wing and sent him to school in town in January 1819. With Salanueva as his patron, Benito made rapid progress. He entered Oaxaca's new Scientific and Literary Institute in August 1828 to study law. Four years later, he was a practicing attorney. He entered politics, rapidly rose from state to federal legislator, then Supreme Court judge, finally being unanimously elected governor by Oaxaca's legislature on 12 August 1849.

From a successful term as governor, Juárez returned to national prominence. He was elected Mexico's president for two separate terms, both interrupted, first by civil war during the latter 1850s and then by the French Intervention from 1862 to 1867. Victory over the French finally brought peace, and Juárez was elected president for the third time, in October 1871. He toiled day and night to realize his dreams for Mexico, but he died from exhaustion on 18 July 1872.

BOB RACE

Guelatao

A government-constructed monumental **Plaza Cívica** has converted this modest mountain town on Hwy. 175 two miles south of Ixtlán into a shrine for beloved President Benito Juárez, who was born nearby on 21 March 1806.

Juárez's timeless credo, *"El respecto al derechos ajenos es la paz"* ("Respect for the rights of all is peace") marks the museum, on the plaza, two blocks uphill from the town highway crossing. Inside, glass cases preserve a few precious mementos: a photograph, Juárez's death mask, a letter, a diary, a graduation certificate from the seminary in Oaxaca, and a model of the renowned black carriage in which Juárez for years, fulfilled his duties of office, one jump ahead of his enemies.

Also on the plaza is a bronze of Juárez's mother, Brigida Garcia, and, at the *presidencia municipal,* a bust of Juárez, together with the historic letter that Juárez wrote to his ambassador in the United States, opposing United States' meddling in Mexican affairs.

Just north of the plaza, a shady path borders the petite spring-fed lake from which the town derives its name, in Zapotec, Guelatao (gooay-lah-TAH-oh), which translates as "Enchanted Lagoon." On the lakeshore, see the famous sentimental bronze sculpture of young Benito, the humble shepherd boy, tending his flock.

The local community joins with the entire country in celebrating the memory of Benito Juárez, "Benemérito de las Américas" ("Hero of the Americas"). Yearly, on 21 March, Mexico's president and Oaxaca's governor kick off a six-day fiesta of tournaments, fireworks, and a whirl of traditional dances by performing groups from a host of Zapotec communities.

Accommodations and Food

Viajes Ecoturísticos recommends the local, competently managed **Casa de Huéspedes La Soledad,** with about twelve clean basic rooms (two with private baths, the rest with shared bath) $7 s, $9 d, and $12 t. Reserve at Calle Francisco Javier Mina, Barrio de la Soledad, Ixtlán de Juárez, Oaxaca 68725, tel. 955/361-71.

Also recommendable is the **Hotel Casa del Cielo,** with four rooms, with hot water, above the back patio. Rates run about $13 s, $15 d, $17t. It's on Servidio Hernández, across from the Jiménez grocery, just downhill from the plaza's southwest corner. Reserve by telephoning the hotel, tel. 955/361-19.

Ixtlán offers several food possibilities. Stock up on fruits and vegetables during the Monday **market,** on the town plaza. Otherwise, for some fresh items and a pretty fair grocery selection, go to **Abarrotes Jiménez,** on Servidio, just downhill from the plaza's southwest corner.

The town supports a restaurant or two. Best is Restaurant Jiménez (open daily 8 A.M.–8:30 P.M.). Guelatao, two miles downhill, also has a few restaurants, such as **El Tio,** across the street from the plaza and museum. After hours, eat at the taco stands around the plaza.

Services

Nearly all of Ixtlán's services are available near the plaza. The bank, **Bancrecer,** changes money Mon.–Thurs. 9 A.M.–3 P.M., Fri. 9 A.M.–5 P.M., tel. 955/366-66 or 955/362-18, at the corner of Revolución and 16 de Septiembre, a block uphill from the plaza. You can also visit the town *biblioteca* (library) next door to the bank.

The *correo,* open 9 A.M.–1 P.M., 3–6 P.M., is also next to the bank. For public fax and money orders, go to *telégrafos,* open Mon.–Fri. 9 A.M.–3 P.M., at the plaza's northeast corner. After hours you can also send a fax at the Jiménez long-distance telephone and fax, tel./fax 955/360-97 or 360-98, next to the Jiménez grocery.

If you get sick, go to the *centro de salud* (government health clinic) on Revolución behind the *presidencia municipal,* open 24 hours. Alternatively, consult one of the towns **private doctors.** Your choices are Dr. Javier Salazar Ventura, hours Mon.–Thurs. 4–8 P.M., across Revolución from the *centro de salud,* or Doctora Ofelia Maldonado Ruiz, at her **Farmacia La Soledad,** open 8 A.M.–3 P.M. and 4–9 P.M., tel. 955/360-03, at 16 de Septiembre 17A, two blocks uphill from the plaza.

Both the *gasolinera* (gas station) and the **bus station** are on Highway 175, about three blocks west of the plaza. The second-class line **Cuenca de Papaloapan** provides several daily connections south with Oaxaca City and north with Valle Nacional, Tuxtepec, and intermediate destinations.

INTO THE PAPALOAPAN

Humid, tropical air, moving gently westward from the Gulf of Mexico, cools, clouds, and drops a deluge of rain on the northern slope of the Sierra Madre de Oaxaca. The water collects and cascades down the mountains, gathering into great, rushing rivers that finally deepen and wind slowly through a grand tropical lowland plain called the Papaloapan (pah-pah-loh-AH-pahn), after the river system that drains it. The rivers are the region's prime asset—the Tonto, the Santo Domingo, and the Valle Nacional join near the town of Tuxtepec to form the Río Papaloapan. At high elevations on the Sierra's northern slope, the waters nourish vast, thick forests: pine-oak at the higher elevations and a fantastically lush, tropical hardwood rain forest that spreads downhill into the valleys. There, farmers have replaced the forest with rich fields of corn and tobacco, great thickets of rubber trees, and, in the shady underlay, plantations of shiny-leafed coffee bushes. The government, moreover, has tamed and harnessed the rivers, gathering them into a pair of immense reservoirs—Temascal and Cerro de Oro—for irrigation, recreation, and electric power.

VALLE NACIONAL: LAND OF SPRINGS

As the rainwaters make their way to the valleys, they sometimes well up as crystalline, mountain-foot springs before they gather into rushing rivers. One of the loveliest of these spring-fed rivers collects at the foot of the Sierra Chinantla, a spur of the Sierra Madre de Oaxaca. It rushes downhill past the town of Valle Nacional, where it's called the Río Valle Nacional.

Valle Nacional (pop. 8,000) is interesting mostly as a springboard to the lush valley and water country that winds north 20 miles (32 km) from its outskirts. The town itself is a commercial service center for the local *ranchos* and *fincas* (farms). Although Valle Nacional is an important coffee-producing center, it would be much easier to get an irrigation pump here than a cappuccino. Lunch table talk centers mostly around crop prices and government plans for repairing the Oaxaca highway. Although nearly everyone in town has abandoned the original Chinantec tongue for Spanish, things change on Sunday during the big weekly *tianguis* (native market). Then you'll most likely rub shoulders with plenty of Chinantec-speaking people, including women in colorful, striped, local *huipiles*.

Besides Sunday, other good times to arrive in Valle Nacional (officially San Juan Bautista Valle Nacional) are during the local fiestas, in memory of Saint John the Baptist around 24 June, and, even bigger, the **Fiesta de San José,** celebrated for three days beginning 18 March. During these times, *calendas* (processions) and floats block the street, fireworks boom overhead, masses fill the church, and merrymakers dance in the plaza.

Valle Nacional Springs

A pair of nearby **balnearios** (developed springs) are perfect for a relaxing afternoon picnic or a pleasant camping overnight. **Arroyo Blanco,** one of the prettiest of the valley springs, is near kilometer marker 42, just about four miles (six km) north of Valle Nacional and about 17 miles (27 km) south of Tuxtepec. Watch for the small sign on the river side of Hwy. 175. It is the private paradise of friendly Diego Alonzo Francisco and his family. They have a several grassy acres shaded by big old trees, with a few chickens and turkeys pecking around, dogs, and lots of *toronjas* (grapefruit) and mangos in season.

Best of all is their big beautiful blue spring, which wells up deep from the underground, becoming a cool, clear river. On Sunday folks crowd in, but on any other day you'd have the place nearly to yourself for half a dollar per person. Señor Alonzo also invites **camping.** Put up your tent, or pull in your self-contained RV, for about $3 a day. Señora Alonzo furnishes all of the drinks and home-cooked food you can eat in the adjacent restaurant. If you prefer, try your luck by fishing for *mojarra* or *pepesca* in the spring for your dinner. The family (or a neighbor) might have a spare room to put you up in for the night if you have no RV or tent.

Another of the valley's springs, not so homey but much more renowned, is **Balneario Zuzul,** a name everyone from Valle Nacional to Tuxtepec knows fondly. Part of the fun is getting there, because you have to ferry over the swift-flowing Río Valle Nacional by motor launch. Once across, you see what the attraction is: a big, round, stone-edged blue pool of clear, cool spring water, which wells up from the depths for everyone's enjoyment, a perfect antidote for a hot afternoon.

Surrounding the pool is a shady, grassy park, great for **tent camping.** If no one seems to be in charge, you might still ask if it's OK to camp. Ask *"¿Es bueno campar?"* You might have to look around for a while before someone understands you, because the standard dialect at Zuzul is Chinantec. Bring your food and drinking water (although on weekends folks will probably be around, selling what you need).

Get there via a gravel turnoff road (signed in

Zuzul is among the most popular balnearios of the many lovely springs in Northern Oaxaca's Water Country.

the southerly direction) between kilometer markers 36 and 37, about seven miles (11 km) north of Valle Nacional, or 15 miles (24 kilometers) south of Tuxtepec. Follow the turnoff about .2 mile (.3 km) to a house on the right and driveway on the left. The closest boat landing is straight ahead 100 yards at the river bank. Alternatively, turn left and continue for .75 mile (1.3 km) to the end of the road. Walk straight ahead to the boat landing on the river.

Practicalities

Valle Nacional has one main business street, Hwy. 175, locally called Av. Benito Juárez, where you'll find most basic services, except for a bank. The town plaza (which accommodates few businesses, however) is on the right side, northbound, approximately at the center of town.

Of the town's three hotels, the best appears to be the downscale **Hotel Valle,** at Calle 2 Poniente 3 (3 West Second Street), Valle Nacional, Oaxaca 68480, on a side street a few blocks south of the plaza, three doors from the highway, no telephone. It offers 16 bare-bulb but acceptably clean rooms in a two-story tier, with baths with room-temperature water (tepid in warm Valle Nacional). Rates are $6 s, $8 d.

Stores along the main street, notably **Frutería Las Mexicanas,** sell plenty of luscious fruits, while *abarroterías,* such as **Las Triunfada,** sell lots of groceries, and a parade of *taquerias, loncherías* and *refresquerías* supply plenty more.

One of the town's best restaurants is the very clean, refined **Desgarenes,** at Juárez 29, tel. 287/740-05, beneath the luxurious big *palapa* on the left side of the street a few blocks north of the plaza.

Find the *correo* (post office), open Mon.–Fri. 9:30 A.M.–1 P.M. and 4–6 P.M., and the *telégrafos* (money orders and fax), open Mon.–Fri. 9 A.M.–3 P.M., at the *presidencia municipal* on the plaza.

For a doctor, go to the town **centro de salud,** tel. 287/741-26; turn east at the sign at the north (Tuxtepec) end of town; continue a block, off the highway.

Getting There and Away

The best way to reach Valle Nacional is on a Cuenca de Papaloapan second-class bus. From the bus station in the middle of town, buses connect north with Tuxtepec and south with

Oaxaca, including many intermediate destinations. From Oaxaca, drivers should follow federal Hwy. 175 about 110 miles (177 km) north, via Ixtlán, to Valle Nacional. The route, although well-maintained much of the way, winds nearly continuously, with a number of steep grades, along most of its length. Furthermore, at this writing, severe ruts and worn pavement slow traffic significantly for about 30 miles around the summit between Ixtlán and Valle Nacional. Allow about five hours, either direction, for the entire trip from Oaxaca.

SANTA MARÍA JACATEPEC

In between Valle Nacional and Tuxtepec, Jacatepec (pop. 3,000) is a village of friendly, frankly curious, Chinantec-speaking folks. Well worth a stop, it's tucked on the far side of the river, once accessible only by boat or a *puente colgante* (pedestrian suspension bridge). Now, a new automobile bridge connects Jacatepec to the main road, but it's still a quiet little place, fine for a *refresco* and a stroll around town. Also, be sure to walk across the hanging bridge. You'll see it about 100 yards upstream from the highway bridge. If you like the place, ask around for a room for the night. Say *"¿Hay cuarto para la noche?"* and someone may be able to oblige. Like most of the houses, it will probably be a clean abode with a cement floor, surrounded by a yard full of leafy plants; it might even have a sturdy, thatched palm-leaf roof.

While you're there, take a look inside the church at the far end of the town main street. You'll see a rare surrealistic Catholic altar, set with Jesus on the cross amid an apocalyptic landscape, with the town's patron, the Virgen de la Concepción, the only apparent ray of hope, floating above. Jacatepec is about 11 miles (18 km) north of Valle Nacional, or the same distance south of Tuxtepec.

SAN JOSÉ CHILTEPEC

Chiltepec is a friendly little Chinantec town with lots of thatched houses surrounded by yards abloom with bananas, red and yellow hibiscus, and crimson torch ginger. Chiltepec is a ripe

prospect for an overnight, mainly because of its inviting hotel and pair of riverside *balnearios.* Visitors also enjoy a sprinkling of *comedores* and a modicum of services, including post office, long-distance telephone, health center, doctor, and pharmacy.

The **Balnearios Mingo** and **Cocos** are relaxed local-style places on the winding Río Valle Nacional, with food *palapas* and plenty of shoreline for sunning, frolicking and splashing. They're best during the warm winter-spring season, when the water is clear and inviting. During the summer rains, the high, sometimes muddy river water sends most bathers to Balnearios Zuzul or Arroya Blanco (see above). Get to the Mingo from the highway by following the signed side road at the south end of town through town. Cocos is just off the highway; turn at the sign about a mile north of town. It has plenty of grassy space beneath a palm grove, perhaps just right for tenting or parking your RV.

The hotel **Posada Chinanteco,** right in the middle of town at Benito Juárez 17, San José Chiltepec, Oaxaca 68456, tel. 2/875-33-84, ext. 134, would be fine for an overnight. Guests enjoy a shady *palapa,* with comfortable chairs for sitting, set in a flowery garden patio. Six clean, thoughtfully decorated rooms, with baths and fans, rent for about $5 s, $8 d.

TUXTEPEC: RIVER COUNTRY

Tuxtepec (pop. 140,000), Oaxaca's second largest city, is the administrative and commercial center of the rich governmental district of the same name. For at least a millennium, the town, at its strategic river-junction location, has been an important trading center. Archaeologists believe that the Popoluca people, direct inheritors of the ancient Gulf Coast Olmec mother culture, first settled Tuxtepec perhaps 2,000 years ago.

History
The name Tuxtepec is the Spanish version of the town's Aztec label, Tochtepec, or "Hill of the Rabbits," which probably describes the town's original site, atop some low hills about a mile and a half west of present downtown Tuxtepec.

At that vital spot, Tuxtepec's early Popoluca people became traders and transporters for the valuable goods—cacao, feathers, gold, copper, cotton—of upstream producers, notably the Mazatecs and Chinantecs. Both still occupy their ancestral homelands: the Mazatecs (People of Mazatlán, "Land of the Deer") between the rivers Santo Domingo and Tonto, west of Tuxtepec, and the Chinantecs (People Atop the Mountains) in the basin of the Río Valle Nacional, to the southwest.

The ambitious Aztec emperors, expanding their domain in the 1400s, saw strategic Tuxtepec as a key to realizing their dreams of grandeur. Aztec forces under Moctezuma I subdued Tuxtepec in the 1460s. They built a ceremonial pyramid, known locally as the Castillo de Moctezuma, which still stands in a west-side residential neighborhood.

Aztec governor-generals commanded a Tuxtepec garrison of several thousand warriors for two generations, putting down rebellions and enforcing tribute from Tuxtepec's many subject towns. The codex Mendocino recorded the yearly spoils, including: "eight hundred loads of . . . red and white blankets . . . eighty bundles of quetzal feathers . . . twenty loads of clear amber, set in gold . . . twenty loads of quartz, enameled and finished with gold . . . 200 loads of cacao . . . twenty thousand rubber balls. . . ."

Hernán Cortés, almost immediately upon marching into the Aztec capital in 1519, asked Moctezuma II of his empire's source of gold. Moctezuma told him, "In Tochtepec the people wash the soil in bowls with water, and afterward, small grains of gold remain." He went on to say, "Not far from Tochtepec are some mines, said to be worked by Zapotecs and Chinantecs, who are not our subjects. If you desire to send soldiers to investigate, I will furnish emissaries to accompany them."

Cortés immediately dispatched his first gold-searching expedition outside of the Valley of Mexico, to Tuxtepec. They eventually brought back what was estimated to be 1,000 pesos' worth—perhaps a small sackful—of gold dust and small nuggets.

In late 1521, Gonzalo de Sandoval, after passing through the Valley of Oaxaca, took possession of Tuxtepec for Spain. Cortés instructed him to found a new town at Tuxtepec and name it Medellín, after the town in Spain where Cortés was born. Although the name Medellín didn't stick, Cortés persuaded the Spanish king to award him Tuxtepec as part of his Marquesate.

Tuxtepec was only a minor player in Mexican colonial and Independence history until it jumped onto the national stage in 1876 when Porfirio Díaz "pronounced" against the re-election of President Lerdo de Tejada. Díaz, a war hero and liberal ally of the revered late President Benito Juárez, threatened civil war. A group of his supporters organized in Tuxtepec, where they formulated the **Plan de Tuxtepec,** which re-asserted the principles of the Reform Consti-tution of 1857 and invented the slogan "¡No Reelección!," opposing reelection of the president, a principle that remains as Mexico's law of the land to the present day.

Lerdo de Tejada nevertheless refused to step down. So, with the entire state of Oaxaca behind him, Díaz marched on Mexico City. Soon Tejada fled the country and Díaz took brief de facto control of the government on 28 November 1876. Soon, Congress endorsed his action. Díaz served as legal president until 1880, as governor of Oaxaca from 1880 to 1884, then resumed the presidency, ignoring ¡No Reelección! until revolution forced him into exile in 1911.

Orientation

Tuxtepec is a modern town that spreads for two or three miles along the steep bank of the broad Río Papaloapan, which flows nearly due east past Tuxtepec's busy downtown. The main business streets begin at the Hwy. 175 bridge at the west end and continue for about a mile east to the town plaza. Moving away from the river, the main streets are Independencia, 20 de Noviembre, 5 de Mayo, and Libertad. A fifth street, quieter, river-view boulevard El Muro also runs parallel to the river, beginning at the east end of Independencia and gradually curving northerly, then westerly, until its course is completely reversed as it runs west along the north side of town.

Unlike most Mexican towns, Tuxtepec's main plaza, the **Parque Benito Juárez,** is not at the center of Tuxtepec, but rather at the east end, where the presidencia municipal and the town church, **Templo de San Juan Bautista,** face adjacent sides of the plaza.

A Walk along the River

Although Tuxtepec owes its existence to the Río Papaloapan, the town has pretty much turned its back on the river ever since trucks and trains have replaced the rafts, canoes, and barges that used to carry small mountains of cotton, rubber, coffee, and lumber from the upstream hinterlands. Nevertheless, a walk along the river is an entertaining route to enjoying Tuxtepec. Avoid the heat by starting out in the morning or late afternoon from the de facto town center—judging by the hustle and bustle—at the corner of Libertad and Matamoros, three short blocks from the river, about halfway between the highway and the plaza. Here, buses arrive and depart with loads of passengers. While people wait, a host of vendors hawk a varied assortment of goods, from CDs and socks to mangos and machine screws. A number of street-front *comedores* and *loncherías* provide hearty meals and snacks.

From there, head along Matamoros toward the river. At the end, Independencia, turn left to the small riverfront square, **Paso Real,** nearly immediately on the right. Here you can enjoy the river view, the breeze, and, if it's evening, perhaps a radiant sunset mirrored from the river's glassy surface. Descend the stairs to the dock, and, for fun, ride the riverboat that ferries folks across to La Esperanza village on the opposite bank.

Continue east along Independencia two more blocks to the **market** (biggest on Sunday). Find the stairs (inside, on the left) and climb to the second level. Here, take a view table at one of the *fondas* and enjoy a snack while feasting on the river view.

You can continue walking east, to the end of Independencia, and continue straight ahead along riverfront boulevard El Muro. Follow along as the river bends northerly to the *puento colgante* (hanging bridge) to San Bartolo. On the other side, you enter San Bártolo Tuxtepec, a sleepy village of yesteryear. Turn right at the first street and stroll up to the town *jardín* and library, where spreading, shady trees frame the view back across the river. One of the few times that San Bartolo wakes up is during its fiesta on 23 and 24 August, when, besides the feasts, fireworks, processions, and masses, the town sponsors musical performances, often including marimba and local-style *música cuenqeuña*.

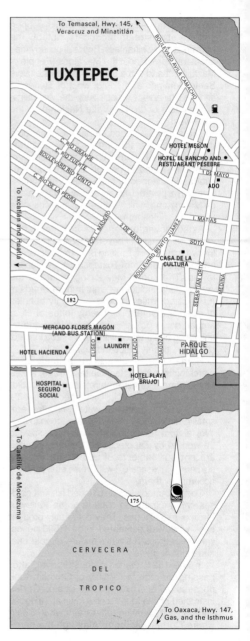

San Bartolo

PUENTE COLGANTE

PLAZA

LIBRARY AND CENTRO CULTURAL

MURO

BOULEVARD

13 DE SEPT.

AV. BONFIL

DISCO PASSY

AV. MANCILLA

AV. ROBERTO COLORADO

AV. 18 DE MAYO

CINEMA TUXTEPEC

PEDRO CASTILLO

JORGE TAMAYO

ALDAMA

MORELOS

ARTEAGA

BENITO JUÁREZ

RAYON

MIGUEL HIDALGO

GUERRERO

NICOLAS BRAVO

DIAZ MIRON

AV. CARRANZA

AUTOBUS TROPICO

AU

TELECOM

AV. LIBERTAD

OCAMPO

MATAMOROS

AV. 5 DE MAYO

PARQUE BENITO JUÁREZ

H. GALEANA

AV. 20 NOVIEMBRE

RESTUARANT CAPORALES

TEMPLO DE SAN JUAN BAUTISTA

AV. INDEPENDENCIA

MURO

BOULEVARD

FERRY TO LA ESPERANZA

MERCADO CENTRAL

SEE DETAIL

Río Papaloapan

LA ESPERANZA

200 yds

200 m

DETAIL

DEGOLLADO

AV. 5 DE MAYO

OCAMPO

MATAMOROS

ALDAMA

FARMACIA MODERNA

MORELOS

CENTRO MEDICO

CAFE INTERNET

ARTEAGA

AV. LIBERTAD

BENITO JUÁREZ

RAYON

HIDALGO

ALLENDE

CAMARA DE COMERCIO

PARQUE BENITO JUÁREZ

GUERRERO

AV. 20 DE NOVIEMBRE

JIMENEZ

BANCO SERFIN

PRESIDENCIA MUNICIPAL

PANIFICADORA

FARMACIA CRUZ VERDE

HOTEL TUXTEPEC AND RESTAURANT

RESTAURANT CAPORALES

BANAMEX

CORREO

AV. INDEPENDENCIA

HOTEL CENTRAL

BANCO INTERNACIONAL

PASEO REAL

HOTEL MIRADOR

BANCOMER

MERCADO CENTRAL

VIEWPOINT

FERRY TO LA ESPERANZA

Río   Papaloapan

© AVALON TRAVEL PUBLISHING, INC.

El Castillo de Moctezuma

This is a 15th-century unreconstructed ceremonial pyramid uncovered around 1916, now the centerpiece of a small neighborhood park in a Tuxtepec west-end suburb. Archaeologists believe that despite its *castillo* label, it was not built as a castle or fortress, but probably served as both a signal post and a ceremonial site for the populous Tuxtepec Aztec colony from around 1460 to 1520.

El Castillo rises gradually from the west side in three steps, to a height of about 25 feet (eight meters), and drops precipitously on the east side. Its surface is littered with crumbling masonry walls, which, on the north side, appear to open to a niche or tunnel.

Get there via Calle Reforma, the last street, Tuxtepec side, before the Hwy. 175 bridge. Turn right and continue three blocks; turn left at the T. Continue four more blocks to a store with a big blue Pepsi sign. That's Calle Ruinas; turn right and continue one block to the park and ruins at the corner of Calles Ruinas and Tabasco.

the hanging bridge over the Río Papaloapan to San Bartolo Tuxtepec

Accommodations

Tuxtepec accommodates its many business visitors with a number of good hotels. The fancier establishments are in the suburbs, by the highway. The cheaper, more workaday accommodations are in the busy downtown.

Of the downtown good choices, the best is probably the **Hotel Central,** which occupies a choice riverfront perch at Independencia 565, Tuxtepec, Oaxaca 68300, tel. 2/875-0966 or 2/875-0913, fax 2/875-0801. Of the hotel's 23 rooms, get one along the airy upper walkway, overlooking the river. Rooms themselves are plain but clean, with bath, TV, phone, a/c or fan, parking, and a good restaurant downstairs. Rates are about $15 s, $17 d, with fan, $16 and $18 with a/c; credit cards are not accepted.

A few doors west and passably good is the **Hotel Mirador,** also right on the river, next to the Paso Real ferry dock, at Independencia 531, Tuxtepec, Oaxaca 68300, tel./fax 2/875-0652, 2/875-0500 or 2/875-0797. Of the 51 plain but clean rooms, reserve one of the second-floor ones, numbers 219 through 223, along the upper river-view corridor. Rentals run about $17 s or d with a/c, $13 fan only, with TV, phone, hot water bath, and parking; credit cards not accepted.

Half a block west is the **Hotel Tuxtepec,** Matamoros 2, Tuxtepec, Oaxaca 68300, tel. 2/875-0934, a few steps off Independencia in the middle of downtown. Lacking a river-view location, the Hotel Tuxtepec management makes up for it by trying harder. Past the reception and invitingly airy street-front restaurant, the small but attractive lobby, set around a bubbling fountain, leads upstairs to 40 immaculate, comfortably furnished rooms. Rentals run a reasonable $12 s or d fan only; $14 and $15 with a/c, all with baths, hot water and parking, but credit cards not accepted.

Moving west half a mile, three blocks from the highway and somewhat up the economic scale, try the renovated four-star **Hotel Playa Bruja** at Independencia 1531, Tuxtepec, Oaxaca 68300, tel./fax 2/875-0325. The hotel's 40 clean, comfortably furnished rooms rise in three stories around a small inner pool patio. Rates are about $20 s, $23 d, $25 t with a/c, TV, phone, parking, and a restaurant-bar. Credit cards are accepted.

On the highway, a block from the bridge, stands Tuxtepec's best, the four-star **Hotel**

Hacienda at Blvd. Benito Juárez 409, Tuxtepec, Oaxaca 68300, tel./fax 2/875-1500, 2/875-1621, 2/875-1732, 2/875-1998. Past the entrance and parking, relegated thoughtfully to the outer periphery, the reception leads to a cool, air-conditioned restaurant bordering a relaxing pool patio and tropical garden. The 60 semi-deluxe rooms in three-story tiers are secluded, clean, and comfortable. The most attractive rooms have small balconies overlooking the garden. For such amenities, these rent for a reasonable $28 s, $32 d, and $38 t, with a/c, hot water bathrooms, cable TV, phone, parking, and credit cards accepted.

Nearly as good is the refined, but motel-style **Hotel El Rancho,** 435 Blvd. Avila Camacho, Tuxtepec, Oaxaca 68300, tel./fax 2/875-0722, 2/875-0469 or 2/875-0704, email: elrancho@tuxcom.net.mx. The hotel, in a mixed residential-business neighborhood, just a block west of the ADO first-class bus station, surrounds a pleasant tropical pool and parking patio. The hotel's only drawback appears to be the room arrangement on exterior corridors, where guests must unfortunately draw blinds for privacy. Inside, the 49 semi-deluxe rooms are immaculate and thoughtfully and comfortably furnished. Rates are $28 s, $32 d, $39 t, with a/c, bath, TV, parking, good restaurant-bar (see below), and limited wheelchair access. Credit cards accepted.

In third place among Tuxtepec's semi-deluxe choices is **Hotel Mesón,** on the highway about a mile from the river, at Blvd. Benito Juárez 1684, Tuxtepec, Oaxaca 68300, tel. 2/875-1200, 2/875-1369, or 2/875-1292, email: elrancho@ tuxcom.net.mx. Here the architect has ingeniously packed three stories of 65 rooms into a small space. The little pool, unfortunately relegated to a cramped upstairs patio, seems like an afterthought. The rooms inside, however, are clean, private, spacious, tiled, and furnished with comfortable 1980s-standard amenities. Rentals cost about $28 s, $32 d, 37 t, with a/c, bath, TV, phone, restaurant-bar, and parking. Credit cards are accepted.

Food

Tuxtepec visitors enjoy plenty of good food. The two town markets, the Mercado Flores Magón on 20 de Noviembre, by the highway, and the central market, on Independencia in the town center, by the river, are the best sources of groceries, fruits, and vegetables. At the central market, *fondas* upstairs serve economical, wholesome *comidas* at luxuriously airy river-view tables.

For good baked offerings, go to the **Panificadora Principal,** tel. 2/875-0755, open Mon. –Sat. 7 A.M.–9 P.M., Sun. 7 A.M.–1P.M., at 20 de Noviembre, corner of Degollado, about five blocks from the highway; or **Petit Cafetería y Pastelería,** open Mon.–Sat. 9 A.M.–8:30 P.M., Sun. 10 A.M.–4 P.M., at 689 5 de Mayo, tel. 2/875-4742, nearer the center of town.

A longtime favorite downtown restaurant, famous for its local-style food and relaxed atmosphere, is **Caporales,** tel. 2/875-4405, open Mon.–Sat. 8 A.M.–8 P.M., Sun. A.M.–6 P.M., in the center of town at Independencia 560, upper floor, across the street from the Hotel Mirador. Moderate.

Second choice downtown, half a block west, goes to the immaculate restaurant of the **Hotel Tuxtepec,** tel. 2/875-0934. Enjoy a good breakfast, lunch, or supper every day 7 A.M.– 11 P.M. Budget.

Three stars for refined ambience and attentive service go to the restaurant **El Pesebre,** tel. 2/875-0722 or 2/875-0469, at the Hotel El Rancho, at 435 Blvd. Manuel Avila Camacho, about a mile diagonally northwest of downtown, two blocks from the highway. Here you can escape from the heat and the hubbub into a cool, air-conditioned TV-free atmosphere and select from a professionally prepared international-style menu of salads, pasta, eggs, fish, fowl, and meat. Moderate.

Entertainment and Events

Tuxtepec's biggest party is the **Feria Tuxtepec,** which runs for about a week during late May or early June, when local people pull all of the rabbits out of their collective hat: election of a queen, grand parade of floats, horse and cowboy parade, cockfights, fireworks, a big commercial exposition, and a folkloric dance festival, including Tuxtepec's own charming **Danza de la Flor de Piña** (Dance of the Pineapple Flower).

If you're in town on 23 and 24 July, during the **Fiesta de San Juan Bautista,** be sure to get in on some of the fun around the plaza, including processions, *marmotas* (dancing giants), fireworks, and a community dance.

Tuxtepec folks also make a big celebration of the **Día de los Muertos** (Day of the Dead) on 1 and 2 November. At the *panteón* (cemetery) three blocks east of the plaza's northeast corner, whole families arrive in the early evening to clean up and decorate the graves with flowers, candy, candles, and the favorite foods of the deceased, then settle down for an all-night vigil.

Tropical Tuxtepec is warm all year-round, and especially so during the warm spring dry season, when folks enjoy the many local *balnearios* (river swimming beaches and natural springs). Some of the best are scattered along Hwy. 175 south of town. (See Valle Nacional and San José Chiltepec in the preceding sections.)

As the heat climaxes in May, folks get relief by participating in the **aquatic competitions,** such as fishing, water-skiing, and motorboat racing, held on the Rivers Tonto and Papaloapan and the Cerro de Oro and Temascal Reservoirs. Check with the chamber of commerce on the plaza for more information.

Services and Information

Tuxtepec has several banks, all with ATMs. The long hours (Mon.–Sat. 8 A.M.–6 P.M.) of **Banco Internacional** (Bital) make it a good choice, at 805 Independencia, tel. 2/875-2111, between Degollado and Jiménez, about three blocks west of the town center. Alternatively, moving east, try **Bancomer,** tel. 2/875-0576, at Independencia 647, next to the market; **Banco Serfin,** tel. 2/875-3844 or 2/875-3955, at 20 Noviembre and Morelos, one block farther from the river; or **Banamex,** tel. 2/875-1974, three blocks farther east, at Independencia and Rayón. After bank hours, try the money changer, **Agencia de Divisas Greco,** at Independencia 289, west end of Independencia near Banamex, open Mon.–Fri. 9 A.M.–6 P.M., Sat. 9 A.M.–2 P.M., tel. 2/875-0100.

Find the **post office** half a block past the east end of Independencia, on the left at Muro 39, open Mon.–Fri. 8 A.M.–7 P.M., Sat. 9 A.M.–1 P.M. *Telecomunicaciones* provides public fax, 2/875-3577, and money orders, Mon.–Fri. 8 A.M.–6 P.M., Sat 9 A.M.–noon, at the corner of Carranza and Morelos. From the downtown market, walk four blocks from the river, inland, along Morelos.

Cafe Internet, at Morelos 204, provides Internet service (email: tuxnet@ns .intertux.com.mex), Mon.–Sat. 9 A.M.–9 P.M., tel. 2/875-3219.

Doctors are plentiful in Tuxtepec. Ask at your hotel desk for a recommendation or go to the **Consultorio Médico** at 252 Morelos, southeast corner of Libertad, consultations Mon.–Fri. 9 A.M.–1:30 P.M., and 4:30–8 P.M., Sat. 9 A.M.–1 P.M., tel. 2/875-0392, emergency 2/875-4537. After hours in emergency, have a taxi take you to the **Hospital Regional Civil,** at Sebastián Ortiz 310, tel. 2/875-0023; or the **Hospital Seguro Social,** on Hwy. 175 on the town side of the river.

For nonprescription medicines and drugs, go to a *farmacia,* such as (moving easterly from the downtown west side): **Farmacia Cruz Verde,** 908 Independencia, across from Banco Internacional; or 24-hour **Farmacia Albatros,** tel. 2/875-2582, fax 2/875-3219, at 20 de Noviembre 881.

For police or fire emergencies, contact the *preventiva* (municipal police) at the *presidencia municipal,* tel. 2/875-3166.

The local **Cámara Nacional de Comercio** (National Chamber of Commerce) at the plaza's northeast corner (of Libertad and Allende) will try to answer your questions. Alternatively, travel agents such as **Viajes Sotelo,** at Morelos 118, tel./fax 2/875-2656, at the center of town, a block from Independencia and a block west of the market, are usually willing to answer travel-related queries.

Getting There and Away

Bus lines from a number of different stations provide connections with both Oaxaca and national destinations.

First-class **Autobuses del Oriente (ADO)** and associated lines, tel. 2/875-0473, operating out of their terminal at the corner of Sebastián Ortiz and 1 de Mayo (one block south, one block behind highway-front Hotel del Mesón), connect south with Oaxaca via Valle Nacional and Ixtlán de Juárez, and northwest with Orizaba, Puebla, and Veracruz, and northeast with Minatitlán and Coatzacoalcos.

Mostly second-class **Autobuses Unidos (AU), Cuenca de Papaloapan,** and **TRV** buses, tel. 2/875-0873, operating cooperatively from their station on Matamoros between Libertad and Carranza, connect south with Oaxaca via Valle Nacional and Ixtlán; southeast with Isthmus destinations of Matías Romero, Juchitán, Tehuantepec, and Salina Cruz; and northwest with Temascal, Orizaba, Córdoba, Veracruz, Puebla, and Mexico City.

Additionally, **Autobuses Unidos** (AU) second-class buses, operating out of a second terminal at the Flores Magón market on 20 de Noviembre, just east (town side) of Hwy. 175, connect west several times daily with Mazateca destinations of Jalapa de Díaz and Huautla de Jiménez.

Small, second-class line **Autobuses Trópico,** tel. 2/875-2895, from its terminal at Libertad 1215, a block and a half west of Matamoros, connects six times daily with Oaxaca via Valle Nacional and Ixtlán.

For drivers paved roads (some good, some not) connect Tuxtepec with Oaxaca and national destinations. Hwy. 175 connects south with Oaxaca via Valle Nacional and Ixtlán, over the Sierra Madre, in about 132 miles (213 km). However, steep, winding grades and a seriously rutted (unrepaired at this writing) 30-mile section near the Sierra summit can slow traffic to a crawl. Allow about six hours for safety in either direction.

Combined National Hwys. 147 and 185 connect Tuxtepec southeast with Tehuantepec, via Matías Romero and Juchitán. The nighttime robberies and hijackings that used to plague the lonely, northern, Hwy. 147 leg of this route have fortunately abated. To be sure, stop at the Hwy. 175-Hwy. 147 intersection gas station to check if the highway remains secure. Allow about five hours road time, either direction, for this 189-mile (304-km) trip.

A good paved route, Hwy. 182, connects Tuxtepec with Huautla de Jiménez in the high Mazateca, via Jalapa de Díaz. Allow about four and a half daylight hours westerly, four hours easterly, for this exhilaratingly scenic 74-mile (119-km) trip.

TEMASCAL AND MIGUEL ALEMÁN DAM AND RESERVOIR

Temascal (pop. about 5,000) is the town where the Mexican government, under the leadership of President Miguel Alemán (1946–52) began building a huge dam to control and harness the waters of the Río Tonto in 1946. The project, officially the Miguel Alemán Dam, was complete in 1955. A subsequent project, the Cerro de Oro Dam and Reservoir, was completed a generation later. The entire Papaloapan basin benefits from the reservoirs, now connected, which provide irrigation water, low-cost electric power, and relief from flood devastation. On the negative side, the dam's social cost was high. Many thousands of Mazatec, Chinantec, and Mixe indigenous campesino families suffered. Thousands had to be moved, some forcibly, from their land and relocated in new, unfamiliar locations.

Today the Miguel Alemán Dam, towering hundreds of feet, just upstream from the town of Temascal, is the project's most visible reminder. It compares in magnitude with the great hydroelectric projects of the American West. Its reservoir stretches about 20 miles long and 15 miles wide (32 by 24 km) and totals about two cubic miles of water, with an average depth of around 40 feet (12 meters). The reservoir's maximum flow can generate about 500 megawatts of electric power, more than enough for the entire state of Oaxaca and nearly enough for a U.S. city the size of San Francisco.

Sights and Activities

Follow the road through Temascal town and continue another half mile uphill to a T intersection. Turn right for the Temascal *embarcadero,* where *palapas* serve fresh fish *comidas* and motorboats on the shoreline wait for passengers. The lake is especially lovely considering that it's artificial. Fortunately, adequate water flows ordinarily keep the level constant and thus avoid the appearance of an ugly bathtub-like ring. From the *embarcadero,* the lake appears to stretch endlessly, invitingly blue and smooth, among green hills and small islands.

The shoreline restaurants specialize in lake bass *(mojarra)* and shrimp *(camarón)* dinners. Boatmen offer to take you on a two-hour *recorrido* (tour) around the lake for around $25 per boat, holding up to about eight. Save money by doubling up with others. The prime destination, besides a number of shoreline hamlets, is Soyaltepec, one of the few villages, along with Ixcatlán, that didn't get swallowed up by the reservoir. (See Ixcatlán, below.)

Besides boat rides and swimming, **fishing**

for bass (typically about a quarter pound) is a major local diversion. You can launch your own boat for free if you check with the *capitán del puerto,* in the center of the adjacent village, uphill from the *embarcadero.*

Parking a self-contained RV or setting up a tent is welcomed anywhere around the *embarcadero* (although level spots appear to be scarce.) A small store at the road, just above the *embarcadero,* could supply water and basic food items. Better stocked stores in Temascal could supply even more.

Before you leave, reverse your path and instead of turning left for the town, head straight along the dam-level road and take a look at the **Monument to President Miguel Alemán,** on the right before the dam. The main attraction, besides the heroic statue of Alemán, is the big mural in the open building atop the staircase. Here government artists have tried their best to dramatize the planned benefits of the dam project. A big mural shows two contrasting worlds: before the dam, a forbidding landscape of disease, superstition, poverty, and starvation, and the bright busy modern world—natives reading, surgeons operating, scientists experimenting, engineers building, teachers teaching, farmers harvesting—after the dam.

Getting There and Away
You can reach Temascal by second-class AU or TRV bus from either Tierra Blanca, Veracruz (north nearby), or Tuxtepec, from west-side Flores Magón market. Drivers, from Tuxtepec follow Hwy. 175 north. After about eight miles (13 km) turn left at the Ciudad Alemán sign. Continue approximately another half hour, or 16 miles (26 km), and turn left at the Temascal sign. After another 13 miles (21 km) continue through the town to the dam, a total of 37 miles (60 km) from Tuxtepec.

SAN PEDRO IXCATLÁN AND THE ISLANDS

An alternate gateway to the Miguel Alemán reservoir shoreline is through Ixcatlán, a prime spot for a country stay. The town stands at the eastern boundary of the Mazateca, where many townspeople and nearly everyone in the

Mazatec thatched house on Isla Soyaltepec

surrounding countryside speak Mazatec, and women wear the bright blue-and-white horizontally striped local *huipil.* The road to town leads through gently rolling, pastoral country—once dense rain forest, now undulating, parklike green pasture, sprinkled with palms and leafy trees. Thatched, whitewashed country houses appear atop the hills and around the bends. This is country where an unknown vehicle is an event. If you're driving, wave as you go by and the people will wave back.

Ixcatlán perches atop a long hill, surrounded by picture-perfect vistas of the verdant countryside, the deeply indented, island-dotted reservoir, and in the background, the precipitous silhouette of Cerro Rabón, the Mazatecs' holy mountain. Besides all this, Ixcatlán has an inviting small hotel, a sprinkling of country *comedores,* services, and excursions to even more remote, even uninhabited, islands.

Isla Soyaltepec
If it's no later than 3 P.M., you're early enough for the trip to Isla Soyaltepec. Once a small isolated town, Soyaltepec (pop. 500) is even more

isolated since the reservoir has confined it to an island where most of its friendly, frankly curious inhabitants speak only Mazatec. The only way to go is by boat, which you can bargain for (figure $15–20 for a two-hour round-trip for up to about six people) at the *embarcadero* on Ixcatlán's west lakeshore (below the Ixcatlán church). Beforehand, ask for boatman Fidel Alto Hermengildo. He's the Soyaltepec elementary schoolteacher and will help you find lodging if you decide to stay overnight on his island.

The six-mile trip takes about half an hour. Along the way butterflies flutter, herons stalk their prey, and clouds billow above the mirror-smooth lake surface. On the western horizon rises the towering massif of **Cerro Rabón,** often cloaked in a blanket of clouds. Along the way you pass through a fleet of little islands, some with small wooded crowns, perfect for an afternoon or overnight soaking in the scenery and solitude. If you do opt for an overnight, be prepared with a tent and mosquito repellent. Have your boatman return to pick you up at an appointed time.

At Soyaltepec, climb (one hour, round-trip) to the old village and church on the island hilltop. Half a dozen kids will probably accompany you. Halfway up, you scale a preconquest-appearing, ponderous stone staircase. At the top, take a look inside the venerable (1744) church, gaze westerly over the many-island lake vista, and get a *refresco* at the hilltop store.

Practicalities

Hotel Nanguina would be a pleasant surprise anywhere, but here in little, out-of-the-way Ixcatlán, it seems even more so. The hotel is a labor of love of its friendly owner, Patricia Sarmiento Castillo, who rents six immaculate, thoughtfully furnished rooms for $7 s or d, 11 t, with fans and room-temperature baths. She has made the hotel even more inviting with a top-level view porch from which guests can enjoy Ixcatlán's dramatic lake-view panorama. Write for a reservation: Hotel Nanguina, Calle Benito Juárez s/n, Ixcatlán, Oaxaca 68450, or leave a message with the town operator, tel. 287/720-88, 287/720-89, or 287/720-93.

The reservoir, whose waters Ixcatlán escaped because of its hilltop perch, has brought fresh fish to Ixcatlán. A scattering of country *comedores* serve good lake bass dinners, notably the homey, clean **El Vaquero** *palapa,* on main street Benito Juárez just past the church.

Plan your visit to coincide with Ixcatlán's main festival honoring **San Isidro Labrador** (Saint Isador the Farmer) 13–15 May. The fiesta's highlight is the traditional dance La Puta Chichi (Chichi the Prostitute).

Visitors to Ixcatlán can count on a number of basic services, including a doctor, a *centro de salud* (health center) at the town entrance, grocery stores, post office, and long-distance telephone.

Get to Ixcatlán by **Autobuses Unidos** (AU) bus bound for Huautla de Jiménez or Jalapa de Díaz from Tuxtepec's west-side Flores Magón market. Ride to the Ixcatlán side road, then taxi, catch a ride, or walk the four miles to town.

Drivers, from Tuxtepec, turn left (west) from Hwy. 175 onto Hwy. 182 at the Jalapa de Díaz sign at the traffic circle, just three blocks north of the Río Papaloapan bridge. Continue along Hwy. 182 west 34 miles (about 55 km) to the signed Ixcatlán right turnoff. Continue four miles (six km) to town.

SAN LUCAS OJITLÁN

While on your way to or from Ixcatlán, you might detour to San Lucas Ojitlán at the signed junction, 27 miles (43 km) west of Tuxtepec and six miles (10 km) east of the Ixcatlán turnoff. Ojitlán is the *cabercera* (head town) of a medium-size Chinantec-speaking *municipio.* Its main street bustles so continuously that few stores take the customary afternoon siesta.

Ojitlán's main establishments front the town's single main street, Independencia. They include a private doctor; *correo* (post office); *telecomunicaciones* (money orders and public fax); long-distance telephone; *centro de salud* (health clinic), tel. 287/760-02; and a number of grocery stores, notably the friendly general store **Centro Comercial del Sureste,** known locally as Tienda de Tinito, right in the middle of town.

Textiles make up the principal local handicraft, mostly colorful *huipiles* which some women weave. One of them is Juana Muñoz; many people, especially the proprietor of Tienda de Tinito, know her and can direct you to her house.

If she's not home, people will most likely know someone else.

Ojitlán's hubbub overflows on Wednesday, the regular day of *tianguis* (native street market), when hosts of country folk, including Chinantec- and Mazatec-speaking women in their brilliant *huipiles,* flock into town.

Local excitement peaks during the big fiesta in honor of Santa Rosa, on 28–30 August. Santa Rosa's popularity is a curiosity, since San Lucas, rather than Santa Rosa, is the official town patron. Community frustration over the local liturgy seems to have led to the preference for Santa Rosa. It turns out that a majority of faithful prefer the service to be in Spanish, but the local priest and the bishop in Tuxtepec insist on Latin, which no one understands.

Townsfolk do celebrate San Lucas, but with only a token fiesta. You can see evidence of the community preference inside the old church atop the hill, at the end of the main street. Behind the altar, notice the all-female cast of saints, with Santa Rosa in the middle, and San Lucas conspicuous by his absence.

THE MAZATECA

JALAPA DE DÍAZ AND VICINITY: THE LOW MAZATECA

By the time you arrive at Jalapa de Díaz, you're well into Mazatec country; walk a mile from town in any direction and you'll hear little, if any, Spanish spoken. For women here, wearing the *huipil* is the rule rather than the exception. Local women distinguish three grades of *huipil:* everyday, fancy, and super-fancy. The latter are beautifully crocheted all by hand, often displaying a glittering throng of birds and animals, fit for a bride.

You'd have little trouble finding Jalapa even if you had no Hwy. 182 to guide you. Jalapa de Díaz stands at the foot of the pinnacle of **Cerro Rabón** (elev. about 7700 feet, 2350 meters), arguably Oaxaca's most uniquely prominent landmass.

Sights

The most colorful times to arrive at Jalapa are Thursday and Sunday, for the big country *tianguis,* when sellers' awnings cover half the town, thronging with native folks. Another good time to arrive is during either of the two patronal fiestas, in honor of San Sebastián (19–20 January) and San Antonio de Padua (12–13 June).

The **Cañon del Río Santo Domingo,** which you can begin to appreciate about five miles up the highway from Jalapa, is one of Mexico's little-known wonders. The road climbs, rounding the foot of Cerro Rabón, and enters a vast cirque of verdant, jungle-clad ramparts on one side and the deep, plunging canyon on the other. At about 10 miles (16 km) uphill from Jalapa, you begin to cross rushing creeks, first Arroyo Blanco, then Arroyo Caballo, then finally the blue, boiling **Río Uluapa.** Walk the path to the right of the river half a mile uphill and see the river first flow from a cave, as a pure, pristine spring, then drop in a foaming waterfall.

For handicrafts, go to the store of **Fausto** (real name Roberto Osorio), on the highway about a block (Tuxtepec direction) from the entry road. He'll be happy to show and sell you examples of the lovely rainbow-hued heirloom *huipiles* that he, his wife, and his friends craft.

Climbing Cerro Rabón

At first glance, Cerro Rabón appears tempting to climb. In fact, many local people do it every day. They tend fields on the mountainside and walk down to town afterward. The net rise amounts to about 6,500 feet and should be attempted only by fit hikers, with a guide, who start at the crack of dawn with good shoes, food, and a jacket against cold. If the weather turns sour, go back or get shelter in someone's house. Lightning and cloudbursts up there could spell disaster. Clouds without rain are OK; they cap Cerro Rabón most of the time. This has resulted in the **cloud forest** coating the mountaintop—a Pleistocene remnant ecosystem of tree ferns, hanging moss, bright liquidambar trees, spiny bromeliads, and orchids.

Pack something to drink, although springs along the way should suffice for most of the water. You must get formal permission from the authorities at the *presidencia municipal,* who can probably suggest a guide, such as the experienced Antonio Bravo or the earnest young Juan de Dios de Tejada, who lives in the part of town called simply *sección 1,* and whom everyone there knows.

Accommodations and Food
Most of Jalapa's business establishments line the main street, Benito Juárez, which leads about a quarter mile from the highway to the town plaza, bordered by the *presidencia municipal* on one side and the church, the Templo de San Sebastián, on the other.

Right in the middle of everything is the town's one lodging house, the family-run **Casa de Huéspedes Robertina,** at Calle Benito Juárez s/n, Jalapa de Díaz, Oaxaca 68460, tel. 287/720-09. The grandmotherly owner rents plain but clean rooms for $7 per person, with bath down the hall.

Buy fruits and vegetables at the several curbside market stalls (which multiply into a big native *tianguis* Thursday and Sunday). Groceries are available at street-front *abarroterías,* such as Abarrotes del Centro, open Mon.–Sat. 7 A.M.–8 P.M. and Sun. 7 A.M.–3 P.M. A sprinkling of *comedores* along Juárez supply wholesome, local-style *comidas.*

For good restaurant food, try the locally recommended **Restaurant Ari** at the first *tope* (speed bump) on the Tuxtepec end of Hwy. 182 through town.

Services
If you get ill, go to the friendly town doctor, Abelardo Cruz Abejo, near the highway. For nonprescription drugs, try one of the basic *farmacias* on the main street. The town *correo* (post office) and *telecomunicaciones* (money orders and public fax) are next to the *presidencia municipal.*

Getting There
Bus passengers get to Jalapa just as from Ixcatlán and Ojitlán. Ride second-class **Autobuses Unidos** (AU) or **TRV** east from Huautla de Jiménez or west from Tuxtepec's market Flores Magón bus terminal. From Tuxtepec, drivers proceed exactly as for Ixcatlán (see preceding) but continue 11.5 miles (18.5 km) past the Ixcatlán turnoff to Jalapa de Díaz, a total of 44 miles (71 km) west of Tuxtepec or 32 miles (53 km) east of Huautla de Jiménez.

HUAUTLA DE JIMÉNEZ AND VICINITY: THE HIGH MAZATECA

Huautla de Jiménez (pop. 20,000), tucked on a high Mazateca mountainside, was put on the world map during the 1960s by María Sabina, a local Mazatec-speaking *curandera* who, like many others, used hallucinogenic mushrooms as part of her bag of remedies. The word somehow got out, and a small army of Love Generation devotees of hallucinogens from the United States and Europe, known locally as *gippis* (HEE-pees), quickly descended on Huautla. With them soon came a continuous stream of doctors, journalists, and anthropologists.

María Sabina seemed to enjoy her renown. She was invited far and wide to testify to the

Local folks gather for a protest meeting in the church basketball plaza in Huatla de Jiménez.

HUATLA DE JIMÉNEZ

PANIFICADORA LA SEÑORA DE OJAITLLAN

To Hwy. 182

FLETES Y PASAJES
(SECOND-CLASS BUS)

PANADERIA
LA GIRALDA
(BAKERY)

COMEDOR
KARINA

CASO

POSADA SAN
ANTONIO AND
GROCERIES

DR. SAUL
MARTÍNEZ AND
PHARMACY

ANTONIO

HUIPILES
VICTORIA
ENRIQUEZ

HOTEL
DE MAYO

PANADERÍA
GIRALDA

GARCIA

LARGA
DISTANCIA

FARMACIA
PINEDA

ABARROTES EL
SURTIDOR
(GROCERY)

DR. LÁZARO
P. GARCIA

AUTOBUSES UNIDOS
(SECOND-CLASS BUS)

RESTAURANT
GEMENIS

BANCO
INTERNACIONAL

FARMACIA
FENIX

JUAREZ

5 DE MAYO

RESTAURANT
ROSITA

HOTEL AND
RESTAURANT
RINCONCITO

HOTEL
OLÍMPICO

MERCADO

TEMPLO DE
LA NAVIDAD

BENITO

CUAUHTÉMOC

PROVEEDORA
DEL HOGAR
(GROCERIES)

PRESIDENCIA
MUNICIPAL

PLAZA

SCHOOL

CORREO

TELECOM

50 yds

50 m

0

0

© AVALON TRAVEL PUBLISHING, INC.

efficacy of her remedies at learned international medical conferences. But after a generation of fame, she passed away in 1985 at the age of 90, leaving Huautla to slumber again.

Her legacy, however, remains plainly visible in Huautla today, in the several businesses and institutions that carry her name, such as the María Sabina Cultural Center, the Comedor María Sabina, and the Farmacia María Sabina.

Besides such obvious reminders, many new-generation *curanderos* carry on María Sabina's mission. Notable among them are two of her grandsons, Filongonia Garcia and Eduardo Valladares, now both middle-aged. Eduardo, who was a constant companion of his grandmother during her heyday, was asked by author Juan Garcia Carrera of his thoughts concerning death. He replied, "By offering you enlightenment, my mushrooms also resign you to the reality of death."

In-Town Sights

Although the town itself spreads over a broad mountainside, the business and service center is concentrated mainly along a few downtown streets. Most important is the east-west street Calle Benito Juárez. Addresses start at number one on Juárez and increase to the east. Just downhill from the west end of Juárez are the town market, *presidencia municipal,* and the church, dedicated to the Virgin of the Nativity—all situated around the town plaza-basketball court *(cancha).* A second street, Cuauhtémoc, downhill from the plaza, runs parallel to Benito Juárez to its intersection with a third street, Antonio Caso, which angles diagonally west, downhill from its intersection, at the east end of Benito Juárez. Highway 182 contours along the mountainside three or four blocks downhill from the town plaza.

The most colorful times to arrive in town are during the patronal celebration **Fiesta de la Virgen de La Natividad** (7–8 September) and the **Feria Comercial** (the Friday before Good Friday, or 11 days before Easter Sunday). The Feria Comercial is attended by a host of villagers who crowd in from the surrounding mountains to watch their favorite traditional dances, including the Flor de Naranja (Orange Flower), Flor de Piña (Pineapple), Flor de Lis, (Heaven), and Anillo de Oro (Ring of Gold). If you miss these, at least try to be present on Sunday for the big *tianguis,* when vendors' awnings fill the entire center of town.

Casa María Sabina and Cerro de Adoración

El Fortín, the east-end ridgetop *barrio* where María Sabina lived, is revered by many Huautlecos. Her house, a simple rust-roofed white dwelling, has been unoccupied for years. It's in the neighborhood just beyond the government hospital not far from the highway. Ask for Casa María Sabina, and most likely a child will lead you there.

From there, continue to sacred site Cerro de Adoración along the path heading gradually upward along the right-hand (western) slope of the ridgetop. Your destination is just beyond the highest hill along the ridgetop, where, after a half-hour climb, you'll reach the pinnacle called Cerro de Adoración. Here, you'll find a monument with four crosses where local folks carry offerings, especially around 3 May, La Día de la Santa Cruz (The Day of the Holy Cross). Besides meeting folks along the trail carrying wood or herding goats, your reward will most likely be a cool breeze and a breathtaking panoramic vista of billowing clouds and rugged peaks, sprinkled with a dozen seemingly Lilliputian villages on their slopes.

Out-of-Town Sights

The area around Huautla, a dramatically folded green landscape of mountains and deep valleys hides a number of natural wonders, the best known of which include two limestone caves and a twin waterfall.

Easiest to get to and see is **Las Regaderas,** a pair of waterfalls not far west along Hwy. 182 from Huautla. Get there by car or white local minibus at Puente de Fierro bridge, four miles (6.6 km) west, Teotitlán direction, from Huautlaq. Just before the bridge, turn right on to a gravel road and continue .6 mile (one km) to the falls.

Las Regaderas (The Showers) plummet 100 feet (30 meters) out of a jungle cliff into a wild, tumbling river. Great trees resembling California sycamores shade both banks. An aging steel cable suspension walkway crosses the river next to an apparently abandoned rustic riverside house. Access to the rocky foot of the falls is steep and slippery, however. Bring a rope to steady your steps and avoid a nasty fall. Unfortunately, few, if any, camping spots are visible along the steep-walled riverbank. Security may also be a problem. Drunkenness seems to be a major local pastime.

Even more spectacular is **Nindo-Da-Gé** (Broad Spring Mountain) cave, first explored completely in 1905, near the little town of San Antonio Eloxochitlán. You probably can explore a majority of its 19 galleries—some gigantic, some petite—in a few hours inside the cave. The seemingly endless procession of dripping limestone formations, which have names such as The Infernal Hill, The Fort, The Snail, and Marimba, are even more fun if you dream up your own names.

The town invites visitors to both camp locally (town stores can supply food and water) and explore their cave. Recently authorities have partially completed a road most of the way to the cave, which can be reached from town in about two kilometers by road, and only another kilometer by foot trail.

The only obstacle to exploring the cave is the reasonable one that for safety reasons you must have a guide recommended by civic authorities. (The guide receives no money; he serves as part of his community service obligation. However, do offer a donation, perhaps about $20, in a sealed envelope, to the *ayuntamiento*—city government.)

A town committee, at this writing consisting of Isidro Beseril, Octavio Nieto, and Alonzo Nieto, are in charge. Another good person to contact for information is former cave committee member and friendly school teacher Professor Froilan Ríos, whose house stands on the left side of the paved road as you enter town. He recommends Alonzo Nieto as the best guide. If you're really serious about exploring the cave, notify Alonzo by leaving a message at the Elochotitlán long-distance telephone operator, tel. 2/37801-26, 800-27, detailing when you're planning to arrive. Do not fail to keep the appointment. Bring at least two strong (four-celled or more) flashlights, good traction shoes, and enough hard hats (hard plastic construction type) for everyone.

Get to San Antonio Eloxochitlán by bus or car seven miles (11 km) along the Teotitlán (west) direction on Hwy. 182, to the San Antonio turnoff gravel road on the right (north). Continue 4.8 miles (7.7 km) to the town church and plaza.

Cave enthusiasts might also enjoy hiking to the **Sotano de San Agustín** (Hidden Cave of San Agustín), near the village of San Agustín, on Hwy. 182 a few miles northeast of Huautla. The cave was only discovered during the 1990s. With a single half-mile (about 800-meter) drop, the San Agustín cave is considered the second deepest in North America. You can reach the cave entrance accompanied by a local guide (inquire at the San Agustín *presidencia municipal*) via the steep downhill trail from near the town church. As for exploring the cave itself, only super-equipped and experienced speleologists should apply to local authorities for permission to enter.

Accommodations

Huautla's best hotel is the **Hotel Rinconcito,** Juárez 8, Huautla de Jiménez, Oaxaca 68500, tel. 2/37801-36, across Juárez from the market. Friendly husband-wife owners Leonardo Altamirano and Catalina Casamiro rent eight plain but clean rooms for $14 s, $19 d, $25 t, with hot water baths. The best are in front, with views of the market below and the mountains in the distance.

Running a distant second two blocks west is the rough but clean **Hotel 1 de Mayo,** at Juárez 30, Huautla de Jiménez, Oaxaca 68500, tel. 2/37800-76. The three stories of approximately 20 bare-bones rooms rent for about $7 s, $9 d, with hot-water baths.

Third choice goes to the extremely basic (emergency only) **Hotel Olímpico,** next door to the Hotel Rinconcito; tel. 2/37801-73, $9 s, $10 d.

Food

Go to the **market** for the freshest fruits and vegetables. Get groceries either at the market or at **Proveedora del Hogar** (Home Supplier) at Juárez 3, across the street from the *presidencia municipal,* or **Abarrotes El Surtidor** at Juárez 27, one block east, corner of Juárez and Garcia González.

For fresh-baked goods, try **Panadería Giralda** two blocks east, at 2 Garcia González, the street that angles uphill a few doors east of the Hotel Rinconcito. Alternatively, go to **Panadería La**

Señora de Ojatitlán, three blocks farther east, at the corner of Caso and Juárez. Find snacks, such as hamburgers, hot dogs, and *tortas,* at the stand in front of the Hotel Rinconcito, across Juárez from the market.

Huautla's best restaurant is in the **Hotel Rinconcito,** upstairs. Guests enjoy a light and spacious dining room with view windows overlooking the colorful market scene below and the cloud-capped green mountains in the distance. Friendly owner Catalina Casamiro serves a simple but tasty menu of eggs, toast, and pancakes for breakfast, and sandwiches, soups, and stews for lunch and dinner. Open daily 8 A.M.–8:30 P.M. Budget.

Alternatively, try the humbler but also friendly *comedor* **La Karina** on Juárez, two blocks east, open daily 8 A.M.–9 P.M., or the **Restaurant Gemenis,** open about the same hours, at Cuauhtémoc 11, downhill from the plaza. In the same vicinity, Señora Catalina Casamiro recommends **Restaurant Rosita,** half a block downhill west, behind and below the school.

Shopping for Handicrafts

Huautla offers some opportunities to shop for its well-known **textiles.** Around the market especially, you'll see women in handmade *huipiles,* adorned with bright embroidered birds, fruits, flowers, and rainbows of pink-, yellow-, and blue-striped satin. **Victoria Enríquez,** at her shop (on Juárez, just east of the Hotel 1 de Mayo), crafts and sells *huipiles* daily except Sun. 8 A.M.–4 P.M. and 6–9 P.M. In addition to the *huipiles,* women craft and decorate blouses, shirts, skirts, tablecloths, and napkins in floral and animal designs. Buy them at either market stalls or a few street-front shops, such as Catalina Casamiro's restaurant-shop in the Hotel Rinconcito, upstairs, or the small handicrafts shop, Artesanías Julieta, on the plaza, west side, lower level. You might be able to see more examples at the homes of individual craftswomen; ask around at the market.

Services

For money, go to the **Banco Internacional** (Bital), open Mon.–Sat. 8 A.M.–6 P.M., tel. 2/37800-29, across Juárez from the market. After hours, use its ATM.

A pair of **doctors** maintain offices on Juárez.

Moving east, first comes **Dr. Lázaro Pérez García,** open Mon.–Sat. 8:30 A.M.–3 P.M. and 5–9 P.M. and also available on call at Juárez 12, upstairs. A block farther east, you'll find **Dr. Saul Martínez,** at his pharmacy and 24 hours on call, tel. 2/37802-57. Nonprescription medicines and drugs are available at other **pharmacies** on Juárez, such as Farmacia Fenix, at Juárez 210, corner of Caso, south side of the street.

The *correo* (post office) and *telecomunicaciones* (public fax and money orders) stand side by side on the plaza's west side, above the shops, across the street (west) from the *presidencia municipal.*

Long-distance telephone is available at both the Hotel Rinconcito, daily 8 A.M.–9 P.M., and a block east at the *larga distancia* and sandwich shop at Juárez 22.

Getting There and Away

Buses operate out of a pair of terminals on Calle Antonio Caso, which runs diagonally downhill from Calle Juárez. Second-class **Fletes y Pasajes** buses, tel. 2/37804-06, connect west with Teotitlán del Camino, thence south with Oaxaca via Cuicatlán and northwest with Mexico City via Tehuacán and Puebla. Second-class **Autobuses Unidos** (AU) buses connect east with Tuxtepec via Jalapa de Díaz; northwest with Mexico City via Teotitlán, Tehuacán, and ·Puebla; and south with Oaxaca, via Teotitlán and Cuicatlán. Local-class white **Transportes Regionales Sierra-Cañada-Teotitlán-Oaxaca** minibuses connect south with Oaxaca, via Teotitlán and Cuicatlán.

For drivers, paved Hwy. 182 connects Huautla east with Tuxtepec via Jalapa de Díaz, along 76 miles (122 km) of winding but breathtakingly scenic mountain road. For safety, allow 2.5 hours eastbound, downhill, or three hours westbound, uphill. In a westerly direction, Hwy. 182 connects Huautla east with Teotitlán del Camino in 41 miles (66 km) of paved, downhill-winding, scenic mountain road. (From Teotitlán, Hwy. 135 connects south an additional 100 miles, 161 km, about 3.5 hours, with Oaxaca.) Allow two hours downhill (westerly), 2.5 hours uphill (easterly).

Unleaded gasoline is available at the Pemex gas station on the highway a few blocks south, downhill from the town center.

THE CAÑADA: CANYON COUNTRY

Shadowed from rain by mountains on all sides, the dry, tropical Cañada canyonland comprises one of Oaxaca's major geo-cultural regions. It encompasses the Cuicateca—the land of the Cuicatecs—a Mixtec-related people who, for longer than anyone can remember, have scratched out a living from their homeland's warm, desert canyon bottoms and steep mountain slopes. Reclusive and traditional, Cuicatec people generally venture out from their home villages only infrequently, mostly to trade at the market towns—sometimes Teotitlán del Camino, more often at Cuicatlán.

TEOTITLÁN DEL CAMINO

Just shy of Oaxaca's border with the state of Puebla stands Teotitlán del Camino (pop. 5,000), the jumping-off point for the Mazateca highlands to the east. Teotitlán's elevation, 3,600 feet (1,100 meters), places it about a mile lower and many degrees warmer than sometimes-chilly Huautla de Jiménez, in the Mazateca highlands. Teotitlán's fortunate combination of warmth, sunshine, and abundant spring water nourishes a local oasis of mangos, bananas, lemons, oranges, and avocados.

Sights
Despite Teotitlán's significance as the capital of the sprawling governmental district of the same name, it nevertheless feels much like a small town, with a modicum of stores and services within a block or two of the central plaza. Streets run approximately east-west (uphill-downhill) and north-south. The church is southeast of the town plaza. The three main east-west streets are Hidalgo, the Hwy. 135 ingress street that runs along the plaza's north side; José Silones, between the plaza and the church; and 5 de Mayo, a block south of the plaza along the church's south side. The main north-south streets are Josefina Ortiz, which runs along the west side of the plaza; Juárez, behind and east of the church; and Independencia, the Hwy. 1–682 ingress from Huautla, one block farther east uphill.

The town's pride is its church, the **Templo de San Miguel Arcángel,** built by Franciscan padres during the 17th century. Outside, an image of angel San Miguel decorates the pinnacle of its Roman-Doric-columned facade. Inside, the ceiling is a cheery sky blue, with bright paintings of Saints John (Juan), Matthew (Mateo), Luke (Lucas), and Mark (Marcos) around the central cupola overhead. The broad church atrium is usually very quiet, except around 29 September, when local folks honor San Miguel with processions, fireworks, and floats ridden by children dressed as angels.

Take a stroll around the adjacent town plaza, where big, shady trees provide a welcome refuge from the warm afternoon sun. At night the plaza becomes the town's central meeting ground, where couples stroll and people relax on benches attractively decorated with bright Puebla tile.

If it's Wednesday or Sunday, another focus of activity is the **market** on Independencia, about two blocks south of the plaza. The big Teotitlán market structure was obviously built for better times. It's presently empty as a tomb five days a week.

Accommodations and Food
The town has three acceptable hotels and one highly recommended restaurant. The best hotel is **Hotel Doña Ofelia,** three blocks west (downhill) and north from the plaza at Calle Ricardo Flores Magón 39, Teotitlán del Camino, Oaxaca 68540, tel. 2/372-0220. (From the plaza corner of Hidalgo and Josefina Ortiz, walk two blocks downhill past the secondary school to Pino Suárez, then turn right and continue one block north to Flores Magón and the hotel). Its six rooms in two stories are clean and comfortably furnished. Best of all, they open onto a shady, homey garden, with chairs and tables for relaxing. In the morning especially, birds sing, and rarely does anything disturb the tranquillity. Rentals run $11 s, $15 d, $16 t, with fan and hot water shower bath. The hotel, the best along Hwy. 135 between Oaxaca and Tehuacán, is often full; be sure to call ahead for a reservation.

The town's second-best but newer hotel has both the same name and the same kindly owner, Ofelia Mesa Muñoz. The newer hotel occupies the corner of Independencia and José Silones, a block and a half uphill east of the plaza. It's not as tightly managed, since Ofelia stays at her favorite, original hotel. The rooms, however, are just as clean and are attractively painted and highlighted with fine Puebla tile. Rooms open to an inviting shaded garden patio. And it's the only hotel in Oaxaca with an irrigation aqueduct (albeit a small one that gurgles quaintly past the edge of the patio). Unfortunately, the location suffers from noisy trucks and buses, which seem to run past the front door every few minutes during the morning. Despite the noise, this is a good second choice. Prices are the same, $11 s, $15 d, $16 t, with fan and shower bath with hot water. Reserve through the address and telephone number for the Hotel Doña Ofelia, above.

Third choice goes to **Hotel Isabel,** at Colonia 7, Teotitlán del Camino, Oaxaca 68540, tel. 2/372-0097, two blocks north of the plaza. The rooms, in an apartment-style block on the quiet edge of town, which rent for about $9 d, are plainer and not as clean, with none of the garden amenities as Ofelia's hotels. Find it two blocks downhill west, to Colonia (at the secondary school), then two blocks north of the plaza.

On the other hand, budget travelers may prefer the plain but homey **Casa de Huéspedes Mary,** $6 s, $7 d, diagonally across the street from the plaza's southwest corner.

The inviting, family-run **Restaurant Silvia** on Juárez, a block east and around the corner from the plaza, lives up to its high local reputation. Although busily patronized by *rancheros,* businesspersons, and occasional tourists, you can usually retreat to the relaxing, airy patio section in the rear. Open daily for *desayuno, comida,* and *cena,* 7:30 A.M.–10 P.M.

Services

Teotitlán plaza-front establishments can supply most emergency needs. Start with the ***correo*** (post office), open Mon.–Fri. 9 A.M.–1 P.M. and 3–6 P.M., at the northeast corner, end of Hidalgo. Diagonally opposite, at the southeast plaza corner, is the small grocery, **Abarrotes Santa Lucia.** One block south, at J. Ortiz 12, you'll find the ***telégrafos,*** open Mon.–Fri. 9 A.M.–3 P.M., tel. 2/372-0171, offering money

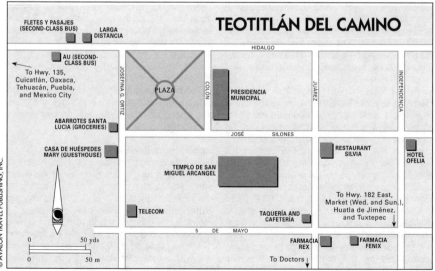

TEOTITLÁN DEL CAMINO

FLETES Y PASAJES (SECOND-CLASS BUS)
LARGA DISTANCIA
HIDALGO
AU (SECOND-CLASS BUS)
To Hwy. 135, Cuicatlán, Oaxaca, Tehuacán, Puebla, and Mexico City
JOSEFINA G. ORTIZ
PLAZA
COLÓN
PRESIDENCIA MUNICIPAL
JUÁREZ
INDEPENDENCIA
ABARROTES SANTA LUCIA (GROCERIES)
JOSÉ   SILONES
CASA DE HUÉSPEDES MARY (GUESTHOUSE)
RESTAURANT SILVIA
HOTEL OFELIA
TEMPLO DE SAN MIGUEL ARCANGEL
To Hwy. 182 East, Market (Wed. and Sun.), Huatla de Jiménez, and Tuxtepec
TELECOM
TAQUERÍA AND CAFETERÍA
5   DE   MAYO
0   50 yds
0   50 m
FARMACIA REX
FARMACIA FENIX
To Doctors

© AVALON TRAVEL PUBLISHING, INC.

orders, telex, and telegraph, but no fax. Try the *larga distancia* on Hidalgo by the bus station, half a block downhill from the plaza, for fax.

For medicines, go to the **Farmacia Rex,** behind the church at the corner of Juárez and 5 de Mayo, open daily 7 A.M.–11 P.M., tel. 2/372-0374. If the Rex doesn't have what you need, continue uphill along 5 de Mayo half a block to Farmacia El Fénix.

As for doctors, visit either **Dr. Sergio Mendoza,** general practitioner, or **Doctora María Teresa Noriega,** family medicine, tel. 2/372-0154, who at this writing were maintaining joint offices in their home at Juárez 50, next to the state water office, about three blocks south of the center of town. Alternatively, go to the **Seguro Social** clinic, tel. 2/372-0139, downhill several blocks on the highway.

Getting There and Away
Second-class buses operate out of a pair of terminals on Hidalgo, a block downhill from the plaza. **Fletes y Pasajes** buses connect south with Oaxaca via Cuicatlán, northwest with Mexico City via Tehuacán and Puebla, and east with Huatla. Second-class **Autobuses Unidos** (AU) buses, tel. 2/37200-61, connect south with Oaxaca via Cuicatlán, northwest with Mexico City via Tehuacán and Puebla, and east with Huautla. Additionally, local-class white minibus **Transportes Regionales Sierra-Cañada-Teotitlán-Oaxaca** buses connect south with Oaxaca, via Cuicatlán, and east with Huautla.

For drivers, paved Hwy. 182 connects Teotitlán east with Huautla in 41 miles (66 km) of scenic but winding uphill mountain road. For safety, allow 2.5 hours (or two hours in the opposite, downhill, direction). In a southerly direction, Hwy. 135 connects with Oaxaca in a winding but easy (with caution) 100 miles (161 km). Allow about 3.5 hours' driving time, either direction. In a northerly direction, Hwy. 135 connects with Tehuacán (39 miles, 63 km, one hour). From there you can continue northwest to Puebla via Hwy. 150 in an additional three-hour, 70-mile (93-km) trip.

Unleaded gasoline is available at the Pemex *gasolinera* on the highway, about a mile northwest of the town plaza.

CUICATLÁN

Cuicatlán (pop. 10,000) is the commercial capital of the Cañada, the emporium for the entire high Sierra hinterland that rises immediately east of town. Cuicatlán, like Teotitlán, owes its wealth to abundant sunshine and water. In Cuicatlán, water is synonymous with the Río Grande, the river that passes west of the highway, just west of town. After nourishing a local oasis of fruit, vegetables, and grain, the Río Grande continues its good work downstream. It joins with the swarm of tributaries draining the entire Cañada basin, becoming the Río Santo Domingo, the major electrical power source at the Miguel Alemán dam. The river unites with the Río Papaloapan past Tuxtepec, finally feeding thirsty crops and people all the way to the Gulf of Mexico.

Sights
Cuicatlán (Place of Song) is home to a busy market, often packed with Cuicatec-speaking people, especially women, wearing their handmade *huipiles.* Head there via the turnoff road from Hwy. 135, which, as it becomes Av. Hidalgo, Cuicatlan's main business street, leads a mile north to the plaza at the town center. There stands the church, the **Templo de San Juan Bautista,** on the plaza's east side. A block farther east is the *presidencia municipal.* Across the street from the *presidencia* is the **market.** Although it's lively enough most days, the market is especially big on Sundays and overflowing around 24 June, when merrymakers crowd the streets and celebrate the **Fiesta de San Juan Bautista** with costumes, parades and floats, community feasts, fireworks, and traditional dances.

Accommodations and Food
Cuicatlán offers a pair of acceptable hotels, a good restaurant, and a number of essential services. The best hotel, in a parklike setting by the Río Grande, is named, appropriately, the **Hotel Oasis.** (Unfortunately the once-beautiful Hotel Oasis has been allowed to run down. But perhaps the owners will have cleaned and fixed the place up by the time you read this.) It's right on the highway, address Carretera Federal, San Juan Bautista Cuicatlán, Oaxaca

68600, tel. 2/37402-66. The approximately 20 plainly furnished rooms rent for about $11 s or d ($17 for two beds), with hot water shower baths, fans, restaurant, pool, and parking. Credit cards are not accepted. A splash in the pool, in the adjacent garden, or in the river nearby, might provide a cooling diversion during a hot Cañada afternoon.

In town, a couple of blocks from the bus station, bus travelers might find the **Casa de Huéspedes Dani,** Calle Hidalgo, San Juan Bautista Cuicatlán, Oaxaca 68600, tel. 2/374-0091, too convenient to pass up. It offers about 10 plain rooms around a parking patio for about $7 s, $9 d, with fans and hot water showers outside the rooms. Credit cards not accepted.

As for food, you'll find the freshest fruit and vegetables in the market and the best grocery selection at the **Super El Molino** grocery at the plaza's southeast corner, across the street from the church.

Cuicatlán's most highly recommended place to eat is the airy *palapa* of the clean, seafood-specialty **Restaurant Boringuen,** two blocks east of the plaza, across the street from the *presidencia municipal.* Enjoy the relaxing open-air atmosphere and fresh fish fillet or shrimp for lunch or dinner. Open 8 A.M.–8 P.M.

Services

Most of Cuicatlán's service establishments are either on the town plaza or along Calle Hidalgo, the north-south Hwy. 135 ingress street. Although at this writing Cuicatlán still had no bank, you might be able to cash a small traveler's check (or at least a US$20 bill) at the grocery store **Super El Molino,** at the town plaza's southeast corner. A long-distance telephone is available at the small *caseta larga distancia* on the plaza at the east corner of Hidalgo.

For nonprescription medicines and drugs, cross to the west, plaza-front side, of Hidalgo to **Farmacia San Juan,** tel. 2/37400-98. If, however, you need a doctor, see **Dr. Rudolfo Reyes Escalante** at his Farmacia San Ramón, tel. 2/37400-33, at Centenario 30. (From the plaza, walk two blocks down Hidalgo to Centenario, then turn right half a block.) Alternatively, go to the public *centro de salud* clinic and hospital on Hidalgo, three blocks downhill from the plaza.

Buy stamps or mail a letter at the *correo,* diagonally across the street from the plaza's southwest corner, second floor.

Getting There and Away

Fletes y Pasajes and **Autobuses Unidos** (AU) long-distance buses operate out of separate stations on Hidalgo, about four blocks downhill from the plaza. They both offer departures connecting north with Mexico City via Teotitlán, Tehuacán and Puebla, and south with Oaxaca.

For drivers, Highway 135 connects south with Hwy. 190 at Telixtlahuaca, thence with Oaxaca, a total of 63 miles (101 km). The route, paved and in good condition but winding, requires at least two hours for safety.

In the northerly direction, Hwy. 135 connects with Teotitlán del Camino in about 37 miles (60 km). Allow about an hour and a quarter for this winding but easy (with caution) trip.

THE ISTHMUS: LAND OF PLENTY

A trip to the Isthmus from the Oaxaca central highlands sometimes seems like a journey to another country. At the Isthmus, the North American continent narrows to a scarce 100 miles in width; the mighty Sierras shrink to mere foothills. The climate is tropical, the land is fertile and well-watered. Luxuriant groves hang heavy with oranges, mangos, avocados, almonds, and coconuts. Rivers wind downhill to the sea, springs well up at the foot of mountains, and swarms of fish swim offshore. The Isthmus is a land of abundance, and it shows in the people. Women are world-famous for their beauty, spirit, and their incomparably lovely flowered skirts and blouses, which young and old seem to wear at any excuse.

And they have excuses aplenty, for the Isthmus is the place of the *velas,* called fiestas in other parts of Mexico. But in the Isthmus, especially in the towns of Tehuantepec and Juchitán, where *istmeño* hearts beat fastest, *velas* are something more special. Most every *barrio* (neighborhood) must celebrate one in honor of its patron saint. A short list names 20 major yearly *velas* in Juchitán alone. The long list, including all the towns in the Isthmus, numbers more than 100.

This all climaxes in the town of Tehuantepec on 26 December, in a grand one-day celebration, the **Vela Tehuantepec,** when everyone dresses up, women in their spectacular flowered *trajes* and men with their diminutive Tehuantepec sombreros, red kerchiefs, sashes, and machetes. The entire town celebrates all night, dancing to the beautiful melody of the *Sandunga,* which, once you've been captured by its lovely, lilting strains, will always bring back your most cherished Isthmus memories.

SANTO DOMINGO TEHUANTEPEC AND VICINITY

HISTORY

Although strictly connected only with a single location, the name Tehuantepec (Hill of the Jaguar) is, in many minds, synonymous with the entire Isthmus region: thus the label the "Isthmus of Tehuantepec." The connection is historical, for Tehuantepec's dominance was born in events of long ago.

The earliest known settlers in the Isthmus left Olmec-style remains, which archaeologists date from as early as 4000 B.C. Much later, around 500 B.C., the Olmecs' inheritors, probably the ancestors of present-day Mixe- and Huave-speaking people, occupied the Isthmus lands. But times changed, and by A.D. 500 the Isthmus had become a strategic funnel: a trade gateway between the great civilizations, such as Teotihuacán and Monte Albán, of the Mexican central highlands and the rich Mayan cultures of Chiapas, Yucatán, and Guatemala.

Eventually, the more populous Zapotec-speaking people displaced the Mixe and Huave in the Isthmus. By A.D. 1400, the Zapotec kings of Zaachila in Oaxaca's central valley controlled the Isthmus gateway with a mountaintop fort at Guiengola, which guarded their Isthmus capital at the present-day town of Tehuantepec.

The ambitious Aztec emperors also coveted the Isthmus gateway. In the 1440s they sent armies to Oaxaca to pressure the Mixtec and Zapotec kingdoms, who allied themselves against the Aztecs. But forced by Aztec victories in 1486, many Zapotec people, including their king Cosijoeza, retreated from Zaachila and took refuge in Tehuantepec. There, together with the Mixtecs under King Dzahuindanda, the Zapotecs, attacking from their stronghold at Guiengola, held off the Aztecs, who offered Emperor Moctezuma's daughter in marriage to King Cosijoeza as part of a peace pact.

With tranquillity established, Cosijoeza returned to reign once again over Zaachila, leaving his son, Cosijopí, as king of the Isthmus, with his court at Tehuantepec. Later, when the Spanish arrived, King Cosijopí joined with Cortés against the Aztecs. After Aztec power was erased, Cosijopí, along with thousands of his subject-inhabitants of Tehuantepec, converted to Christianity.

SIGHTS

Orientation

Although the Río Tehuantepec splits the Tehuantepec town (pop. 52,000) along a roughly north-south line, the west-side portion, across the river via the Puente Metalico (Metal Bridge), first built for locomotives around 1900, seems like a mere suburb of the town center, east of the river. On the central plaza itself, the *presidencia municipal* (city hall) occupies the south side, along Calle 5 de Mayo; the main market, **Mercado Jesús Carranza,** lies on the plaza's west, river side, along Calle Juana C. Romero; and to the northeast, past the end of main north-south street Benito Juárez, about a block and a half northeast of the plaza, stands Tehuantepec's most venerable monument, the **Church and Ex-convent of Santo Domingo.**

Around the Plaza

First, take a stroll around the plaza, where you'll find some interesting sculptures, including noble likenesses of Miguel Hidalgo (the Father of Mexican Independence) and a pair of Tehuantepec heroes. On the north side, look for the bronze of a seated **Doña Juana Catalina Romero (1855–1915),** a Tehuantepec legend. She is famous partly for her good works, establishing schools for Tehuantepec children during the days when public education was a rarity in Mexico.

On the plaza's west (market) side, you'll find the bronze bust of **A. Maximino Ramón Ortiz,** the first and only governor of the Isthmus, when it was separated from Oaxaca as the territory of Tehuantepec for a few years during the 1850s. Politics, however, were not Ortiz's first love. He is best remembered as the composer of the *Sandunga,* Tehuantepec's beloved theme. His

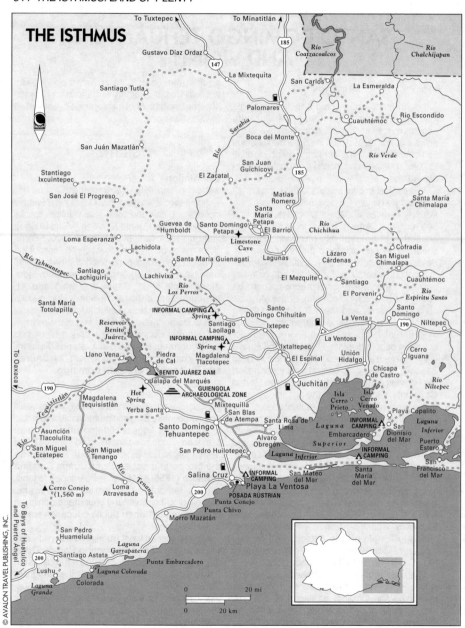

THE ISTHMUS

To Tuxtepec

To Minatitlán

Gustavo Díaz Ordaz

Río Coatzacoalcos

Río Chalchijapan

185

147

La Mixtequita

San Carlos

La Esmeralda

Santiago Tutla

Palomares

Cuauhtémoc

Río Escondido

Río Sarabia

Boca del Monte

San Juán Mazatlán

Río Verde

Stantiago Ixcuintepec

San Juan Guichicovi

185

El Zacatal

San José El Progreso

Matias Romero

Santa María Chimalapa

Guevea de Humboldt

Santa María Petapa

Santo Domingo Petapa

El Barrio

Río Chichihua

Loma Esperanza

Río Tehuántepec

Lachidola

Limestone Cave

Lagunas

Lázaro Cárdenas

Cofradia

San Miguel Chimalapa

Santiago Lachiguiri

Santa María Guienagati

Lachivixa

El Mezquite

Santiago

Cuauhtémoc

El Porvenir

Río Espíritu Santo

Santa María Totolapilla

Río Los Perros

Santo Domingo Chihuitán

Santo Domingo

Niltepec

190

INFORMAL CAMPING ⛺
Spring

Santiago Laollaga

Ixtepec

La Venta

Reservoir Benito Juárez

Llano Vena

Piedra de Cal

INFORMAL CAMPING ⛺
Spring

Magdalena Tlacotepec

Ixtaltepec

El Espinal

La Ventosa

Cerro Iguana

Unión Hidalgo

Río Niltepec

To Oaxaca

190

BENITO JUÁREZ DAM

Jalapa del Marqués

Chicapa de Castro

GUIENGOLA ARCHAEOLOGICAL ZONE

Juchitán

Magdalena Tequisistlán

Hot Spring

Yerba Santa

Mixtequilla

Isla Cerro Prieto

Isla Cerro Venado

Playa Copalito

Laguna Inferior

Río Tequisistlán

San Blas de Atempa

Santa Rosa de Lima

INFORMAL CAMPING ⛺

San Dionisio del Mar

Puerto Estero

Asunción Tlacolulita

San Miguel Ecatepec

San Miguel Tenango

Santo Domingo Tehuantepec

Alvaro Obregón

Laguna Superior

Embarcadero

San Francisco del Mar

San Pedro Huilotepec

Laguna Inferior

INFORMAL CAMPING ⛺

Santa María del Mar

Río Tenango

Salina Cruz

⛺ **INFORMAL CAMPING**

San Mateo del Mar

▲ Cerro Conejo (1,560 m)

Loma Atravesada

200

Playa La Ventosa

POSADA RUSTRIAN

Punta Conejo

To Bays of Huatulco and Puerto Ángel

San Pedro Huamelula

Punta Chivo

Morro Mazatán

Santiago Astata

Laguna Garrapatera

Punta Embarcadero

200

Lushu

La Colorada

Laguna Colorada

Laguna Grande

0   20 mi

0   20 km

© AVALON TRAVEL PUBLISHING, INC.

ageless melody seems to perfectly capture the essence of the Isthmus in a gracefully drowsy rhythm that swings slowly, yet deliberately, like the relaxed sway of lovers in a hammock beneath the deep shade of a Tehuantepec grove.

Templo y Exconvento de Santo Domingo

From the plaza's northeast corner, walk north along Calle Hidalgo one block to the venerable Santo Domingo church, behind its broad fenced atrium, on the right. The aging landmark (to the left of the new church) is interesting, partly because it was one of the few, if not the only, Christian churches in Mexico financed by a native ruler. Cosijopí, the last king of the Zapotecs, who was baptized as Juan Cortés de Cosijopí, after his friend and ally Hernán Cortés, paid for the construction with both cash and the labor of thousands of his subjects. The building was erected under the supervision of Fray Fernando de Albequerque, vicar of Tehuantepec, between 1544 and 1550.

Given the warm relations between King Cosijopí and the Spanish, it is ironic that the Inquisition authorities burned Cosijopí at the stake a generation later for continuing (and for encouraging his people) to worship the old gods.

Enter through an interior side door, off the left-aisle of the very attractive new church. Inside, old Santo Domingo's most remarkable feature is its lovely wooden *tabla* (altarpiece), with an unusual ebony Lord of Creation perched on its crest, with a dog, turtle, and deer in tow.

The convent section, on the old church's north side, was abandoned not long after the Reforms of the late 1850s forced the Dominicans from Mexico. It had crumbled into a virtual ruin by the mid-20th century, when local people rolled up their sleeves and restored it in 1953. The convent, rebuilt a few years later, became the **Casa de la Cultura** in 1982. Now in the evenings it resounds with the noises of young musicians and dancers at practice.

To take a look inside the restored convent (open Mon.–Fri. 10 A.M.–2 P.M. and 5–8 P.M., Sat. 10 A.M.–2 P.M.), retrace your steps out across the atrium, turn right at Calle Hidalgo, and walk north. After two short blocks turn right at Guerrero. Walk one long block. Just after the *centro de salud* turn right into an alley, which leads south to the Casa de la Cultura and the old convent.

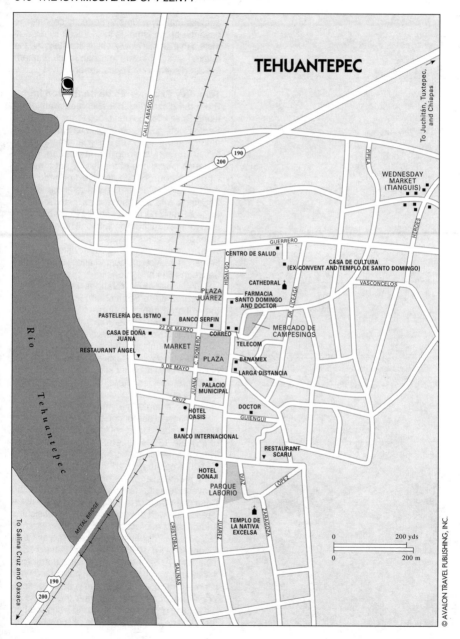

TEHUANTEPEC

CALLE ABASOLO

To Juchitán, Tuxtepec, and Chiapas

200
190

PIPILA

WEDNESDAY MARKET (TIANGUIS)

HEROES

GUERRERO

CENTRO DE SALUD

CASA DE CULTURA (EX-CONVENT AND TEMPLO DE SANTO DOMINGO)

HIDALGO

CATHEDRAL

VASCONCELOS

PLAZA JUÁREZ

FARMACIA SANTO DOMINGO AND DOCTOR

DE LICEAGA

PASTELERÍA DEL ISTMO

BANCO SERFIN

22 DE MARZO

CORREO

MERCADO DE CAMPESINOS

CASA DE DOÑA JUANA

MARKET

C. ROMERO

TELECOM

RESTAURANT ÁNGEL

PLAZA

BANAMEX

5 DE MAYO

LARGA DISTANCIA

JUANA

PALACIO MUNICIPAL

CRUZ

DOCTOR

HOTEL OASIS

GUIENGUI

BANCO INTERNACIONAL

RESTAURANT SCARU

HOTEL DONAJI

DIAZ

LOPEZ

PARQUE LABORIO

ZARAGOZA

Río

Tehuantepec

METAL BRIDGE

CRISTOBAL

SALINAS

JUAREZ

TEMPLO DE LA NATIVA EXCELSA

0   200 yds
0   200 m

To Salina Cruz and Oaxaca

190
200

© AVALON TRAVEL PUBLISHING, INC.

Inside the Casa de la Cultura, look for the faded but still-visible flower and animal motifs Cosijopí's long-gone artists painted on the walls three and a half centuries ago. See if you can get the administrative secretary (ground floor, in the cloister) to let you go upstairs, where the ancient wall decorations appear as fresh as if they were painted only a generation ago. In other upstairs rooms you'll see a host of historical mementos, from ancient Olmec-style figurines to a lovely jade necklace, once scattered, but excavated piece by piece and finally reassembled here.

Markets

The most colorful downtown action goes on at the **Mercado Jesús Carranza,** just across Romero from the plaza. At midday, the market overflows with life. The center of everything is the corridor street on the market's north side, which connects the plaza with the businesses along the railroad tracks behind the market.

People, especially women in *traje,* tend to be apprehensive of rubber-necking strangers with cameras in hand. A good strategy is to blend in. Get a *refresco* at one of the food stalls and find a low-profile spot in the shade where you can take in the passing scene.

Get some relief from the heat and bustle inside the roofed market building itself. If you're in the mood for shopping, plenty of handicrafts are available. On the bottom floor, stalls offer the gold filigree jewelry that the Tehuantepec women love to wear. Look farther for lots of woven goods, such as baskets, string bags of *ixtle* fiber, hand fans, and hammocks. Upstairs via the stairway on the southwest corner by the railroad track, you'll find Tehuantepec's pride—the beautiful embroidered *tehuana* flowered blouses and skirts. Look around, decide what you want, then bargain for it. Asking prices for the prized, embroidered flower-design blouses run as much as $30, a whole outfit about $100.

Behind the market runs the railway track, which has the distinct appearance of being abandoned, because dozens of vendors regularly set up where trains should come roaring through. Shopkeepers, however, report that trains actually use the track occasionally, when everyone scatters with their goods—from bananas and melons to shrimp and hammocks.

Pottery, including many big, homely items—pots, griddles, bowls, planters—is for sale at the second downtown market, the lackluster Mercado 5 de Febrero, sometimes known as the **Mercado de Campesinos,** tucked at the plaza's northwest corner. Smaller for-sale items include pots painted with bright flowers as well as woven goods, such as baskets, fans, and handmade brooms.

Besides the two aforementioned permanent daily markets near the plaza, country people flood into town for *tianguis,* street markets, on Wednesday and Sunday. Visit the Wednesday *tianguis,* set up along north-side **Calle Héroes,** most easily by riding a *motocarro* from the plaza. Alternatively, from the plaza, walk north along Hidalgo past the church. Two blocks from the plaza, turn right at Guerrero and continue several blocks to the blue-trimmed San Juan Bautista church, where you turn left at Héroes. After a few blocks, you'll see the awnings stretched along side streets.

The Sunday *tianguis* is much bigger, so much so that it's held on the west side across the river, by the highway to Oaxaca in the open space behind the Hotel Gueixhoba.

The House of Doña Juana Catalina Romero

The railway track so intimately close to the market is due to the speculated intimate relationship between aging President Porfirio Díaz and local beauty Doña Juana Catarina Romero. Doña Juana Catarina lived in the French-style mansion, now white with fancy blue window awnings, that rises by the tracks. Her octogenarian granddaughter, who occasionally enjoys receiving visitors, still lives in the mansion.

La Cueva

If sometime you feel like an early morning or late afternoon walk, head for La Cueva (The Cave), as local folks call it. It's visible most of the way up the hill called Liesa, across the river about two miles (three km) west of town. La Cueva has been hallowed ground for as long as anyone remembers. Local folks tell stories about the existence of a secret passageway somewhere at the back of the cave that leads all the way to Guiengola, the "old town," now a mysterious ruin on the

VELAS OF THE ISTHMUS

The Isthmus *velas* amount to a near-continuous regional party. People stay up all night, sometimes for days on end of feasting, drinking, dancing, and parading with family and friends, many of whom return from afar to renew cherished old relationships. What follows is a short list that includes only the most important Isthmus *velas*.

Date	Place	Title
18–21 January	Jalapa del Marqués	San Sebastián de las Flores
First Friday of Lent	San Pedro Huamelula	Carnaval
20–25 February	Matías Romero	Vela San Matías
first days of April	San Pedro Tehuantepec	Feria de Mango (Mango Fair)
15 April	Juchitán	Vela Ique Guia (Festival of the Chief)
25 April	Juchitán	Vela Ique Guidxi (Of the People)
27 April	Juchitán	Vela Paso Cru (Stations of the Cross)
3 May	Juchitán	Vela Guzebenda (Of the Fisherfolk)
3–6 May	Salina Cruz	Santa Cruz
5 May	Juchitán	Vela Quintu
8 May	Juchitán	Vela Guigu Dixta
10 May	Juchitán	Vela San Pedro Cantarito
13 May	Juchitán	Vela San Isidro Guete
15 May	Juchitán	Vela Guela Bene
16 May	Juchitán	Vela Iguu
The last 15 days of May	Juchitán	Fiesta de San Vicente Ferrer
	Juchitán	Vela Biadxi
	Juchitán	Vela Calvario
	Juchitán	Vela Angelica Pipi
	Juchitán	Vela San Isidro Labrador
	Juchitán	Vela San Vicente Chico
	Juchitán	Vela San Vicente Grande
	Juchitán	Vela de Cheguigo
Last week of May	Tehuantepec	Vela Sandunga
16 June	Juchitán	Vela San Antonio
24 June	Juchitán	Vela San Juan Bautista
	Juchitán	Vela Taberneros
	Juchitán	Vela Coheteros
24–30 June	San Pedro Huamelula	Fiesta del Apóstol San Pedro
27–30 June	San Pedro Tapanatepec	Fiesta Patronal de San Pedro
21–29 July	Santiago Laollaga	Fiesta de Santiago Apóstol
July	Juchitán	Vela de los Niños
13 August	Juchitán	Vela Asunción
15 August	Juchitán	Vela San Jacinto
13–16 August	Jalapa del Marqués	Fiesta de la Asunción
13–18 August	Tehuantepec	Fiesta Patronal del Barrio de Santa María Reoloteca
31 August–11 September	Tehuantepec	Fiesta del Laborio
3 September	Juchitán	Vela de la Familia Pineda
4 September	Juchitán	Vela de la Familia López
5 September	Juchitán	Vela del Triunfo del Batallón Juchiteco de 1866
	Juchitán	Vela Superior
1–4 October	San Francisco Ixhuatan	Vela del Santa Patrón
26 December	Tehuantepec	Vela Tehuantepec

mountain 10 miles to the west. (See Excursions West of Tehuantepec, below.)

La Cueva still draws virtually everyone in town for a pilgrimage during both Semana Santa (Holy Week) and 3 May (Día de la Cruz). It's best not to try the climb during the heat of the day (allow at least an hour for the whole excursion). In order to get a head start, spend a dollar or two on a taxi or *motocarro* (the motorcycle-driven carts buzzing near the market) to take you to the base of the hill.

Other Sights

A number of smaller plazas dot Tehuantepec's several *barrios* (neighborhoods). If you head south along Juárez two long blocks, you'll arrive at **Plaza Laborio** and its adjacent blue-trimmed, storybook **Templo de la Natividad Excelsa.** Before you go inside to look around, notice that the right bell tower is tilted at a crazy angle, not unlike the Leaning Tower of Pisa. Laborio (the name of the church's *barrio*) residents don't seem to worry. "It's been like that for years," they say.

Plaza Laborio is mostly sleepy, except during the 31 August–11 September **Fiesta Laborio,** when residents and visitors celebrate with a long menu of feasts, dancing, fireworks and *calendas* (processions).

Also worth a visit, across the river, is the **Barrio de Santa María.** (Get there by bearing left at the street heading diagonally left from the highway, a block or two west of the river bridge; after about two more blocks, go left again.) The main community pride and joy is the (also bright blue and white) **Templo de la Virgen de la Asunción.** The church, by the same architect who built the famous pilgrimage church in Juquila, is the focus of a busy round of *barrio* events. The bustle climaxes during the 13–18 August **Fiesta Patronal del Barrio de Santa María Reolotoca,** with a *calenda* (procession), a parade of flower-decorated bull-drawn carts, and earsplitting popular dances on three successive nights. Bring your earplugs.

ACCOMMODATIONS

Tehuantepec offers visitors at least three hotels, one of them, semi-luxurious, in the west suburb,

and a humbler but acceptable pair downtown. Best choice downtown is the **Oasis,** a block south from the plaza hubbub, behind the *presidencia* at Melchor Ocampo 8, Tehuantepec, Oaxaca 70760, tel. 971/500-08, fax 971/508-35.

Although at first glance the Oasis doesn't appear very exciting, a closer examination reveals the talents of the owner, friendly, English-speaking artist Julin (hoo-LEEN) Contreras, whose art decorates the hotel's restaurant wall. She also was commissioned to do the mural in the council chamber on the second floor of the *presidencia municipal.*

She offers 28 plain but clean and comfortable rooms, with colorful, thoughtfully selected bedspreads and curtains. In some rooms of the four-story tier, windows open to garden, mountain, and river views. Pottery and plants selected by the owner decorate niches and corridors. In the room-tier courtyard, a towering *chico zapote* tree stretches skyward. Other trees around the yard supply all of the seasonal grapefruits and mangos that guests can eat. A parking lot provides security for cars. All this for

the leaning tower of Templo de la Natividad Excelsa

$9 s, $9 d, $14 t with hot water, fans, and good, relaxed, Restaurant Almendro (Almond Tree). Credit cards are not accepted. For lovers of the way Mexico "used to be," this is the place.

Second choice downtown goes to the **Hotel Donaji** (named for Oaxaca's beloved Zapoteca heroine), two blocks south of the plaza on quiet Plaza Laborio, at Juárez 10, Tehuantepec, Oaxaca 70760, tel. 971/500-64. The 48 rooms, in a big two-story block, are plain but clean enough for an overnight. They rent for about $10 s, $14 d fan only, $14 s, $18 d with a/c; with parking, but credit cards not accepted. The Donaji's pluses are air-conditioning (desirable in warm Tehuantepec) and its location on the tree-shaded, drowsy (except during the 31 August-11 September fiesta) Plaza Laborio.

By far the most comfortable hotel in town is the four-star **Hotel Guiexhoba** (ghee-ay-SHOW-bah), which deserves extra points simply for its Zapotec label, the name of a locally abundant white flower with a fragrant scent reminiscent of jasmine. The hotel has a specimen bush, which blooms during the summer rainy season, by the front entrance. Find the hotel on Hwy. 190, inbound from Oaxaca on the right before the bridge, at Carretera Panamericana Km 250.5, Barrio Santa María, Tehuantepec, Oaxaca 70760, tel./fax 971/51-710 and 971/50-416.

The Guiexhoba's 36 spacious, clean, and comfortable rooms, in two stories, enfold a parking courtyard that fortunately shields rooms on its north side from highway noise. Staff are generally attentive, competent, and courteous. The upstairs rooms away from the highway are quiet and have fewer people walking past the windows; unfortunately, you must draw drapes for privacy. Rates run a reasonable $26 s, $29 d, $31 t, with pool, parking, good cable TV, a/c, hot water shower baths, and the very good Restaurant Guiexhoba.

FOOD

Groceries, Breakfasts, and Treats

Tehuantepec's freshest fruit and vegetable sources by far are the luscious mounds of bananas, mangos, avocados, pineapples, lettuces, radishes, carrots, and much more in the plaza market (be sure to scrub with soap and/or pool before eating). Likewise, find the best grocery sources, such as the **Abarrotes El Centro** permanent stall, also in the market, in the covered section on the ground floor.

Breakfasts you'll probably find most conveniently at your hotel, such as the Restaurant Almendro of the Hotel Oasis and the restaurant at the Hotel Guiexhoba. Otherwise (or if you're staying at Hotel Donaji), go to Tehuantepec's best, the delightfully refined **Restaurant Scaru** (see below) three blocks south of the plaza.

Satisfy your sweet tooth with the baked offerings of the **Super Panadería y Pastelería del Istmo,** open daily 7:30 A.M.–8:30 P.M., tel. 971/508-08. Find it on the railroad tracks, just north of the market, on the left. For evening snacks, fill up at the food stall lineup on the plaza's east side.

Restaurants

Tehuantepec offers a sprinkling of good sit-down restaurants. By far the best is the showplace **Restaurant Scaru,** at south-side cul-de-sac Callejon Leona Vicario 4. Here in a graceful, airy setting, owners lovingly portray picturesque aspects of traditional Isthmus life. Walls bloom with murals of fruit, festivals, and lovely *tehuanas* in their bright, flowery costumes, while patios are sprinkled with hammocks and sheltered overhead by luxurious handcrafted *palapas*. Friday, Saturday, and Sunday afternoons 2–6 P.M., a marimba band will play the *Sandunga* to your heart's content. After such a luscious introduction, the food, from a very recognizable menu of eggs, salads, soups, meats (including some game), fish, fowl, and pastas, is no less than you would expect. Open daily 8 A.M.–11 P.M., tel. 971/506-46. Moderate; credit cards accepted.

Get there from the plaza by walking two long blocks south along Juárez to Plaza Laborio. Turn left and walk one block to Callejon Leona Vicario on the left; the restaurant is on the uphill side of the street.

Second choice goes to the good but the more ordinarily picturesque restaurant at the **Hotel Guiexhoba** across the river. The food, from a typical but tasty menu of breakfasts (eggs and pancakes), lunches (hamburgers, soups, and stews), and dinners (meat, fish, fowl, and spaghetti) sometimes comes with a flaming crepe Suzette flourish. Open daily 7:30 A.M.–10 P.M., tel. 971/517-10. Moderate; credit cards accepted.

Back downtown, seafood lunches and dinners are the tour de force of **Restaurant Ángel,** tel. 971/516-28, on the highway corner entrance to town, at 5 de Mayo 1. You can have the best of the day's catch of *camarones, langosta, ostiones,* *pulpo, calamar, pescado* (shrimp, lobster, oysters, octopus, squid, fish), and much more. The air-conditioning is a plus. Although open daily (8 A.M.–11 P.M.) for breakfast, the staff doesn't seem to wake up until about noon. Moderate; credit cards accepted.

SERVICES

Money and Communications

Tehuantepec offers several banks, all of which have ATMs. The long money-changing hours (Mon.–Fri. 9 A.M.–5 P.M., Sat. 9 A.M.–2 P.M.) of the **Banco Internacional** (Bital), at J.C. Romero 60, tel. 971/522-91, a block and a half south of the plaza, make it a good first choice. Alternatively, go to **Banamex** (Mon.–Fri. 9 A.M.–3 P.M.), tel. 971/523-83, on the plaza's west side, or **Banco Serfin** (Mon.–Fri. 9 A.M.–5 P.M.), tel. 971/509-16, on the plaza's northwest side, corner of Romero.

The *correo* (open Mon.–Fri. 8 A.M.–3 P.M., including rapid, secure **Mexpost** service), tel. 971/501-06, and *telecomunicaciones* (money orders and public fax 971/501-59, open Mon.–Fri. 8 A.M.–7:30 P.M. and Sat. 9 A.M.–noon), stand side by side at the north end of Juárez, at the plaza's northeast corner.

Long-distance telephone and photocopies are available at **Papelería La Esfera,** tel. 971/500-42, fax 971/504-60, open Mon.–Sat. 8 A.M.–8 P.M. and Sun. 9 A.M.–1 P.M., at the plaza's southeast corner next to Banamex.

Medical and Emergencies

A number of town **pharmacies** provide nonprescription medicines and drugs. Perhaps the best is **Farmacia Santo Domingo,** open Mon.–Sat. 8 A.M.–10 P.M., tel. 971/500-80, run by Dr. Leopoldo Vasquez, who prescribes on the spot. Find him on Romero, one block north (from Banco Serfin) of the plaza's northwest corner.

If you need to consult a doctor you can always find one at the ***centro de salud*** (health center),

---

MOTOCARROS

The city of Tehuantepec's public transportation system was long ago preempted by the city's regiment of *motocarros*—small, motorcycle-driven flat-bed trucks that buzz, putt, squeal, and skid around town continuously. The center of the action is the railroad track behind the market, where all Tehuantepec *motocarros* faithfully return for passengers and cargo.

Motocarros have thus become the end-all answer to how to get around in Tehuantepec's heat. Long ago, everyone (excepting mad dogs and Englishmen) learned that too much midday walking can produce a considerable sweat at least and sunstroke at worst. If you get overheated, do as Tehuantepec people do and take a seat in the shade and cool down with an *agua* or *refresco.* Later, continue your extended tour via *motocarro.* Fares run less than half a dollar for an entire circuit of the town.

take a motocarro *to the market*

JUANA CATALINA ROMERO

Why Tehuantepec's main downtown streets, which carry such nationally renowned labels as "Cinco de Mayo," "Juárez," and "Hidalgo," should include "Juana C. Romero" among them is a question nearly all adult townsfolk can immediately answer. "Doña Juana," they say, is Tehuantepec's heroine because she "built schools and helped the children of Tehuantepec." Some go on to say that she "got lots of help for Tehuantepec from her friend, Presidente Porfirio Díaz."

When pressed, most Tehuantepec folks acknowledge that she had a close (some even say intimate) relationship with Porfirio Díaz. Juana Catalina was an 18-year-old blue-blooded beauty when first introduced to Díaz in 1873. At that time he was the celebrated general who beat the French at Puebla on 5 May (Cinco de Mayo) 1862 and heir apparent to the late President Benito Juárez. Although he must have been charmed by her beauty at their first meeting, most certainly nothing immediate came of it, since he was both middle-aged and married and she had her upper-crust reputation to preserve.

Whatever passed between them during later years has been the subject of endless gossip. In any case, she never married, and Don Porfirio, it is speculated, had the railroad tracks laid right past her house in downtown Tehuantepec so he could hop off the train and visit her with no fuss or muss.

---

three blocks from the plaza at Guerrero 19. Get there by walking from the Banco Serfin at the plaza's northwest corner. After two blocks, turn right at Guerrero and continue a long block to the *centro de salud* on the right.

Alternatively, consult with general practitioner Dr. José Manuel Vichido, open Mon.–Sat. 9 A.M.–1 P.M., tel. 971/508-62, on Calle Guietiqui. From the plaza's southeast corner, walk south one block along Juárez; turn left at the first street, Guietiqui. The doctor's office is half a block down on the left.

Police service is available from at least two sources in Tehuantepec. Call either the *policía municipal*, tel. 971/500-01, or the *preventiva*, tel. 971/123-46.

GETTING THERE AND AWAY

By Bus

The main bus station, tel. 971/501-08, is on the highway, with official address Carretera Panamericana Km 20. It's at the highway intersection at the end of Calle Héroes, about a mile northeast of downtown. Get there by taxi or *motocarro* from the plaza.

Four major bus lines, first-class **Autobuses del Oriente** (ADO) and **Cristóbal Colón** (CC) and second-class **Sur** and **Autobuses Unidos** (AU), offer many connections north across the Isthmus, northwest with Oaxaca, southwest with the Oaxaca Pacific Coast, and east with Chiapas. Direct departures connect north via Juchitán with Tuxtepec, Villahermosa, Palenque, Minatitlán, and Coatzacoalcos; northwest with Oaxaca, Puebla, and Mexico City; southwest with Salina Cruz, Bahías de Huatulco, Pochutla (Puerto Ángel), and Puerto Escondido; and east via Juchitán with Tuxtla Gutiérrez, San Cristóbal las Casas, and Tapachula at the Guatemala border.

In addition to the above, a pair of reliable second-class cooperative lines, **Oaxaca Istmo** and **Fletes y Pasajes**, stop on the highway by the bus station. Oaxaca Istmo offers connections northwest with Oaxaca and southwest with Bahías de Huatulco, Pochutla (Puerto Ángel), and Puerto Escondido, while Fletes y Pasajes offers connections northwest with Oaxaca, southwest with Salina Cruz, and northeast with Juchitán.

By Car

Paved roads fan out from Tehuantepec in four directions. Hwy. 190 connects northeast with Juchitán (17 miles, 27 km), then splits north as Hwy. 185 at La Ventosa and continues north Matías Romero and Minatitlán all the way to the Gulf of Mexico at Coatzacoalcos, a total of 166 miles (267 km). Allow about 4.5 driving hours, either way, for this relatively easy trip.

For Tuxtepec, from Hwy. 185 turn onto Hwy.

147 at Matías Romero and continue northwest a total of 189 miles (304 km). Allow about five hours driving time from Tehuantepec. **Warning:** Some robberies have occurred on the long, lonely Hwy. 147 Matías Romero-Tuxtepec leg. Authorities advise drivers to restrict their travel to **daytime only** on this stretch.

Highway 190 connects Tehuantepec northwest with Oaxaca along 155 miles (250 km) of well-maintained but winding highway. Allow about five hours Oaxaca direction (uphill), 4.5 hours in the opposite direction.

Highway 200 connects Tehuantepec southwest with the Oaxaca Pacific Coast, via Salina Cruz (nine miles, 15 km), Bahías de Huatulco (100 miles, 161 km, three hours), Pochutla-Puerto Ángel (124 miles, 200 km, four hours), and Puerto Escondido (170 miles, 274 km, five hours) of paved, lightly traveled, but secure highway.

Hwy. 190 connects Tehuantepec east via Juchitán (17 miles, 27 km) and Niltepec to Tapanatepec (78 miles, 126 km) near the Chiapas border. A badly rutted 30-mile stretch around Niltepec slows traffic to a crawl. Allow about 3.5 hours driving time to Tapanatepec.

Drivers should fill up with **gasoline** at the Pemex *gasolinera* on the west side of the river, about a mile west of the bridge, where the road splits southwest to Salina Cruz, northwest to Oaxaca.

EXCURSIONS WEST OF TEHUANTEPEC

The interesting destination trio of Guiengola, Jalapa del Marqués, and Tequisistlán can be combined into a full-day auto or taxi excursion (two days by bus) west of Tehuantepec. Along the way enjoy a vigorous hike through pristine forest to the regal ruined fortress-city at Guiengola, a breezy boat ride on the Jalapa de Marqués reservoir, a soak in the community hot (actually just warm) spring, and a stop at the marble factory at Tequisistlán.

Guiengola—Mountain Fortress
Guiengola (ghee-ayn-GOH-lah), "Big Rock" in Zapotec, may have been abandoned before the Spanish arrived, but it was never forgotten. Local

people refer to it as the "old town" and often hear voices when up there. If so, they rush down the mountain before dark.

Ghosts notwithstanding, an excursion to Guiengola is a chance to get some fresh air into your lungs as you enjoy the Isthmus tropical forest up close—fluttering butterflies, spiny cactus, flowery trees, and fireflies and hoot owls (if you return at dusk). At the end of the rough motor road that winds about four miles up Guiengola Mountain, you continue on foot via a sometimes steep two-mile (three-km), one-hour hike through summer-green (but brown in spring) tropical woodland. If you start early, you might see *venado* (deer), *javelin* (wild pigs) and, if you're lucky, a *león* (mountain lion).

You know you're getting close to the ruins when the trail straightens out and you see a continuous series of vegetation-covered mounds and walls on both sides. You are following a regal street, lined with ruined houses of the nobility. Next, break out into the open, where a four-tiered unreconstructed noble pyramid, called the Pyramid of the Sun, rises at the right. On the opposite side, across a spreading, flat ceremonial plaza, another, even taller, five-tiered Pyramid of the Moon stands on your left. To the extreme left rises a big ball court, so well preserved that it appears as if a dozen persons could spend a weekend with machetes and a few shovels and put the place in order for a tournament on Monday.

What you see immediately around you is only the ceremonial center. Beneath the surrounding forest are dozens of mounds, remains of temples, ceremonial patios, and homes. The state of preservation is exceptional, partly because of the site's isolation. These structures of stone and mud mortar are delicate and mostly unexplored; please refrain from climbing on them.

Guides and Getting There: Arrive early, by 9 A.M., to avoid the midday heat and give you time to contact a guide, most likely either José Luis Toral Sánchez or Feliciano Gonzáles Mendez, whom the government has certified as official guardians of Guiengola. You will probably find one or both of them at the **Comedor Gema** or one of the other highway-front *palapas* that provide lunches (sometimes of armadillo, venison, iguana, coati and other game), drinks, and bottled water (very necessary, since no water is available along the route). Once you've contacted your guide, you could either continue to Guiengola immediately or detour with your guide to Jalapa de Marqués and Tequisistlán and return to explore Guiengola in the late afternoon. **Warning:** Exploring the ruins without a guide could be hazardous, and could also get you into *mucho* trouble with the authorities.

By car, get there by driving your own vehicle or a rental car (agents in Oaxaca, Salina Cruz and Juchitán) to the blue signed right turnoff that runs right past the Comedor Gema, about 10 miles (16 km) west, Oaxaca direction, along Hwy. 190 from Tehuantepec. Otherwise, get to the crossing by sharing a taxi, or, most cheaply and easily, via the blue-and-white **Autotransportes Jalapa de Marqués** buses, which leave the Tehuantepec plaza in front of the market about every half hour.

Visitors are welcome to bathe (in a bathing suit) in the warm community spring at Jalapa del Marqués.

Jalapa del Marqués

During Mexico's big-dam boom during the 1950s, planners decided to conserve and control some of the trillions of gallons of water that flow via the Río Tehuantepec into the sea. A good idea, thought most, for flood control and irrigation during the long winter and spring drought.

The result is **Benito Juárez dam and reservoir,** which provides irrigation water, fish, and a tourist attraction for Jalapa del Marqués (pop. about 3,000), the biggest town on the reservoir.

The cost for all this was that the Jalapa de Marqués, originally on the bank of the Río Tehuantepec, had to be moved five miles uphill to its present location next to Hwy. 190, about 18 miles (30 km) west of Tehuantepec. Now the people have everything new—wide paved streets, church, and a Casa de la Cultura.

People in Jalapa del Marqués eat a lot of fish—specifically, *mojarra* (freshwater bass). A number of restaurants cook it up and serve it for visitors; try Del Camino and El Gorda at the east, Tehuantepec, edge of town.

The next thing to do is go fishing or take a **boat ride** on the lake. This is good anytime of year, but is best in the dry winter or spring, when the silt from the summer rains has settled and the lake is invitingly clear. Arrive early enough to find one of the boatmen down at the lake before they go home for the day. A good man to ask for is Alejandro Oliveras, who charges about $12 for a two-hour ride or fishing trip. Bring your own pole, unless you want to fish by line or net as the locals do.

A popular excursion destination is **Tres Picos,** a Zapotec ruin on the far side of the lake. There you can explore a trio of conical stone pyramids, about 30 feet high, and a submerged ball court. Also, if the water is low and clear enough, perhaps your boatman will take you to see the site of the submerged old Jalapa del Marqués, where you'll be able to see the old church beneath the water or even sit on its bell tower, which at low water protrudes from lake surface.

Before or after your boat excursion, take a look inside the **Casa del Pueblo,** on the town plaza about .1 mile downhill from the highway. Besides a number of giant animal bones, apparently mastodon, it has a big collection of locally gathered preconquest pottery, including some very phallic-looking figurines.

Get to the plaza and the lakeshore boat landing by the paved main street, marked by a huge concrete welcome *(bienvenidos)* portal on the highway. Continue downhill, past the central plaza (.1 mile, Casa del Pueblo on the right, uphill plaza corner). Pass a playground and traffic circle (.4 mile, .6 km); after another 1.4 mile (1.9 km) mostly on a dirt road, you arrive at the beach and boat landing. At least go swimming (in your bathing suit) and enjoy a lakeside picnic.

Finally, join the folks in the community *agua caliente* (warm spring) about half a mile uphill from the highway. People begin arriving about six in the morning, when it's cool. They bring their soap and clothes to be washed, and stay for hours, playing in the hot-tub warm water (about 102° F, 39° C). Wear your bathing suit. If you don't have one, just go in with your clothes on like everyone else. Skinny-dipping, unless you're under three, is liable to land you in jail besides reinforcing the local people's stereotypical view of the "loose" foreigner. **Get there** via the dirt street that heads uphill at the highway long-distance bus stop, a few blocks, west (Oaxaca direction) of the town entrance portal. After two blocks uphill, bear left, then turn right and pass a big electrical transformer station. Continue uphill to a low ridge, where on the right side, you'll see the women washing clothes in big tanks inside an enclosure (to keep animals out). The women are friendly and also careful to keep their waste water from the lower basins where you'll be welcome to bathe. (The basins outside the enclosure are for animals only.)

By bus, get to Jalapa del Marqués via either the Tehuantepec central bus terminal or second-class blue-and-white **Autotransportes Jalapa del Marqués** bus from in front of the Tehuantepec market.

Tequisistlán

This little *municipio,* officially Santa María Magdalena Tequisistlán, was on ground too high to get gobbled up by the reservoir. The huge-in-summer (and muddy) Río Tequisistlán continues to run right next to town. During the dry, hot spring this river might appear very inviting for a dip into its clear, gurgling water.

Take a look inside at the old church in the center of town. Here folks enjoy the church's completely marble-floored atrium in front, especially handy for dancing during the 20–24 July festival in honor of Santa María Magdalena. On the church's side you'll find the kicker: probably the world's only *marble* basketball court.

You can see the source of all this by going to the community **marble factory,** on Hwy. 190 about a mile west (Oaxaca direction) of the town highway crossing. If you arrive during working hours (about 9 A.M.–2 P.M. and 4–7 P.M.), get someone to show you around. You'll see dozens of men and machines working beneath a shady open-air roof, cutting, grinding, and polishing dozens of beautiful pieces of marble.

In the nearby office, feast your eyes on the beautifully polished finished products. The factory will custom-make anything you want—such as the lovely marble bathroom top you've always wanted, a statuesque marble cat, or some other favorite animal.

Get there by car, or by bus from the Tehuantepec station. Get off at the Tequisistlán crossing and hop on the local Tequisistlán bus, which shuttles folks the two miles to and from the highway about every 10 minutes.

JUCHITÁN AND VICINITY

Isthmus people associate the name Juchitán with both the town, Juchitán de Zaragoza, and the governmental district that it rules—a domain larger in extent than either the Distrito Federal or each of the four smallest Mexican states. The district of Juchitán (Place of Flowers) ranges from the Chimalapas, the roadless jungle refuge of dozens of Mexico's endangered species, south to the warm Pacific and the rich lagoons that border it.

But like any empire, Juchitán is the sum of its small parts—hidden slices of Mexico that few outsiders know, from the crystalline springs of Tlacotepec and Laollaga to the seemingly endless groves of the "world mango capital" at Zanatepec and the vibrant market and near-continuous community festivals—the *velas*—of busy, prosperous Juchitán de Zaragoza.

SIGHTS

Orientation
Juchitán (pop. 80,000) bustles with commerce all the daylight hours. Main streets 16 de Septiembre and 5 de Septiembre steadily conduct a double stream of traffic to and from the north-side highway crossing. A few blocks to the west, the Río Los Perros (River of the Dogs, for the otters that hunt for fish in the river) courses lazily southward, marking downtown Juchitán's western boundary. Traffic focuses about a mile south of the highway at the town plaza, the **Jardín Central Benito Juárez,** the town's commercial and governmental nucleus. On Calle 16 de Septiembre, on the plaza's east side, the long, white classical arcade of the *palacio municipal* fills the entire block, from Calle Efrain Gómez bordering the plaza's north edge to Calle Benito Juárez on the south. Governmental offices occupy the upper floor of the *palacio,* while businesses, crafts booths, and food stalls spread across the bottom. Behind the facade, taking up the entire city block east of the plaza, is the town market, **Mercado 5 de Septiembre.**

Around the Plaza
A fun spot to start off (or end) your day exploring Juchitán is at a table in the graceful old-Mexico patio of **Restaurant Casa Grande** on Calle Benito Juárez, on the plaza's south side. Here a hearty breakfast or a cool lunch will invigorate you for yet another few hours of relaxed plaza sightseeing.

Stroll out and admire the fine busts of Benito Juárez on the plaza's east side and Margarita Maza, his wife, on the west side, by Calle 5 de Septiembre. On the plaza's north side find the Monument to the Battle of 5 September 1866, where a Mexican eagle and a heroic Benito Juárez commemorate the victory of the ragtag local battalion over a superior French imperial force.

Step east, across Calle 16 de Septiembre, to the **crafts stalls** beneath the northerly (left) half of *palacio municipal* arcade. What you don't find downstairs you'll find in an upstairs market foyer. Stroll the aisles and choose from a host of excellent items customarily including, besides the famous Isthmus embroidered skirts and blouses, handwoven cotton *hamacas* (hammocks), leather huaraches and *bolsas* (purses), woven palm and reed baskets, mats, and hats (*canastas, petates,* sombreros), and gold-filigree jewelry *(joyería).*

For **pottery,** walk west along Calle Juárez (which borders the plaza's south side) to the block just west of the plaza. There along the old town church's rear wall, a lineup of stalls offers an assortment of ceramics, mostly practical traditional housewares, from huge round red *ollas* (jars) and flat *comales* (griddles) to brightly painted piggy banks and flower vases.

San Vicente Ferrer Church and Casa de la Cultura
While you're in the vicinity, visit the town's pride, the Templo de San Vicente Ferrer. Reach it by circling the block; continue west on Calle Juárez, go immediately left at 5 de Mayo, then after one block turn left again at Belisario Domínguez, to the church on the left. Although the church's early history is shrouded in mystery, the present

construction appears by its style to date from the mid-19th century. Its dedication to San Vicente Ferrer, patron of survivors of the sea, appears connected to Juchitán's original founding as a refuge for survivors, perhaps of some ocean disaster, such as a terrible tsunami or hurricane, some time shortly before the conquest. Present-day Juchitecos, inheritors of their patron's zeal and ferocity, celebrate his memory with gusto to match, with no less than eight consecutive *velas,* beginning on the first Saturday of the last 15 days of May.

Across the street from the church, you might linger for a few minutes in the shady side plaza, **Parque Helidoro Charis Castro.** Here stands

the bronze bust of Castro, the beloved Juchitecan *maderista* general who led the 13th Juchitecan Battalion in its bloody, but ultimately successful, revolt against dictatorial forces, from 1910 to 1914.

Afterward, look around inside the **Casa de la Cultura** (open Mon.–Fri. 10 A.M.–3 P.M. and 5–8 P.M., Sat. 10 A.M.–3 P.M., tel. 971/132-08) next door, west of the church. The building, originally a Catholic school, became the Casa de la Cultura in 1972, through the efforts of celebrated painter Francisco Toledo. Rooms around the graceful, old-Mexico patio accommodate a café, a small archaeological museum, an art exposition gallery, and a children's library. The

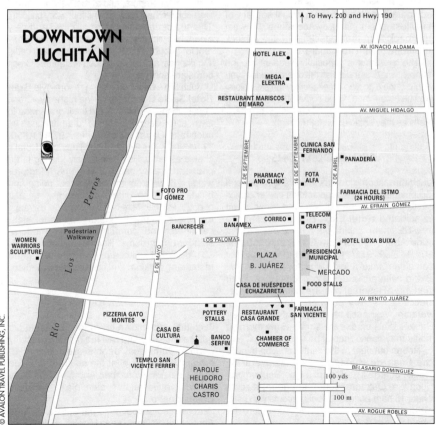

DOWNTOWN JUCHITÁN

To Hwy. 200 and Hwy. 190

AV. IGNACIO ALDAMA

HOTEL ALEX

MEGA ELEKTRA

RESTAURANT MARISCOS DE MARO

AV. MIGUEL HIDALGO

CLINICA SAN FERNANDO

PANADERÍA

PHARMACY AND CLINIC

FOTA ALFA

FARMACIA DEL ISTMO (24 HOURS)

AV. EFRAIN GÓMEZ

FOTO PRO GÓMEZ

5 DE SEPTIEMBRE

16 DE SEPTIEMBRE

2 DE ABRIL

CORREO

TELECOM

BANCRECER

BANAMEX

CRAFTS

LOS PALOMAS

HOTEL LIDXA BUIXA

Pedestrian Walkway

WOMEN WARRIORS SCULPTURE

Los Perros

PLAZA B. JUÁREZ

PRESIDENCIA MUNICIPAL

MERCADO

5 DE MAYO

CASA DE HUÉSPEDES ECHAZARRETA

FOOD STALLS

AV. BENITO JUÁREZ

PIZZERIA GATO MONTES

POTTERY STALLS

RESTAURANT CASA GRANDE

FARMACIA SAN VICENTE

CASA DE CULTURA

BANCO SERFIN

CHAMBER OF COMMERCE

Río Los

TEMPLO SAN VICENTE FERRER

PARQUE HELIDORO CHARIS CASTRO

BELASARIO DOMINGUEZ

0   100 yds

0   100 m

AV. ROGUE ROBLES

© AVALON TRAVEL PUBLISHING, INC.

reception staff sell a few Spanish-language books of local history and folklore.

The Women Warriors

As an interesting downtown side-street diversion, walk across the Río Los Perros for a look at the intriguing *Woman Warriors* sculptures on the west riverbank. Head west along Juárez. Two blocks west of the plaza, from the middle of the river bridge, notice the two tall sculptures of women (in Juchiteca skirts and blouses) about two stories high, in what appears to be a small neighborhood park.

Local residents seem to know little about them, except that "they are guarding the people from the river." Get a better view of the sculptures (which, close-up, you'll see are of stainless sheet steel) by accessing the west riverbank from the pedestrian bridge a block upstream (north) from Juárez.

The riverbank is especially pleasant around sunset, when, standing on the Juárez bridge, you might catch a cooling breeze, enjoy the sky colors, and be entertained by the flocks of grackles flying overhead and scrapping and cackling in riverbank trees as they settle down for the night.

ACCOMMODATIONS

Juchitán accommodates visitors with several acceptable hotels. A popular town-center choice is the once semi-deluxe, but now a bit dilapidated **Hotel Lidxi Buixa** (LEED-shee boo-EE-shah), behind the *palacio municipal* at 2 de Abril 79, Juchitán, Oaxaca 70000, tel. 971/112-99, 971/113-90. The 26 rooms (not too clean, take a look) rent for about $16 s, $20 d, with a/c, cable TV, phones, pool, and parking. (Reservations are necessary here, because it's very popular with out-of-town vendors, who arise around 5 A.M. to tend their market stalls across the street. Early morning noise may consequently be a problem.)

Rough but right at the center of everything is the **Casa de Huéspedes Echazarreta,** on Benito Juárez just west of 16 de Septiembre, Juchitán, Oaxaca 70000, no phone. It rents about 15 bare-bones, but clean, rooms with bath, around an invitingly tranquil inner courtyard, for about $8 s or d.

Moving two blocks north from the plaza along 5 de Septiembre, past Miguel Hidalgo, you'll find the inviting **Hotel Don Alex Lena Real,** at 16 de Septiembre 48, Juchitán, Oaxaca 70000, tel. 971/110-64, fax 971/138-82. The 14 very clean rooms with king-size beds rent for about $14 s, $22 d, with a/c, phones, TV, and restaurant, but street-only parking. Credit cards are not accepted.

Three more blocks north (a total of five blocks from the plaza) rises the Don Alex's sister hotel, the **Hotel López Lena Palace,** at 16 de Septiembre 70, Juchitán, Oaxaca 70000, tel. 971/113-88, fax 971/113-89. Designers have packed a modicum of extras, such as potted plants, airy corridors, and attractively decorated rose-colored hallways, into the four-story building. The 40 spartan-chic rooms are tiled and very clean, but with bare-bulb reading lamps. They rent for about $22 s, $28 d, and $35 t, with cable TV, phones, a/c, bar, and good restaurant. Credit cards are accepted.

Juchitán's best hotel is the resort-style **Gran Hotel Santo Domingo,** on the highway across from both the bus station and the ingress road to town, at Crucero, Carretera Panamericana s/n, Juchitán, Oaxaca 70000, tel. 971/110-50, 971/136-42, fax 971/119-59. The Gran Hotel's choice attraction is a luxuriously inviting large pool and grassy patio, a welcome refuge for winding down from the heat, street noise and bustle. The approximately 40 rooms, in a pair of double-storied tiers beyond a tropical entrance foyer, are spare but clean, spacious, high-ceilinged, and comfortable, with modern-standard bathrooms. Rentals run about $27, $31 d, $38 t, with a/c, TV, phones, good restaurant, parking, and credit cards accepted.

FOOD

Juchitán's downtown plaza food stalls do big business all day and half the night. Especially popular with local people are the market *fondas,* bottom level at the south (right) side of the *palacio municipal.* Another, less busy *fonda* spot is on the side plaza Helidoro Charis Castro.

For baked goods, go to **panadería,** on 2 de Abril, between Gómez and Hidalgo, a block east and half a block north of the of the plaza's northeast corner. For pizza and snacks try **Pizzería Gato Montes** (Wildcat Pizza), Colón 7, tel. 971/139-45, open daily 7 P.M.-midnight, a block west of the church between Belisario Domínguez and Juárez.

The class-act downtown restaurant, perfect for a midday break, is the refined **Restaurant Casa Grande,** in the inner patio of an ex-mansion, at Juárez 12, tel. 971/134-60. The mostly business and upper-class patrons choose from an international list of soups, salads, sandwiches, meats and pastas, and a number of Oaxacan regional specialties, such as *chilequiles con tasajo* (chilied tortillas with beef), *enchiladas de mole negro* (enchiladas with black mole sauce), and *chile relleno de picadillo* (chili stuffed with spiced meat). Open daily 8:30 A.M.–8 P.M. Moderate.

On the other hand, local fish lovers frequent seafood restaurant **Mariscos de Marlo,** at the corner of 16 de Septiembre and Hidalgo, for its long, very correctly Mexican menu of seafood and more. Have it all, including a plethora of clam, oyster, and shrimp cocktails; soups, both clear and creamed; octopus, squid, lobster, and shrimp (cooked 10 ways); and seven styles of *cucarachas* (cockroaches). One block north of the plaza, at 16 de Septiembre 22, tel. 971/119-07, open daily 8 A.M.-11 P.M. Moderate.

Alternatively, escape temporarily from Mexico at the coffee shop-style **Restaurant Santa Fe,** tel. 971/115-45, at the highway crossing next to the bus station. In the air-conditioned Denny's-like atmosphere, enjoy fresh coffee and fruit, followed by tasty eggs, waffles, and pancakes for breakfast, several hamburgers or salads for lunch, and finally, soups, spaghetti, beef, chicken, and fish for dinner. Open daily 24 hours. Moderate.

ENTERTAINMENT AND EVENTS

Juchitán's substantial excess wealth goes largely to finance an impressive round of parties, locally called *velas,* in honor of a patron saint or a historically or commercially important event. The *velas* are organized and financed by entire *barrios* (neighborhoods), and led by *mayordomos,* usually a well-to-do male head of household, but also including his spouse, children, and all relatives and friends, who usually add up to a major fraction of the population of an entire Juchitán *barrio.* The *mayordomo* family, together with male and female *capitanes* and their closest friends, make up the *mayordomía,* the core committee responsible for carrying off the celebration.

Customary activities include blossom-decorated church masses, parties in the house of the *mayordomo,* community barbecues, a parade of fruit and flower-laden floats, from which the *capitanas,* dressed like brides in their stunningly embroidered Tehuantepec outfits, throw fruit and gifts to the street-side crowds.

In all, Juchitecans celebrate 20 in-town *velas,* which fill streets with merrymakers during the last half of April, virtually the entire month of May, and several days each in June, July, August, and September, a total of about 50 days of celebrating for the entire year. This wouldn't be too excessive if it were not for the approximately 20 obligatory national holidays and the other 30 unmissable *velas* in neighboring Isthmus communities. (See the special topic *Velas* of the Isthmus.)

Local folks sometimes offer droll commentaries about all this celebrating: "If you go to a *mayordomo* house, I'll tell you what you'll find . . . . no bed, no stove, no shoes, just happy people and lots of friends."

Lacking a local fiesta, you might want to take in a film at the genteel **Cinema Casa Grande,** on the plaza, south side. Enter past the patio Restaurant Casa Grande.

SERVICES

Money and Communications

A number of downtown banks, which all have **ATMs,** help manage Juchitecos' money. They'll also change your money into pesos or U.S. dollars. Best choice for its long hours is **BanCrecer** (GrowthBank), open Mon.–Fri. 9 A.M.–5 P.M., Sat. 10 A.M.–2 P.M., at Efrain Gómez 19, half a block west of the plaza's northwest corner, tel. 971/111-60, 971/134-82. Also open long hours is **Banco Internacional** (Bital), open Mon.–Fri. 9 A.M.–5 P.M.

and Sat. 9 A.M.–2 P.M., at 16 de Septiembre 52, three blocks north of the plaza. Third choice goes to **Banco Serfin,** tel. 971/120-00, open Mon.–Fri. 9 A.M.–3 P.M., Sat. 10 A.M.–2 P.M. at the corner of Belasario Domínguez and the extension of 16 de Septiembre, one block south of the *palacio municipal.*

The *correo* (post office) tel. 971/112-72, is open Mon.–Fri. 8 A.M.–7 P.M., Sat. 9 A.M.–noon, at the plaza's northeast corner, just west of the *palacio municipal.* *Telecomunicaciones* (public fax and money orders), tel. 971/110-40, also open Mon.–Fri. 8 A.M.–7 P.M., Sat. 9 A.M.–noon, is across the street, at the corner, beneath the market portal.

Photo and Cameras
A trio of downtown camera shops sell and develop film and stock some cameras and photo supplies. Try **Foto Facil,** at 16 de Septiembre 26, inside the big Mega Elektra store, west side of the street, a block and a half north of the plaza; or **Foto Alfa** on the same street, east side, just north of the plaza; or **Foto Pro Gómez,** a block west and a block north of the plaza, on 5 de Mayo, west side, a few doors north of Efraim Gómez.

Medical Needs
A ready source of nonprescription medicines and drugs is the 24-hour **Farmacia del Istmo,** tel. 971/109-94 and 971/103-16, at Efrain Gómez and 2 de Abril, one block behind the north side of the *palacio municipal.* Alternatively, go to the big drugstore-style **Farmacia San Vicente,** open daily 7 A.M.–9:30 P.M., diagonally across from the south corner of the *palacio municipal,* tel. 971/132-59.

A number of **doctors** maintain offices near the plaza. For example, general physician-surgeons Dr. Ruben Calvo López and Dr. Carlos Alonso Ruiz and gynecologist Doctora Anabel López Ruiz, gynecologist, have regular consulting hours at Clínica San Fernando, tel. 971/115-69, on 16 de Septiembre between E. Gómez and Hidalgo, half a block and a half north of the plaza's northeast. Alternatively, go to pharmacy and **Clínica Nuestra Señora de Exaltación,** tel. 971/113-78, with about six specialists on call, at 5 de Septiembre, east side of street, half a block north of the plaza.

In **emergency,** follow your hotel's recommendation or have a taxi take you to the General Hospital Dr. Macedonio Benítez Fuentes, tel. 971/114-41 or 971/119-85, downtown on Efrain Gómez near the plaza.

INFORMATION

The local **Cámara Nacional de Comercio** (National Chamber of Commerce), under the supervision of friendly director Cristóforo Vásquez Pineda, will try to answer your queries (in Spanish). Find him on the second floor, above Banamex, corner of 5 de Sept. and E. Gómez, open Mon.–Fri. approximately 9 A.M.–1 P.M. and 4–7 P.M., tel. 971/115-97.

Alternatively, try travel agent **Zarymar,** at 5 de Septiembre 100B, several blocks north of the plaza, tel. 971/107-92 or 971/128-67 for information, airline tickets, and auto-"mobile rentals.

GETTING THERE AND AWAY

By Bus
A modern long-distance *camionera central* (central bus station), at the Hwy. 190 crossing north of downtown, is the point of departure for all of the first-class and most of the second-class connections with both Oaxaca and national destinations. Both first- and second-class lines service customers from separate waiting rooms (first-class on the left, second-class in the right). The busy but clean station has snack stores and luggage check service. Long-distance telephone and fax is available at a small office in the second-class waiting room.

Autobuses del Oriente (ADO) and affiliated lines, tel. 971/125-65, offer direct first-class connections north with Gulf of Mexico destinations of Minatitlán, Coatzacoalcos, Villahermosa, Palenque, and Ciudad del Carmen; northwest with Oaxaca, Mexico City, Veracruz, and Tampico. Additionally, first-class carrier **Cristóbal Colón** (CC), tel. 971/125-65, and its luxury-class subsidiary, Plus, offer connections northwest with Oaxaca, Puebla, Mexico City, and Veracruz; southwest with Salina Cruz, Bahías de Huatulco, Pochutla (Puerto

Ángel), and Puerto Escondido; and east with Chiapas destinations of Tuxtla Gutiérrez, San Cristóbal las Casas, and Tapachula, at the Guatemala border.

Second-class carriers include **Autobuses del Oriente** (ADO), which offers connections north with Coatzacoalcos; southwest with Tehuantepec and Salina Cruz; and east with Tapanatepec, including all intermediate destinations. Additionally, **Autobuses Unidos** (AU) offers second-class connections northwest with Puebla, Mexico City, Orizaba, Veracruz, and Tuxtepec; and southwest with Tehuantepec and Salina Cruz, including all intermediate destinations. Moreover, **Sur** offers second-class connections north with Coatzacoalcos, northwest with Oaxaca, southwest with Bahías de Huatulco, and east with Tapanatepec and Tapachula, including all intermediate destinations.

Semi-local bus connections with adjacent towns are available via the green-white-and-yellow **Autotransportes Istmeños** across the side street, south less than a block toward town from the *camionera central*.

By Car

Drivers have the same highway choices and destinations as listed at the end of the Tehuantepec section, preceding. Simply subtract 30 minutes driving time (and 17 miles, 27 km distance) for northerly and easterly trips; add the same for northwesterly and southwesterly trips. In Juchitán, fill up with **gasoline** at the Pemex *gasolinera* at the Hwy. 190–town ingress crossing.

NORTH OF JUCHITÁN

A number of uniquely interesting destinations await travelers willing to venture into the foothill hinterland northwest and north of Juchitán. Foremost among them are the storied former royal Zapotec bathing **springs** that well up, blue and crystalline, at Tlacotepec and Laollaga, an hour's travel northwest of Juchitán.

Equally ripe for exploring is the stalactite-studded **limestone cave** near the town of Santo Domingo Petapa, together with the singularly successful cooperative company town at Lagunas, about an hour and a half north of Juchitán.

Each of these excursions can be enjoyed from Juchitán in a leisurely day by car or a long day by bus.

THE SPRINGS AT TLACOTEPEC AND LAOLLAGA

Both of these bathing resorts were part of the territory of the Zapotec royal family of King Cosijoeza. He often used the springs as a refuge during his protracted war with Aztec emperor Ahuitzotl during the 1490s. A famous traditional story recounts how love resolved the bloody conflict. Tiring of the struggle, Ahuitzotl proposed a peace pact. In exchange for allowing Aztec traders and envoys to pass through the Isthmus lands, Cosijoeza would receive Aztec princess Coyollicatzin in marriage. One day, meditating over the proposition while bathing in the Tlacotepec spring, Cosijoeza was awestruck by a stunning apparition of Coyollicatzin. Despite his apprehension, Coyollicatzin's apparition enchanted him with her beauty. Thus persuaded, Cosijoeza soon took Coyollicatzin in marriage, sealing the pact between the two nations.

Their marriage was a happy one. Children resulted, and Cosijoeza passed the springs at Tlacotepec and Laollaga to their son Cosijopí, the king of the Isthmus lands, and their daughter, Princess Donaji, both of whom continued to exercise authority after the conquest.

Magdalena Tlacotepec

Storied Princess Donaji (see the special topic The Story of Donaji in the Oaxaca City chapter), who after the conquest was baptized as Magdalena Donaji, donated both her Christian name and the springs and royal park at Tlacotepec to the local community, still known as Magdalena Tlacotepec.

Today the town's springs and surrounding sanctuary are a unique asset for all Istmeño families to enjoy, which they do en masse on sunny Sundays and holidays. The source, a clear, cool underground river, wells up from a rocky basin and fills a long, meandering, aqua blue swimming hole. Shoals of little fish that nibble and tickle your feet hide in crannies and flit along the sandy bottom. Shady mango trees overhang the bank and spread into a rustic public strolling ground on one side. On the other, entrance side, food stalls surround a parking area.

Here you can park your (self-contained) trailer or RV or set up a tent and stay a spell, walking into the surrounding hills in the morning to enjoy wildlife and wildflowers and splashing in the cool spring in the afternoons. Custodial personnel who keep the site clean and secure collect nominal fees for parking and camping.

Santiago Laollaga

Laollaga (lah-oh-YAH-gah) springs mark the northern boundary of the petite *municipio* of Santiago Laollaga, which you pass through on your way to the springs. A big parking lot overlooks the main series of pools (concrete basins) built into the rocky downhill channel of the Río Laollaga. Shady trees overhang the pools, and a pair of permanent open-air *comedores* on the riverbank serve drinks and food.

Visitors equipped with a self-contained trailer or RV might enjoy a stay, parking in the lot for a day or two. Fees run only a few dollars a day. Unfortunately, the water at the main pools is sometimes a bit tainted by soap from folks washing clothes upstream. You can assure pure water by following the river a quarter mile upstream to its source, a natural *ojo de agua* spring welling from the base of the hills. Here great shady trees spread over a sandy riverbank, ripe for tent camping if you don't mind sharing the spot with a few townsfolk on weekdays, more on weekends.

Laollaga diversions might include strolls around the town and along dirt roads and trails, into the summer-lush native tropical woodlands. By local bus or car, you could explore farther afield, along the good gravel road (where you made your last turn left) threading the green-forested Río Los Perros valley and foothill country 15 miles (25 km) northwest to remote Santa María Guienagati.

Arrive during the last 10 days in July and join Laollaga's big **Fiesta de Santiago Apóstol**

Laollaga spring water runs through a series of pools (shown) about a half mile downstream from its crystalline source.

(20–30 July), which includes four separate *velas,* with fireworks, carnival rides and games, *regada* (fruit-throwing), dances, and *mojigangos* (giant dancing figures).

Small town stores can supply basic groceries. Pharmacies, a private doctor, a *centro de salud,* a post office, and a *caseta larga distancia* can provide basic services.

Getting There and Away

Get to Tlacotepec and Laollaga from Juchitán via Ixtepec. By bus, take by one of the Ixtepec-labeled buses that frequently head northwest from the Hwy. 190 crossing, across the street from the *camionera central*. Half an hour later, at Ixtepec, transfer to the red and white Tlacotepec- or Laollaga-labeled local bus.

By car, from the Hwy. 190 crossing at Juchitán, mark your odometer and head across Hwy. 190 northwest through Ixtaltepec (five miles, eight km) to the railroad tracks at Ixtepec

(9.7 miles, 15.6 km). Immediately after crossing the tracks, turn left. After about 300 yards or three blocks, turn right at Ixtepec's main street, Calle 16 de Septiembre. Continue .3 mile (.5 km) and fork left at the Balneario sign (10 miles, 16.3 km). Turn left at a second sign (10.4 miles, 16.7 km), then left again at an unsigned T-intersection (10.7 miles, 17.2 km). Finally a mile farther at a Y-intersection (11.7 miles, 18.8 km), go left and continue, following the Balneario signs to Tlacotepec, a total of about 18 miles (29 km). Alternatively, bear right at the Y and continue through Chihuatán (turn left at town corner, at 16.2 miles, 26.1 km) to Santiago Laollaga town center (19.2 miles, 31 km). Turn right and continue through town. At a total of 19.7 miles (31.7 km), just before the road becomes gravel, turn left to the *balneario,* whose entrance you'll see after about three blocks.

LAGUNAS: COMPANY TOWN

If success can be measured by longevity, the industrial cooperative town of Lagunas, which began producing cement in 1942, has earned its plaudits. Moreover, the unique experiment it represents seems as robust as ever. The idea began back in the 1930s, when investors were eager to exploit a mountain of local limestone that towered conveniently beside the cross-isthmus rail line. The era was, however, that of reformist President Lázaro Cárdenas, when the star of socialism was rising over Mexico from the east. The enterprise must be a cooperative, the government demanded. Investors, realizing the project's unique prospects, agreed, and Cruz Azul, a uniquely Mexican private-public cooperative, was born.

Today, the great mill beside the railroad tracks hums all day and night, producing millions of tons of cement yearly for projects from Chile to Canada. Moreover, besides supporting the livelihoods of thousands of families in the entire local hinterland, the Lagunas mill (judging from the tidy, dust-free town) appears to produce little of the debilitating cement dust that has shortened the lives of cement mill workers the world over.

At the town center, across the tracks from the mill, a monument erected by the workers (the Cooperadores de La Cruz Azul) honors Guillermo Alvarez, Cruz Azul's guiding light, with pair of eternally flickering electric lamps.

Along Av. Cooperativismo facing the plant stand the town Banamex branch, the post office, the public telecommunications office, and the plant superintendent's office. Badged workers, all in pressed khakis and hard hats, walk with purpose along the sidewalks. Some turn and continue along the town's main street, Av. Cruz Azul, and continue past the hamburger shop, *centro comercial* (company store), an immaculate bakery, and the big church, dedicated the Virgin of Guadalupe. From the commercial center, tree-lined residential streets extend past schools, a hospital, and tidy concrete houses with some of Mexico's rare, American-style unfenced yards with lawns.

Accommodations
If you want to stay, Cruz Azul will probably be able to accommodate you in the semi-deluxe **Casa de Huéspedes Club Deportivo Social y Cultural.** Rooms are immaculate, with comfortable (some king-size) beds, shiny furnishings and modern-standard bathrooms. They rent for about $8 per person, with a/c or fans, and the restaurant is good. Credit cards are not accepted. Friendly hotel manager Miguel Ángel Hernández, tel. 972/603-46, says that they don't accept drop-in guests. You must reserve in triplicate. Send one copy to Lic. Guillermo Alvarez Cuevas, Director General, Cooperative "La Cruz Azul," S.C.L., Torres Alidad No. 517, Colonia del Valle, Mexico, D.F., tel. 01 5/687-2030; a second copy to the plant superintendent, Ing. Pablo Resendiz Garcia, Gerencia de Planta, Lagunas, Oaxaca 70380; and a third copy to Alvarado's boss, Sr. Jose L. Tapia Olguin, Gerencia Regional, Club Deportivo "Cruz Azul," A.C., Lagunas, Oaxaca 70380. It may help to explain that you have been referred by the *Oaxaca Handbook* and that you intend to explore the caves at Petapa and would like an overnight room.

SANTO DOMINGO PETAPA: LIMESTONE CAVE

Several miles past Lagunas, Santo Domingo Petapa (pop. about 2,000) marks the end of the pavement. Unless you arrive during a national holiday or the 1–4 August town festival in honor of Santo Domingo, Petapa will appear like a typical Oaxaca country town. Petapa does have, however, at least one claim to fame, and that is the grand limestone cavern on the mountainside two miles beyond the town.

Head straight to the *presidencia municipal* and ask for a guide to show you around inside the cave. Be sure to write a letter in advance, in Spanish, addressed to the Presidente Municipal, Santo Domingo Petapa, Oaxaca, 70350, telling your date and time of arrival and that you'd be happy to pay (say $10) for an experienced guide to show you the cave. Alternatively, two or three days in advance you could ask the desk clerk at your hotel to leave a message at the Petapa *larga distancia*, tel. 971/135-50, making the same request.

These preparations will give you a good chance of seeing the inside of the cave. Come equipped with sturdy shoes, hard hats (at least plastic), and, if possible, super-bright three- or four-celled flashlights. The cave, between one- and two-hours' walk west of town, is large, with a towering, cathedral-like entry portal and a river flowing from its mouth. Your exploration inside will take about two hours and extend past stalagmites and stalactites approximately half a mile into the mountainside.

EAST OF JUCHITÁN

From south to north, the grand Isthmus landscape east of Juchitán gradually changes through three distinctive panoramas. In the south, at the Pacific Ocean, the Isthmus begins as three grand, glassy, wildlife-rich lagoons—the Laguna Superior and Inferior on the west side and the Mar Muerto (not the "Dead Sea" but the "Calm Sea") on the east. This is the home ground of the Huave people, driven to the Isthmus' salty edge an age ago by the Zapotecs, to make their living mostly from the sea. North of that lies the fertile, most prized crescent of pastures, fields, orchards, the sizable towns of Niltepec, Zanatepec, and Tapanatepec, and the Panamerican Highway, which connects them all. Farther north rise the trans-isthmus mountains, the Sierra Atravesada, heartland of the Chimalapas, a wild kingdom of sylvan forests, rushing rivers, and deep, shadowed canyons, a final refuge of rare, endangered, and yet-to-be-discovered species of plants and animals.

First access to all this is by the Panamerican Highway east of Juchitán, then by side roads north and south from junctions such as La Venta, Zanatepec, and Tapanatepec.

LA VENTA

La Venta (The Windy Place), about 18 miles (29 km) east of Juchitán, lives up to its name, so much so that the Comisión Federal de Electricidad has installed seven towering wind generators at the very spot. The ultramodern, gleaming windmills, visible from the highway, whir obediently, doing their good work.

A side road leads to the windmills' base, where a display explains the project. So far the seven 10-story generators have been able to average a continuous 500 kilowatts of power, enough for a modern Mexican village of 500 family homes. Currently, 500 kilowatts of electric power sells for about $1,000 per day, implying that each of the 500 families would have to fork out about $2 a day, $60 a month, for such power. Thus the experiment appears to be showing that although not presently affordable for most Oaxacans, Mexican wind power appears promising for industry now and for home use in a future, more prosperous Mexico.

A rough but mostly paved side road leads north from La Venta to the backcountry **Chimalapas** jumping-off point villages of San Miguel Chimalapa (14 miles, 23 km) and Cuauhtémoc (17 miles, 27 km). The immense million-acre Chimalapas de facto wilderness is the communal property of two Zoque-speaking indigenous communities headquartered, respectively, at San Miguel Chimalapa and the more remote San Martín Chimalapa, 30 rough miles (48 km) north from the Hwy. 185 junction at El Mezquite.

The Chimalapa Zoque people are rightly

suspicious of strangers, especially now that their lands have become one of Mexico's few remaining storehouses of valuable tropical hardwoods, endangered animal pelts, and minerals. Legitimate visitors to the Chimalapas wilderness, if any are allowed at all, are strictly licensed by state and local authorities and must be accompanied by community guides. If you're interested in hiking and camping in the Chimalapas, first contact federal-state tourism in Oaxaca City (607 Independencia, tel. 951/421-55, email: turinfo@gob.mx) for information on how to proceed.

UNIÓN DE HIDALGO

This fair-sized *municipio* is one of the main gateways to the rich fishing grounds and tiny, Huave-speaking beach villages of the **Laguna Superior.** At the end of an approximately seven-mile (11-km) mostly paved but bumpy road, you'll arrive at the big town plaza. In the vicinity you'll find groceries (**Abarrotes Sánchez,** Altamirano 12, tel. 971/382-59), a neglected hotel (the **Diush'i nga' a naroohba'a,** at the corner of Leona Vicario Sur and Matamoros Oriente), a pharmacy (**Farmacia San Isidro,** Nicolas Bravo 13 Oriente, tel. 971/382-27), police (at the *palacio municipal,*), a post office, and a *telecomunicaciones* (public fax and money orders) office.

Although you'll most likely be passing through Unión de Hidalgo on the way to somewhere else, you can join the festivities (processions, mass barbecues, dancing, fruit- and gift-throwing *regadas,* carnival games and rides) if you arrive during one of the several town *velas.* The fun begins in April with the **Vela de los Pescadores** (Festival of the Fisherfolk) and continues, on 3 May with the **Vela de Santa Cruz;** during the second 15 days *(quinceana)* of May, *velas* honor of San Vicente Chico and San Vicente Ferrer Grande. Later come the *velas* in honor of San Isidro the Farmer, Santa María Santísima, and San Pedro Apóstol, 26–30 June. During the first days of August, townsfolk honor Santo Domingo de Guzmán, and 27–30 September, they celebrate the town's founding. Finally, they celebrate Santa Cecilia on 22 November and the Virgin of Guadalupe on 12 December.

PLAYA COPALITO AND SAN DIONISIO DEL MAR

From Unión de Hidalgo, continue south through Chicapa de Castro, a total of about 23 miles (37 km) to Playa Copalito (Little Copal Tree Beach), a tiny (but with electricity) fishing village of thatched houses and poor but friendly Huave-speaking folks. A long sandy beach built of myriad wave-washed mussel and clam shells winds along the oft mirror-smooth Laguna Superior. Motorboats and *canoas* recline lazily on the beach. A few scraggly shoreline trees provide a bit of shade, and grassy spaces appear fine for RV parking or tent camping.

Here, the main work for locals and diversion for visitors is fishing. *Lanchas* routinely return with a dozen one- or two-pound *lisa* (mullet), *sierra* (mackerel) or pompano. Fishermen are willing to take visitors on a half-day fishing excursion or exploration for about $15.

Since Playa Copalito is an idyllic but isolated little place, campers should arrive well equipped with tent, food, and water. Bring insect repellent; mosquitoes may be fierce certain times of the year (although they weren't a problem one wet September). Village stores might supply some essentials, but don't count on it.

While you're in the vicinity, the pilgrimage town of **San Dionisio del Mar** (two miles past the Playa Copalito turnoff, also accessible directly from the highway from the south-headed turnoff about 11 miles, 18 km east of La Venta) might be worth a visit. The miraculous image of San Dionisio at the town church attracts thousands of pilgrims yearly, mostly around the 6–8 October festival. A guesthouse is available for overnight accommodation.

Get to La Venta by eastbound **ADO, Cristóbal Colón,** or **Sur** bus, from either of the central terminals at Tehuantepec or Juchitán. At La Venta, transfer to a local bus or *colectivo* south to Unión de Hidalgo, then transfer to the San Dionisio-bound *verde* (green) bus, via Chicapa. About 45 bumpy minutes later, get off at the Playa Copalito (walk one mile) right turnoff (dirt) or continue ahead to San Dionisio.

By car or RV drive east from Juchitán to La Venta (19 miles, 31 km). Set your odometer and turn right (south), heading for Unión de Hidalgo.

At 7.2 miles (11.6 km) make your way through the town, asking townsfolk *"¿El camino a Chicapa?"* ("The way to Chicapa?"). Arrive at Chicapa del Castro (11 miles, 17.5 km), where you turn left, heading toward San Dionisio. After a total of 22.6 miles (36.4 km), turn right at the dirt road toward Playa Copalito (one mile farther) or continue to San Dionisio del Mar, a total of about 24 miles (39 km).

SANTO DOMINGO ZANATEPEC

The important town of Santo Domingo Zanatepec (pop. about 10,000), on Hwy. 190 about 54 miles (87 km) east of Juchitán, is the point of departure for the wild and spectacularly steep Zanatepec River Canyon. There, accompanied by a guide, you can bask in a hot spring and hike to a pair of wilderness lakes.

Zanatepec, moreover, has a restaurant and hotel. For a break, stop by the mango-shaded **Restaurant Nadxielly** (I Love You), tel. 972/100-49, where for a pittance you can eat all the mangos you want during April and May. The family-run establishment, well marked on the highway's north side, offers home-style *comidas* daily 6 A.M.-midnight.

Next door stands the basic **Hotel San Rafael,** Santa Domingo Zanatepec, Oaxaca 70160, same telephone as the restaurant, tel. 972/100-49. The 20 plain but clean rooms rent for about $12 s, $16 d with fan, $20 s, d, or t with a/c, with parking.

Zanatepec can provide a number of goods and services through establishments located mostly along main street Hidalgo, north of the highway. Get groceries at Abarrotes Eli, Hidalgo s/n, tel. 972/101-44; medicines and medical consultation the at the farmacia of Dr. Ricardo Hernández, Hidalgo s/n, open Mon.–Sat. 8 A.M.–2 P.M. and 4–6 P.M. tel. 972/101-92; *telecomunicaciones* (public fax and money orders), tel. 972/101-42, open Mon.–Fri. 9 A.M.–3:30 P.M. and *correo* (post office), both at Hidalgo 200 next to the *presidencia municipal;* and *policía* (police), tel. 972/100-74, at Hidalgo 198, the *presidencia municipal.*

Into the Río Zanatepec Canyon
The hotel also serves as contact point for guide **Hermillo Toledo,** who takes parties for excursions into the Río Zanatepec Canyon during the December–May dry season. During the rainy season the river may be too high. Access from the highway is by a rough gravel road to the village of Agua Caliente (nine miles, 14 km); from there, visit the hot spring, then continue walking (about two hours) up the canyon to a pair of lakes, the Lago del Sol (Lake of the Sun) and Lago de la Luna (Lake of the Moon). Options include expert-level rock climbing, wildlife viewing, fishing, and wilderness camping by the river or the lakes. Expect to pay Hermillo about $30 per day for his services.

SAN PEDRO TAPANATEPEC

"Mango Capital of the World" San Pedro Tapanatepec, besides being a main access point for Rincón Juárez on the Mar Muerto (Calm Sea), also has a number of highway-side hotels, restaurants, and services.

Accommodations and Food
One of the best bets for a meal in Tapanatepec is the relaxing open-air restaurant at the **Hotel Misión,** open daily 8 A.M.–9 P.M., on the south side of the highway. An inviting plus is the pool, if it's in running order.

The adjoining hotel, at Carretera Panamericana Km 925, San Pedro Zanatepec, Oaxaca 70180, tel. 972/181-33 or 972/180-09, offers around 20 basic rooms with hot water shower baths for about $16 s or d, $30 t with fan, $20 s or d, $35 t with a/c. Any time other than the Feria del Mango (Mango Fair, first week of April) or the Fiesta Patronal de San Pedro (27–30 June) you could probably bargain successfully for less. If not, take a look at some of the three or four other hotels, such as the **Casa Blanca** (tel. 972/180-39, $27 d with a/c), the **Cruz,** and the **Flor** (tel. 972/180-47, $16 d), on the highway nearby.

Services
Most of Tapanatepec's service establishments are either on the highway or along the main business street, Calle Martín Melendez, parallel and just south of it. For groceries, go to **Abarrotes La Flor,** on the highway, tel. 972/182-

82; for money, to **Banamex,**, at M. Melendez 48, open Mon.–Fri. 9 A.M.–3 P.M.; for medicines, either **Farmacia López,** on the highway, tel. 972/183-73, or **Farmacia Espinoza,** at M. Melendez 78, tel. 972/181-92; a doctor, the **Seguro Social** clinic, 16 de Septiembre 47, tel. 972/181-19; *correo* (post office), tel. 972/182-15, open Mon.–Fri. 9 A.M.–3 P.M., and *telecomunicaciones* (public fax and money orders), tel. 972/181-60, same hours, both on Av. Juárez, by the *presidencia municipal;* and the Policía Federal de Caminos (Federal Highway Patrol), tel. 972/183-13, on the highway.

RINCÓN JUÁREZ AND THE CALM SEA

For a look at what Istmeños call the Mar Muerto (not because it's *muerto,* literally dead, but because it's much calmer than the Mar Vivo, the open ocean), head south about 14 miles (23 km) by a good paved road to Rincón Juárez village (pop. about 500). Three or four seafood *palapas* line a sandy beach lapped by the gentle waves of a spreading, silvery sea. Life follows the drowsy rhythms of daylight and darkness, weather, and tides. Mornings, early, fishermen load their nets and paddle silently out in canoes or buzz out in motorboats to try their luck. Usually they return with about a 20-pound catch, possibly including jumbo shrimp, clams, or fish for sale to the wholesalers whose trucks arrive in the afternoon.

Visitors can also enjoy their own quiet routine, enjoying sunrises and sunset, watching the flocks of pelicans, cormorants and herons, and exploring the lagoon either on foot or by boat. Fishermen are willing to take parties out for wildlife-viewing or fishing excursions (expect to pay about $20 for half a day). Be prepared with your own binoculars and tackle.

Alternatively, launch your own boat or inflated raft right on the beach. Camping would be fine, by tent or RV, right on the spacious shoreline. A restaurant-store, **Los Cocos,** provides home-cooked *comidas* and basic groceries.

Get to Rincón Juárez by bus (Tapanatepec-bound first- or second-class) from either the Juchitán or Tehuantepec central terminals. Continue by the approximately hourly local bus from Tapanatepec. Alternatively, ride the blue-and-white **Transportes Rincón Juárez** bus, which leaves the Juchitán market daily at 1 P.M. (or five minutes later turns right at the Hwy. 190 crossing corner by the Pemex gas station—verify at the station). The same bus departs Rincón Juárez for Juchitán daily at 8 A.M.

By car, the Rincón Juárez trip requires about three hours from Juchitán. Set your odometer at the Hwy. 190 crossing by the Pemex gas station. Continue east along Hwy. 190 about two hours to Tapanatepec. After 67 miles (108 km) (or 13 miles (21 km) from Hotel San Rafael in Zanatepec), in the middle of Tapanatepec you reach the paved right highway turnoff road for Rincón Juárez. Continue through the town and over the only river-crossing bridge. Continue along another 14 miles (23 km) of paved road to Rincón Juárez, about 74 miles (119 km) from Juchitán.

SALINA CRUZ AND VICINITY

Salina Cruz was important long before the conquest. The *salinas* (salt-producing ponds) where many generations of native people had been harvesting salt for trade attracted Hernán Cortés very soon after his arrival in Mexico. He also recognized Salina Cruz's strategic position on the Isthmus, where the long-sought route to China was accessible, not by a torturous trans-Sierra journey but by a short, easy passage over the narrow, low Isthmus. Cortés lost no time in acquiring the *salinas* as part of his personal domain and building ships on nearby Playa La Ventosa with which to explore the Pacific.

His efforts have been amplified by successive generations. Beginning in the 19th century and continuing to the present day, the Isthmus regularly tempts canal builders wanting to carve a sea route between the Atlantic and Pacific. President Juárez's government settled for a rail connection, begun by the American Louisiana railroad company in Salina Cruz around 1870. President Porfirio Díaz presided over the project's climax, with up-to-date Salina Cruz port facilities built by the British company Iglesias, Pearson and Son, Ltd., around 1900.

Since the 1960s Petroleos Mexicanos (Pemex) and other government authorities have greatly extended those early efforts with a hefty trans-isthmus pipeline funneling Gulf crude oil to a grand petrochemical complex as well as elaborate new shipping docks. From these, great loads of chemicals, crude oil, gasoline and other fuels, minerals, fruit, and much more move out via truck, train, and ship to Mexico and the Pacific. Salina Cruz has thus become the industrial engine of the southern Mexican Pacific, employing more than 10,000 workers whose wages directly and indirectly support many tens of thousands more.

SIGHTS

Salina Cruz (pop. 80,000), Oaxaca's third city, outstrips both Juchitán and Tehuantepec in hustle and bustle. In Salina Cruz, enterprise reigns and people are working. Crowds with money to spend support a host of town-center markets, stores, offices, hotels, and restaurants. If you need to buy something, Salina Cruz is the place in the Isthmus that you're most likely to get it.

Salina Cruz's big downtown stretches in a mile-long rectangle north and south from the town plaza. Some of the north-south streets change names at the plaza, others don't. On the plaza's east side, 5 de Mayo becomes Héroes south of the plaza, while on the plaza's west side, Avila Camacho retains the same name its entire length. West another block and north of the plaza runs Wilfredo Cruz, which becomes Tampico on the south side, while a block east of 5 de Mayo, Puerto Ángel remains the same both north and south of the plaza. Thankfully, east-west streets do not change. From a block north of the plaza, moving successively south, are Guaymas, Mazatlán, Acapulco, and finally, Coatzacoalcos, a block south of the plaza.

Town activity focuses at the very pungent and busy market northeast of the plaza, between Guaymas and Mazatlán. Several blocks south of the plaza are the container docks along the Calle Miramar, which leads to the drowsy beach village of Playa Ventosa (see below).

Once you've gotten your fill of the sights and sounds around the plaza and market, head west to breezy harbor vista point **Faro del Marina.** Drive or ride a Salina-labeled bus or a taxi west along Acapulco, the plaza's south-side street. First you pass *dique* (DEE-kay, dry dock) no. 1 and the naval compound, then cross beneath the great rack of pipelines conducting a small river of oil and chemicals over the road. Continue, winding uphill to the summit parking lot on the right. On the harbor's near side stands the fishing fleet; on the opposite side are the smart gray naval frigates and destroyers. On the right, at the outer pier, great supertankers take on lakes of crude oil, most likely bound for Japan and the United States.

Continue west downhill to Barrio Salinas, named after Hernán Cortés's salt-producing ponds, the **Salinas del Marqués.** Although the

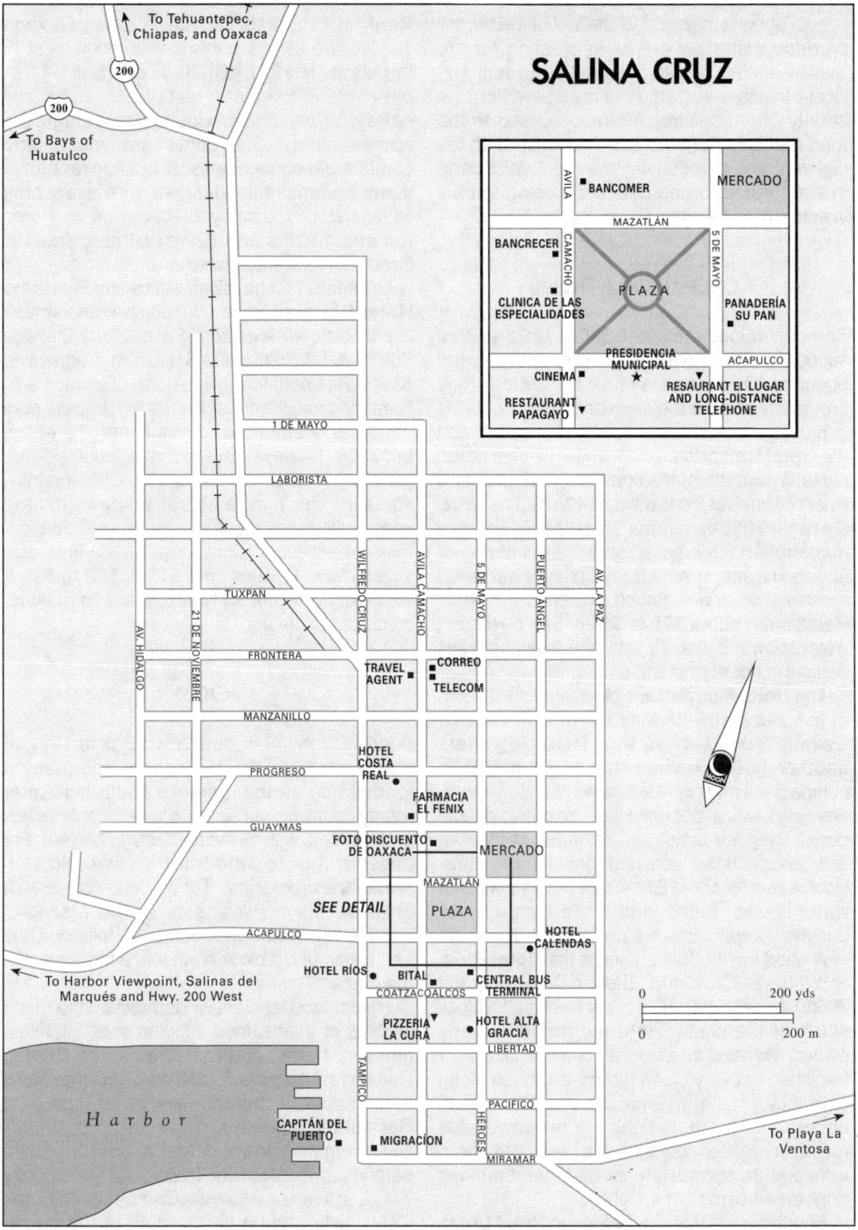

SALINA CRUZ

To Tehuantepec, Chiapas, and Oaxaca

200

200

To Bays of Huatulco

Inset detail map:

AVILA

BANCOMER

MERCADO

MAZATLÁN

CAMACHO

5 DE MAYO

BANCRECER

PLAZA

CLINICA DE LAS ESPECIALIDADES

PANADERÍA SU PAN

ACAPULCO

PRESIDENCIA MUNICIPAL

CINEMA

RESAURANT EL LUGAR AND LONG-DISTANCE TELEPHONE

RESTAURANT PAPAGAYO

Main map labels:

1 DE MAYO

LABORISTA

WILFREDO CRUZ

AVILA CAMACHO

5 DE MAYO

PUERTO ANGEL

AV. LA PAZ

TUXPAN

AV. HIDALGO

21 DE NOVIEMBRE

FRONTERA

TRAVEL AGENT

CORREO

TELECOM

MANZANILLO

HOTEL COSTA REAL

PROGRESO

FARMACIA EL FENIX

GUAYMAS

FOTO DISCUENTO DE OAXACA

MERCADO

MAZATLÁN

SEE DETAIL

PLAZA

ACAPULCO

HOTEL RÍOS

BITAL

HOTEL CALENDAS

To Harbor Viewpoint, Salinas del Marqués and Hwy. 200 West

COATZACOALCOS

CENTRAL BUS TERMINAL

PIZZERIA LA CURA

HOTEL ALTA GRACIA

LIBERTAD

TAMPICO

PACIFICO

HEROES

Harbor

CAPITÁN DEL PUERTO

MIGRACIÓN

MIRAMAR

To Playa La Ventosa

0   200 yds

0   200 m

© AVALON TRAVEL PUBLISHING, INC.

ponds, about a mile west of the foot of the hill, still produce salt, they are as interesting for the wildlife—flocks of waterfowl, both resident and local—that they sustain. People also live from the bounty of the *salinas.* Afternoons, next to the road that cuts north across the marshes to the highway you can usually see men waist deep in the pond, throwing nets and hoping to haul in something for dinner.

ACCOMMODATIONS

The continuous crowd of Salina Cruz visitors supports several hotels. With the exception of the beachfront hostelries in Playa La Ventosa they are nearly all near the town center.

Moving clockwise around the plaza, start with the **Hotel Calendas,** one long block east of the plaza, just south of the corner of Acapulco and Puerto Ángel, at Puerto Ángel 408, Salina Cruz, Oaxaca 70600, tel./fax 971/445-74. Savvy managers have created an inviting lodging of about 20 clean, spacious, thoughtfully furnished rooms in two stories around a quiet interior patio. Rentals run about $25 s, $28 d, $32 t, with hot water shower baths, TV, a/c, and parking. Credit cards are not accepted.

The **Hotel Altagracia,** a block and a half south of the plaza at 5 de Mayo 520, Salina Cruz, Oaxaca 70600, tel./fax 971/407-26, offers another good choice. The 18 rooms, in a compact but invitingly decorated two-story block, are clean, with either one king-size or two double beds. They are tastefully decorated in modern '90s style, with tile floors and some marble baths. Rooms rent for about $19 s, $22 d, $24 t, with hot water shower baths, and a/c, but street-only parking. Credit cards are not accepted.

A good low-budget choice is the **Hotel Ríos,** at Wilfredo Cruz 405, Salina Cruz, Oaxaca 70600, tel. 971/403-37, a block west, half a block south of the plaza. Here the grandmotherly owner maintains three stories of about 20 plainly furnished but very clean rooms, arranged along corridors around an interior patio. Choose an upper room for more light and privacy. Rates run a very reasonable $9 s or d, with bath (room temperature shower), fans, and street parking only; credit cards not accepted.

Fourth choice downtown goes to **Hotel Costa**

Real, at Progreso 22, Salina Cruz, Oaxaca 70600, two blocks north, half a block west of the plaza, tel. 971/428-70, fax 971/451-11. A plus here is the clean restaurant, especially handy for breakfast. Upstairs, although the approximately 30 rooms are clean and comfortable enough, they do not appear particularly well-maintained. Make sure everything works before you pay your money down. Rates run about $26 s and $29 d, with a/c and TV. Credit cards are accepted.

Convenient for travelers with cars or RVs is the **Hotel El Parador,** at Carretera Transistmica Km 6, Colonia Aviación, Salina Cruz Oaxaca 70670, tel./fax 971/629-51. On the highway's east side, about four miles north of town, the El Parador's major attraction is its big, tropical pool patio, perfect for relaxing at the end of a warm, busy day. However, the rooms, although clean, generally lack light and ventilation. Consequently, some rooms may smell of mildew *(moho),* especially during the summer-fall rainy season. Inspect various rooms until you find one satisfactory. Rentals cost $17 s, $22 d, $25 t, with a/c, hot water shower baths, and parking; credit cards not accepted.

FOOD

Food is plentiful in downtown Salina Cruz. If you're on a budget, the ***fondas*** (permanent food stalls) on the market's south side offer hearty country-style soups, stews, rice, tamales, and seafood, with all the tortillas you can eat. For dessert, go to one of the two close-in ***panaderías*** (bakeries). Try Su Pan (Your Bread) on 5 de Mayo, west side of the plaza; or Pastelería Internacional, corner of Wilfredo Cruz and Guaymas, a block north and a block west of the plaza.

Health food fanciers will appreciate the many shelves of grains, food supplements, vitamins, ginseng, herbs, and remedies at the **Centro Naturista Aquarius**. Find it on Camacho, half a block south of the cinema corner, just past Restaurant Papagayo.

Among the town center's best sit-down eateries is **Restaurant Papagayo,** open daily 7 A.M.–11 P.M., at Avila Camacho 407, tel. 971/420-84, half a block south of the plaza-corner cinema. Here Chinese-Mexican owners carry on their traditions with Hong Kong decor and some Chinese cuisine (2–7 P.M. only), but mostly Mexican and international specialties. Here, customers enjoy good breakfasts (hotcakes, bacon, eggs), lunches, or dinners (hamburgers, tortas, soup, salad, fish, chicken) daily 7 A.M.–11 P.M.

Second choice near the plaza is **Restaurant El Lugar** (The Place), where customers enjoy a view perch above and away from the sidewalk hubbub, especially good for breakfast or a late snack. Beneath a squadron of cooling ceiling fans, choose from a tasty, familiar menu of soups, sandwiches, chicken, meats, eggs, and fish. It's open long hours, daily 7–2 A.M., tel. 971/408-63.

If you're in the mood for pizza, try the tidy (but often noisy, ask them to turn down the TV) **Pizzería La Cura,** open daily about 1–8 P.M., a block and a half south of the plaza on Avila Camacho, between Coatzacoalcos and Libertad.

For a modicum of tranquillity and plain good food, try the dining room of the Hotel Costa Real, open daily 7:30 A.M.–10:30 P.M., at Progreso 22, two blocks north, half a block west of the plaza.

ENTERTAINMENT AND EVENTS

True to Tehuantepec tradition, Salina Cruz folks sometimes abandon their workaday habits for fiestas. First comes the **Fiesta de la Santa Cruz,** on 3 May, in a blast that includes coronation of a queen, full-costumed traditional dances, fruit-and gift-throwing *regada* parade, carnival rides and games, and fireworks.

If you miss the above, you might be lucky and get in on one later, such as the **Fiesta del Pueblo,** an all-purpose town fiesta, for several days beginning 9 May; the **Fiesta de Santa Rosa de Lima** (26 August–2 September); the **Fiesta de San Francisco Asis** (3–5 October); and the **Fiesta de San Diego,** 11–16 November.

If, sadly, you miss all the fiestas, at least console yourself by going to the curiously labeled **Cinema Sección 38,** right on the plaza-front, southwest corner of Acapulco and Avila Camacho, tel. 971/420-36, where you can enjoy programs of mostly first-run American action-adventure and romantic comedy films.

SERVICES AND INFORMATION

Money
Several banks, all with ATMs, serve downtown customers. A good first choice is **Banco Internacional** (Bital), with long hours Mon.–Sat. 8 A.M.–7 P.M., tel. 971/444-76, a block south of the plaza, northeast corner of Avila Camacho and Coatzacoalcos. Alternatively, also on Avila Camacho, try **Bancomer,** open Mon.–Fri. 8:30 A.M.–5:30 P.M., Sat. 10 A.M.–2 P.M., tel. 971/400-32, on the east side of the street a few steps north of the plaza; or **Bancrecer,** open Mon.–Fri. 9 A.M.–5 P.M., Sat. 10 A.M.–2 P.M., on the west side of the street a block north of the plaza.

Communications
The town *correo* (post office, with Mexpost secure mail service), tel. 971/400-40, open Mon.–Fri. 8 A.M.–7 P.M., Sat. 9 A.M.–1 P.M., and *Telecomunicaciones* (public fax and money orders), tel. 971/407-60, open Mon.–Sat. 8 A.M.–7:30 P.M., Sun. 9 A.M.–2 P.M., stand side by side four blocks north of the plaza, east side of Avila Camacho, corner of Frontera. Moreover, a 24-hour *larga distancia* (long distance) telephone serves customers at the plaza's southeast corner, below Restaurant El Lugar.

Travel Agent and Car Rentals
Travel agents, besides selling tickets and renting cars, are sometimes ready sources of information. Try the **Agencia de Viajes Grupo Azul,** four blocks north of the plaza at Avila Camacho 205B, west side, corner of Frontera, tel. 971/432-66 or 971/436-66, open Mon.–Sat. 8 A.M.–8 P.M.

Immigration
Being a port of entry, Salina Cruz has a **Migración** (Immigration Office). Go there, at the foot of Tampico, four blocks south of the plaza, if you lose or need an extension on your tourist permit. It's open Mon.–Fri. 9 A.M.–2 P.M., tel. 971/402-42 and 971/428-72.

If you arrive by **private boat** and have inspection documentation from another Mexican port, present it for check-in at the Capitán de Puerto, located just west of Migración, across Tampico. If you arrive without Mexican inspection documentation, first go to Migración for an inspection, then to the Capitán del Puerto.

Medical and Emergencies

Several pharmacies sell medicines and drugs near the plaza. For discounts, go to the big **Farmacia El Fénix,** tel. 971/402-99, at the northwest corner of Avila Camacho and Guaymas, a block north of the plaza, open Mon.–Sat. 8 A.M.–10 P.M. If it can't supply you, try **Farmacia de la Cruz** at the southeast corner, diagonally across the intersection.

Of the several downtown doctors' offices, the **Clínica de Especialidades Médicas** (Medical Specialties Clinic), tel. 971/441-07, at Avila Camacho 306, west side of the plaza, offers several choices: gynecologist (Mon.–Sat. 10 A.M.–1 P.M.), pediatrician (Mon.–Fri. 5–8 P.M.), orthopedist (Mon., Wed., Thurs., 6–8 P.M., Sat. 10 A.M.–1 P.M.), and general practitioner (Mon.–Fri. 5–8 P.M.).

Alternatively, at neighboring offices in the same block, west of the plaza, are an internist, Dr. Jaime Castro Castellanos, tel. 971/441-07, office hours Mon.–Fri. 6–9 P.M., Sat. 9 A.M.–2 P.M., and an orthopedist, Dr. Mauricio Ramos Garduño, tel. 971/433-42, office hours Mon.–Fri. 6:30–9 P.M., Sat. 10 A.M.–1 P.M.

In emergency, either follow your hotel recommendation or have a taxi take you to Sanatorio del Carmen on Calle Francisco Villa 16, tel. 971/443-34. In a police emergency, contact the **municipal police,** tel. 971/405-23.

Photos and Laundry

Best town source of film (Kodak, Konica and Fuji), developing, cameras, and supplies is **Foto Discuento de Oaxaca,** open Mon.–Sat. 9 A.M.–8 P.M., on Avila Camacho, half a block north of the plaza, tel. 971/443-00. Get your laundry done at **Lavandería Anabel,** tel. 971/404-90, and 971/622-02, open Mon.–Sat. 8 A.M.–1:30 P.M., 4–7:30 P.M. at Tampico 53, between Progreso and Guaymas, west side of street, a block west and a block and a half north of the plaza,.

GETTING THERE AND AWAY

Bus travelers, go to the *camionera central* (central bus terminal), tel. 971/402-59, on 5 de Mayo, half a block south of the plaza. **Cristóbal Colón (CC), Plus,** and **Autobuses del Oriente** (ADO) offer luxury and first-class service; **Autobuses Unidos** (AU) and **Sur** offer second class.

Cristóbal Colón departures connect northwest with Mexico City via Tehuantepec and Oaxaca; southwest with Bahías de Huatulco, Pochutla (Puerto Ángel), and Puerto Escondido; east with Juchitán, Zanatepec, Tuxtla Gutiérrez, San Cristóbal las Casas, and Tapachula on the Guatemala border. Its subsidiary line Plus offers luxury-class connections northwest with Oaxaca, Mexico City, and Veracruz, and southwest with Bahías de Huatulco.

ADO offers first-class connections north with Tehuantepec, Juchitán, Minatitlán, Coatzacoalcos, Villahermosa, Palenque, Ciudad del Carmen, Tuxpan, Veracruz, and Tampico.

AU offers second-class connections northwest with Oaxaca, Puebla, Mexico City, Orizaba, and Veracruz, and north with Tehuantepec, Juchitán, and Tuxtepec.

Sur offers second-class connections north with Tehuantepec, Juchitán, and Coatzacoalcos; east with Zanatepec and Tapanatepec, and southwest with Astata and Bahías de Huatulco.

Drivers have the same highway choices and destinations as listed at the end of the Tehuantepec section, preceding. Simply add 20 minutes to the driving time (and nine miles, 15 km distance) for northerly, northwesterly, and easterly trips; subtract the same for southwesterly trips. Fill up with **gasoline** at the Pemex *gasolinera* on the highway, Tehuantepec direction, about four miles (six km) north of downtown.

PLAYA LA VENTOSA

Playa La Ventosa is Salina Cruz's sleepy little beach village on the historic Bahía de la Ventosa (Windy Bay) where Hernán Cortés built his first caravels to explore the Pacific. Get there by car, taxi, or white or orange Ventosa-labeled bus running west along Calle Miramar next to the container docks, four blocks south of the plaza. Drivers, bear left at the fork at the end of Miramar and continue winding over the hill toward the beach. After about two miles, you get a good view of the petrochemical plant on the left, belching a swirling, hellish plume of pollution. Fortunately for Salina Cruz (but not for other towns downwind), prevailing breezes blow the smoke away from town.

About four miles from downtown you arrive at Playa La Ventosa. One of the best places to land is **La Palapa de Chava,** the beachfront restaurant at the end of the main street through town. Friendly, knowledgeable owner Salvador Mendoza likes to tell visitors about Playa La Ventosa. He says that wood for Cortés's ships was cut inland and floated downstream via the **Río Tehuantepec,** which empties into the bay's east (left facing the ocean) side. There the summer rainy-season flood stains the entire Bahía Ventosa a muddy brown while depositing piles of driftwood on the east-side beach. In the dry winter and spring the river dries slows to a clear trickle and the bay becomes clear and blue.

Shift your view west and notice what appears to be a tower atop the headland, a mile or two beyond the foreground bay and beach. This tower has been known for longer than anyone remembers as **El Faro de Cortés,** The Lighthouse of Cortés. The tower's builders cut a window on the seaward side, where historians believe they placed an oil lamp to guide ships to the harbor.

If the story is true, the lighthouse would be nearly five centuries old. How could this be? Without maintenance, mortar crumbles and bricks usually fall after two or three centuries. Restaurant owner Salvador Mendoza answers that experts believe that Cortés built the tower of bricks and mortar, mixed with egg whites and yolks instead of water, which made mortar durable enough to keep the lighthouse standing straight, without any repairs, until the present day.

Activities
Wander the beach, rocky in the rainy summer and fall, sandy in the dry winter and spring. On the east side, by the river's mouth, collect shells and driftwood, watch the antics of the pelicans, seagulls, and cormorants, and, with your binoculars, look for rarer species. On the west side, explore the tide pools beneath the rocky headland, then head inland and hike the headland's forested arroyos up to the breezy hilltop for a close-up view of Cortés's Lighthouse.

On another day, go on a fishing excursion and catch a load of silvery *mojarra* (sea bass), *lisa* (mullet), and *sierra* (mackerel) for a feast for everyone in the neighborhood. Go in your own boat or hire a boatman (figure on about $40) to take you out for half a day.

Accommodations
For accommodation, either park your RV, set up a tent, or stay in one of the Playa Ventosa beachfront lodgings. On the far west side of the beach, beneath the headland, is a secluded, level grassy spot that appears fine for tenting. RV-equipped travelers could simply park at one of a number of likely spots down by the beach.

Otherwise, stay at La Ventosa's best, **Posada Rústrian,** so relaxing that it's worth reserving well ahead of time if you plan to arrive during high-occupancy times around Christmas, Easter, weekends, and Jan.–April. Posada Rústrian amounts to a downscale mini-resort, perched on a breezy rise with a palm-fringed beach view. Watch for the sign on the left as you're entering town. No TV, no phones, simply about 10 plain but clean and comfortable rooms and a breezy, shaded vista restaurant with chairs and hammocks for resting and reading. Rooms rent for about $8 s or d, $17 t, with fans and room temperature private shower baths. Write or call for a reservation, Posada Rústrian, Playa Bahía la Ventosa, Salina Cruz, Oaxaca 70600, tel. 971/404-50.

Three or four alternate lodgings do exist, although none so inviting as Posada Rústrian. For example, try **Casa Limones** across the main town street from Posada Rústrian, or Posada Miramar, a block farther, near the end of the street on the right just before Palapa La Chava.

EXCURSION EAST OF SALINA CRUZ: HUAVE COUNTRY

The country due east of Salina Cruz, is one of the low-lying, barrier sand spits to which many of Oaxaca's Huave-speaking people were marginalized by the more populous Zapotecs long before the Spanish arrived. The Spanish simply continued the segregation that was already in place.

The Huave appear to have grudgingly

accepted their lot. They subsist, mostly off of the cattle that graze whatever brush, grass, and cactus that grow in the sand, and the fish and shrimp that they can catch in the ocean and the lagoons.

San Mateo del Mar (pop. around 2,000), seat of the *municipio* of the same name, with a uniquely picturesque church and a native market, is the major destination of this eastern excursion. Get there (18 miles, 29 km) one hour east from the jumping-off spot on Hwy. 200, near marker Km 17.

The plaza-center of San Mateo del Mar is a block or two south (turn right) from the entrance road. The main sights are the market, which takes up much of the town plaza; the lagoon, past the plaza, a block south; and the church, just to the east of the plaza. When I was there a sullen sacristan (church keeper) didn't let me enter, claiming that the church was closed. Its colorful facade, however, is unique.

The market is where most of the town action is. Women are the actors and Huave is the language. Dress appears to be the dividing line: the women who wear *traje,*—red blouse, dark skirt, striped cloth headdress trailing a bright ribbon—seem to be the ones who speak Huave only. Besides a few vegetables, they mostly sell the local fish and shrimp that their husbands have caught and they've dried in the sun.

Despite their historical shyness (most likely based on a communal memory of hard experience), you might get a smile when you say *"Buenos dias"* or *"Buenas tardes."* The Huave reticence shows directly in the way they build their homes. Notice the walls, the older of sticks or brush, now increasingly of concrete, that surround each family compound. In some country lots, concrete walls appeared to me to have been built even before any buildings. (This of course, is not unlike a significant fraction of town Mexicans themselves, especially the well-to-do, who have historically surrounded their houses with brawny fences and encased their windows with steel bars.)

Santa María del Mar

If you have time, continue another 10 miles (16 km) to smaller Santa María del Mar (pop. 500). Here you'll find a sleepier town plaza and a humbler church. For a bit of action, turn north (left) from the plaza to the *embarcadero,* on the Laguna Inferior beach, about a mile from town. A detachment of marines guards the beach, apparently to keep order among the locals. The guards seemed unconcerned with me as I drove past their post.

A battalion of fishing *lanchas* lines a broad, breezy beach. Gentle waves wash the shallow shoreline, and dogs laze in the sun. With the added security of the marines, this appears to be an especially good spot for prepared tenters or RVers (bring water and food). The most exciting time is mid- to late afternoon, when the fishermen bring in their catches. They sell whatever they can to buyers who arrive with trucks, and load the rest on wheelbarrows which they push home for drying. The good shrimp price that the buyers were paying—about $2.50 per pound at this writing—reflects both local and world demand.

beached Huave fishing boats on the Laguna Inferior at Santa María del Mar

Gettting There: Go by bus (ask for a "San Mateo del Mar" bus at the Salina Cruz market) or by car. The road, initially paved but potholed, finally good, all-weather gravel, takes off from near the Hwy. 200 Km 17 marker about three miles north of town. Turn right (or catch a San Mateo del Mar-marked bus) at the highway traffic signal and road that heads east, by the big electrical sub-station. Drivers set your odometer. After about five blocks, follow the traffic left; continue straight about two miles, passing through the traffic circle at the Pemex refinery gate. Cross the Río Tehuantepec at mile 4.7 (7.6 km). After the river bridge, follow the right road fork, and continue for about another 13 miles (21 km) through a couple of hamlets, just before San Mateo del Mar, 18 miles, 29 km from Hwy. 200.

RESOURCES:

GLOSSARY

Many of the following words have a social-historical meaning; others you will not find in the usual English-Spanish dictionary.

abarrotería—grocery store

aguardiente—Mexican "white lightning": cheap distilled liquor made from sugarcane

alcalde—mayor or municipal judge

alebrije—fanciful wooden animal, mostly made in Arrazola and Tilcajete villages

alfarería—pottery

andando—walkway, or strolling path

antojitos—native Mexican snacks, such as tamales, *chiles rellenos,* tacos, and enchiladas

artesanías—handicrafts

artesano, artesana—craftsman, craftswoman

asunción—the assumption of the Virgin Mary into heaven (as distinguished from the *ascención* of Jesus into heaven)

atole—a popular nonalcoholic drink made from corn juice

audiencia—one of the royal executive-judicial panels sent to rule Mexico during the 16th century

ayuntamiento—either the town council or the building where it meets

barrio—a town or village district or neighborhood, usually centered around its own local plaza and church

bienes raices—literally "good roots," but popularly, real estate

boleto—ticket, boarding pass

brujo, bruja—male or female witch doctor or shaman

caballero—literally, "horseman," but popularly, gentleman

cabercera—head town of a municipal district, or headquarters in general

cabrón—literally a cuckold, but more commonly, bastard, rat, or S.O.B.; sometimes used affectionately

cacique—local chief or boss

camionera—bus station

campesino—country person; farm worker

canasta—basket of woven reeds, with handle

cantera—local volcanic stone, widely used for colonial-era Oaxaca monuments

Carnaval—celebration preceding Lent, called Mardi Gras in the U.S.

casa de huéspedes—guesthouse, usually operated in a family home

caudillo—dictator or political chief

charro—gentleman cowboy

chingar—literally, to "rape," but is also the universal Spanish "f" word, the equivalent of "screw" in English

Churrigueresque—Spanish Baroque architectural style incorporated into many Mexican colonial churches, named after José Churriguera (1665–1725)

científicos—literally, scientists, but applied to President Porfirio Díaz's technocratic advisers

coa (estaca)—digging stick, used for planting corn

Cocijo—Zapotec god of rain, lightning, and thunder

cofradia—Catholic fraternal service association, either male or female, mainly in charge of financing and organizing religous festivals

colectivo—a shared public taxi or minibus that picks up and deposits passengers along a designated route

colegio—preparatory school or junior college

colonia—suburban subdivision-satellite of a larger city

comal—a flat pottery griddle, for heating tortillas

compadrazgo—the semiformal web of village and *barrio compadre* and *padrino* relationships that determine a person's lifetime obligations and loyalties

compadre—a semi-formalized "best friend" relationship that usually lasts for life

comunal—refers to the traditional indigenous system of joint decision-making and land ownership and use

Conasupo—government store that sells basic foods at subsidized prices

correo—post office

criollo—person of all-Spanish descent born in the New World

cuaresma—Lent

curandero, curandera—indigenous medicine man or woman

damas—ladies, as in "ladies room"

Domingo de Ramos—Palm Sunday

ejido—a constitutional, government-sponsored form of community, with shared land ownership and cooperative decision-making

encomienda—colonial award of tribute from a designated indigenous district

farmacia—pharmacy, or drugstore

finca—farm

fonda—foodstall or small restaurant, often in a traditional market complex

fraccionamiento—city sector or subdivision

fuero—the former right of clergy to be tried in separate ecclesiastical courts

gachupín—"one who wears spurs"; a derogatory term for a Spanish-born colonial

gasolinera—gasoline station

gente de razón—"people of reason"; whites and mestizos in colonial Mexico

gringo—once-derogatory but now commonly used term for North American whites

grito—impassioned cry, as in Hidalgo's Grito de Dolores

hacienda—large landed estate; also the government treasury

hamaca—hammock

hechicero—a "wizard" who leads community propitiatory ceremonies

hidalgo—nobleman; called honorifically by "Don" or "Doña"

hojalata—tinware

indígena—indigenous or aboriginal inhabitant of all-native descent who speaks his or her native tongue; commonly, but incorrectly, an Indian *(indio)*

jacal—*native label for thatched, straw, and stick country house*

jejenes—"no-see-um" biting gnats, especially around San Blas, Nayarit

judiciales—the federal "judicial," or investigative police, best known to motorists for their highway checkpoint inspections

jugería—stall or small restaurant providing a large array of squeezed vegetable and fruit *jugos* (juices)

juzgado—the "hoosegow," or jail

larga distancia—long-distance telephone service, or the *caseta* (booth) where it's provided

licencado—academic degree (abbrev. Lic.) approximately equivalent to a bachelor's degree in the U.S.

lonchería—small lunch counter, usually serving juices, sandwiches, and *antojitos*

machismo; macho—exaggerated sense of maleness; person who holds such a sense of himself

mano—the stone roller used to grind corn on the *metate*

mayordomo—community leader responsible for staging a local Catholic religious festival

mescal—alcoholic beverage distilled from the fermented hearts of maguey (century plant)

mestizo—person of mixed Indian-European descent

metate—a slightly concave, horizontal stone basin for grinding corn for tortillas

milagro—small religious wish medal, often pinned to an altar saint by someone requesting divine intervention

milpa—a small, family-owned field, usually planted in corn

molcajete—a stone mortar and pestle, used for hand-grinding, especially chiles and seeds

mordida—slang for bribe; "little bite"

olla—a pottery jug or pot, used for stewing— vegetables, meats, beans, coffee

padrino, padrina—godfather or godmother, often the respective *compadres* of the given child's parents

palapa—an open, thatched-roof structure, usually shading a restaurant *panela*—rough brown cane sugar, sold in lumps in the market

panga—outboard launch *(lancha)*

papier-mâché—the craft of glued, multilayered paper sculpture, centered in Tonalá, Jalisco, where creations can resemble fine pottery or lacquerware

Pemex—acronym for Petróleos Mexicanos, the national oil corporation

peninsulares—the Spanish-born ruling colonial elite

peón—a poor wage-earner, usually a country native

petate—all-purpose woven mat, from palm fronds

piciete—wild tobacco

piñata—papier-mâché decoration, usually in animal or human form, filled with treats and broken open during a fiesta

plan—political manifesto, usually by a leader or group consolidating or seeking power

Porfiriata—the 34-year (1876–1910) ruling period of president-dictator Porfirio Díaz

pozole—stew of hominy in broth, usually topped by shredded meat, cabbage, and diced onion

presidencia municipal—the headquarters, like a U.S. city or county hall, of a Mexican *municipio,* county-like local governmental unit

preventiva—state-funded local police

principal, anciano—a respected elder, often a member of a council of elders, whom the community consults for advice and support

pronunciamiento—declaration of rebellion by an insurgent leader

pueblo—town or people

pulque—the fermented juice of the maguey plant, approximately equivalent to strong beer or wine in alcoholic content

puta—whore, bitch, or slut

quinta—a villa or country house

quinto—the colonial royal "fifth" tax on treasure and precious metals

regidor—a community official, often a town council member, responsible for specific government functions, such as public works

retorno—cul-de-sac

rurales—former federal country police force created to fight bandidos and suppress dissent

Sabi—Mixtec god of rain

Semana Santa—Holy Week, the week before Easter

servicios—the ladder of increasingly responsible public tasks that, if successfully performed, leads to community approval, prestige, and leadership for a given individual by middle age

tapete—wool rug, made in certain east-side Valley of Oaxaca villages

taxi especial—private taxi, as distinguished from *taxi colectivo,* or collective taxi

telégrafo—telegraph office, lately converting to high-tech *telecomunicaciones,* or *telecom,* offering telegraph, telephone, and public fax services

temascal—a traditional indigenous sweat room, rock-enclosed and heated by a wood fire, usually used for healing, especially by women after childbirth

tenate—basket of palm

tepache—a wine, fermented from *panela* (sugarcane juice)

tequio—an obligatory communal task, such as local road work, street sweeping, or child care, expected of all adult villagers from time to time

tianguis—(tee-AHN-gees) literally, "awning," but usually the weekly native town market, where vendors and buyers bargain beneath the *tianguis*

tono—a usually benign animal guardian spirit

topil—lowest municipal job, of messenger, filled by youngest teenage boys

vaquero—cowboy

vecinidad—neighborhood

yanqui—Yankee

zócalo—town plaza or central square

PRONUNCIATION GUIDE

Your Oaxaca adventure will be more fun if you use a little Spanish. Mexican folks, although they may smile at your funny accent, will appreciate your halting efforts to break the ice and transform yourself from a foreigner to a potential friend.

Spanish commonly uses 30 letters—the familiar English 26, plus four straightforward additions: *ch, ll, ñ,* and *rr,* which are explained below.

Accent

The rule for accent, the relative stress given to syllables within a given word, is straightforward. If a word ends in a vowel, an *n,* or an *s,* accent the next-to-last syllable; if not, accent the last syllable.

Pronounce *gracias* GRAH-seeahs (thank you), *orden* OHR-dayn (order), and *carretera* kah-ray-TAY-rah (highway).

Otherwise, accent the last syllable: *venir* vay-NEER (to come), *ferrocarril* fay-roh-cah-REEL (railroad), and *edad* ay-DAHD (age).

For practice, apply the accent ("vowel, *n,* or *s*") rule for the vowel-pronunciation examples below. Try to accent the words correctly without looking at the "answers" to the right.

Exceptions to the accent rule are always marked with an accent sign: (á, é,í, ó, or ú), such as *teléfono* tay-LAY-foh-noh (telephone), *jabón* hah-BON (soap), *rápido* RAH-pee-doh (rapid).

Vowels

Once you learn them, Spanish pronunciation rules—in contrast to English—don't change. Spanish vowels generally sound softer than in English. (Note: The capitalized syllables below receive stronger accents.)

Pronounce *a* like ah, as in "hah": *agua* AH-gooah (water), *pan* PAHN (bread), *casa* CAH-sah (house).

Pronounce *e* like ay, as in "may": *mesa* MAY-sah (table), *tela* TAY-lah (cloth), and *de* DAY (of, from).

Pronounce *i* like ee, as in "need": *diez* dee-AYZ (ten), *comida* ko-MEE-dah (meal), and *fin* FEEN (end).

Pronounce *o* like oh, as in "old": *peso* PAY-soh (weight), *ocho* OH-choh (eight), and *poco* POH-koh (a bit).

Pronounce *u* like oo, as in "cool": *uno* OO-noh (one), *cuarto* KOOAHR-toh (room), *usted* oos-TAYD (you).

When *y* is used as a vowel, as in the conjunction *y* (and) or at the end of a word, pronounce it as *i* (ee, as in "need").

Consonants

Seventeen Spanish consonants, *b, d, f, k, l, m, n, p, q, s, t, v, w, x, y, z,* and *ch,* are pronounced almost as in English; *h* occurs, but is silent—not pronounced at all.

As for the remaining seven *(c, g, j, ll, ñ, r, and rr)* consonants, pronounce *c* hard, like *k* in "keep": *cuarto* KOOAR-toh (room), Tepic tay-PEEK (capital of Nayarit state). **Exception:** Before *e* or *i,* pronounce *c* soft, like an English *s,* as in "sit": *cerveza* sayr-VAY-sah (beer), *encima* ayn-SEE-mah (atop).

Before *a, o, u,* or a consonant, pronounce *g* hard, as in "gift": *gato* GAH-toh (cat), *hago* AH-goh (I do, make). Otherwise, pronounce *g* like *h* in "hat": *giro* HEE-roh (money order), *gente* HAYN-tay (people).

Pronounce *j* like an English *h,* as in "has": *jueves* HOOAY-vays (Thursday), *mejor* may-HOR (better).

Pronounce *ll* like y, as in "yes": *toalla* toh-AH-yah (towel), *ellos* AY-yohs (they, them).

Pronounce *ñ* like ny, as in "canyon": *año* AH-nyo (year), *señor* SAY-nyor (Mr., sir).

The Spanish *r* is lightly trilled, with tongue at the roof of the mouth like the British r in "very" ("vehdy"). Pronounce *r* like a very light English *d,* as in ready: *pero* PAY-doh (but), *tres* TDAYS (three), *cuatro* KOOAH-tdoh (four).

Pronounce *rr* like a Spanish *r,* but with much more emphasis and trill. Let your tongue flap. Practice with *burro* (donkey), *carretera* (highway), and Carrillo (proper name); then really let go with *ferrocarril* (railroad).

ENGLISH-SPANISH PHRASEBOOK

A profitable route to learning Spanish in Mexico is to refuse to speak English. Prepare yourself (instead of watching the in-flight movie) with a basic word list in a pocket notebook. Use it to speak Spanish wherever you go.

Basic and Courteous

Courtesy is very important to Mexican people. They will appreciate your use of basic expressions. (Note: The upside-down Spanish question mark merely warns the reader of the query in advance.)

Hello—*Hola*
How are you?—*¿Cómo está usted?*
Very well, thank you.—*Muy bien, gracias.*
okay, good—*bueno*
not okay, bad—*malo, feo*
and you?—*¿y usted?*
(Note: Pronounce *"y,"* the Spanish "and," like the English "ee," as in "keep.")
Thank you very much.—*Muchas gracias.*
please—*por favor*
You're welcome.—*De nada.*
Just a moment, please.—*Momentito, por favor.*
How do you say . . . in Spanish?—*¿Cómo se dice . . . en español?*
Excuse me, please (when you're trying to get attention).—*Excúseme, con permiso.*
Excuse me (when you've made a boo-boo).—*Lo siento.*
good morning—*buenos días*
good afternoon—*buenas tardes*
good evening—*buenas noches*
Sir (Mr.), Ma'am (Mrs.), Miss—*Señor, Señora, Señorita*
What is your name?—*¿Cómo se llama usted?*
Pleased to meet you.—*Con mucho gusto.*
My name is . . .—*Me llamo . . .*
Would you like . . . ?—*¿Quisiera usted . . . ?*
Let's go to . . .—*Vámonos a . . .*
I would like to introduce my . . .—*Quisiera presentar mi . . .*
wife—*esposa*
husband—*esposo*
friend—*amigo* (male), *amiga* (female)
sweetheart—*novio* (male), *novia* (female)

son, daughter—*hijo, hija*
brother, sister—*hermano, hermana*
father, mother—*padre, madre*
See you later (again).—*Hasta luego (la vista).*
goodbye—*adiós*
yes, no—*sí, no*
I, you, he, she—*yo, usted, él, ella*
we, you (pl.), they—*nosotros, ustedes, ellos*
Do you speak English?—*¿Habla usted inglés?*

Getting Around

If I could use only two Spanish phrases, I would choose *"Excúseme,"* followed by *"¿Dónde está . . . ?"*

Where is . . . ?—*¿Dónde está . . . ?*
the bus station—*la terminal autobús*
the bus stop—*la parada autobús*
the taxi stand—*el sitio taxi*
the train station—*la terminal ferrocarril*
the airport—*el aeropuerto*
the boat—*la barca*
the bathroom, toilet—*el baño, sanitorio*
men's, women's—*el baño de hombres, de mujeres*
the entrance, exit—*la entrada, la salida*
the pharmacy—*la farmacia*
the bank—*el banco*
the police, police officer—*la policía*
the supermarket—*el supermercado*
the grocery store—*la abarrotería*
the laundry—*la lavandería*
the stationery (book) store—*la papelería (librería)*
the hardware store—*la ferretería*
the (long distance) telephone—*el teléfono (larga distancia)*
the post office—*el correo*
the ticket office—*la oficina boletos*
a hotel—*un hotel*
a café, a restaurant—*una café, un restaurante*
Where (Which) is the way to . . . ?—*¿Dónde (Cuál) está el camino a . . . ?*
How far to . . . ?—*¿Qué tan lejos a . . . ?*
How many blocks?—*¿Cuántos cuadras?*
(very) near, far—*(muy) cerca, lejos*
to, toward—*a*
by, through—*por*
from—*de*

the right, the left—*la derecha, la izquierda*
straight ahead—*derecho, directo*
in front—*en frente*
beside—*a lado*
behind—*atrás*
the corner—*la esquina*
the stoplight—*la semáforo*
a turn—*una vuelta*
right here—*aquí*
somewhere around here—*acá*
right here—*allí*
somewhere around there—*allá*
street, boulevard, highway—*calle, bólevar, carretera*
bridge, toll—*puente, cuota*
address—*dirección*
north, south—*norte, sur*
east, west—*oriente, poniente (oeste)*

Doing Things

Verbs are the key to getting along in Spanish. They employ mostly predictable forms and come in three classes, which end in ar, er, and ir, respectively:

to buy—*comprar*
I buy, you (he, she, it) buys—*compro, compra*
we buy, you (they) buy—*compramos, compran*

to eat—*comer*
I eat, you (he, she, it) eats—*como, come*
we eat, you (they) eat—*comemos, comen*

to climb—*subir*
I climb, you (he, she, it) climbs—*subo, sube*
we climb, you (they) climb—*subimos, suben*

Got the idea? Here are more (with irregularities marked in bold).

to do or make—*hacer*
I do or make, you (he she, it) does or makes—
hago, hace
we do or make, you (they) do or make—
hacemos, hacen

to go—*ir*
I go, you (he, she, it) goes: *voy, va*
we go, you (they) go: *vamos, van*

to love—*amar*

to swim—*nadar*
to walk—*andar*
to work—*trabajar*
to want—*desear*
to read—*leer*
to write—*escribir*
to repair—*reparar*
to arrive—*llegar*
to stay—*quedar*
to look at—*mirar*
to look for—*buscar*
to give—*dar* (regular except for *doy,* I give)
to have—*tener* (irregular but important: *tengo, tiene, tenemos, tienen*)
to come—*venir* (similarly irregular: *vengo, viene, venimos, vienen*)

Spanish has two forms of "to be." Use *estar* when speaking of location: "I am at home." "*Estoy en casa.*" Use *ser* for state of being: "I am a doctor." "*Soy una doctora.*" *Estar* is regular except for *estoy,* I am. *Ser* is very irregular:

to be—*ser*
I am, you, you (he, she, it) are—*soy, es*
we are, you (they) are—*somos, son*

At the Station and on the Bus

I'd like a ticket to . . .—*Quisiera un boleto a . . .*
first (second) class—*primera (segunda) clase*
roundtrip—*ida y vuelta*
how much?—*¿cuánto?*
reservation—*reservación*
reserved seat—*asiento reservado*
seat number . . .—*número asiento . . .*
baggage—*equipaje*
Where is this bus going?—*¿Dónde va este autobús?*
What's the name of this place?—*¿Cómo se llama este lugar?*
Stop here, please.—*Pare aquí, por favor.*

Eating Out

A *restaurante* (rays-tah-oo-RAHN-tay) generally implies a fairly fancy joint, with prices to match. The food and atmosphere, however, may be more to your liking at other types of eateries (in approximate order of price): *comedor, café, fonda, lonchería, jugería, taquería.*

I'm hungry (thirsty).—*Tengo hambre (sed).*

menu—*lista, menú*
order—*orden*
soft drink—*refresco*
coffee, cream—*café, crema*
tea—*té*
sugar—*azúcar*
drinking water—*agua pura, agua potable*
bottled carbonated water—*agua mineral*
bottled uncarbonated water—*agua sin gas*
glass—*vaso*
beer—*cerveza*
dark—*obscura*
draft—*de barril*
wine—*vino*
white, red—*blanco, tinto*
dry, sweet—*seco, dulce*
cheese—*queso*
snack—*antojo, botana*
daily lunch special—*comida corrida*
fried—*frito*
roasted—*asada*
barbecue, barbecued—*barbacoa, al carbón*
breakfast—*desayuno*
eggs—*huevos*
boiled—*tibios*
scrambled—*revueltos*
bread—*pan*
roll—*bolillo*
sweet roll—*pan dulce*
toast—*pan tostada*
oatmeal—*avena*
bacon, ham—*tocino, jamón*
salad—*ensalada*
lettuce—*lechuga*
carrot—*zanahoria*
tomato—*tomate*
oil—*aceite*
vinegar—*vinagre*
lime—*lima*
mayonnaise—*mayonesa*
fruit—*fruta*
mango—*mango*
watermelon—*sandía*
papaya—*papaya*
banana—*plátano*
apple—*manzana*
orange—*naranja*
fish—*pescado*
shrimp—*camarones*
oysters—*ostiones*
clams—*almejas*

octopus—*pulpo*
squid—*calamare*
meat (without)—*carne (sin)*
chicken—*pollo*
pork—*puerco*
beef, steak—*res, biftec*
the check—*la cuenta*

At the Hotel
In beach resorts, finding a reasonably priced hotel room ordinarily presents no problem except during the high-occupancy weeks after Christmas and before Easter.

Is there . . . ?—*¿Hay . . . ?*
an (inexpensive) hotel—*un hotel (económico)*
an inn—*una posada*
a guesthouse—*una casa de huéspedes*
a single (double) room—*un cuarto sencillo (doble)*
with bath—*con baño*
shower—*ducha*
hot water—*agua caliente*
fan—*abanico, ventilador*
air-conditioned—*aire acondicionado*
double bed—*cama matrimonial*
twin beds—*camas gemelas*
How much for the room?—*¿Cuánto cuesta el cuarto?*
dining room—*comedor*
key—*llave*
towels—*toallas*
manager—*gerente*
soap—*jabón*
toilet paper—*papel higiénico*
swimming pool—*alberca, piscina*
the bill, please—*la cuenta, por favor*

At the Bank
El banco's often-long lines, short hours, and minuscule advantage in exchange rate make a nearby private *casa de cambio* a very handy alternative:

money—*dinero*
money-exchange bureau—*casa de cambio*
I would like to exchange traveler's checks.—*Quisiera cambiar cheques de viajero.*
What is the exchange rate?—*¿Cuál es el cambio?*

How much is the commission?—*¿Cuánto cuesta el comisión?*
Do you accept credit cards?—*¿Aceptan tarjetas de crédito?*
money order—*giro*
teller's window—*caja*
signature—*firma*

Shopping

Es la costumbre—it is the custom—in Mexico that the first price is never the last. Bargaining often transforms shopping from a perfunctory chore into an open-ended adventure. Bargain with humor, and be prepared to walk away if the price is not right.

How much does it cost?—*¿Cuánto cuesta?*
too much—*demasiado*
expensive, cheap—*caro, barato (económico)*
too expensive, too cheap—*demasiado caro, demasiado barato*
more, less—*más, menos*
small, big—*chico, grande*
good, bad—*bueno, malo*
smaller, smallest—*más chico, el más chico*
larger, largest—*más grande, el más grande*
cheaper, cheapest—*más barato, el más barato*
What is your final price?—*¿Cuál es su último precio?*
Just right!—*!Perfecto!*

handicrafts—*artesanías*
craftsman, craftswoman—*artesano, artesana*
fanciful wooden animal—*alebrije*
mask—*máscara*
tinware—*hojalata*
basket (of reeds, with handle)—*canasta*
basket (of palm)—*tenate*
wool rug or hanging—*tapete*
doll—*muñeca*
cutlery—*cuchillería*
knife—*cuchilla*
sword—*espada*
vase—*florera*
cup—*tasa*
bowl—*escudilla*
pot—*olla*
pitcher—*jarro*
furniture—*muebles*
jewelry or gem—*joya*
filigree jewelry—*filigrana*

candlestick—*candelero*
tablecloth—*mantel*
napkin or place mat—*servilleta*
embroidery—*bordado*
skirt—*falda*
blouse—*blusa*
shirt—*camisa*
dress—*vestido*
purse or bag—*bolsa*
wallet—*cartera*
wool—*lana*
maguey fiber—*ixtle*
leather—*cuero, piel*
cotton—*algodón*
copper—*cobre*
silver—*plata*
gold—*oro*
iron—*hierro*
pewter—*peltre*
glass—*vidrio*
wood—*madera*
black clay—*barro negro*
red clay—*barro rojo*
onyx—*onix*
wraparound skirt—*enredo, pozahuanco* (on the coast)
belt—*cinturón*
shawl—*rebozo*

Telephone, Post Office

In smaller Mexican towns, long-distance connections must be made at a central long-distance office, where people sometimes can sit, have coffee or a *refresco,* and socialize while waiting for their *larga distancia* to come through.

long-distance telephone—*teléfono larga distancia*
I would like to call . . .—*Quisiera llamar a . . .*
station to station—*a quien contesta*
person to person—*persona a persona*
credit card—*tarjeta de crédito*
post office—*correo*
general delivery—*lista de correo*
letter—*carta*
stamp—*estampilla*
postcard—*tarjeta*
aerogram—*aerograma*
air mail—*correo aero*
registered—*registrado*
money order—*giro*

package, box—*paquete, caja*
strlng, tape—*cuerda, cinta*

Formalities
Although crossing into Mexico is relatively easy, many experienced travelers find it among the most exotic of destinations—more so than either India or Japan.

border—*frontera*
customs—*aduana*
immigration—*migración*
tourist card—*tarjeta de turista*
inspection—*inspección, revisión*
passport—*pasaporte*
profession—*profesión*
marital status—*estado civil*
single—*soltero*
married, divorced—*casado, divorciado*
widowed—*viudado*
insurance—*seguros*
title—*título*
driver's license—*licencia de manejar*
fishing, hunting, gun license—*licencia de pescar, cazar, armas*

At the Pharmacy, Doctor, Hospital
For a third-world country, Mexico provides good health care. Even small Oaxaca towns have a pharmacy or two and a basic hospital or clinic.

Help me, please.—*Ayúdeme por favor.*
I am ill.—*Estoy enfermo.*
Call a doctor.—*Llame un doctor.*
Take me to . . .—*Lleve me a . . .*
hospital—*hospital, sanatorio*
drugstore—*farmacia*
pain—*dolor*
fever—*fiebre*
headache—*dolor de cabeza*
stomach ache—*dolor de estómago*
burn—*quemadura*
cramp—*calambre*
nausea—*náusea*
vomiting—*vomitar*
medicine—*medicina*
antibiotic—*antibiótico*
pill, tablet—*pastilla*
aspirin—*aspirina*
ointment, cream—*pomada, crema*
bandage—*venda*

cotton—*algodón*
sanitary napkins (use brand name)
birth control pills—*pastillas contraceptivos*
contraceptive foam—*espuma contraceptiva*
diaphragm (best carry an extra)
condoms—*contraceptivas*
toothbrush—*cepilla dental*
dental floss (bring an extra supply)
toothpaste—*crema dental*
dentist—*dentista*
toothache—*dolor demuelas*

At the Gas Station
Some Mexican gas station attendants are experts at shortchanging you in both money and gasoline. If you don't have a locking gas cap, either insist on pumping the gas yourself or make certain the pump is zeroed before the attendant begins pumping. Furthermore, the kids who hang around gas stations are notoriously light-fingered. Stow every loose item—cameras, purses, binoculars—out of sight *before* you pull into the *gasolinera.*

gas station—*gasolinera*
gasoline—*gasolina*
leaded, unleaded—*plomo, sin plomo*
full, please—*lleno, por favor*
gas cap—*tapón*
tire—*llanta*
tire repair shop—*vulcanizadora*
air—*aire*
water—*agua*
oil (change)—*aceite (cambio)*
grease—*grasa*
My . . . doesn't work.—*Mi . . . no sirve.*
battery—*batería*
radiator—*radiador*
alternator, generator—*alternador, generador*
tow truck—*grúa*
repair shop—*taller mecánico*
tune-up—*afinación*
auto parts store—*refaccionería*

Numbers and Time
zero—*cero*
one—*uno*
two—*dos*
three—*tres*
four—*cuatro*
five—*cinco*

six—*seis*
seven—*siete*
eight—*ocho*
nine—*nueve*
10—*diez*
11—*once*
12—*doce*
13—*trece*
14—*catorce*
15—*quince*
16—*dieciseis*
17—*diecisiete*
18—*dieciocho*
19—*diecinueve*
20—*veinte*
21—*veinte y uno,* or *veintiuno*
30—*treinta*
40—*cuarenta*
50—*cincuenta*
60—*sesenta*
70—*setenta*
80—*ochenta*
90—*noventa*
100—*ciento*
101—*ciento y uno,* or *cientiuno*
200—*doscientos*
500—*quinientos*
1,000—*mil*
10,000—*diez mil*
100,000—*cien mil*
1,000,000—*milión*
1999—*mil novecientos noventa y nueve*
one-half—*medio*
one-third—*un tercio*
one-fourth—*un quarto*

What time is it?—*¿Qué hora es?*
It's one o'clock.—*Es la una.*

It's three in the afternoon.—*Son las tres de la tarde.*
It's 4 A.M.—*Son las cuatro de la mañana.*
six-thirty—*seis y media*
a quarter till eleven—*un cuarto hasta once*
a quarter past five—*un cuarto después cinco*

Monday—*lunes*
Tuesday—*martes*
Wednesday—*miércoles*
Thursday—*jueves*
Friday—*viernes*
Saturday—*sábado*
Sunday—*domingo*

January—*enero*
February—*febrero*
March—*marzo*
April—*abril*
May—*mayo*
June—*junio*
July—*julio*
August—*agosto*
September—*septiembre*
October—*octubre*
November—*noviembre*
December—*diciembre*

last Sunday—*domingo pasado*
next December—*diciembre próximo*
yesterday—*ayer*
tomorrow—*mañana*
an hour—*una hora*
a week—*una semana*
a month—*un mes*
a week ago—*hace una semana*
after—*después*
before—*antes*

SUGGESTED READING

Some of these books are informative, others are entertaining, and all of them will increase your understanding of both Mexico and Oaxaca. Some are easier to find in Oaxaca than at home, and vice versa. Take a few along on your trip. If you find others that are especially noteworthy, let us know. Happy reading.

HISTORY

Calderón de la Barca, Fanny. *Life in Mexico, with New Material from the Author's Journals.* New York: Doubleday, 1966. Edited by H.T. and M.H. Fisher. An update of the brilliant, humorous, and celebrated original 1913 book by the Scottish wife of the Spanish ambassador to Mexico.

Chance, John K. *Conquest of the Sierra.* Norman: University of Oklahoma Press, 1990. Professor Chance uses archival sources to trace the evolution of colonial society, principally the northern Sierra Zapotec communities and how they adapted their religion, customs, and settlement patterns in response to the pressures of Spanish rule.

Collis, Maurice. *Cortés and Montezuma.* New York: New Directions Publishing Corp., 1999. A reprint of a 1954 classic piece of well-researched storytelling, Collis traces Cortés's conquest of Mexico through the defeat of his chief opponent, Aztec Emperor Montezuma. He uses contemporary eyewitnesses—notably Bernal Díaz de Castillo—to re-vivify one of history's greatest dramas.

Cortés, Hernán. *Letters from Mexico.* Translated by Anthony Pagden. New Haven: Yale University Press, 1986. Cortés's five long letters to his king, in which he describes contemporary Mexico in fascinating detail, including, notably, the remarkably sophisticated life of the Aztecs at the time of the conquest.

Díaz del Castillo, Bernal. *The True Story of the Conquest of Mexico.* Translated by Albert Idell. Garden City: Doubleday, 1956. A soldier's still-fresh tale of the conquest from the Spanish viewpoint.

Garfias, Luis. *The Mexican Revolution.* Mexico City: Panorama Editorial, 1985. A concise Mexican version of the 1910–1917 Mexican revolution, the crucible of present-day Mexico.

Gugliotta, Bobette. *Women of Mexico.* Encino, CA: Floricanto Press, 1989. Lively legends, tales, and biographies of remarkable Mexican women, including several from Oaxaca.

León-Portilla, Miguel. *The Broken Spears: The Aztec Account of the Conquest of Mexico.* New York: Beacon Press, 1962. Provides an interesting contrast to Díaz del Castillo's account.

Meyer, Michael, and William Sherman. *The Course of Mexican History.* New York: Oxford University Press, 1991. An insightful, 700-plus-page college textbook in paperback. A bargain, especially if you can get it used.

Novas, Himlice. *Everything You Need to Know About Latino History.* New York: Plume Books (Penguin Group), 1994. Chicanos, Latin rhythm, La Raza, the Treaty of Guadalupe Hidalgo, and much more, interpreted from an authoritative Latino point of view.

Ridley, Jasper. *Maximilian and Juárez.* New York: Ticknor and Fields, 1999. This authoritative historical biography breathes new life into one of Mexico's great ironic tragedies, a drama that pitted the native Zapotec "Lincoln of Mexico" against the dreamy, idealistic Archduke Maximilian of Austria-Hungary. Despite their common liberal ideas, they were drawn into a bloody no-quarter struggle that set the Old World against the New, ended in Maximilian's execution, insanity of his wife, and the emergence of the United States as a power to be reckoned with in world affairs. The defeat of France and Maximilian in Mexico was aided by U.S. support of the Juarez government. The Monroe Doctrine became a reality. Never again would a European power invade Mexico or any other country in the Americas.

Ruíz, Ramon Eduardo. *Triumphs and Tragedy: A History of the Mexican People*. New York: W.W. Norton, Inc., 1992. A pithy, anecdote-filled history of Mexico from an authoritative Mexican-American perspective.

Simpson, Lesley Bird. *Many Mexicos*. Berkeley: The University of California Press, 1962. A much-reprinted, fascinating broad-brush version of Mexican history.

ARCHAEOLOGY

Flannery, Kent, and Joyce Marcus. *The Cloud People*. New York: Academic Press, 1983. Eminently authoritative authors trace the divergent evolution of the Zapotec and Mixtec peoples as revealed by the archaeological record.

Marcus, Joyce, and Kent Flannery, contributor. *Zapotec Civilization*. New York: Hudson and Thames, 1996. Recent finds shed light on the roots of Oaxaca's dominant linguistic group. The book includes in-depth discussions and aerial photos of many Oaxaca archaeological sites.

Paddock, John, ed. *Ancient Oaxaca*. Palo Alto, CA: Stanford University Press, 1966. Eminent Oaxaca archaeologist edits a richly illustrated compendium of articles by major discoverers of Zapotec, Mixtec, and other antiquities.

Winter, Marcus. *Oaxaca, the Archaeological Record*. Mexico, D.F.: Minutiae Mexicana, 1992. A distinguished Oaxaca resident investigator skillfully traces a concise history of the Oaxaca's preconquest inhabitants, based on finds at Monte Albán, Mitla, and dozens of other Oaxaca Valley and mountain sites.

UNIQUE GUIDE AND TIP BOOKS

American Automobile Association. *Mexico Tourbook*. Heathrow, FL: AAA, 1995. Published by the American Automobile Association, offices at 1000 AAA Dr., Heathrow, FL 32746-5063. Short sweet summaries of major Mexican tourist destinations and sights. Also includes information on fiestas, accommodations, restaurants, and a wealth of information relevant to car travel in Mexico. Available in bookstores or free to AAA members at affiliate offices.

Forgey, Dr. William. *Traveler's Medical Alert Series: Mexico, A Guide to Health and Safety*. Merrillville, IN: ICS Books, 1991. Useful information on health and safety in Mexico.

Franz, Carl. *The People's Guide to Mexico*. Santa Fe: John Muir, 11th edition, 1998. An entertaining and insightful A-to-Z general guide to the joys and pitfalls of independent economy travel in Mexico.

Freedman, Jacqueline, and Susan Gersten. *Traveling like Everybody Else: A Practical Guide for Disabled Travelers*. New York: Adama Books, 1987. A thoughtful guide for travelers with disabilities.

Graham, Scott. *Handle with Care*. Chicago: The Noble Press, 1991. Should you accept a meal from a family who lives in a grass house? This insightful guide answers this and hundreds of other tough questions for persons who want to travel responsibly in the third world.

Jeffries, Nan. *Adventuring with Children*. San Francisco: Foghorn Press, 1992. This unusually detailed book starts where most travel-with-children books end. It contains, besides a wealth of information and practical strategies for general travel with children, specific chapters on how you can adventure—trek, kayak, river-raft, camp, bicycle, and much more—successfully with the kids in tow.

Martinez, Felipe, et al. *The State of Oaxaca*. Oaxaca: Government of the State of Oaxaca, 1996. Although its English translation is rough, the text of this show-and-tell book of Oaxaca provides the reader with interesting details to accompany its many beautiful color photos. Available at craft shops and the federal/state tourist information office on the plaza in downtown Oaxaca.

Schroeder, Dirk G., ScD, MPH. *Staying Healthy in Asia, Africa, and Latin America*. Emeryville, CA: Avalon Travel Publishing, 2000. This Volunteers in Asia book is full of tips for anyone going to the developing world, with an overview of the most common health problems and advice on how to avoid them or treat them if you do fall ill.

Weisbroth, Ericka, and Eric Ellman. *Bicycling Mexico*. New York: Hunter, 1990. These intrepid adventurers describe bike trips from Puerto Vallarta to Acapulco, coastal and highland Oaxaca, and highland Jalisco and Michoacán.

Werner, David. *Where There Is No Doctor: A Village Health Care Handbook*. Palo Alto, CA: Hesperian Foundation, 1992. How to keep well in the backcountry. Although travelers may not agree with some of the authors' advice, many of the thousands of tips might save you money, time, and trouble in Mexico. Available from the Hesperian Foundation, P.O. Box 1692, Palo Alto, CA 94302.

FICTION

Bowen, David, ed. *Pyramids of Glass*. San Antonio: Corona Publishing Co., 1994. Two dozen-odd stories that lead the reader along a month-long journey through the bedrooms, the barracks, the cafés and streets of present-day Mexico.

Fuentes, Carlos. *Where the Air Is Clear*. New York: Farrar, Straus, and Giroux, 1971. The seminal work of Mexico's celebrated novelist.

Fuentes, Carlos. *The Years with Laura Díaz*. New York: Farrar, Straus, and Giroux, 2000. A panorama of Mexico from Independence to the 21st century through the eyes of one woman, Laura Díaz, and her great-grandson, the author. As one reviewer said, that she ". . . as a Mexican woman, would like to celebrate Carlos Fuentes; it is worthy of applause that a man who has seen, observed, analyzed and criticized the great occurrences of the century now has a woman, Laura Díaz, speak for him." Translated by Alfred MacAdam.

Jennings, Gary. *Aztec*. New York: Atheneum, 1980. Beautifully researched and written monumental tale of lust, compassion, love, and death in preconquest Mexico.

Peters, Daniel. *The Luck of Huemac*. New York: Random House, 1981. An Aztec noble family's tale of war, famine, sorcery, heroism, treachery, love, and, finally, disaster and death in the Valley of Mexico.

Porter, Katherine Ann. *The Collected Stories*. New York: Delacorte, 1970.

Rulfo, Juan. *The Burning Plain*. Austin: University of Texas Press, 1967. Stories of people torn between the old and new in Mexico.

Traven, B. *The Treasure of the Sierra Madre*. New York: Hill and Wang, 1967. Campesinos, *federales,* gringos, and *indígenas* all figure in this modern morality tale set in Mexico's rugged outback. The most famous of the mysterious author's many novels of oppression and justice set in Mexico's jungles.

Villaseñor, Victor. *Rain of Gold*. New York: Delta Books (Bantam, Doubleday, and Dell), 1991. The moving, best-selling epic of the gritty travails of the author's family. From humble rural beginnings in the Copper Canyon, they flee revolution and certain death, struggling through parched northern deserts to sprawling border refugee camps. From there they migrate to relative safety and an eventual modicum of happiness in Southern California.

ARTS AND CRAFTS

Barbash, Shepard, and Vicki Ragan. *Oaxaca Wood Carving*. San Francisco: Chronicle Books, 1993. Ragan's luscious color images and Barbash's interesting, authoritative text highlight the best of Oaxacan wooden *alebrijes,* masks, dolls, toys, and much more.

Fishgrund, Andrea Stanton. *Zapotec Weavers of Teotitlán*. Santa Fe: University of New Mexico Press, 1999. Authoritative, richly color-illustrated description of the history, economics, and techniques, both traditional and contemporary, of the textile weavers of Teotitlán del Valle, in the Valley of Oaxaca.

Muller, Robert J., The Architecture and Sculpture of Oaxaca, 1530s to 1980s. Tempe: Arizona State University, 1995. An informative stone-by-stone guide to Oaxacan monumental buildings, mostly churches. The author's solid commentary vivifies visits to every church of note in Oaxaca state and transforms what might be humdrum sightseeing for the reader-traveler to recognition, understanding, and appreciation.

Sandoval, Judith Hancock. *Shopping in Oaxaca*. Oaxaca: Government of Oaxaca, 1998. The serious shopper's and wholesaler's guide to Oaxacan crafts, even including some food. The author both illustrates a plethora of examples in black and white and authoritatively lists nearly every source of Oaxacan folkcraft, from individual artisans to nearly every established crafts shop in the entire state. Available at crafts stores and the federal-state tourist information office on the plaza in Oaxaca City.

Sayer, Chloë. *Arts and Crafts of Mexico*. San Francisco: Chronicle Books, 1990. All you ever wanted to know about your favorite Mexican crafts, from papier-mâché to pottery and toys and Taxco silver. Beautifully illustrated by traditional etchings and David Lavender's crisp black-and-white and color photographs.

PEOPLE AND CULTURE

Augur, Helen. *Zapotec*. New York: Doubleday and Co., 1954. One woman's view of Oaxaca's history and culture: a tapestry of Oaxacan tradition from the Mixteca to the Isthmus and ancient Monte Albán to present-day Oaxaca City.

Baird, Joseph. *The Churches of Mexico, 1530-1810*. Berkeley: University of California Press, 1962. Mexican colonial architecture and art, illustrated and interpreted, with many monumental examples from Oaxaca.

Castillo, Ana, ed. *Goddess of the Americas*. New York, Riverhead Books, 1996. Here a noted author has selected from the works of seven interpreters of Mesoamerican female deities as visions that range as far and wide as Sex Goddess, the Broken-Hearted, the Subversive, and the Warrior Queen.

Cohen, Jeffrey. *Cooperation and Community: Economy and Society in Oaxaca*. Austin: University of Texas Press, 1999. A pithy, authoritative account of the history, economy, politics, and folkways of the Santañeros—the people of the weaving village of Santa Ana del Valle, in the Valley of Oaxaca. Here, time-honored customs—*compadrazgo, guelaguetza, promesas*—fuse with latter-day realities to produce a culture simultaneously modern and traditional.

Cordrey, Donald, and Dorothy Cordrey. *Mexican Indian Costumes*. Austin: University of Texas Press, 1968. A lovingly photographed, written, and illustrated classic on Mexican native peoples, including many Oaxacan groups.

Covarrubias, Miguel. *Indian Art of Mexico and Central America*. New York: Knopf, 1957. A timeless work by the renowned interpreter of *indígena* art and design.

Edinger, Steven T. *The Road from Mixtepec*. Fresno, CA: Asociación Cívica Benito Juárez, P.O. Box 12320, Fresno, CA 93706, 1996. A compassionately researched and photographed account of the people of San Juan Mixtepec, in the Mixtec Alta region of Oaxaca. The author, through his solid anecdotal narrative, relates the story of how the people whose means of existence have been gradually degraded for the past four hundred years maintain their lives, spirit, and traditions only by repeated emigration to work as marginal farm laborers in northern Mexico and the United States.

Greenberg, James. *Blood Ties: Life and Violence in Rural Mexico.* Tucson: University of Arizona Press, 1993. The author reveals, with a wealth of personal anecdotes, the cultural underpinnings beneath decades of deadly feuding between two leading Chatino towns in Oaxaca's southern Sierra.

Leslie, Charles M. *Now We Are Civilized.* Detroit: Wayne State University Press, 1960. A now-classic anecdotal study of the worldview and ways of the Zapotec people of Mitla, Oaxaca.

Martinez, Zarela. *The Food and Life of Oaxaca.* New York: Macmillan, 1997. Martinez, a New York restaurateur, leads her readers on an intriguing tour of Oaxacan folkways by way of the palate. Features chapters on Oaxaca's seven *moles,* 150 recipes, and two dozen photos of finished gastronomical creations.

Nader, Laura. *Harmony, Ideology, Justice, and Control in a Zapotec Mountain Village.* Palo Alto, CA: Stanford University Press. How some northern Sierra Zapotecs solve disputes, using religion-based ideas of harmony to achieve social control.

Chinas, Beverly Newbold. *Isthmus Zapotecs: A Matrifocal Culture of Mexico.* New York: Harcourt-Brace-Jovanovich, 1997. How a female-dominant culture functions in Oaxaca.

Palmer, Colin A. *Slaves of the White God: Blacks in Mexico.* Cambridge, MA: Harvard University Press, 1976. A scholarly study of why and how Spanish authorities imported African slaves into America and how they were used afterward. Replete with poignant details taken from Spanish and Mexican archives describing how the Africans struggled from bondage to eventual freedom.

Romney, Kimball, and Romaine Romney. *The Mixtecs of Juxtlahuaca.* Huntington, NY: Robert E. Krieger Publishing Co., 1966. Authors study the contemporary Mixtec culture of the western Mixteca. Pithy examples, especially of the organization of fiestas, still ring true despite the generation elapsed since the research was done.

Stephen, Lynn. *Zapotec Women.* Austin: University of Texas Press, 1992. Study of how women run much of the local economy and a significant fraction of the politics in the Oaxaca Isthmus districts of Tehuantepec and Juchitán.

Toor, Frances. *A Treasury of Mexican Folkways.* New York: Bonanza Books, 1947, reprinted 1985. An illustrated encyclopedia of vanishing Mexicana—costumes, religion, fiestas, burial practices, customs, legends—compiled during the celebrated author's 35 years' residence in Mexico in the early 20th century.

Trilling, Susana. *Seasons of My Heart.* New York: Ballantine Publishing Group, 1999. The celebrated Oaxaca author, chef, and cooking teacher leads her readers on a culinary journey of the seven regions of Oaxaca. Along the way they stop by market towns, mountain hamlets, shoreline villages, and lush highland valleys, visiting the friends with whom she refined the dozens of recipes that introduce the best of Oaxacan cooking. *Seasons of My Heart* is the companion volume to Trilling's National Public Television series on Oaxacan cooking.

Wauchope, Robert, ed. *Handbook of Middle American Indians.* Vols. 7 and 8. Austin: University of Texas Press, 1969. Authoritative but aging surveys of important native-speaking groups in northern, central (vol. 8), and southern (vol. 7) Mexico.

GOVERNMENT, POLITICS, AND ECONOMY

Campbell, Howard. *Zapotec Renaissance: Ethnic Politics and Cultural Revival in Southern Mexico.* Albuquerque: University of New Mexico Press, 1994. A history of how the Zapotecs around Juchitán, Oaxaca, fought city hall and won.

Murphy, Arthur D., and Alex Stepick. *Social Inequality in Oaxaca.* A sociopolitical history of grassroots underclass activism in Oaxaca City during the '60s, '70s and '80s.

Poleman, Thomas T. *Agricultural Development in the Mexican Tropics.* Palo Alto, CA: Stanford University Press, 1964. The successes, failures, and consequences of Mexico's great dam project in Oaxaca's Papaloapan basin.

Rubin, Jeffry W. *Decentering the Regime.* Winston-Salem, NC: Duke University Press, 1997. Ethnicity, radicalism, and democracy in Juchitán, Oaxaca.

FLORA AND FAUNA

Goodson, Gar. *Fishes of the Pacific Coast.* Stanford, CA: Stanford University Press, 1988. Over 500 beautifully detailed color drawings highlight this pocket version of all you ever wanted to know about the ocean's fishes (including common Spanish names) from Alaska to Peru.

Leopold, A. Starker. *Wildlife of Mexico: The Game Birds and Mammals.* Berkeley: University of California Press, 1959. Classic, illustrated layperson's survey of common Mexican mammals and birds. Out of print.

Mason Jr., Charles T., and Patricia B. Mason. *Handbook of Mexican Roadside Flora.* Tucson: University of Arizona Press, 1987. Authoritative identification guide, with line illustrations, of all the plants you're likely to see in the Oaxaca region.

Morris, Percy A. *A Field Guide to Pacific Coast Shells.* Boston: Houghton Mifflin, 1974. The complete beachcomber's Pacific shell guide.

Pesman, M. Walter. *Meet Flora Mexicana.* Globe, AZ: D.S. King, 1962. Delightful anecdotes and illustrations of hundreds of common Mexican plants. Out of print.

Peterson, Roger Tory, and Edward L. Chalif. *Field Guide to Mexican Birds.* Boston: Houghton Mifflin, 1973. With hundreds of Peterson's crisp color drawings, this is a must for serious birders.

Wright, N. Pelham. *A Guide to Mexican Mammals and Reptiles.* Mexico City: Minutiae Mexicana, 1989. Pocket-edition lore, history, descriptions, and pictures of commonly seen Mexican animals.

INTERNET RESOURCES

A number of websites may be helpful in preparing for your Oaxaca trip:

MEXICO IN GENERAL

www.visitmexico.com The official website of the public-private Mexico Tourism Board; a good general site for official information, such as entry requirements. It has lots of summarily informative sub-headings, not unlike an abbreviated guidebook. If you can't find what you want here, call the toll-free information number 800/44-MEXICO (800/446-3942).

www.mexonline.com Very extensive, well-organized site with many subheadings and links to Mexico's large and medium destinations, and even some in small destinations. For example, Oaxaca City is typical, with about 50 connections, including about 15 hotels and rentals. Excellent.

www.mexconnect.com A very good work in progress; with dozens upon dozens of subheadings and links, especially helpful for folks thinking of working, living, or retiring in Mexico.

www.amtave.com This is the website of the Mexican Association of Adventure and Ecotourism. Lists contact addresses, telephones, and emails of dozens of ecotourism operators in virtually all Mexican states. Good.

www.go2mexico.com An aspiring commercial site that covers the Pacific Mexico destinations of Mazatlán, Puerto Vallarta, Ixtapa-Zihuatnejo, Acapulco, Huatulco, Oaxaca, Guadalajara, and Manzanillo (including current weather reports). However, several of these destinations are incomplete at this writing. A work in progress, potentially good if completed.

www.mexicodesconocido.com The site of the excellent magazine *Mexico Desconocido* ("Undiscovered Mexico") that mostly features stories unusual and off-the-beaten-track destinations. Presently the site covers only a

few locations; hopefully it will expand in the future. Good.

www.travel.state.gov The U.S. State Department's information website. Lots of subheadings and links of varying completeness. (For example, the subheading listing medical care available worldwide listed only about a dozen doctors and hospitals.) Other links, however, have plenty of solid information, especially consular advice, such as travel advisories or accessing U.S. citizens arrested overseas. Does not seem to contain many specifics on Mexico, however. Fair to good.

OAXACA DESTINATIONS

Oaxaca City

www.oaxaca.gob.mx/sedetur Website of the Oaxaca Secretary of Tourism. Good Tourist Guide section with archaeological sites, recipes, churches, museums, festivals, myths and legends, recipes, murals, handicrafts, and more. Good.

www.oaxaca.com Commercial community guide to Oaxaca City with loads of noncommercial information. It has links to a long list of Mexico websites and much, much more. The Oaxaca "Tourist Guide" section would probably be of most use to someone planning a Oaxaca trip. Good.

www.oaxaca4less.com English-language commercial site useful for the two or three dozen hotels, bed-and-breakfasts, and rental apartments that it lists. Good.

Huatulco

www.baysofhuatulco.com.mx Restaurants, hotels, general information, events, tour operators, water sports, land sports. A work in progress with lots of hotels with prices. The hotel association sub-site is functioning well. Only in Spanish at this writing, however. Good.

ACCOMMODATIONS INDEX

Ángel del Mar, Hotel: 201
Aguirre, Hotel: 182
Altagracia, Hotel: 370
Amakal, Hotel: 217
Antonio's, Hotel: 135
Apoala Tourist Yu'u: 270
Arco Iris, Hotel: 237
Bahía de la Luna: 201
Barceó Huatulco: 218–219
Beach Hotel Inés: 237–238
Benito Juárez Tourist Yu'u: 312
Beyafrey, Hotel: 308
Calendas, Hotel: 370
Calesa Real, Hotel: 136
California, Hotel: 304
Camino Real: 137
Campamento del Monte: 315
Carmona, Hotel: 258–259
Casa Arnel: 140
Casa Blanca: 366
Casa Blanca, Hotel: Huajuapan 289; Puerto Escondido 237
Casa Bugambilias: 139–140
Casa Caruso: 139
Casa Colonial: 141
Casa de Huéspedes Capy: 200
Casa de Huéspedes Club Deportivo Social y Cultural: 363
Casa de Huéspedes Dani: 341
Casa de Huéspedes Echazarreta: 358
Casa de Huéspedes Gundi y Tomás: 200
Casa de Huéspedes La Soledad: 319
Casa de Huéspedes Mary: 339
Casa de Huéspedes Rincón Sabroso: 200
Casa de Huéspedes Robertina: 333
Casa de Mis Recuerdos: 140
Casa del Cielo, Hotel: 319
Casa Limones: 373
Casa Oaxaca: 139
Casas de Playa Acali: 237
Casona de Llano, Hotel: 138
Castillo Huatulco, Hotel: 218
Central, Hotel: 326
Cliserio, Hotel: 303
Club Med (Bays of Huatulco): 219
Costa Real, Hotel: 370
Cruz: 366

Díaz, Hotel: 257
del Carmen, Hotel: 250
Diana, Hotel: 297
Dom Pedro, Hotel: 273
Don Alex Lena Real, Hotel: 358
Donaji, Hotel: 350
Doña Ofelia, Hotel: 338–339
El Danzante, Cafe and Posada: 277
El Parador, Hotel: 370
El Portal, Hotel: 300
El Rancho, Hotel: 327
Flor: 366
Fortín Plaza, Hotel: 138
Francia, Hotel: 135
Gala, Hotel: 135–136
Gala Resort: 219
Garcia Peral, Hotel: 289
Gilda, Hotel: 273
Gran Hotel Santo Domingo: 358
Grifer, Hotel: 217
Guelaguetza *ramada:* 262
Guiexhoba, Hotel: 350
Hacienda, Hotel: 326–327
Hidalgo, Hotel: 273
Hierve el Agua Tourist Yu'u: 174
Hotel and Restaurant Regis: 169
Hotel 6: 180
Isabel, Hotel: 339
Juquila, Hotel: 266
Juquila Plaza, Hotel: 250
Juvi, Hotel: 276
La Buena Vista, Hotel: 200
La Cabaña, Hotel: 201
La Conchita, Hotel: 250
La Gloria Coffee Farm: 227–228
Laredo, Hotel: 289
Las Gaviotas: 259
Las Golondrinas, Hotel: 137–138
Las Palmas, Hotel: Crucecita 217; Puerto Escondido 236–237
Las Rosas, Hotel: 134
La Zapoteca, Hotel and Restaurant: 174
Lidxi Buixa, Hotel: 358
Lo Cósmico: 202
Lola's: 201–202
López Lena Palace, Hotel: 358
Loren, Hotel: 236

Los Mangos: 294
Maela, Hotel: 140
Magnihotel: 219
Marina Sol, Hotel: 279
Marisa, Hotel: 259
Maris, Hotel: 257
Marlin, Hotel: 218
Marques del Valle, Hotel: 135
Meigas Binneguenda, Hotel: 218
Mesón, Hotel: 327
Mexico, Hotel: 301
Mirador, Hotel: 326
Misión de Los Angeles, Hotel: 138–139
Misión, Hotel: 366
Mitla, Hotel and Restaurant: 173–174
Mixteco, Hotel: 297
Monte Albán, Hotel: 135
Nanguina, Hotel: 331
Nayar, Hotel: 236
Nieto 1, Hotel: 308
Oasis: Tehuantepec 349–350
Oasis, Hotel: Cuicatlán 340–341
Oaxaca Trailer Park: 141
Olímpico, Hotel: 336
1 de Mayo, Hotel: 336
Palacio del Chatino, Hotel: 247
Paraíso Escondido, Hotel: 236
Paraíso Río Grande, Hotel: 254
Penelope's: 200–201
Pepe's: 259
Pérez, Hotel: 257
Playa Bruja, Hotel: 326
Plaza del Ángel, Hotel: 289
Pochutla, Hotel: 209
Posada Cañon Devata: 201
Posada Catarina: 134
Posada Chinanteco: 322
Posada de Chencho: 14o–141
Posada del Parque, Hotel: 217
Posada los Ángeles: 250
Posada Michelle, Hotel: 217
Posada Nopala: 247–248
Posada Primavera: 218

Posada Rancho Cerro Largo: 203–204
Posada Rústrian: 373
Principal, Hotel: 136
Puerto Mexico, Hotel: 273
Puesta del Sol, Hotel: 210
Quialana Tourist Yu'u: 170
Ríos, Hotel: 370
Real de Antequera, Hotel: 135
Regis, Hotel and Restaurant: 169
Rinconcito, Hotel: 336
Rincón del Pacífico, Hotel: 237
Rivera del Ángel, Hotel: 134–135
Roca Blanca cabañas: 255
Rockaway: 238
San Mishell's, Hotel: 300–301
San Nicolas, Hotel: 250
San Rafael, Hotel: 366
San Sebastián de Las Grutas Tourist Yu'u: 181
Santa Ana Tourist Yu'u: 168
Santa Fe, Hotel: 237
Santa Monica, Hotel: 254
Santa Rosa, Hotel: 135
Santillan, Hotel: 265–266
Sarita, Hotel: 266–267
Señorial, Hotel: 134
Shambala: 202–203
Siete Mares, Hotel: 254
Soraya, Hotel: 199–200
Suites Begonias, Hotel: 217
Teotitlán Tourist Yu'u: 167
Tlapazola Tourist Yu'u: 170
Tourist Yu'u Tlacolula: 169
Trailer Park and Villa Relax: 238
Trailer Park La Palmera: 204
Tuxtepec, Hotel: 326
Valle, Hotel: 321
Victoria, Hotel: 138
Villa de León, Hotel: 138
Villa Florencia, Hotel: 200
Villa Flores, Hotel: 266
Villa María: 141
Yacautzi: 312
Zaashila Resort, Hotel: 219

RESTAURANT INDEX

Ángel, Restaurant: 351
Albert, Restaurant: 309
Altro Mundo, Restaurant: 239
Amarantos: 143
Ari, Restaurant: 333
Arrecife, Restaurant: 204
Art and Harry's Surf Inn: 240
Boringuen, Restaurant: 341
Bruno's: *see* Cafecito
Burger Bonny: 259
Cafe and Posada El Danzante: 277
Café La Antigua: 145–146
Café La Olla: 145
Cafe Capuchino: 238
Cafecito, Restaurant: 240
Cafe Huatulco: 220
Cafe Oasis: 220
C and S Café: 309
Caporales: 327
Casa de la Abuela: 143
Casa del Pueblo: 314
Casa Grande, Restaurant: 359
Catedral, Restaurant: 144
Centeotl, Restaurant: 169
Claudia, Restaurant: 267
Coffee Beans: 142
Comedor Familiar Gonzales: 309
Comedor Juquila: 220
Comedor Tere: 297
Coqui, Restaurant: 273
Crotos, Restaurant: 239
Del Jardín: 143
Desgarenes: 321
Don Memo, Restaurant: 309
El Asador Vasco: 143
El Calvario, Restaurant: 303
El Che: 145
El Dorado, Restaurant: 289
El Giardino del Papa: 220
El Laurel: 145
El Lugar, Restaurant: 371
El Mesón: 144
El Naranjo, Restaurant: 146
El Pesebre: 327
El Sagrario, Restaurant: 144–145
El Tio: 319
El Vaquero: 331

Esther, Restaurant: 210
Eunice, Restaurant: 276
Fonda Toñita: 259
Frutería Angelita: 220
Frutería Las Mexicanas: 321
Gemenis, Restaurant: 337
Guelaguetza *ramada:* 262
Hostería Alcalá: 142
Hotel Beyafrey restaurant: 309
Hotel Costa Real restaurant: 371
Hotel del Carmen restaurant: 250
Hotel Garcia Peral restaurant: 289
Hotel Guiexhoba restaurant: 350–351
Hotel La Buena Vista restaurant: 204
Hotel Misión restaurant: 366
Hotel Rinconcito restaurant: 337
Hotel Santa Fe restaurant: 239–240
Hotel Tuxtepec restaurant: 327
Hotel Villa Florencia restaurant: 204
Juanita, Restaurant: 301
Junto del Mar, Restaurant: 239
La Angelita: 250–251
La Antigua, Restaurant: 142
La Brew: 142
La Cafetería: 143
La Casita: 143
La Flor de Oaxaca: 146
La Galería, Restaurant: 239
La Karina: 337
La Manantial Vegetariana: 145
La Montaña: 314
La Muralla, Restaurant: 145
La Zapoteca, Hotel and Restaurant: 174
Leyvis y Vicente: 204
Lo Cósmico: 205
López Pizza: 297
Los Angeles, Restaurant: 146
Los Arcos, Restaurant: 292
Los Mangos restaurant: 294
Los Portales, Restaurant: 301
Los Portales Taco and Grill: 220
Los Reyes, Restaurant: 209
Manantial, Restaurant: 304
Marcelina's Big Burger: 259
Mariscos de Marlo: 359
Mariscos Jorge: 146
Mary, Restaurant: 180

Mitla, Hotel and Restaurant: 173–174
Nadxielly, Restaurant: 366
Nikos, Restaurant: 289
Noemi, Restaurant: 273
Panadería Bamby: 143
Panadería Carmen: 238
Panadería Giralda: 336
Panadería La Señora de Ojatitlán: 336–337
Panadería San Alejandro: 220
Panificadora Principal: 327
Papagayo, Restaurant: 370–371
Pastelería La Vasconia: 143
Perla Flameante, Restaurant: 239
Petit Cafetería y Pastelería: 327
Pizza Nostrana Spaghettería: 145
Pizzería Gato Montes: 359
Pizzería La Cura: 371
Posada Rancho Cerro Largo restaurant: 205
Primavera: 143
Quickly, Restaurant: 145
Rayito del Sol, Restaurant: 210

Rebe: 297
Rincón de Gon: 301
Río Grande, Restaurant: 254
Roma: 267
Rosita, Restaurant: 337
Sabor de Oaxaca, Restaurant: 220
Sammy's Place: 309
San Ángel, Restaurant: 209
Santa Fe, Restaurant: 359
Sardina de la Plata, Restaurant: 238–239
Sarita: 248
Scaru, Restaurant: 350
Shambala: 204–205
Silvia, Restaurant: 339
Super Panadería y Pastelería del Istmo: 350
Susy's: 204
Tartamiel Pastelería Frances: 143
Terranova: 143
Tito's, Restaurant: 309
Tlamanalli: 167
Tres Coronas, Restaurant: 303

INDEX

A

abeto: 11
achiote: 7
accommodations: 82–88; *see also* Accommodations Index, camping, *specific place*
Achiutla, San Miguel: 304–306
African-Mexicans: 52, 252
African tulip tree; 9
aguardiente: 91
Aguas Blancas massacre: 40–41
Aguas Termales Atotonilco: 235
ahuehuete: 8
airlines: 92
air transportation: around Oaxaca 102; to Oaxaca 91–93; *see also specific place*
alcaldes mayores: 26–27
alcoholic beverages: 90–91
alebrijes: 80
Aléman, Miguel: 36
Alvarez, Luis Echeverría: 38
A. Maximino Ramón Ortiz statue: 343–345
Amialtepec: 250
amphibians: 16–17
Amusgos: 65
Amusgos, San Pedro: 261
Andador de Macedonio Alcalá: 131
animals: 12–17; *see also specific place*
animas: 55–56
Antequera: 23
antojitos: 88
apartments: 83; *see also* Accommodations Index, specific place
Apoala, Valley of: 269–271
"Apostle of the Indians": 24
Arco de Yagela: 317–318
arid tropical scrub zone: 10–11
armadillos: 12
Arquitos, Los: 132–133
Arrazola: 182–183
Arroyo Blanco: 320
Arte de Oaxaca: 151
artesanías: 76–81; *see also* handicrafts, *specific place*
Artesanías de Palma: 285
Artesanías y Industrias Populares de Oaxaca (ARIPO): 151
art galleries: Arte de Oaxaca 151; Galeria Art Mexicano 151; Galería Indigo 151; Galería Nancy Canseco 131; Galería Quetzalli 151; Monedas y Antiguidades 152; Museo de Arte Contemporaneo de Oaxaca 131
arts: 76–81; *see also specific place*
Asociación de Comuneros de Mazunte: 207
Asociación Pro Desarrollo Sociocultural y Ecologíos de Bahías de Huatulco: 225
Astata, Santiago: 228
Asunción Cuyotepeji: 291
Asunción Tlaxiaco: 298–302
ATMs: 110; *see also specific place*
Atotonilco Hot Springs: 235
ATVs: 72
Atzompa, Santa María: 188–189
aullador: 13
authentic jewelry: 111–113
automobile travel: *see* car travel
Aztec parakeet: 15
Aztec pine: 8

ARCHAEOLOGICAL SITES

Achiutla, San Miguel: 304–306
Cerro de la Campana: 192
Cerro de las Minas Archaeological Zone: 285–288
Cerro La Iglesia: 247
Cuquila, Santa María: 307
Dainzu: 164
El Castillo de Moctezuma: 326
El Fortín archaeological site: 275
El Mogote, San José: 189–190
Guiengola: 353–354
Huamelulpan, San Martín: 306–307
Lambityeco: 164–165
Mitla: 170–174
Monte Albán: 18–19, 184–188
Monte Negro Archaeological Zone: 268–269
Pueblo Viejo archaeological site: 275
San Miguel Progreso: 307–308
Teotihuacán: 19
Tilantongo Archaeological Zone: 268–269
Xatachio archaeological zone: 272–273
Yagul Archaeological Zone: 169–170
Yucuita: 267–268

Aztecs: 20–21
Aztlán: 20–21

B
backcountry camping: 85–88; *see also specific place*
baggage: airlines 93; buses 104
Bahía Cacaluta: 216
Bahía Chachacual: 216
Bahía Chahue: 215
Bahía Conejos: 215
Bahía El Maguey: 216
Bahía El Organo: 216

BEACHES

Bahía Cacaluta: 216
Bahía Chachacual: 216
Bahía Chahue: 215
Bahía Conejos: 215
Bahía El Maguey: 216
Bahía El Organo: 216
Bahía San Agustín: 216–217
Bahía Tangolunda: 215
La Bocana: 215
Mar Muerto: 367
Playa Bachoco: 231–232
Playa Barra de Colotepec: 234
Playa Brasil: 229
Playa Cangrejo: 229
Playa Carrizalillo: 231
Playa Cerro Hermosa: 253
Playa Chacahua: 254
Playa Copalito: 365
Playa Corralero: 261–262
Playa del Amor: 197
Playa Entrega: 215–216
Playa Estacahuite: 196–197
Playa La Ventanilla: 199
Playa La Ventosa: 372–373
Playa Marinero: 231
Playa Mazunte: 197–198
Playa Oso: 196
Playa Panteón: 196
Playa Principal: Puerto Ángel 196; Puerto Escondido 230–231
Playa Puerto Angelito: 231
Playa San Agustinillo: 197
Playa Zicatela: 231
Playa Zipolite: 197
Roca Blanca: 254–255

Bahía San Agustín: 216–217
Bahía Tangolunda: 215
Balaa Xtee Guech Gulal: 166
Balneario Atonaltzin: 272–273
Balneario Cocos: 322
Balneario El Paraíso: 209–210
Balneario Mingo: 322
Balneario Zuzul: 321
bandidos: 97
banks: 110; *see also specific place*
barba amarilla: 15
bargaining: 111
bargains, accommodations: 82
Barrio de Santa María: 349
barro negro: 81, 175
Basilica de Nuestra Señora de la Soledad: 130
basketry: 76–77
bats: 12
Bays of Huatulco: *see* Huatulco, Bays of
beach buggies: 72
beachcombing: 68; *see also specific place*
Becari Language School: 155
bed-and-breakfasts: 82–83; *see also* Accommodations Index *specific place*
Bee Nu'u: 276–277
beer: 91
behavior, tourist: 117–118
Benito Juárez Birthday: 73
Benito Juárez dam and reservoir: 354
Benito Juárez town: 312–314
Ben Zaa: 59–60
bicycling: *see* mountain biking, *specific place*
birds/bird-watching: 14–15; Bays of Huatulco 222; Lagunas de Chacahua National Park 252–254; Río Copalita wildlife sanctuary 215; Salinas del Marqués 368–370
birth: customs 52–53
black pottery: 81
boating: 72, 74-75; *see also specific place*
booklist: 385–390
bookstores: Bays of Huatulco 225; Oaxaca City 151, 156; Puerto Escondido 244
border crossing: 96
Border Industrialization Program: 38
bravo: 91
bread: 91; *see also specific place*
bribes: 100
bromeliads: 11
brown pelicans: 14–15
bullfighting: 76
burbuja: 78

business: 42–47
bus transportation: around Oaxaca 102–104; to
    Oaxaca 93–95; see also specific place
butterfly farm: 197

C

Cárdenas, Lázaro: 35
Cañon del Río Santo Domingo: 332
Cacahuatepec: 261
Cacaluta, Bahía: 216
caiman: 16
calabaza: 6
calendar, Mesoamerican: 52–53
Calles, Plutarco Elías: 34–35
calling: using Mexican telephones 113
Calm Sea: 367
Calpulalpan: 318; birthplace 319
Camacho, Manuel Avila: 35–36
Campamento del Monte: 315
camping: 84–88; backcountry camping 85–88;
    Apoala 270; Bays of Huatulco 219–220;
    Benito Juárez town 312–314; Campamento
    del Monte: 315; Cascada Esmeralda 304;
    Cuajimoloyas 312–314; Laguna Encantada
    296–297; Oaxaca City 141–142; Pinotepa
    Nacional 259; Playa Copalito 365; Puerto
    Ángel 204; Puerto Escondido 238; Temascal
    330; Tonalá 294; Valle Nacional 320–321
canastas: 76
candelabra cactus: 11
candelabro: 11
Cano, Edmund Sánchez: 36
caoba: 10
Capilla de la Virgen de Guadalupe: 291
Capilla del Sagrario del Señor de los Corazones:
    285
Capilla del Señor de Tlacolula: 168
car-rental agencies: 106; see also specific place
car travel: around Oaxaca 104–105; permits
    108–109; to Oaxaca 95–100; see also specific
    place
Carnaval: 73; Juxtlahuaca 296; Pinotepa Don
    Luis 261; Putleco 308
Carranza, Jésus: 34
Carranzistas: 34
carrizo: 76
carving (wood): 79–80
casa de cambio: 110
Casa de Cortés: 131
Casa de Cultura Rudolfo Murales: 177
Casa de Juárez: 132

CAVING/CAVES

Cave of Serpent: 269–270
La Cueva: 347–349
Nindo-Da-Gé: 336
Petapa: 363–364
San Sebastián de Las Grutas: 181
Sotano de San Agustín: 336

Casa de la Cacica: 275–276
Casa de la Cultura: Juchitán 357–358;
    Tehuantepec 345–347
Casa del Pueblo: Benito Juárez town 312; Jalapa
    del Marqués 354–355
Casas, Bartolomé de las: 24
casas de huéspedes: 82–83; see also specific
    place, Accommodations Index
cascabeles: 15
Cascada Chorro Conejos (Juquila): 250
Cascada del Diablo: 227
Cascada de San Juan Lachao (Nopala): 247
Cascada Esmeralda: 303–304
Catedral de la Virgen de Guadalupe: 285
Catedral de Oaxaca: 127
Catholicism: 55–56
cattle egret: 14
Caujimoloyas: 312–314
Cave of Serpent: 269–270
caves: Petapa 363–364
caves: San Sebastián de Las Grutas 181
cecina: 144
Centro Comercial del Sureste: 331
Centro Cultural de Santo Domingo: 131
Centro de Difusión del Conocimiento de la Grana
    Cochinilla Tlapanochestli: 175–176
Centro de Fotografía Alvarez Bravo: 132
Centro de Idiomas: 155
ceramics: 80–81
ceriman: 9
Cerro de Atole: 246–247
Cerro de La Caja: 292
Cerro de la Campana: 192
Cerro de las Minas Archaeological Zone:
    285–288
Cerro del Fortín: 126, 149
Cerro La Iglesia: 247
Cerro Rabón: 331, 332–333
Cerro Volado: 306
ceviche: 89

Chacalapa, San José: 209–210
Chachacual, Bahía: 216
Chagas' disease: 115–116
Chahue, Bahía: 215
Chalcatongo: 303
chango: 13
Charquito Atotonilco Hot Springs: 255
Charro Day: 74
Chatinos: 64–65
Chazumba, Santiago: 292
Chiapas rebellion: 39
chicle tree: 10
chicozapote: 10
children, traveling with: 109, 119
Chiltepec, San José: 322
Chimalapas: 364–365
Chinantecs: 62–63
chocolate tree: 10
Chocos: 66
Chontals: 67
church: 55–56; historical influence 23–24
Church and Ex-convent of Santo Domingo: 131–132
churches: construction 178–179
Científicos: 33
Cinco de Mayo: 73; history 30
climate: 3–4; see also specific place
clothing: handmade 77–78; indigenous 54; packing 121
cloud forest: 11–12, 317; Cerro Rabón 332
Coalición de Obrero, Campesino, y Estudiantil del Istmo (COCEI): 37
Coalición de Oreros, Campesinos, y Estudiantes de Oaxaca (COCEO): 37
coatimundis: 12
cochineal: 10
cochineal dye: 26
cochineal farm: 175–176
cocodrillo: 16
coconut palms: 6
Codex Nutall: 277
codices (of Oaxaca): 19–20
coffee farm: see La Gloria Coffee Farm
Coixtlahuaca: 279–280
Cola del Serpiente: 270
colectivo taxi: 105
colonial Oaxaca: 24–27
Comisión Estatal de Derechos Humans: 41
communications: 113–114
compadrazgo relationships: 52–53, 249
conduct: 117–118

CHURCHES/CATHEDRALS

general discussion: 178–179
Basilica de Nuestra Señora de la Soledad: 130
Catedral de la Virgen de Guadalupe: 285
Catedral de Oaxaca: 127
Church and Ex-convent of Santo Domingo: 131–132
Crucecita church: 213
Parroquia de la Virgen de la Asunción: 168
Parroquia de San Miguel Arcángel: 280–281
San Andrés Huayapan church: 315
Santuario de Nuestra Señora de Juquila: 249
San Vicente Ferrer Church: 356–357
Templo de la Asunción: Nochixtlán 265; Tlaxiaco 300
Templo de la Natividad Excelsa: 349
Templo de la Natividad: Chalcatongo 303; Ejutla 179–180; Tamazulapan 271–272
Templo de la Virgen de la Asunción: 349
Templo de Los Reyes Santo Magos: 247
Templo de Nuestra Señora de la Concepción: 227
Templo de San Juan Bautista (Cuicatlán): 340
Templo de San Mateo: 318
Templo de San Miguel Arcángel: 338
Templo de San Pedro: Huamelula 229l; Pochutla 209
Templo de Santa Catarina: 316
Templo de Santiago Apóstol: Huajolotitlán 291; Jamiltepec 256; Juxtlahuaca 295
Templo de Santo Domingo: Ocotlán 177–179; Tonalá 294
Templo de Santo Domingo de Gúzman: 283
Templo de Santo Tomás Apóstol: 316–317
Templo Santiago Apóstol: 303–304
Templo y Exconvento de San Jerónimo: 163
Templo y Exconvento de San Juan Bautista: 279
Templo y Exconvento de San Miguel Achiutla: 305
Templo y Exconvento de San Pedro y San Pablo: 274–275
Templo y Exconvento de Santiago Apóstol: 273
Templo y Exconvento de Santo Domingo: 345–347
Templo y Exconvento de Santo Domingo de Guzmán: 278
Tequisistlán church: 355

Conejos, Bahía: 215
coniferous forest: 11–12
congregaciones: 24–25
consejo de ancianos: 49
Constitution Day: 73
Constitution of 1857: 30
Constitution of 1917: 34, 47
consulates: Oaxaca City 154–155
coral snake: 16
Corazón del Pueblo: 151
correos: 113; *see also specific place*
corrida de toros: 76
Cortés, Hernán: 21–24
Cosijoeza, King: 188
Cosijopí, King: 22–23
Costa Chica: 252; *see also specific place*
costeños: 252
Costoche, Finca: 247
Coyotepec, San Bartolo: 175–176
crafts: 76–81; *see also* handicrafts, *specific place*
Creaciones Alberto: 242
credit cards: 111
criollos: 27, 51
crocodiles: 16
crocodile hatchery (Lagunas de Chacahua): 253
Crucecita: 213
cuatro carices: 15
Cueva de la Iglesia: 281
Cuicatecs: 66
Cuicatlán: 340–341
Cuilapan de Guerrero: 182
Cuquila, Santa María: 307
currency: 110–111
customs: border regulations 109; of people 52–55, 117–118
cutlery: 80
Cuyotepeji, Asunción: 291

D
Dainzu: 164
Danza de la Flor de Piña: 327
Danzantes: 184
death: customs of 53
deep-sea fishing: 72; *see also* fish/fishing, *specific place*
de Gortari, Carlos Salinas: 38–39
Democratic Revolutionary Party: 49
demographics: 3
de la Madrid, Miguel: 38
de las Casas, Bartolomé: 24
de Ordaz, Diego: 22

Día de Candelaria: 73
Día de los Muertos (Tuxtepec): 327
Día de los Reyes: 73
Día de San Antonio Abad: 73
dialects: 57
diarrhea, traveler's: 114
Díaz, Porfirio: 30–33
Diego, Juan: 56
disabled travelers: 119–120
distritos: 48
doctors: 116–117; *see also specific place*
Dominican missionaries: 23–24, 271; *see also specific place*
Donaji: 188
Doña Juana Catalina Romero: house 347; statue 343
dress: of locals 54
drinking water: 114–115
drinks, alcoholic: 90–91
driving: *see* car travel
Dueñas, Ignacio J. del Río: 175–176

E
Eco Escondido: 244
economy: 42–47; colonial times 25–27
eco-tours: Bays of Huatulco/Río Copalita 222
eco-travel: 118
Ec Solar: Puerto Ángel 199, 207; Puerto Escondido 244
eels: 16
egrets: 14
8-Deer of the Tiger Claws: 19–20, 268–269
Ejército Popular Revolucionario (EPR): 40–41
Ejército Zapatista Liberación Nacional: 39
ejido lands: 47
Ejutla de Crespo: 179–180
El Aguacate: 256

ECOLOGICAL PROJECTS

Asociación de Comuneros de Mazunte: 207
Asociación Pro Desarrollo Sociocultural y Ecologíos de Bahías de Huatulco: 225
Eco Escondido: 244
Ec Solar: Puerto Ángel 199, 207; Puerto Escondido 244
Iguana Nursery: 235
turtle sanctuary: Playa Escobilla 244; Puerto Escondido 235

El Castillo de Moctezuma: 326
Elderhostel: 101, 120
elder travelers: 120–121
El Día de la Cruz: 272
electricity: 114
El Faro de Cortés: 373
El Fortín archaeological site: 275
El Grito de Dolores: 28
El Llano: 138
El Maguey, Bahía: 216
El Mogote, San José: 189–190
El Organo, Bahía: 216
El Señor de los Corazones: 284
El Tule: 8; Santa María del Tule 163; Yucunama 277
embroidery: 77–78; see also specific place
emergency evacuation: 116
Empresa Ecoturística Comunitaria: 314
encomenderos: 24
encomienda system: 24
enredo: 54, 77; see also specific place
Enriquez, Victoria: 337
Escalera del Fortín: 149
escorpión: 16
Español Interactivo: 155
Estados Unidos Mexicanos: formation of 28–29
ethnic groups: 51–52; see also specific group, place
Etla: 190–191
evacuation, air: 116
Exconvento de Santa Catalina: 131
Exconvento de Santiago: 182
EZLN (Ejército Zapatista Liberación Nacional): 39

F
Fábrica Ecología de Cosmeticos Naturales de Mazunte: 199
facts, Oaxaca: 3
faja: 54
fake jewelry: 111–113
Faro del Marino: 368
fauna: 12–17; see also specific place
Federación Estudiantil de Oaxaca (FEO): 37
female travelers: 117–118
fer-de-lances: 15
Feria Comercial: 335
Feria del Mango: 73
Feria Tuxtepec: 327
Festival of San José: 190

festivals: 73–76; see also specific festival, place
velas
Field Guides tour: 101
fiestas: 73–76; see also festivals and events, specific place
filete de pescado: 89
Finca Costoche: 247
first aid: 69; kits 116
fish/fishing: 16–17, 70–71, 72–76; deep-sea fishing 72; licenses 74–75; Bays of Huatulco 223; Jalapa del Marqués 354; Lagunas de Chacahua National Park 252–253; Laguna Superior: 365; Mar Muerto: 367; Playa Copalito: 365; Playa La Ventosa 373; Puerto Ángel 206; Puerto Escondido 241; Temascal 329–330
flora: 4–12; see also specific place
flowers: see flora, specific variety
flying: see air transportation
folk dance shows: Oaxaca 148
folk dancing: Tuxtepec 327
food: 88–91, 144; see also Restaurant Index, specific place
Food Harvest Center of Hope: 157
forests: cloud 11–12; coniferous: 11–12; pine-oak 7–8; tropical deciduous 6–7; tropical evergreen 8–9; see also specific place
Fox, Vicente: 41–42
frangipani: 7
frigate birds: 14–15
Frissell Museum: 173
fruits: 89–90
fueros: 30

G
gachupines: 27
Gadsden Purchase: 30
Galeria Art Mexicano: 151
Galería Indigo: 151
Galería Nancy Canseco: 131
Galería Quetzalli: 151
Galo Sánchez turtle sanctuary: 235
garrobo: 16
garzas: 14
gasoline: 97
geckos: 16
geography: 1–4; see also specific place
Gila monsters: 16
glass manufacture: 78
glossary: 375–377
gold jewelry: 78–79
golf: 72; see also specific place

FESTIVALS AND EVENTS

general discussion: 73–76
Benito Juárez Birthday: 73
Carnaval: 73; Juxtlahuaca 296; Pinotepa Don Luis 261; Putleco 308
Charro Day: 74
Cinco de Mayo: 73; history 30
Constitution Day: 73
Día de Candelaria: 73
Día de los Muertos (Tuxtepec): 327
Día de los Reyes: 73
Día de San Antonio Abad: 73
El Día de la Cruz: 272
Feria Comercial: 335
Feria del Mango: 73
Feria Tuxtepec: 327
Festival of San José: 190
Fiesta Costeño: 240
Fiesta de Santo Domingo de Guzmán: 74
Fiesta de la Natividad (Putla): 308
Fiesta de la Preciosa Sangre de Cristo: 74
Fiesta de la Santa Cruz: 294
Fiesta de la Santa Cruz de Huatulco: 73
Fiesta de la Virgen de Juquila: 251
Fiesta de la Virgen de La Natividad: 335
Fiesta de la Vírgen de La Navidad: 74
Fiesta de la Virgen de la Asunción: 257
Fiesta de la Virgen de los Remedios: 74
Fiesta del Apóstol de San Pablo: 73
Fiesta de la Virgen del Rosario: 74
Fiesta del Barrio de Santa María Relatoca: 74
Fiesta del Dulce Nombre de Jesús: 181
Fiesta de los Rábanos: 148
Fiesta del Santa Cristo de Tlacolula: 168–169
Fiesta del Señor de La Natividad: 166
Fiesta del Señor del Perdón: 73
Fiesta del Señor de Misericordias: 73
Fiesta del Señor de Piedad: 228
Fiesta de Octubre: 300
Fiesta de San Antonio de Padua: 74
Fiesta de San Bartolomé: 170, 175

Fiesta de San Isidro Labrador: 74
Fiesta de San José: 320
Fiesta de San Juan Bautista: 327–328
Fiesta de San Marcos: 170
Fiesta de San Mateo: 318
Fiesta de San Miguel: 305
Fiesta de San Miguel Arcangel: 74
Fiesta de San Pablo y San Pedro: 74
Fiesta de San Pedro: 229
Fiesta de San Pedro Mártir de Verona: 277
Fiesta de San Sebastián: 73
Fiesta de Santa María de la Asunción: 291
Fiesta de Santa María Magdalena: 74
Fiesta de Santa María Santísima: 74
Fiesta de Santa Rosa de Lima: 74
Fiesta de Santiago Apóstol: 362
Fiesta de Santo Domingo: 294
Fiesta de Santo Tomás Apóstol: 317
Fiesta Laborio: 349
Fiesta of Jesus the Nazarene: 73
Fiesta of the Coronation of the Virgin of the Rosary: 73
Fiesta of the Precious Blood of Christ: 74
Fiesta of the Virgen de Soledad: 240
Fiesta Patronal del Barrio de Santa María Reolotoca: 349
Fiesta Principal del Apóstol de San Pablo: 173
Independence Day: 74
Juegos Florales: 148
Lunes del Cerro: 147
Lunes del Tule: 148
New Year's Day: 73
Sábado de Gloria: 73
San Isidro el Labrador: 74
Semana Santa: 73
Vela de los Pescadores: 365
Vela de Santa Cruz: 365
Vela Tehuantepec: 342
Virgin of Carmen day: 147
Week of Ramos: 73
see also specific place, velas

Gortari, Carlos Salinas de: 38–39
gourd tree: 6
government: 47–49
Grassroots: 157
gratuity: 111
great blue heron: 14
Green Angels: 96–97
green parakeet: 15

Guelaguetza: 58
Guelatao: 319
guerita: 16
Guerrero, Vicente: 28
guesthouses: 82–83; see also Accommodations Index, specific place
Guiengola: 353–354
guitars: 80

HANDICRAFTS

general discussion: 76–81, 111
Atzompa: 188–189
Crucecita: 223–224
Huajuapan: 285
Huautla de Jiménez: 337
Huazolotitlán: 257
Jalapa: 332
Jamiltepec: 256
Juchitán: 356
Juquila: 251
Juxtlahuaca: 295–296
Mitla: 173
Oaxaca City: 150–151
Ocotlán: 176–177
Ojitlán: 331–332
Puerto Ángel: 206
Puerto Escondido: 241–242
San Martín Tilcajete: 176
San Pedro y San Pablo Tequixtepec: 292
Santa Ana del Valle: 168
Santo Tomás Jalieza: 176
Tehuantepec: 347

H
Hacienda del Cacique: 189–190
"Halls of Montezuma": 29
handicapped travelers: 119–120
healers: 56
health: 114–117; *see also specific place*
heliconia: 9
Heredia, Mayoral: 36
heron, great blue: 14
Hidalgo, Father Miguel: 28
hieroglyphic rock paintings: 281
hieroglyphics: 19–20
Hierve el Agua: 174–175
highways: from the United States 99–100
hiking: Bays of Huatulco: 222; Cerro de La Caja: 292; Cerro Rabón: 331, 332–333; Hierve el Agua: 174; Parque Comunal de San Felipe: 133; Picacho: 166–167; Puente Colosal: 283–284; Tonalá Canyon: 293–294; *see also* caving/caves
historical sites: Achiutla, San Miguel 304–306; Casa de la Cacica 275–276; Cerro de las Minas Archaeological Zone 285–288; Codex Nutall 277; Cueva de la Iglesia 281; El Castillo de Moctezuma 326; Exconvento de Santiago 182; Guiengola 353–354; Huamelulpan, San Martín 306–307; Mitla 170–174; Monte Albán 18–19, 184–188; Monte Negro Archeaological Zone 268–269; Ñuiñe glyphs 288; Palacio de Gobierno (Oaxaca City) 126; Peña de los Guerreros 281; Puente Colosal 283–284; Tilantongo Archaeological Zone 268–269; Tres Picos 354; Xatachio archaeological zone 272–273; Yagul Archaeological Zone 169–170; Yucuita 267–268
history: 17–42; *see also specific place*
hitchhiking: 106
Holy Cross of Huatulco: 127
homestays: 82–83; *see also* Accommodations Index, *specific place*
Horizons: 101
horseback riding: Bays of Huatulco 221–222; Oaxaca City 149; Puerto Escondido 241
hospitals: 116–117; *see also specific place*
hotels: 82; local 84; *see also* Accommodations Index, *specific place*
howler monkeys: 13
Huajolotitlán, Santiago: 291
Huajuapan de León: 284–291
Huamelula, San Pedro: 229
Huamelulpan, San Martín: 306–307
Huatulco, Bays of: 211–229; accommodations 217–220; entertainment 221; food 220–221; history 211–212; information 225; services 224–225; shopping 223–224; sights 212–217; sports and recreation 221–223; transportation 225–226; upland excursions 226–229; *see also specific bahía, place*
Huautla de Jiménez: 333–337
Huaves: 66–67
Huaxpaltepec, San Andres: 257
Huazolotitlán, Santa María: 257
Huerta de Juquila: 284
huipiles: 54, 77; *see also specific place*

I
Iguana Nursery: 235
iguanas: 16
immunizations: 115
import rules: 109
Independence Day: 74
independence, Mexican (history of): 27–30
indígenas: 27, 51–52, 58–59
indigenous groups: 58–67; *see also specifc group, place*
industrialization: 38

injuries: 116
Institutional Revolutionary Party (PRI): 35, 47–48
institutions, civil: 55
Instituto de Artes Gráficos de Oaxaca: 132
Instituto de Comunicación y Cultura: 155
instruments, musical: 80
insurance: car 96, 105; travel 93
Internet: 114; see also Appendix, specific place
ironwork: 80
Isla Soyaltepec: 330–331
Isthmus, the: 342; see also specific place
Iturbide, Emperor Agustín: 28–29
Ixcatecs: 66
Ixcatlán, San Pedro: 330–331
Ixtepeji, Santa Catarina: 315–316
Ixtlán de Juárez: 316–319
ixtle: 77

J
jabalí: 12
jabillo: 6
Jacatepec, Santa María: 322
jaguars: 13
jaguarundis: 13–14
Jalapa de Díaz: 332–333
Jalapa del Marqués: 354–355
Jalieza, Santo Tomás: 176
Jamiltepec, Santiago: 256–257
jet skiing: 71–72; see also specific place
jewelry: 78–79; buying 111–113
jogging: Bays of Huatulco 221; Oaxaca City 149;
    Puerto Ángel 205; Puerto Escondido 241
Juárez, Benito: 29, 30–31, 123–125, 318
Juárez, Benito town: see Benito Juárez town
Juchitán de Zaragoza: 356–361
Juegos Florales: 148
jugería: 90
juices, fruit: 89–90
Juquila, Santa Catarina: 248–251
Juxtlahuaca, Santiago: 295–298

KL
Kansini, King Fane: 67
kayaking: 70–71; see also specific place
kids, traveling with: 109, 119
La Bocana: 215
La Capilla del Pedimento: 249–250
La Cueva: 347–349
Ladatel card: 113
La Gloria Coffee Farm: 227–228
Laguna Colorada: 229

Laguna de Manialtepec: 235
Laguna Encantada: 296–297
Laguna Garrapatera: 229
Lagunas: 363
Lagunas de Chacahua National Park: 252–254
Laguna Superior: 365
La Mano Mágico: 151
Lambityeco: 164–165
land: 1–4
language courses: Oaxaca City 155
languages: 56–57
Laollaga, Santiago: 362
La Peña Donde Murió El Aguila con Dos
    Cabezas: 270
Las Campanas: 288
Las Dos Peñas Colosales: 270
Las Regaderas: 335–336
Las Vigas: 314
latifundistas: 30
Latziruetze: 317
La Venta: 364–365
La Virgen Morena: 56
laws: 118
leather: 78; see also specific place
leoncillo: 13–14
Léon, Colonel Antonio de: 28–29
Ley Iglesias: 30
Ley Juárez: 30
Ley Lerdo: 30
Library of Francisco Burgoa: 131–132
Librería de Bibliofiles de Oaxaca: 156
Librería Universitaria: 156
Libros Amate: 156
licenses, fishing: 74–75
lipstick tree: 7
literacy rate: 3
Llano de las Tarjeas: 312–314
Los Arquitos: 132–133
Los Pozuelos: 317
Luna Azul: 221
Lunes del Cerro: 147
Lunes del Tule: 148

M
México: 20–21
machismo: 117
Madero, Francisco: 31–33
Madrid, Miguel de la: 38
Magdalena Peñasco: 302–303
Magdalena Tlacotepec: 361–362
Magna Sin plomo: 97

maguey: 11
mahogany: 10
mail: 113; see also specific place
maíz: 88
Majolica pottery: 81
mala mujer: 7
male travelers: 118

MARKETS/TIANGUIS

Cacahuatepec: 261
Astata: 228
Atzompa: 188–189
Chalcatongo: 303
Crucecita: 223–224
Cuicatlán: 340
Ejutla: 179
Etla: 190–191
Huajuapan: 285
Huamelula: 229
Huautla de Jiménez: 335
Huaxpaltepec: 257
Jalapa: 332
Juchitán: 356
Juquila: 251
Juxtlahuaca: 295
Magdalena Peñasco: 302–303
Mercado de Artesanías: 150
Mercado Juárez: 127, 149–150
Mitla: 173
Ocotlán: 176–177
Ojitlán: 332
Pinotepa Nacional: 258
Pochutla: 208
Puerto Ángel: 206
Puerto Escondido: 241–242
Putla: 308
Salina Cruz: 368
San Antonio Castillo Velasco: 176
San Martín Tilcajete: 176
San Mateo del Mar: 374
Santa María Huatulco: 227
Santa María Xadani: 227
Santo Tomás Jalieza: 176
Tehuantepec: 347
Teotitlán del Camino: 338
Tepelmeme: 283
Tlacolula: 168–169
Tlaxiaco 298, 300
Tuxtepec: 324
Yosundua: 303–304

mandil: 77
manglar: 6
mangle colorado: 6
mangrove wetland area: 6
marble factory (Tequisistlán): 355
margays: 13–14
mariposario: 197
Mar Muerto: 367
marriage: 54
masks: 79–80
massage: Puerto Escondido 243
matapalo: 9
mata ráton: 7
Mateos, Adolfo López: 36–37
Maximilian I, Emperor: 30
mayordomía: Juchitán 359; Suchilquitongo 191
Maza, Margarita: 124–125
Mazatecs: 61–62
medical care: 116–117; see also specific place
medical tags: 116
medications: 115
Memorias de Yucundaayee: 291–292
Mercado de Artesanías: 150
Mercado de Campesinos: 347
Mercado Jesús Carranza: 347
Mercado Juárez: 127, 149–150
mescal: 91
Mesoamerica: 50, 52–53
mestizos: 27, 51
metalwork: 80
Mexican-American War: 29
Mexican fan palm: 6
Mexican juniper: 11
Mexican white pine: 8
Mexi-Maya tour: 101
Mexpost: 113
Miguel Alemán Dam and Reservoir: 61, 329–330
missionaries: 23–24
Mitla: 170–174
Mixes: 63–64
Mixteca: 60, 263; see also specific place
Mixtecs: 60–61
"Moctezuma's revenge": 114
Moctezuma II: 21
moles: 144
Molinos, San Pedro: 303
Monedas y Antigüedades: 152
money: 110–111; see also specific place
money exchange: 110; see also specific place
monkeys: 12–13
mono de araña: 13

Monte Albán: 18–19, 184–188
Monte Albán hill: 126
Monte Negro Archeaological Zone: 268–269
Montezuma pine: 8, 11
Monument to President Miguel Alemán: 330
mordidas: 100
Morelos, José María: 28
morenos: 252
Morro Mazatán: 229
motocarros: 351
motos: 72
mountain biking: Bays of Huatulco 222
Mujeres Artesanías de las Regiones de Oaxaca (MARO): 150–151
municipios: 48–49
murciélagos: 12
Museo Arte Prehispánico e Rufino Tamayo: 130–131
Museo Comunitario: 191
Museo Comunitario Ihitalulu: 306
Museo de Arte Contemporaneo de Oaxaca: 131
Museo de Artesanías Oaxaqueñas: 224
Museo de la Soledad: 130–131
Museo Philatelica de Oaxaca: 132
Museos Comunitarios de Oaxaca: 162, 167; *see also specific place*
museums: Balaa Xtee Guech Gulal 166; Bee Nu'u 276–277; Casa de Cortés 131; Casa de Juárez 132; Casa de la Cultura (Juchitán) 357–358; Casa de la Cultura (Tehuantepec) 345–347; Casa del Pueblo (Benito Juárez town) 312; (Casa del Pueblo) Jalapa del Marqués 354–355; Centro de Difusión del Conocimiento de la Grana Cochinilla Tlapanochestli 175–176; Centro de Fotografía Alvarez Bravo 132; Cerro de las Minas 288; Cuquila, Santa María 307; Frissell Museum 173; Hacienda del Cacique 189–190; Instituto de Artes Gráficos de Oaxaca 132; Memorias de Yucundaayee 291–292; Museo Arte Prehispánico e Rufino Tamayo 130–131; Museo Comunitario 191; Museo Comunitario Ihitalulu 306; Museo de Arte Contemporaneo de Oaxaca 131; Museo de Artesanías Oaxaqueñas 224; Museo de la Soledad 130–131; Museo Philatelica de Oaxaca 132; Museum and Cultural Center (Teposcolula) 275–276; Museum of the Cultures of Oaxaca 131–132; Niace 283; Shan Dany 167–168; Templo de la Preciosa Sangre de Cristo 166; Templo y Exconvento de Santo Domingo de Guzmán 278; Tequixtepec 280; turtle museum (Mazunte) 199; Yucuita 267–268
Museum and Cultural Center (Teposcolula): 275–276
Museum of the Cultures of Oaxaca: 131–132
musical instruments: 80

N
NAFTA: 38–39
nagual: 64
Nahuas: 67
National Action Party: 49
native people: 58–67
nauyaca: 15
negros: 27, 52
New Laws of the Indies: 24
New Spain: 22–24
New Year's Day: 73
Niace: 283
Nindo-Da-Gé: 336
Niños Héroes: 29
Nochixtlán: 265–267
Nopala, Santos Reyes: 246–248
¡No Reelección!: 31–32
northern jacana: 14
Ñuiñe glyphs: 288
nuts: 90
Nyu-u Sabi: 60–61

O
Oaxaca de Juárez (Oaxaca City): 122–159; accommodations 134–142; food 142–146; entertainment and events 147–149; history 122–125; other practicalities: 153–157; shopping 149–152; sights 126–133; sports and recreation 149; transportation 157–159
Oaxaca State Human Rights Commisson: 41
Oaxaca wedding dress: 78
Obregón, Alvaro: 34
ocelots: 13
ocote macho: 8
Ocotlán: 176–179
oil: discovery 38
Ojitlán, San Lucas: 331–332
onyx: 78
orchids: 11
Ordaz, Gustavo Díaz: 37
Oro de Monte Albán (Puerto Escondido): 242
Oro de Monte Albán: 79, 151
Ortiz, A. Maximino Ramón: statue 343–345

Otomanguean: 56–57
oyamel: 11

P

packing: 121
Palace of Columns (Mitla): 172
Palace of Six Patios (Yagul): 169
Palacio de Gobierno (Oaxaca City): 126
Palacio de las Gemas: 150
palanca: 15
palapas: 84–85; see also Restaurant Index,
    specific place
palma real: 6
Pancho Villa: 32–33
Papaloapan: 320; see also specific place
Papaloapan Project: 61
papier-mâché: 80
Parador Yosocuta: 293
parakeets: 15
parasailing: 71–72; see also specific place
Parque Comunal de San Felipe: 133
Parque Helidoro Charis Castro: 357
Parque Paseo Juárez: 138
Parque Recreational: 312
Parroquia de la Virgen de la Asunción: 168
Parroquia de San Miguel Arcángel: 280–281
parrots: 15
Partido Acción Nacional (PAN): 49
Partido Revolucionario Democratico (PRD): 49
Partido Revolucionario Institucional (PRI): 35,
    47–48
Paso Real: 324
passport: 107
pastries: 91; see also specific place
patron saints: 56
Pax Porfiriana: 31
pay phones: 113
Peña de los Guerreros: 281
Peña Larga: 312
peccaries, collared: 12
pelícano: 14–15
pelota mixteca: 296
peninsulares: 27
people: 50–67; see also specific people, place
People's Revolutionary Party: 40–41
péricos: 15
permits: boat 74–75; car 108–109
pescado frito: 89
pescado veracruzana: 89
peso: 110; crisis 40
Petapa, Santo Domingo: 363–364

petate: 76
petrol: 97
Petróleos Mexicanos (Pemex): 35
pets: 109
phones: 113; see also specific place
photographs: of people 64
phrasebook: 378–384
Picacho: 166–167
pictures: of local people 64
pinabete: 8
piñanona: 9
piñatas: 80
pine trees: 7–8; see also specific variety
pine-oak forest: 7–8
pino real: 8
Pinotepa Don Luis: 260–261
Pinotepa Nacional: 258–260
pinturas rupestres: 281
Pizarro, Hernando: 22
Plan de Iguala: 28
Plan de Tuxtepec: 323
Planetarium: 149
Plan of Casa Mata: 28–29
plantlife: 4–12; see also specific place
Plateria Taxco: 242
Plato de Taxco: 224
playas: see beaches
Playa Bachoco: 231–232
Playa Barra de Colotepec: 234
Playa Brasil: 229
Playa Cangrejo: 229
Playa Carrizalillo: 231
Playa Cerro Hermosa: 253
Playa Chacahua: 254
Playa Copalito: 365
Playa Corralero: 261–262
Playa del Amor: 197
Playa Entrega: 215–216
Playa Estacahuite: 196–197
Playa La Ventanilla: 199
Playa La Ventosa: 372–373
Playa Marinero: 231
Playa Mazunte: 197–198
Playa Oso: 196
Playa Panteón: 196
Playa Principal: Puerto Ángel 196; Puerto
    Escondido 230–231
Playa Puerto Angelito: 231
Playa San Agustinillo: 197
Playa Zicatela: 231
Playa Zipolite: 197

plumeria: 7
Pochutla: 196
Pochutla, San Pedro: 208–209
poinsettia: 7
police: 118; bribing 100
politics: 47–49
Popolucas: 66
population: 3; 50–51; *see also specific place*
porfiriato: 31
Portillo, José López: 38
Posada Rancho Cerro Largo: 203
post office: 113; *see also specific place*
pottery: 80–81
pozahuancos: 77, 259; *see also specific place*
Pozo de Santa Cruz: 227
Presas de Huayapan: 315
prescriptions: 115
presidents: 47–48; *see also specific president*
prickly pear: 10 11
PRI (Partido Revolucionario Institucional): 35, 47–48
Programa Nacional de Solidaridad: 39
pronunciamientos: 28
pronunciation guide: 378
Proveedora Escolar: 156
Pueblos Mancomunados: 314
Pueblo Viejo archaeological site: 275
Puente Colosal: 283–284
Puente Morelos: 293
Puerto Ángel: 194–210
Puerto Escondido: 230–245
pulque: 91
Punta Arena: 215
Putla de Guerrero: 308–310

QR
quechquémitl: 54, 77
quesillo a la plancha: 144
Quetzalcoatl: 19–20
Quialana, San Bartolomé: 170
rabo de mico: 11
rafting: Bays of Huatulco 215
rail transportation: 104
rainforest, tropical: 9–10
Rancho Alegre: 210
Rancho Caballo del Mar: 221–222
rates, hotel: 82; *see also specific place*
rattlesnakes: 15
Rebellion of La Noria: 31
rebozo: 54

recreation: 68–76; *see also specific place, specific activity*
red mangrove: 6
regulations, entry/exit: 107–109
religion: 55–56
rental, car: 104–106; *see also specific place*
rental, house: 83; *see also specific place*
repairs, car: roadside assistance 96–97; shops 97–99
repartmiento: 26–27
reptiles: 15–16
reservations, airline: 92, 93; *see also specific place*
resorts: 84; *see also* Accommodations Index, *specific place*
resources: Internet 391–392; print 385–390
responsible travel: 118
restaurant price key: 88
Reyes, Marcelino López: 235
Rincón Juárez: 367
Río Arena: 259
Río Bamba Valley: 229
Río Copalita wildlife sanctuary: 215
Río Grande: 254
Río Mixteco Valley: 291
Río Tehuantepec: 373
Río Uluapa: 332
Río Verde: 1
rituals (customs): 52–55; *see also specific place*
road signs: 105
robbery: 110; gas station 97
Roca Blanca: 254–255
Romero, Doña Juana Catalina: 352; house 347; statue 343
ropa típica: 78
rosa amarilla: 7
Rosa, Doña: 175
routes: bus: 95; car 99–100
rubber tree: 10
Ruiz textile stand: 242
RV travel: 95–100; *see also* Accommodations Index, *specific place,* trailer parks

S
Sábado de Gloria: 73
Sabina, María: 333–335
sabinera (Tonalá): 294
sabino: 8
sacred fir: 11
safety: driving 96, 118; pedestrian 118; water 69

sailing: 70–71; *see also specific place*
saints, patron: 56
Salina Cruz: 368–372
Salinas del Marqués: 368–370
San Agustín, Bahía: 216–217
San Andres Huaxpaltepec: 257
San Andrés Huayapan: 315
San Antonio Castillo Velasco: 176
San Bartolo Coyotepec: 175–176
San Bartolo Tuxtepec: 324
sandbox tree: 6
San Dionisio del Mar: 365–366
San Felipe del Agua: 132–133
San Isidro el Labrador: 74
San José Chacalapa: 209–210
San José Chiltepec: 322
San José del Pacífico: 210
San José El Mogote: 189–190
San Juan Colorado: 261
San Lucas Ojitlán: 331–332
San Martín Huamelulpan: 306–307
San Martín Tilcajete: 176
San Mateo del Mar: 374
San Mateo Peñasco: 303
San Miguel Achiutla: 304–306
San Miguel Progreso: 307–308
San Miguel Tequixtepec: 280–282
San Pedro Amusgos: 261
San Pedro Huamelula: 229
San Pedro Ixcatlán: 330–331
San Pedro Molinos: 303
San Pedro Pochutla: 208–209
San Pedro Tapanatepec: 366–367
San Pedro Tututepec: 225
San Pedro y San Pablo Tequixtepec: 291–292
Santa Ana del Valle: 167–168
Santa Anna, Antonio López de: 29–30
Santa Catarina Ixtepeji: 315–316
Santa Catarina Juquila: 248–251
Santa Catarina Ticúa: 303
Santa Cruz de Huatulco: Oaxaca City 127; Santa
   María Huatulco 227
Santa Cruz de Huatulco town: 213
Santa María Atzompa: 188–189
Santa María Cuquila: 307
Santa María del Mar: 374–375
Santa María del Tule: 163
Santa María Huatulco: 227
Santa María Huazolotitlán: 257
Santa María Jacatepec: 322
Santa María Xadani: 227

Santiago Astata: 228
Santiago Caballerito: 291
Santiago Chazumba: 292
Santiago Huajolotitlán: 291
Santiago Jamiltepec: 256–257
Santiago Juxtlahuaca: 295–298
Santiago Laollaga: 362
Santiago, Pepe: 182–183
Santo Domingo Petapa: 363–364
Santo Domingo Tehuantepec: 343–353
Santo Domingo Tonalá: 294–295
Santo Domingo Zanatepec: 366
Santos Reyes Nopala: 246–248
Santo Tomás Jalieza: 176
Santuario de Nuestra Señora de Juquila: 249
San Sebastián de Las Grutas: 181–182
San Vicente Ferrer Church: 356–357
saraguato: 13
savanna: 6
scorpion: bites 115–116
scrub land, arid tropical: 10–11
scuba diving: 69–70; Bays of Huatulco 222–223;
   Puerto Ángel 205–206; Puerto Escondido 241
seafood: 89; *see also specific place,* Restaurant
   Index
sea grape: 6
sea snake: 15–16
seasons: 3–4; *see also specific place*
sea turtles: 16
Semana Santa: 73
senior travelers: 120–121
Señor de Misericordias: 227
Señor del Perdón: 292
service, vehicle: 96–98
Shan Dany: 167–168
shellfish: 89
shopping: 111–113; *see also specific place*
sialing: Puerto Ángel 205
Sierra Madre del Sur: 193
signs, road: 105
silk cotton tree: 7
silver jewelry: 78–79
snakes: 15–16
snorkeling: 69–70; Bays of Huatulco 222; Puerto
   Ángel 205–206; Puerto Escondido 241
snowy egret: 14
socially responsible travel: 118
Sociedad Cooperativa Nueva Punta Escondida:
   241
Sociedad Cooperativa Punta Escondida: 234

Sociedad Servicios Turísticos Bahía Tangolunda: 223
socioeconomic statistics: 43
Sola de Vega, San Miguel: 182
Solidaridad: 38–39
sopa de guias: 144
Sotano de San Agustín: 336
Soyaltepec, Isla: 330–331
Spanish: phrases 378–384; *see also* language courses, *specific place*
speed limits: 96
spelunking: *see* caving/caves
spicy food: 88–89
spider monkeys: 13
sportfishing: *see* fish/fishing
sports: 68–76; *see also specific place, specific sport*
springs: *see specific* balneario
stonework: 78
strangler fig: 9
Suchilquitongo: 191–192
sunburn: 114
sunset spots: Puerto Ángel 205; Puerto Escondido 240
surf fishing: 72; *see also specific place*
surfing: 70–71; *see also specific place*
swimming: Bays of Huatulco 222; Laollaga 362; Oaxaca City 149; Puerto Ángel 205; Tamazulapan 272

T
Talavera pottery: 81
talleres mecánicos: 98–99
Tamazulapan: 271–274
Tangolunda, Bahía: 215
Tangolunda Golf Course: 221
Tapanatepec, San Pedro: 366–367
tarjetas turísticas: 107
taxis: 105–106
Teatro Alcalá: 131
Tehuantepec, Santo Domingo: 343–353
tejon: 12
Tejupan: 273
telegraph service: 113–114; *see also specific place*
telephones: 113; *see also specific place*
temascal: 56
Temascula: 329–330
Templo de la Asunción: Nochixtlán 265; Tlaxiaco 300
Templo de la Natividad Excelsa: 349

Templo de la Natividad: Chalcatongo 303; Ejutla 179–180; Tamazulapan 271–272
Templo de la Preciosa Sangre de Cristo: 166
Templo de la Virgen de la Asunción: 349
Templo de Los Reyes Santo Magos: 247
Templo de Nuestra Señora de la Concepción: 227
Templo de San Juan Bautista (Cuicatlán): 340
Templo de San Mateo: 318
Templo de San Miguel Arcángel: 338
Templo de San Pedro: Huamelula 229l; Pochutla 209
Templo de Santa Catarina: 316
Templo de Santiago Apóstol: Huajolotitlán 291; Jamiltepec 256; Juxtlahuaca 295
Templo de Santo Domingo: Ocotlán 177–179; Tonalá 294
Templo de Santo Domingo de Gúzman: 283
Templo de Santo Tomás Apóstol: 316–317
Templo Santiago Apóstol: 303–304
Templo y Exconvento de San Agustín: 126–127
Templo y Exconvento de San Jerónimo: 163
Templo y Exconvento de San Juan Bautista: 279
Templo y Exconvento de San Juan de Dios: 127
Templo y Exconvento de San Miguel Achiutla: 305
Templo y Exconvento de San Pedro y San Pablo: 274–275
Templo y Exconvento de Santiago Apóstol: 273
Templo y Exconvento de Santo Domingo: 345–347
Templo y Exconvento de Santo Domingo de Gúzman: 278
tenate: 76
tennis: 72; Bays of Huatulco 221; Oaxaca City 149; Puerto Escondido 241
Teotihuacán: 19
Teotitlán del Camino: 338–340
Teotitlán del Valle: 165–167
Tepelmeme de Morelos: 282–284
Teposcolula: 274–276
tequila: 91
Tequisistlán, Santa María Magdalena: 355
Tequistlatec: 67
Tequixtepec, San Miguel: 280–282
Tequixtepec, San Pedro y San Pablo: 291–292
textiles: Teotitlán 165–166
theater: Oaxaca City 148
theft: 97, 110

tianguis: 112; *see also* markets/*tianguis, specific place*
Ticúa, Santa Catarina: 303
Tienda de Tinito: 331
Tiger Claw: 19–20
tigre: 13
tigrillo: 13
Tilantongo Archaeological Zone: 268–269
time zone: 114
tinware: 80
tipping: 111
Tlacochahuaya, San Jerónimo: 163
Tlacolula: 168–169
Tlacotepec, Magdalena: 361–362
Tlapazola, San Marcos: 170
Tlaxiaco, Asunción: 298–302
Tom's Garden: 210
Tonalá Canyon: 293–294
Tonalá, Santo Domingo: 294–295
tonos: 56
Topiltzín: 19
tourism: 46–47
tourism boards: 108
tourist cards: 107
tourist Yu'u: 83–84; *see also* Accommodations Index, *specific place*
tours: 100–101; Apoala 269–270; Bays of Huatulco/Río Copalita 222; Ixtlán vicinity 317–318; northern Sierra mountains 314; Oaxaca City 153–154; Puerto Escondido 234, 235–236; Río Zanatepec Canyon 366; Tequixtepec 281–282; Valley of Oaxaca 161–162; Zapotec Tours 101
town names: 162
trailer parks: 86–88; *see also* Accommodations Index, camping, *specific place*
train travel: 104
traje: 77; *see also specific place*
"Transparency Commission": 42
transportaton: around Oaxaca 102–106; to Oaxaca 91–101; *see also specific mode of transportation, specific place*
Travel Adventures into Art: 101
travelers with disabilities: 119–120
travel insurance: 93
Treaty of Guadalupe Hidalgo: 29
tree ferns: 11
trees: *see* flora, *specific variety*
Tres Picos: 354
Trigarantes ("Three Gaurantees"): 28
Triques: 65–66

tropical deciduous forest: 6–7
tropical evergreen forest: 8–9
tropical rainforest: 9–10
turista: 114
turtle museum (Mazunte): 199
turtle sanctuary: Playa Escobilla 244; Puerto Escondido 235
turtles, sea: 16
Tututepec, San Pedro: 225
Tuxtepec: 322–329

UV
Unión de Comunidades de la Region del Istmo (UCIRI): 39
Unión de Hidalgo: 365
Valle Nacional: 320–322
vegetarian food: 89; *see also* Restaurant Index, *specific place*
vegetation zones: 4–12
velas: Isthmus 348; *see also* festivals and events, *specific place*
Vela de los Pescadores: 365
Vela de Santa Cruz: 365
Vela Tehuantepec: 342
Viajes Ecoturísticos Schiaa Rua Via: 317
Vigil, Garcia: 34
Villa, Francisco (Pancho): 32–33
Villa Temazcalli: 243
Vinigulaza Language and Tradition: 155
Virgen de los Remedios: 255
Virgin of Carmen day: 147
Virgin of Guadalupe: 56
visas: 107
voltage: 114
volunteer work: Oaxaca City 157

W
walking: Bays of Huatulco 221; Oaxaca City 149; Puerto Escondido 233–234, 241; Tuxtepec 324
War of the Reforms: 30
water, drinking: 114–115
water-skiing: 71–72; *see also specific place*
weather: 3–4; *see also specific place*
weaving: 76–77
wedding dress, Oaxaca: 78
Week of Ramos: 73
wildlife: 12–17, 68; *see also specific place,* tours
windsurfing: 70–71; *see also specific place*
wine: 91
Woman Warriors: 358

WATERFALLS

Cascada Chorro Conejos (Juquila): 250
Cascada del Diablo: 227
Cascada de San Juan Lachao (Nopala): 247
Cascada Esmeralda: 303–304
Cola del Serpiente: 270
Hierve el Agua: 174–175
Huerta de Juquila: 284
Jamiltepec: 256
Las Regaderas: 335–336
Parque Comunal de San Felipe: 133
Santa María Xadani: 227

women travelers: 117–118
woodcarving: 79–80
wool weavings: 81
woven crafts: 76–77

XYZ
Xatachio archaeological zone: 272–273
Xochicalco: 19
Yagul Archaeological Zone: 169–170
Yanhuitlán: 278
Yegui: 164
Yosocuta Reservoir: 293
Yosundua: 303–304
Yucuita: 267–268
Yucunama: 276–278
Yu-uku Chakuaa: 256
Zaachila: 183
Zanatepec, Santo Domingo: 366
Zapata, Emiliano: 32–34
Zapatistas: 39
Zapotalito: 252–253
Zapotec temple: 166
Zapotecs: 59–60
Zapotec Tours: 101
Zedillo, Ernesto: 39–41
Zimatlán: 180–181
Zoques: 63–64
Zumárraga, Archbishop: 56

ABOUT THE AUTHOR

I N THE EARLY 1980s, the lure of travel drew Bruce Whipperman away from a 20-year career teaching physics. The occasion was a trip to Kenya that included a total solar eclipse and a safari. He hasn't stopped traveling since.

His dream drew him to the Earth's beautiful, hidden corners: Kilamanjaro's icy heights, Malaysia's sylvan jungles, Kashmir's golden meadows, Japan's subarctic Summer Islands, and now Oaxaca's regal ruined cities, its feast of crafts, and its colorful native markets.

Bruce has always pursued his travel career for the fun of it. He started with slide shows and photo gifts for friends. Others wanted his photos, so he began selling them. Stranded one time in Ethiopia, he began to write. A dozen years later, after scores of magazine and newspaper feature stories, *Moon Handbooks: Pacific Mexico* became his first book. Next came *Moon Handbooks: Puerto Vallarta*, and now, *Moon Handbooks: Oaxaca*.

Travel, after all, is for returning home, and that coziest of journeys always brings a tired but happy Bruce back to his friends, son, daughter, and wife Linda in Oakland, California.

For him, travel writing heightens his awareness and focuses his own travel experiences. He always remembers what a Nepali Sherpa once said: "Many people come, looking, looking; few people come, see." Bruce invites *Moon Handbooks: Oaxaca's* readers likewise to "come, see"—and discover and enjoy—the delights of Oaxaca with a fresh eye and renewed compassion.

U.S.~METRIC CONVERSION

1 inch = 2.54 centimeters (cm)
1 foot = .304 meters (m)
1 yard = 0.914 meters
1 mile = 1.6093 kilometers (km)
1 km = .6214 miles
1 fathom = 1.8288 m
1 chain = 20.1168 m
1 furlong = 201.168 m
1 acre = .4047 hectares
1 sq km = 100 hectares
1 sq mile = 2.59 square km
1 ounce = 28.35 grams
1 pound = .4536 kilograms
1 short ton = .90718 metric ton
1 short ton = 2000 pounds
1 long ton = 1.016 metric tons
1 long ton = 2240 pounds
1 metric ton = 1000 kilograms
1 quart = .94635 liters
1 US gallon = 3.7854 liters
1 Imperial gallon = 4.5459 liters
1 nautical mile = 1.852 km

To compute celsius temperatures, subtract 32 from Fahrenheit and divide by 1.8. To go the other way, multiply celsius by 1.8 and add 32.

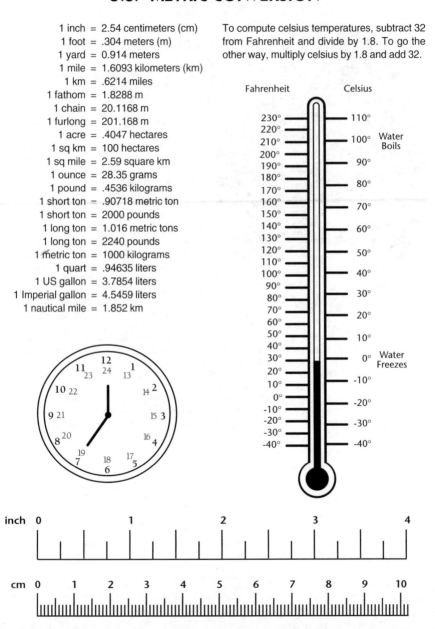

AVALON
TRAVEL
publishing

How far will our travel guides take you? As far as you want.

Discover a rhumba-fueled nightspot in Old Havana, explore prehistoric tombs in Ireland, hike beneath California's centuries-old redwoods, or embark on a classic road trip along Route 66. Our guidebooks deliver solidly researched, trip-tested information—minus any generic froth—to help globetrotters or weekend warriors create an adventure uniquely their own.

And we're not just about the printed page. Public television viewers are tuning in to Rick Steves' new travel series, *Rick Steves' Europe*. On the Web, readers can cruise the virtual black top with *Road Trip USA* author Jamie Jensen and learn travel industry secrets from Edward Hasbrouck of *The Practical Nomad*.

In print. On TV. On the Internet.

We supply the information. The rest is up to you.

Avalon Travel Publishing

Something for everyone

www.travelmatters.com

Avalon Travel Publishing guides are available at your favorite book or travel store.

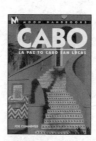

Will you have enough stories to tell your grandchildren?